1 MONTH OF
FREE
READING

at
www.ForgottenBooks.com

By purchasing this book you are eligible for one month membership to ForgottenBooks.com, giving you unlimited access to our entire collection of over 1,000,000 titles via our web site and mobile apps.

To claim your free month visit:

www.forgottenbooks.com/free271182

ISBN 978-0-483-03299-6
PIBN 10271182

ORIGINS

IN

WILLIAMSTOWN

BY

ARTHUR LATHAM PERRY, LL.D.

PROFESSOR OF HISTORY AND POLITICAL ECONOMY IN WILLIAMS COLLEGE,
MEMBER OF THE MASSACHUSETTS HISTORICAL SOCIETY, AND
PRESIDENT OF THE BERKSHIRE HISTORICAL
AND SCIENTIFIC SOCIETY

NEW YORK
CHARLES SCRIBNER'S SONS
1894

To

THE PERPETUAL MEMORY

OF

Colonel Benjamin Simonds and Captain Nehemiah Smedley

BOTH OF THEM PROMINENT AMONG THE EARLIEST SOLDIERS AND
SETTLERS IN WEST HOOSAC
BOTH OF THEM PATRIOT OFFICERS IN THE WAR OF THE
REVOLUTION
AND (WHAT IS MUCH LESS WORTH THE MENTION)
BOTH OF THEM GREAT-GREAT-GRANDFATHERS OF MY CHILDREN

PREFACE.

THE first time I ever heard of Williamstown and Williams College was in the early autumn of 1843, a month or so after the Semi-centennial of the College, which fell on the 16th of August of that year. Rev. Phineas Cooke, an alumnus of the College of 1803, and forty years later a pastor of the church in Lebanon, New Hampshire, had attended this celebration with one of his sons; and a short time afterwards exchanged pulpits with the pastor in my native village of Lyme, New Hampshire. My mother was the widow of the previous pastor there, and as such, was well known to Mr. Cooke, who came into our house after the afternoon service, as was customary with him, and related to my mother at length his recent experiences at his *alma mater* in Massachusetts. I was then a boy of thirteen years, and listened intently but not over-intelligently to this talk. Phineas Cooke was an immensely tall man, six feet and six inches in height; he was also an immensely solemn man in his manner of speaking, employing a sort of cluck of the tongue at the close of each sentence deemed important; and on account of both these peculiarities, he was popularly known in that region as *the high priest of New Hampshire.* He was a native of old Hadley on the Connecticut, and naturally enough passed over the Hoosac Mountain to Williamstown for his college education. But in the forty years from his graduation he had never revisited the place. Great changes had taken place here in that time, as a matter of course. His son, who came with him hither in 1843 from Lebanon, had, in the mean time, grown up and been graduated at Dartmouth. The two were entertained at the Semi-centennial by an elderly lady, Mrs. Amasa Shattuck, who, as a girl, had waited at table on Cooke in her father's, William Smith's, house in Water Street; and now both father and son were waited on at table by Mary Shattuck, a granddaughter of the hostess, Mrs. Smith, of more than forty years before. All this, and much more than this, of a similar kind, was oracularly given out in the way of reminiscence to my mother on that sunny Sunday afternoon. It soon passed out of a small boy's head, although not irrecoverably.

Nearly five years later, when my own preparation for college was about completed, my own pastor in Lyme, Rev. Erdix Tenny, who was my father's successor there, chanced to ask me where I was expecting to go to college. I answered, "Dartmouth," — which was but nine miles distant from my home, and, as I supposed, the only institution accessible to me in my poverty. He himself was an alumnus of Middlebury, and had, on several grounds, a strong prejudice against Dartmouth, and kindly suggested to me whether Williamstown might not be a good place for me to go to. He mentioned Mark Hopkins as the popular and efficient president there, — a name that somehow settled down into my memory. After I had gone back to Thetford Academy, which was just across the Connecticut River from my native village, and in plain sight on its hilltop, I thought over at my leisure what the minister had said, and remember now that the name " Hopkins " seemed to have then a sort of solid sound. I wrote to him for a catalogue of the college; which he forwarded at once, and with it a copy of a pretty thick pamphlet entitled "Sketches of Williams College," just then written and published by David A. Wells of the class of 1847. The catalogue impressed me less than the pamphlet, for there was some striking history in the latter, and some romance; some little account of the old French and Indian wars along the upper Hoosac, and of Fort Massachusetts and its capture by the French in 1746; and a little sketch, too, of Colonel Ephraim Williams, who wrote his last will and testament, as it were, in his life blood. I concluded to try Williams College.

A fellow-passenger with me in the stage from Greenfield, over the Hoosac Mountain to North Adams, when I made my initial journey to Williamstown as a prospective freshman in September, 1848, was Waldo W. Ludden, then a member of the sophomore class. He was courteous and intelligent and won my confidence, and never afterwards lost it, although I was even then aware that a sophomore is a sort of natural enemy of a freshman. The story was told in the stage, that there "used to be" a notice-board to passengers at the foot of the mountain, *Walk up if you please*, and another upon the summit, *Ride down if you dare*. Somewhat as an echo of this last, when we reached the west descent of the mountain, Ludden proposed to me that we leave the stage and take a short cut adown, which, he said, was an old war-path of the Indians, and as straight as a gun-barrel. This statement excited my interest at once, and I accepted the proposal with alacrity, plying him with questions, which he could not answer, as to what Indians frequented this old trail, and when, and why. When we reached the foot of the mountain, which was a considerable time before the stage reached it, I was struck with the position and beauty of the valley. About ten miles to the west of where we stood, the Taconics loomed up to defend the valley on that side, very much as the Hoosacs, over which we had just passed, stood guard over it on the east; while all the huge tumbles that constitute the Greylock range formidably flanked it on the south, as the Dome and the Domelet overlooked it frowningly on the north. The two branches of the Hoosac River, which the Indians had named respectively the *Ashuwillticook* and the *Mayunsook*, on the angle between which we were standing, united in the village of North Adams to form a stream, which, while it cannot compare in beauty with my native Connecticut in its long upper reaches, may yet claim something of the eulogy long ago poetically paid to that: —

"No watery gleams through happier valleys shine,
Nor drinks the sea a lovelier wave than thine."

In short, the *Genius loci* touched me at the very first; and has never since loosened, but only tightened, its genial hold.

During my college course of four years, I managed to find out all that anybody here then knew, which was very little indeed, about old Fort Massachusetts and the local events falling in the old French and Indian wars. I made the pleasant acquaintance of the old farmer who then owned the broad meadow along the Hoosac, on which the fort once stood, and who had ploughed over its rude lines time and time again, and whose son had once accidentally thrown off by his ploughshare the flat stone covering the well of the fort, and had looked down for a moment or two upon the rubbish of old utensils and whatnot, with which its depths were more than half filled up. He repeatedly visited the spot with me; gave me permission to transport to the College the last headstone remaining legible in the little " God's Acre " just to the west of the site of the fort; and at length, when I wished to set a memorial tree on the very site of the fort itself, he took pains to point out what he believed to be the middle of the parade-ground within the original enclosure or block-house. The large elm now growing there was planted in 1859 by my own hands in the precise spot thus indicated by Clement Harrison. I wish here to acknowledge publicly the courtesy of the Young Men's Christian Association of North Adams, in which township falls the site of the fort, who, as I understand it, with unanimity and even enthusiasm, voted many years ago that that tree should in future be known as "Perry's Elm."

Throughout the whole of my mature life, now no longer short, all of it spent in Williamstown as my home and the place of varied labors, my early and constant interest in its original military occupatiou, — no other town in Massachusetts (I think) had such purely military beginnings; my later curiosity as to its successive civil establishments and development; the circumstances under which it became still later the seat of a venerable and influential College; my close and vital connection, through marriage and otherwise, with many of the remarkable persons and families among its earliest settlers and their descendants; — all those have served to deepen and broaden the gladdening researches made into the earlier and later facts relating to my town and College. Some of the results of this longtime interest and investigation are now presented to the public, in this volume. A mass of still unused and mostly subsequent material, large portions of it concerning the origin and exigences and successes of the College, has already been slowly gathered and partially classified; and should a kind Providence but spare my life and strength a few years longer, the hope is fondly indulged that I may be able to give to my townsmen generally, and especially to my fellow-alumni, another volume which may be probably entitled "Williamstown and Williams College," some indirect references to which may here and there be found in the text of the present work.

A. L. P.

February 27, 1894.

TABLE OF CONTENTS.

—•◦•—

CHAPTER I.

ORIGINS IN WILLIAMSTOWN.

———◦◦◦◦◦◦———

CHAPTER I.

SITUATION.

"Beautiful for situation, the joy of the whole earth, is Mount Zion, on the sides of the north." — Psalms xlviii, 2.

WILLIAMSTOWN lies in the northwest corner of Massachusetts. Its northern line of five miles in length is, for that distance, the southern line of Vermont. The entire northern line of Massachusetts was long in controversy between that state and New Hampshire, and was finally settled on by the Privy Council in England, March 10, 1740, in these words: "That the northern boundary of Massachusetts be a curved line pursuing the course of the Merrimack River at three miles distance, on the north side thereof, beginning at the Atlantic Ocean and ending at a point due north of Pawtucket Falls, *and a straight course drawn from thence due west,* until it meets with his Majesty's other governments."

This line was actually run the next year by a surveyor named Richard Hazen, a prominent citizen of Haverhill, on the Merrimack, and accordingly is sometimes called "Hazen's line," and has never since been altered. Pawtucket Falls are the rapids on which the city of Lowell was long afterwards built; but by some means the line to be drawn "due west," from a point three miles north of them, was really drawn about 1° 45′ *north* of due west; so that Massachusetts, so far as Williamstown is concerned, gained thereby more than one-third of the area of the town; otherwise the meadows of the Hoosac, the site of the College, the slopes of Prospect, and all the lands north of a line about midway between the two villages, would have been adjudged to New Hampshire, and afterwards have fallen

1

to Vermont. It was indeed a blessed error of the compass that kept this fine strip of country within the jurisdiction of Massachusetts.[1]

When Richard Hazen ran his line in 1741, he did not know precisely at what point to the westward to stop; for the boundary between New York and Massachusetts had not then been definitely settled, and the authority under which he acted ordered the line to be extended west "until it meets his Majesty's other governments." There had been, however, a general understanding ever since the Dutch "New Netherland" had been conquered by the English in 1664, that that Province extended twenty miles east of Hudson's River. Indeed, a futile attempt had been made by the very commissioners, who took possession of the Province in the name of King Charles the Second, to draw, on that understanding, the western boundary line of Connecticut. So far as Massachusetts was concerned, such a line would correspond pretty nearly with the summits of the Taconic Hills. Accordingly, Hazen carried his line westward over the top of this range, calling that part crossed by the line "Mount Belcher," from the name of the governor under whose commission he was surveying, and supposed that the ultimate New York boundary would run along those summits, but, for the sake of convenience, he continued the line "to Hudson's River, at about eighty poles from the place where Mohawk River comes into Hudson's River." [2]

Yet misunderstandings, as between New York and Massachusetts in relation to their boundary line, began early, and continued until 1773; some of the New York patroons claimed that their land-grants reached over into the valley of the Housatonic. A few Dutch pioneers had crept up the Hoosac from the westward, very near to the point where Hazen's line crosses that river. In 1739 the first committee from the government of Massachusetts, that came into this valley to survey it, complained in their report of "the great opposition we met with from sundry gentlemen from Albany," and the committee of the General Court to which this report was referred recommended "that the government of New York be informed by proper letters of the resolution of this Court herein, and that we are ready to join commissioners with such as shall be appointed by them for the stating and perambulating the bounds between each province." The same committee refer to "the better securing the undoubted right this government have to those and other lands thereabout," and also refer to the lands as those "whereon some few

[1] Original Surveys of Williamstown, as copied by Tutor Coffin in 1843; Williams' *Vermont*, p. 211; and Palfrey's *New England*, v. 4, p. 558.
[2] See Hazen's Journal of this Survey, first printed in 1879.

people have already got and inhabit"; again, in 1749 another committee " are further of opinion that a letter be sent from this government to the government of New York once more, to press them to join commissioners with such as shall be appointed by this Court for settling the boundaries between this government and that of New York"; but at length, in 1773, all these anxieties were quieted by a Board of Mutual Commissioners, who, with the governors of the two provinces, met at Hartford, Connecticut, and agreed on the line substantially as it now runs, although the line was not drawn and finally established till the summer of 1787, while the Federal Convention that framed our National Constitution was in session at Philadelphia, both parties in the meantime having appealed to the Congress of the Confederation to appoint commissioners for that purpose.

The persons thus appointed were John Ewing, David Rittenhouse, and Thomas Hutchins, all distinguished men, the first two citizens of Philadelphia, and the last, who did the work and made the report in the name of the three, was the first prominent American geographer. He had been assisted in the survey by Professor Samuel Williams of Harvard College, afterwards a citizen and the first historian of Vermont. The line as thus settled by national authority is a straight line north by east, and its length as stated in the report was "fifty miles, forty-one chains, and seventy-nine links." A small equilateral triangle of land at its extreme southwest corner has since been granted by the state of Massachusetts to the state of New York, but with this insignificant exception the boundary-line between them is still Hutchins' line of 1787. It so happened that this line did not coincide at all with the west line of Williamstown as laid out in 1749 by a committee of the General Court of Massachusetts, but ran 446 rods to the west of the southwest corner of the town as then laid out, and gradually approached the old line as it ran northwards, and crossed it about a mile and a half south of Hazen's line, which line it struck at last about half a mile east of the top of the Taconic Ridge. This point is now the northwest corner of the town of Williamstown, of the county of Berkshire, and of the state of Massachusetts. It is also the southwest corner of the state of Vermont; and it cuts into two very nearly equal parts the eastern line of the state of New York. It is marked at present by a small marble monument, which was probably set when the line was run in 1787. Its latitude is 42° 44', and its longitude 73° 13' west from Greenwich. Not far from 150 acres of the original town of Williamstown was in this way cut off from its northwest corner and thrown into New York, while a gore of land on the southwest of the old town was thrown into Massachusetts, and fifty years later (April 9, 1838) annexed to Williamstown. The present western line of the town, accordingly, is Hutchins' line for that distance, and is very nearly eight and one-fourth miles in length, and is in direction N. 20° 15′ E., keeping all the way pretty near to the highest points of the Taconic Range.[1]

The southern line of Williamstown, including, since 1838, the baseline of "the Gore," makes a straight course of very nearly six and three-fourths miles in length, and in direction a little south of east from the New York boundary to the western line of the present town of Adams. This course, bounding Hancock and New Ashford on the north, descends from the ridge of the Taconics, passes across the narrow valley of the Hancock Brook, runs over "Stratton Mountain" so-called (a huge wedge almost closing up the Williamstown valley on the south), so as to bring into the town the finely rounded northern face and summit of that mountain, next crosses the still narrower valley of the Ashford Brook, and then climbs up the steep side of Saddle Mountain, to strike the Adams line but little to the south of the peak of Greylock.

From this lofty point, the eastern boundary of the town, which is the only one of its four sides meeting with no change since Colonels Partridge and Choate and Captain Dwight traced the town's limits as a committee of the General Court in 1749, runs its course of about eight and one-fourth miles slightly to the east of north, at first high up along the western slope of Greylock, — about sixty rods from its highest summit, — and so along the western slopes of Mounts Fitch and Williams, all three of whose high heads are in what was the old township of East Hoosac, and then obliquely over the strong shoulder called "Wilbur's Pasture," which serves to unite Mount Williams with Mount Prospect, and then adown the gorge between these and diagonally across the valley of the Hoosac, — just cutting in twain the long woollen-mill in Blackinton,—and then climbing the slope of East Mountain to the north of the river, and passing along its western side more than half-way up to its summit, hits Hazen's line at last, and makes the northeast corner of the town.

Within these four lines are enclosed as nearly as may be forty-seven square miles, or 30,000 acres, of wonderfully varied surface.[2]

[1] Mass. Arch., v. 114, pp. 314, 315; Hildreth's U. S., v. 2, pp. 44, 572, v. 3, p. 531; Professor Dewey in Field's Berkshire, p. 9; Drake's Biog. Dict., arts. "Samuel Williams" and "Thomas Hutchins"; Rev. John Norton's Redeemed Captive; and Coffin's Map of Williamstown. In these matters of angles and distances, I have had the help of my mathematically gifted colleagues, Professor Safford and Professor Dodd.
[2] The exact mathematical direction of the southern and eastern town-lines cannot be given till another accurate survey be had; nor can the exact length of any of the

It is time now to try to convey to readers who have never seen the Williamstown valley, to those who have sometimes seen it but now live at a distance from it, and even to those who live within it but have not had the leisure or the taste to examine it in detail, clearer conceptions of its grand outlines and delightful features. Perhaps this may best be done by following out what the Germans call the "river-and-mountain-system" of the region. In its broader sense this valley lies enclosed between the Taconics on the west and the Hoosacs on the east, the tips of the two crests at this point are as nearly as possible twelve miles apart, the courses of the two mountain ranges are pretty nearly north and south, the valley is accordingly an east and west one, and the Hoosac River flows through it on its northern edge in that general direction. The north branch of the Hoosac, called by the Indians *Mayunsook*, washes the western slopes of the Hoosacs as they bound the valley at its northeast corner; and the south branch, named by the aborigines *Ashuwillticook*, flows northerly through a narrow valley of its own between the Hoosacs and Saddle Mountain, draining the adjacent sides of the two at the southeast corner of the valley; and then these two river-branches unite in the village of North Adams to form the *Hoosac*, along whose northern bank throughout the Williamstown valley, and so on to the Hudson, ran for one hundred years in the historical times ending in 1759 (and no one can tell for how much longer) the great eastern war-trail of the Six Nations from their homes on the Mohawk (and to the west of it) to the Deerfield and the Connecticut. The Canada Indians, also, in conjunction with their French allies, trod the same war-path to reach Fort Massachusetts and the valleys beyond the Hoosac Mountain.

The village of Williamstown is just west from that of North Adams, at five miles' distance, but the two are mostly out of sight of each other owing to an intervening ridge through which the Hoosac has forced its way to the westward, namely, the easternmost of the three lobes of Saddle Mountain, which is called the "Raven Rock," and which slopes gradually down to the south bank of the Hoosac,

four lines be given till then. Correction for the variation of the needle was made for the west line, — that is, exactly N. 20° 15′ E.; but corrections for variation were not made in the original survey of 1749, and the results for the three lines were stated then as follows : north line, " S. 82° E., 1583 rods "; east line, " S. 9° 50′ W., 2600 rods "; south line, " N. 80° 30′ W.; 2126 rods." To the length of this line 446 rods have since been added. As the measurement of the lots within the lines was originally understated, as a rule, so it is probable that lengths as then measured were understated also. The town-area given in the text must be very nearly right. See Field's *Berkshire*, pp. 9, 397. My fellow-townsmen, William Torrey and J. A. Eldridge, surveyors, have given me information on these points.

and is penetrated near the stream by the "Little Tunnel" of the railroad, while from the north bank there rises up at once a spur of the Green Mountains extending northerly into Vermont. To one looking due east from any part of the village of Williamstown or from the highlands to the westward of that clear to the top of the Taconics, the view is limited by a long and low arc of a circle, the southern tip of which is the summit of Mount Williams (the northern point of the central lobe of Saddle Mountain), and the northern tip of which is the summit of Smedley Height (the south end of the Green Mountain spur just referred to), and the centre of which is the tops of the Hoosacs. These tops, though some miles more distant than the slopes of the other two, form, to the eye of a · Williamstown observer, one bended line with them, and constitute the arc within which the sun rises throughout the year, and within which are the visible risings of the moon also. The grandest sight vouchsafed the dwellers on this part of the Hoosac is the sun of a cloudless morning rising in its strength in some part of this long arc, and the most beautiful sight is the full moon ascending the blue from some point within it. At the summer solstice the sun rises directly over the Smedley Height, and the point of dawn shifts daily to the southward, till at the winter solstice it is just over that part of the line made by the lower slope of Mount Williams. The writer's eastern piazza happens to front the middle part of this slightly concave line, and he has watched with delight, for many years, the annual passage of the sun back and forth between these extreme points, and also the corresponding movements of the moon; and this middle part happens to be just that point of the ridge of the Hoosacs under which passes the famous "Hoosac Tunnel."

The Hoosac River from the junction of its two branches flows nearly due west three-quarters of a mile, and then bending southerly has upon its right bank the spacious meadow on which Fort Massachusetts once stood, and then turning slowly to its westerly course again, through narrower meadows on either side, trends suddenly to the northward at about four miles' distance from the junction, and thence flows through meadows, growing for the most part broader in a general northwesterly direction, till at length it meets the Hudson. This sharp bend of the river at the southwestern foot of Smedley Height brings into view the Williamstown valley in its secondary sense as a valley extending north and south. Just after this bend is taken the Hoosac receives its largest tributary in this part of its course; namely, the so-called Green River, which is formed at South Williamstown village by the junction of the Ashford and

Hancock brooks, both of which enter Williamstown from the south, the first washing the eastern foot, and the second the western foot, of Stratton Mountain.

The head-springs of both these brooks are on the same watershed, and on the same parallel of latitude, about five miles apart, and about ten miles south of the point where the Green River strikes into the Hoosac. The Ashford Brook rises just near the town-line between New Ashford and Lanesboro, at an altitude 1300 feet above tide-water; and within a few rods of the spring is the swamp whose drainage forms the northernmost branch of the Housatonic River, whose course ends in Long Island Sound. The Hancock Brook rises on a swell of the Taconics, very near the state-line between Massachusetts and New York, and soon turning at right angles to the north, flows in that direction through a narrow but very fertile valley, to its junction with the other. On the same swell of the Taconics with the source of this brook, and only a short distance to the south of it, lies the source of the Kinderhook creek, which, flowing southerly through the Hancock valley and Stephentown, reaches the Hudson at Schodack. Five miles long is the Green River, and the point at which it pours into the Hoosac just above the railroad station is only about 585 feet above tide-water. A mile lower down the main river comes in another tributary from the southward, which is called Hemlock Brook; and it is these four streams together, with the lower reach of the Hoosac in the town, which form the "Williamstown valley" in its narrower sense; that is to say, the latitudinal valley lying wholly within the town limits, in contrast with the longitudinal valley of about the same length comprising the northern parts of both Williamstown and North Adams.

At the point where the old county road from Pittsfield to Bennington crosses the Hoosac at the Moody bridge, the river, which has kept an almost straight northwest line from the junction of the Green, flows due west till it. takes in the waters of the Hemlock, then curves pretty sharply for a due north course for a while, and then bends eastward till it touches the county road again just before both of them leave the town altogether. Thus the road between these two points subtends what is very nearly a semicircle of river, which encloses the "River Bend Farm," so-called, of which we shall hear more by and by, because it was a French and Indian station in the old French wars, and because it became the home of Colonel Benjamin Simonds for many years; the same arc encloses also six of the original Meadow Lots, three of the original Pine Lots, two of the original fifty-acre Lots, as these were early divided by and among the " proprietors "; and it encloses also the mouth of the Broad Brook, a very considerable tributary of the Hoosac coming into it on the east side at right-angles, whose two branches, uniting a little north of the town and state line at a place called the " Forks," drain a small section of southern Vermont. All the pine timber of the original town grew on or near the banks of the Broad Brook, the first saw-mill of the town was carried by its water, and its site enclosed within the semicircle, and some young pines are now growing up again on these lands divided in 1765 into sixty-three " pine lots" of three acres and sixty rods each. Just beyond the Vermont line the Hoosac receives also on the east side the water of Ware's or Rattlesnake Brook, a small stream that comes tumbling down the hillside. The bridge over this stream on the old county road, which is also here the old Indian trail, is the beginning of the " Dug Way" so-called, a very narrow road cut into the hill for a mile or so in Pownal right along the right brink of the Hoosac. The only other affluents of our river received in Williamstown of any account are two small brooks flowing down the north sides of Saddle Mountain and hitting the stream close together just after it enters the town from North Adams.

Of course the lowest point of land in Williamstown, since all the running water of the valleys and hillsides drains into the Hoosac, is the place where the river cuts the north line of the town into two equal parts and pours into Vermont. This point is about thirty-five feet lower than the river level at the Noble bridge near the railroad station. When they were running the north line of the state of Massachusetts, Richard Hazen and his helpers crossed the river at this point on Sunday, the 12th of April, 1741. " With difficulty we waded it and lodged on ye West side that night. It Clouded over before Night and rained sometime before day, which caused us to stretch Our blankets and lye under them on ye bare ground, which was the first bare ground we laid on after we left Northfield." This interesting lodging-place of the sturdy surveyor, who was a God-fearing man notwithstanding he continued his survey through the wilderness on Sunday, is on the broad and beautiful meadow once owned by John Bascom, and is within plain sight and a stone's throw of the " Line House" so-called on the public highway. Indeed, Hazen's line bisects both the house and the meadow. From the Hoosac at this lodging-place the old surveyor found it twenty-one miles and sixty rods to the Hudson River, — "at about Eighty poles from the place where Mohawk river comes into Hudson's river."

There is not a single lake or pond within the limits of Williams-town, and, consequently, except as dams have been thrown across the streams for purposes of utility or beauty, there is no expanse of water anywhere. This is the only fault that has ever been found with the region as one of picturesque beauty. Along the Hoosac and the lesser streams there is considerable alluvial land, much of which was originally cut into "meadow lots," and which is natur-ally very fertile land; of swampy or marshy land there is very little in the town, although the mosses and ferns, which are pretty sure signs of a soil too wet and cold to be productive, are not wanting in the hill pastures and poorer meadows; upland of a moderate height above the streams, and easily tilled and fairly productive, constitutes by much the larger part of the surface; and a good deal of the rest is pretty steep and sometimes pretty stony hillsides. There is almost no land in the whole circuit that will not bear forest trees, and forest trees in their due proportion are as profitable a crop as can be raised. There are perhaps 2500 acres of ground which has once been cleared and tilled, which would have been, and would be now, more productive in forest than as ploughed or pastured, and some of this is being allowed to grow up again to trees, although systematic tree-planting to any considerable extent in fields has never yet been practised here, as surely it might profitably be done. When first explored and surveyed, the town was splendidly wooded in every part, of which the evidence is the direct testimony of the surveyors and early settlers, and also the early division among the householders of the "pine lots" and the "oak lots." Of more than one of the early land-buyers and home-seekers trustworthy tradition reports that he came in "and went to chopping."

The curve of the Hoosac that we have been following from its entrance on the east to its exit on the north, cuts off from the rest of the town its remarkably picturesque northeast corner, which con-tains about one-ninth of its entire area, and which has had a history and development somewhat distinct from that of the rest of it. We are concerned at present only with the physical features of this iso-lated part. From the first settlement of the town it has borne the designation of the "White Oaks," and it is almost certain now to carry this name onwards till the end of time. All the original "oak lots" were within this curve; of white oak timber in the other parts of the town there was little or none; and when, in 1866, the unique and self-denying labors of Professor Hopkins had estab-lished a church on the Broad Brook, he christened it the "Church of Christ in White Oaks." This organization shows no signs of

decay, the memory of the great and good man who breathed it into
form gives no sign of getting dim, and the name that had been
attached to the locality for a century has now accordingly been fastened to it by a new tie of gratitude and religion.   The lands of this
section consist of the pretty broad and very fertile bottoms along
the right bank of the Hoosac, and some intervale along both banks
of the lower Broad Brook; of about a thousand acres of tolerably
level upland, mostly on what is called Oak Hill; and for the rest, of
the rather steep slopes of that spur of the Green Mountains which
has already been referred to.   This spur is very irregular in shape,
and, with its connecting mountains further north, forms a striking

"EAST MOUNTAIN."

I. Mount Hazen.   2. Hudson's Height.   3. Mount Emmons.   4 Smedley Height.

feature in the landscape of southwestern Vermont; but the part of
it with which we shall have most to do, which is commonly called
as a whole "East Mountain," in relation to the village and the
College, and which rises up sharply from the north bank of the
Hoosac as it enters the town into a noble ridge (running north) on
the average about 1600 feet above the stream, has none of its four
summits in Williamstown, and only about two-thirds of its western
slopes.
   Of these four summits, which are tolerably distinct from each other
as seen from the westward, the northernmost and highest, which
has been appropriately named "Mount Hazen" in honor of the
old surveyor of 1741, who ran his line over this ridge and just at the
foot of this rise, rests wholly in Vermont, and curves to the west
from the general direction of the ridge as if to do obeisance to

the majestic "Dome," and slopes down rapidly northwards to the "Forks" already mentioned. This peak of Mount Hazen, which closes up the view from our village to the northeast, is 2500 feet above sea by careful estimation from the known heights of neighboring peaks. "Hazen's Rock," an immense boulder first noticed and named and marked by the writer and his eldest son, stands about nine rods north of the "line" and about three rods west of the crest of the ridge; and it is possible, if not probable, that Hazen stood upon this rock when he saw what he describes in his "Journal" under April 12, 1741. The next swell to the south of this, and perhaps 250 feet lower, has been well called "Hudson's Height" in memory of Captain Seth Hudson, the last survivor of the original proprietors of Williamstown and of the officers, and probably also of the soldiers, of Fort Massachusetts. He was at one time, as we shall see by and by, the surgeon, and at another the commander, of Fort Massachusetts in its decline. The third summit is a beautifully rounded one, free from trees and other obstructions to the view, 2276 feet above the sea-level, and the only place in the region where the primeval gneiss rock comes to the surface, while there are huge boulders scattered over the entire ridge, from several of which, and especially from Hazen's Rock, almost the entire lines of the town and nearly its whole area can be seen at one view. Into the solid rock on this third height was sunk, many years ago, for scientific purposes, a copper bolt, and the height itself has been justly designated "Mount Emmons" by one who was once a pupil and later a colleague and always an admirer of the distinguished Professor of Natural History in the College, Ebenezer Emmons. He was the author and founder of what he named the "Taconic System" in geology, which became famous in the annals of that science, and he used often to take his students to this local point of advantage to show them the gneiss — the foundation rock of his science — and to display to them as best he could the relations of his "system" to the other and then better known geological strata. The south peak of this ridge of East Mountain has already been spoken of as "Smedley Height," so named in honor of that family which first cleared up the acres at its foot, and owned the oak lots stretching up towards its summit, and cultivates to this day, by some of its descendants, a part of these ancestral fields. Smedley Height is 1917 feet above tide-water according to hypsometric measurements made by John Tatlock, then a student in the College, in 1881.

The present view in summer-time from any one of these four summits, of which the three last named are in the town of Clarksburg, is such as to well reward the zeal and sweat of the climber. Cultivated farms fill up the valley and the lower uplands for the most part, green pastures with patches of second-growth forest occupy the mountain slopes, the Hoosac and its main tributaries glance and glimmer in the sunlight, the scalloped crests of the Taconics, deeply dented at four points for the passes over them, and covered mostly with forest trees, bound the view to the westward, while the three lobes of Saddle Mountain with its spurs and the finely rounded front of Stratton Mountain, with a brook at either foot, limit the southern view. Even Richard Hazen was struck with admiration, cold-blooded mathematician though he were, and unopened yet by axe or fire as were the primeval forests of the valleys and the hillsides, when he and his men came upon this ridge in the early springtime. "At the End of three miles we Came upon the top of an Exceeding High Mountain [East Mountain], from whence we discovered a large Mountain which lyes Southwesterly of Albany [the Catskills], as also a Row of large mountains on Each side of us bearing North and South nearest [Saddle Mountain and Green Mountains] and a Ridge of exceeding high Mountains three or four miles before us bearing the same Course [the Taconics] and a fine valley betwixt them and us on Each side of the line [Hazen's line] big enough for Townships [Hoosac valley]."

This ridge of East Mountain, to one or all of the rounded points of which it is much to be hoped that a carriage road from the valley will sometime be laid, since by utilizing existing roads this may be done without too great difficulty, bounds the White Oaks region on the east; and it is bounded on the north by the lower slopes of the "Dome," the largest and finest mountain that is in plain view from the valley. Greylock is not visible to the dwellers on the Hoosac and Green rivers and Hemlock Brook, nor from either of the villages of Williamstown, owing to the height of Mount Prospect and Bald Mountain, which together form the western lobe of Saddle Mountain; while the Dome rises gradually up in silent and solemn majesty from the brink of Broad Brook to a height of at least 3000 feet above the tides of the sea, and is visible from every quarter of the town, and is, perhaps, the most striking feature of its landscape, which it limits on the north. The name was most appropriately given to it by Professor Hopkins, from its form. The most of it's mighty mass is in Vermont, and it has companion piles to the north and east of ·it, particularly in the "Haystack," which seems to overtop it, while itself falls gracefully down on the south and west in fertile swells and charming fields to the brook and to the river. Half-way down towards the west a little knob, called the "Domelet," protrudes its head, as if to exhibit by way of contrast the gigantic proportions of the other; and still farther down in the same direction a wholly cleared and very fertile swell of land, named "Mason's Hill," carries the gladdened eye clear down to the Hoosac.

On the southern foot of the Dome, at a few yards above Broad Brook and drawing into it, gushes up out of the sand, from a clear bottom, a copious thermal spring, which has been called the "Sand Spring" from the beginning of the town. Its water has a mean temperature throughout the year of 71°, and is not only warm, but soft also, owing to the absence of limestone in that locality. This spring has something of a history, and we shall hear more about it

I. The Dome.   2. The Domelet.

by and by. There is only one other thermal spring within the town boundaries, and that is on the other side of the Hoosac, about a mile west of this one and on the same parallel, though its mean temperature is something like 10° lower than the Sand Spring. Professor Bascom, who once owned this smaller spring and the meadow through which its water finds a short way to the Hoosac, believed that its average temperature for the year was not less than 64°. In comparison with these thermal springs, Professor Hopkins found the mean temperature of the water of his well, and presumably of other ordinary springs and wells in the town, to be 47°, which he also found to be the mean temperature of the air above his well, as a result of personal observations made three times a day throughout an entire year.

Before leaving the "White Oaks" for good in this cursory description of its physical features, we must just note the historical fact

that its main road, following in general the course of the river on
its north side, which we shall call the "Hoosac Road," since it has
been so named certainly from the time when the captives of Fort
Massachusetts passed over it in 1746, is a part of the old Mohawk
war-path, by which the Five Nations and the Canada Indians (as
well) passed to their raids and battles on the Deerfield and the Connecticut. We must also note the fact that nearly all of the sandy
land in the town is found in this locality. Pines like the sand, and
while the oaks and other deciduous trees clung to the sides of East
Mountain to its very crest, the sandy levels on Oak Hill, and patches
here and there partly on Broad Brook and partly on the Hoosac,
grew up originally to lofty pines. A special road was very early
laid out, branching off from the road up Broad Brook, which itself
left the Hoosac Road at right angles, "to convean the pine lots."
This road ran up northeasterly almost to Hazen's line, and stopped
on the last range of pine lots which butted on that line. Memorials
of these old pines appear at the present day in the beautiful grove
in front of the Sand Spring Hotel, in the fine grove of young pines
opened up in 1883 as a pleasure resort by John M. Cole, near the
railroad station, and called the "Garden of Eden," and in clusters of
small pines scattered over almost the whole of the old pine area.
Back from the river land has always been cheap in the White Oaks,
partly because it is poor land, and partly because it has always had
a poor population; but a sort of half-weird and half-Hebrew glory
was thrown over the whole region by the labors, and especially by the
recreations, of Professor Hopkins, who named, for example, his own
farm on Broad Brook "Steepacres," the pine level of Oak Hill the
"land of Goshen," and a huge rock a little to the east of the summit
of the Dome "White Face"; and whose inexhaustible humor entertained almost without end the young ladies of his "Alpine Club,"
as well as any casual fellow-walker (reverend or gay) over his favorite tramping-grounds, with quaint names and odd Scripture allusions
and bits of old superstition. The very stones of Broad Brook assumed,
through his imagination, strange shapes and took on queer names
and preached grotesque sermons, and the flora of the hills became
redolent of far-off lands, and even the maples of the spring-time
reminded him of the cedars of Lebanon which were "full of sap."

Now if we cross over the Hoosac on Hazen's line, and tarry just
long enough on the meadow where that worthy "slept on ye bare
ground" to christen it in passing, and yet in permanence the
"Bascom Meadow," since John Bascom, long a citizen of Williamstown and a successful teacher in the College and always deeply

interested in the history and prosperity of both, once owned the meadow for many years; and if we climb up the steep ascent abutting on the meadow, we shall shortly find ourselves on the crest of North West Hill, one of the four foot-hills of the Taconic Range in this town, lying in a line north and south on the western side of the valley. North West Hill has greatly declined in its importance. from the early time, and would hardly delay us at present for much description, were it not that it became then very populous, that the principal road to Bennington ran along its crest, and that the land and woods upon it and upon the shallow-dish valley that connects it with the much higher parent ridge, and upon that parent ridge itself drew out again the admiration of our "noted and ingenious surveyor of land" (*Boston Gazette*, February 19, 1754). Richard Hazen wrote in his "Journal," April 13, 1741, "This Mountain was Exceeding good Land, bearing beech, Black birch, and Hemlock, some Bass wood. Over this Mountain we concluded the line would run betwixt New York Government and these whenever it should be settled, and therefore nam^d it Mount Belcher that it might be as Standing a Boundary as Endicutt's Tree." About in the centre of this broadly dish-shaped valley a small brook rises in some bits of springy and swampy land, which holds its semicircular course of about two miles through deep glens for the most part, and then falls into the Hemlock Brook, just before the latter drops silently into the Hoosac. This little brook is well called the "Ford Brook" in memory of good old deacon Zadock Ford, the edge of whose farm was washed by it; and the deepest and darkest stretch of glen through which the brook bickers along is called "Ford's Glen." This brook completely bounds North West Hill on the south. The North West Hill Road, which starts at right angles from the west end of the Main Street and skirts along the last house lot of the northern tier, soon crosses Ford Brook and begins to climb the hill. The hill is a short two miles long in Williamstown, and then falls abruptly off to the Hoosac in Pownal. The original road ran pretty straight over the hill lengthwise, generally a little to the west of its highest crest, but the northern half of it has been discontinued for travel for many years, on account of its steepness and liability to wash out, and the branch road, which turned off to the west to reach the farms on the flat, and then bent north parallel to the old road to strike the Hoosac by a shorter and somewhat less precipitous descent (though still steep) is now the only road. There are eight of the original 100-acre lots, and three of the fifty-acre lots of the first division, on this hill proper; and from time to time several poor families have pushed quite over the broad level upon the sixty-acre lots on the final slope of the Taconics.

Before Hazen's line makes its final mount to cross the Taconics it runs up into a hollow of the mountain side, which goes by the name of the "Moon Hollow," from the name of a poor family that lived within it for three-quarters of a century or more. Here corner two states flanked by a third. The New York line that Hazen supposed would run along the crest of "Mount Belcher," as he himself named the swell of the Taconics at this point, as a matter of fact came further east in 1787, and runs across this hollow, so that the Moon house (now occupied by a man named Haley) and a part of the little farm are in the state of New York. A small marble monument marks the corners of Vermont and Massachusetts; and one of the long-legged Moons once slept in summer-time astraddle of this stone, and afterwards boasted that he had lodged in three states the same night. This monument has been thrown out of plumb by the roots of a tree underneath which it stands, and has otherwise a rather forlorn appearance; but it has served its rude purpose for a century, and deserves perhaps this passing notice of one who has often mused upon the spot. There is nothing special to distinguish Mount Belcher from the rest of the noble ridge of which it forms a part, although the resuscitation of the name after 140 years of inanition in the "Journal" of Richard Hazen brings worthily to memory again a remarkable man of the last century, Jonathan Belcher, an American-born colonial governor of three states, and the real founder of the College of New Jersey at Princeton.

The second of the foot-hills of the Taconics in order southward has been called "Buxton" from immemorial time, probably from Buxton in England, though what the tie of connection be (if any) has not been ascertained. Buxton is a much lower and smaller hill than the other three, and differs from them also in having been completely cleared in every part from forest trees. North West Hill is about 600 feet in its highest parts above the Hoosac at its base: Buxton is in no part over 300 feet above the two brooks which almost completely encircle it. It has the Ford Brook on the north, and the Buxton Brook on the west and south. Buxton Brook, a beautiful stream in its whole course of three miles, rises in the very northwest corner of the town in two branches, the springs of both being just under the New York line, one of them in the Moon Hollow, and the other in a gorge a little to the south of it; and these small branches unite only a few rods south of the springy hollows in which Ford Brook takes its rise, and then flow on a considerable stream flanking the Buxton farms, receiving a small tributary called "Birch Hill Brook" on the southern side, and then striking the northern tier of House Lots at the west end of the Main Street divides them into two nearly equal portions till in House Lot number 10 it empties into the larger "Hemlock Brook," which latter now hurries out of the House Lots to its junction with the Hoosac. A little above the junction of the Buxton with the Hemlock, there is, in the former, a shaded pool, which has long gone by the name of "Diana's Bath," a designation so far as this inappropriate, that the pool is quite too small and shallow to correspond with the person of that goddess as she is usually represented in Greek and Roman art. No part of the original House Lots should be considered as in Buxton, although a considerable part has long been popularly so reckoned: only that is Buxton proper, which lies west of the northern range of House Lots and within the two brooks so often already mentioned.

In the angle between Buxton Brook and its small tributary, Birch Hill Brook, there lies one of the oldest farms in Williamstown, commonly called the "Red House Farm," owned since 1782 for a century by the Sherman family, and owned before that by Joel Baldwin. This farm runs back towards the west into a conical hill, which has been repeatedly ploughed to its very top, though apparently never seeded down, and which has upon its summit about a quarter of an acre of level ground, whence may be had in all directions one of the finest views in Williamstown. Perhaps we may properly call this hill "Joel's Sentry," for it overlooks and is a part of Joel Baldwin's original farm, and it overlooks also every part of his later farm adjoining on North West Hill, on which he died in 1808. The Red House Farm is not a part of Buxton, nor is it strictly a part of Birch Hill; it lies west of the one and north of the other; Joel's Sentry is not itself of sufficient size to be enumerated as a separate foot-hill of the Taconics, and it slopes down sharply to the west into a shallow valley separating it from them. This valley runs north, under and parallel with the Taconics, quite up to North West Hill. Through the entire length of this narrow valley there ran a private way in old times from the Petersburg Road at Donahue's to the North West Hill Road not far from Baldwin's. In this valley once lived the Fowler family, and later the Welch family intermarried with that, and still later Russell Pratt and others. There are no dwellers in that valley now, though the Fowler house and a barn or two are still standing within it. There are also one or two deserted houses on the upper stretch of Buxton Brook not far off. By means of this "Fowler Vale" accordingly, and especially by the common shoulder of the Taconics in which all the brooks here take their rise, North West Hill and Buxton and "Joel's Sentry" farm are closely connected together, and are separated from the hills to the southward by Birch Hill Brook and by a still higher shoulder of the Taconic range.

This strong shoulder is common to the two remaining hills on the western side of the Williamstown valley, namely, "Birch Hill" and "Bee Hill," the former named from its prevailing forest tree (prevailing now also, as well as a century ago), and the latter undoubtedly from the abundance of wild honey found upon it by the early settlers. This shoulder strikes out southeastwardly from the general trend of the Taconics, and becomes the means of reaching readily from this side the first practicable pass over them into the state of New York. We have seen that Surveyor Hazen honored his official superior, the governor of Massachusetts and New Hampshire, by naming the northern reach of the mountain-chain over which his own chain ran "Mount Belcher," but that reach is all the way abrupt, and gives no chance for a road over it; while this connecting shoulder unites the mountain at a point where itself is considerably depressed with two comparatively high foot-hills, which may be gradually ascended, and so a relatively easy passage be found over the mountain by what may best be called the "Petersburg Pass," from the name of the New York town on the other side. What we have called the Petersburg Road is the continuation of the main street of the village at its west end, where the North West Hill Road leaves it at right angles, and runs almost due west for about a mile, at first up the Buxton Brook, and then from its junction with that up the Birch Hill Brook to Donahue's in the old 100-acre lot number 63. Both of the small branches of this brook rise in that lot or just over its outer lines and unite within it, so that the brook and the road that flanks it are the northern boundary of Birch Hill. In common speech the "Red House" and the Donahue house have always been reckoned as on Birch Hill, and so they may be well enough considered, for they are on the road that follows up the brook which itself is the natural boundary between the hills. At Donahue's the road turns south at a right angle and runs straight for more than half a mile, to strike the shoulder on which to find a means of exit at the Petersburg Pass. Just at the point at which the road turns northwest again to pursue its gradual climb towards the Pass, namely, on the old sixty-acre lot number 54, which is commonly called the "Prindle Place," there is a junction of the road at the corner with a narrow and pretty steep valley running due east, through all the lower part of which glides the "Glen Brook" so-called, which falls into the Hemlock Brook only a few rods south of the southwestern quarter of the House Lots. This valley and brook, up which a broken road once ran, was always called in old-fashioned times the "Gully," but is now more euphoniously and appropriately denomi-nated the "Glen," and is for our present purpose the picturesque border line between Birch and Bee hills.

Before describing the latter we will follow our Petersburg Road to the Pass. For a mile or more now the road runs strongly north-west, just under the ridge of the shoulder, for the Pass is exactly due west of Donahue's, and the road direct from his house takes the traveller much to the south for the sake of an easier and more uniform climb, and this space must be regained by a northerly trend, which brings one at length on a level with the Pass and oppo-site to it about a half-mile off. There is at first, with a sharp turn to the west, a slight descent from this final point of the shoulder, and then a little further ascent brings the traveller or scene-hunter directly upon the main Taconic in the well-rounded Petersburg Pass. This is a natural depression (shaped just like a saddle) below the general height of the main ridge in this part of it of perhaps 150 feet; the centre of it is 2075 feet above the sea-level, the top of "Leet Hill" directly to the south of it is 459 feet higher, the gap is entirely free from trees on both its approaches, so that sight is unobstructed for-wards and backwards; the land on both its rising flanks was long ago cleared, and has been often ploughed; the winds that sweep through it are such that a new forest growth will but slowly recover its hold on the soil; and the view that one gains from the centre of it towards the west is such as baffles all description. Tumbled hills just below in the valley of the "Little Hoosac"; innumerable farms on and be-tween these hills; roads like white ribbands leading through the valleys; higher ridges, broken and beautiful, filling the breadth be-tween these and the valley of the Hudson; apparently rising grounds beyond that river, both fertile and wooded, lying "green and still," and stretching as far as the eye can reach; the dim outline of the Catskills to the southwest beyond Albany; and far to the northward the dark evergreen peaks of the Adirondacks mingling with the sky, — are elements in a view never to be forgotten by those who have seen it even once under favorable conditions. The writer, who has seen it perhaps twenty times in all seasons, was gazing on it in company

with a dear friend, July 26, 1879, when vast masses of white mist
were seen gathering in the valley below, which rose slowly up the
sides of the mountain and soon completely cut off all vision to the
westward, and which, rising higher and higher, borne by the usual
sweep of the winds up and over the Pass, wholly encircled and
covered the observers, bringing to them with a damp and chill a
sense of aerial unsteadiness and a sort of wonderment not un-
mingled with awe.

Buckwheat and other grains were growing that day (though
small) just over the western brow of the Pass, and the scene to the
west shows more fertile land than that to the eastward; but our concern at present is more with Massachusetts than with New York, and
more with Williamstown than with Petersburg, a pleasant village
in the valley of the "Little Hoosac," which gives its name to the
Pass, and down into which the Pass road winds at first abruptly and
then more gently between swelling hillocks and fertile farms on
either side. The resemblance of this great gap in the Taconics to
a saddle may be carried out even into details; for there rises up on
the north immediately from the road a regular knob 100 feet high
which may well be regarded as the pommel, and on the south a
gentler, higher, more rounded arc, which well serves the fancy as
the cantel. This imaginary cantel is the actual northern face of
Leet Hill, a symmetrical swell of the Taconics at this point, 2534
feet above the level of the ocean, at whose southeastern foot is a
mountain farm that was occupied uninterruptedly for more than a
century by four generations in succession of one family bearing that
name. The farm was sold out of the family in the spring of 1885.
Of "poor old Jared Leet," who cleared up this farm on the hillside,
singing rude songs of his own to while away his toil, specimens of
which may enliven a future page, a grandson of Governor William
Leet of Connecticut, who befriended the regicides in their direst
need, we shall know more in the sequel.

The scene to the eastward from the summit of the gap, from the
pommel above it, or from a point in the road about a quarter of a
mile below it, is essentially the same in all its grand features,
and is perhaps the noblest view anywhere to be seen in this region:
Treadwell Hollow widens out before the eye like a huge boat, and
the broad lands between the two villages of Williamstown seem at
that altitude like levels, and the eye is carried forward in a straight
line into the Hopper and up the sides of Prospect and Bald
mountains till old Greylock itself satisfies while it limits the vision.
It cannot be less than seven miles from the Pass to the summit of

Greylock; and it seems most like standing on the stern of an enormous steamer, whose sides swell out at the centre to contract again
in the distance, and whose prow is pressed up into a gigantic peak
bearing streamers!

When David Dudley Field, the distinguished legist and publicist,
was seventy-five years of age, he drove to this Pass in company with
his classmate of 1826, Rev. Dr. Durfee, his son-in-law, Sir Anthony
Musgrave, then British governor of Jamaica, and one of the professors of the College. Although a graduate, and a frequent visitor
to Williamstown all his life, he had never before climbed to any
pass of the Taconics. He took in the majestic scene right and left,
but said little; and then proposed to the Professor that they clamber
on foot to the top of the pommel. Straight as an arrow, six feet
and one quarter in height, showing few signs of age, he reached the
top with scarcely quickened breath. Though born and reared in
New England, and Massachusetts was then his summer home, his
companion observed that his quick glances towards the Hoosacs
returned to linger fondly on the Adirondacks and the Catskills and
the regions between and beyond them, and down towards the city
where his more than fifty years of successful legal life had been
passed; and, with the single expression on his lips, "It is the Empire
State!" he returned to his carriage.

The stretch of the Taconics to the north of the pommel as far as
Hazen's line and beyond it, may well be included in the general
designation of Mount Belcher, for the reason already indicated;
there is, indeed, much that is distinctive and more that is beautiful
in this part of the range, in the way of swell and fall and curve, till
the range itself sinks gradually down to the intervale level at the
junction of the Little Hoosac with the Hoosac at North Petersburg;
and a carriage road might run without any great difficulty along or
near the summit of the range from the Pass itself to this junction,
following in general the path by which students and others have
long frequented the "Snow-Hole," so-called, a rocky gorge on the
eastern slope not far from the corner of the states, in which snow is
usually found in August and sometimes in September. In the very
Pass itself is the point where the New York line of 1787 bisected
the original west line of Williamstown drawn in 1749. South of
that point is the acute angle of the "Gore" broadening to its base
of 446 rods of the present south line of the town, and north of it is
the small triangle already described as cut off from Williamstown
by the line of 1787, and thrown into the state of New York.

We must now give a moment's attention to the etymology of the

Indian name, by which is designated this fine range of hills that forms the western wall of the entire county of Berkshire, just fifty miles in length, as well as of its northwesternmost town just a little over eight miles in length. To the euphonious form "Taconics" have we finally curtailed and softened down the aboriginal word full of consonants. The archives of Massachusetts give about forty different spellings to this original Mohegan word; nevertheless its derivation and signification are reasonably certain, according to J. Hammond Trumbull of Hartford, the only trustworthy authority in this century for the Mohegan dialects. He says: "There is no interpretation which I can affirm is certainly right: the least objectionable is 'forest' or 'wilderness,' the Delaware *Tachanizen*, which Zeisberger translates as 'woody,' 'full of woods,' from *Tokone*, 'the woods,' literally 'wild land,' 'forest.' A sketch of Shekomeko (Dutchess County, New York) by a Moravian missionary in 1745, shows to the eastward in the distance a mountain summit, recognizable as the Mount Washington group, marked '*K'takanatshan*,' 'the big mountain,' a name which resolves itself into *Ket-Takone-Wadshu*, 'great woody mountain,' that is, great Taconic mountain."

So far as these great wooded hills flank the town of Williamstown, they are about 1500 feet above the level of the streams that skirt their base, and there are but four passes leading over them into the valleys beyond; the range, however, is not by any means a sheer wall on either side, but has its spurs and spines and hollows on its flanks, and peaks and gaps and plateaus on its top. As seen from the valleys, its horizon line is wonderfully varied, curved, and billowy; as a general thing it is clothed to the very tops with deciduous trees, particularly birch, beech, maple, and chestnut; and the tints of the spring and autumn foliage on these aspiring, swelling, indefinitely varied summits, invite inspection by so much the more as they certainly do beggar description.

Down such a water-shed as this is many streams will flow as a matter of course, and if there be passes over it and roads over them, these will naturally follow up the courses of the streams, — the human road-makers finding that Nature has been before them working out in long ages a path for the footsteps of men. Such a stream is the northerly branch of Hemlock Brook, which takes its rise just over the Massachusetts line, and just south of our Petersburg Pass, and flows down the whole length of Treadwell Hollow to unite at Brookman's with the southerly branch that rises also just over the New York line at the "Berlin Pass," the second of our natural roadways over the great Taconic wall. Now, as by much the longest

stretch of stream under a single designation within the town; as
constituted by these two branches, which descend respectively from
these two northern passes, over which all the direct travel from
Williamstown goes into the state of New York; as helping by
means of these branches, both of which rise in that great state, to
make easy friendly intercourse between the two states, by making
passable the lofty barrier that divides them; and as having many
secrets of the hills and of the woods to whisper to its companion
stream, Buxton Brook, at their junction in the northwestern quarter
of the House Lots, — the Hemlock Brook, though small, is lifted
into the region of high respectability. After the junction of its two
branches at the foot of Treadwell Hollow, the stream runs southeastwardly for a mile or more around the "Torrey Woods," and then
bends suddenly northward, receiving at this point, as a tributary, the
"Sweet Brook," which comes down from the "Kidder Pass," the
third of the Taconic gaps, and then flowing due north a couple of
miles through the valley of the "Hemlocks," unites with the bickering "Buxton" for another mile of curving flow to find the Hoosac,
having described a nearly perfect semicircle in a course of six miles.
Thus in a few plain lines has honor due been done to a country
brook, which probably was never sung in poetry, or described before
in prose.

Treadwell Hollow, down which tumbles, from the Pass, the northern branch of Hemlock Brook, and up which runs a second rude
and steep roadway to the Pass itself, swarmed with people at the
end of the last century and at the beginning of this, constituting
then a large school district with a schoolhouse of its own; but after
1850 it became gradually deserted of human habitations, and the
last one of the old houses within the valley burned down March 4,
1885, — the inauguration day of President Cleveland. This was
the house of Agur Treadwell, who gave his name to the Hollow,
and who reared there a large family of daughters, many of whose
descendants "are with us unto this day." Abandoned sites of log-
huts or cellars of rude houses may still be traced in considerable
numbers on both sides of the road almost up to the Gap, while the
people and their dwellings for the most part disappeared long ago.
At the time the Treadwell house burned down there were left but
three dwellings within the valley, and these comparatively modern
ones. The Leet house was one, just then sold out of the family
with the farm, which was the original sixty-acre lot number 40, the
house standing some distance to the west of the road and the
stream over a rise of ground; the Brookman family kept watch and

ward at the entrance of the Hollow from below, cultivating a quite tolerable hillside farm, and illustrating the outward success that almost always keeps step with the forthputting of the moral and Christian virtues; and between these two, on the opposite side of the road, was one other little homestead, then occupied by an Irishman named Fleming.

Now we come to the fourth and last of our secondary hills that hang on the flank of the Taconics, namely, to "Bee Hill," which has played first and last no insignificant part in the history of Williamstown. All four of these hills are really attached to the main stem by a single shoulder, that one by which the Petersburg road winds up into the Pass. The Glen Brook, which, in its due easterly fall, drains some low and moist lands that slope down from that shoulder, divides Birch Hill from Bee Hill; and the Hemlock Brook, springing from near the same shoulder, runs completely around the base of Bee Hill on its western and southern and eastern sides to the point at which the Hemlock receives the Glen. Bee Hill is shaped like an old-fashioned sugar-loaf of gigantic size lying on its side, base towards the southeast. Its western slope rises up sheer and lofty from the bottom of Treadwell Hollow; its southern side is the Torrey Woods skirting the brook lower down, and its eastern acclivity is the "Hemlocks," in which lie the limestone quarries.

The original road over Bee Hill started from the Main Street at right angles near its western end, and ran due south along the limit of House Lot number 29 to the bridge over the Glen Brook, whose place has never been substantially changed from its first building, and then crawled over the sugar-loaf just as and where it does now, in the form of a bow, to the entrance of Treadwell Hollow. The first part of this road as far as the Glen Bridge was long ago discontinued, and was replaced by the hypothenuse of the right-angled triangle beginning at the Mansion House and running diagonally across the House Lots to John Sherman's, and thence to the bridge. This comparatively new road to the Glen Bridge from the Main Street may well be called the "Glen Road." Though a belt of limestone edges the eastern base of Bee Hill, the hill as a whole is a slaty formation, and holds accordingly much warm and fertile land, that is easily tilled and constantly renewed; and on this account it was occupied early by a set of enterprising farmers, and in particular by the Hickox family, who have owned and tilled first and last most of the arable land of the hill, so that it is every way appropriate that its highest eminence, directly overlooking Treadwell Hollow, and conspicuously seen from every part of the village by those looking up through the Glen, should be now christened and hereafter known as " Hickox Height." That sightly point was long owned by the family, and if an enterprise had prospered which they conceived and set on foot and partly carried out, they would have deserved still more a lasting memorial on Bee Hill, — one as lasting as the hills themselves; for at the time when their neighbors of Birch Hill and others were pushing the present Petersburg road towards the Pass, the Bee Hill people stoutly claimed that a nearer and better road to the same place could be wound around their hill upon the east side of Treadwell Hollow; and so they set to work with a will to make such a way, and to get it through to the common shoulder first; and one can trace to this day about half-way up the slope the track of their road, unfinished because one of the rude land-owners beyond them forbade the use of his land for that purpose. The consequent delay gave the Birch Hill fellows the victory in point of time, which was virtually the point of victory in the whole matter. Agur Treadwell permitted them to cross his lot, but Amos Birchard put up the bars. At Birchard's boundary, accordingly, all traces of that road begun fade out upon the hillside. Henry Hickox, then an octogenarian, related these facts to the writer many years ago, and added that he himself had rendered a small boy's help to this worthy but futile endeavor of the family.

The Bee Hill road, already described as reaching to the entrance of Treadwell Hollow, became in 1799 a part of a public Turnpike, connected in North Adams with another Turnpike chartered by the state two years before to run over the Hoosac Mountain to the Deerfield River, making one continuous road; so that it became necessary at that time to repair and in some parts to rebuild an old road running up the south branch of the Hemlock Brook from the point where it unites with the Treadwell Hollow Brook to the second of the great passes over the Taconics; namely, to the " Berlin Pass," long so-called from the name of the New York township on the other side of the barrier. Under Massachusetts authority, accordingly, the turnpike was completed to the line of New York, and was then carried forward under the auspices of that state up to and over the Gap and down into the valley of the Little Hoosac, and the toll-gate was located at a house only a few rods this side the line on the " Gore," which was then indeed a part of Massachusetts, and forty years later was annexed to Williamstown. This last stretch of the old turnpike from the forks of the brook, which we always call the " Berlin Road," though it is continuous with the Bee Hill road, and also with the " Hemlock Road " from John Sher-

man's up Hemlock Brook to the forks, runs almost due west and
pretty steadily up hill past three farms, each of which has an interesting history, for one mile and a half in Massachusetts and fully
another mile in New York to the Berlin Pass.

On the right hand as one trudges up this road there rises a lofty
conical hill, beautiful in outline, around whose base the road winds
from the point where the New York line is crossed to the spring of
water at the foot of the last ascent leading up to the Pass. This
almost mathematically symmetrical hill as seen from a distance is
in fair continuation of the much larger Leet Hill, the two together
filling up the whole space between the two passes, with the Leet

"BERLIN PASS."

1. Mount Hopkins.   2. Dodd's Cone.   3. Leet Hill.

farm nestling between the two hills. Among all the varied summits
of the Taconics in this part of their range this particular cone is
unique; and it has been known for some time to a narrow circle of
friends, and the present writer strongly desires that it may be known
for all time in the widest manner, as "Dodd's Cone"; in perpetual
recognition of Cyrus Morris Dodd of the class of 1855, long Professor of Mathematics in the College, a man of exact knowledge, elegant taste, perfect temper, Christian patience, thorough kindness of
heart, and a genuine courtesy of mien consequent upon that. As a
long-time colleague watching his fidelity to duty, as a trustful friend
seeing him victor in recurring adversities, the writer pays with
heartfelt pleasure this little tribute which may perhaps be remembered when both are dead.

There have been times when a tin cup might be seen hanging to
a stake set by public authority or private benevolence near the little

spring that bubbles up at the base of the last lift before the Pass is reached. Foot-travellers and others usually refreshed themselves here often in ways more primitive and perhaps more satisfactory than drinking from the public cup. Even a leisurely walker will pass in ten minutes from this point to the desired summit, which is 2192 feet above tide-water. The resemblance to a saddle is not so marked in this mountain depression as in the more northern one, although the land on both sides the road, and on both acclivities for a considerable distance, is completely bare of trees and is smooth and cultivable meadow or pasture. Open and ploughable ground to the north rises gradually up in the rear of Dodd's Cone, but there is no knob in it comparable to a pommel; and similar land slopes up from the road on the south towards Mount Hopkins, but there is no arch in it at the right distance which the fancy can frame into a cantel. But the Pass is a grand and noble spot on this old earth. The scene to the westward and southward is broader and lovelier than at Petersburg; cultivated fields and patches of orchard and wooded hilltops and pastures dotted with grazing cattle fill the nearer view in summer time; in contrast with the green fields and green woods, the country roads shimmer and glisten like long strips of white ribbands; with the sun at the proper angle in the western sky, the brooks dancing from their uplands towards the central valley gleam and shine at intervals like ribs of molten silver; and the observer fortunate in the time of his visit may say of these quiet homesteads and long reaches of sleeping and beautiful landscape, as Whittier said of his lower years when the height of his life was reached, how these —

> Now lie below me green and still
> Beneath a level sun!

Two or three other characteristic differences between the Berlin and Petersburg passes will put us into still better possession of the peculiarities of the former. Thus the northern one is exactly in the line of the highest peaks of the Taconics, along its own part of the ridge both north and south; while the southern one is out of range with its nearest summits, being decidedly west and back of these as one approaches from Williamstown. Moreover, Petersburg is half and half between the two states, the line crossing the very ridge of the Pass; while Berlin is wholly in New York, a full mile west of the line. Then two passable roads converge at the former gap, the one running up Treadwell Hollow, also the usual Petersburg road creeping along the shoulder of the foot-hills; while there is but one road can take the passenger up to and over the Berlin Pass.

Also the access to Petersburg, whichever road be chosen, is through woods and waste lands and past uncovered cellars and signs of desolation and abandonment; but the Berlin road goes past pretty good farms on either hand, and the last one (the old toll-gate farm) became noted for its productiveness under the ownership of Alexander Walker and the industry of his family, canny Scotch people from Aberdeenshire: the parents married there Aug. 7, 1856. Mr. Walker could handle the fiddle-bow and the surveyor's instruments with about equal facility; but as the lines fell to him in this country in prosy times and non-piping localities, the Scotch reels and strathspeys, of which he was a master and even a successful composer and publisher, slumbered for the most part upon the bridge of his fiddles, of which he invented and perhaps patented a prized improvement. Nevertheless, his residence at the head of the gorge, where the Fosters had lived for three generations, threw a sort of halo of music and good cheer up and down the valley, and proved to many persons a kind of subtle attraction not only for the Pass, but also for Mount Hopkins beyond it. Even the New York land to the very top of the gap has seen its days of fertility; for Enos Briggs, whose well-walled cellar is still conspicuous on the left of the road above the spring, was so successful in the culture of turnips on that side hill during the first two decades of this century, that he long went by the name of "Turnip Briggs"; and persons were still living in Williamstown in 1885 who remembered clearly seeing this humble vender of vegetables sell his savory wares along the single village street. It is but fair to add, that the ashes of the heavy hard woods burned on the clearings gave a quickness and strength to that soil for a time, of which it was long since deprived. And lastly, no wagon road leads from the Petersburg Pass either north or south, though there is a foot-path running north to the Snow-Hole; but from the Berlin Pass a comparatively well-trodden road for common vehicles turns off to the left towards a notable and so frequented objective which will shortly engage our attention for a little.

In the meantime let us take our last look from the Gap itself. To the eastward and over the entire valley of the Green River stands in almost startling distinctness the whole range of Greylock, or "Saddle Mountain," as it has long been, and is also best, named. We are indeed on ground 1343 feet lower than the highest peak of that range, which is properly called "Greylock," and 411 feet lower than the summit point of Bald Mountain, and also 405 feet below the centre peak of Prospect, and yet all that is most worth the seeing in this remarkably isolated group that holds the highest mountain in Massachusetts is quite under our eye from the Hoosac River to Pontoosuc Lake. Saddle Mountain may well be compared to a human left lung with its three distinct lobes. If one will conceive of such a lung magnified to mountain size, and lying lengthwise to the observer with the due depressions between the lobes, and the top of each of these puckered up into peaks at the proper points, and that one of the lobes nearest the beholder parted in the middle in such a way as to display the central and highest lobe from top to bottom through the cleft, he will have before his mind's eye a fair image of Saddle Mountain as it appears from Berlin Pass and as it is in reality.

"THE HOPPER," FROM BERLIN PASS.

1. Greylock.	4. Mount Moore.	7. Bald Mountain.
2. Mount Williams.	5. Mount Griffin.	8. Simonds Peak.
3. Mount Fitch.	6. Slope Norton.	9. Mount Chadbourne.

The western lobe of this huge mass of correlated mountain is cut into two parts by the "Hopper" so-called, a sharp-cut opening through the middle of it down to the base of Greylock itself, which is the majestic crown of the second and central lobe, so that as seen through the Hopper there is displayed to the on-looker from the Taconics the imperial western front of Greylock from very bottom to very top. The northern half of this first lobe thus bisected in some great convulsion of Nature is "Prospect" proper; and from the Hopper Brook that bathes the foot of both the halves, the jagged pasture and forest land shoots up at an angle of thirty-three degrees into "Simonds Peak," 2600 feet above tide-water more or less. Simonds Peak is clearly seen from several of the prominent streets of Pitts-

field, and indeed it was named thus in commemoration of our Revolutionary colonel by the gifted historian of that town, Dr. Smith.
From this its highest point, Mount Prospect declines towards the
north at a pretty steady angle for a mile or more, and then falls
sharply off into the so-called "Slope Norton," which carries the hill
down gradually to that intervale of the Hoosac on which stood old
Fort Massachusetts. "Bald Mountain" heads the southern half of
the western lobe, and lifts itself up from the Hopper Brook quite
as steeply, though not quite so high, as its fellow-mount across the
gorge; but the rest of this part is not quite parallel with the central
lobe, and is not in strict continuation therefore of Mount Prospect,
but bends decidedly towards the west, and after a long and comparatively low depression from the summit of Bald Mountain, it rises
gracefully again and ends grandly, though not loftily, in "Mount
Chadbourne." The writer ventures to apply this name to the beautifully rounded and wooded height that terminates the western lobe
of Saddle Mountain, in future memory of the fifth president of
Williams College, with whom, as colleague, professor, and president,
he was intimately associated for thirty years. Chadbourne loved
the hills and the trees and the rocks and the flowers. He knew
every nook and corner of this fair town. No species of plant, no
form of animal life, no geological peculiarity, escaped his eye. No
name has ever before been given to this bluff and full yet human and
tender height. Shall we, then, friends living and to come, call it
once and for all Mount Chadbourne?

It must not be inferred from what has just been said, that at all
times one can have a clear vision through the Hopper to the base of
Greylock, even from such an elevated lookout as the Berlin Pass.
Sometimes the white clouds fill up the opening from top to bottom,
cover Bald and Simonds with a fleecy mantle that never felt the
loom, rise and wholly envelop old Greylock himself, or hang like
Burns's "haffets" on either side of his hoary head, as the name
implies, then float along in rolls and folds (as they did this morning),
rising and falling, tarrying and hesitating, concealing and then revealing all the peaks of the group, and at last ascend from their transient
resting-places between the lobes and from along the slopes and tops
into the sunny or starry sky. After such a morning it often happens
that the atmosphere becomes the most transparent, the vision into
the Hopper the most penetrating, and the grand outline of the
mountain the sharpest against the opposing sky. Sometimes, again,
the summer shower-clouds and the wilder storm-clouds of rain, or
snow, or hail pack the Hopper to its fullest capacity, and press down

into the shallow valleys between the lobes, and burden the broad mountain tops, till, like an over-cargo filling a ship's hold, and spread upon the deck also, they seem to sink the mountain to the water's edge! Oftener than appear these cloud and storm effects, however, and especially in the gala months of June and October, such a clear and blessed light is thrown into this hollow of hollows (one might almost write holy of holies) that it seems as if the trees and even the limbs might be counted one by one as they clothe the steep hill-side; and when the early frosts have painted the leaves of the deciduous trees in every color of the rainbow, and the evergreens scattered everywhere among them set off by way of contrast the gorgeous colors, to look in upon the three sides of the great Hopper from the west, each vying with the other two in splendor, or to look down upon them all at once from the summit of Bald or of Simonds, is such a sight that its impression never fades out from the mind of any lover of natural beauty, and no one seeing it ever expects to see it surpassed this side of the new Jerusalem.

But our footing at the Gap is exalted enough to overlook alto-gether the first parallel of Saddle Mountain, and to enable us to see something of the broad shoulders and shallow valleys (disjointed by the Hopper) connecting that line with the second and loftier one, and also visually to take in from end to end the middle lobe of our Titanic lung. It is at least five miles as the bird flies from Mount Williams, the northern height of this central battlement, to the point of "Mount Griffin," its southern height. The eye first takes in the meadow on which Fort Massachusetts once stood; runs up Slope Hawks, which connects the site of the fort with Mount Wil-liams, itself a magnificent protuberance of mountain, dominating the valley of the Hoosac, and the rampart on one side of the "Ther-mopylæ of New England," as that valley was once called by Edward Everett; glances on to "Mount Fitch," the next and only high peak of that ridge to the north of Greylock, receiving its appropriate name many years ago from the Hopkins Alpine Club in memory of the first president of the College; rests then for a little on the tow-ering point of Greylock, an immemorial name; then drops some-what to an even stretch of mountain ridge, only broken by two slight swells close together with a little rift between them, which we have called "Mount Moore," to commemorate the second presi-dent of the College; and at last rests to return on the southmost point of the central ridge, which drops off very sharply into the foot-hills encircling Pontoosuc Lake, and which has been named Mount Griffin, in perpetual honor of the third president of the Col-

lege. As fronting the Taconics, old Greylock is grandly flanked on
the right by Fitch and Williams; on the left by Moore and Griffin;
and in his front are Simonds, Bald, and Chadbourne. Fitch and
Moore are nearly equi-distant from Greylock on either hand, and
so again are Williams and Griffin nearly equi-distant from the other
two on either hand, and from Greylock itself. President Moore, as
we may perhaps learn at length on a future page, was doubtful
whether the College could ever flourish in so inaccessible a place as
Williamstown then was; and his thoughts wavered during the six
years he was here, between the valley of the Connecticut and the
valley of the Hoosac as the true position for the College; and he at
last went to Amherst to become the first president there, and took a
large portion of the students with him; for which reasons his portrait is not with the rest in the gallery of this college, and his name
has been rarely mentioned of late years in connection with its history; but it is certain that he was actuated by honorable motives in
those transactions from first to last, and his name deserves respect-
ful recognition in the memorials of this college, and so far as the
present writer can secure that result, it will rest for all time upon
the not inconspicuous twin peaks already designated; and any one's
fancy may play, if it will, between the two neighboring peaks as
outward tokens of the mind of good Dr. Moore wavering between
Berkshire and Hampshire.

"Wilbur's Pasture" is the mountain farm, though there were
never homestead buildings upon it, which occupies the shoulder
uniting Prospect with Mount Williams, in short, the seat of the
saddle that gave the entire mountain its name to those who travelled up and down the Hoosac by the old path of the Mohawks.
"Harrison's Farm," on the other hand, which had upon it a good
house and a large barn, and was very fertile in the early days, is
the uniting shoulder and valley between Bald Mountain and Greylock; and rude and early wagon roads, that are still travelled in
summer-time more or less, led from some of the thoroughfares of
Williamstown to these sky farms. The first circled around Mount
Williams from the "Notch Road," so called, into Wilbur's Pasture,
and the other, starting from the west side of the mountain, wound
through the Hopper and up Bald Mountain to Harrison's Farm;
and these immense pastures and the woods bordering on them fill
up for the most part the interval between the first and second lines
of the mountain, and each furnished a route to the summit of Greylock, but only sinewy pedestrians or audacious horseback riders
essayed this final stage of the journey.

This casual mention of the "Notch Road" may serve to introduce all that needs now be said about the third lobe of Saddle Mountain. This is the eastern parallel of the mountain, is much lower than either of the others, has been called from immemorial time "Raven Rock"; the Ashuwillticook or south branch of the Hoosac washes the whole length of its eastern flank; the valley between it and the Greylock ridge is wider and more cultivable than the shoulder valleys on the other side, and it extends considerably further north than the other ridges. Indeed, it dips down in "Furnace Hill" to the very brink of the Hoosac at the junction of the Ashuwillticook and the Mayunsook. It is over this ridge that the sun rises in winter to the folks in the village of Williamstown, its height being such as to hide from them the much higher range of the Hoosacs; it also hides from the same the houses of their neighbors in North Adams; and the "Little Tunnel" of the great Hoosac Tunnel Railway passes under it just as it loses itself on the river's brink. The valley between Raven Rock and Greylock is the "Notch," and the southern end of it, of remarkable construction, is the "Bellows-Pipe." It lies wholly in the old township of East Hoosac; the farms within it were early settled; the Wilburs, by whom the pasture above was owned and cleared, and from whom it is named, were perhaps the principal family in the Notch; and the graphic fitness of the name "Bellows-Pipe" will be seen when it is said, that the northern winds and storms sucked and pushed through the long and narrow Notch escape from it with a bound and a burst and a howl over the rising shoulder at the southern end (seeking in vain to confine them) into the broad open beyond.

Our visual excursions from the Berlin Pass are now over. It only remains, from this Pass as a standpoint, because the rude road diverges here that leads up to "Mount Hopkins," to give some account of this loftiest bulge of the Taconics within sight of the town and the college, to unfold the grounds on which it has been sought for many years to attach an honored name to this particular mountain, and to commend in fair but strong terms to all lovers of natural scenery (both transient and resident) repeated visits to this chief glory of the Taconics — this never-humbled pride of the Williamstown valley — before they leave the region for good, or suppose that they have seen all of its wonders. Because this Pass is a mile back from the general trend of the Taconics in this part of their course, the road leading from it to Mount Hopkins must regain that distance to the eastward before this summit is gained, which stands about in line with Dodd's Cone and Leet Hill. Only stopping now to fling out an exhortation or two to the authorities that are to be in the future to construct a good road from the Pass to the summit, and just to say that the present bridle-path turns first south and then sharp southeast and east for the mile and a half between the points, we may find ourselves shortly upon a broad patch of cleared land nearly level, that has often felt the plough and the harrow and the hoe, and doubtless yielded full returns to the husbandman's toil and sweat, and that is 2790 feet above the sea-level, and 2082 feet above the old astronomical observatory on the College grounds.

About the beginning of the present century, a man by the name of Macomber owned and cleared up this land, and had his dwelling and barn upon it, and used to carry down upon his back a bag of grain now and then to a mill on the Little Hoosac, in or near what is now the village of Berlin, New York. The mountain came thence to be known as the " Macomber" Mountain, and was commouly so designated in Williamstown during the first quarter of the century. If this name had become firmly fixed to the mountain on both sides of it, the present writer would have been the last man in the world to try to dislodge it, for he not only believes that civilization rests on the plough, but also that no other man's name is so fit to be fixed on any patch of ground anywhere as *his*, who has subdued and replenished it. But Macomber was not so fortunate as this. Gradually on the other side it came to be called the "Williamstown" Mountain, and on this side (queerly enough) it came to be generally named the "Berlin" Mountain, neither of which names had any significance or appropriateness ; and under these circumstances, to christen the height became a lawful privilege to any one who could establish a claim to be godfather, either in his own behalf, or in that of another. The turnpike over the Pass made the place accessible from both sides; Macomber had a sort of farm road from the turnpike to his homestead ; doubtless a few students may have clambered up there from time to time, but it was not the custom in the early days of the College, as it has happily become since, for the students to explore all the hills and to dive into all the valleys, — a pilgrimage or two to Greylock quite sufficed the average student for his college course; and so it came about that Harry Hopkins, the president's eldest son, who was graduated in 1858, and who became a fearless and efficient chaplain in the Union army during the Civil War, discovered, or rather rediscovered, this splendid outlook for west and south and north and east. He experienced the joy of having found something new, something at least practically unknown in his own time. He went there often himself, and also took his friends thither. Among others he took up his uncle, Albert Hopkins. The veteran naturalist was delighted. He, too, began to frequent the place in his leisure hours. He even extemporized an observatory there to broaden, or rather to deepen, the view to the east; but the unchecked winds dealt roughly with the structure, as with so many others of similar character in the neighborhood.

But let the good man himself describe a little, and propose a little in his own words.

One peculiarity in the Taconic range is the spurs which it sends out. Look at the Hoosac range, east of Adams ; how uniform it is. On the other hand, let one ride from Williamstown to Hancock, and notice the mountains on his right. He is continually passing buttresses or spurs, which push their roots out almost to the highway. Between these he sees valleys, or perhaps they ought to be called gorges or ravines, pushing their way far in toward the backbone of the chain. From a foot-path south of the Berlin summit, you will emerge into an open place, where you will for a time forget that there is anything higher or finer to be sought. At this point you have the full effect of these spurs which you will now perceive are an appendage of the west as well as of the east flank of the mountain, and which appear (to use rather a vulgar comparison) like hogs' backs. The effect of these sub-chains as seen from the point I am now speaking of, is heightened by the fact that they jut out nearly at right angles to the general trend of the mountain on whose crest we are walking. Nature does not often deal in right angles. Hence we are more struck by an appearance of geometrical precision when we observe it in the grouping of natural objects. Having inserted our gimlet into a dead beech, and swung our barometer with its basin as nearly as possible on a level with the summit, we walked here and there to get the views. The Katskills could certainly be seen ; though I had great difficulty in convincing my friend, Dr. N. H. Griffin, of the fact. He would still insist that the "faint pencillings" on the sky, which I pointed out to him as *terra firma*, lay in cloud land. To me they were masses, lofty, grand, substantial; to him they were like the "baseless fabric of a dream," a mirage, which some change in the atmosphere would melt up, or some gust of wind would topple over. One thing we saw which was remarkable. It was a very bright light, evidently beyond the Hudson, which occasionally flashed up and then disappeared. My explanation of it (perhaps incorrect) was this : the sky being partly overcast, the sun's rays fell at intervals on the roof of some glass structure, some greenhouse, perhaps, between Troy and Albany, and hence this alternating light. I cannot enter into particulars ; but will say in general that the view from this point more nearly resembles that from Greylock than any other in the neighborhood. It was first brought into notice by Chaplain Hopkins, with whose name I should like to see it associated. The matter of names, however, is rather a delicate and difficult one. When we reached the usual summit crossing on our return, I told my friend to clap down and look at the landscape backward with his head inverted. The experiment seemed new to him, and I introduce it here because, though really an old

experiment, as old at least as the days of my grandfather [Curtis], who taught
it to me on Sky Lot [in Stockbridge], yet the philosophy of it, I mean of the
effect, I have never seen fully explained ; and am in doubt whether it is a question for the professors in optical science or physiology to explain.

However much Chaplain Hopkins may have been pleased with
this pleasant token of his uncle's good-will, he was too modest and
too meritorious a man not to see at once that, if the name "Hopkins" were to be permanently affixed to the mountain, it must be on
the ground of the merits of men older and greater and more conspicuous than himself. And there were two such men at hand
bearing the name, who had spent long and useful and far-out-reach-
ing lives under the shadow of the mountain, — his uncle and his
father. The former, the first·proposer of the name in behalf of
another, was on the whole himself the most worthy to have his
worth perpetuated till the end of time in the name of one of those
"everlasting hills," to which he was so fond of referring in talk and
sermon. He was an intense lover of Nature, a more intense and
devoted lover of mankind, and a most intense and consecrated
lover of God. But why not have the name of the mountain
commemorate for all time his brother also, and his nephew too,
as he himself originally proposed ? For fifty years Mark Hopkins
was the pride and the pillar of the College ; for forty years Albert
Hopkins was in holy charge of the Ark of God both in the College
and the town ; and for many years Harry Hopkins was a Christian
frontiersman in the valley of the Missouri, an efficient organizer
and father of new churches, a bishop indeed within that fold and
form of Christianity whose boast it was and is to be "a church
without a bishop and a state without a king." He carried Williamstown ideas and Williams College influences into the great valley of
the continent in its germinating time, and scattered them there
widely and wisely.

To any one approaching the Taconics from the eastward, or looking at them from any eminence on that side, there are twin peaks
on this particular swell, of which the northern one is indeed the
highest as measured by the barometer, but the other one appears as
high from many points as measured by the eye. It is, however,
one mountain, one Mount Hopkins, with two predominating points,
one for each of two brothers, *par nobile fratrum*, of whom it is difficult to say which were the greater, so different were they in their
temperament and in the tenor of their lives. And between these
mountain peaks, as always in such cases, there is a connecting link,
part valley and part shoulder, all one mountain still ; and so, why

may not this lower height, this link touching each and uniting both, be a fit symbol of the younger and less gifted, yet not less loving man, who reached his full hand and great heart to his bereaved uncle when the latter's only son fell in battle for his country, without withdrawing one tittle of filialness as the first-born son of his own father? So let it be. One mountain, one name, three persons, one family, no designated part to commemorate any particular one, an earthly trinity in unity, locally fixed and bound to endure.

It happened that the writer was travelling a few days ago in Washington County, New York, and was facing over what is called "Oak Hill" on the old stage road between Albany and Whitehall, a few miles north of *Tyashoke* on the Hoosac, and so was enabled to gain a fair view of the northern Taconics in general and of Mount Hopkins in particular from distant and elevated points to the northwest. The truth is, the people in the Williamstown valley are too near the Taconics to be able to appreciate fully their height and their beauty and their wonderful variety. To see them on their New York side and from twenty miles away is to get a new impression of, and feel a higher respect for, this mountain barrier, that has divided in the minds of men since 1664 the old Province of the Massachusetts Bay and the still older Province of New Netherland. The same remark may be made, and with still greater emphasis, of Saddle Mountain with all its lobes and peaks. Here, too, in a certain sense "distance lends enchantment to the view." The high road over the Oak Hill of Washington County, at whose base flows the old Dutch stream of Owl Kill, up whose sluggish current lay the weary march in 1746 of the captives of Fort Massachusetts towards Canada, also gives clear and splendid views of Greylock and Williams and Fitch and Bald and Simonds, as well as of the whole mass together and of the huge cleft in its western side. Moreover, Mason's Hill, in Pownal, and Mount Anthony, in Bennington, offer superb views of Saddle Mountain from the north. The old "Indian Path" over the Hoosacs, and the turnpike that crossed and recrossed that, hold out grand points of view from the east; and there are hills in Rowe and Windsor and Ashfield, and doubtless many other towns in Berkshire and Franklin counties that are bold enough to overlook the Hoosacs sufficiently to present to a good eye Greylock certainly, and less distinctly its neighbor peaks on either hand.

Since the eastern and southeastern foot of Mount Hopkins broadens down into some tolerably level land, on which a part of the original second division of fifty-acre lots was laid out; and since John and William Torrey, brothers, from Middletown, Connecticut, settled on some of these lands about 1766, and numbers of their descendants have been living ever since upon the same and neighboring farms, we will venture to call this strip of land the "Torrey Plateau," because this was from the first a family of marked characteristics, and deserved to have, as will fully appear on later pages, their name commemorated locally in the section of the town which their toil helped to clear of its primeval forest. When the President's house, that had been formerly occupied by the Whitmans, was being repaired for the residence of Dr. Carter, in 1881, a bit of time-stained paper was found in the rubbish, with many other similar ones of like purport signed by other parties, inscribed as follows:

WILLIAMSTOWN Aug 20 1803

Mr Whitman Sir please to send me by the Bearer two Quarts of your Best rum and charge the same to me and in so doing you will Oblige your friend and humble Servant

JOHN TORREY JR

This John Torrey was born Dec. 11, 1774, on the Torrey Plateau. The handwriting was fair, and the spelling was good, but there was an entire absence of punctuation-marks, probably because he was in a hurry for his beverage!

The next loop of the Taconics south of Mount Hopkins is "McMaster Mountain"; and the Pass that divides the two, and furnishes a way for the third road over the barrier and into the state of New York, has now been called for sundry years the "Kidder Pass." The two earliest settlers in the southwest of Williamstown were Robert McMaster and Moses Rich, both from Palmer or its immediate neighborhood, and both taking up their lots near each other, in the spring of 1763, on the brook which flows down this Pass in two branches, uniting just on the original west line of Williamstown. The Pass itself, and the road leading up to it between these two branches, and the mountain to the south of it, were all on the "Gore," so called; and there were several men living in Williamstown 123 years after McMaster and Rich built their first houses on the brook below, who remembered that in their boyhood this whole hollow, and the mountain to the left of it, was called "Mac's Pattin." Among those still living who remember that designation are James Smedley, Eaton Johnson, and B. F. Mills. What the word "pattin" meant, nobody seemed to know or care. That is the way the boys heard it, and so the old men pronounce it. One thing makes it all clear: All the town lots were deeded in the ordinary way; but this land was on the Gore, and so belonged to the Commonwealth; and the instrument conveying rights of possession was called a "patent," as proceeding from the sovereign authority. McMaster was an enterprising farmer, as became a Scotch-Irish Presbyterian, and added to his home lot lying in Williamstown a huge patch of mountain land that had belonged to the state; and his name has thus been perpetuated in connection with that purchase. "McMaster Mountain," accordingly, is well designated; and we leave it to our readers to affix the name beyond all possibility of change.

This "pattin" brook, after an easterly course of two miles and a sudden lurch to the north, falls into the Hemlock Brook just as that, too, takes its final bend northwards. This junction of the two brooks is right at the corner of the "Torrey Woods," as these are entered from the Hemlock road. There was a road very early laid out to "convean" the fifty-acre lots of the second division, which ran due west in continuation of the Green River road, when that abandoned the stream at some distance above the "Krigger Mills" and passed over Stone Hill, crossing the old county road at right angles and forming "Woodcock's Corner," so called, and then dropped down into the valley of this brook and up the stream towards the Pass. Most of the way the present road follows this old line into the northern end of "Oblong Road," so called, while the Kidder Pass road, now but little travelled, is a much later extension, continuing the old road over the Taconics and down into the village of Berlin, New York. The best house along this old road was built in 1804 by a family of the name of "Sweet," and it was long occupied by them, but towards the end of the century was long owned and lived in by Dan Phelps. The name of the proprietor, through whose farm the brook flowed, became gradually and properly attached to the brook itself, and so it is and always will be called the "Sweet Brook."

McMaster early opened a farm road up between the two little branches of Sweet Brook into his patent on the Gore. In process of time, two or three small and rude farms worked themselves out of the forest into the light upon the side hills along these brooklets. Although the cellar of the homestead, one of the most indestructible memorials of human habitation in such places, is still visible enough, the lowest of these farms was long ago abandoned to a forlorn pasture; but the upper one, near the summit of the Pass, is still more or less cultivated, and, indeed, has been divided into two, and two poor houses, or rather shanties, one on either side of the road, send

up from time to time their smoke into the sky.   George Kidder and
his wife, after whom the Pass is named, lived in one of these shanties forty years and more.   She was the widow of James Richards,
who died here in a January when the Pass was terribly drifted, and
lies buried near the shanty beneath an unlettered headstone.   Shall
we give a moment here to the short and simple annals of the poor?
George Kidder, a native of Townsend, a carriage painter by trade,
found his way to Troy, New York; he had lost his wife, and having
a bad felon on his finger, and supposing he had lost the use of his
hand, wandered rather than went to the village of Berlin; and coming over the Pass one day, he found Mrs. Richards trying to gather
in her corn all alone; he took hold and helped her what he could

"JOHNSON PASS"; "KIDDER PASS."

I. Martin's Mount.   2. Comstock Heights.   3. Mount Mills.   4. McMaster Mountain.

"with the gleanings," as he said; he got dirt into his sore, she
washed it out and dressed it; "she told me she had this little
place, __ some debt on it then, — we paid it up, and we've lived here
ever since."   Kidder was three years in the late war as a private
soldier in the 37th Massachusetts, Colonel Richards, was ruptured
in the service, wore a truss ever after, "never got any pension, — if
Dr. Duncan had lived, he would have helped me get it."   The
Kidders had no children, but they adopted and brought up a boy,
Albert Brooks, to whom, when he married, they gave twenty acres
of poor land near their own place, and he built a shanty there for
himself.   "Two children and well on for another," Kidder once told
the writer, in reference to the new family.   "Albert is working now
on t'other side the mountain, getting out ash for Wood's mowers
and reapers at Hoosac Falls.   The oldest boy used to come over

here last summer a good deal, — *I sot everything on him.*"   An amus-
ing incident is well authenticated in connection with the marriage
of Albert Brooks: he brought his girl to a minister here in the village, of a Sunday evening, and paid him one dollar for performing
the ceremony; a shower having sprung up, he borrowed, to protect
his bride, an umbrella that had just cost two dollars: the umbrella
was not returned, which may be said to have made the whole service unprofitable to the minister in a pecuniary point of view.   To
portray the Kidders truthfully, it must be added, that the husband
became increasingly intemperate after the war; and the last time
the writer saw the pair together, he was lying on the bank of the
Sweet Brook, nearly insensible, while the faithful wife sat in the
shade of a neighboring tree, waiting till he should recover enough
to climb with her the steep and rough path to their home.

As the Gore was annexed to Williamstown in 1837, and as the
summit of this Pass is within the west line of the Gore, while the
summits of the other three are all in a neighboring state, we may
perhaps claim the "Kidder" as a peculiar possession of our own,
and justify the long digression over its name.   It is also noteworthy
as being in a special sense face to face with Greylock, which is
here disclosed through the Hopper from its high crown to its broad
roots; and there are those who think that the very best views of
the valley and the range are to be gathered from this lofty and tor-
tuous path; and it is certain that no one has ever seen either to its
absolute perfection who has not climbed on foot or horseback to this
particular spot, and turned, as he rested a little from stage to stage,
to take long and wide glances backward.

One more touch, and we leave the Taconics as a range, to return
to them not again in further description.   The last of the four
passes in Williamstown, and about like the others in height, follows
up a little brook between the southern end of McMaster Mountain
and the next main loop of the Taconics, of which the high northern
face is named "Mount Mills."   The Pass itself has long been called
the "Johnson Pass," in commemoration of Lieutenant David Johnson, of whom we shall hear a good deal in the sequel, a man of note
among the early settlers, whose farm and home lay at the foot of
the Pass, and who helped to construct the rude road over it (still
travelled somewhat) in 1813.   The farm adjoining Johnson's was at
that time owned by Charles Sabin, son of Lieutenant Zebediah
Sabin, who was a comrade of Johnson's in Arnold's famous expedition up the Kennebec in 1775, and who lost his life upon that expedition; and the farm adjoining Sabin's on the Oblong road, and also

adjoining on the north Lieutenant Sabin's farm, then occupied by his grandsons, was owned by Captain Samuel Mills. These three men, Mills and Johnson and Sabin, were the prime movers in the building on this side of the road up the hollow and over the watershed; and some of the enterprising farmers of Berlin did their share of the work at the same time by building the road from that village up the New York slope to the summit. In fact, all the roads over the three southern passes enter that village, as the road over the northern Pass enters the village of Petersburg.

It throws a clear and pleasant light on the state of things in this region at that time, that one motive on both sides for building the road over the Johnson Pass was to accommodate Dr. Samuel Porter, who lived then on Stone Hill, a famous doctor and bonesetter of his day, who had patients in a wide circuit of country. So far as Captain Mills was concerned, it was another ground of interest in the road, that it opened up a large tract of land belonging to him (and still owned by his grandson), out of which he had already developed a sort of mountain farm, which after his death, in March, 1814, was carried on for many years by Walter Converse, who had previously been an inmate of his family. The barn is still standing in the hollow; and the cellar wall of the house close by the road, the only house ever built in that mountain valley, serves to remind the passer-by that life and love, parents and children, seed-time and harvest, at one time relieved the otherwise utter desolateness of those steep slopes and dismal woods. Olive Converse, afterwards the wife of Justin Torrey, was born in that house; and Harriet Converse, later the wife of Myron Torrey, spent the first dozen years of her life there, except a few months of its opening; and she told the writer in 1885, that their nearest neighbors on the one hand were the Comstocks, who lived in the last house in Williamstown on the Hancock road, and on the other hand, Henry Green's family, who lived in a deep gorge of McMaster Mountain, corresponding in many respects to their own. The farm lay wholly on the Gore, and the family made special arrangements for the schooling of the children in the Sherwood district in Williamstown proper.

From the summit of the Johnson Pass, of which a wide strip was long ago completely cleared of woods to feed the capacious maw of a charcoal kiln whose foundations still crown the highest point, any one may see distinctly and grandly, looking to the north, the much higher and smoother and more rounded Berlin Pass, with its neighbors, Dodd's Cone and Leet Hill, overtopping it as perpetual sentinels. Much nearer by may be seen the place where the Kidder

Pass also overcomes the range; but that road, both on the summit and on the sunset slope, is concealed from this point of observation by thick woods. The Johnson top is considerably further west than the Kidder, and a little further west than the Berlin, and gives, of course, no such broad views in any direction as does the latter; for this is comparatively a humble Pass, and commemorates as its promoters and the users of its road comparatively humble men, though Johnson and Mills and Sabin were all brave soldiers on the right side in the battle of Bennington, and on other fields besides of patriotic fight. The finely arched northern brow of the mountain to the south of the Pass, which is in plain sight from the colleges and from most of the lifting points within the valley of Williamstown, we desire to have called in perpetuity " Mount Mills," because it overlooks the good captain's valley-farm now deserted, and the entire road on either slope on which he and his neighbors wrought for the public good and their own.

The late Dr. Henry L. Sabin, who died in February, 1884, aged fourscore years and three, once told the writer that he himself, a boy of thirteen, carried refreshments to his uncle, Charles Sabin, and others, while they were at work building the road up this Pass. What these refreshments were in the detail did not at that time transpire, except that they were the ordinary "baiting" or dinner, accompanied, of course, by the then customary stimulus, of which Charles Sabin and his two sons, who then carried on the old Sabin place, were quite too fond. The constant prominence of this family in the town, however, and especially the sturdy patriotism of Lieutenant Zebediah Sabin and the excellent character of Anna Dwight, his wife and widow, and the high position of their descendants here, make it every way fitting that this name be affixed to some one of those rock-ribbed hills at whose feet their life work was done. Accordingly, will present contemporaries and coming posterity unite to make current, that the twin egg-shaped hills projecting above the general level of the Taconics to the south of Mount Mills and near the south line of the town be called " Sabin Heights " hereafter ? These close-nestling hills, too, may be seen from many parts of the main village, in whose homes Dr. Sabin also made himself dear by fifty years of medical ministry.

May it please the reader, we will now retreat from the Taconic peaks and ravines, which have detained us perhaps too long already, by the old road, of which the Johnson Pass road was but a western continuation, which led straight from the New Ashford road on the east to the Hancock road on the west, between the southern tier of the 50-acre lots of the second division and the adjoining 100-acre lots. The part of this road eastward from Austin Blair's has been of late years discontinued. Beginning at the end of the long Oblong, it passed over the gentle and fertile slope of Stratton Mountain, giving at first the traveller going east a fine view on his right of "Point Young" and "Martin's Mount" and the other peaks of Jericho Ridge, which is the western side of the mountain mass of which Stratton Mountain is the northern front. The whole is a huge wedge thrust into the Williamstown valley from the south, and flanked on the east by the Ashford Brook and on the west by the Hancock Brook, which two unite at South Williamstown to form Green River. The town of Hancock in the olden time was called "Jericho"; and Martin's Mount is so designated in order to commemorate Martin Townsend, one of the first settlers of that town, and one of its sturdiest and most picturesque citizens. Williamstown has no claim upon him, though the two towns have had many points of interesting contact; but his son, Nathaniel, born in 1781, spent a long and honored life here; and his three grandsons, Rufus M., Martin I., and Randolph W., are all graduates of the College, in '30, '33, and '36, respectively. Martin's Mount is the highest peak on Jericho Ridge, and is nearly opposite the old farm in the valley, which Martin Townsend and Susannah Allen, his wife, (married in 1773, when he was seventeen and she but fourteen), cleared and cultivated, and upon which they grew rich and old. They spread their first meal in their new home on the top of a barrel, and their lodging-place at first was more primitive than was usual for white folks even in these forests primeval. He was a loyalist in the Revolution, as he had a right to be, and so were several others of the chief men of Jericho. It stands upon a town record of October, 1777, that eleven men, of whom he was the first named, " have all of them returned from the enemy, with whom they have been in battle against us." The reference is to the battle of Bennington; but it has never been exactly cleared up, and never will be, precisely in what capacity or in what degree of active toryism they were in or near that battle. Townsend died on his farm in May, 1848. On his tombstone are these words: "Incomprehensible Infinity! In Him all is right."

Passing over this cross-road, accordingly, to the Ashford road at Aaron Deming's old place, and up the Ashford road a quarter of a mile or so, we come to an old road on the left hand that goes up alongside "Roaring Brook" (so called from immemorial time). Roaring Brook falls into the Ashford Brook on the right of the main road a few rods above this turn. The brook and its many branches drain a wide hill country to the south of Greylock and Bald Mountain. As this brook road is one way to reach the "Heart of Grey-lock," as it was called by Professor Hopkins and his Alpine Club, a place on the upper reaches of the brook, where three of its tributaries pour down into a wonderfully hidden recess in the depths of Saddle Mountain, we will follow up the road as far as it goes towards that objective point. For vehicles, at present the road ends at the junction on the left of the first large tributary with the main brook, or, as it has been called for a half century or more, at "Goodell's"; although formerly one road extended up from this point the steep flanks of Bald Mountain, to the Harrison farm between that summit and Grey-lock, and another followed up the main stream some distance further. About 1830 there were seven or eight poor houses along this road and brook, and nearly the same number on nearly the same sites about 1890. Daniel Kinney, a substantial citizen,

1. Starling Daniels, his point. 2. Ard Roberts, his point. 3. " Gell's," his point.

CENTRAL LOBE OF GREYLOCK (SOUTHERN END).

early made his home near the entrance to the brook road on the left-hand side of it. This is still called the "Kinney Place." It is on the 100-acre lot No. 24. One of his daughters married a Comstock, and they had a home in East Street, and became the parents of the late Mrs. Reed Mills. Zenas Roberts, born Sept. 21, 1781, son of Ard Roberts and Miriam, lived in one of these houses on the brook before and after 1830. The elder Roberts, whose name is on many a Revolutionary muster-roll, and who was in the battle of Bennington, and who used, at the beginning of this century, to spay sows and render other like services to his neighbors, lived on the Ashford road a few rods above the turn, on 100-acre lot No. 25, a place still occupied by his descendants. Starling Daniels, of whom we shall hear more by and by, lived during the last part of his life in one of these houses up Roaring Brook, and his widow and children after him. Some one or more families of the name of Goodell have lived on that road during most of the present century. Mrs. Thompson, a lady of excellent Christian character, lived on the Kinney Place, with her son-in-law, for many years, about 1880. Beautiful house-plants adorned the windows of that old house during her residence in it.

At Goodell's a considerable tributary falls into Roaring Brook on the left hand as one goes up, and this branch it is that drains the whole region between Bald Mountain and Mount Chadbourne, and the southern flanks of both of these. We may call this, if we please, "Goodell Brook." Then, following up the main stream, at first along what was once a wagon road, and afterwards along steep banks without any sign of path, we come into a rough and wild and dark gorge, adown which pours over rocks and old roots and fallen trunks our roaring brook, "and hears no sound save his own dashings." The thick woods on the high hillsides right and left have been repeatedly cut off, to be burned into charcoal to feed the furnace fires of the Lanesboro Iron Company. But woods in such places renew their youth like the eagle's. Some trees are always left standing on account of their inaccessibility, and some on account of their comparative uselessness for furnace purposes; the soil is dank, and is annually enriched by leaves falling thick on the spot and blown in from the upper hillsides; sprouts and saplings of all kinds push up with vigor under these circumstances, and it is but a few years after a cutting when the whole scene seems as dense and wild as it did before the woodman's axe echoed at all up and down the hollow. Less than two miles' ascent brings one from Goodell's into the "Heart of Greylock," well so called; that is, into an elongated basin tipped at an angle, in the depths of the forest; into this there tumbles first on the left hand, from some sixty feet above, a strong stream, white with friction from its rocks; a couple of rods ahead there falls into the same, from the right-hand side, a larger brook, though from a lower height, that has drained in its course a part of the "Berry Patch," that is, the lower western slopes of mounts Moore and Griffin; while just in front, the main brook dashes down the steep rocks some thirty feet or more into the upper quarter of the basin, having drained from a longer distance the upper and more marshy flanks of the same mountains. Here, then, is the "Heart." This the receptacle and reservoir of the life-blood of this giant mass of mountain.

A dialogue between Albert Hopkins and one of the young ladies of his Alpine Club, written out by him afterwards, and doubtless somewhat replenished and embellished beyond the actual conversation had on the spot, will give the reader a deeper and pleasanter impression of the seclusion and grandeur of the place than any possible words of the present writer. It is the lady who opens the dialogue, and the respondent is the Professor himself.

How still it is! I have not dared to whisper since we came here. I suppose this is the Heart of Greylock.

If great Nature is silent, we may well be.

Does not this remind you, sir, of that place we read of, — "which the vulture's eye hath not seen"?

I was thinking of that other passage, — "the earth with its bars is about me forever." It is something to be confronted by great rocky strata, as we are here.

Since you have spoken, another passage has occurred to me, — "The strength of the hills is His also."

You may well be reminded of that; and also of the place where it says, — "If I speak of strength, lo! He is strong." When we see great rocks interlaminated, and twisted together like these, we feel our littleness; we are sure that He who disposed, cemented, and piled them so high above us, could "take no pleasure in the legs of a man or the strength of a horse."

I wish, sir, you would repeat to me the rest of that passage from Job; for I have forgotten it. I think I should better understand its meaning here.

I will repeat the commencement of it. It needs to be read with a commentary; not, as you suggest, that of learned critics or theologians, but of vast objects such as we see around us. The passage would bear to be read by the seaside, or by starlight, as you will see before I have finished repeating it : —

"He is wise in heart and mighty in strength; who hath hardened himself against Him, and prospered?.
Which removeth the mountains and they know not; which overturneth them in his anger;
Which shaketh the earth out of her place, and the pillars thereof tremble;
Which commandeth the sun and it riseth not, and sealeth up the stars;
Which, alone, spreadeth out the heavens, and treadeth upon the waves of the sea;

Which maketh Arcturus, Orion, and Pleiades, and the chambers of the south ;
Which doeth great things past finding out ; yea, and wonders without number.''

I do not think, sir, I ever heard that passage before.

Probably not. You had heard it read from a dry wooden desk ; and, perhaps, by some lily-fingered clergyman, who never went into the Heart of
Greylock, or into the heart of anything. But you will confess to me now the
value of a good commentary.

Let me ask you, sir, whether you think my reference to the passage which
speaks of the "vulture's eye and the lion's whelps" was out of place ?

Perhaps not, though some critics refer that passage to the operations of the
miner; which were on a grand scale anciently, as now.

I will give you another translation ; and to interest you the more in it, I will
tell you that it is by a lady [Louisa Payson Hopkins], — one who once looked
upon Greylock, and also ascended it. At the top of the manuscript is written
in pencil, "very literal"; and though no Hebraist myself, I have reason to
believe the translation very exact. You will notice that in this translation the
poetical form of the original has been preserved, which has not been done by
our translators.

> " As to the earth, out of it cometh bread,
> And under it is turned up as it were fire.
> Her stones are the place of sapphires,
> And her dust is gold for him (man), (or gold is dust for it, — the
>   sapphire).
> The bird of prey knoweth not the path to it,
> And the vulture's eye hath not seen it.
> The sons of pride (wild beasts) have not trodden it,
> The lion hath not passed over it.
> (Man) layeth his hand upon the flint,
> He upturneth mountains from their roots,
> He causeth streams to break out among the rocks,
> And his eye seeth every precious thing.
> He restraineth streams from trickling (in the mines),
> And that which is hid he bringeth to light.''

I had hardly supposed so grand a description could refer to the works of
man.

So it might seem. Yet you remember when I showed you into the Tunnel
the other day, we reached a place which no vulture's eye could ever have seen,
nor lion's whelps could ever have passed. Whereas, here, methinks, I can even
now hear a vulture screaming over us ! Did I tell you that in a chasm near
by, or rather, overhanging us, there is a golden eagle's nest ?

I should think, too, the wild beasts might congregate here in the night season.
And as to the Tunnel, I am sure it seemed to me, when we were there, that the
work was almost superhuman. It was frightful, too, so that, if we had not had
the chief engineer to pilot us in, I should never have dared to attempt it. But
probably in Job's day they knew little of such excavations.

I am not sure of that. Think of that vast channel or tunnel forty leagues in
length, 300 feet wide, and part of it at least cut through the solid rock, cut, too,

in Job's day, perhaps. If our engineers can undertake and perform almost superhuman things, so could those of King Moeris.

I think there is one thing, however, which, if Job went to visit King Moeris, as according to your suggestion he may have done, to see his hydraulic works, the engineers of the king could not have shown him.

I see, I presume, what you are about to say, but go on.

I think they could not have shown him, as Mr. Granger and Mr. Stowell showed us, how to blast rocks by gunpowder and touch off the blasts by lightning.

To say nothing of drilling by compressed air. Well, no doubt science has made great strides since then. But human labor was cheap in old times ; and they pecked away till they accomplished in longer time the same things which we do. But are you sure it is so still here ?

I thought it was perfectly still. But I think I can hear the wind in those spruces, though they are so high up. I fancy no birds are ever heard here, unless it may be owls or whippoorwills.

You are mistaken in that. We should not expect to hear meadow larks or bobolinks in this deep gulf ; but had we made our visit a few weeks since, we should have heard several sweet singers,— among them the solitary thrush.

I should like to hear the note of the thrush now. It chimes in so well in great solitudes like these.

I am glad to see that you distinguish the notes of birds ; even of those that are not very familiar. I do not suppose there are half a dozen young ladies in Williamstown or Adams, and I might go on to Cheshire, Pittsfield, and so on down the County, who ever heard a solitary thrush ; or what amounts to the same thing, who know that they ever heard one.

Do not speak so disparagingly, sir, of us.

Of course, I make you an exception ; and a few others, whose education has been conducted on something like rational principles.

Excuse me, sir, please, but there are a thousand things here I am eager to examine, and I see the afternoon is wearing away.

You are afraid of the wild beasts, perhaps, who might be prowling around, if nightfall should overtake us here. But I must detain you a little while longer ; for this subject of the abuses of what is popularly termed "education" has been running lately in my mind, and must have vent somewhere.

Allow me, sir, to say that, if we can ever climb back over these frightful "bars" as you call them, the same good things, which I know you wish to say, might be spoken before a larger audience.

And a more appreciative one, I fancy. Very well, we will not break friendship ; especially here in the "Heart" of Greylock. But look ! How the shadows lengthen ! Is it possible that is the sun, which we see through the gap, so near to the summit of the Taconics ? These "bars" cannot be let down, so we must hasten and scramble over them, or the "sons of pride" will be upon us before we catch a glimpse of Williamstown or White Oaks.

Like the Professor and his fair band, we, too, must now beat a retreat from the Heart of Greylock ; but as belonging to a younger generation than they, we will, like Wolfe's men at the Heights of Abraham, scramble up the almost perpendicular banks of the brook

already described, that pours itself foamy into the left auricle of
the Heart; because that route, though rough, will bring us directly
up to the now famous Camping-Ground, that lies on the skirts of
the Harrison farm upon the high shoulder-valley between Bald
Mountain and Greylock.   The head spring of this brook is on the
flank of Greylock, a little north of the camping-place, and a little
east of the cleared ground of the farm; and a small tributary of it
rises in another spring that gushes up within the beat of the camp
itself; and here on Williamstown ground, ever after about the year
1870 till the present writing, various parties from the leading
families of this village have spent a month or two in the summer-
time, camping out on one· or the other of the tiny tines of this fluent
fork; outdoor life at such an elevation and amid such wonders and
solitudes of Nature is found to be at once restful and exhilarating;
all the points of interest in the neighborhood of the camp, and in
the great Hopper to the north of it, have been constantly visited,
and appropriately christened, and often vividly described, by these
parties, consisting about equally of young ladies and gentlemen;
the "Vista," for example, to the north of the camp, situated near
the watershed, whence the head stream of the "Bacon Brook"
flows north into the Hopper, and that of the "Camp Brook" also
rising close by flows south into the Heart, as we have already seen,
is one of the chief points of interest, whence, adown between Bald
Mountain and Simonds Peak, a distant and enchanting view is
gained across the whole Williamstown valley in a northwest direction, and so across the west end of the village in the line of the
Mansion House and the Kappa Alpha Lodge, and so on towards the
"Golden Gate," — the point at which the Hoosac lapses into
Vermont; although it is said, that of late years the undergrowth
near to the Vista has shown more vigor in shooting up so as to
obstruct the view, than the thews of the young men, namely, the
successive guardians and champions and laborers of the camp, have
shown in cutting it down, and so keeping the long and weird view
open.
    The Harrison farm, to which reference was just now made, has
been connected in its history with two of the early and prominent
families of the town, namely, the Harrison and Bacon families. Jacob
Bacon, son of Nathaniel 2d, both of Middletown, Connecticut, came
here a young yeoman about 1766, perhaps a little later; his father
had given him some lots of land in Lanesboro as early as 1761, and
he himself bought land there in June, 1766; Aaron Bacon and
Daniel Bacon, from Middletown, believed to be his brothers, were

landowners here in 1766, holding first division fifty-acre lots 61 and 63; and Jacob Bacon at any rate became an important citizen here, and died in December, 1819, in his eightieth year. His daughter, Jerusha, married Almon Harrison, son of Titus Harrison, another well-to-do citizen; and while the Bacons had previously held land in or near the Hopper, Harrison bought, towards the end of the last century, of a great land-grabber in his day, Ephraim Seelye, 1300 acres, including the whole high plateau between the Bluffs of Bald Mountain and the present camping-grounds. The purchase money was $1000. The present Bacon farm in the Hopper had been settled very early by Elkanah Parris, an old soldier of Fort Massachusetts; and Harrison now pushed a rude road past that place, perhaps wholly upon his own land, up the steep flank of Bald Mountain and across the flat to the point where the camps are now pitched. He cleared the land on the top, burnt the timber, raised at first great crops of wheat, built a log-house for tenants by the side of Camp Brook, the cellar and under-pinning stones of which are plainly visible to this day; and built a large barn also to the north of the house, all signs of which have long been obliterated. It has been credibly transmitted to our own times, however, that there were men enough present at the "raising" of the barn to lift the big beams into place by sheer human strength. It must have been a day of interest and probably of jollification to the men in the valley below, who were summoned to the old-fashioned raising amid the half-burned stumps of the mountain top; for there was not then, and never has been since, a framed building within two miles of the spot; and there must have been, accordingly, a novelty about it, a sort of prospective elevation of spirits, that made that particular call to a "raising" popular in the farmhouses along Green River and its branches. There was indeed no fee or reward for such a service rendered by one's neighbors; but the summoner was expected to furnish "refreshment" while the tug of the lifting was going forward, and especially when the beams and rafters were all in position, and the white oak pins had been well driven in; it was the part of the boys that were present at a raising to distribute the pins; and Almon Harrison was not a man to grudge the entertainment usual on such occasions in this locality, which was "good old" St. Croix rum; he liked it himself; and it throws a little shading over the pleasant picture of the barn-raising beneath the Bluffs, — a shading that real life often gives to its apparently most joyous scenes, — that, a decade or two later, when cider-brandy stills became the style in Williamstown, Harrison set up one on the banks of Green River near "Taylor's Crotch," that he became a drunkard, and that the Judge of Probate appointed Deacon Levi Smedley guardian over his old age, lest he should squander the patrimony of his children.

Under these circumstances the Harrisons sold the 1300 acres to Stephen Bacon, son of Jacob Bacon, and brother-in-law of Almon Harrison, who paid for the property about the same as Harrison had paid for it before, improved the former Hopper road to the mountain farm, while about the same time a second road had been run up to it from Goodell's on the other side, continued to cultivate the land there for many years, thus and otherwise permanently attached the name of Bacon to the region of the Hopper, and left to his son, Stephen Bacon 2d, born in 1804, to pass the whole of a long life on or near the paternal acres, though the Harrison farm had gone meantime into other hands. Tenants by the name of Valet, and Cottrell, and others, occupied in succession the log-house by Camp Brook. At length Stephen Bacon 3d, great-grandson to Jacob, rather through purchase than inheritance from his father, came to be a large landowner and successful farmer within the Bacon circuit, living in the last third of the century in the old house of Elkanah Parris, of which the remark was often made that its beams were of white oak, of which not a tree was ever found in the Hopper or within two or three miles of it, leaving the fair implica- tion that Parris hauled the frame of his house from the White Oaks proper. These general facts justify the designation of what is now a poor pasture annually growing smaller by the crowding in of the woods all around its outskirts as the "Harrison Farm"; and they also fully justify the naming of the brook and its branches that rises near the Vista, and drains the whole south side of the Hopper, as "Bacon Brook." The Bacon and Harrison families occupied the same pew in the old village meeting-house, built in 1796, and the two are likely always to be associated in the traditions and history of the Hopper. An anecdote well authenticated, that comes down to us from the beginning of the century, throws some light on the state of things in Williamstown at that time, and on the degree of intelligence then had among the common cultivators of the soil : — When Schuyler Putnam, son of the General, was the landlord of the Mansion House, a travelling showman brought a single tiger to be exhibited there for so much a sight. Among many others who came to see this small fraction of a menagerie, and duly paid their money, came Jacob Bacon and his wife Lois.

After looking at the animal as long as they liked, the wife said to the husband, "Come, Jacob, go get your money back, and let's go home; it's nothing but a tiger-cat!"

Before we finally leave the Harrison farm and its associations to descend into the Hopper by the Bacon Brook, we may do ourselves the pleasure of quoting and reading a fine passage descriptive of Bald Mountain and the Hopper, from the pen of Albert Hopkins : —

The spot to which I refer is Bald Mountain in Williamstown, near the Ashford line. This mountain, as a whole, resembles a lion couchant, with his head to the east, guarding seemingly the outlet of the Hopper. The sentinel is quite in keeping with the passage or gap, which he seems to protect. In fact his huge shoulder and mane form one side of the gap itself. If I have been rightly informed, Bald Mountain must bear a striking resemblance to the celebrated Rock of Gibraltar. The material, however, of which it is composed, is less beautiful than the Gibraltar stone. Like most of the group to which it belongs, it is slate, talcose, and mica, with modules of white or milky quartz intermixed.

Our mode of ascent (keeping up the figure of the lion) was on foot, and up the middle of the back. And if your readers will bear in mind the difference between a lion couchant and a lion dormant, they will see what we found to our cost to be true, that when we had reached the top of the monster's back, the greater part of the climbing remained to be done. However, we stood about twelve o'clock on his bald pate. And had we not been prepared for the view by having repeatedly seen it before, we should have been lost in absolute astonishment. But though there was less of astonishment, there was not less of wonder, as we gazed at the immense mountain masses which upheaved themselves before us. In fact we enjoyed an advantage which would have been secured by no other approach to the look-off, — that of emerging suddenly from the inconveniently thick and tangled covering of our fancied animal, into an open space where all that Greylock has of grandeur stood confronting us in a moment.

I will indicate a few points of interest, in the first place, in regard to the "Hopper," as the pioneers of Fort Massachusetts memory agreed to call this remarkable and unique indentation in the Greylock chain, — a "Clove" it would be called among the Catskills. It would seem as if some tremendous throe of Nature in the primitive ages essayed at this point to break the chain in two, but only succeeded with the weaker or western half of the link. Not content with this, it would seem that this primeval force directed its fury eastward, determining to grapple with the strength of Greylock itself; and how nearly successful it was in this audacious and almost impious attempt, those can testify who have penetrated into the true Hopper, or Hopper within the Hopper, as it might be called, a point not visible to the traveller as he passes up from Pittsfield by the usual route.

Overlooking this frightful chasm, an eagle has built his nest. Here the slanting rays of the sun scarcely penetrate, even at noon. In this gloomy fissure clouds have broken at times, so tradition reads, and so the people believe. Here are landslides 1000 feet high, one of them fresh, and apparently the result of that immense and unexampled burden of snow, which, during the past winter, loaded our mountain sides. Certain lady readers will doubtless turn pale at this part of my letter. Nothing would tempt them to set their feet in so awful a place. To such let me say that the Alpine Club, composed mostly of ladies, have not only penetrated here, but actually made the ascent to Greylock up this nearly vertical escarpment.

Prospect Mountain appears nowhere so finely as from Bald Mountain. It abuts out in a most imposing manner. Higher than Bald, it cuts off the horizon on the northeast ; but it more than compensates for what it conceals by its grand pyramidal outline ; and also by the fact, that it makes, with Mount Williams opposite, a superb setting for a beautiful landscape which appears between, contrasting finely in its azure tinge with the deep green of the nearer mountain slopes. This picture has for its floor that lofty table-land known as Wilbur's Pasture, — now growing up, by the way, into a fine evergreen park, worth being seen.

Through a gap in the opposite direction appear the Catskills. It is well for us here in the valleys to get our heads lifted up, at least once a year, high enough to see the outline of these ever to be admired summits. If I had spoken my mind freely, I should have said at least once a month. Another point of interest is the view southward. Here we see the Pittsfield valley, with its western lake, a beautiful sheet of water ; and, what interested us particularly, Monument Mountain, in Stockbridge, not projected, as from Greylock, like an undulating thread along the flank of Taconic, and hence not recognized from there except by those well posted up in south county scenery, but here Monument Rocks stand out distinctly against the sky. I thought I could see a rock called the " Haystack " under Bald Peak, but may have been mistaken. Monument Rocks are famous, having been immortalized by Bryant, and it is rather a nice point to see them from this distance. I had the pleasure of pointing them out, a few weeks since, to a party of ladies, from a point still more distant, in Clarksburg, where we spent a night pleasantly on the Green Mountain range ; and were able, after watching Greylock bathing himself, or clothing himself, in sunlight, — a process which required more than half an hour to perform, — after this we could see not only Monument Rocks, but could actually detect their white, chalk-like tints as seen from Stockbridge Plain.

I cannot close this brief sketch of a pleasant day's ramble on Bald Mountain, without referring to my last visit there. It was, perhaps, twenty years since, in company with a party, among whom was Miss Catherine Sedgwick. It was in the fall of the year, a little earlier than I should have chosen to visit the spot for the sake of the autumnal scenery. But Miss Sedgwick had selected that time purposely ; because she preferred the woods when the green, if it did not preponderate over the more brilliant colors, was at least fairly represented ; and her preference was justified by the view, than which nothing could be finer, since the forest immediately under Bald Mountain, on the east, and in front, is composed mostly of deciduous trees.

Miss Sedgwick was a native of Stockbridge, and a great admirer of its beautiful scenery, but she owned the power of our loftier mountains and more ample forests ; and would often bring her distinguished friends here, to have pointed out to herself and them what could not be found in the more quiet landscapes and woodlands of Southern Berkshire.

No one admired the scenery of our county more appreciatively than Miss

Sedgwick, so no one, not even Bryant, has done more to turn the eyes of others towards it. It happened to her to reach a period in life when the outward senses are less keen, and impressions from Nature less vivid; but her sensibilities were never more wakeful to suffering than during her latter years. Her patriotism and her charities were conspicuous during the war; and since then she has been full of sympathy with every good work. Among her latest gifts were some valuable books, in the title-page of one of which, entitled "The Charities of Europe," she wrote a few lines, closing with the prayer "that it may be blessed on its holy mission to the *Dear Boys in the White Oaks*."

One may descend to the Hopper from Bald Mountain, whence and in relation to which these striking observations by Professor Hopkins were made, either by the Harrison farm-road, or, if he be firm-footed, by the Bacon Brook, which unites its water near the bottom of the vast gorge with "Money Brook," so-called, another stream that drains with its branches all the northern sides and recesses of the Hopper, as Bacon Brook draws the drainage of its southern sides. In one of the deep and dismal gorges far up on this northern side of the Hopper, where the roots of Mount Fitch and Simonds Peak and the Wilbur Pasture all intertwine, remote and inaccessible, where the foot of man in any age has but very seldom trod, and will tread but seldom till the end of time, a small gang of counterfeiters, not long after the year 1800, had a concealed den by the side of the brook for their work of fraud. Tradition still tells many a tale about these criminals, which the prudent man will receive with caution, or not at all; but the main fact rests on firm historical grounds, and has very properly given a euphonious name to the mountain brook. Giles B. Kellogg, of Troy, a native of the town and a graduate of the College, in his old age repeatedly told the writer, and afterwards put the statement into writing for its better authentication, that, when he was a boy in his father's house, there was an old chest in one of the chambers that contained the tools and other apparatus of these counterfeiters, which had been found in the Hopper, and brought to his father as a Justice of the Peace to be used as evidence against the men in case they could be apprehended. The gang had either abandoned their work and tools, or at least had escaped the officers; but one man was arrested on suspicion that he had belonged to it, and was brought before Justice Samuel Kellogg; there was no legal evidence against the accused, and the court broke up, when a single witness had appeared and testified, that, as he was hunting in the Hopper, he had heard the sound of hammering, — "Kling, kling, kling!" and then turning to the prisoner, the witness exclaimed, "That was you, Michael, hammering out the dollars!"

No reader of these pages would ever forgive the present writer, nor would he ever forgive himself, if he should purposely omit to quote at this very point, and pretty fully too, the alleged dialogue between Professor Hopkins and one of the lady members of his Alpine Club, ostensibly held between the two as the club were climbing Money Brook in June, 1869, and as the dialogue was written out from memory for publication by the former a few days after the jaunt. Some lines on "Wawbeek Falls" will also be appended, although the name of their student author, then a member of the club, will be prudently withholden, since it is not certain that he would now be willing, after such an interval of time, to father the poem, which he might now deem to be wild and crude. The names of the two "falls" in Money Brook referred to in the conversation have a strong South Berkshire flavor, and emanated undoubtedly from the memory of the Professor, whose early life in Stockbridge and vicinity beautifully colored his later life in Williamstown.

It seems fortunate, does it not, sir, that the Wawbeek Falls should be discovered just as the Cascade was losing something of its former prestige ?

It was quite a timely discovery ; since the Cascade, even in its palmiest days, could not compete with these new falls.

There will be quite a quarrel about the honor of discovering them, I suppose.

Undoubtedly. It is already whispered round that a bear hunter in the latter part of the last century came across them. And more recently it is said that they have been heard in the distance by some foresters.

On the other hand, sir, the honor of making this fine discovery belongs, I claim, exclusively to the club. I well remember as we were returning last autumn from the Heart of Greylock ; we came over Bald Mountain ; and you took occasion from there to point out to us a shoulder in the group of mountains opposite, saying at the same time that that must be among the earliest explorations of the spring. You said you had an idea that there was something worth seeing there. Any one who went there, you said, would find a " huge world."

I recollect the circumstance ; still a mere proposal to visit a spot so wild and difficult of access did not make us discoverers. It was only when we had penetrated into it, it was only when our eyes had actually seen the recesses of the gorge, when we stood confronted by the great abutment which closes it in, and saw in place of dry ledges, as we feared, or at most, ledges covered with moss, a beautiful ribbon of foam let down in festoons from one shelf to another,—then it was that we might, as we did, regard ourselves as real *bona fide* discoverers.

Do you recollect, sir, who caught a glimpse of the falls first ?

Modesty forbids me to answer that question, but I accord to you the credit of being the second to see them. In fact, had you been in front, you might have seen them first.

I shall not soon forget the impressions made by my first glimpse of them, nor the pleasure we had as we ascended the steep mountain side opposite and observed them from aloft at a distance. What a curious effect it has to watch them through the opera-glass, reclining so as to bring one eye directly over the other.

That glass has an immense field of view; and your respect for it will be increased, when I inform you that rays of light from the summit of Chimborazo and the cone of Cotopaxi have passed through its lenses. Let me now ask you how high you judged the falls to be?

Full seventy feet, were they not? Through the glass they seemed hundreds of feet. Do you imagine them to be permanent, sir, or like the March cataracts in the Hopper which are visible only when the snow is melting?

As Money Brook, to which the stream from these falls is a principal tributary, is permanent, no doubt the falls are so likewise. There are seasons, you know, when our western friends are ashamed to exhibit even the Father of Waters. But I must now tell you, what I did not tell you afterwards, nor do any of the club know it, that there are beautiful falls higher up. You noticed, no doubt, that I did not join the returning party till they had reached the falls half or three quarters of a mile below. The cause of my delay was a device to explore the stream still farther up. And I was well rewarded for my pains; for a fifth of a mile, perhaps, above the falls was another cascade scarcely yielding in beauty to the one below. The quantity of water was less, for in the interval the stream had forked again; but it dashed along over a succession of benches after a fashion to have drawn many exclamations, had the rest of the party been able to ascend so far. These falls are probably about 1800 feet high.

Are you in earnest, sir?

I am. This cascade is nearly on a level with the Harrison farm on Bald Mountain, and must be, therefore, seventeen or eighteen hundred feet above the valley. From this point the ground slopes back gently towards Mount Fitch on the east, and towards the rim of the Hopper on the south. I think I will ask you to guess the name of these upper falls.

Sky Falls!

You are correct. They are, no doubt, the highest falls in the State. We should not, however, pronounce certainly on the point till we have explored more thoroughly the sources of Money Brook. At least one of the club has volunteered to undertake that exploration, and it should be done at once; for the forthcoming book of Washington Gladden will, no doubt, attract swarms of tourists in this direction. Whatever laurels, therefore, the club expects to win in the line of discovery, it behooves them to gather soon.

Do you not think, sir, that some more feasible route might be devised to reach the Wawbeek Falls? Otherwise, I fear that few outside the club will ever see them.

They might be reached by the way of Wilbur's Pasture. Tourists from the East would find this way the most convenient. They would then commence their explorations at the top of Sky Falls, and follow the stream downwards. But we are not to expect that ordinary tourists will do any such thing, simply for the reason that it would be impossible. The falls are real, yet they are in a dell so deep and lonely, and so at right angles to everything, that to most persons they are destined, no doubt, to remain forever among the myths of Greylock.

WAWBEEK FALLS.

Nature tripping over Greylock,
   Threw her velvet mantle down,
And clasped its green folds on his shoulder
   With a jewel from her crown.

A gem with the diamond's lustre,
   And the opal's fitful light,
Which blended the pearl's soft iris
   With the shadowy chrysolite.

And the mountain's giant sentries,
   Round the priceless treasure fold,
As the dragons in the garden,
   Watched the fabled fruit of gold.

Gently as a maiden's tresses
   Brush against her rounded cheek,
O'er the time-worn, moss-grown boulders
   Glide the waters of Wawbeek.

Dancing on the sloping sunbeams,
   Sadly sweet, yet weirdly strong,
Thro' earth's emerald arched temple,
   Floats its mystic, dreamy song.

Breaks it first in filmy silver
   Like a bride's soft veil of lace,
Crowned with flowers made fairer, purer,
   By the roses of her face.

Then bubbling, laughing, sighing, singing,
   Pours it from the glittering ledge,
Gleaming like a Naiad's tresses,
   Silvered with the kiss of age.

As the sun rolls down towards evening
   O'er it steals a golden glow,
Like a conflagration sweeping
   Thro' a forest thick with snow.

And the gold blends with the ruby
   Till the water seems like wine,
As if Bacchus on the mountain
   Had o'erturned his cup divine.

Then calmer, slower, softer, clearer,
   Glides it o'er the argent-sand,
Like some life, its youth's joy ended,
   Sweeping toward the Better Land.

Money Brook and Bacon Brook join their streams in murmuring acquiescence on one of the lower slopes of the huge Hopper, and so form the Hopper Brook, which, after a devious course of two miles or so, falls into Green River at Taylor's Crotch.

It now only remains, to complete this opening chapter on the "Situation" of Williamstown, to devote a few elementary paragraphs to its geology, its diversities of soil, its natural productions, and its unique beauty as a whole.

The central valley of the town is underlaid throughout by limestone. This is true in general of the narrow east and west portion along the Hoosac, and more exactly true of the broader valley north and south along the courses of the Green River and the Hemlock Brook. Now limestone is a good rock for all practical purposes. It seems to give the right proportion of "grit" to both the men and the beasts who live above and upon it. The Blue Grass region in Kentucky, which is a limestone section, breeds horses of the best bottom and the greatest speed of any in the United States; and Vermont, which is also full of limestone rock, stands next after Kentucky in that regard. We shall see on many a sequent page, that the men of Williamstown at any rate, whether the same be true of other localities or not, have shown from the very first good courage and firm stamina in five successive wars, as well as in many a moral conflict. It is probably true, accordingly, that a bit of limestone in one's daily bread does no harm to the digestion, or the subsequent action of mind and body; and limestone water also, to those who are well used to it, is the most wholesome water in the world.

An excellent quarry of limestone lies along the lowest edge of Bee Hill by the Hemlock Brook, and the ledge extends diagonally across the brook and reappears in masses on the southern slopes of Stone Hill. The materials for the building of the second College chapel in 1859 came from this quarry, and then Goodrich Hall was built from the same in 1861, next Clark Hall in 1880, then Morgan Hall in 1882, and the new Gymnasium also in 1885. These and all the other College buildings, without exception, have as their underlying foundation, in whole or in part, the living limestone rock. Previous to the erection of the first College chapel in 1827, now called Griffin Hall, masses of this rock rose up, ragged and twice as high as a man's head, on the main street in front of that building. These masses were broken down by gunpowder and thrown into the foundations of that building, and the ground in front was smoothed off much as it is at present; but when the trees were planted there,

about 1850, earth was brought from a distance to cover to a sufficient depth for their growth the then almost naked limestone rock,
which even now appears here and there above the surface. The
Records of the Trustees, under date of August 3, 1785, which was
the second meeting of that body, reveal the fact, that there had been
long before a lime-kiln near where the Soldiers' Monument now
stands; because they passed a vote at that time to erect their first
building for the Free School either "upon the eminence south of
Mr. William Horsford's house [where the West College now
stands], or upon the eminence further east in the northwest corner
of Captain Isaac Searle's lot [where Clark Hall now stands], *opposite the old lime-kiln*, as the Corporation shall hereafter determine."

At present the only place in the village, or near it, in which the
native rock stands out boldly, is directly in the rear of the chapel,
where the western wall of the hill itself is a picturesque and perpendicular mass of limestone about fifteen feet high, full of scars and
cracks and crevices and old geologic wrinkles.

In the autumn of 1884 the writer had the pleasure and profit of
studying this limestone formation carefully, under the personal
instruction of Professor Dana, of New Haven, then, and for a long
time previous, the foremost geologist in the United States. He
exhibited the proofs on the spot and in detail, that this bed-rock
not only covers all the central valleys of Williamstown at no great
depth beneath the surface, but also that it crowds up into the clove
of the Hopper, and there dips under the range of Greylock, and
reappears upon the other side in the town of Adams, where the
inclination is towards the west, while the dip on this side is pretty
uniformly towards the east.

"Most limestones have been formed from shells and corals ground
up by the action of the sea, and afterwards consolidated. The composition is usually the same as carbonate of lime, except that
impurities, as clay or sand, are often present. Carbonate of lime
is one of the most universal of minerals. It is the ingredient of a
very large part of the limestones of the world, and these include
the various true marbles. When free from impurities, it consists
of carbonic acid forty-four parts, and limestone fifty-six parts. In
common limestone, oxygen is forty-eight per cent of the whole."
(Dana.) These simple facts of science account for much in the
soil, and for something in the history, of central Williamstown.
The soil of course is calcareous, that is, a soil full of lime, and there
is also much iron in it, partly because there is iron in the limestone,
and partly because there is a large deposit of iron ore, which was

once profitably worked on the slope of Mount Williams, and such ore was doubtless more or less diffused in the region. The presence of oxygen and iron and lime in and upon the rock frets it continually. Oxidation is followed by disintegration, and gives rise to the reddish-brown dust which always covers the limestone boulders embedded in the soil, and which constantly enriches and strengthens it for the purposes of agriculture. This our limestone soil, consequently, is good, has a body to it, takes kindly to other fertilizers, grows unsurpassed grasses and vegetables, and though for some reason no longer favorable to wheat, is still as good for corn as any land in the world.

Carbonic acid is two parts oxygen and one part carbon. All that is needful in order to burn pure limestone into lime, is to throw off the carbonic acid by heat, which leaves a pure lime. The limestone here, however, has too many of the impurities spoken of above to make a good lime; and this is undoubtedly the reason why the "lime-kiln" in the main street, spoken of as "old" even in 1785, was abandoned.

. The rock next in importance to this limestone of our valleys, which itself extends uninterruptedly to the north and becomes the great central marble belt of Vermont, is the mica schist of all our encircling hills. The Taconics and their lower eminences towards the valley, the whole mass of Saddle Mountain in every part of it, and for the most part the East Mountain also, with its four uplifts already described, are composed of this slaty and schistose and most useful rock. Its constituents are the same as those of granite and gneiss, containing, however, relatively more quartz and more mica and less feldspar than these. Since common clay is a mixture of powdered feldspar and quartz, and is composed of just one-half of oxygen, and the sand which comes from quartz is more than one-half of oxygen, and feldspar only a little less than one-half, these two things follow as a matter of course from the great abundance and lofty place of mica schist in all the mountains round about; namely, first, that clay must be a large ingredient in the soil of all the contiguous valleys and farms; and second, that substances so largely composed of oxygen as clay and sand are, will easily burn and fuse, and consequently that common bricks have naturally been burned and built with in almost every part of this town from the first. All the early College buildings, for example, as well as many farmhouses and other dwellings, were built of brick burned out of the clay and sand of the immediate localities.

In the course of ages, vast beds of clay have slipped down from the sides and gorges of these schistose mountains; for example, adown the three sides of the Hopper and the slopes of Mount Prospect and Mount Williams: and there they lie to-day, underneath the farms and roads of a large part of our territory. One such deposit of clay from the cleft between Williams and Prospect, and which lies near the Baker Bridge and the east line of Williamstown, furnished for nearly a century materials for brick-burning, and for a time also for a coarse pottery work made at the east end of the village by a Mr. Faxon, of Hartford. Clay roads are uncomfortable in the springtime when they are heaved up by the frost, and sometimes even dangerous by means of breaking through the lifted crust; but for the summer and autumn they are the best roads in the world, — hard and smooth, Nature's own aluminated pavement.

These slaty slopes and hilltops, reinvigorated by the constantly disintegrating rocks above them and underneath them, make very early and very fertile land. Sometimes the very plough manures the soil as it traces the furrow. The farms on Bee Hill, for example, and on the slopes of Prospect south of Blackinton, are perhaps a week earlier in springtime than the colder calcareous lands along the river bottoms; but the latter are, after all, a stronger and heartier soil, — lime and iron are good for the land, — while, nevertheless, these rough and slaty uplands grow warm in the sun, drain easily, partially renew themselves from the fretting rock beneath; and, when the clays are not too stiff, are worked without difficulty, and bountifully reward the farmer's toil by all the crops adapted to such a soil.

There is but one other native rock in Williamstown besides these two, and that is confined to a narrow belt along the north side of the Hoosac River, and to a still narrower section upon the highest parts of Stone Hill, namely, quartzite. There are quartzite boulders of all sizes, locally called "hardheads," scattered all over the area of the town, even to the tops of the highest hills, and these were doubtless brought hither from a distance in the period of the glaciers; but quartzite *in situ* is only now to be found in the two places just indicated. Dana defines quartzite as "a hard, compact rock, consisting of quartz grains or sand, and usually either white, gray, or grayish red in color. It is but a step removed from ordinary sandstone, and owes its peculiarities to metamorphic agencies." When the railroad was built west from North Adams through Williamstown, it became needful to make a deep cut at Braytonville through this hard quartzite, and several successive contractors are said to have been ruined through gross underestimates of its hardness and difficulty in working. Long afterwards, however, the broken rock from this cutting and from other cuttings instituted for the purpose, was found to be the most useful material obtainable for ballasting the entire road.

Quartzite is especially associated with sand, as mica schist is with clay, and nearly all the sandy land in Williamstown is found to the north of the Hoosac, and in more or less connection with this species of rock. There are, however, no great deposits in town of white sand, once disintegrated from this rock, or once the source whence the rock was formed, whichever of the two views be the right one in geology, as there are in the neighboring towns of Lanesboro and Cheshire, where such deposits have long been utilized in the manufacture of glass products on the spot, and been exported also for that purpose to great distances and in immense quantities. It is probable that there may be a small deposit of white sand in some connection with the quartzite somewhere in the White Oaks, because the "Ballous," a noted family there, brought sand into the street for scrubbing purposes for several generations; and when one or another were asked where they got it, their half-witted answer commonly was, "Oh! we fine it!" But it has been the opinion of many that they rather pounded it from the partially pulverized rock, than found it free in any special deposit, which, if it exist, was never reported as seen by other inhabitants of that locality.

Much more local interest attaches to this odd "Ballou" family, pronounced as if it were "Blue," whitish mulattoes, as some have said, very dark whites, as has been asserted by others, extremely dirty in either case, than whether there be free white sand in some corner of the White Oaks. "Are the Blues blacks, or blue-blacks?" has been a long-standing conundrum with the generous and inquisitive people of Williamstown.

Aaron Ballou was a poor cripple nearly doubled together, his head almost between his legs, who was often seen in the street selling sand, or, more rarely, begging, and who died on Oak Hill, May 30, 1876. His brother Amasa, with others, was frozen to death in the road over the Petersburg Pass the night of the 16th of April, 1857. A brother of these two was named after good Deacon Deodatus Noble; and that the whole family have been underwitted may be illustrated by what was said to him by another brother of still a third one: "Date, Dan's sick as hell, — can't live, 'fore mornin'." Another member of the family, an uncle of these just mentioned, so far as relationships can be made out in a family given to miscegenation, a strong man, used to do little jobs

in the street as occasion offered. Old Christopher Penniman, a
wholesale butcher, who dealt in salt and salted meat as well as
cattle, sometimes employed him. One day a load of salt in bags
had to be taken from the wagon; and Harvey and Chester Penniman, sons of the proprietor, and young bucks of the town, mounted
the wagon to lay on the stout shoulders of the White Oaker the
heavy bags. Tossing one in sport pretty vigorously to its destination, they were rewarded by this ejaculation sputtered out from
between gritted teeth, "I, gy! more buk there 'n heft!"

Notwithstanding its great abundance only a few miles to the south,
there is comparatively little pure sand to be found within the town's
limits, and it has sometimes proven difficult to procure sand even
good enough and abundant enough for the purposes of the stone
mason and plasterer. The Sand Spring, as its name implies, bubbles
up profusely through fine sand; and it was along the course of
Broad Brook, which flows near to this spring, that the only pine
timber of consequence was found by the early settlers, so close is
the native affinity between pines and the sand; and pines of a later
growth are starting up again at present over a sandy hill along the
Hoosac, north and east of the mouth of that brook, where two pine
lots were located in 1765, and to some extent in other places north
of the Hoosac; and there is a large sandy hill east of the Green
River and over against Water Street, and another on Hemlock Brook
near the west end of the village, and there is some sandy or rather
gravelly soil between the two main tributaries of Green River at the
south part of the town; and some of the alluvial land along the
Hoosac may perhaps be called sandy, as, for instance, on the old Kellogg farm, now owned by F. G. Smedley, whence of late years some
sand has been brought to the village for use in making mortar.

From the three species of native rock, to which attention has now
been called, the materials of the soil have been so well mixed together by Nature, — the clay and sand and lime and iron have been
so well adjusted into loam, — that the land is generally productive,
and might be made far more so than it is, by a more skilful and
laborious husbandry. The lower slopes of North West Hill, as they
approach Birch Brook and Hemlock Brook, have always been
esteemed among the best lands in the town : the farm cleared up
by Joseph Tallmadge, and now owned by Colonel A. L. Hopkins, has
generally been regarded the best grain farm in town; while the
farm along the Green River, which began to be cleared by Ichabod
Southwick as early as 1763, and is now owned and tilled by Deacon
Stephen Hickcox, may hardly be reckoned under his efficient culture

as inferior to the best. There is more of excellent land on the southerly slope of Stone Hill, and the northerly slopes of Prospect, on the slaty rolls of Birch and Bee hills, as well as on the limestone levels of the central uplands and the alluvial levels of the two main rivers. [1]

Now, as the soil in general is good, so the seasons are commonly favorable to the crops cultivated in this region. Indeed, the spring season opens earlier than one would suppose from the looks of things here in midwinter; for on the first day of April, 1868, Albert Hopkins found in bloom the trailing arbutus (epigera), the silverleaf (hepatica), the aspen, and the alder. This was a little earlier than is usual, while in the course of that month blossoms are always found on the elm, the soft maple, the willows, the leatherwood, the coltsfoot, the bloodroot, the spring-beauty, the wake-robin, and the violets. The birds, too, come early, the bluebirds within a day or two of March 15, the robins in considerable numbers about the same time, the sparrows and blackbirds and meadow larks in the last days of March or first days of April.

There is usually no lack and no excess of rain for the best purposes of agriculture. Occasionally a season will be so dry as to have the term "drought" applied to it by those who cultivate the more sandy or gravelly lands; sometimes, too, the springtime will seem to be wet and backward, as when, for instance, the average temperature of the 11th of June, 1869, was as low as fifty-two degrees; but a late spring does not import a deficient harvest, because Nature has the knack of making up for lost time; and all these matters of heat and moisture seem to be attempered to the average needs of our soil and crops. Wheat is no longer much raised on the farms in Williamstown, nor rye; corn, oats, buckwheat, and barley are the principal cereals, while grass, potatoes, and the edible roots pretty much round out the circle of the agriculture; as orchards, small fruits, and garden vegetables are the main items of the horticulture. It is true that an impatient farmer in haying-time, or a gardener whose weeds are getting the start of his plants, may sometimes take up the burden, if not the words, of Shakspeare, — "And the rain it raineth every day"; but in the whole upshot of the season it is generally allowed by all, that the climatic influences of all sorts are wisely ordained, even in reference to the requisites of the average products of the soil; and in all kinds of seasons, early or late, dry

[1] See the Lowell Lectures entitled "Agriculture," of Deacon Alexander Hyde; Chester Dewey, in Introduction to Field's *Berkshire*; and I have derived information as to soils from my colleague, Chadbourne, and my father-in-law, James Smedley.

or wet, warm or cold, it is the joy of the springtime to watch the vegetation creep slowly up the sides of the mountains to their top. Mount Williams, for example, rises about 2400 feet directly up from the Hoosac and the meadow on which Fort Massachusetts once stood; and there is room, accordingly, for many zones of vegetation between the valley and the summit, and in a late season the foliage on the trees at the very top is not visible in the valley before the 8th of June.

Ephraim Williams, Senior, who officially traversed many parts of the present town of Williamstown in 1739, then in its primeval wildness, in obedience to a Resolve of the General Court of Massachusetts, did not put upon record in his report to that body any detailed description of its territory, or any transcript at length of his own impressions in regard to it; and just about the same may be said of Richard Hazen, surveyor for Massachusetts and New Hampshire, who looked down upon its area, certainly with admiration, from what we now call Mount Hazen, two years later than that, in 1741; still we fortunately possess from the polished pens of three gentlemen of times long subsequent to theirs, all of them comparatively strangers to the place, and each of them differing widely from the others in social position and general standpoint, their personal impressions received by casual views of our valley and of its environment; and this initial chapter of our book on Williamstown will now be brought to a conclusion by the use of a quotation from each of these three gentlemen, of whom but one was a native of this country, and one of the other two only a transient traveller through it in 1883, recording afterwards in a pleasant volume what he saw and what he thought about it at the time.

James McCosh, a Scotchman till 1868, then a long time president of the College of New Jersey and resident of Princeton, wrote of Williamstown as follows: "It is placed on a knoll in the heart of a capacious hollow, surrounded with imposing mountains. It struck me as a spot at which the Last Judgment might be held, with the universe assembled on the slopes of the encircling hills."

Daniel Pidgeon, F.G.S., an English tourist, with a sharp eye in his head for natural objects, and with an uncommon faculty for interpreting the social conditions of the New World, thus frankly jots down his own impressions: —

A charming stage ride of four miles, following the Hoosac River past the foot of Greylock, brought me to Williamstown, which peaceful and academical village lies buried, like Adams, among mountains, here enclosing a lovely triangular valley, where the Green River joins the Hoosac in its course to the Hudson.

The town is built on a boldly undulating plateau of limestone, which, rising to a considerable height from the lower ground, affords magnificent views of the encircling hills, whose forest-covered crests tower to heights of three and four thousand feet. The valley is wholly settled by farmers; there is not a manufactory and hardly a retail shop in the village, whose pretty white bungalows rise from park-like and elm-shaded stretches of turf, while the undulating main street is bordered at intervals by the halls, chapel, museum, and library of Williams College. The college buildings are for the most part plain and without any academic air, but, spite of a chapel like the conventicle of an English country town, a very unpretentious library, and a number of barrack-like "halls" where the men live, its romantic situation, park-enfolded homes, and peaceful atmosphere, place Williamstown easily ahead of every other New England village for beauty. The "secret societies" are nothing more than students' clubs, which affect a little mystery in their organization, and are distinguished by cryptogramic titles, whose meaning is only known to the members. Thus the letters, Α, Δ, Φ, carved on the façade of the meeting-room of one of the largest societies, may possible signify αεν δεινοι φαγειν (always terrible eaters), although nothing beyond examples, it is said, supports this view of the case. Some of these clubs are wealthy institutions; old members, who have succeeded in life, delighting to bring liberal offerings to the lares and penates of their college days, so that many of them are now housed in spacious and handsome temples.

The Sabbath evening was still and peaceful, and I sat on the veranda of the hotel, looking, by turns, up to the wooded summits of East Mountain, the Dome, and Greylock, already tinged with sunset pink, around upon the white, lawn-bordered homes of farmers and professors, or down the dusty Hoosac valley, where a silver thread of water wound about, and was finally lost sight of in the folds of Taconics' forest robe. In the porch of the "terrible eaters'" lodge, just opposite, a group of students, picturesquely disposed, was singing the evening hymn in harmony, while above the great gray hills a rising moon hung her silver shield against the sunset's crimson. Thus the May night fell, lightly as sleep, upon a scene of singular beauty and purity, closing a day made delightful to me by rest from labor and labor questions, by some pleasant glimpses of American youth, and by the bright anticipations for its manhood to which those glimpses gave rise.

The last quotation is from Nathaniel Hawthorne, written in 1838, when he described himself as "the obscurest man of letters in America." He became, perhaps, the most illustrious man of letters in America. At any rate he was an American, in birth, in training, in sympathies, in atmosphere, in everything.

Greylock was hidden in clouds, and the rest of Saddle Mountain had one partially wreathed about it; but it was withdrawn before long. It was very beautiful cloud scenery. The clouds lay on the breast of the mountain, dense, white, well-defined, and some of them were in such close vicinity that it seemed as if I could infold myself in them; while others, belonging to the same fleet, were floating through the blue sky above. I had a view of Williamstown, at the distance of a few miles, — two or three, perhaps, — a white village and steeple in a gradual hollow, with high mountainous swells heaving themselves up, like immense, subsiding waves, far and wide around it. On these high mountain-waves rested the white summer clouds, or they rested as still in the air above ; and they were formed into such fantastic shapes that they gave the strongest possible impression of being confounded or intermixed with the sky. It was like a day-dream to look at it ; and the students ought to be day-dreamers, all of them, — when cloud-land is one and the same thing with the substantial earth. By degrees all these clouds flitted away, and the sultry summer sun burned on hill and valley.

CHAPTER II.

"My sentence is for open war; of wiles
More unexpert, I boast not: them let those
Contrive who need, or when they need, not now."
— MILTON.

IN the summer of 1609 remarkable historical events took place a little to the west and northwest of the Hoosac valley, events that served to color its after history throughout, and that became in the way of preparings and developments the ground and occasion of the long-subsequent building of Fort Massachusetts. On the one hand, Henry Hudson, an Englishman sailing under Dutch authority, was navigating that summer the river since called by his name, in a small yacht christened the "*Half Moon*," as far up as the present site of Albany; one of his boats, moreover, running up further to the upper mouth of the Mohawk, where the old town of "Half Moon" still commemorates the name of the craft that lay anchored below. The mouth of the Hoosac is about ten miles still further up the river upon its other bank. Before the yacht turned to descend the stream, never till then touched by the keel of white men, Hudson handsomely entertained on board his ship the chief men of the Indians of the region, especially of the Iroquois or Six Nations, who then inhabited and controlled both banks of the main stream to a good distance inland, and also of its tributaries, the Hoosac and the Batten Kill. The story of this feast lingered clear in the traditions of the Iroquois for two hundred years, and for nearly as long a similar tradition was current among the Mohegans, whose chief seat in historical times was at Schodack at the mouth of Kinderhook Kill, somewhat lower down the river.

Three at least of the white men on board the *Half Moon* kept a sort of journal of events, and some of these also note the fact, that Hudson gave the chiefs "much wine and *aqua vitæ*"; that then first the northern Indians saw a drunken man; that the rest "did not

69

know how to take it," thinking the man bewitched, and bringing
their charms to save him from the strangers' arts; and that when
the old chief promptly recovered the next day, after "sleeping all
night quietly," and professed himself much delighted with the
experience, they held the whites in high honor and made Hudson
"an oration" after their well-known manner in later times.

Among the results of this fortunate discovery and exploration
of the "Great River of the Mountains," as the Indians called it, was
the gradual establishment of the province of New Netherlands by
the Dutch, a fort and the beginnings of a settlement on Manhattan
Island, dating from 1613, and Fort Orange and a settlement on the
present site of Albany, dating from 1623. In 1650, under the Dutch
governor Stuyvesant, the beginnings of a boundary line between
New Netherlands and New England were determined on at Hartford; namely, to start on the west side of Greenwich Bay about four
miles from Stamford, the line to run thence up into the country
twenty miles, provided it did not come within ten miles of the
Hudson River, the Dutch agreeing not to build within six miles of
such line. When the English took forcible possession of the New
Netherlands in 1664, and rechristened the province "New York," and
Fort Orange "Albany," after the two titles of the King's brother,
later James the Second, to whom the province had been assigned by
Charles the Second, there was a meeting between commissioners of
Connecticut and parties representing the Duke of York and Albany
in relation to a permanent boundary line between the two provinces.
Good feeling prevailed on both sides, and a general understanding
was reached and maintained, that the line should be run about
twenty miles to the east of Hudson River. Nothing was expressly
stipulated about the line further north, as between Massachusetts
and New York, but the impression strongly prevailed in the former
colony that the latter had virtually agreed to extend the same line
northwards, and so to make the west line of Massachusetts also
about twenty miles from the Hudson. Unfortunately, however,
more than a century elapsed before this boundary was definitely
established in 1787, and in the mean time mutual fears and jealousies,
conflicting claims and baffled negotiations often attempted, became
one main reason for the building of Fort Massachusetts in 1745.
The Dutch had kept the good-will of the Six Nations for the most
part, and transferred the same with the province to the English, a
circumstance that had a controlling influence upon historical events
for a century, that is, until the end of the French and Indian
wars.

On the other hand, during this same summer of 1609, Samuel
Champlain, who the year before had laid the first foundations of
Quebec, in the name of King Henry IV., of France, was sailing
further up the St. Lawrence under a royal commission, in company
with about sixty Indian warriors from the neighborhood of Quebec,
and from the Ottawa and its tributaries, — Montagnais and Algonquins and Hurons, — and then to the south up the river Richelieu
into the beautiful lake then first named by himself "Champlain."
His motive was exploration, description to his king, and the extension to the southward of the dominion of France; and their motive
was now to attack to better advantage, with the help of Champlain
and his two French companions, each of the three armed with the
arquebus, a weapon then utterly unknown in the wilderness, their
hereditary and traditional enemies, the Iroquois of central New
York. The first time Champlain had entered the St. Lawrence in
1603, he had found encamped near the mouth of the Saguenay,
at Tadousac, a large number of these northern savages, estimated
at a thousand, who had just returned from, and were celebrating
a great victory over, the Iroquois, near the mouth of the Richelieu;
and he had learned in the mean time, and indeed was never afterwards allowed to forget, that the region of that stream and of the
lake that drains through it to the St. Lawrence was and had been
for many generations, perhaps for many centuries, the neutral and
uninhabited battle-ground between these ever hostile tribes and races
on the St. Lawrence and its northern and western tributaries, and
those tribes on the Mohawk and the lakes back of it and the Hudson
above it, where, in all probability, on each returning summer they
met in deadly conflict, with alternating successes and defeats. It is
interesting to note that for this time, the summer of 1609, the battle
took place upon that rounded point at the junction of the waters
of Lake George with those of Lake Champlain, where nearly a century and a half afterwards the French built their little fort Carillon,
and the British their famous and gigantic fortress Ticonderoga.
The Mohawks numbered two hundred and the northern Indians but
sixty, yet the presence of the three Frenchmen with firearms more
than made up the difference; and the tumultuous joy of the latter
over their victory that ensued, issuing, as usual, in nameless cruelty
to their captives, is set in the graphic pages of Champlain over
against the sudden flight and utter dismay of the former at the
strange and deadly weapons of their foes.

Again and yet again in later years Champlain accompanied similar
war parties of the Hurons and Algonquins and Montagnais against

their brave and more civilized enemies of the Five Nations of New York, the second time in 1610, to a battle near the mouth of the Richelieu, whence not a single Mohawk returned to tell the tale of disaster and death; and the third time in 1615, after an immense circuit with a host of savages up the Ottawa and by Lake Nipissing and Georgian Bay and Lake Ontario, to a wholly unsuccessful attack on the central stronghold of the Iroquois, probably located near the foot of Seneca Lake at what is now Perryville, New York; and, as Hudson gained for the Dutch and English, by kind treatment, the lasting friendship of the Mohawks and their allies, so Champlain and his French successors acquired the lasting enmity of the same, just about in proportion to their remarkable success in holding firm the confidence and allegiance of the Indians of Canada. In all the great wars that followed between England and France, so far as their respective colonists in America took part in them, the Iroquois almost uniformly sided with the English, and the great northern tribes cast in their lot for better and worse with the French, even after the fall of Quebec in 1759, and until the death of Pontiac, the great Ottawa chief, in 1769.

1. The first of these wars is commonly called "King William's War." It began when the news of the English Revolution, and the continued recognition of James II. nevertheless by Louis XIV., reached the wilderness in 1689; and it was terminated by the Peace of Ryswick in 1697. In August of the first-mentioned year fifteen hundred of the Iroquois surprised the French town of Montreal at break of day, set fire to the houses, and engaged in indiscriminate massacre. In September, commissioners from New England held a conference with the Mohawks at Albany, and asked for an alliance and for help in fighting the Abenakis of Maine. "We have burned Montreal," they replied; "we are allies of the English; we will keep the chain unbroken." But they would not consent to invade the Abenakis. On the other hand, in a vain attempt to gain the esteem of the Five Nations by a display of prowess, to win them to neutrality at least, if not to friendship, Frontenac, the French governor of Canada, planned and executed a triple descent of French and Indians into the English provinces; one of which struck Schenectady at midnight, with the usual horrors of warwhoop and massacre and conflagration; another, Salmon Falls, on the Piscataqua, where women and children to the number of fifty-four were either murdered or carried captive; and the third, the fort and settlement in Casco Bay, further to the eastward. So it went, back and forth, to the weary close of this great war.

2. The next of these colonial struggles has long been named "Queen Anne's War." It arose in 1703, and subsided with the Peace of Utrecht in 1713. Vaudreuil, now governor of Canada, resolved to conciliate the Five Nations for this war at any cost, and so made a formal treaty with the Senecas, which was commemorated by two strings of wampum; and to prevent any rupture of this agreement, he determined to send no war parties against the English on the side of New York at all, so that it was the province of Massachusetts that was chiefly desolated this time by savage forays from Canada. Deerfield had been warned by friendly Mohawks that danger would hang over it in the winter of 1704; and thereafter there was not a night but the sentinel was abroad, not a house but was fortified by its little circle of palisades; when, on the morning of the first day of March, the snow lying four feet deep and crusted, a war party of 200 French and 142 Indians who had come on the crust all the way from Canada, after the unfaithful sentinels had retired at the approach of dawn, raised their infernal yell, set the village on fire, so that only the church and one dwelling escaped, killed outright forty-seven of the people, and made captives of 112, including the minister and his family. "The Redeemed Captive," written by this minister, John Williams, after his return from Canada, became famous and acquainted everybody in the colonies before the next war broke out with a touching tale of Indian manners and atrocities. Four years later, the destroyer of Deerfield, Hertel de Rouville, led a similar horde of French and Indians to a second and more ruthless sack of Haverhill on the Merrimac, which had also suffered similarly in the previous war. No wonder the brave Peter Schuyler, of Albany, sent the following message to Governor Vaudreuil: "I hold it my duty towards God and my neighbor to prevent, if possible, these barbarous and heathen cruelties. My heart swells with indignation when I think that a war between Christian princes, bound to the exactest laws of honor and generosity, which their noble ancestors have illustrated by brilliant examples, is degenerating into a savage and boundless butchery. These are not the methods for terminating the war."

3. "King George's War," with which our present chapter is specially concerned, commenced in 1744, and was provisionally interrupted rather than definitively concluded by the Peace of Aix la Chapelle in 1748. During this interval the line of forts between the Connecticut and the Hoosac was established and constructed. Fort Massachusetts was the westernmost and chiefest of the whole line; and all were built and manned under the authority and at the

expense of the General Court of the colony. In this brief interval
also the particular fort just mentioned was besieged and taken by
the French and Indians, was then burnt by them, its entire garrison
taken captive to Canada, and then afterwards rebuilt and regarri-
soned by the colony, more indeed as it turned out for actual service
in the following than in the present war. By much the greatest
event, however, in King George's War was the capture from the
French, chiefly by Massachusetts troops, of the Fortress of Louisburg
on the island of Cape Breton in 1745. This fortress had been pronounced by competent engineers to be impregnable. It was even
called the "Gibraltar of America." Obtaining in the General Court
a majority of but one vote in favor of the enterprise, William
Shirley, royal governor of the colony from 1741 to 1756, projected
and organized and carried through under the immediate command
of William Pepperell, of Maine, an expedition, comprising men of
the New England colonies and a few from the middle colonies;
which, under a motto suggested by Whitefield for the purpose, —*nil
desperandum Christo duce*, — completely reduced the renowned French
fortress in less than two months, when, at the hearing of the news,
Boston bells rang out their thankful peals, while the people humbly
exclaimed, "God has gone out of the way of his common providence
in a remarkable and most miraculous manner." As we shall see in
the sequel, the story of the taking of Louisburg connects itself
intimately with the story of the line of forts in western Massachusetts, insomuch as William Williams, the builder of Fort Shirley,
and the rebuilder of Fort Massachusetts, and the commander of the
line of forts, enlisted men out of its garrisons to take them as
soldiers to Louisburg at Shirley's command, though he arrived there
too late to be of service in the reduction.

4. The last and most decisive of the great wars carried on in the
wilds of America between France and England, with some parts of
which our coming story will be intimately blended, is best named
in America, also what it has long been called in Europe, the "Seven
Years' War." It was not precisely the same seven years in the two
cases, but it was the same war, and carried on with largely the same
motives in the double participants on each side. France and Canada
were Catholic and Jesuit, England and the colonies were intensely
Protestant; besides, for a century and a half the two powers had
been contending by sea and by land for territorial supremacy in
America. In 1613 Captain Argall, from Virginia, had broken up the
French settlement on the island of Mt. Desert, which gave rise to
an intercolonial war on the Atlantic at the very time Champlain was

operating against the Five Nations from his base of Quebec. As early as 1535, Cartier had sailed up the St. Lawrence as far as Montreal, which he named. The French had a valid claim by exploration certainly, and in a partial sense by Christianization also to by far the largest part of the present United States east of the Mississippi, and they controlled that river to its mouth, and its northern tributaries to their sources. The Seven Years' War began on this side the water in the valley of the upper Ohio in May, 1754, when Washington, bearing a commission from the governor of Virginia, captured a French detachment under Jumonville and killed the commander; while indeed the war was not openly declared in Europe between the two great powers till 1756; and the Peace of Paris in 1763 closed the war for good and all, so far as French claims in America went, by the surrender of Canada and the great West to Great Britain, and made peace for many years in Europe also as between the two main combatants. Now it is curious to notice that the chief campaigns in this war, beginning in 1755, were fought out on the old neutral battle-ground of the Iroquois and Algonquins. The upper Hudson and Lake George were a war-path for the English and Mohawks to Lake Champlain and Canada, and the Richelieu and upper St. Lawrence were routes for French and Indians to Lake George and Oswego. It is these immemorial routes and battle-grounds of the Indians, and later of their civilized confederates on the one side and the other, that connects the valleys of the Hoosac and the Deerfield and the line of forts flanking the two with the vast events and issues of the last two French wars.

At the outbreak of King George's War in 1744, to which we now turn back to take up causes and effects in their historical order, the colony of Massachusetts was naturally enough intensely anti-French and zealously anti-Catholic. Father Râle, a Jesuit priest, a man of much vigor and scholarly cultivation, had been established in a French mission among the Abenakis at Norridgewock, on the upper Kennebec, as early as 1695. He accompanied these Indians on their hunting and fishing excursions, and obtained a large influence over them. Many of them became neophytes and counted their beads and said their Ave Marias. And he was believed by the New Englanders to have instigated various Indian forays against the settlements along the coast. The whole network of Jesuit missions on the St. Lawrence, on the Chaudière, and on the Kennebec excited a fearful animosity in Massachusetts, whose people ascribed all Indian hostilities to their machinations. Râle was specially singled out for vengeance, and a price was set upon his head. His forest chapel at Norridgewock was burned down in 1705; a second expedition in 1722 pillaged his cabin and chapel, which had been in the meantime rebuilt, carrying off among other papers, which certainly confirmed the English suspicions, his dictionary compiled by himself of the Abenaki language, now preserved as invaluable in the library of Harvard College; and at last in 1724 another English party surprised the place, killed the priest at the foot of his mission cross, disgracefully mutilated his body, killing also seven chiefs who had tried to protect his sacred body by covering it with their own.[1] Twenty years later, accordingly, when the next formal war broke out between England and France, Massachusetts carried into it not only an hereditary enmity against Frenchmen, but also a fierce crusading spirit against Catholics and Jesuits.

An entirely distinct set of causes from these, however, contributed to the great exertions made by Massachusetts throughout King George's War, and especially to the building of the line of forts westward from the Connecticut River. The original charter of Massachusetts extended the limits of the colony to a point "three miles north of the Merrimac River." But what part of Merrimac River? The colony claimed that it meant *any* part of that river, and that the river was known by that name from the point of junction of its two main branches in what is now Franklin, New Hampshire; but the colony of New Hampshire, which had been mostly united with Massachusetts under one government from its first settlement in 1623 to its final separation in 1741, claimed in general that the charter intended a point three miles north of the *mouth* of the river; and a great deal of acrimony attended, from first to last, this controversy about the boundary line. New Hampshire was still feeble and poor, and had declined to assume the expenses of an independent administration of government; and yet, looking forward to that goal, steadily pushed its claim to jurisdiction over many townships which its southern neighbor had founded and defended on the territory in dispute. Unluckily, as this boundary question pressed towards its final solution through all the manifold phases that always attend such controversies, the General Court of Massachusetts became odious to the home government in England for persistently refusing to vote a stated salary to the governors appointed by the Crown, and other

[1] The bell of Râle's chapel has been preserved in a wonderful way, and is exhibited in the rooms of the Maine Historical Society in Portland. It was probably caught in its fall from the little tower when the chapel was burned, by the crotch of a pine tree, which gradually grew into it and over it and almost covered it, and thus preserved it till it was discovered in a log rafted to market and about to be sawed. I saw it at Brunswick some years ago in a transverse section of the log.

similar reasons, and New Hampshire sent unscrupulous agents to England who well knew how to inflame the jealousy that had long existed and was now intense between the Crown and the larger colony. It might, therefore, have been easily foreseen that the Privy Council, to which the boundary matter had been referred for final settlement, would favor New Hampshire in their award. As a matter of fact, their decision, which was ultimate, took away from Massachusetts a strip of territory fourteen miles in width and fifty in length, passing it over to New Hampshire, although that colony, in the previous controversy, had never dared even to advance such a claim.

Both colonies would probably have compromised with tolerable content on a point three miles north of the mouth of the Merrimac, and a line drawn thence due west till it met the west line of New York; but ignorance of geography on the part of the Privy Councillors, the ill repute of Massachusetts with the home government, and the lack of conscience in the New Hampshire agents, conspired to bring in the atrocious award, which was never afterwards modified, namely, that neither the head nor mouth of the river, but its very southernmost bend at Pawtucket Falls (now Lowell), was meant in the charter, and the boundary line should run due west from a point "three miles north" of that particular spot. Accordingly, Jonathan Belcher, then governor of both provinces, ordered a surveyor named Richard Hazen to run the line thus in the spring of 1741, and it was done, and the boundary has remained unaltered to this day. This wretched affair bore such fruits of ill-will as between the two provinces, and of consequent embarrassments to the Crown, that Belcher was recalled from his double government, and New Hampshire became a separate province, receiving Benning Wentworth as first royal governor in 1741.

Under this condition of sore feeling towards the neighbor colony and the mother country, under the acute sense of having been grossly wronged by them both, the magnanimity of Massachusetts towards them both at the time King George's War broke out three years later is beyond all praise and all precedent. New Hampshire professed herself pecuniarily unable to defend the towns and man the forts on the newly gained territory against the French and Indians, and appealed to Massachusetts to continue to do in these matters just as she would were the territory still her own, and the General Court responded to this request promptly and liberally, not only throughout this war, but through the next also. Massachusetts had built for the defence of her towns in the valley of the

Connecticut in 1724, in connection with the troubles and hostilities arising about the operations of Father Râle, Fort Dummer on the west bank of that river a little below the present village of Brattleboro; and by Hazen's line this fort was now thrown into New Hampshire; yet the General Court hastened to garrison it with Massachusetts men, in connection with several smaller forts on or near the river south of the line. Much more than this, in the very teeth of French and Indian hostilities in the region, Massachusetts defences were pushed up the river thirty miles from Fort Dummer, and a fort built on the east bank called Fort Number Four, now Charlestown, New Hampshire. Captain Phineas Stevens, of Sudbury, was sent thither in 1746 with a company of brave men. He and they showed such conduct and gained such successes in that neighborhood on several occasions during this year and the two next, that the British Commodore, Charles Knowles, then off our coast with a fleet, sent Captain Stevens in recognition a valuab-e sword, which incidentally occasioned the renaming of Number Four as *Charlestown*, although the old name stuck to the spot more or less for a century, especially in the mouths of later settlers in the upper Connecticut valley, for whom the place was the base of their early supplies. Stevens commanded there till 1750, and died there in 1756.

Massachusetts at the same time, instead of nourishing her grudge against England on account of the undoubted wrong received, fitted out the expedition against Louisburg in 1745, and laid at the King's feet in triumph, the strongest French fortress in America.

As each one in the direct line of forts built west of the Connecticut River in this war was located within two or three miles of Hazen's line, it is difficult to resist the conclusion that the colony, curtailed as it had been in its territory, was now determined to maintain what was left to it at all hazards and against all comers.

And there was a third consideration that had to do with the building of Fort Massachusetts, and one still further west projected but never built. The boundary line between New York and Massachusetts was still unsettled. Surveyor Hazen was directed to carry his line west till it should meet "his Majesty's other governments." When he reached the top of the Taconics two miles west of Williamstown, he supposed his duty was fulfilled, although for convenience he extended his line to the Hudson; and, as a matter of fact, forty-six years later the official New York line crossed his own very near the spot where he supposed it would; but for all that, in all the years of these French wars, and especially after her experience of 1741, Massachusetts' was nervous and anxious about her western

boundary. Commission after commission was raised by the General
Court to sit with similar commissions raised by the sister colony to
lay for good, if possible, this troublesome specter, but no progress
seemed to be gained by all the pains; in the meantime Dutch farmers owning allegiance to New York, were creeping up the Hoosac
into what is now Petersburg and Pownal, and Livingston's Patent
was held to extend over into the valley of the Housatonic, and Dutch
and other settlers had cleared lands within that valley which Massachusetts was sure were her own; and when, accordingly, the westernmost fort was erected in 1745, there was doubtless some tinge
of defiance as well as of determined colony pride in its christening, — FORT MASSACHUSETTS.

The first martial note raised by the Massachusetts colony in King
George's War, was the appointment of a committee of three by Governor Shirley to build a line of forts "from Colrain to the Dutch settlements." Shirley had succeeded Belcher on his recall in 1741,
and, as British-born and Boston-trained, became a loyal and active
and able colonial governor for fifteen years, though for about half
that interval he was absent in England, when Spencer Phips, as lieutenant-governor, acted wisely in his stead. The chairman of this
committee was John Stoddard, of Northampton, who practically
came to do all its work, though nominally associated with him were
Oliver Partridge, of Hatfield, and John Leonard, of a noted colonial
family to the eastward. Stoddard was the leading figure and controlling spirit at the west throughout this war. He was the Colonel
of the Hampshire militia till his death in 1748, at the time when
"Hampshire" covered all the colony west of the Connecticut River.
In a multitudinous public service as legislator, military officer, and
judge, he showed himself to be a vigorous man, as he belonged also
to a vigorous race. His grandfather was Anthony, who emigrated
from London to Boston in 1639, with Mary Downing his wife, sister
of Sir George Downing, after whom the present Government Street
in Westminster is named. His father was Reverend Solomon, long
the noted minister of Northampton, a successful preacher and a
theological controversialist, three of whose daughters married into
the Williams family; one other became the mother of Jonathan
Edwards, and one other the mother of Joseph Hawley; so that
Colonel John Stoddard was own uncle to the Captain William
Williams soon to be spoken of, and also to the two other celebrated characters soon to be spoken of. We shall see in these
chapters that nepotism played a great part in the colonial period,
and particularly in the Williams family.

July 20, 1744, Stoddard wrote a letter from Northampton to Captain William Williams, which is still extant, in his own hand, and which till now has never been printed, on the top of the sheet of which stands this memorandum : —

The fort 60 feet Square Houses 11 feet wide Mounts 12 feet Square 7 feet high 12 feet High the fort roof of ye Houses to be shingled the Soldiers Employed to be allowed the Carpenter nine shillings others six shillings a day Old Tenor.

Then follows the letter itself, which is the foundation document in the history of northwestern Massachusetts : —

Sir you are hereby Directed as soon as may be to Erect a fort of the Dimensions above mentioned, and you are to employ ye soldiers under your Command, viz such of them as are effective men and to allow them by ye day in manner as above expressed and in case your soldiers chuse rather to undertake to build sd fort for a sum in Gross or by ye Great you may promise them Two Hundred pounds old Tenor Exclusive of the Nails that may be necessary the fort is to be erected about five miles and a half from Hugh Morrison's house in Colrain in or near the line run last week Under the direction of Col⁰ Tim⁰ Dwight by our order and you are hereby further directed as you may have Opportunity to Search out some Convenient places where two or three other forts may be Erected Each to be about five miles and a Half Distance upon the line run Last week as above mentioned or the pricked line on the platt made by Col⁰ Dwight you will have with you.

and further you are to order a sufficient Guard out of the men under your Command to guard such persons as may be Employed in erecting sd fort and further you have liberty to Exchange of the men under your command for those that are und^r the Command of Capt. Elijah in case there be any such that will be proper to be Employed in building sd fort you will take care that the men be faithful in their business, they must be watchful and prudent for their own safety.

there must be good account kept of the various Services in case men work by the day.

JOHN STODDARD.

To CAPT. WILLIAM WILLIAMS.
NORTHAMPTON, July 20, 1744.

Accompanying this letter was the following certificate of the same date, written in Stoddard's own hand, with the autograph signatures of Partridge and Leonard : —

We the Subscribers being appointed by his Excellen^cy to build a Line of forts from Colrain to the Dutch Settlements &c. Do approve of the building of a fort in ye place above mentioned and also of the manner of building the same and the pay to be allowed therefor.

JOHN STODDARD,
OL. PARTRIDGE, } Committee.
JOHN LEONARD,

The Colonel Timothy Dwight referred to in the above letter was a citizen of Northampton, the father of the afterwards famous President Dwight of Yale College, and soon to be related by marriage to the Stoddards, inasmuch as his wife was a daughter of Jonathan Edwards. Different members of this celebrated Dwight family, all descended from the early immigrant, Timothy of Dedham, will run across our path at distant intervals as we go on with our story. President Dwight was repeatedly at Williamstown, and left on record for us valuable local information; but it may well be doubted whether he himself knew that his father, as a comparatively young man, surveyed the line parallel to Hazen's line at about two miles' distance, on which the line of forts was shortly afterwards located. Captain Nathaniel Dwight, of Belchertown, had much to do with our valley as a surveyor and as a soldier at a later day; and still later, Anna Dwight Sabin became "a mother in Israel" in South Williamstown.

In accordance with the ample authority conveyed in this letter, Captain Williams set himself promptly upon building FORT SHIRLEY, as the blockhouse was named, when completed, after the popular and enterprising Governor of the colony. It was built of the dimensions prescribed to him, and placed at the spot indicated to him in the letter, which was in what is now the northern part of the township of Heath, near the upper reaches of a small brook that finds its way to the Deerfield at Shelburne Falls. As this was the first considerable work of defence in the line of forts westward, and became the model for the construction of others both on the Connecticut and the Hoosac; as all the items in the expenses of construction are still extant, the bulk of them in Williams's own handwriting; as current rates of wages at that time, and prices current of many of the necessaries of life, may be easily gathered from these items, as well as the prevailing depreciation of Massachusetts paper money both in the "New Tenor" and the "Old Tenor"; as six nearly entire timbers of the original fort are still well preserved in Heath, from which the mode of erection and of interlocking at the corners can be certainly deduced; and as the site itself at present, which the writer has repeatedly visited and studied, and especially the old well within the enclosure, yield something in addition of instruction as to the way of doing things in "ye olden time"; the reader will perhaps willingly pardon some minuteness of detail at this point, and some needful delay in the flow of the general narrative.

In about three months Fort Shirley was finished, for on the 30th of October, Captain Williams commenced to billet himself within it, charging the "Province of the Massachusetts Bay" twenty-five shillings a week "to March ye 4th being 17 weeks and 5 days." Pine trees at least a foot and a half through were cut down in the neighborhood and drawn to the site of the blockhouse that was to be; scorers at six shillings a day in forty-eight days' works in all reduced the logs to something like the required shape, and then hewers in twenty-four days' works in the aggregate at nine shillings a day wrought them down smooth to fourteen inches by six; and when put into place, the timbers rested on their six-inch side, and augur-holes were bored into them at intervals, into which dowel-pins of red oak were driven in such a way as that each course of timbers was strongly dowelled to the one above it. In October, 1885, the present writer pulled out with his own hands a couple of these pins from the extant timbers, in which they had then quietly rested just 141 years. As the fort was ordered to be built twelve feet high, there must have been ten of these courses, one above another; and each end-piece was dovetailed at the corners, with the corresponding one at right angles to it, in a way that is clearly indicated at the ends of four of the timbers still preserved. The fort was sixty feet square. Two reaches of the pines, accordingly, each thirty feet long, would have covered a side; but, for the sake of strength, the joints of each course would doubtless be broken by the layer above, so that in many cases at least there would be three timbers in a layer. Nothing certain can be inferred from the lengths of the timbers remaining, for although some of these are long, we cannot be sure that they are entire; while we may be sure that four of the six were at a corner, because they show the framing at the ends necessary for the interlocking.

This, then, was a blockhouse, so-called. For "framing and raising" it Captain Williams charged the colony in wages paid out £22 10s. As is common in such matters, at least one false mortise was made by a careless carpenter in the framing, for there may be seen at present in Clark Hall a bit of red oak taken out from such a mortise very long after it had been filled in and smoothed over. This unknown carpenter undoubtedly supposed that he had thus obliterated forever all traces of these false strokes of his chisel, yet Orsamus Maxwell, owner of the timber in which the ancient fault had hidden itself, did not need the reminder of the present writer, when the two together discerned it in 1885, that "there is nothing covered that shall not be revealed, neither hid that shall not be known."

Strong as these walls would be as just described, they were ren-

dered very much stronger by two mounts twelve feet square and
seven feet high erected on two of the opposite corners above and
upon the regular walls. The following is an item in the Captain's
monetary account rendered to Colonel Stoddard: "To Hewing the
mount Timbers £6. 6s." It is plain that if there were to be any
fighting by the soldiers within the fort, it could only be on and from
these mounts, for there were no orifices through the walls of the
fort itself. And so it actually fell out a little afterwards in the
siege of Fort Massachusetts, similarly built with two similar mounts.
But no organized war parties of French and Indians ever appeared
at Fort Shirley. Small bands of the red men lurked repeatedly in
the encircling forest, but more for observation and for picking off
single men than for purposes of attack. Continual watch and
ward was held, nevertheless, on these Shirley mounts, sometimes
by a single man only, till the fort was abandoned in the next war.

Within these walls and resting back upon them, houses or barracks
were built eleven feet wide for the use of the officers and soldiers
and their families, — "roof of ye houses to be shingled." If the
"eleven feet wide" prescribed by Colonel Stoddard, meant, as is
presumed, extension towards the centre of the interior, and if the
houses were on one side of the square only, there would still be an
open parade forty-eight feet by sixty. If the houses were on two
sides (and there could hardly have been more, though we have no
exact information upon this point), there would still have been an
open court forty-eight feet square. There is good evidence that the
roofs of the houses slanted up to the top of the wall, the wall of the
fort making the back wall of the house, and the houses all fronting
the hollow square in the centre of the fort, which was doubtless used
for and called "the parade." Such a roof was called in those days
a "salt-box" roof. The shingles were certainly rived from sections
of pine logs perhaps larger than those hewn down for the timbers,
and they cost at any rate, according to the return, £24, and for
"Joynting and laying ye Shingles £3" additional were charged.
Captain William Williams with his officers and men passed the
winter of 1744–45 in these barracks; in one of them were the headquarters of Captain Ephraim Williams, the founder of the town and
the College, from Dec. 10, 1745, to Dec. 10, 1746, in which time
he had 350 men "under his particular charge and government" in
the several forts east and west; and in one of these houses also
dwelt Mrs. John Norton with her little family, wife of the chaplain of the line of forts, from August, 1746, to August, 1747, while
her husband was in captivity in Canada.

There were two separate accounts rendered to Colonel Stoddard for moneys expended in building Fort Shirley; the first, which follows, for the heavier expenses of the main construction, and the second, to be given later, for the more numerous items of finishing and furnishing: —

Hewing out sides of ye fort	{ Hewers 24 days } { Scorers 48 " }	£10	16s.
To hewing insides of ye houses		6	6
To Hewing the mount Timber		6	6
partitions		1	10
floors		20	0
shingles		24	0
spars and framing Door		1	0
ribs and laying		3	0
Joynting and laying ye shingles		3	0
Braces		2	0
Framing and Raising		22	10
		£114	16

Next to the shingles, the largest single item in this bill is for the "floors." This, in connection with the fact that the ground on which the fort stood is wet at the present time and in all likelihood was quite as wet at that time, and taken in connection, too, with certain curious marks and a hole apparently burnt in on one of the extant timbers, as if much worn by the tread of feet, and possibly placed near to an oven or old-fashioned fireplace, makes it probable, if not certain, that the whole interior of the fort was floored over with pine timbers similar to those in the walls. Another item in this bill makes it probable, also, that the " insides of ye houses," that is, the sides parallel to the exterior walls, were built of similar hewed stuff, and either framed into the flooring upright or laid up in order like the outer walls; and still another item gives some color of truth to the conjecture that the " partitions " between the houses, namely, the subordinate interior divisions to these, were of lighter and cheaper materials. The " braces " referred to in this bill may have been the rafters of the houses binding the tops of the " insides of ye houses " to the higher outer wall, in which case they would likely be poles from the woods near by, costing little, and supporting the shingles as well as bracing the interior wall; or they may have been supports from below of the " mounts," or possibly parts of their structure above. On one or two of the extant timbers.

there are incisive framings on a bevel for braces or for something else, which the writer with his present knowledge cannot interpret to his own satisfaction.

But however this may be, the old well of the fort is able thoroughly to interpret itself to this day. Beyond any reasonable question, it occupied one of the corners of the fort enclosure, so as to be accessible to the garrison at all times, whether besieged or not, and at the same time be removed from the "parade." Even the story of the mode of its making may be easily and pretty certainly recovered by any one accustomed to put together facts of this kind constructively. Almost three half-centuries have already passed since the well was dug and the water first drunk by the thirsty workmen around it, and yet the risk is very slight in predicating for substance, that four forest staddles about six inches in diameter, one for each corner of the well, were set upright on the ground, and then ash planks, rived from a log about five feet long, were pinned or spiked on the outside of these staddles, beginning at the bottom; and this frame being placed on the ground where the well was to be, the earth was thrown out over the sides, and so the well was gradually sunk to the required depth, the plank siding being gradually added upward as the shaft was lowered. These rived planks and the tops of the four corner-poles, that can now be seen and fingered less than two feet below the surface of the ground, were not very uniform in thickness, and of course have rotted off at the top by time and exposure; but enough of both has been preserved till this time by constant submergence in the water and in the unusually moist soil above it to reveal the nature of the materials used and the mode of their employment. One of the corner-posts was a black birch, and the bark on it was in a good state of preservation at and below the surface of the water in 1886. Several pieces of this ash plank, a number of fractured brick from the chimney or oven, and a bit of the birch bark, are among the modest treasures of Clark Hall at present.

On Captain Williams's first rough record of expenses on the fort as rendered to Colonel Stoddard, there stands the following significant "N. B. Nothing reckoned for Chimneys or Drawing ye Timbers nor Nails Gates and Doors." This note was a sufficient intimation that a more formal and formidable bill of particulars would be forwarded to headquarters in due time; and it was forwarded accordingly, and has been preserved, drawn up in another and more careful and more practised hand than that of Captain Williams, as follows : —

AN ACCOUNT OF THE LABOUR AND EXPENSES IN BUILDING THE BLOCK HOUSE IN THE LINE OF FORTS WEST OF COLRAIN.

		£	s	d
To Serg^{t.} Jonathan Drown	For 10½ Days Work at 6/	3	3	
" Corp^{l.} Forginson	" 5 days and a piece	1	11	6
" Jo. Alexander	" 21 Days	6	16	
" Ezra Brown	" 2 Days		11	
" Valentine Wheeler	" 5 Days	1	9	
" Nathan Harris	" 8½ Days	2	1	
" Stephen Eddy	" 11 Days and a piece	3	8	
" Roger Kelly	" Odd jobs	2	7	
" Jo. Lovereighn	" 6 Days	1	15	
" Enoch Kelton	" 9 Days and a piece ·	2	11	
" Cyrus Church	" 4 Days	1	3	6
		£26	16	
" John Lynham	" 1½ Day		9	
" Hezekiah Tynkam	" 2 Days		12	
" Jno. Lakeman	" 17 Days	4	12	
" Eph^m Bullen	" 2 Days and a piece		13	
" Saml Clark	" 18 days	4	1	6
" Joseph Hill	" 3 days and a piece	1		
" Isaac Underwood	" 9 days and a piece	3	1	
" John Alexander	" 14 days and a piece	4	6	
" Oliver Thayer	" 5 days and a piece	1	2	3
" John McClatick	" 2 days		12	
" Oliver Stanley	" 1 day		4	6
" Peter Montague	" 25 days	7	11	6
		£28	4	9
" Phineas Smith	" 5 days	1	9	
" Samuel Root	" 7½ days	2	11	
" James Gray	" odd Jobs		14	
" Hezekiah Elmer	" 11 days	2	19	
" Moses Webb	" 1 day		5	
" Simon Rouse	" 2 days		11	
" Job Nimrod	" 2 days and a piece		12	
" John Foster as Carpenter	" 35 days at 9/	15	15	
" John Rugg as ditto	" 30 Days at 9/	13	10	
" Serg^t Coss	" drawing Timber and Stones 9½ days at 50/	23	15	
" Ebⁿ Wells	" Drawing Timber 4 days at 50/	10		
" Saml Osborn	" 13½ days at 6/	4	2	9
" Saml Chamberlain	" 16½ days	5	1	3
" Eph^m Twitchell	" 9½ days	2	7	
" George Williams	" 5 days	1	6	6
		£ 85	8	6
	Carried over	£140	9	3

		£	s	d
To Amos Alexander	For 7 days and a piece	£2	5	9
" John Stratton	" 14 " " "	3	19	
" Paul Field	" 7 " " "	2	2	9
" Jno. Kennedy	" 8 " " "	2	8	
" Natⁿ Butterworth	" 32½ "	9	3	
" Benj. Randall	" 30 "	9		
" Moses Brooks	" 4 "	1	4	
" Sergt Peck	" 1½ "		9	
" Sergt Garfield	" 6 "	1	6	
" Ebʳ Stebbins	" 6 "	1	6	
" Stephen Stimson		5	7	6
" Andrew Smith	" 8 days making ye chimneys at 10/ per day			
" Alexander Herren	" laying the Stones of 2 of the Chimneys 3½ days at 12/ per day	2		
		£40	8	6

	£	s	
To Joseph Brooks Building the other 2, 6 days at 10/	3		
To Chamberlain and others digging the clay Carrying the mortar and stones making the Catts &c	10		
" David Twitchell for 10 days	3		
" Boarding the Chimney Makers	2		
" 9 Horse loads of straw for the Chimneys	4	10	
" 5 Horse loads of Hay for the Cattle	2	16	
	2	10	
" Making the lath for shingling upon	3		
" Laying the Floor of the parade	8		
" making 12 Thousand shingles	20		
" 2 mill Board nails at 45/	4	10	
" 16 mill shingle Do at 18/	14	8	
" 5 ct of 20d Do	1	15	
" 5 pʳ Hooks and Hinges			
" 5 Hasps and Staples			
" 3 pad Locks		15	
" 2 pʳ Small Door Hinges			
To Hewing Scoring &c 4774 feet of Timber at 21/ for every 120 feet is	45	15	

The whole amount of money charged in this second bill, including £2 16s. apparently foisted in under the item "Hay for the cattle," reaches £306 11s. 9d., old tenor. Something of what is charged in the first bill, namely, £114 16s. in the aggregate, seems to be covered by some of the items of the second, especially the scoring and hewing of the wall timbers; but of this we cannot be absolutely sure; and perhaps the safest way to compute the whole cost of the fort is to add the two amounts together, making in all £421 7s. 9d. But we must remember that all this was reckoned in old tenor paper money of Massachusetts, first issued in 1690 for King William's War, and which, depreciating from the first, as such money always does, became worth, during the four years of King George's War, about four to one in sterling silver. In 1737, a "new tenor" paper money was also issued by Massachusetts, which soon settled into the ratio with "old tenor" of one to four, and both thereafter depreciated together in that proportion. In 1750, the ransom money for the capture of Louisburg having been received from England in specie, the wise colony redeemed all its paper of both kinds reckoned as old tenor, at about eleven paper for one silver, and for the next twenty-five years enjoyed the unspeakable blessings and prosperity of a sound money. The whole cost of Fort Shirley, accordingly, reckoned in silver sterling in the year of our Lord 1744, was not far from £50.

The fact, as demonstrated by this bill, that Fort Shirley had four stone chimneys, makes it nearly or quite certain that "ye houses," or barracks, were on two sides of the enclosure, since the chimneys with their fireplaces were for the use of the barracks for cooking purposes the year round, and for the warmth of the occupants in winter. The foundations of some of these chimneys remain on the site unstirred to this day, and the position of the remains of all of them is consistent with the supposition, that the barracks were on two sides of the enclosure, and that each chimney accommodated two of the rooms. It is possible, but not likely, that each chimney stood against the interior wall of each side of the fort; in which case there would naturally be two houses on each side, eight in all, which arrangement would at once clutter the parade and also make the houses less defensible in case an enemy penetrated the fort. That Williams was not quite satisfied with these Shirley barracks, howsoever they may have been placed, seems to be proven by his order in 1747 in regard to the new barracks at Fort Massachusetts on its rebuilding under his direction. This time he had the barracks put wholly outside the enclosure, "within five feet of the north side of the fort, and at equal distances from the east and west ends." But it is every way probable that the chimneys there, though there were to be but two of them, had the same general adjustment to the rooms as they had before at Fort Shirley. What this adjustment was, appears clearly from Williams's further order to his subordinate: "Place a chimney in the centre of the east part with two fireplaces, to accommodate those rooms. In the west part, place the chimney so as to accommodate the two rooms, on that part," etc. By one of these fireplaces at Fort Shirley, Captain William Williams passed the winter of 1744–45, conducting his correspondence with Colonel Stoddard, with Fort Dummer to the northward, and Fort Pelham to the westward; probably in the same chimney-corner, certainly within the same fort, Captain Ephraim Williams passed the winter of 1745–46, watching over the scouting from fort to fort, and attending to the wants and duties of the "three hundred and fifty men under his particular charge and government in the Line of Forts"; and by the side of one of these Shirley fireplaces, too, Mrs. John Norton, wife of the chaplain of the line of forts, passed the dreary winter of 1746–47, her husband in captivity in Canada, and she caring as best she could for the wants of her little ones, sick or well, one of whom, Anna, she laid away to rest in the August following, under a rude headstone in Shirley-field.

Captain Elijah Williams was at this time acting as sub-commissary under Colonel Israel Williams, commissary for the "western department" of the Province; and in this capacity during the last week in July and the month of August, 1744, he despatched to Fort Shirley twenty-one men with horses, bearing 1520 pounds of pork, 1052 pounds of biscuit, twelve bushels of peas, twenty-eight gallons of rum, two brass kettles, chalk lines and chalk, grindstone, gouge, auger, frow, adz, steelyards, dividers, spade, broad hoe, and stub hoe. W. L. Cook, who has owned for many years the farm of which Shirley-field is a part, found there an old stub hoe with every mark of antiquity upon it, and sent it as a veritable relic of the fort to George Sheldon, of Deerfield, who thought it likely to be the very one spoken of in this record, and as such deposited it in the Pocumtuck Memorial Hall, where it may now be seen.

Many of the men to whom moneys were paid according to the foregoing bill of accounts, are shown by their names to have been Scotch-Irish people, probably for the most part from the nearest settlement to Fort Shirley, namely, Coleraine, about five miles to the eastward. August 4, 1718, five shiploads of Scotch Protestants from Londonderry and its neighborhood in the north of Ireland, where they and their fathers had been colonized in the room of displaced Celtic Irish for two generations or so, sailed into Boston Harbor, whence they scattered, not so much as individual families, as in considerable sections together as churches; one part moving that autumn to Worcester, and settling there for the present; another part tarrying in Boston, where they soon established a Presbyterian church; still another division migrating to Andover Hill; and perhaps the largest division of all continuing their voyage after a little to the coast of Maine, where many families permanently settled, and whence more returned in the following spring to found their famous town of Londonderry in New Hampshire. Those immigrants of 1718, with others of a like strain of blood and faith who followed them later, have perceptibly colored the whole history of Massachusetts since, and much more the whole history of New Hampshire. More or less they have hung together from generation to generation as families, as churches, at least as acquaintances, reknitting from time to time the old ties, and keeping in good memory the *auld lang syne.*

Most of those who went to Worcester, being depreciated there as Irish, and even persecuted as Presbyterians, either fared on in the course of a few years into towns of their own, as Pelham, Blanford, and Coleraine, or became a leading element in the population of many other towns, as Brookfield, Ware, and Warren. Those who settled Coleraine in 1736, designated it after their native or adopted town of the same name on the Bann Water in the county of Derry. Eight years after this settlement, at that time the extreme settlement in the northwest of the colony, though Charlemont and Pittsfield had been granted at the same date, 1735, when France and England mutually declared war, and there was a call in Massachusetts for men to build forts and for soldiers to man them, these comparatively new-comers now scattered over New England, who hated popery as they feared the devil, responded promptly to the Protestant calls, enlisted for the line of forts for the siege of Louisburg, and for the expeditions against Crown Point and Canada. The famous corps of partisans, known as "Rogers' Rangers," were mostly made up from them, and Rogers himself was a brave and enterprising Scotch-Irishman. The prominent families in Coleraine from the first were the Morrisons, Clarks, Pennells, McCowens, Herrouns, Cockrans, and Hendersons; and our later story will be sprinkled over here and there by the representatives of these families, and of many other Scotch-Irish families of the immigration of 1718, and we shall then see, perhaps, that these were of such stuff as men are made of.

A very few families of purely Celtic blood and Irish nativity, and notably among these the numerous Young family, came in company and good-fellowship with the otherwise pretty thorough Scotch people of this remarkable immigration from Ulster into New England of 1718. "We are surprised," wrote the pastor of Londonderry in 1720 to Governor Shute, "to hear ourselves termed Irish people, when we so frequently ventured our all for the British Crown and liberties against the Irish papists, and gave all tests of our loyalty which the government of Ireland required, and are always ready to do the same when required." A few of these immigrants, particularly Abraham Blair and William Caldwell, had taken a brave hand in the memorable defence of Londonderry in 1689; and, as an honorary testimonial of this great service to the Crown amid starvation and death, they enjoyed at home and brought with them to America a personal exemption from British taxation. Aside from their valuable characteristics as colonists, the immigrants as a class made two important contributions to the useful industries of their adopted land. Potatoes as an article of food were first introduced into New England by them. These were planted simultaneously in the spring of 1719 by the Youngs in Worcester, and by Nathaniel Walker in Andover. Distrusted at first as poisonous by some of the people of Worcester, to whom a few tubers were presented that spring for planting by members of the Young family, and said to have been thrown away into a swamp by the recipients, rather than planted by them, this delicious esculent under the lead of the strangers soon came to be and continues an essential necessity for the American -table and farm. "Irish potatoes," in distinction from "sweet potatoes," derive their designation from this circumstance of their origin in this country. Again, these Scotch-Irish first introduced the domestic manufacture of flax fabrics into the colonies. Says Belknap in his "History of New Hampshire": "They brought with them the necessary materials for the manufacture of linen; and their spinning-wheels, turned by the foot, were a novelty in the country."

These people were generally quite poor, but a very small proportion of them only were illiterate; they were for the most part frugal, industrious, and deeply religious in a certain narrow and half-mechanical way; like most Scotchmen of all ranks, they were too fond of stimulating and alcoholic beverages, both men and women, which some of the latter euphemistically and conscientiously denominated "cordials"; as a rule, they were untidy (not to say filthy) in their personal habits and general housekeeping; in some cases certainly, probably in many, there were no ordinaries in connection with their dwellings for two or three generations after they came; and it is altogether likely, though no direct contemporary testimony on the point is known to the writer, that this lack of neatness in their persons and houses was one distinct ground of dislike in which they were held by their neighbors. Lincoln in his "History of Worcester" uses words about this as follows: "Differences of language, habits, and ceremonial, laid the foundation of unreasonable hatred, and the strangers were not treated with common decency by their English neighbors. Their settlements, in other places, were approached by bodies of armed men, and their property, in some instances, wantonly destroyed. They were everywhere abused and misrepresented as Irish, a people then generally, but undeservedly, obnoxious; a reproach peculiarly grievous to the emigrants. The jealousy, however, with which they were first regarded, finally yielded to the influence of their simple virtues and sterling worth."

There is fortunately extant among the Williams papers, in the Athenæum at Pittsfield, a letter from Captain John Stevens stationed at Fort Dummer to Captain William Williams stationed at Fort Shirley, the letter bearing date Feb. 14, 1745, which indicates pretty clearly the nature of the duties falling to the commander of each line of forts, as well the line running up the Connecticut River from Northfield to No. 4, as the line running at right angles to that from Northfield to the Hoosac River. Williams had just written a letter to Captain Josiah Willard in command on the other line, in relation to the scouts kept constantly passing back and forth, from fort to fort in each line, and also from line to line, keeping the two in communication, proposing himself shortly to visit Fort Dummer, and to perfect with Willard mutual arrangements of this sort. This letter was sent by Sergeant Smead, who brought back to Shirley the letter of Captain Stevens. The latter wrote, that he himself was about " to set out for No. 4," but invited Williams to come as proposed to Fort Dummer and confer with Captain Willard about matters of mutual concern. These scouts were provided with snowshoes in winter at the public expense, were usually in little squads commanded by a corporal or sergeant, and their zeal in service was stimulated by a handsome bounty from the colony treasury for Indian scalps. This bounty for 1745 was £100, *new tenor*. In the autumn of 1744, the General Court had " Ordered, that twelve men out of each of the five snow-shoe companies in the western parts, amounting to sixty in all, be detached and sent out under a captain commissioned for that purpose, to scout and range the woods, for the four months next coming, their march to be from Contoocook on the Merrimac River to the westward as far as the Captain-General shall think best." The proposed visit of Captain Williams to Fort Dummer was on business connected with this vote.

The rations allowed the troops at this date were: *In garrison,* one pound of bread, one-half pint of peas or beans per day, two pounds pork for three days, one gallon molasses for forty-two days. *On the march,* one pound bread, one pound pork, one gill of rum per day.

Five years before Hazen's line was drawn, that is, in 1736, Massachusetts, justly supposing the territory was all her own, laid out four townships on and east of the Connecticut River, and numbered them, going up stream from Northfield, 1, 2, 3, 4, respectively. These townships corresponded in general with the present Chesterfield, Westmoreland, Walpole, and Charlestown, New Hampshire. As these early lay-outs were numbered, so they were popularly named; and as early as 1740 a settlement was commenced at No. 4 by three families of the name of Farnsworth from Lunenburg; and these, reinforced by a few other families from below, and particularly by Captain Phineas Stevens, of Sudbury, who became the hero and patriarch of the region afterwards, built a corn-mill in 1743 and a fort for their own protection, which also was designated from the township as No. 4, and which during two wars became a frontier fortress of the utmost importance both to the colony as a whole and to the local settlers. What Fort Massachusetts was during these wars to the Hoosac settlements, such was Fort No. 4 to those of the upper Connecticut. Even the corn-mill became famous. For about forty years in those troublous times of war and poverty it was the source of supply to the scattered settlers above even as far up as Thetford and Lyme. The writer himself in his childhood used to hear the stories from some of the veterans of the latter town, the town of his nativity, of the toil and hazard of bringing grists on sleds up the river on the ice from " Old Number Four."

. While Williams and Willard were thus passing the winter each in his isolated fort, one on the windy mountain-top in what is now Heath, and the other upon the half-cleared intervale of the Connecticut, sending out and receiving their snow-shoed scouts and keeping in military communication with each other, much bigger matters than these were revolving in the minds of Governor Shirley and the Great and General Court in Boston. Shirley had conceived the idea that the French fortress of Louisburg might be surprised and captured by Massachusetts militiamen : the proposal was carried in the legislative body by just one vote; and the following letter from Colonel Stoddard to Captain Williams will explain itself to the reader, who will yet doubtless notice that the objective of the expedition is not named in the letter, probably for fear it might thus be prematurely betrayed to the French, and perhaps, also, lest the mention of the distant Cape Breton might deter the men from enlisting.

NORTHAMPTON, Feb. 25, 1745.

We are raising two or three Companys of Volunteers for the Expedition, Capt Pumroy is beating up for men in the upper part of the County, I was provoked (when we mustered) to see how few appeared after so much pretension to List but since that time some others have appeared and am ready to think there will be 18 or 20 in this town. What appearance there will be in other places I can't yet tell.

I imagine that some of your men will readily List, and if they will go they shall be entitled to everything as other men are, and restored to their places in the Garrison at their return if they desire it.

it would be best immediately to know their minds, and let me have a List of them, I hope there will appear 15 or 16 of them, which we may make use of only in case there do not a sufficient number appear elsewhere, and I will take effectual care to supply their places.

the thing is of weight with me and you must be thorough in it

I am your servant JOHN STODDARD

Capt. Williams

Since I wrote the above, I rec^d a letter from the Gov^{nr}, who depends on my getting some companies you must not fail on your part J. S.

Interests and movements begin to thicken in and around Fort Shirley. Without doubt, on receipt of this letter the irrepressible Captain "immediately" consulted with his men in order "to know their minds" about "the Expedition"; as a result, a certain number soon enlisted, which he calls "a company," probably about as many as Stoddard specified in his letter; the Captain accompanied these to Boston in hopes that he himself would receive a suitable commission and be allowed to sail for Louisburg; but his services to the westward were regarded by Governor Shirley as then too important to be dispensed with, and he shortly went back to his fort; meanwhile the expedition, consisting of 3250 men, sailed from Boston, April 4; and when, early in June, Governor Shirley became anxious to send on reinforcements to Louisburg, several things happened concerning the Captain, which we will leave him to describe in his own graphic way. In a letter from Louisburg, dated Oct. 3, 1745, Williams writes as follows: —

Upon the war with France our Govr and General Assembly thinking it would be prudent to send a Number of Soldiers into our Western Frontiers gave me a Maj^{rs} commission (first a capt^s then while the work was in progress a major's) to command the several Companies sent thither; When the Govenour saw twas requisite to send supplies to Gen. Pepperell while in the siege, an Express was sent me 150 miles to raise recruits; which I did with such Dispatch that in 6 days tho' at that distance I was in Boston with 74 able bodied men. As I did in the spring raise a company but was not suffered to come with them

for this reason that my presence and command would be more for His Majesty's
service where I was.   But now the utmost Dispatch being requisite they pitched
upon the men they tho't would soonest raise the Leiveis they proposed to send.
Upon my arrival in Boston the Govenour gave me a Lieut Col⁰ commission in
the Regiment of which Col⁰ John Choate is Chief &c.

That William Williams possessed the knack of putting good
speed into his work is proven by better evidence than his own
testimony, unimpeachable as that may be.   A comparison of dates
sometimes yields remarkable truths.   Colonel Stoddard's letter,
dated February 25, compared with the following bill of accounts,
dated March 4, of itself demonstrates the haste with which the first
batch of volunteers for Louisburg was started from Fort Shirley to
Boston, and even their places in garrison supplied by impressed men.

CAPT. WILLIAM WILLIAMS ACCᵀ MARCH 4, 1745.
PROVINCE OF THE MASSACHUSETTS BAY TO W. W. MARCH 4, 1745.
DR.

To his billeting himself from Oct. 30 to March ye 4ᵗʰ being
17 weeks and 5 days at 25/ per week £22 3/
To cash paid David Field for the entertainment of Eleven
Impressed men sent to the Fort since the enlistment for
Cape Bretton . . . . £ 2 8/ 8d.
To ditto paid Aaron Danieur's and John Lucas for ditto . . £ 2 15/
To 23 days work of the Soldiers in Clearing and Mending
the Road from ye Fort to Colrain at 4/ per day . . . . £ 4 12

Old Tenor . . . . £31 18/ 8d.
New Tenor [¼] . . . . . . £ 7 19 8

Fort Shirley, March 4ᵗʰ
1745 Errors Excepted
per Wᵐ Williams.

Two days after this little bill was made out, Colonel Stoddard
penned the following letter to Captain Williams, which relates to
what was afterwards called "Fort Pelham," the second in the
"Line of Forts" to the westward: —

NORTHAMPTON, March 6, 1745.
To CAPT. WILLIAM WILLIAMS
OF FORT SHIRLEY

Sir you are hereby fully authorised and Impowered In ten days after this Date
to employ so many of the soldiers under your Command as you Judge necessary
In finishing a fort in the place where the Comᵗᵉᵉ for Building a Line of Block
Houses &c agreed with Capt. Moses Rice to Build one and employ for that pur-
pose the Timbers the sd Rice has drawn together (the sd Rice having Desired sd
Timber may be employed for that purpose) you are to allow to a Carpenter Nine

Shillings and other Effective men Six Shillings a Day Old Tenor you are to finish sd fort with all convenient speed provided the sd Rice do not within sd ten days take effectual care to your Satisfaction that he will finish it.

JOHN STODDARD

We the Subscribers Together with Col⁰ Stoddard who subscribes the foregoing being the May'ʳ Part of the Comᵗᵉᵉ above mentioned   We agree to the Order made to sd Capt Williams So far as it respects us in sd Capacity

OL. PARTRIDGE } Comᵗᵉˢ
THOS. INGERSOLE }

Now it is almost certain that Surveyor Dwight, in running by Stoddard's order the July preceding the new military line to the westward, on which it was expected in general there would be forts every five or six miles, carried the same parallel with Hazen's line at about two miles south of it from the site fixed upon for Fort Shirley to the next main mountain swell (as the brooks flow there), on which Fort Pelham was now ordered to be built.   Shirley is five miles and a half west of Morrison's in Coleraine, and Pelham is very nearly the same west of Shirley.   It seems from the above letter that Stoddard had already made a sort of bargain with Captain Moses Rice, who had settled with his family in the spring of 1743 on the upper Deerfield in what is now Charlemont, to build this second fort on that spot.   Moses Rice was an enterprising farmer from Rutland, Worcester County, who bought in April, 1741, 2200 acres of land in the valley of the Deerfield, on which, two years later, he put up his first cabin under a buttonwood that is still standing; and on which, a little to the east of this, stands the formal monument to his memory near the grave with its original headstone.   June 11, 1755, Captain Rice was killed and scalped by Indians near the spot where his ashes still repose.   His family was the first settled in the valley of the Deerfield west of Coleraine. He had indeed two or three grown-up sons and a son-in-law, and perhaps also a very few neighbors along the intervale, in 1745, when Colonel Stoddard agreed with him to draw the timbers and erect a new fort on the hill-top in the present township of Rowe; but it would seem clear to the present writer beforehand, that, had it been the design of the committee to erect at this spot another blockhouse jointed at the corners and lifted twelve feet high, like "Shirley," already built, or "Massachusetts," soon to be built further west, no contract would have been entered into with a mere farmer and innholder like Captain Rice, and a man, too, having so limited a control over human hands.   We shall shortly see good reasons for believing that Fort Pelham was never an elaborate blockhouse, like the two others, but only a palisaded fort, or stockade, formed of forest staddles set upright in a trench, touching each other around the four sides of a parallelogram, and then these uprights pinned or spiked firmly together once or more above and the earth thrown back into the trench below, a work much more easily and roughly constructed than a blockhouse, and one also naturally enclosing more land.

The present writer first critically examined the site of Fort Pelham in the autumn of 1878, and in company with John H. Haynes, a native of Rowe and a graduate of the College in 1876, and the second time more carefully in the summer of 1885 and in special company with his son, Carroll Perry, who had just then entered the College as a freshman; the general state of things there, the location of the oldest road from Fort Shirley past Pelham, one or two miles further due west, and especially the condition of the fort-ground situated in an open pasture and apparently wholly unchanged for more than a century, emboldened him to draw the following inferences and conclusions in regard to Fort Pelham, with a practical certainty of their substantial correctness: (1) That Pelham was a purely palisaded fort constructed of upright posts or forest staddles sunk into the ground and bound together in contact with each other above, and not like Fort Shirley and the two bearing in succession on the same site the name "Massachusetts," a jointed blockhouse of hewn timbers; (2) that it was in form a parallelogram twelve rods by twenty-four in extent, thus enclosing more than an acre and a half of dry ground on the swell of a broad hill; (3) that a trench, perhaps a foot deep, was dug around the four sides, and posts of a pretty uniform size (perhaps hewed) were set upright into the trench, unless natural trees of the right dimensions were already growing in line, and then the earth thrown back into the trench and upon both sides of the staddles, which now forms the pillow of turf that can be traced almost unbroken, particularly on the south and east sides; (4) that the well of the old fort was near the middle of the enclosure and upon the highest ground within it, and that the removal of four or five large stones that now choke the opening would practically restore the digging of 1745, and discover with certainty whether it were originally walled up within or constructed with corner-posts like the corresponding well at Shirley; (5) that the considerable circular depression a little northwest of the old well either indicated that the magazine of the fort was in part, at least, a substructure, or that the beginning of an unfinished well there was thwarted by

a ledge, and a thorough excavation at that point might reveal which
of the two, and possibly a stone floor or some remains of side walls;
(6) that the main opening into the parade of the fort was, undoubtedly, on the north side, along which, at some distance further north,
on account of the head of a swamp in the direct line east and west,
the military road from Fort Shirley certainly passed in a northerly
curve to the west, the straight west line being resumed about a half-
mile further on; (7) that the fort was placed where it was by the
rude engineers of the time near the head waters of what came in
consequence to be called Pelham Brook, in order to guard against
access to the Deerfield by means of one of its many tributaries by
parties of French and Indians coming from the north with hostile
intent; (8) that the mount (or mounts) of the fort gave to the sentinel a wide survey of glorious mountain scenery in every direction, and
that to the west Greylock itself, then, as now, towered with bended
arch above the long range of the Hoosacs; and (9) that the barracks
of the men posted at Fort Pelham, of whom twenty was about the
complement during King George's War, were within the pickets and
probably at the corners in connection with the mount or mounts,
although, naturally enough, there are no such remains of chimneys
and ovens and bricks there as fairly clutter the ground at Fort Shirley.

There can be no reasonable doubt, that the old public road (long
ago discontinued) that passed by Pelham to the west in the line of
the road still travelled from Shirley to Pelham, connects itself historically with Colonel Stoddard's original order to Captain Williams
in July, 1744, directing him to construct Fort Shirley: — "and you
are hereby further directed as you may have Opportunity to Search
out some Convenient places where two or three other forts may be
Erected Each to be about five miles and a Half Distance upon the
line run the Last week as above mentioned or the pricked line on
the platt made by Col° Dwight whᶜ platt you will have with you."
If this line had been continued due west, it would have hit the
Deerfield River at the point where the modern towns of Monroe
and Florida corner upon it.   From Readsboro, Vermont, to the east
end of the tunnel, the Deerfield flows west of south, but from that
point it turns sharply east and holds that course in general till it
strikes the Connecticut.   Now all the streams in Rowe flow south
to the Deerfield; and consequently, there was a strong temptation,
to which it ultimately succumbed, for this original east and west
road to turn off south and so reach the Deerfield.   When Captain
Moses Rice agreed with Colonel Stoddard to draw the timber for
Fort Pelham, there must have been some kind of a path from his

house to the chosen site of the fort; and a year or two later, as we shall see, there was a travelled road between the two points, down which Chaplain Norton, Dr. Thomas Williams, and fourteen soldiers marched on their way to Fort Massachusetts. A good road now runs down Pelham Brook from the site of the fort near the little village of Rowe to the railroad station, Zoar, upon the Deerfield. A third good road drops down southwesterly from the west end of the old military road that followed Dwight's line, and passing by " Pulpit Rock " to the right, and thus the heights dissuading Dwight in 1744 from a due west course, through Swiss scenery magnificent to behold, strikes the Deerfield at Hoosac Tunnel station. There is indeed in modern times an east and west road through Rowe, passing a little to the north of Dwight's military line and road, through the upper end of the straggling village, by the Unitarian meeting-house, and so on to cross the Deerfield (here flowing south) into the primitive and diminutive Monroe. A pretty fair country road, and since 1883 a narrow gauge railroad, climb up alongside the Deerfield from Hoosac Tunnel station into the almost unbroken woods of southern Vermont.

It is a matter of complex inference, and yet of nearly absolute historical certainty, that Fort Pelham was built under the direction of Captain William Williams, by the soldiers under his command in the springtime of 1745. His headquarters were then at Fort Shirley. He had spent the winter there. Captain Moses Rice, two years before this, the first settler in Charlemont, who could not probably control the services of over a half-dozen effective men, had failed to come to time in his stipulations with the always prompt Colonel of Hampshire. The latter empowered Williams to go ahead with the work, " to employ so many of the soldiers under your command as you judge necessary," to finish said fort, " and employ for that purpose the Timbers the said Rice has drawn together," "you are to allow to a Carpenter Nine Shillings and other effective men Six Shillings a Day old Tenor," "you are to finish sd fort with all convenient speed," "provided the sd Rice do not within sd ten days take effectual care to your satisfaction that he will finish it." This letter sounds like business; it was addressed to a man who liked business; and who wrote six months after in protest to Governor Shirley against being left to do garrison duty at Louisburg, that he and other officers of his regiment " were not undertakers in the Expedition at first, *but generously threw down their tools*, left their business and their friends to suffer, and ran to the assistance of the Colony," etc.

About the middle of March, Captain Williams sent to Boston a small "company" of volunteers from the men under his command to take part in the siege of Louisburg. If he could have had a commission to suit him, he would gladly have gone with them, and sailed with the rest on the 4th of April. But both Shirley and Stoddard then thought his services indispensable on the western frontiers. About the first of June, however, Shirley sent a messenger 150 miles to Williams with such inducements to enlist others and to volunteer himself, that in six days he was in Boston with seventy-four able-bodied men for the reinforcement so loudly demanded. He made up his muster-roll of the soldiers in the line of forts till the 9th of June, 1745, and he sailed for Cape Breton on the 23d.

A new character now appears upon the western scene, and one destined to color it in its essential features till the end of time. His name is Ephraim Williams. He is a second cousin to his predecessor at Fort Shirley, three years younger than he, though one generation nearer to their common ancestor, Robert Williams, of Roxbury. Ephraim was now thirty-one years old. He was not directly related to the Stoddards, but his half-cousin, Israel Williams of Hatfield, five years his senior, and now commissary to the line of forts, was own cousin to John Stoddard. Ephraim came forward under the auspices of Israel, though his own father of the same name had been an influential citizen in Stockbridge after 1739. Aside from his own merits, which were considerable, the fame and fortune and influence of Ephraim Williams were much promoted by his personal relations with the three famous "river gods" of the Connecticut valley, and with other leading families of western Massachusetts.

The sources for the further history of these forts and of Fort Massachusetts are meagre and much scattered, but are genuine and original: old letters from the chief actors in those scenes, filed away and endorsed perhaps by their recipients, or accidentally preserved as family heirlooms, and particularly the collections which came down through the families of Israel Williams of Hatfield, and William Williams of Pittsfield; petitions for pecuniary relief or public recognition of some sort sent in to the General Court by almost everybody who was in the public service in those days, and the action or non-action of the court on these petitions, all preserved in good order in the Secretary's office in Boston, and the military muster-rolls of the old French wars, preserved in the same place, indexed and accessible, — have proved the principal memoranda from which our narrative has been constructed. Certain private journals, like that of

Chaplain Norton; the public records of land-grants made to individuals, and in some cases the registry of the more ancient deeds of land;
and always, when possible, personal and repeated visits to the localities of consequence to the development of events, — have aided and
guided and corrected the slow building up of the story as now told.

The name that was applied to the new colony-fort in the spring
of 1745, and later to the little brook that flows by it, christened the
same, whether given by Governor Shirley, or Colonel Stoddard, or
William Williams himself, — and the last is perhaps most likely,
for he was a man that kept the run in a small way of what was
going on in England, — is a curious instance of an Old-World name,
transiently prominent, but now well-nigh forgotten there, becoming
perpetuated by accident, in a remote corner of the New World.
Henry Pelham was nobody in particular except the brother of the
Duke of Newcastle, but he became a first lord of the British Treasury in 1743, and was virtually prime minister of England thereafter
till his death in 1754, when William Pitt, whose gradual introduction into high public place by Pelham was the latter's greatest
service to his country, stepped boldly though tentatively into the
chief control of affairs, and in five years put an end to French
domination in America. The rustic colonial politicians were wont
to keep a sharp eye on the drift of things in England, and knew
who the rising statesmen were over there whenever any such seemed
to show up their heads. Besides this, it is said that Henry Pelham
made a personal tour of Massachusetts a little before the outbreak
of King George's War; and, at any rate, the old county of Hampshire, for one or both of these reasons, exhibited to the world a
township, a fort, and a mountain stream, all called after his name at
just about the same time.[1]

So soon as it was known, accordingly, that Major William Williams was to leave Fort Shirley and his present command of the
line of posts for Louisburg, with whatever men he could muster at
the west, Ephraim Williams, Junior, received a commission as
captain, doubtless from Colonel John Stoddard, with authority to
enlist a company and to take command of the forts in his cousin's
place, with headquarters at Fort Shirley. Our primary evidence
for this fact is a sentence as follows in a petition of John Perry
to the General Court made a couple of years later: "Whereas
your Honours Humble Petitioner Enlisted in the service of the
Country under the Command of Captain Ephraim Williams in
the year 1745," etc. There is also extant an original muster-roll

[1] Charles Knight's *England*, VI. 111, 112, 178, 183, 197.

"of the Company in his Majesty's Service under the Command of
Ephraim Williams, Jun'r, Captain," which, although it does not
bear the usual endorsement with the date of its rendering, contains
the following significant note appended to the name of Samuel
Barnard: "Omitted on Capt. William Williams Spring Roll ending
June 9, 1745." This note on a roll holding the names of twenty-
three men, among them Moses Rice, then well settled at Charlemont,
also six men who had been up at No. 4 under Captain Stevens, and
returned, proves conclusively that Captain Ephraim took the command of the forts already erected June 9, 1745; and it also explains
the fact that that date and December 10, just six months from
the first, were the two hinges of time on which things turned at the
forts for two or three years, inasmuch as most of the extant muster-
rolls for that interval bear these two dates, particularly the latter
one, which was the natural time for the ending of the Fall Roll, as
June 9 under these circumstances was the natural date of the Spring
Roll. For example, besides the dates of the individual rolls, we
find these words in William Williams's own handwriting among his
papers in Pittsfield: "The Indent of Capt. Epraim Williams, commander of the Line of Forts, viz. Northfield, Falltown, Colrain,
Fort Shirley, Fort Pelham, Fort Massachusetts, and the soldiers
posted at the Collars, Shattucks, Fort Bridgman's, Deerfield, Rhode-
town and New Hampton from Dec. 10, 1745, to Dec. 10, 1746. In
which time he has had three hundred and fifty men under his particular Charge and Government."

Some of these men who manned the forts both at this time and
later on did not voluntarily enlist in the service of the colony, but
were forcibly impressed into it, whenever the volunteers were insufficient in number to make up the designated quota. June 3, 1744,
Governor Shirley ordered Colonel Stoddard to impress or enlist 100
able-bodied men "out of the Regiment of militia under your command for the defence and protection of his Majesties subjects in the
Western frontiers of this Province against the enemy, to be posted
and disposed of in such manner as I shall farther order." Enlistments were stimulated by the offer of bounties for Indian scalps.
For 1745 the bounty voted by the General Court was £100, *new
tenor*. This offer was renewed more than once. For example, Feb.
23, 1748, it was voted that £100 be paid the men taking the scalp
of an Indian enemy, *the scalp to be presented to the Government at
Boston*. About a month after Captain Ephraim Williams assumed
the command at Fort Shirley, Colonel Stoddard directs Major Israel
Williams to impress or cause to be impressed three men from Hat-

field, who were to report at once to Captain Williams at Fort Shirley, "the commander there." It so happens that the earliest extant paper of Ephraim Williams, whether military or other, is dated at Fort Shirley on the same day that this order was given from Northampton, namely, July 17, 1745, and runs as follows: —

I am heartily glad that Ens. Stratton is enlisted: I look upon him as a fit man to have ye command of ye men posted at Northfield, and appoint him to have ye charge of them and to appoint another under him in his absence. I have ordered Corp. Alexander back to Fall-town by reason his family is there.

EPHRAIM WILLIAMS.

A couple of orders to this Hezekiah Stratton of Northfield were sent by the Captain at just about the same time, as follows: —

To Ensign Stratton, Sr.: I desire you to see that ye soldiers lodge at ye forts and likewise desire you and the commanding officers to consult in what manner is best to guard ye people in their business, and conduct accordingly till further orders, who am yⁿ to serve.

E. WILLIAMS.

Ensign Stratton: If you have no man among you that is fit to head a scout as Alexander, send for him, for he shall have corporal's pay whether he does any more than have a care of the scout. He has been in ye service you know a great while. I know nothing but he has behaved well.

EPHᴹ WILLIAMS.

This last reference to Alexander as having been in the service "a great while," concerns, beyond much doubt, the organization of snow-shoe companies in those parts two or three years before. Colonel Stoddard wrote a letter to Governor Shirley dated July 12, 1743, making recommendation of certain men as worthy to become the officers "of the three companies of snow-shoe men ordered to be in the County of Hampshire." Eleazer Porter and Israel Williams also sign this letter to the Governor, which is in Stoddard's own handwriting. They recommended for Captains, Elijah Williams, Seth Dwight, and Seth Pomeroy; for Lieutenants, John Catlin, Junior, Joseph Billing, Supply Kinsley; and for Ensigns, William Wright, Moses Marsh, John Clap. All the signers of this letter, as well as some of those recommended in it, became in later times distinguished men; and, as the following narration will have much to do with some of them, it will be best to delay a little here for the purpose of giving a brief account of the more famous among them.

John Stoddard was born in Northampton in 1681, and was the son of Rev. Solomon Stoddard, for sixty years a very successful preacher there. He was a young soldier in Queen Anne's War, and was one of the guard in the house of Rev. John Williams, of Deerfield, on the memorable night of the sack of that town by the Indians in February, 1704. In 1728, he was commissioned by Governor Burnet, Colonel of the regiment of militia within the county of Hampshire, and Captain of the first company within the town of Northampton. Thereafter he was the chief director of civil and military events in the western parts of the colony till his death in 1748.

Israel Williams was the son of Rev. William Williams, of Hatfield, who was the minister there for fifty-six years, dying in 1741. This Rev. William was half-brother of Ephraim, Senior, both sons of Isaac, of Roxbury; and so Israel, who was born in Hatfield in 1709, and died there in 1789, was half-cousin to Ephraim, Junior, the founder of the College. He was also own cousin to John Stoddard, whose sister had become the minister's second wife, and so Israel's mother.

This Israel was a very able and independent and influential man, perhaps the most so of all the Williamses; and he was commissioned by Governor Shirley, Oct. 18, 1744, commissary of the "Western Forces" with the rank of Major, and continued in this post till the death of Stoddard, when he succeeded the latter as Colonel of the Hampshire regiment. As commissary he was under the orders of J. Wheelright, of Boston, Commissary-in-chief.

Elijah Williams, who lived in Deerfield and died there in 1772, aged sixty years, was a son of the Rev. John Williams, famous as the "Redeemed Captive" of 1704, the first minister of Deerfield, who continued for forty-three years as the faithful preacher and pastor of that frontier town. Elijah served as an under-commissary with the rank of Captain to his cousin, Major Israel, throughout King George's War. He wrote the following letter from Deerfield to Colonel William Williams, who had in the meantime returned from Louisburg to the scenes of his former activity, dated March 3, 1747: —

I think at this time it would be advisable to have a constant scout maintained either to Hoosack or Pontoosuck for the protection of these towns [meaning the towns on the Connecticut]. I should have sent a scout yesterday but could not get Indian shoes in this town, therefore have not sent. I would be glad of your direction in this affair; and if you direct me to send a scout I would entreat you to prevail with Maj [Israel] Williams to send me by the Bearer as many Indian shoes as you think necessary to be employed in that service. These with duty to you and Madam

from yours to command

ELIJAH WILLIAMS.

This letter is endorsed under the same date as follows: —

Received of Maj. Is. Williams ten pairs Indian shoes which I promise to deliver to Capt. Elijah Williams of Deerfield.

his
CHARLES ø COOTS.
mark.

Seth Pomeroy, the last of those recommended by Colonel Stoddard and others for militia officers in 1743, whom it is needful for us to characterize at present, was son of Ebenezer and grandson of Deacon Medad Pomeroy, all of Northampton, and was born there in 1705. He was a gunsmith by trade, an ingenious and skilful mechanic, who worked by his forge nearly all his life in the intervals of his military services. He bequeathed trade and skill and success to his son, Lemuel, who was forty years in the Legislature of Massachu-. setts, and who died in 1819, aged eighty-two. He was commissioned a Captain in the militia in 1744, no doubt in consequence of the recommendation of the previous year. He was a Major in the successful colonial expedition against Louisburg in 1745. Ten years later he became Lieutenant-colonel in Colonel Ephraim Williams's regiment in the expedition against Crown Point, and commanded the regiment throughout the battle of Lake George after the fall of his chief in the "bloody morning scout," whom he caused to be buried the next day under the tall pine by the side of the military road (just cut) from Fort Edward to Lake George. Of him as he was twenty years later, Bancroft writes as follows in his account of the battle of Bunker Hill: "The veteran, Seth Pomeroy of Northampton, an old man of seventy, once second in rank in the Massachusetts army, but now postponed to younger men, heedless of the slight, was roused by the continuance of the cannonade, and rode to Charlestown Neck; there, thoughtful for his horse, which was a borrowed one, he shouldered his fowling-piece, marched over on foot, and amidst loud cheers of welcome, took a place at the rail fence." A few days after this, he was appointed by Congress the senior brigadier-general in the new continental army; but the appointment causing some difficulty in the adjustment of questions of rank, he declined it and retired to his farm. Always, however, a zealous and devoted patriot, on the news the next year of the military disasters in New Jersey, he headed the militia of his neighborhood and marched to the Hudson River, and died at Peekskill in February, 1777.

Shortly after the completion of Fort Shirley in the late summer of 1744, while Captain William Williams was new in command there,

Captain Elijah Williams as acting under-commissary sent up from Deerfield the following supplies to the fort in charge of twenty-one men with horses; namely, 1520 pounds of pork, 1052 pounds of biscuit, twelve bushels of peas, twenty-eight gallons of rum, two brass kettles, chalk lines and chalk, a grindstone, gouge, auger, a frow [an instrument for splitting cask-staves], an adz, a pair of steelyards, dividers, a spade, and a broad hoe and stub hoe. About 1880, William L. Cook, who then owned the farm on which Fort Shirley was situated, found the remains of a stub hoe not far from the fort, which is quite likely to have been the one here mentioned, and which he sent in that belief to the Pocumtuck Historical Society in Deerfield, where it is now exhibited in their Memorial Hall.

The rations allowed the troops on the frontiers at this date were as follows: —

In Garrison
{
One lb. of bread per day
One half pint peas or beans per day
Two lbs. of pork for three days
One gallon molasses for 42 days.
}

On the March
{
One lb. bread per day
One lb. pork per day
One gill rum per day.
}

At a later date, covering the year from Dec. 10, 1745, to Dec. 10, 1746, we find a memorandum in the handwriting of Colonel William Williams as follows: —

AT EACH OF THE FORTS FOR THE USE OF THE SICK

12 gallⁿˢ Rum	60 in yᵉ Whole	at 18/
14 lbs Rice	70 " " "	at
1 Bushel Oatmeal	5 " " "	at
20 lbs candles	100 " " "	at 3/
2 lbs Pepper	10 " " "	at 15/
14 lbs Sugar	70 " " "	at 3/
4 Buckets	20 " " "	at 3/
2 Axes	10 " " "	at 28/.

Interesting as they are, we must now turn our main attention away from these two forts on the hills, to take notice only incidentally of their later fortunes, in order to glean the details of the story of a far more important military work in the valley of the Hoosac River. Whose eye it was that first picked out the site of Fort Massachusetts, and whose authority it was that first designated that as the proper place for defence against French and Indians approaching from the west, is not now certainly known, and probably never can be certainly known. In this respect the two earlier forts of the line stand in marked contrast with the later and more significant one. John Stoddard had indeed written to William Williams in July, 1744, "to search out some convenient places where two or three other forts may be erected, each to be about five miles and a half distance upon the line run the last week as above mentioned," that is, the line westward from forts Shirley and Pelham; perhaps Williams had executed this commission in whole or in part before he left for Louisburg in June, 1745; he had at any rate from his headquarters at Shirley superintended the erection of Fort Pelham in the spring of that year; the thoughts, however, of his superiors, Governor Shirley and Colonel Stoddard, and his own thoughts also, during that winter and spring, had been strongly drawn eastward towards Louisburg, rather than westward into the wilderness; and at any rate there is no direct proof that he selected the site of Fort Massachusetts. *Who did?*

Ephraim Williams was unquestionably in command of the line of forts when the first tree was cut down on that fine meadow of the Hoosac, and the ground was cleared for the laying up of the timbers of the first fort there. This is plain from John Perry's "petition" already quoted, for he says that he "enlisted in the service of the country under the command of Captain Ephraim Williams in the year 1745"; and it further appears, that he enlisted as a carpenter at nine shillings a day, old tenor, to help build the new fort. It is plain also, from a letter written at Fort Massachusetts, soon to be quoted entire, that Williams at least stood in this relation to the new fort, that work on it began about a month after he became commander of the line, and that the man then, and long after, in charge of the work and of the subsistence of the enlisted workmen on the spot, was Lieutenant John Catlin, Junior, second in command at Fort Shirley, Williams's own headquarters. Still, all this does not prove that Williams himself had any direct supervision over the erection of the fort, and still less, that he had chosen its site. It makes for the contrary, that William Williams had sole charge of the rebuilding of the fort in 1747, after its destruction in August, 1746. On the whole, and after patient researches in many places, this question must be left for the present, and probably forever, unsettled. It is, in fact, more curious than important.

About one mile from the junction of the *Ashuwillticook* and the *Mayunsook* in the present town of North Adams, the resultant Hoosac pursues its course westerly, till it strikes a strong cliff of quartzite, which deflects it sharply to the south, to form in its return to the west a broad semicircular arc enclosing the meadow on which stood Fort Massachusetts. The famous Indian trail of the Five

Nations (immemorial in its origin) between the Hudson and the Deerfield, crossed the Hoosac by a ford, which is still occasionally used as such, at the eastern end of this arc. The fort was so located as to command this ford, and also the old Mohawk war-path across the meadow ; moreover, directly to the north and within long musket-shot range, jutted out.the high and rough quartzite rocks, making it difficult to outflank the fort on that side, while the bending river strengthened the position on the south. To the west and northwest of the site of the fort, there were then as now, and then more than now, stretches of low and swampy ground. Considering the methods of warfare then in vogue in the New World, the traits of the French and the habits of the Indians, and even the hostile tests to which the fort itself was actually subjected, it must be admitted that its position was well chosen for the ends for which the work was built. Edward Everett, in an oration at the College, aptly characterized this pass of the Hoosac between its cliffs on either side as a *Thermopylæ*. Such indeed it proved to be.

Who it was that brought on to this meadow the first hardy band of choppers and hewers, — who it was that marked out on and among the primeval trees that grew there the rude lines of a rude fortification destined soon to become famous, — is a matter to guess at rather than to record. It may well have been John Catlin, of Deerfield, who wrote the following letter from the fort — so far as now appears the first public paper emanating thence — on August 3d of the same summer. Catlin was at any rate, during all that time, second in command at Shirley under Ephraim Williams, and, later, became captain and commander at Shirley when Williams transferred his headquarters to Massachusetts. We do not know the names of the hard-handed men who felled and squared and lifted and pinned up the heavy timbers for the first fort on the Hoosac, as we fortunately happen to know from the contemporary record the names of those who tugged at the green timbers at Shirley the previous year; but there is every reason for concluding that the new fort was substantially a copy of the older one in all its modes of construction. The detailed story of its siege and capture in the following year gives some positive evidence, as we shall shortly see, that the manner of building the two blockhouses was practically identical. Moreover, while it is almost certain that some of the men who helped to build Fort Shirley came over the Hoosacs with Catlin to help build Fort Massachusetts, John Perry, carpenter of Falltown (now Bernardston·), is the only man known *certainly* to have worked on it ; and John Perry, with Michael Gilson, Philip Alexander, and others, who are known to have been soldiers in the east and west line of forts, assisted ten years later to build on the "Great Meadow" in what is now Putney, Vermont, a blockhouse in the north and south line of forts, which is described as follows in Thompson's "Vermont," a description that shows it to have been essentially like Fort Shirley, and inferentially like Fort Massachusetts also: "This fort was 120 feet long by 80 wide, and was built of yellow pine timber, hewed 6 inches thick, and laid up about 16 feet high. The houses within were built against the wall, with a roof slanting up (called a salt-box roof) to the top of the wall, the wall of the fort making the back wall of the house, and the houses all fronting the hollow square in the centre of the fort." We have already learned from the extant timbers of Fort Shirley, that they were hewed down to six inches by fourteen. It may well be that the larger pines on the intervales of the Connecticut yielded to Perry and Gilson a plenty of sticks six inches to eighteen, so that ten courses would make a fort fifteen feet high.

Now to return to the incipient Fort Massachusetts. Lieutenant Catlin in charge of the work found it no easy problem to handle his commissariat. To bring supplies for his soldiers and carpenters over the Hoosac Mountain from Deerfield, was difficult and dangerous; there was no road but the old Mohawk trail, which can still be traced nearly over the line of the modern Hoosac Tunnel; he had evidently been ordered by the commissary, Major Israel Williams, of Hatfield, to try his luck in getting provisions further down the Hoosac among the Dutch farmers, who had been creeping up that river towards the mountains for a generation or two; and after going thither on that errand, he wrote back to his chief the following extremely interesting letter, although it must be confessed that the early education of the writer in spelling and grammar had been sadly neglected.

FORT MASSACHUSETTS.

Augt ye 3, 1745.

Hond Sir these are to informe that I have perseuant to your desier ben Down to ye Duch and in the first place made up a Counts With Mr Vanasee & find deu to him 2-4-6 in there mony he hath disposed of but tow hids and the tallow Sir I pos to informe you the Surcomstances we are in I carried With me 258^{lb} Weight of Pork and found in ye Stores thirtee pounds of Beaf and Brad to last to ye 22 of July I found three Skipel of flour in the Stores and sence found Whare Bardwell had brought 20 Skipel more we have fetched up 17 all-Ready Sir I find that the Rum hath ben very Slipry trade but how much hath ben Sold to perticulr men I Cant yet tel. Sir the ox we kild on ye 29 July the Weight 475^{lb} the quntity of Pork that Bardwell Spake of I have ben to see and find that thare is about 400^{lb} weight Which is the Whol I can

Sight of att preasant the price three pence half peny per pound Mr Vannees
will Let me have 800ᵗᵇ Weight in December att the same price further I have
tried the best of my skill to git Wheat and shall now Let you know how I Can
have it .Mr Vannees demands 29 per Skipel he giting it ground & delivering
it att his house the pay may be made to his Son att New York in Rum or any
other att the markit price. further Mr Hawk att the firt house will Let me
have one 100ᵗᵇ skipel of old Wheat att 2ˢ 6ᵈ per skipel and Will git it ground
and Brought to his house a mile nier to us his pay must be in money Saveing
2 pare of Stocings and 2 pare of Shoes : Sir I now Wait for your orders which
to take the Last Whet mentioned is Chepist but thare is no man that Can
Supply in all we want like Vannees ; Sir the price of Rum I Cant yet know but
in a fornits time Vanase Son will be up from New York and he will then let me
know. the Want of money oblidges me to stand with my finger in my mouth
ware the money hear things might be had much chepier Plese to send Bardwell
as soun as possiable for the Care of the work att the fort and giting the provisions I find is hard Sir there is dificulty Respecting yᵉ Wheat that Bardwell
Bought forsbury sayeth that he was to take the wheat before it was ground and
Charges 3 pence per Bushil for giting it ground & brought to his house Salt
cant be had on this Albany and brought one horse Sir we are all in health &
yours att Command

JOHN CATLIN 2ᴺᴰ.

This precious letter, originally directed to "Majʳ. Isˡ Williams att
Hatfield," is preserved, among other invaluable papers of that
recipient, in the library of the Massachusetts Historical Society. It
has never before this been printed, and it was copied for the present
use at the kind instance of Mr. Librarian Green. It would be difficult to pack into so few words more varied and important information to a local posterity than this monstrously misspelled missive
indirectly conveys. In the first place, we learn from these lines
(if we will only read between the lines) that it had already dawned
on men's minds what a huge obstruction to travel and transportation was the watershed between the Deerfield and Hoosac rivers.
In the military circles of Massachusetts the Hoosac Mountain began
to be talked about in 1744; it came first into writing apparently in
this letter of 1745; a rude road over the mountain took the place of
the Indian trail not far from the time of Wolfe's great battle at
Quebec in 1759; just at the close of the century a turnpike was constructed to connect through Williamstown with a turnpike over the
Taconics into the state of New York; about 1830, a descendant of
the "Mr. Hawk" spoken of in this letter, a citizen of Charlemont,
conceived the idea of a canal under the mountain to unite for commercial purposes the waters of the two streams; at the middle of
the present century a tumult of voices induced the state of Massachusetts to embark in the enterprise of excavating a tunnel under

the mountain, which was accomplished after long delays and at vast expense; and the talk of men about that mountain as an obstacle to intercommunication, which began in 1744, finally ceased in 1887, when the Hoosac Tunnel and all the approaches to it on either hand were purchased by and confirmed to the Fitchburg Railroad Company.

"The firt house," referred to above by Lieutenant Catlin, was the house of Eleazar Hawks, born in Deerfield in December, 1693, and who was consequently fifty-two years old when he negotiated with Catlin for the sale of the wheat. He was an older brother of Sergeant John Hawks, who distinguished himself at Fort Massachusetts the next year, and was the common ancestor of all the Hawks families in Charlemont, some of whom were still residing in 1887 on the lands of their fathers. His house was the westernmost house in Charlemont, and was of course the first house reached in the Deerfield valley by one coming over the mountain from Fort Massachusetts. His lands lay on both sides of the Deerfield, his house stood on the south side of the river, and his lands were bounded on the east by the lands of Captain Moses Rice, the first and most prominent settler in that exposed valley, of whom we have already learned something in connection with the building of Fort Pelham.

It seems almost certain from this old letter, that Captain Rice, or one of his sons, had already built some sort of a grist-mill on his own lands; for Catlin writes to the commissary, that Hawks agreed to get the stipulated wheat ground and "Brought to his house a mile nier to us," that is, nearer to Fort Massachusetts, where the letter was written. Unless there were in 1745 a grist-mill about a mile east of Hawks's house, which would put it on Rice's land and near the brook, on which a grist-mill and saw-mill certainly stood a few years later, the sentence in question does not appear to yield any sense whatever. This was before the " Propriety " of Charlemont was completed, and the mill, if it existed, was Rice's private property, and he could charge whatever he pleased for grinding; another passage in the letter indicates that "3 pence per Bushil for giting it ground" was about the current rate; but in 1753, after the legal organization of the place, it was voted to pay " Mr. Aaron Rice, who hath built a corn-mill in said town, which is allowed by the proprietors to be of public use for the town, £170 old Tenor, in part satisfaction for building said mill, provided the said Aaron Rice will give a sufficient obligation to the Propriety to keep said mill in repair, and grind at all convenient times for the proprietors, taking one-sixteenth part for toll, and no more." Later in the same month of January the proprietors also voted " to give said Aaron Rice the saw-mill irons belonging to yᵉ proprietors, and to compleat the set, he engaging to build a saw-mill on the brook he hath built the corn-mill on, and to saw bords for the proprietors at yᵉ same prices, and to sell bords at yᵉ same price that they are sold for at Deerfield, for yᵉ space of ten years next ensuing." [1]

The " Bardwell " several times mentioned by Catlin in this letter was undoubtedly Thomas Bardwell, of Hatfield, who had already been up the Deerfield and probably over the watershed to the Hoosac in the interest of the commissary department, and whose further assistance Catlin desired in his own heavy responsibilities. "Plese to send Bardwell as soun as possiable for the Care of the work att the fort and giting the provisions I find is hard." Some one or more of this family of Hatfield afterwards migrated to the Deerfield in the present town of Shelburne, and gave name to a ferry and then to a bridge over the river, called perhaps for a century " Bardwell's Ferry," and at length the name has been permanently attached — " Bardwells " — to the local station on the Fitchburg Railroad.

The chief interest, after all, of this ancient and goodly epistle of the illiterate Lieutenant is his honest report of what he brought back, when he had " ben Down to yᵉ Duch perseuant to your desier." The people of Massachusetts had been very jealous for a generation of the gradual approach of the Dutch farmers of New York towards the western line of the former colony, and of the alleged encroachments of the Dutch beyond that line. There had been mutual complaints and reproaches a plenty as between the adjoining colonies, as has already appeared in these pages ; and it is quite curious, though natural enough, that the first substantial intercourse between those who had so long looked at each other askance, was in the interest of a friendly exchange of commodities for the reciprocal advantage of both parties. It is curious, also, that the first advances were made by the agents of the colony, which was then building a fort fronting the Dutch almost as much as it did the French, for the subsistence of the soldiers manning that fort; and menacing, too, any further creeping up of the Hoosac by those, some of whom were already supposed to have overpassed the line. Catlin went down the river at the instance of his supe-

---

[1] These quotations from the old records of Charlemont are taken from the admirable " Discourse at the Centennial Anniversary of the Death of Moses Rice," delivered at Charlemont, June 11, 1855, by my excellent and now (1887) venerable friend, Joseph White.

riors to see Dutchman Van Ness about buying from him com. missary supplies. for the rising work on the upper river, designed in part to inhibit him and his neighbors from crowding themselves further eastward. Who was Van Ness, and who were his neighbors in 1745 ?

Here we must go back a little, for we are on extremly interesting historical ground.

But before we go back for this purpose, we must insert another interesting letter from Catlin to Israel Williams, his commissary superior, written only two days after the first, and showing the gen. eral interest excited among the Dutch on the middle Hoosac by the appearance among them of a Massachusetts lieutenant seeking supplies.

FORT MASSACHUSETTS.

Aug't ye 5, 1745.

Sir Since I wrote the account of my procedings consarning the wheat Mr. Vanness has been with me, and tels me that if you will take all the wheat you want of him that he will take our money and the same price as mentioned before. Sir, I have this day a large family from the Duch, and one man offers me whete for 2 : 5 per skipel ither one or 200 skipel to be delivered in flower at the first house [undoubtedly Van Der Verick's, now Petersburg Junction]. Another of them will let me enough to pay for a sute of broad cloth for 2 : 6 per skipel to be delivered at the same house in flower.

As good care of the beafe hath been taken as if your honour were hear, but for the want of salt I feare some of it will spile.   One skipel of salt is the howle we can git till we go to Albany for it.

We are informed by an Indian from Crown Point that one of the sculks that kiled Phips at the greate meadow received his death wound and died att Crown point.   We are all well and in good spirits, and make tho we scout every day no discovery att present.

Sir, I am yours to serve

JOHN CATLIN 2D.

In the year of our Lord 1688, the year of the great and final English Revolution, though James II. was still on the English throne and the grant was made as by his authority, there was granted at Albany by Governor Dongan to four persons, two of them dwellers at Albany, and one at Catskill, and one in the city of New York, the so-called "Hoosac Patent." This grant included about 70,000 acres of very fertile land, extending from the easterly bounds of Schaghticoke "on both sides of a certain creek called Hoosac, being in breadth on each side of the said creek two English miles, and as in length from the bounds of Schaghticoke aforesaid to the said place called Nochawickquask." The only pecuniary consideration expected on either side to be rendered for this princely domain, was an annual quit-rent of ten bushels of "good sweet merchantable winter wheat" to be delivered at the city of Albany. One of these four grantees was Hendrik Van Ness, of Albany. But neither he nor any one of the others made any movement for settlement on these fine lands for almost forty years. The reason was, the track lay directly on the great war-path between Canada and the English colonies. King William's War broke out the very next year after the "Hoosac Patent" was signed. Queen Anne's War was only closed up by the Peace of Utrecht in 1713. Garret Van Ness, a descendant of the original patentee of that name, made the first permanent lodgement within the limit of the Patent in 1725. He is the landed proprietor, with whom Lieutenant Catlin negotiated twenty years later for wheat and other supplies for Fort Massachusetts. He was born in December, 1702, and his homestead was on the north bank of the Walloomsac not far from its mouth, while his farm lay on both banks of that stream and extended two miles or more to the northwest along the northeast bank of the Hoosac, nearly to the mouth of the Owl Kill, or Eagle Bridge. Some portions of this estate remained in the Van Ness family until 1818. Four, at least, of his grandsons of the same name had large landed estates upon the Hoosac and the Walloomsac.

Just ten years after this settlement of Van Ness, and ten years before the commercial visit of Catlin to that region, Barnardus Bratt, an heir by marriage of another of the four proprietors under the Patent, and a purchaser of the rights of other heirs, established his home at what we now call Petersburg Junction. His great wealth and his assumption of manorial rights gave him a distinguished social position and the title of "Patroon of Hoosac." Directly south of him, and adjoining, another Dutchman, Van Der Verick, had established himself before Catlin's visit as the proprietor of the broad meadows at the junction of the "Little Hoosac" with the Hoosac River. Bratt had already erected a grist-mill and a saw-mill, the first in the district, on a little stream that flowed past his dwelling down through a lateral valley to the eastward. This grist-mill gave considerable significance to Catlin's regrets that he had not the ready money wherewith to buy the "good sweet merchantable winter wheat" of Van Ness.

The figures of these Dutchmen appear upon the scene of the middle Hoosac district, and solid down to our own day. But long before these men put in their substantive, if not picturesque, appearance along the two streams, more shadowy and more traditionary forms of men flitted over the beautiful region, yet left no trace upon it except *a name,* which no lapse of time, no religious hatreds, no competing and conflicting designations, have even yet sufficed to obliterate. *That name is St. Croix.* The name is French, and must, therefore, have been given by Frenchmen. The name is eminently Catholic, and must, then, have been bestowed by devotees of the Old Church. When? By whom? Under what circumstances? No answer ever comes to these questions often lifted. They appeal to the imagination, they call up attractive pictures, but they evoke no reply from any contemporary record. Jesuits from Canada, however, founded mission stations among the Indians all along the St. Lawrence and its tributaries, from the Kennebec to the waters of the upper Mississippi. Father Jogues, from Quebec as a centre, began Christian work among the Hurons in 1636, continued it from 1642 among the Chippewas in Michigan, visited repeatedly by different routes what is now the state of New York, was captured and tortured by the Mohawks in 1643, named what we now call Lake George "Saint Sacrament" on a final missionary journey, and was soon after murdered by the Mohawks in 1646. Some have thought it likely that Father Jogues himself in one of these journeys passed up the Hoosac and the Walloomsac, and determined to establish a future mission there, and gave the district the name of the "Holy Cross"; but Parkman, in his copious account of the travels of this Father, seems to allow no room for such an ancillary operation as this; and there is no need of any violent hypothesis; French missionaries from Canada discovered Lake St. Sacrament long before Father Jogues christened it; and all that we certainly know is this, that some of these, at some time, visiting the place with a missionary intent, were struck with the beauty of the Walloomsac and with its conveniences of access, and left a sweet name upon it which more than two centuries have not effaced.

It is a cherished opinion of the writer, and one originally suggested by personal observation at the two localities concerned, that the name "St. Croix" was given by the French missionaries to the district on account of the fact that the Walloomsac strikes the Hoosac exactly at right angles, — making a perfect Egyptian cross, — and that the Little White Creek strikes the Walloomsac a mile or more above its mouth in precisely the same manner, except for a turn a few rods above the junction. It is very remarkable, at any rate, that the term "St. Croix," while it was often applied in a general way to a narrow strip of country extending from Eagle Bridge on the west to the first battle-field of Bennington on the east, affixed itself much more definitely and tenaciously to these two points of river junction. Long before the Revolutionary War there was a village of St. Croix on the north bank of the Walloomsac just above its junction with the larger stream ; two railroads are now making junction on the south bank within a stone's throw (almost) of the site of the ancient church of St. Croix, which itself disappeared before the opening of this century, but several of the moss-grown headstones in the church-yard were legible a few years ago ; although every other memorial of the meeting-house or other building along that part of the old road is utterly gone. The original homestead of Garret Van Ness, where Catlin was doubtless entertained while doing his errand, was about half a mile up the stream from the church, and afterwards became the tavern of St. Croix. The mills of the hamlet were about half a mile further up, on the Little White Creek, just where their successors stand to-day, — the present grist-mill having been built in 1776, and is noted as the spot where the battle of Bennington both began and ended the next year. The tendency of the name " St. Croix," to attach itself to these rustic mills and to the little village on the opposite bank of the Walloomsac, and gradually to withdraw itself from the west end of the strip where the church stood, and from the east end where the main battle was fought, is very noticeable. The present little village of North Hoosac is the modern representative, both as to place and name, of the ancient St. Croix. The corruptions to which this French name was subjected in the course of a century in English mouths is something amazing. *Sancoick* is perhaps the most common and the most natural of all. Governor De Lancey of New York spelled it *Sink-haick.* The variations are innumerable. Almost all of the contemporary accounts of the battle of Bennington use the word in some form as a designation of place, and it is difficult to say whether the Americans or the British or the Germans mouth it worst.

Evidently well pleased with the hospitality of the Dutch and with the looks of their country, and with the policy of getting his supplies on this side rather than the other of the Hoosac Mountain, Lieutenant Catlin returned to his fort and made his report to his superior officer. What Major Williams thought about these matters, what further orders he gave concerning them, is not recorded, nor is it important. The fort doubtless went steadily forward towards its completion. The reference of Catlin to the wheat (800[lb] Weight), which " Mr Vannees will Let me have in December att the same price," demonstrates that it was intended that the fort should be occupied in a military way during the winter to come. It was so occupied. Fortunately we possess the muster-roll of the

common soldiers or sentinels who garrisoned it from the 10th of
December to the 9th of June following.

A MUSTER ROLL OF THE COMPANY IN HIS MAJESTY'S SERVICE UNDER THE
COMMAND OF EPHRAIM WILLIAMS, JUN'R CAPTAIN, VIZ.

MEN'S NAMES	QUALITY	TIME OF ENTRANCE	TILL WHAT TIME
Jonathan Bridgman	Cent'l	Dec'r 10	June 9.
Moses Scott	"	"	"
John Perry	"	"	"
Eben'r Dickinson			Feb. 28.
John Danelson			"
Elijah Graves			June 9.
Samuel Goodman			"
Joseph Kellogg			"
Aaron Kidder			
Zebulon Allin			
Nath'l Ranger			"
Jonathan Stone			Feb. 27.
John Guilford			June 9.
Stephen Stow			"
Daniel Smead			"
Samuel Taylor	"		Feb. 11.
David Warner	"		Feb. 24.
Luke Smith	..	"	Feb. 20.
Elear Hawks, Jun'r		Feb. 21	June 9.
Gad Corse		Dec. 10	Feb. 24.
Nathaniel Brooks		April 15	June 9.
Connewoon Hoondeloo		Dec. 10	Feb. 24.
Eben'r Miller, Jun'r		"	"
Gershorn Hawks		Feb. 20	June 9.
John Mighills		Dec. 10	"
Moses Adams		"	"
Joseph Petty		"	Feb. 15.
Patrick Ray			June 9.
Amos Stiles			"
Barnard Wilds			"
Jedidiah Winehall			Feb. 15.
Aaron Ferry			"
Parker Pease			Feb. 26.
Thomas Miller			"
Abner Aldrich			June 7.
Ezekiel Foster			June 9.
John Cochran			"
Thomas Foot			Jan. 30.
John Newton		"	Mar. 30.
Richard Wallis		Mar. 31	June 9.
John Conally		Dec. 10	Feb. 27.
Samuel John		"	June 9.

These forty-three men were the garrison of Fort Massachusetts during its first winter, 1745–46. There is a fair sprinkling of Scotch-Irish among them, Danelson, Cochran, Conally, Wallis, and others; for the immigration of 1718, into Massachusetts, from Londonderry and its neighborhood, was already beginning to color (as it has never yet ceased to color) the state of things in New England. Throughout this and the next French and Indian war, these Scotch enlisted largely from Worcester and Pelham and Brookfield, and other towns, into which they had scattered, partly because they were intense Protestants and hated the French, and partly because they were becoming numerous and continued poor. Several of the names in this list will confront us again in the sequel, some of them repeatedly and interestingly. Ezekiel Foster became one of the original proprietors of the town of West Hoosac. John Perry was one of the next year's captives to Quebec. Eleazar Hawks was son of him with whom Catlin bargained for wheat in Charlemont, and was himself killed by the Indians at the " Bars Fight " in Deerfield, Aug. 25, 1746. Gershom Hawks was his brother, and was wounded by the Indians near Massachusetts Fort two days after this muster-roll was made up, that is, June 11, 1746. John Mighills, while riding near the fort with his sergeant, John Hawks, both on one horse, was fired upon by skulking Indians and was wounded, but made his escape to the fort. This was May 9, just a month before the roll was made out. Sergeant Hawks was worse wounded than the soldier by the same volley, and fell from the horse; but as two Indians ran to scalp him, he recovered and presented his gun, which so scared the savages, that one jumped down the bank, and the other got behind a tree and called for quarter. John Hawks, uncle to Gershom and brother to him who was nearest neighbor on the east to the fort, had doubtless been in the fort all winter as a petty officer, and so had John Catlin as Lieutenant commanding.

Captain Ephraim Williams had his headquarters for that winter in Fort Shirley, and had with him in all forty-seven men. Happily we have that muster-roll also among the extant papers of the commissary, Israel Williams. It is made up as between the same extreme dates as the other, namely, December 10 to June 9. It is evident that there was a shift of men from Shirley to Massachusetts at the latter date, and probable also, that Captain Williams shifted his headquarters at the same time to the same place; for Elisha Nims, who is put down on the Shirley roll as present to June 9, was killed two days later at Fort Massachusetts. Some of the soldiers were at work near the fort on that day, when a party of Indians fell upon them, killed and scalped Nims, and wounded Gershom Hawks as already related. A part of the Indians had laid an ambush to cut off the retreat of any of the soldiers who might attempt to regain the fort; and though the ambush rose to carry out their plan, a sharp fire from the fort prevented its execution. They took captive, however, Benjamin Taintor of Westboro. This party of Indians came of course and returned by St. Croix and the Hoosac, and nearly 100 cattle belonging to the Dutch and English farmers of the valley were killed by them. The body of one of the Indians was found a few days after buried in the bank of the river not far from the fort, and some long cords were also found, supposed to have been brought along by which to lead their captives to Canada.

The last rude headstone remaining standing in the little graveyard attached to Fort Massachusetts stood over the grave of Elisha Nims. One hundred years after his death the students of the College obtained permission of Captain Harrison, the then owner of the meadow, to exhume the skeleton. The leaden ball that killed him was found embedded in one of the vertebræ of the back. That portion of the spinal column was brought to the College, and is still to be seen in the museum in Clark Hall. In the spring of 1852 the present writer obtained leave from Captain Harrison to bring the headstone itself to the College. It was then lying upon ploughed ground, and the inscription was fast becoming illegible. That too is preserved in the museum. The inscription is as uncouth as the stone on which it was cut by some illiterate soldier, who mistook both the year and the day. It runs as follows: —

June 12
1745
Elisha Nims
A 26 Y

We are merely told that the soldiers were "at work" near the fort, when the Indians fell upon them, and killed Nims and wounded Hawks and "captivated" Taintor, as the phrase ran in those days. Of course it is only a matter of conjecture what the soldiers were doing; but as corn was growing two months later when the fort was besieged, between the stumps round the fort, and especially on the side towards the bend of the river, it is no very violent guess, that the soldiers were planting, or possibly hoeing, corn that morning. There had been little, or nothing, to do through the winter; and it is noticeable from the muster roll how many of the poor fellows got sick, or homesick, or furloughed, along the last of February. As the spring opened, and as time hung heavy on his hands, one of the soldiers, a carpenter, picked himself out a piece of wild land on the north bank of the river, about a mile west of the fort (it lay at the east end of the present village of Blackinton), and fenced it off, and even built him a house on it. This was John Perry, the picturesque, the irrepressible. There was no pre-emption law in those days, and the Great and General Court of Massachusetts could not be brought to recognize any valid title to said land as vested in said Perry, although he afterwards argued with them in the following terms : —

And upon ye encouragement we had from ye late honorable Col. John Stoddard, which was that if we went up with our Families he did not doubt but ye Court would grant us land to settle on, whereupon I your Honours Humble petitioner carried up my family there with my household stuf and other effects and continued there till we was taken when we was obliged to surrender to the French and Indian enemy August the 20 1746. The losses your Humble petitioner hath met with together with my captivity hath reduced me to low circumstances, and now humbly prayeth your Honours of your goodness to grant him a grant of land to settle upon near ye fort where I fenced which was about a mile west of ye fort, or elsewhere, where your Honours pleaseth and that your Honours may have a full reward hereafter for all your pious and charitable Deeds your Honours Humble petitioners shall alwais pray.

Perry wrote out his petition with his own hand, and the original in the Massachusetts Archives is dated Nov. 5, 1747, shortly after he returned from his captivity in Quebec; but there is some anachronism about this, as well as a trifle too much piety and sycophancy, because he speaks in the body of the petition of "ye late honorable Col. John Stoddard," while that worthy deceased June 19, 1748. Perry's house was up and stocked when the French and Indians took and burned the fort in August, and on their return they naturally burned the humble dwelling that stood by the side of their warpath, and it was then the only house in the valley of the Hoosac within the limits of Massachusetts. Mr. and Mrs. Perry prized their new home and its contents, and apprised the General Court of their value, as follows : —

I would humbly lay before your Honours the losses I sustained there, which are as followeth, a house I built there for my family 80 pounds two feather beds with their furniture 100 pounds two suits of apparel apiece for me and my wife 150 pounds two Brass Kettles a pot and pewter with tramel tongs fire slice and knives and forks to ye balance of 20 pounds one cross cut saw 20 pounds and one new broad ax 6 pounds three new narrow axes 8 pounds and one adds 2 pounds two steel traps 14 pounds two guns 32 pounds one pistol 5 pounds one 100 weight of suggar 20 pounds, total 457 pounds with a great many other things not named.

If the carpenter's appraisement of the separate pieces of his property seem to us ridiculously excessive, we must remember that he reckoned in " Old Tenor," which was then just one quarter of "New Tenor," which itself was depreciated compared with silver.

The Shirley muster roll, already alluded to, has interesting features and interesting names. The three rolls, including a subordinate one of twenty-three names, probably of men that occupied Fort Pelham from the early spring to the common date of termination of all three, namely, June 9, 1746, show that enlisted men passed pretty freely from one fort to another in the line of forts, according to various exigencies and especially to expectation of hostile attack. No hostile Indians had been near Fort Shirley now for two winters. Pelham had not even been approached by an enemy. All the indications of the spring and summer so far pointed out Fort Massachusetts as the exposed position. The first demonstration against it was made May 9, and the second, still feeble, June 11; and whether Captain Williams went down there in person or not, a number of his men from the hill forts went down. Among others went down from Shirley Benjamin Simonds, just turned of twenty, enlisted from Ware River, destined to play a great part in the Hoosac valley till the very end of the century. Six of the men who went up with Captain Phineas Stevens to No. 4 early in March, returned to their service at Pelham in about three weeks, for ten weeks and four days, till June 9. These were Sergeant Daniel Severance of Deerfield, Aaron Belding of Northfield, Celeb Chapin of Springfield, Phinehas Nevers, and Samuel Severance and Joseph Petty, both of Northfield. The last two were in Captain Melvin's scout to Lake Champlain in May, 1748. He had but eighteen men with him. When nearly opposite Crown Point, he discovered two canoes on the lake with Indians, one of them about sixty rods from the shore. Going in plain sight of the fort, he boldly, but imprudently, fired several volleys into the canoe. These Indians in the canoes, by the way, were just returning from a raid made against Fort Massachusetts. A gun from the fort gave the alarm, and no less than 150 Indians started in pursuit. Melvin eluded them on his retreat over the Green Mountains for six days, when suddenly, while some of his men were lunching and others shooting with their guns the salmon passing up West River, the Indians poured in a volley upon them from behind logs and trees, not more than forty feet distant. Six of the party were killed outright, among them our Samuel Severance; our Joseph Petty was so severely wounded as to be unable to retreat with the rest; his comrades got him to a spring, where they put some pine boughs for him to lie on, and setting up other boughs as a sort of wind-break, placed a pint cup of water within his reach, *and told him to live if he could* till they should come back with help. As he was one of the most respected citizens of Northfield, sixteen of his townsmen (one of them a doctor), so soon as they learned the facts, resolved to learn his fate. They started on horseback, found his dead body and buried it, and were out four days. The place was about thirty-three miles from Fort Dummer up West River. Hall, in his "Eastern Vermont," locates it within the limits of Londonderry.

Our old friend, Moses Rice of Charlemont, who contracted to build Fort Pelham, but did not, was in that fort as a "centinel" from May 8 to June 9, 1746. John Smead of Sunderland, one of the later captives of Fort Massachusetts, whose strange and tragic story must be told in brief in the sequel, was in Fort Shirley all winter and till the shift of June 9. So was Aaron Denio of Deerfield, a Scotch-Irishman, of whom we shall hear more by-and-bye. So, also, was John Burk of Falltown, one of its earliest settlers in 1738, before whom, as soldier and townsman, there lay a useful and conspicuous career. But we must no longer delay on these first muster rolls of the three western forts, but give our attention now to the westernmost, a crisis in whose story was drawing near at midsummer of 1746.

Unluckily for Fort Massachusetts, and apparently, also, for the military reputation of Ephraim Williams, the summer and fall of 1746 was much confused and distracted in New England as regarded the French War. The capture of the fortress of Louisburg the year before by the raw levies of Massachusetts had astonished the mother country and even the colonists themselves; the former was glad and the latter were proud. Accordingly in April, the British ministry sent orders to the colonies to enlist fresh troops, which the King would pay, for a combined attack on Canada. The New England levies were to be joined at Louisburg by a fleet and army from England, with a view to capture Quebec, while the levies from the other colonies were to rendezvous at Albany to operate in the rear against Montreal. In spite of the previous mortality at Louisburg, Massachusetts raised 3500 men, Connecticut 1000, New Hampshire 500, Rhode Island 300, New York voted 1600, New Jersey 500, Pennsylvania 400, Maryland 300, and Virginia 100. The southern troops, with those from Connecticut, assembled at Albany under Governor Clinton, but the feeble British ministers changed their minds. No fleet and no army appeared as towards Quebec, and 1500 of the Massachusetts men were marched to Albany to join Clinton. Instead of the expected English squadron, a French fleet of forty ships of war, with 3000 veteran troops on board, sailed for the American coast under D'Anville, exciting the greatest alarm throughout New England. Boston was believed to be the great object of the French fleet and army. The advance on Montreal was put a stop to, owing to the failure of English co-operation, the fear of D'Anville, and other difficulties. Five companies of a regiment under Colonel Joseph Dwight of Brookfield, to which Lieutenant-Colonel Williams was assigned, both recently from Louisburg, recruited for the Canada campaign chiefly in the Connecticut valley, not without draining more or less from the garrisons of the line of forts, were sent to Boston, and the other five to the most exposed western frontier of Hampshire County. *In the meantime the knowledge in Canada that D'Anville's fleet was off the coast, that part of it had anchored in the harbor of Halifax, and that fear and turmoil were the consequence in New England, stimulated unwonted activity in fitting out parties of French and Indians to depredate on the English colonies at exposed points, and especially the uncommonly large party that captured and burned Fort Massachusetts in August.* But at last, in the good providence of God, the September gales crippled the French fleet, D'Anville died of grief at Halifax, his successor in command committed suicide over accumulated disasters, and only a shattered remnant of the proud armament crept back to France in November.

As we fortunately possess from the pen of an eye-witness and active participant a detailed account of the siege and capture of Fort Massachusetts and of the captivity that followed it, it is now the purpose to print in order the essential parts of this account, with such additions as have been derived from other contemporaneous records, and with such comments as have been suggested by local investigations, and may serve to help frame the entire picture as completely as is possible at this late day. As the present is the very first attempt to elaborate a history of Massachusetts and its associate forts, so it is the belief of the writer that no future effort will ever be made to glean from the original sources patiently, piece by piece, the obscure yet fascinating story. Both of these considerations have stimulated to long-continued and conscientious studies of the broken fragments in order to make up an imperfect whole.

John Norton, the author of the record now to be quoted, was born in Berlin, Connecticut, in 1716, was graduated at Yale College in 1737, and in November, 1741, was ordained in Deerfield to become the first minister in Falltown, a new township just then organized west of Northfield. A small church was formed at the same time and place with the ordination. But the times were unsettled. War with France soon became imminent. In about two years Fort Shirley was built a few miles to the westward. It was no use; church and congregation could not be kept together. Norton flung up in Falltown, and was appointed chaplain to the line of forts in 1745, with his spiritual headquarters at Shirley. He was two years younger than Ephraim Williams, and the two probably took up their residence in Shirley at just about the same time. Norton took his family with him. Williams was a bachelor. Undoubtedly it was the plan of their superiors that both, in the exercise of their diverse functions, should pass occasionally from Shirley to Pelham and Massachusetts, and backwards to the less formal forts and garrisons nearer to and on the Connecticut River.

The full title of Norton's pamphlet, printed in Boston in 1748, "and sold opposite the prison," is "'The Redeemed Captive,' being a narrative of the taking and carrying into captivity the Reverend Mr. John Norton, when Fort Massachusetts surrendered to a large body of French and Indians, August 20th, 1746. Written by himself." The title, "Redeemed Captive," was unfortunate, for it provoked comparison with a much more important narrative with the same heading of the sack of Deerfield in 1704, and of the captivity of Rev. John Williams, the first minister of Deerfield, and of his family and flock, which soon became a famous book, and has remained so ever since. Mr. Norton had no literary ability at all, and apparently very little practice as a writer, though truthful and accurate in his statements to the last degree; while the printer, who refrained from putting his own name upon the performance, did his work in a very shabby manner, the pamphlet being full of typographical and other errors. There is no evidence that it ever had much, if any, circulation; and, at any rate, it had become extremely scarce and almost wholly unknown, when Drake reprinted it in his "French and Indian War," published by Munsell in 1870. We will now listen to the worthy chaplain telling his own story in his own way.

Thursday, Aug. 14, 1746.—I left Fort Shirley in company with Dr. Williams, and about fourteen of the soldiers; we went to Pelham fort, and from thence to Capt. Rice's, where we lodged that night. Friday, the 15th, we went from thence to Fort Massachusetts, where I designed to have tarried about a month.

The Dr. Williams referred to here was Thomas, uterine brother of Captain Ephraim, and four years younger. The two were the only children of Ephraim Williams by his first wife, Elizabeth Jackson. There were other children, fruits of a second marriage, of whom more will be told in the sequel. These two brothers, as is usual in such cases, seem to have been specially fond of each other; and it is an easy conjecture, for which there is some foundation, that the step-mother was a bad element in the early home life of these two boys, in Newton, where they were born, the one in February, 1714, and the other in February, 1718. Dr. Thomas was the surgeon in the line of forts, probably becoming such about the same time that Ephraim became the captain, and John Norton the chaplain. Pelham was about five miles west of Shirley, and Captain Rice's about four miles south of Pelham. Rice had moved his family from Rutland, Worcester County, to the upper Deerfield, in the early spring of 1743. The position of his house, when Norton and Williams and the fourteen soldiers lodged in and around it, is well known to this day. It stood near a buttonwood tree now growing close by the road, a few rods west of his grave with its original headstone, and of his monument, dedicated Aug. 2, 1871. The only house then built west of Rice's in the Deerfield valley, and between that and Fort Massachusetts, was Eleazar Hawks', already referred to. Catlin says, "one mile nier us." The distance from Rice's to the fort, the second day's march, over the mountain by the old Indian trail, was not far from fourteen miles.

Saturday, 16th. — The doctor with fourteen men went off for Deerfield, and left in the fort Sergeant John Hawks with twenty soldiers, about half of them sick with bloody flux. Mr. Hawks sent a letter by the doctor to the captain, supposing that he was then at Deerfield, desiring that he would speedily send up some stores to the fort, being very short on it for ammunition, and having discovered some signs of the enemy; but the letter did not get to the captain seasonably. This day also, two of our men being out a few miles distant from the fort discovered the tracks of some of the enemy.

Dr. Thomas Williams had received from Yale College a degree as Master of Arts in 1741, and Norton had received his second degree probably the year before; and it is diverting to think of these two men taking this two days' tramp together through the wilderness, followed by fourteen soldiers, or preceded, — it makes but little difference which, — passing but two human dwellings in the whole march, and perhaps relieving the tedium of the long path by college reminiscences, or speculations as to their own or other classmates' futures, as their successors at Yale of a hundred later classes have been doing at New Haven, on the occasion of their reunions, ever since. Beyond a doubt, the fourteen men from Shirley were brought down to reinforce the garrison of the western and more exposed work, but the Doctor took away with him, the next day, the same number that he brought, though undoubtedly not the same men. The need of ammunition and other supplies was very great, and the detachment that went off with the Doctor went doubtless as a military guard to bring back the stores. Sergeant Hawks sent also a letter to Captain Ephraim Williams, supposing that he was then at Deerfield, unfolding the low circumstances at the fort, and informing that some signs of the enemy had been discovered. These signs multiplied the next day. No wonder such signs were discovered! It has never been precisely cleared up, and never will be, why Captain Williams was absent from all his forts at this particular juncture, and why the most advanced one — the very outpost — was left with only a sergeant in command, and virtually with no means of offence or defence in case of attack, in men, or stores, or ammunition. It is certain that he was in unbroken command of the line of forts, twelve in all, including Deerfield, from Dec. 10, 1745, to Dec. 10, 1746, — "in which time he has had 350 men under his particular charge and government." All that can truthfully be said is, that the expedition to Canada was uppermost in the minds of the authorities of Massachusetts during that summer; that an entire regiment under Colonel Joseph Dwight and Lieutenant-Colonel William Williams was recruited for that service within hearing, as it were, of the tap of the drum of those forts; that 1500 Massachusetts levies were sent to Albany early in the season, and many others later, after the news of D'Anville's disasters had reached Boston ; and that Captain Williams's absence from his post was somehow or other connected with these movements, proposed or actual, towards Albany, though there is no evidence known to the writer that Williams himself went to Albany in this campaign, either before or after the capture of Fort Massachusetts. It has often been stated and printed that he was absent at Albany when the siege took place. Sergeant Hawks "supposed that he was then at Deerfield." Hawks's letter reached him, indeed, but not "seasonably." Nevertheless, it was an unlucky miss for the Captain in a military point of view, that he happened to be absent from the post of danger at the head of a fair garrison, with fair supplies, in August, 1746. Such a chance to gain military reputation was never renewed to him afterwards.

As Dr. Williams filed out of the gate of Fort Massachusetts, with his fourteen men, for Deerfield, he and they fell immediately into an imminent hazard, of which they had at the time no intimation at all. The fort was already encircled by its enemies from Canada! Close by the road leading down to the ford of the Hoosac already described, a part of Vaudreuil's forces had secreted themselves in the brakes and bushes, and so near were they to the little detachment headed east, that they could actually have touched them with their guns; "but rather than attempt to seize them, which would have brought on a fire, and apprised the garrison of their proximity, they suffered the surgeon and his men to pass without interruption." (Hoyt.) After the surrender of the fort, this fact was communicated in detail to the garrison by the French themselves. This was Saturday, the 16th.

Lord's Day and Monday, 17th and 18th. — We met with no disturbance, nor did we discover any enemy; but the sickness was very distressing; for though some began to amend, yet there were more taken sick. Eleven of our men were sick, and scarcely one of us in perfect health; almost every man was troubled with the griping and flux.

The meadow on which the fort stood was and is low ground; the river was then much larger than now, and time had not then worn its channel so deep as it is now; consequently, the drainage of the ox-bow must have been then very imperfect, and the swamp to the northwest must have been broader and wetter than it is at present. It was, therefore, an unwholesome place for garrisoned men to occupy in August, and we do not need to look further for causes of the distressing sickness of which the good chaplain complains; and though the fort stood on the highest ground enclosed in the bend of the river, where the elm tree has been growing since 1859, that itself is but little lifted above the general level. In 1885 most of the meadow, including the site of the fort, was surveyed into streets and building lots; but the general impression of lowness and imperfect drainage in part prevented for several years the taking up of the lots by householders. An elevated railroad embankment also runs across the meadow from east to west on its northern side, and, of course, disfigures it.

Tuesday, 19th. — Between eight and nine o'clock in the morning, when, through the good providence of God, we were all in the fort, twenty-two men, three women, and five children, there appeared an army of French and Indians, eight or nine hundred in number, commanded by Monsieur Rigaud de Vaudreuil, who, having surrounded the fort on every side, began with hideous acclamations to rush forward upon the fort, firing incessantly upon us on every side.

Considering that the investment of the fort was really made on Saturday, the French concealed themselves remarkably well till Tuesday forenoon. The sickness within the fort accounts for the fact that the men were not stirring, and that new signs of an enemy were not discovered. So far as the present writer can help to secure that result, the names of the thirty persons within the fort during this memorable siege will not be forgotten by posterity.

Sergeant JOHN HAWKS,	Deerfield.
Chaplain JOHN NORTON,	Falltown.
JOHN ALDRICH,	Mendon.
JONATHAN BRIDGEMAN,	Sunderland.
NATHANIEL EAMES,	Marlboro.
PHINEAS FORBUSH,	Westboro.
SAMUEL GOODMAN,	Hadley.
NATHANIEL HITCHCOCK,	Brimfield.
THOMAS KNOWLTON,	Town unknown.
SAMUEL LOVATT,	Mendon.
JOHN PERRY;	Falltown.
AMOS PRATT,	Shrewsbury.
JOSIAH REED,	Rehoboth.
JOSEPH SCOTT,	Hatfield.
MOSES SCOTT,	Falltown.
STEPHEN SCOTT,	Sunderland.
JACOB SHEPHERD,	Westboro.
BENJAMIN SIMONDS,	Ware River.
JOHN SMEAD,	Athol.
JOHN SMEAD, JR.,	Athol.
DANIEL SMEAD,	Athol.
DAVID WARREN,	Marlboro.

The women and children were Mary, wife of John Smead, and their children, Elihu, Simon, and Mary; Miriam, wife of Moses Scott, and their children, Ebenezer and Moses; and Rebecca, wife of John Perry.

Turning now from the mere handful of the defenders of the fort, half of them sick and none of them well, and eight of them women and children, to the "army of French and Indians eight or nine hundred in number," who attacked and reduced it, it is to be said in the first place, that we are not shut up to Norton's narrative and Hawks's journal and the other contemporary English accounts for our knowledge of the make-up of this army, but luckily we have also the contemporaneous and official French accounts, the originals preserved in the Archives of Paris. It is in itself a curious thing, and it makes a curious phase of the semi-civilization of French

America, that a careful record was made of the numbers and destination of even the smaller parties sent out into the English country for plunder and scalps before they started, as well as a summary of the results after the party had returned from its raid. So considerable a hostile incursion as that of Vaudreuil would, of course, under such a custom, find conspicuous antecedent and subsequent remembrancers; and from these and associated documents, we learn that not Canada Indians alone, but Indians from the upper lakes also, Ottawas from Detroit, Sauteurs from Mackinaw, Hurons, and even Pottawatamies, were in Vaudreuil's detachment. We learn that seventeen Mississaguer from the head of Lake Ontario, who left Vaudreuil before the capture of the fort, went eighteen miles below Albany, struck a blow, and brought back four scalps. We find that Vaudreuil left Montreal on the 3d of August, and that his force consisted at the start of "2 captains, 1 lieutenant, 3 ensigns, 2 chaplains whereof one is for the Indians, 1 surgeon, 10 cadets of the regulars, 18 militia officers, 3 volunteers, and about 400 colonists and 300 Indians, including those domiciled and those from the Upper country." In another quarter of these documents we discover that Lieutenant Demuy left Montreal the 16th of July for Crown Point with a party of 470, mostly Indians, thence for Wood Creek, scouting and "felling the trees on both sides to render its navigation impracticable to our enemies." Demuy was ordered to wait at the "River au Chicot" [Wood Creek] for the party commanded by Vaudreuil, which he did, and whom he joined. Wood Creek flows from the south into the head of Lake Champlain at what is now Whitehall, and the Poultney River, or "East Bay," as it used to be called, in which the boats of Vaudreuil's detachment were left, finds its way into the lake from the northeast at almost the same point. The doubt as to the numbers with which Vaudreuil invested Fort Massachusetts hinges mainly on the doubt as to the number that Demuy contributed to the force at Wood Creek. Vaudreuil left Montreal with 740 men. In the detailed account of his expedition further on, seventeen Indians are mentioned as having left his party "before the capture of the fort." Demuy left Montreal a fortnight earlier with 470 men for preliminary operations on Wood Creek, but with special orders to wait for and join the later party, which he did. "Several of these Indians have formed parties and been out on excursions," reads the record. The more natural interpretation of this language is, that they had returned and rejoined Demuy before he joined the larger war-band for the South. If only half of Demuy's men came with him to the Hoosac, the whole party would have mounted up to 950. That is probably about the number. Norton's "eight or nine hundred" is a moderate and credible statement.

In still another part of these Paris documents is the following, which is quite truthful in the main, although shaky in spots:—

It having been deliberated, in a council held with the Canadians and Indians, that an attack should be made on the fort called Massachuset, after the name of that Province, Sieur de Rigaud [Vaudreuil] arrived after a march of ten days in the neighborhood of this fort. He commenced the attack on it on the morning of the 30th of August, keeping up an incessant fire from both sides until the following day, when the garrison surrendered at discretion. Three women and five children were found in it. The loss on the part of the English was not ascertained, as they had buried all their dead, except one. The French loss was one man killed and twelve wounded. Sieur Rigaud was among the latter. The fort was burnt on the same day, and the prisoner having stated that a reinforcement was to arrive from Dierfil, Sieur Rigaud detached sixty Iroquois and Abernakis on the route they were to come. These Indians having met this reinforcement, which consisted only of nineteen men, defeated it and brought in four prisoners only, all the remainder having been killed.

This last is a distortion of the "Bars Fight" in Deerfield, which will presently be related as it was. The accuracy of Norton's words describing the Indian yell as "hideous acclamations," and their method of rushing forward towards an enemy and then instantly back again to cover, and of "firing incessantly upon us on every side" without aim or reference to the probability of doing execution, is confirmed by the accounts of other sieges and battles in the French wars and particularly by the scene at Braddock's Defeat.

Mr. Hawks, our officer, ordered that we should let them come without firing at all at them, until they should approach within a suitable distance, that we might have a good prospect of doing execution. We suffered them to come up in a body till they were within twenty rods of us, and then we fired; upon which the enemy soon betook themselves to trees, stumps, and logs, where they lay and fired incessantly upon us; some taking opportunity to run from one tree and stump to another, and so drew nearer to the fort. This they did in a very subtle manner, running so crooked that it was very difficult to shoot at them with any good prospect of success, until we observed that when they came to a stump, they would fall down; which we observing, prepared to catch them there as they fell down by the stumps; and this we did probably with success; for they soon left off this method.

John Hawks was born in Deerfield, Dec. 5, 1707, and died there June 24, 1784; and the headstone above. his grave was still standing legible more than a century after his death, in the old and aban-

doned God's Acre at Deerfield. His courage and conduct at the
siege of his fort and afterwards, deeply impressed the susceptible
French, and loaned him much influence at Montreal and Quebec.
In February, 1748, he had occasion to go to Canada with a flag of
truce for an exchange of prisoners, and was treated very handsomely
there. His young nephew, Samuel Allen, captured at the Bars
Fight, had become so attached in two years to the Indian mode of
life in Canada, that he would not voluntarily return with his uncle,
and the latter was suffered to use force to compel him; and besides,
the Governor of Canada sent six Frenchmen and two or three
Indians as a guard of honor to accompany the Sergeant home, and
they came with him as far (almost) as No. 4. Hawks continued
useful in the service until the conquest of Canada, and was conspicuous on the right side at the opening of the Revolution, while his
pastor and more influential neighbors on both sides the Connecticut
were Tories. "In Memory of Col. Hawks," etc., runs his epitaph. The reference in Norton's text to trees, stumps, and logs,
gives a vivid picture of the ground around the fort in August, 1746.
These were the stumps of the pines, whose hewn trunks pinned
together and locked at the corners formed the walls of the fort;
others were stumps of trees cut down in order to let the sun in on
ground where corn could be planted and grown; deciduous trees
were doubtless mingled in with the pines, and had been cut down
for fuel and other purposes, and the trunks and branches would
naturally more or less strew the ground; and, unless later indications along the Hoosac interval are deceptive, spruces were the
trees growing in the swamp to the west and northwest. Remarkably cool and level-headed under the circumstances were the Sergeant and the Chaplain and the Sharpshooters, that they should
calculate by inference to fire where the Indians would probably
be in an instant, rather than where they actually were at the
instant.

About this time we saw several of the enemy fall and rise no more; among
which was the captain of the St. Francis Indians, who was one of the foremost,
and called upon the rest to press on upon the fort. Sergeant Hawks got an
opportunity to shoot him into the breast, which ended his days. At the beginning of the engagement, the General sent his ensign with his standard (which
he, standing behind a tree about thirty rods distant from the fort, displayed),
the General also walked up the hill within about forty rods of the fort, where
he stood and gave his orders; but being discovered he had a shot or two fired at
him; upon which he moved off; but presently after comes to his ensign, where
being discovered, he received a shot in his arm, which made him retreat with his
ensign to their camp.

The St. Francis Indians, the pride and courage of whose captain was thus brought low by the skilled aim of Sergeant Hawks, were Mission Indians, as they were called, — that is, heathen who had been baptized, in contradistinction from the unmitigated heathen, in whose company they fought and scalped in all their incursions. These particular Indians were Abenakis from the region of our Maine, who had been domiciliated by the French missionaries of the order of St. Francis for more than half a century on the river named after their saint a few miles above its opening into the Lake St. Peter, which is an immense broadening-out of the St. Lawrence about halfway between Quebec and Montreal. The river St. Francis rises very near the source of the Connecticut, in the Height of Land between New Hampshire and Canada. The village of that name, where these Indians lived, which was destroyed in 1759 by Robert Rogers, the famous partisan ranger, in one of the most daring and successful raids ever made on this continent, had been the pride of the French Jesuits, and was perhaps the most influential of their stations in New France. Says Parkman of these Indians: "They were nominal Christians, and had been under the control of their missionaries for three generations; but though zealous and sometimes fanatical in their devotion to the forms of Romanism, they remained thorough savages in dress, habits, and character. They were the scourge of the New England borders, where they surprised and burned farmhouses and small hamlets, killed men, women and children without distinction, carried others prisoners to their village, subjected them to the torture of running the gantlet, and compelled them to witness dances of triumph around the scalps of parents, children and friends."

To any one familiar with the lay of the land around Fort Massachusetts, there is very little difficulty in determining with exactness the local movements of General Vaudreuil and his ensign, as they are graphically described at this stage of the siege by the keen-eyed Chaplain. The investing force had formed two camps, one to the northwest of the fort, where the General had his headquarters, and the other to the southeast, on the bank of the Hoòsac, where its course is southwest. The carriage road on the north of the fort, which probably follows very nearly the line of the old Indian trail, hugs the edge of the quartzite hill just within the ordinary range of the old "queen's arm" of those days; and to one passing east from the site of the French camp there was then and is now a shoulder of the hill jutting down to the swamp, and when the General "walked up the hill within about forty rods of the fort, where he stood and gave his orders," he was walking up on this shoulder, and the place where he stood may be pointed out to-day, certainly within a rod or two. Presently venturing down on the low ground, where his ensign stood with the lilied banner of France, he received a shot in his arm, the scar of which the Chaplain had a chance to see afterwards upon a nearer view.

The enemy still continued to fire almost incessantly upon us, and many of them crept up within a dozen rods of the fort. We were straitened for want of shot. Several of our men being newly come into the service, and for want of bullet moulds, had not prepared for any long engagement, and therefore the sergeant ordered some of our sick men to make bullets, another to run some shot, having shot-moulds. This put him upon taking particular notice of the ammunition, and he found it to be very short, and therefore gave orders that we should not fire any more than we thought necessary to hold the enemy back, unless when we had a very good opportunity and fair prospect of doing execution ; so that we fired but little. We had sometimes very fair shot, and had success. We saw several fall, who, we are persuaded, never rose again. We might have shot at the enemy almost any time in the day, who were in open view of the fort, within fifty or sixty rods of the same, and sometimes within forty and less ; the officers sometimes walking about, sword in hand, viewing of us, and others walking back and forth as they had occasion, without molestation, for we dare not spend our ammunition upon them that were at such a distance.

The men characterized by Mr. Norton as having "newly come into the service," were beyond question some or all of the fourteen who came in with Dr. Williams the Friday night before ; and the Chaplain's language seems to imply that it was the business of the men to run bullets, each for himself, and so be "prepared for any long engagement"; but as the sentence is not grammatical, so neither is it quite intelligible. Only eight of the men were in health, fourteen were sick, and the good policy of the French officers in letting the fourteen stout hearts pass by on the road to Deerfield the Saturday previous now vindicated itself; they had no interest to prevent the depletion of the fort, but every motive to further it; still, some of the sick were not so sick but they could use the bullet moulds, and others run some buckshot, having moulds for that purpose, though it appears in the sequel that it was not in accordance with the unwritten military law of the wilderness to make use of shot in such warfare. Sergeant Hawks then first became fully aware how short were his stores of ammunition. It was to replenish these that he had sent out the fourteen men. No doubt he wished them back ; but in any case he must have realized that all that could now be done was to prolong the siege as much as possible before the inevitable surrender of the fort. The orders that he gave to spare the ammunition were cool and prudent. So were the lessened shots, that were " very fair and had success." " We saw several fall who never rose again." Our brave narrator belonged to an orthodox church militant. To him the only good Indian (on the French side) was a dead Indian. The French officers seen " walking about sword in hand, viewing of us," were already noted men, and destined to become exceedingly noteworthy on both sides the ocean before the surrender of Quebec in the next decade. Besides Vaudreuil, of whom we shall learn something significant later, there were Demuy and La Corne : each of these, and especially the last, had before him a conspicuous career until the downfall of New France.

Towards evening the enemy began to use their axes and hatchets. Some were thoughtful that they were preparing ladders in order to storm the fort in the night ; but afterward we found our mistake, for they were preparing fag- gots in order to burn it. This day they wounded two of our men, viz., John Aldrich they shot through the foot, and Jonathan Bridgman with a flesh wound the back side of the hip. When the evening came on the sergeant gave orders that all the tubs, pails, and vessels of every sort, in every room, should be filled with water, and went himself to see it done ; he also looked to the doors, that they were made as fast as possible. He likewise cut a passage from one room to another, that he might put the fort into as good a posture of defence as might be, in case they should attempt to storm it. He distributed the men into the several rooms. While he was thus preparing, he kept two men in the northwest mount, and some in the great house, the southeast corner of the fort, to watch the enemy and keep them back.

The chief interest of this passage is the clear though indirect way in which is shown the mode of construction of Fort Massachusetts. Evidently it was an exact pattern of Fort Shirley, of which our knowledge happens to be so full and particular. Of course the well was inside of the walls, and probably, as at Shirley, in one corner. The barracks, or rooms, were built against the inside wall, with a salt-box roof, as at the Putney fort on Great Meadow, which John Perry later helped to construct as he helped to construct this. These rooms were continuous so far as they went, for Hawks " cut a passage from one room to another," and "distributed the men into the several rooms." The "mount," of which Norton here speaks, was a feature of all the blockhouses built in those times, and was a sort of platform of boards or plank thrown across the upper tier of hewn timbers at one of their four angles. On this was constructed a rude watch-box, a place for a sentinel somewhat protected, as the platform around it was the place to fire from and protect the fort.

There were no loopholes in the walls, which were six inches thick, of hewed pines, so that the only places of offence were these mounts. It was from this northwest mount, built towards the enemy's approach and the camp of Vaudreuil, that the latter had been wounded, the captain of the St. Francis Indians killed, and the shots been fired that "had success"; and it was while standing here that Aldrich and Bridgman were wounded, and Thomas Knowlton was killed the next day. The blockhouses usually were furnished with two of such mounts, on opposite angles, but the language here seems to imply that the first Fort Massachusetts had but one; and in place of the other, on the opposite angle, there was "the great house," the upper story of which rose above the walls and served the purpose of both mount and watch-box. "He kept two men in the northwest mount, and some in the great house, the southeast corner of the fort, to watch the enemy and keep them back." The lower story of the "great house" was in all probability the officers' quarters, and perhaps also the storehouse of provisions and ammunition, while above it constituted a somewhat safer watch-box and place of offence than the other. It becomes pretty plain, as the narrative proceeds, and as one is able to put things together and draw the proper inference, that the soldiers' barracks and the great house were built against the south wall of the fort, while the "parade" occupied the interior space on the north side, and the gate with its strong doors was an opening in the north wall, and the well with its two posts (either for well-sweep or other means of hoisting the water) was near the northeast corner. It was no new device, but already an old one, for Canada Indians to prepare and to use faggots to burn defended houses and forts in New England from the outside; and when one remembers that the exterior walls of this fort were pine logs with a twelvemonth seasoning, it makes the Sergeant's pails, tubs, and vessels of every sort, filled with water, seem ridiculously inadequate for extinguishing the possible conflagration, although the precaution was praiseworthy.

I was in the mount all the evening; it was cloudy and very dark the beginning of the evening. The enemy kept a constant fire upon us, and, as I thought, approached nearer and in greater numbers than they had in the daytime. We had but little encouragement to fire upon the enemy, having but the light of their fire to direct us, yet we dared not wholly omit it, lest they should be emboldened to storm the fort. We fired buckshot at them, and have reason to hope we did some execution, for the enemy complained of our shooting buckshot at that time, which they could not have known had they not felt some of them. They continued thus to fire upon us until between eight and nine at night, then the whole army (as we supposed) surrounded the fort, and shouted, or rather yelled, with the most hideous outcries, all around the fort. This they repeated three or four times. We expected they would have followed this with a storm, but were mistaken, for they directly set their watch all around the fort; and besides their watch they sent some to creep up as near the fort as they could, to observe whether any persons attempted to make their escape, to carry tidings to New England.

It seems odd, that the good Chaplain should have located the fort in his mind as outside of New England, especially as its very name had been given to emphasize the fact that it was within the jurisdiction of the colony of Massachusetts, and, as Sir William Johnson said afterwards of Lake George, "to ascertain its undoubted dominion here." But his passing over by the old Indian path of the Hoosac Mountain, that gigantic water-shed between the valleys of the Deerfield and the Hoosac, and his being immediately plunged into the confusing scenes of a siege by 800 French and Indians, more or less, may well excuse this single perturbation in his geography; and we shall see in the sequel, that in his journey to Canada he manifested an uncommonly correct topographical sense, though he was in all probability wrong in the instance when he differed from Sergeant Hawks as to the location of a petty stream affluent to Wood Creek. The Chaplain stood in his lot, and shirked no military duty; he was in the mount in the early evening when it was very cloudy and dark, and the latter part of the night he kept the regular watch there. What was he thinking about during that, to him, momentous night before the surrender of the fort? The conjecture may safely be hazarded, that one topic of his thoughts was his wife and two little girls left behind in Fort Shirley. He had intended to tarry in Fort Massachusetts about a month, but in less than a week there was no Fort Massachusetts to tarry in; as a matter of fact he saw neither wife nor child for more than a year; as a matter of prospect during that cloudy night on watch, the chances of life at all were scarcely worth looking at. But he did not bate a jot of heart or hope. His was the true New England grit. Hawks and Norton bore off most of the honors that Fort Massachusetts ever yielded to mortal men.

In a well-known passage the Roman historian Tacitus writes, that in all battles it is the *eyes* that are first conquered. Not on that principle did the Indians fight, but on the principle that the *ears* are first conquered. According to all accounts the Indian battle yells were the most terrifying sounds ever erupted from human throats: as painted and daubed and bedevilled the looks of these creatures were enough to strike terror to the boldest hearts;

and when, superadded to this, their unearthly gutturals and infernal screeches assailed the ears from all points of the compass at once, the bravest men that ever bore a musket, even if they did not yield to fright, carried the sound of the war-whoops till the day of their death. One of Braddock's officers wrote three weeks after his defeat at the Monongahela, where there were fewer French and Indians than at the siege of Fort Massachusetts, — "I cannot describe the horrors of that scene; no pen could do it. The yell of the Indians is fresh on my ear, and the terrific sound will haunt me till the hour of my dissolution." Even our slow-going and adjective-sparing narrator reiterates the epithet "hideous," as applied to the war-whoops that he heard around the fort, three or four times on as many of these pages.

The body of the army then drew back to their camps; some in the swamp west of the fort, the other part to the southeast, by the river side. We then considered what was best to be done : whether to send a post down to Deerfield or not. We looked upon it very improbable, if not morally impossible, for any men to get off undiscovered, and therefore the Sergeant would not lay his command upon any to go ; but he proposed it to several, desired and encouraged them as far as he thought convenient ; but there was not a man willing to venture out. So the Sergeant having placed the men in every part of the fort, he ordered all the sick and feeble men to get what rest they could, and not regard the enemy's acclamations ; but to lie still all night unless he should call for them. Of those that were in health, some were ordered to keep the watch, and some lay down and endeavored to get some rest ; lying down in our clothes, with our arms by us. I lay down the fore part of the night. We got little or no rest. The enemy frequently raised us by their hideous outcries, as though they were about to attack us. The latter part of the night I kept the watch.

Deerfield was the nearest town of any size to the line of forts, the home of many of the officers and men in garrison, the source of most of their commissary supply, and the only hope for reinforcements in case of exigency; accordingly, it is no wonder that the sergeant and the chaplain thought of Deerfield, when they found that the fort was thoroughly invested. Indeed, the Sergeant, in co-operation with the Surgeon, had already sent fourteen men to Deerfield to act as convoy to stores and ammunition, before he knew the fort was to be invested, though he had "discovered some signs of the enemy"; an urgent letter was at the same time sent to Captain Williams at Deerfield, that he "would speedily send up some stores to the fort"; and now the question was between sergeant and chaplain, whether in their now weakened and besieged state, other messengers should be sent after the former, — whether such messengers would be likely to "get off undiscovered," that is, to get through the close lines of the besiegers, — and, if so, whether they would be likely to fetch back succor in season to prevent, if that were possible, the surrender of the fort. The long stretches over the Hoosac Mountain were a minor element in the question, but the chief thing was the hostile camps on either side of the fort, the night watch of the French set all round the fort, and besides "they sent some to creep up as near the fort as they could, to observe whether any persons attempted to make their escape, to carry tidings to New England." It was madness, under the circumstances, to send anybody out; whoever went would by so much lessen the eight men, who alone of the twenty-two, were in tolerable health. The Sergeant, therefore, would not lay his command upon any to go; but he evidently desired that one or more should make the attempt, for he proposed it to several, and encouraged them as far as he thought convenient; but it was in every respect fortunate, that no one could be persuaded to go.

Wednesday 20. — As soon as it began to be light, the enemy shouted, and began to fire upon for a few minutes, and then ceased for a little time. The Sergeant ordered every man to his place, and sent two men up into the watch-box. The enemy came into the field of corn to the south and southeast of the fort, and fought against that side of the fort harder than they did the day before ; but unto the northwest side they did not approach so near as they had the first day, yet they kept a continual fire on that side. A number went up also into the mountain north of the fort, where they could shoot over the north side of the fort into the middle of the parade. A considerable number of the enemy also kept their axes and hatchets continually at work, preparing faggots, and their stubbing hoes and spades, etc., in order to burn the fort. About eleven o'clock, Thomas Knowlton, one of our men, being in the watch-box, was shot through the head, so that some of his brains came out, yet life remained in him for some hours.

Knowlton was the only one of the defenders of the fort who was killed outright during the siege. That the body was not removed from the watch-box and buried, before the surrender of the fort and the consequent mutilation of the remains by the savages and the semi-savage Frenchmen, was owing to the appearance of life still remaining in him till the catastrophe occurred. Why the besiegers should use their stubbing hoes and spades, as well as their axes and hatchets, in preparing faggots, is not quite clear, unless the reason be that the stubs and roots of bushes cut the year before were drier, and so more suitable to their purpose of burning the fort. The reference to the field of corn to the south and southeast of the fort is interesting ; for the planting of it, and the hoeing, must have been prosecuted under difficulties, since it is certain that no trees had been felled on that meadow prior to the spring of 1745, and since Norton's description of the Indians dodging round between the stumps within gunshot of the fort, proves that the planting there did not differ much from that upon many another "burnt piece" in New England before and since. Yet soldiers in garrison, when no enemy is near, find life tedious to the last degree under the most favorable circumstances. The young farmers and mechanics in Fort Massachusetts, in May, 1746, even if they were not put upon it by their officers, would rather work out of doors a part of the time than not. The prospect of a few ears apiece of "roasted" green corn in September may have still further stimulated their zeal, and they were all used to such work at home. It was this tedium, doubtless, as well as a desire to found for himself a home, that led one of the soldiers, John Perry, to fence in a few acres of wild land a mile west of the fort, and build him a loghouse thereon; and perhaps to plant around it a few hills of beans and corn, which he might harvest in the fall, without the leave of the commander at the fort; and, at any rate, conjecture would be vain as to what hands harvested the corn at the fort, in the autumn of 1746. That place was then utterly deserted of men, and continued so for six months, — no human habitation nearer than the house of Eleazar Hawks in Charlemont.

For one, the writer is very thankful for the incidental statement that a number of the besiegers went up into the mountain north of the fort, where they could shoot over the north side of the fort into the middle of the parade; because, along with other evidence, this goes to show the exact situation of things in the interior of the fort. The parade was on the north side of the interior; the gate in the middle of the north wall opened directly into it; the well, with its posts, must have been in the northeast corner, otherwise the parade would have been cluttered with them; and the watch-box, as we know, was over the other corner on that side. The barracks and the "great house," accordingly, must have been built against the south wall, and perhaps also against a part of the walls of the two ends. This was almost certainly the precise state of things in the interior of Shirley also, as the ruins of that fort in Heath pretty clearly disclose to this day; and while in Pelham, which was a stockade, and not a blockhouse like the other two, the well was in the centre of the enclosure, there is good evidence to be found on the spot to this day that the gate was in the middle of the north wall, as it certainly was in Massachusetts.

About twelve o'clock the enemy desired to parley. We agreed to it, and when we came to General Vaudreuil, he promised us good quarter if we would surrender; otherwise, he should endeavor to take us by force. The Sergeant told him he should have an answer within two hours. We came into the fort and examined the state of it. The whole of our ammunition we did not judge to be above three or four pounds of powder and not more lead; and, after prayers unto God for wisdom and direction, we considered our case, whether there was any probability of our being able to withstand the enemy, for we supposed that they would not leave us till they had made a vigorous attempt upon us, and, if they did, we knew our ammunition would be spent in a few minutes' time, and then we should be obliged to lay at their mercy.

This is a good place for us to learn something about this Vaudreuil, with whom Hawks and Norton parleyed, and to whom they shortly afterwards surrendered. He belonged to the most distinguished French family that ever resided in, or held government over, New France. His father, Marquis de Vaudreuil, was Governor of Canada from 1703 till his death at Quebec in 1725. His older brother, who succeeded to the father's title of Marquis in 1748, was born at Quebec in 1698, was appointed Governor of Louisiana at the other extremity of New France in 1743, and became in 1755 the last — and perhaps the best — of all the French Governors of Canada. Our Vaudreuil, who commonly passed by the name of Rigaud de Vaudreuil, was born in Montreal Feb. 8, 1704, became town major of Three Rivers, and, after his exploit on the Hoosac, was almost constantly employed in important services till the downfall of French Canada. Ten years after the surrender of Fort Massachusetts, in conjunction with Montcalm, he captured Oswego with 1600 prisoners, — the greatest triumph that had then been achieved by the French arms in America. "The cries, threats, and hideous howlings of our Canadians and Indians," wrote Vaudreuil, "made them quickly decide." The next year, 1757, he was given by his brother the chief command of a detachment consisting at least of 1600 French and Indians, sent in March to surprise and capture Fort William Henry at the head of Lake George. It was brilliantly conducted, and came near being successful. All the outbuildings of the fort were burnt, — storehouses, hospital, saw-mill, huts of Stark's rangers, a sloop on the stocks, and piles of planks and cord-wood, besides two sloops ice-bound in the lake and a large number of batteaux on the shore. Montcalm, who did not like it that Governor Vaudreuil gave the chief command to Rigaud, wrote, "I worked at the place of the last affair, which might have turned out better, though good as it was. If I had had my way, Levis or Bougainville would have had charge of it. However, the thing was all right and in good hands. The Governor, who is extremely civil to me, gave it to his brother; he thought him more used to winter marches." And the truth was, that the fort was vigilantly watched as against surprise and bravely defended as against assault, the garrison consisting of 346 effective men, — a part of them being Scotch-Irish Presbyterian rangers from New Hampshire under John Stark, — and Major Eyre and the other British officers were resolute and capable men. Later in the same season Vaudreuil was an important commander under Montcalm in the successful siege and destruction of Fort William Henry. In all the subsequent movements for the defence of Montreal and Quebec against Amherst on the one side and Wolfe on the other, both the brothers Vaudreuil were active and persistent to the last, — Rigaud in the field as soldier and Pierre in council as Governor; and when it was all over with New France, the two betook themselves to Paris together, — the Governor to be imprisoned in the Bastille on charges preferred by the friends of Montcalm, though afterwards released and partly exonerated, and dying in 1764, while the soldier-victor at Fort Massachusetts was still living at St. Germaine in 1770.

Had we all been in health, or had there been only those eight of us that were in health, I believe every man would willingly have stood it out to the last. For my part I should; but we heard that if we were taken by violence the sick, the wounded, and the women would most, if not all of them, die by the hands of the savages; therefore our officer concluded to surrender on the best terms he could get, which were —

I. That we should be all prisoners to the French; the General promising that the savages should have nothing to do with any of us.

II. That the children should all live with their parents during the time of their captivity.

III. That we should all have the privileges of being exchanged the first opportunity that presented.

Besides these particulars, the General promised that all the prisoners should have all Christian care and charity exercised towards them; that those who were weak and unable to travel should be carried in their journey; that we should all be allowed to keep our clothing; and that we might leave a few lines to inform our friends what was become of us.

In accordance with this last permission, Norton wrote a letter the next day, though he dated it Aug. 20, 1746, and nailed it on the west post of the well-sweep, the fort having been burned in the meantime by Vaudreuil's orders. Norton does not anywhere give the text of the letter, for the reason doubtless that he kept no copy of it; but it was found a few days afterward and carried to Deerfield, and it ran as follows: —

These are to inform you that yesterday, about nine of the clock, we were besieged by, as they say, seven hundred French and Indians. They have wounded two men and killed one Knowlton. The General De Vaudreuil desired capitulations, and we were so distressed that we complied with his terms. We are the French's prisoners, and have it under the General's hand, that every man, woman, and child shall be exchanged for French prisoners.

The good Chaplain is careful in this letter to give his authority for the statement that the besieging army consisted of "seven hundred": "as they say," that is, the French officers; his own opinion, given much later, after he had marched to Canada in company with this army was, that there were eight or nine hundred; and we have already gathered reasons from the contemporary French documents for believing that even this was an underestimate. When the French officers saw the poverty of the fort and the paucity of its defenders, and realized that they had been held at bay for thirty hours, it was naturally enough their care to belittle their own force. Although Norton does not mention it in connection with the parley, it has come down to us on the authority of Hawks, that the enemy then displayed their own means of capturing the fort, such as axes, hoes, spades, a quantity of fascines ready cut, and a number of grenades.

The military vigor of the Chaplain strikingly appears in the last passage quoted. He was one who "would willingly have stood it out to the last." In this respect there was a strong resemblance between him, the first minister of the gospel who ever exercised his functions in the valley of the Hoosac within the limits of Massachusetts, and his next following settled successor within the same local limits, Rev. Whitman Welch, the first minister of Williamstown, called in July, 1765. The "minute men," who went from here to Cambridge ten years later, were his parishioners; several of these were drafted in the late autumn to go up the Kennebec with Arnold to surprise Quebec. Mr. Welch accompanied these as a volunteer, not as the chaplain of the detachment, — a service that was rendered by Mr. Spring of Newburyport, — but apparently because he liked enterprise and danger and the military life. Zebadiah Sabin and David Johnson, two of his parishioners, were subordinate officers under Arnold in this expedition, and Welch, who was fond of athletic exercises and excelled in them, left parish and wife and two children, exactly as Norton had done, and doubtless with a similar relish, to take the hazards of war; but while Norton returned from his captivity to a parish in Connecticut, Welch died at Quebec in March, 1776, of the small-pox, as did also many of his compeers in that perilous journey through the wilderness.

About three of the clock we admitted the General and a number of his officers into the fort. Upon which he set up his standard. The gate was not opened to the rest. The gentlemen spake comfortably to our people; and on our petition that the dead corpse might not be abused, but buried, they said that it should be buried. But the Indians, seeing that they were shut out, soon fell to pulling out the underpinning of the fort, and crept into it and opened the gates, so that the parade was quickly full. They shouted as soon as they saw the blood of the dead corpse under the watch-box; but the French kept them down for some time and did not suffer them to meddle with it. After some time the Indians seemed to be in a ruffle; and presently rushed up into the watch-box, brought down the dead corpse, carried it out of the fort, scalped it, and cut off the head and arms. A young French cut off one of the arms and flayed it, roasted the flesh, and offered some of it to Daniel Smead, one of the prisoners, to eat, but he refused it. The Frenchman dressed the skin of the arm (as we afterwards heard) and made a tobacco pouch of it. After they had plundered the fort, they set it on fire, and led us out to their camp.

This Daniel Smead, who refused to become a cannibal at the dictation of a semi-savage, or rather double-savage, was one of a family of seven (increased the next day to eight), all taken in the fort and all carried captive to Quebec. They were from Pequaog, what is now Athol. The father, John Smead, this son Daniel, and John Smead, Jr., were paid soldiers. The mother, Mary, and three young children were in the fort in a position of dependence. John, Jr., died a captive in Quebec the next April. "He was taken with me at Fort Massachusetts. He was seized with the distemper in October last, and was bad for a time, and then recovered in some good measure, and after a little time relapsed, and as he did several times, till at last he fell into a consumption, of which he died." This Daniel died also at Quebec a little more than a month later than his brother. "Died Daniel Smead, a young man. He was taken with me, and was son to John Smead. He was first taken sick in November, and by frequent relapses was worn out, and fell into a purging, by which he wasted away and died." The father, John Smead, returned home from his captivity Aug. 31, 1747, probably bringing with him his three younger children; but about six weeks after his return he was travelling from Northfield to Sunderland, when he was killed by an ambush of Indians and scalped.

Vaudreuil had the satisfaction of raising the lilied banner of France — *fleur-de-lis* — on the top of the fort for an hour or two before it was burned. Undoubtedly it was hoisted at the summit of the "great house" in the southeast corner of the fort. Ten years later, when the French captured Oswego and burned the forts and made the place a desert, a tall cross was planted amid the ruins, graven with the words, *In hoc signo vincunt;* and near it was set a pole bearing the banner of France, with the inscription, *Manibus date lilia plenis.* It seems queer to present denizens along the Hoosac, that the French flag should ever have floated even for an hour over its waters!

The contrast between the French officers, who spoke pleasantly and kindly to the prisoners, and the young Frenchman, whether native or Canadian, who practised the barbarities on the body of the dead Knowlton, is one that French society in Canada perpetually presented until its downfall. The exquisite manners of Paris, all the proverbial politeness of France, pitched its tent in and near the residences of the governors of Canada and of such courtly gentlemen as Montcalm, whether in Quebec or Three Rivers or Montreal, while close alongside this refinement, speaking the *patois* of the country, were the cruelty and falsity and barbarism of the *habitans* and fur-traders, surpassing, if possible, in degradation even the Indians themselves. The sight of Knowlton's blood dripping down from the watch-box to the ground, roused the Indians to a fierce desire to scalp and mutilate the body; and the same sight roused the young Frenchman to flay the arm, and roast and eat the flesh of the dead man.

As the fort was now shortly plundered and set on fire and burnt to the ground, and the prisoners led out to the camp of the French a little to the northwest, our last opportunity to get a further glimpse of the mode in which it was constructed is offered us in the passage last quoted. It is evident that it was free space under the watch-box at the northwest angle, for it was there that the Indians saw the blood, before the body had been removed from the mount; which is another circumstance going to show that the north side was the free and open side of the fort, — the space under the watch-box at the west end and the space around the well at the east end of this side really making one space with the parade in the middle of it. This view is confirmed by the fact that the Indians pulled out the loose stones forming the underpinning of the fort, crept within, and opened the gate that was certainly on the north side, "so that the parade was quickly full." Then they shouted as soon as they saw the blood. It is absolutely certain that the well, both at Shirley and Massachusetts, was in the northeast angle. Norton nailed the letter on the west post of the well, which was not burned when the walls of the fort went down under the fire. Drake ["Particular History," p. 120] understands this to mean the west arm of the well-crotch, within which the well-sweep worked.

At any rate, the well-sweep, if there was one, was parallel with the east wall of the fort, and near it; and if there were none, one cannot see why there should be any " west post " of the well at all, on which a letter could be nailed. It will be noticed by the painstaking reader (not by others), that this arrangement put the well as much out of the way as it could possibly be put in the interior of such an enclosure, doubtless very near to the east wall and to the north wall at their junction. It may be only a chance coincidence, or it may indicate a custom obtaining in blockhouses in those times : at any rate it is a fact, that when General Amherst built his great fort at Crown Point, the " big well " was placed in the northeast angle also.

We had been at their camp but a little time, when Mons. Doty, the General's interpreter, called me aside, and desired me to speak to our soldiers, and persuade them to go with the Indians ; for he said that the Indians were desirous that some of them should go with them ; and said that Sergeant Hawks, myself, and the families, should go with the French officers. I answered him that it was contrary to our agreement, and the General's promise ; and would be to throw away the lives of some of our sick and wounded. He said, no ; but the Indians would be kind to them ; and though they were all prisoners to the French, yet he hoped some of them would be willing to go with the Indians.

The French were in close alliance for peace and war with the Indian tribes of Canada and the West, but they were troublesome allies at the best, and in moments of excitement were utterly uncontrollable. Montcalm writes: " You would take them for so many masqueraders or devils. One needs the patience of an angel to get on with them." They abandoned Dieskau to a man in the battle of Lake George. Montcalm himself by his utmost endeavors could not prevent their massacre of his plighted prisoners after the surrender of Fort William Henry. They could not be made to understand, still less to respect, the obligation of pledges. In the case before us, Vaudreuil had promised more than he could perform; he had bitten off more than he could chew. The Indians insisted on their claim to escort the bulk of the prisoners to Canada, to present them to the Governor-General themselves, and so be able the better to claim an expected reward. The spirit, if not the letter, of the capitulation put all the prisoners into the care of the French officers and men ; and this was fully recognized by Vaudreuil in his sending his interpreter to Norton, and asking him to persuade the soldiers to go with the Indians voluntarily. Why did the General send Monsieur Doty to Norton rather than to Hawks, the proper officer ? If an innocent conjecture may be hazarded, it may have been a religious scruple on the part of Vaudreuil, a sense at least of the sanctity of a promise, that would be violated if he sent the prisoners among the Indians; and so, if their religious leader would consent to it and get the consent of some of the soldiers, his own conscience would be the better satisfied. It was a compliment to the Chaplain at any rate, and no disrespect to the Sergeant; but the scheme, whatever its motive, did not work, and the General was left to settle it with his conscience the best he could; the Indians must be placated in any event and so the terms of the surrender were strained, even if not broken.

We spoke to Sergeant Hawks, and he [Doty] urged it upon him. We proposed it to some of our men who were in health, whether they were willing to go or not, but they were utterly unwilling. I returned to Doty, and told him we should by no means consent that any of our men should go with the Indians. We took the General to be a man of honor, and hoped to find him so. We knew that it was the manner of the Indians to abuse their prisoners, and sometimes to kill those that failed in traveling and carrying packs, which we knew that some of our men could not do; and we thought it little better for the General to deliver them to the Indians than it would be to abuse them himself, and had I thought that the General would have delivered any of our men to the savages, I should have strenuously opposed the surrender of the fort, for I had rather have died in fight, than to see any of our men killed while we had no opportunity to resist. He said that the General would see that they should not be abused; and he did not like it that I was so jealous and afraid. I told him I was not the officer, but as he spake to me, so I had freely spoken my mind, and discharged my duty in it, and he had no reason to be offended, and I hoped the General would not insist on this thing, but would make good his promise to all the prisoners.

These were no fancied fears of Norton's in respect to the sick and wounded among the prisoners, for he was familiar with the story of the captivities to Canada that had taken place in Queen Anne's War, and particularly with the "Redeemed Captive," Rev. John Williams's account of the sack of Deerfield in 1704. Of the 112 captives taken from Deerfield at that time, seventeen were killed or died on the march to Canada, and among these was Mrs. Williams, wife of the minister, who was tomahawked at the foot of a hill in what is now Greenfield. Everybody in New England in 1746 was familiar with these facts from the popularity of Williams's little book with the above title, published in 1707, in which he gave an interesting narrative of the adventures of the captives, and which was soon in everybody's hands. Still, it must be owned, that in the present instance these vigorously expressed fears for the feeble captives proved in the issue to be groundless. These captives were extraordinarily well treated, as we shall see. Perhaps Vaudreuil's qualms of conscience, if he had any, over the terms of capitulation, made him all the more scrupulous that no harm should come to the surrendered from the Indians.

He [Doty] went to the General, and after a little time the officers came and took away John Perry and his wife, and all the soldiers but Sergeant Hawks, John Smead and Moses Scott and their families, and distributed them among the Indians. ˙ Some French officers took the care of the families, namely, Smead's and Scott's, and Mons. Demuy took me with him, and M. St. Luc Lacorn took Sergeant Hawks with him, and so we reposed that night, having a strong guard set over us.

The reason why Rebecca Perry and her husband were placed in the care of the Indians, while the other two women with their husbands and the five children were taken charge of by the French officers, seems to have been that they had no children as impediments. The Indians were to go ahead in the march, and the French to bring up the rear. Eleven in all were put with the French, and nineteen were given over to the Indians. The Sergeant and the Chaplain were very honorably treated, for the two highest officers in command, next to the General, took these with them respectively, namely, La Corne took Hawks, and Demuy, Norton. La Corne, like Vaudreuil, was a native Canadian. His father, Captain La Corne, town major of Three Rivers in 1719, started his son, who had received in baptism the name of the third evangelist, St. Luc, into public life the next year, and the same time that the first Governor Vaudreuil was paving a way in life for his own two sons, one of whom became his successor as the last Governor of Canada, and the other distinguished himself first in the capture of Fort Massachusetts. La Corne became during the last fifteen years of New France a successful partisan officer after a type of his own. He was active and able and ruthless and tireless. His intimate knowledge of the Indian languages gave him a wonderful influence over the motley tribes that danced the war-dance at Montreal or Quebec. He seemed to be everywhere where there was council and carnage. Now at Niagara, now at La Chine Rapids, once and again in Acadia, where he was in command of 2500 men, extremely serviceable in the reduction of Fort William Henry, and standing indifferently by while maddened Indians massacred the prisoners surrendered with the fort, wounded at the rapids of Lake Ontario in 1759, and again wounded at the capture of Quebec, shipwrecked on his way to France when all was over in Canada, yet saved from the sea by a miracle, and finding his way back to Quebec by another miracle of physical endurance, where he wrote a journal of the voyage, — his was a figure which only New France in her last days could have produced, or would have tolerated.

Writes Parkman in a memorable passage:[1] —

Worst of all was the fate of the *Auguste*, on board of which was the bold but ruthless partisan, Saint-Luc de la Corne, his brother, his children, and a party of Canadian officers, together with ladies, merchants, and soldiers. A worthy ecclesiastical chronicler paints the unhappy vessel as a floating Babylon, and sees in her fate the stern judgment of Heaven. It is true that New France ran riot in the last days of her existence; but before the *Auguste* was well out of the St. Lawrence she was so tossed and buffeted, so lashed with waves and pelted with rain, that the most alluring forms of sin must have lost their charm, and her inmates passed days rather of penance than transgression. There was a violent storm as the ship entered the Gulf; then a calm, during which she took fire in the cook's galley. The crew and passengers subdued the flames after desperate efforts, but their only food thenceforth was dry biscuit. Off the coast of Cape Breton another gale rose. They lost their reckoning and lay tossing blindly amid the tempest. The exhausted sailors took in despair to their hammocks, from which neither commands nor blows could rouse them, while amid shrieks, tears, prayers, and vows to Heaven, the *Auguste* drove towards the shore, struck, and rolled over on her side. La Corne, with six others, gained the beach, and towards night they saw the ship break asunder, and counted a hundred and fourteen corpses strewn along the sand. Aided by Indians and by English officers, La Corne made his way on snow-shoes up the St. John, and by a miracle of enduring hardihood, reached Quebec before the end of winter.

Lieutenant Demuy, who took Chaplain Norton in charge for the journey to Canada, was son of the Captain Demuy of the French regulars in New France, who was appointed Governor of Louisiana in 1707, and who died on his journey thither to assume that position. The son left an excellent record in Canada, with no word, so far as appears, to mar it. When he was appointed to command at the Lake of the Two Mountains in 1746, he was reported to Paris by his superiors as "a prudent, wise, and sedate man, and a very exact officer in all that appertains to the King's service"; he became afterwards commandant at La Prairie, and still later at Detroit; and he seems to have possessed remarkable influence over the Indians, both over the Mission Indians and those from the farthest west and south.

Thursday, 21. — In the morning I obtained liberty to go to the place of the fort, and set up a letter, which I did, with a Frenchman and some Indians in company. I nailed the letter on the west post. This morning I saw Josiah Reed, who was very weak and feeble by reason of his long and tedious sickness. I interceded with the General for him, that he would not send him with the

[1] Montcalm and Wolfe, v. 2, p. 384.

Indians, but could not prevail. I also interceded with the General for John Aldrich, who, being wounded in the foot, was not able to travel; but the interpreter told me they must go with the Indians, but they should not be hurt; and they had canoes a little down the river, in which the weak and feeble should be carried. We then put up our things and set on our march for Crown Point, going down the river in Hoosuck road. I was toward the front, and within about a half a mile I overtook John Perry's wife; I passed her, M. Demuy traveling apace. I spoke with her, and asked her how she did? She told me that her strength failed her in traveling so fast. I told her God was able to strengthen her. In him she must put her trust, and I hoped she was ready for whatever God had to call her to. I had opportunity to say no more. We went about four miles to the place where the army encamped the night before they came upon us. Here I overtook neighbor Perry, which surprised me, for I thought he had been behind me with the French, but he was with the Indians. I asked him after his health. He said he was better than he had been. I inquired after his wife. He said he did not know where she was, but was somewhere with the Indians, which surprised me very much, for I thought till then she was with the French.

Josiah Read was from Rehoboth in the Old Colony. He was sick of the prevailing distemper before the fort was besieged, and was doubtless treated by the Indians after the surrender with all the consideration that was possible, an Indian carrying him on his back. He died at the place of the first encampment during this (Thursday) night; and though Norton suggests a little later a fear that he may have been murdered, it became perfectly clear after the return of the surviving captives that the man died of his malady. John Aldrich was of Mendon in Worcester County, and was one of the two wounded in the watch-box on the first day of the siege. When the rest of his surviving companions in captivity returned to their several homes the next year, John Aldrich and one other were left sick in Quebec, but these two also returned afterwards, and were paid their wages, twenty-five shillings a month, for the year and more, by the Treasurer of the Colony. The captives started Thursday morning for Crown Point from Vaudreuil's camp near the fort, the Indians in general in front and the French in the rear, though soon more or less commingled on the march, making their way as best they could "down the river in Hoosuck road" towards the first resting-place four miles to the west where there is a decided bend of the river to the north. Norton's use of the term, "road," here, shows that the immemorial Mohawk trail was even then much travelled back and forth. It was a road. After crossing the stream at Fort Massachusetts, it ran thenceforth along its northern bank and usually near to the water, unless the interval were low and wet, in which case the Indians always hugged the edge of the higher land, or unless there were a considerable bend in the stream, in which case the Indians made the short cut as unerringly as a modern engineer. The place where Norton overtook John Perry's wife was near or at the place where her husband had built their house a short time before, and stocked it with the goods to which reference has been had already, and which the struggling Indians bringing up the rear burned in passing. The considerable confusion into which Norton falls in this paragraph concerning the Perrys, betrays the fact that he wrote out his narrative some time after the events, from notes taken at the time; for he tells us expressly a little way back that Perry and his wife, with the bulk of the soldiers, were distributed among the Indians, while here he twice expresses much surprise to find them in the company of the Indians — "for I thought till then she was with the French."

The Hoosac meadow in Williamstown, on which the band of captives rested for a while about noon of the first day's march, has been from that day to this an interesting place. " We went about four miles to the place where the army encamped the night before they came upon us." The place is now called the River Bend Farm. There has been for many years a steam saw-mill where the river begins to bend northward, which has more or less disfigured the meadow, and the tracks of the Fitchburg railroad curving round the bend and requiring considerable cutting and filling, to say nothing of a deposit of gravel which has been carried off in large quantities for ballasting, have still further disfigured and transformed it; but when perhaps for centuries the Indians used to make a sort of camp and stopping-place upon this curve covered with primeval forests, of which enormous pines formed a part, it was one of the loveliest places in all New England; and when about twenty-five years after the present passage, the farm was fairly cleared up, it became, perhaps, the most fertile farm in Williamstown, and certainly the residence and tavern-stand of its most prominent and patriotic citizen. Indian arrow-heads and other Indian relics have always been found in its ploughed fields, and even so late as 1887. And notwithstanding the cut-up and demoralized surface, Samuel Abbott, a graduate of the College of that year, found several valuable relics of Indian occupation on the place. Next to Josiah Read, who died a few miles down the river a few hours later, the sickest of the captives was a lad named Benjamin Simonds, of Ware River, then twenty years old, who lived to own the broad meadow, and to build upon it the stately house still standing, of which, as well as of him, we shall be likely to learn more in the sequel.

Here we sat down for a considerable time. My heart was filled with sorrow, expecting that many of our weak and feeble people would fall by the merciless hands of the enemy. And as I frequently heard the savages shouting and yelling, trembled, concluding that they then murdered some of our people. And this was my only comfort, that they could do nothing against us, but what God in his holy Providence permitted them ; but was filled with admiration when I saw all the prisoners come up with us, and John Aldrich carried upon the back of his Indian master. We set out again, and had gone but a little way before we came up with Josiah Read, who gave out. I expected they would have knocked him on the head and killed him, but an Indian carried him on his back. We made several stops, and after we had traveled about eight miles we made a considerable stay, where we refreshed ourselves, and I had an opportunity to speak to several of the prisoners ; especially John Smead, and his wife, who being near her time, was filled with admiration at the goodness of God in strengthening her to travel so far.

The cause of the shouting and yelling of the savages, here referred to by Norton, may very probably have been the burning of John Perry's premises, at that time the only house in the Hoosac valley till they came down to Dutch Hoosac, where they burned, the next day, seven houses and fourteen barns, and a large quantity of wheat, and slaughtered many hogs and cattle, doubtless accompanying the devastation with similar whooping and outcry. Every vestige of this already thriving settlement at the junction of the Little Hoosac with the Hoosac went up in flames; one of the proprietors named Samuel Bowen was killed, and the loss in that single neighborhood was estimated, at the time, as £50,000 New York currency. The French account of the doings of this party returning from the sack of Fort Massachusetts is not exaggerated as much as usual : " Barns, mills, churches, and tanneries were destroyed, and the harvest laid waste for a distance of thirty or forty miles." Indeed, the small party of French and Indians returning from the attack on Fort Massachusetts two months before, when Elisha Nims was killed, and Gershom Hawks wounded there, slaughtered, in Dutch Hoosac, nearly one hundred animals belonging to the Dutch and English farmers. The valley is this time trod by an army that leaves nothing of value movable or burnable behind it. But we are getting a little ahead of Norton's narrative.

I saw John Perry's wife. She complained that she was almost ready to give out. She complained also of the Indian that she went with, that he threatened her. I talked with a French officer, and he said that she need not fear, for he would not be allowed to hurt her. Mons. Demuy, with a number of men, set out before the army, so I took my leave of her, fearing I should never see her more. After this Sergeant Hawks went to the General and represented her case to him. So he went and talked to the Indians, and he [her master] was kind to her after that. After we had traveled round the fields, I thought he was about to leave the river, which increased my fears. But I found out the reason ; for they only went to look some buildings to plunder, and burn them.

Vaudreuil was true to his after promise, even if he had proved false to the exact terms of surrender. No captives in like circumstances ever had less cause to complain of their treatment on the whole. These conferences were had, and this result was reached, while the slow march was progressing through the present town of Pownal, Vermont, and approaching and passing the present line of the state of New York. The valley of the Hoosac narrows decidedly after passing into Petersburg, and the river turns sharply to the west, till the valley suddenly broadens to receive into itself the valley of the Little Hoosac at the junction of the two streams. These united valleys, at their place of union, are now called, for railway reasons, Petersburg Junction. They were formerly called, from the prevailing nationality of the farmers there, Dutch Hoosac. The meadows here are very broad, and have always been very productive. Here located himself in 1735, Bernardus Bratt, a Dutchman, who married in that year, Catharine Van Vechten, and who built his house very near the present railway station. He built the first saw-mill and the first grist-mill in this district. These mills, and a large quantity of grain, lumber, and other property, both his and his neighbors', were burned by our Indians at this time. "They went to look some buildings to plunder, and burn them." They went up the Little Hoosac and burned every farm-house and barn in what is now North Petersburg. They performed the same pleasing service for the Bovies and Brimmers and Bowens and Van Der Vericks, on whose meadow, directly to the south of Bratt's, the whole army encamped for the night. Dec. 1, of this year, Norton notes in his diary the death at Quebec of Gratis Van Der Verick, who had been a captive for a year, and had been taken at Saratoga, and who may have belonged to the family then occupying what has since been called the " Joseph Case farm," and is now called (1887) from its present owner, the " Edward Green " farm, on which Vaudreuil, with his motley force and his prisoners, made their first night's encampment, after leaving the fort for good.

A little before sunset we arrived at Van Der Verick's place, where we found some of the army, who had arrived before us, but most of them were still behind ; and I had the comfort of seeing the greatest part of the prisoners come up: God having wonderfully strengthened many who were weak ; the French carrying the women. There were some few that tarried behind about two miles, where Mrs. Smead was taken in travail: And some of the French made a seat for her to sit upon, and brought her to the camp, where about ten o'clock, she was graciously delivered of a daughter, and was remarkably well. The child also was well. But this night Josiah Read, being very ill, either died of his illness, or else was killed by the enemy ; which, I could never certainly know, but I fear he was murdered.

From Fort Massachusetts to Van Der Verick's place, the first day's journey towards Canada, was not far from fourteen miles as the river runs. Nature put her seal of beauty and bounty upon the spot, and Providence marked it with displays of graciousness, that doubtless came in answer to prayer; the French showed unwonted kindness to the sick women, bringing Mrs. Scott and Mrs. Perry to the camp, carrying them ; and when Mrs. Smead was taken in travail some two miles back from the camp, it was French officers and soldiers who tenderly tarried for her, made a seat for her to sit upon, and carried her in their arms to the camp on the meadow, which was then made memorable forever by the birth and baptism of a Christian child.

Friday, 22. — This morning I baptised John Smead's child. He called its name *Captivity*. The French then made a frame like a bier, and laid a buck skin and bear skin upon it, and laid Mrs. Smead, with her infant, thereon ; and so two men at a time carried them. They also carried Moses Scott's wife and two children, and another of Smead's children. The Indians also carried in their canoes, Benjamin Simonds and John Aldrich and Perry's wife, down the river about ten miles.

At least two canoes had been brought by the Indians from the head of Lake Champlain, where most of their boats were left to await their return, up to the junction of the Hoosacs, and here they took into these for the next stage of their journey homeward, the sick man, and the wounded man, and the invalid woman, all of whom had been in Indian charge from the start. Their birch-bark canoes and paddles were extremely light, and were easily borne over the shorter or longer carrying-places, which intermitted the water-ways between Canada and the Colonies, by whichever of the usual routes these ways were attempted. There was less land-carriage by Lake George or Wood Creek to the Hudson, or by any one of the three routes over the Green Mountains to the Connecticut, than by the route chosen on this occasion by Owl Kill to the Hoosac.

We had remarkable smiles of Providence. Our men that had been sick, grew better and recovered strength. The enemy killed some cattle which they found in the meadow; so that we had plenty of fresh provisions and broth, which was very beneficial to the sick. I then expressed a concern for the feeble people, understanding that we were to leave the river, and travel through the wilderness near sixty miles; but Mons. Demuy told me I need not fear, for the General had promised those Indians a reward who had the care of the feeble persons, if they would be kind and carry them through the journey. This night I visited most of the prisoners. This night, also, died two Indians of their wounds. The enemy had got four horses.

Scarcely less picturesque than the first was this second night's encampment at St. Croix, the junction of the Walloomsac with the Hoosac. The encampment was on the land of Garret Van Ness, whose acquaintance we have already made in connection with supplies for Fort Massachusetts. The horses obtained for the couriers to carry the good news to Canada, undoubtedly belonged to Van Ness, for he owned two miles or more of the land between the mouth of the Walloomsac and the mouth of Owl Kill, where is now the hamlet of Eagle Bridge. From Van Der Verick's to Eagle Bridge, the second day's more comfortable journey, is pretty nearly ten miles. Here all hands were to leave the line of the Hoosac, and push on nearly due north, into the then unsettled wilderness, now Washington County, to the head of Lake Champlain, where is now the town of Whitehall. The canoes, with the two or three sick ones, might, perhaps, be pushed up the Owl Kill a few miles above its mouth, and then all the rest would be land journey to the lake.

Saturday, 23. — This morning the General sent off an officer with some men to carry news to Canada. This day we left the river and traveled in the wilderness, in something of a path, and good traveling for the wilderness, something east of north, about fifteen miles; the French still carrying Smead's and Scott's wives and children; the Indians finding horses for Benjamin Simonds and John Aldrich. Perry being released from his pack, was allowed to help his wife, and carry her when she was weary. About three in the afternoon they were alarmed by discovering the tracks of a scout from Saratoga. This put them into a considerable ruffle, fearing that there might be an army after them. But I presumed that they need not be concerned about it. The body of the army lodged between two ponds, but part, with a number of the prisoners, were sent forward about two miles, till they crossed Sarratago river; it is there twenty rods wide, but shallow water. This night also died two more Indians of their wounds.

This paragraph is one of extreme importance both historically and geographically, and has been often heretofore, if not always, wholly misinterpreted. So good a geographer and historian as Samuel G. Drake explained the "Sarratago river," as "doubtless the Hudson river." It is, in fact, no other than the Batten Kill. The proof of this, and the reason why Norton, following the usage of the time, called the stream "Sarratago River," as the same much higher up in the hills was also called in Captain Melvin's more famous "Journal," in 1748, will come forth into clear light as we go on. Once and again and again the present writer has gone carefully over every foot of ground covered by this passage, which was the third day's march of the captives, and satisfied himself by personal inspection, not only as to the exact spot of the lodging-place "between two ponds," which is the water-shed between the Hoosac and the Batten Kill, but also as to the exact place of their crossing the river, which is called to this day "the ford." Their route lay directly up Owl Kill on the west side of it, just as the public road now runs from Eagle Bridge to Cambridge, and thence north along the present road to Salem, through what is now Jackson Center, and then, after bending a little to the right between Long Pond and McLean Pond, found the "divide," and there was their camp for the night. Dead Pond, apparently without inlet or outlet, lies just upon the water-shed. Then from Big Pond (just north) there flows a tiny stream through Little Pond to reach the kill below. These are the so-called Jackson Ponds. The ground is low and swampy along this little tributary of the kill, and so the Indian path turned to the left, keeping the higher ground, and then went through a little pass between high hills, and came directly down to the present ford over the Batten Kill at East Greenwich. A substantial farmhouse now flanks the old Indian trail on the west just before the ford is reached. Much narrower now are mountain streams than they were 140 years ago, and Norton's "twenty rods" have shrunk to less than half that width.

The whole of what is now Washington County, and the western slopes of the Green Mountains adjoining it, across both of which the Batten Kill, in a prevailingly western direction, finds its way to the Hudson, was in the early times Iroquois Country, or the hunting grounds of the Six Nations. Lake Champlain was the "Lake of the Iroquois." The river Richelieu draining the lake into the St. Lawrence, and the territory on both sides of the lake and of its outlet, was the mutual battle-ground of the Mohawks with the Canada Indians. Writes Slafter in his "Champlain": "This region occupied a peculiar relation to the hostile tribes on the north and those on the south of the St. Lawrence. It was the battle-field, or war-path, where they had for many generations, on each returning summer, met in bloody conflict. The territory between these contending tribes was neutral ground. Mutual fear had kept it open and uninhabited." Samuel Champlain and two French arquebusiers were the first civilized witnesses and partakers of one of these con-

flicts in 1609, between Mohawks on one side and Montagnais and
Hurons and Algonquins on the other, on a spot since become famous
all the world over, — Ticonderoga. The path, therefore, up which
Vaudreuil led his army and his captives from the Hoosac to Lake
Champlain, was an old Mohawk war-path, less trodden, it may be,
than the great east and west one to which it lay at right angles,
because the Six Nations usually went up to their battles at the
north by the Hudson and its carrying-place to Wood Creek. Norton
says, however, "in something of a path, and good traveling for the
wilderness." Later, when the Six Nations-had dwindled, they gave
over by solemn treaty to the Stockbridge Indians, who were a part
of the Mohegans, with whom the Six Nations were friendly, these
hunting grounds of Washington County and western Vermont.
Annually passed up from southern Berkshire these hunting parties
of the Indians through Williamstown into these gameful forests at
the north, and it is a pleasure to add that their alleged rights in the
lands were respected by the whites, when these lands came to be
settled and subdued. In possession of the writer is the original
manuscript memorandum drawn up at Bennington, Nov. 30, 1767,
with the autograph signatures appended of 101 land owners in the
towns of southwestern Vermont, which reads as follows : —

Whereas the Stockbridge Indian Tribe, Col. Jacobs and others, Challenge
twelve or more Townships of land Situate and being On the West Line of the
Province of New Hampshire, as Chartered by Benning Wentworth Esq. Gov-
cruor of s^d Province, and the s^d Indian Tribe are Willing and will be Ready On
the First day of January next to Treat with us or any one of us Respecting
their Title, and will at that time Likewise appoint a Meeting at which meeting
They will make it Appear That They are the Sole Owners Thereof and have the
only Proper and Lawful Right to Sell and Convey the Same ; and Whereas we
the Subscribers whose names are hereunto Perfixed, being Willing and desirous
to make Sure to Ourselves and Successors a good and Sufficient title to the
Interests which we now Possess, and to make such Addition or Additions
Thereto as Shall be Thought Proper and Conducive to our Several Interests
by $\begin{cases} \text{Mr. JEDIDIAH DEWEY} \\ \text{Capt. JOHN FASSETT \& S. FAY} \end{cases}$ Whome we depute and Elect to Treat
with s^d tribe or Such of them as will be necessary to treat with In order to ye
procurement of a proper title to Such Land and Lands Lying and being as
afores'd, In Consideration of all which we Severally Engage For ourselves
Heirs Ex^{rs} and Administrators to pay or Cause To be paid to the s^d Jedidiah,
John or Stephen the Severall Sum or Sums According to our Proprietorship As
will Appear by ye Charter afores'd both ye Sum and Sums which he or they may
give for s^d Land or Lands and ye Cost and Cost Necessarily Arising by means of
the Procurement of s^d Title and to pay Such Sum and Sums of money Unto
ye s^d Jedidiah John or Stephen at Such time and times as he or they Shall agree
with the s^d Tribe Indian or Indians. Witness Each of our hands &c.

It does one's eyes good to run over these 101 autographs of the earliest settlers of Pownal and Bennington and Shaftesbury and Arlington and Manchester, for they are firm and strong and full of character, every one of them legible after all the foldings and unfoldings of the sheet (written on both sides) during the past century and a quarter. This paper was drawn up by Leonard Robinson, and signed also by Samuel and Moses and Silas Robinson, all four of them sons of Captain Samuel Robinson, founder of Bennington and father of Vermont, who died in London, on business for the settlement, two months before this paper was signed; and of the rest of the signers, almost every one was a marked man in his own locality, and many of them lived to distinguish themselves in one way and another during the Revolutionary War. Dewey, chairman of the committee empowered to treat with the Stockbridges, and both his colleagues, sign among the very first. Perhaps the finest autograph of the whole is that of Moses Robinson, afterwards Chief Justice, Governor, and United States Senator, of Vermont. Seth Warner's autograph is here, and two others of the same family, all spelling their name "Worner"; and Scotch-Irish names, Breakenridges, Stewarts, Cochrans, Armstrongs, Clarks, and others are mingled in with Saffords, Harwoods, Pratts, Rudds, Harmons, and others. Now, this old paper proposing to buy off Indian rights to Iroquois hunting grounds in southern Vermont fully confirms what is otherwise known, namely, that an old Indian hunting trail branched off to the right from the main one leading north, up which our captives are slowly wending their way, probably following up the Batten Kill to its head sources in the Green Mountains.

But why did Norton in 1746 and Melvin in 1748 call the Batten Kill "Sarratago river"? For the first time the means are now at hand, not only satisfactorily to answer this question, but also to give a succinct history of Fort Saratoga, which gave birth to the old name of this stream, but whose site and fate and even name have been a confused uncertainty for a century past.

In the Documentary History of New York, our modern word "Saratoga" is spelled in nineteen separate ways, Indian and Dutch and French and English, and all the different spellings are given in the index. Several distinct derivations of the word from Indian roots have been suggested from time to time, but no one of them seems to be in itself probable, and at any rate no one of them has been generally accepted. Perhaps one reason for this unsuccessful etymological quest after the origin of the word may be found in the uncertainties as to the locality to which it was first affixed as a name.

The earliest ascertainable historical reference to a place bearing this name is found in a Report of Governor Dongan's to his superiors in England in the year 1687, in the course of which he says: —

I have done my endeavors and have gone so far in it that I have prevailed with the Indians to consent to come back from Canada on condition that I procure for them a peece of land called Serachtague lying upon Hudson's river above forty miles above Albany and there furnish them with Priests. Thereupon and upon a petition of the people of Albany to mee·setting forth the reasonableness and conveniency of granting to the Indians their requests I have procured the land for them, altho it has been formerly patented to people at Albany, and have promised the Indians that they shall have Priests and that I will build them a church and have assured the people of Albany that I would address to his Majesty as to your Lordships that care may be taken to send over by the first Five or Six it being a matter of great consequence.

This reference proves that the place so named abutted at least upon the North River. The next significant reference is in Major Peter Schuyler's journal of his military expedition to Canada in 1691, in which, after mentioning his first day's march from Albany "about 24 miles, until we came to the still water in the evening," he continues, "We marched to Saraghtoga, 16 miles distance." This also implies that the place was on the river bank, because Schuyler was on a military march and would naturally take the shortest route, and because his entries make it evident that he did not leave the river till he crossed it to reach Wood Creek. Saratoga, therefore, was on the river, and on the west bank of it.

A later entry of Schuyler's on this same expedition throws further light on the locality in question. He speaks of "a party of 80 Mohawks at a Lake right over Saraghtoga." This must mean what we now call Saratoga Lake, and his phrase "right over Saraghtoga," must mean "right over" west or back from a place then so named, to a place now so named.

The same inferences are even more clearly drawn from the journal of General John Winthrop, during a march of Connecticut soldiers up the North River in 1690. He writes, August 1, "Quartered this night at a place called the Still Water soe named for that the water passeth soe slowly, as not to be discerned, yet at a little distance both above and below is disturbed and rageth as in a great sea, occasioned by great rocks and great falls therein"; and August 2, "Quartered this night at a place called Saratogo, about 50 English miles from Albany, where is a blockhouse and some of the Dutch soldiers." King William's War, in which both Schuyler and Winthrop operated against the French in Canada, was brought to a close by the

Peace of Ryswick in 1697, and in the interval between that and Queen Anne's War there are several notices of Saratoga, of which the most significant dates from 1698 as follows : " Regarding Cheragtoge, a post on the Hudson river, 28 miles north of Halve Moon, I could not get there, though I had set out for that purpose, in consequence of the freshet in the rivers and other impediments, which it was impossible for me to surmount. I shall observe, however, with submission to your Excellency, that I learned, by minute inquiries that I instituted, that the farms, which were only seven in number, as well as the fort which was built there in Leisler's time, have been entirely ruined by the last war; since which time they have never been thought of, and the settlers have never thought of returning thither; and, also, because the French claim this country as dependent on them, notwithstanding we have had possession of it a great many years. I think it would not be useless to have a small fort built there of palisades, with a small stone tower in the centre, to maintain possession, and encourage the settlers to build and take up their residence there again."

When Queen Anne's War began to threaten the colonies, and particularly New York, Lord Cornbury, the Governor, and Robert Livingston, the Patroon, became anxious that Saratoga should be fortified; for the former wrote in 1702 : —

I propose there should be a stockadoed fort at Saractoga, a place Six and twenty miles above the Half Moon upon Hudson's River, and is the farthest settlement we have. If a large stockadoed Fort is made there, it will not only secure our settlements there, but it will be a retreat for our Rivers Indians upon .all occasions, and the charge will be very little over £200. The number of men that, in my opinion, will be necessary for the defence of these places now, in time of War, will be six hundred foot thus to be disposed of : four hundred men at Albany, a captain and one hundred men at Schenectady, forty men at Nustigione under the command of a Lieutenant, a Lieutenant and thirty men at the Half Moon, and a Lieutenant and thirty men at Saractoga, which just makes six hundred men.

And Livingston wrote the next year as follows : —

But if the taking of Canada can not be effected next summer, then it will be highly requisite that the fronteers of Albany be better secured, and that the fort which my Lord Cornbury has begun, be not only compleated with all speed, but that there be a stone fort built at Shinnéctady also, and Stockadoe Forts at Nastagione, Half Moon, Sarachtoge, Skachbooke and Kinderhoek, and garrisoned with soldiers.

So far all historical references to Saratoga have been to a locality on the west bank of the Hudson on both sides of a rocky stream, now called Fish Creek, striking the Hudson at right angles in the present village of Schuylerville. On this stream, near its mouth, the Schuyler family, of Albany, built mills very early; the " seven farms," already alluded to, were on the banks of this creek. The name " Saratoga " attached itself strongly to a straggling village slowly growing up along the bank of the river and on the banks of the creek; and it was here that General Burgoyne burnt the mills of General Schuyler, and finally surrendered his army to General Gates, in 1777; all the operations leading to which surrender are often (though wrongly) called the battle of Saratoga. But in 1709, in the course of Queen Anne's War, Colonel Schuyler, great-uncle to General Schuyler, built a stockade fort directly opposite the mouth of Fish Creek on a moderate elevation upon the *east* bank of the Hudson, in the northwest corner of the present town of Easton, Washington County, and this structure came to be called Fort Saratoga. As the great military route to and from Canada had hitherto been by Wood Creek, Colonel Schuyler seems to have thought that Albany would be better covered by a fort here on the east bank, and another fort was built the same summer higher up on the east bank of the river at " the great carrying-place " to Wood Creek, and named Fort Nicholson, afterwards Fort Edward. Now as Fort Saratoga was built and long maintained about a mile below the mouth of the Batten Kill, and quite in the line east and west of the main stretches of that stream, it is as natural as can be that the stream itself came to be known as " Sarratago River," as both Norton and Melvin called it. Speaking generally for that century, it may be said, that " Saratoga " meant Fish Creek with the land and buildings on either side of it, and " Fort Saratoga" meant the present Corliss Hill and farm on the eastern bank opposite.

Fort Saratoga had a most interesting history, which only comes within our beat incidentally. We should have known nothing of its mode of construction, had it not been for the journey of a Swedish naturalist up the eastern bank of the Hudson in 1749, just forty years after its erection. Peter Kalm, in his "Travels in North America," writes as follows : —

Saratoga has been a fort built of wood by the English, to stop the attacks of the French Indians upon the English inhabitants in these parts, and to serve as a rampart to Albany. It is situated on a hill, on the east side of the river Hudson, and is built of thick posts driven into the ground, close to each other, in the manner of palisades, forming a square, the length of whose sides was within reach of a musket-shot. At each corner are the houses of the officers, and within the palisades are the barracks, all of timber. This fort has been kept in order and was garrisoned till the last war, when the English themselves set fire to it, not being able to defend themselves in it against the attacks of the French and their Indians; for as soon as a party of them went out of the fort, some of these enemies lay concealed, and either took them all prisoners, or shot them. I shall only mention one out of many artful tricks which were played here, and which both the English and French who were present here at that time told me repeatedly. A party of French, with their Indians, concealed themselves one night in a thicket near the fort. In the morning some of their Indians, as they had previously resolved, went to have a nearer view of the fort. The English fired upon them, as soon as they saw them at a distance; the Indians pretended to be wounded, fell down, got up again, ran a little way, and dropped again. Above half the garrison rushed out to take them prisoners; but as soon as they were come up with them, the French and the remaining Indians came out of the bushes, betwixt the fortress and the English, surrounded them and took them prisoners. Those who remained in the fort had hardly time to shut the gates, nor could they fire upon the enemy, because they equally exposed their countrymen to danger, and they were vexed to see their enemies take and carry them off in their sight, and under their cannon. Such French artifices as these made the English weary of their ill-planned fort. We saw some of the palisades still in the ground. There was an island in the river, near Saratoga, much better situated for a fortification.

We may probably estimate Professor Kalm's "gunshot" as forty rods, making the stockade a square enclosing an acre of ground. In 1745, at the opening of King George's War, another Colonel Schuyler, uncle of the General, was engaged to strengthen Fort Saratoga by building six blockhouses within the enclosure of the palisades, — a matter, as all other matters connected with the forts in that war, causing endless wrangling between the Assembly of New York and the Governor, George Clinton the elder. In November of that year, 1745, a famous French partisan officer, Marin, surprised with his Indians the hamlet of Saratoga on Fish Creek, burnt to ashes twenty houses and an old fort there, killed and scalped over thirty persons, and carried off captive more than sixty persons besides. Just before this, Governor Clinton had sent up six eighteen-pounders to Fort Saratoga, which was probably not then molested by Marin; and two or three months later, the New York Assembly voted, at the instance of the Schuyler family, £150 to further strengthen Fort Saratoga by building a new fort, which may have been a little distance removed from the old stockade, or may have been within or in some way attached to that. At any rate, the new fort, which was 150 × 140 feet, was named Fort Clinton after His Excellency the Governor. To finish here the story of this fort, we must anticipate a little the main narrative, and say that the same La Corne St. Luc, who in August, 1746, courteously conducted John Norton as his cap-

tive across "Sarratago River," in June, 1747, conducted a remarkably successful attack by French and Indians upon Fort Clinton, on
whose walls were then mounted six eighteen-pounders and six
twelve-pounders. It was he who practised the stratagem on the
garrison as correctly related above by Professor Kalm. We will
condense La Corne's own account of the attack and its results, as it
is preserved in the Paris documents, and as it is confirmed in all
essential respects from English sources also.

La Corne, with two subordinate officers, about twenty Frenchmen,
and 200 Indians of different nations, started from Crown Point at
midnight, June 23, 1747, "for Sarratau, to endeavor to find a good
opportunity to strike some good blow on the English or Dutch garrison at Fort Klincton, as they call it." They crossed over the
Hudson to the west side, and sent on a scout of eight to see what
was going on at the fort. These reported "that some forty or fifty
English were fishing in a little river [Fish Creek] which falls into
that of Orange [the Hudson] on this side the fort." "I sent St. Ours
to see where the river could be crossed, and to watch the movements
of the fort. He returned to say that he had found a good place, and
that several Englishmen were out walking." The next day the
whole force crossed over to the east side half a league above the
fort, although the Abenaki Indians were opposed to it, doubtless
because they were afraid of the mounted cannon, as all Indians
always were. La Corne promised to give his gun, which was a
double barrel, to the first man who should take a prisoner.

Waited all day to see if any person would come out. Made a feint, to induce
them to come out. Demanded of the chiefs six of their swiftest and bravest
men, commanded them to lie in ambush on the banks of the river, within eight
paces of the fort, at daybreak, to fire on those who should come out of the fort,
and to try and take a scalp, and if the fort returned their fire to pretend to be
wounded, and to exhibit some difficulty in getting off, so as to induce the enemy
to leave the fort. Those who lay in ambush fired on two Englishmen, who
came out of the fort at break of day on the thirtieth [June], and who came
towards them. The fort made a movement to come against our scouts, who
withdrew. About a hundred and twenty men came out in order of battle, headed
by two lieutenants and four or five other officers. They made towards our people,
in order to get nearer to them by making a wheel. They halted at the spot where
our scouts had abandoned one of their muskets and a tomahawk. Sieur de St.
Luc arose and discharged his piece, crying to all his men to fire; some did so, and
the enemy fired back, and the fort let fly some grape, which spread consterna-
tion among the Indians and Canadians, as it was followed by two other discharges of cannon ball. Our men then rushed on them, and routed the enemy,
whom they pursued within thirty *toises* of the fort fighting. Some threw themselves into the river and were killed by blows of the hatchet, and by gun shots.

Forty-five prisoners were taken and twenty-eight scalps. The number of those drowned could not be ascertained. One lieutenant, who commanded, with four or five other officers, was killed, and one lieutenant was taken prisoner. About one hundred and fifty men, as well as they could judge, came out of the fort, without daring to advance. Of the one hundred and twenty or thirty who might have been in the sortie from the fort, some twenty or twenty-five only appear to have re-entered it. The fort might be one hundred and fifty feet long by one hundred wide, with six wooden redoubts for barracks; four in the angles of the fort and two in the centre of the two main curtains, which have been protracted to enlarge the fort that was one half too small when it was first visited by Sieur Marin; but experiencing such harassing from the French and Indians, they apprehended some new attacks from us; however, it had not been rabbeted when M. Marin was there.

This frightful mishap in June, together with perpetual misunderstandings and bickerings with his Assembly, led Governor Clinton in November to order the abandonment and the burning of Fort Saratoga. The cannon were taken back to Albany. When Professor Kalm was on the spot about eighteen months later, apparently all that he saw, at any rate all that he mentioned, were some of the old palisades of 1709 still standing, that had naturally enough escaped the fire that destroyed Fort Clinton. In the course of a century tradition had nearly, if not entirely, lost trace of the fort, of its site, and even of its name, which was usually transferred over to Fish Creek, when Asa Fitch, an antiquarian whose dwelling was on the Batten Kill, reascertained from Kalm that the fort was on the eastern bank of the river, and published the fact in one of the volumes of the "New York Agriculture," that it was located about a mile south of the mouth of the Batten Kill. Whether he ever visited and more definitely determined its site, does not now appear. In 1886, in company with his friend, Isaac Collins, the present writer studied in detail upon the spot the probable location of Fort Saratoga. He satisfied himself beyond any reasonable doubt that the site of the fort was on the ground now occupied by the two houses and farm buildings of the Corliss family, where there is just about an acre of comparatively level land, right upon the bank of the river, as La Corne's description makes necessary, though lifted decidedly above it, as Kalm's term "hill" makes necessary; while the crowning evidence was discovered by him with the assistance of a venerable lady who had spent her life upon the little plateau, in indubitable traces of a very old road, coming up from the river's brink and just skirting the edge of the level, and passing on east towards and into the road to Galesville and Greenwich and Cambridge, where we know there was a Revolutionary road, along which Baum's soldiers

crossing the river at Schuylerville made their way to the battle-field
of Bennington. Trees larger round than a large man's body were
growing in the very bed of this old road up the bank, depressed, as
such roads always are, below the general level of the ground. Up this
old road, beyond a question, were dragged from the landing Clinton's
eighteen-pounders and twelve-pounders to mount upon the walls of
his fort above; and up this old road, equally beyond a question,
were dragged from the same landing the four brass cannon by the
Hessians, that played their part in the battle of Bennington.

The exact relations of Fort Clinton to old Fort Saratoga will
perhaps never be determined. La Corne's references to the enlarge-
ment of Fort Clinton after Marin's first visit there, and to the fact
that it was not "rabbeted" when Marin was there, are enigmatical,
though the probabilities are very strong that Clinton was set up
within or very near the palisades of old Saratoga; because a French
detachment sent out from Crown Point at the end of November,
coming into the neighborhood and hearing that the fort had been
burnt, visited the spot to verify the fact, judged that three weeks
had passed since the burning, and reported that twenty chimneys
were left standing, that some small grenades and a twelve-pound
shot had not been removed, that the well had been infected, that;
judging by the marks of the wheels, the *caston* had been removed,
and that from the ground occupied at the landing by the *batteaux*,
there might have been ninety of these. Now twenty chimneys are
a preposterous number for one small fort, with only "six wooden
redoubts for barracks"; the rest of the chimneys must have belonged
to some or all of the six blockhouses ordered to be built within the
enclosure of the old palisades. The chimneys of Clinton were evidently not distinguishable from the other chimneys left standing
after the burning of the fort; and, therefore, Clinton must have
been a part of old Fort Saratoga.

The news of the destruction, by New York authority, of the Saratoga fort was bad news indeed to the whole colony of Massachusetts.
Their entire frontier towards the northwest was now uncovered to
hostile incursions of French and Indians. Fort Massachusetts had
been rebuilt in the spring of 1747, as we shall shortly learn in detail,
and mutual arrangements were sought to be entered into in July
between the two colonies as represented by Governor Shirley and
Governor Clinton, by which a hundred men should be kept constantly on the scout between Forts Massachusetts and Saratoga. It
was not without bitterness, therefore, and a sense of needless and
pitiless exposure that Massachusetts learned, late in the autumn, of

the voluntary destruction of their only barrier towards the north-west against Crown Point and Canada.

We must now return both in time and place from this long but not profitless digression, to Norton's narrative and our poor captives toiling northward.

Lord's day, 24. — This day we set out in the morning and came to Sarratago river, crossed it, and came to our company, which had been before us. Here we came to a rich piece of meadow ground and travelled in it about five miles. We had good travelling this day. We crossed several pieces of good meadow land. We went about eighteen miles. John Perry's wife performed this day's journey without help from any. Our sick and feeble persons were remarkably preserved to-day; for about two o'clock in the afternoon there fell a very heavy shower of rain, which wet us through all our clothes. Mrs. Smead was as wet as any of us, and it being the third day after her delivery, we were concerned about the event; but through the good Providence of God she never perceived any harm by it, nor did any other person but Miriam, the wife of Moses Scott, who hereby catched a grievous cold. This night we lodged in a meadow, where was a run of water, which makes a part of Wood Creek.

Mr. Norton kept a good eye on all the members of his peeled and scattered flock, but he did not know all that was going on among the French and Indians, his companions. He reports when they all were south of the Batten Kill, that there was a considerable ruffle among them, on discovering the tracks of a scout from Saratoga, as if there might be an army after them. On the other hand, Vaudreuil reports to his superiors in Quebec, that he detached a party of Abenakis to proceed towards Fort Saratoga, that they met seventeen soldiers belonging to the fort, took four of them and scalped four others, and that the rest, pursued by the Indians, who killed some of them, threw themselves precipitately into the fort. Vaudreuil also reported in the same connection the success of about thirty Abenakis, detached by him immediately after the taking of Fort Massachusetts to go to Deerfield, who took, he said, five or six scalps. This was the Bars Fight in Deerfield, in which five persons were killed, one wounded, and one taken captive; two of the Indians were killed also. The fourth day's journey of the captives was the longest yet made by them, — eighteen miles. It is easy to trace the path on the spot, or even by a good map, such as Fitch's map of Washington County. It ran nearly due north from the Batten Kill up on the west side of McNob's Lake, where the present road runs to the little hamlet of Lakeville, and then up on the west side of the large and beautiful Cossayuna Lake, where there is no road at present, but are still "the several pieces of good meadow land," and thence between the hills of the present town of Argyle up into the more open land of the town of Hartford, and still up to the lodging-place for the night, " where was a run of water which makes a part of Wood Creek," that is to say, Mud Creek, so-called, which is a branch of East Creek, which itself falls into Wood Creek, near Smith's Basin, on the present Champlain Canal. All the geographical notes in this part of Drake's " French and Indian War " are utterly wide of the mark. There are no such streams and branches as those copiously referred to in notes on pages 266 and 267.

Monday, 25. — This morning we set out and travelled about eleven miles. We had something rough travelling to-day. We quickly left the small stream we lodged by at our right hand to the east of us, and travelling a few miles over some small hills and ledges, came to a stream running from east to west, about two or three rods in width, and about two feet deep. We crossed it our general course being north. We travelled about two or three miles farther and came to a stream running from southwest to northeast, about six rods in width, which we crossed. And this stream (which we suppose to be Wood Creek) according to the best of my remembrance, and according to the short minute that I made of this day's travel, we left at the right hand to the east of us ; but Sergeant Hawks thinks I am mistaken, and that we crossed it again, and left it at the left hand west of us. I won't be certain, but I cannot persuade myself that I am mistaken. The French and Indians helping our feeble people, we all arrived well at our camp, which was by a couple of ponds. Some few who were· before us went to the drowned land.

This day's journey was the fifth from Fort Massachusetts, and the last performed wholly by land. Its topographical notices are extremely interesting, and enable one to follow the path with absolute certainty. Norton was mistaken, and Hawks was certainly right, in the little matter of geography in dispute between them. In the morning's start they left Mud Creek to the right, and still bearing northeast, they passed over some small slate hills and ledges in the modern town of Granville, and soon struck the Pawlet River in the present village of North Granville. The river runs here from east to west just as the Chaplain describes it, and they crossed it in a due northerly course. Two or three miles further they came to the same stream again in Guilder's Hollow, where it was then, and is still, nearly double the width it has at North Granville, partly because it was lower down in its course, and partly because it was shallower there. It has a course there from southwest to northeast. But the straight and best way to their night's camping-place at what is now East Whitehall, led them to cross the same stream the third time, and then to leave it on the west, just as Hawks said they did. The good Chaplain made his " minute " too soon, or else a bit carelessly, for after the second crossing it would have been .simply impossible for him to reach his night's lodging on the hillside without crossing the third time also. Hawks, too, kept a careful journal of the captivity, which was extant well into this century, but never printed, and long ago disappeared. Both journalists alike supposed the stream they crossed to be Wood Creek, while it was in reality the east branch of that historic stream, uniting with it a mile or so south of the head of Lake Champlain, and contributing, perhaps, as much water to that short stretch of stream as its far more famous fellow of the west. The Indians called the Pawlet River *Mettowee*, a beautiful name, which ought forever to supersede the more prosaic one, especially as it takes its rise in Dorset and not in Pawlet, through which indeed it flows.

The camp at the close of the last day's march was near to what is now East Whitehall, and "Herbert's Pond," so-named, is with very little question one of the "couple of ponds" by which they slept, and there is at the present time a considerable peat bog close by Herbert's, which may well have been the other of the two ponds. If any wonder why Vaudreuil led his force so far to the eastward of his objective, namely, the place where his boats had been left two weeks before in the mouth of the Poultney River, or East Bay, as it used to be called, just before its junction with Wood Creek and the united entrance into Lake Champlain, the ready answer is found in Norton's repeated reference to the "drowned lands." All around the head of Lake Champlain, both up the East Bay and also up Wood Creek for considerable distances, were low and swampy lands, liable to be overflowed, and such as the old Indian trails were always sure to avoid, when possible; by leaving the Mettowee at the west, and skirting along the highlands to the east, they found dry ground at all seasons of the year, and though the distance was decidedly greater, the going was decidedly better.

Tuesday, 26. — This day we took our journey. Our course in the morning something west of north. In travelling about three or four miles we came to a mountain, a steep ascent about eighty or one hundred rods, but not rocky. After we passed this mountain our course was about west, five or six miles, till we came to the drowned lands. When we came to the canoes, the stream ran from northeast to southwest. We embarked about two o'clock; the stream quickly turned and ran to the north. We sailed about eighteen or twenty miles that night, and encamped on the east side of the water.

The writer has twice been over on foot the ground of this last morning's tramp of the captives. The present public road from East Whitehall to Whitehall undoubtedly follows in general the footsteps of General Vaudreuil. The old path, however, turned to the right from the present lay of that road a mile or more from the town, along a little lift of higher ground down to the place (or near it) where there is now a bridge over the Poultney River, or East Bay, and where "the stream ran from northeast to southwest." There most of the canoes had been deposited a fortnight before. The crowd embarked without ceremony, the stream quickly turned to the north, they rowed with the current the afternoon and evening, and encamped that night in what is now Benson, Vermont, and, perhaps, at what is now Benson Landing.

Wednesday, 27. — We embarked about nine o'clock, and sailed to Crown Point, something better than twenty miles. Some of the army went in the night before, and some before the body of the army. The sails were pulled down, and the canoes brought up abreast, and passed by the fort over to the northeast point, saluting the fort with three volleys, as we passed by it, the fort returning the salute by the discharge of the cannon. This was about twelve o'clock. Here we tarried till the 4th of September. I lodged in an house on the northeast point. We all arrived better in health than when we were first taken.

Lakes George and Champlain with their inlets are, of course, within the basin of the St. Lawrence, and formed the only natural route between the colonies and Canada for all their traffic in time of peace, and their military expeditions back and forth in war-time. The shores had been a sort of neutral ground as between French and English ever after King William's War. After the Peace of Utrecht, in 1713, the hostile feeling between the two subsided a good deal, especially in Europe; and Crown Point, a bold northerly projection from the western shore of Lake Champlain, about seventy-five miles north of Albany, became quite an important trading-station as between the English of New York and the northern Indians of Canada until 1731, when the French authorities at Montreal sent a party to occupy Crown Point, and soon built a fort there and made a settlement also on the east side of the water, at a place now called Chimney Point. This movement of the French startled both New York and New England. The Assembly of the former resolved that "this encroachment, if not prevented, would prove of the most pernicious consequence to this and other colonies." They sent formal notice of the intrusion to Pennsylvania, Connecticut, and Massachusetts, and applied for aid to the Board of Trade and Plantations in England. That body supported their complaints, but Robert Walpole, the Minister, counselled peace, and the French quietly occupied both shores of the lake at that point. They called their military work there Fort St. Frederic, which remained in their hands a sharp

and constant thorn in the side of the English throughout two successive wars, until, in 1759, the year of the capture of Quebec, a large
English force, under General Amherst, pushing on towards a junction
with General Wolfe, compelled the garrison there to unite with that
just ousted from Ticonderoga in a common flight down the lake to
its outlet. Crown Point is twelve miles below Ticonderoga.

At the time of this enforced visit to Crown Point by Chaplain
Norton in 1746, Fort St. Frederic was at the height of its military
strength and political domination. Next to Quebec, it was the
strongest post in New France. It had grown from a wooden stockade, authorized to be erected by the French king on the 8th of May,
1731, capable of accommodating a garrison of thirty men only, to a
strong fortress built of limestone, with a tower of three stories,
bomb-proof, capable in 1734 of holding 120 men in garrison, and
subsequently strengthened and enlarged, containing within its walls
a small chapel, whose vesper bell called to their evening prayers the
scarred veteran of France, and the voluble Canadian, and the rude
husbandman whose hut stood outside the fort. The very northernmost point of the cape was occupied by this impressive fortification,
from which the shore falls back a little on both sides, eastward to
the deep channel of the lake, and westward to a broad bay of back
water constituting the cape on that side. This position explains the
ceremony of the salute described by the good Chaplain here. Vaudreuil's boats had already passed in the channel of the lake the
northeast point, where stood a stone windmill, serving also the purposes of a redoubt, and where there were also one or more good
houses; but the main fort must be first saluted, and so "the sails
were pulled down, and the canoes brought up abreast, and passed by
the fort over to the northeast point, saluting the fort with three
volleys as we passed by it, the fort returning the salute by the discharge of the cannon." The Chaplain was lodged with his custodian,
M. Demuy, "in a house on the northeast point," where, evidently,
the best quarters were in the neighborhood of the fort. The land is
high and dry there.

Thursday, 28. — This day I was invited by Monsieur Demuy to go over and
see the fort, which I did. It is something an irregular form, having five sides
to it; the ramparts twenty feet thick, the breastwork two feet and a half, the
whole about twenty feet high. There were twenty-one or twenty-two guns
upon the wall, some four and six pounders, and there may be some as large as
nine pounders. The citadel, an octagon, built three stories high, fifty or sixty
feet diameter, built with stone laid in lime, the wall six or seven feet thick,
arched over the second and third stories for bomb-proof. In the chambers nine

or ten guns; some of them may be nine pounders, and I believe none less than six, and near twenty patararoes. But as my time was short, I cannot be very particular. They have stores of small arms, as blunderbusses, pistols, and muskets. This night proved very cold and stormy.

This detailed description of Fort St. Frederic is the earliest in point of time that has come down to us from any quarter. The French officers were doubtless very glad to exhibit the great strength of the work to Norton and Hawks, in order that they might report the same to their constituent, the colony of Massachusetts, which then and afterwards had a deep interest in its construction and approaches. Very fortunately, we have a parallel and independent account of the fort from the pen of the celebrated Swedish traveller, Peter Kalm, written three years later than Norton's, namely, in 1749.

Fort St. Frederic is built on a rock consisting of black line slates, and is nearly quadrangular, has high and thick walls, made of the same limestone, of which there is a quarry about half a mile from the fort. On the eastern part of the fort is a high tower, which is proof against bomb shells, provided with very thick and substantial walls, and well stored with cannon from the bottom almost to the very top, and the governor lives in the tower. In the *terre plaine* of the fort is a well-built little church and houses of stone for the officers and soldiers. There are sharp rocks on all sides towards the land beyond cannon-shot from the fort, but among them are some which are as high as the walls of the fort and very near them. Within one or two musket-shots to the east of the fort is a windmill, built of stone, with very thick walls, and most of the flour, which is wanted to supply the fort, is ground here. This windmill is so constructed as to serve the purpose of a redoubt, and at the top of it are five or six small pieces of cannon.

July 6, 1889, a beautiful and memorable day, the writer spent alone on the Point in critically examining the present ruins of the fort St. Frederic in its two parts, the main and the windmill redoubt on the northeast point "within one or two musket-shots of the fort." The circular redoubt, on which the windmill stood, was so firmly and scientifically built that the United States had no occasion to stir a stone of the exterior construction, when, one hundred and forty years after the French engineer laid it out, a national light-house was built up in the centre of it, exactly where the windmill stood. The modern engineer indeed dug deep within and erected a structure that looks as if it would last forever, but it will not probably outlast the far older circular rim that encloses it.

· The ruins of the proper fort, perhaps fifty rods to the westward of the lighthouse, show the thorough work of the French in destruc-tion, as well as in original construction. In July, 1759, General Amherst, having captured Ticonderoga, sent forward immediately

200 of Rogers' Rangers to examine the position of the French at Crown Point, with orders to seize and hold, at all hazards, some strong post near the fort. But before the Rangers could reach their objective, the French had utterly destroyed their fort, burned all their surrounding settlements, and joined the retreating garrison of Ticonderoga in a common dropping down the lake to Isle aux Noix. The glory of Fort St. Frederic was gone forever.

With the clear and complementary accounts of Norton and Kalm in one's hand, however, it is not difficult on the spot to reconstruct in the mind's eye the old fortress in its general features. Portions of the tower still frown over the lower desolations of rampart and barrack and chapel. It does not look as if many of the scattered stones had ever been carried away; and there can be but little doubt that thorough excavations there would reveal the breast-work nearly entire, the foundation-walls, at least, of the chapel and barracks, something of the magazine, and perhaps other parts and piles ostentatiously shown to Norton. In less than a week after the departure of the French, Amherst reached Crown Point with his large army of 11,000 men, and immediately traced out the lines of a new fort about 200 yards west of the site of St. Frederic. He had no need to meddle with materials already accursed by Gallic and papistic hands, however accessible they were; for the lime-stone was abundant there even above ground, and he cut a broad ditch entirely around his fort out of the solid rock, and used the fragments taken out to construct the massive barracks that are still standing, as impressive in their lofty desolation as the prostrate ruins of St. Frederic. The whole circuit of Amherst's fort, meas-uring along the ramparts, was a trifle less than half a mile, or, to be exact, 2559 feet. The ramparts were about twenty-five feet thick, and nearly the same in height, and were built of solid masonry, the lime having been burnt on the spot. The curtains varied in length from fifty-two to 100 yards; and in the century and a third since the fort was built and abandoned, — for the conquest of Quebec and Montreal the next year put an end to New France and made useless the fortress, — the grass has grown over the rampart and its bastions, and made of portions of their summit a pleasant promenade. The gate, as usual, was in the north wall; and from the northeast bastion was a covered way, still clearly traceable, leading down to the water. The well within the works was ninety feet deep, eight feet in diameter, cut down with enormous labor into the solid limestone. The fort was never wholly completed, but it is said to have cost the English government about £2,000,000 sterling.

There is at present but a single house upon the Point. Nor is there another on the cape in sight, from the ramparts of the fort. The farmer who occupies the house and owns the land enclosing the old forts, is, curiously enough, a Frenchman, hospitable to the occasional stranger who visits the Point out of historic curiosity, though his wife is an American woman, and his daughters (as befits the local succession of events) speak only English, attending school at Port Henry on the west side of the bay. His cattle graze at will within and without the enclosures of Amherst's fort, and are estopped from falling into the old well by a rude brush heap that covers it over. In contrast with its former turmoils of war, the present peaceful desolations of Crown Point are blessed.

Besides this description of Crown Point as it was in 1746, by the worthy Chaplain from the Hoosac valley, and many subsequent points of contact between the two localities, it is fitting that the historian of Williamstown and Williams College should here call attention to the important scientific labors at Crown Point, and in its neighborhood, of Professor Ebenezer Emmons, who was the indefatigable teacher here of several branches of natural history, particularly geology, between 1833 and 1863. He was the first to apply the term "chazy limestone" to the rock called by the English translator of Kalm's "Travels," "black line slates," and thus to distinguish scientifically a peculiar form of that rock very abundant on the west shores of Lake Champlain, out of which both its great military fortresses of Ticonderoga and Crown Point were constructed, from the common kinds of limestone found almost everywhere. After he was appointed in 1836 one of the commission to make a geological survey of New York, he made careful soundings to ascertain the depth of the water in various parts of Lake Champlain, and found it to be 300 feet four miles north of Westport; he was credibly informed that soundings of 600 feet had been made in other places in that part of the lake; and as the surface of the lake is only ninety-three feet above tide water, he gave it as his opinion that its bottom, in spots, may be at least 500 feet below the ocean level. Professor Emmons also particularly examined the phenomenon of "Split Rock," a few miles above Crown Point, on the west side of the lake, which had always been supposed to be the result of the action of an earthquake, famous in Canada as having occurred in the year 1663; and pronounced the separation to have been probably occasioned by the wearing away or decomposition of an intermediate mass of rock containing a large quantity of pyritous iron. The good Professor was appointed, in 1856, the state geologist of North Carolina, and was busily engaged in that survey when the Civil War broke out, and interrupted his labors. He returned north, and died in 1863. He was for some years a practising physician in Williamstown. The struggle of his life was to maintain the reality and scientific importance of his own discovery of what he named the "Taconic System," referred to in the following terms from Appleton's "Annual Cyclopedia" of 1861: "The assent of geologists to the Taconic System advocated by the late Professor Emmons, after so many years of disbelief, is another instance of the triumph of investigation over preconceived errors."

Friday, 29. — This morning Smead's and Scott's families were brought out of their tents into the house, that they might be more comfortable. It rained and was very cold all the day, and at night the wind was very high.

Captivity Smead, the baby born at the first encampment at the junction of the Little Hoosac with the Hoosac, was now just one week old, and the mother had with her three other children, all young; and Mrs. Moses Scott had two young children also; no wonder these were taken out of their tents into the house, that they might be more comfortable. The south and east winds have a fair sweep over northeast point, where the windmill was and the lighthouse is, and the cry of a new-born child appeals to the humanity of man always and everywhere.

Lord's day, 31. — We had the liberty of worshipping God together in a room by ourselves. This day about twelve o'clock, the enemy who went off from us from Hoosuck the morning after we were taken, returned, and brought in six scalps, viz., Samuel Allen, Eleazar Hawks, Jun., two Amsdels, all of Deerfield; Adonijah Gillet of Colchester, Constant Bliss of Hebron, and one captive, viz., Samuel Allen, son to him who was killed. He was taken with his father and Eleazar Hawks. The Amsdels and Gillet were killed in Deerfield South Meadow, August 25th. The Indians also acknowledged they lost one man there. This lad told us they had not then heard in Deerfield of their taking Fort Massachusetts. A young Hatacook Indian was his master, and carried him to St. François.

This is an indirect but accurate account of the "Bars Fight," so-called, in the southwest Meadow of Deerfield, five days after the taking of Fort Massachusetts. There are several contemporary accounts of this affair. The French account is as follows: "Sixty Abernakis belonging to this force went, after the fight [at Hoosac], to lie in wait for twenty Englishmen who were to come to the said fort, according to the report of the prisoners; but, not meeting with them, went further, and some returned with seven scalps, one Englishman and one negro." The journal of Deacon Noah Wright, of Deerfield, runs in this wise : —

August 25th, 1746. — In the southwest corner of Deerfield meadows a number of Indians came upon our men at work, killed and scalped Samuel Allen, Eleazar Hawks, and one of Captain Holson's soldiers named Gillet, and two of the Widow Amsden's children ; taken captive, one boy of Samuel Allen's, and chopped a hatchet into the brains of one of his girls. They are in hopes that she will recover. One man killed one of the Indians, who got one gun from them and lost three guns by them.

Rev. Benjamin Doolittle, of Northfield, who died in January, 1749, left also a brief record of this fight, which is utilized in Drake's "Particular History." He gives as a reason why the Indians "went further," their "not being satisfied with the spoil" gathered at Fort Massachusetts. He says also of Eunice Allen, who was struck down by a blow of a tomahawk, "which was sunk into her head," that the enemy in their haste omitted to scalp her, and that she afterwards recovered. Indeed, all three of the children of Samuel Allen, who was killed and scalped, were living as late as 1793; this Eunice, Caleb, who was pursued but escaped, and Samuel, the captive whom Sergeant Hawks brought home with him from Canada the next August. "This lad told us they had not then heard in Deerfield of their taking Fort Massachusetts." Norton seems surprised, that what occurred on the west side of Hoosac Mountain, August 20, was not known in Deerfield, thirty miles to the eastward, August 25. As a matter of fact, that news did not reach Deerfield until August 30, as we learn from Deacon Wright's diary : —

August 30, 1746. — A post this day returned to and from fort Massachusetts, and brings us news that the fort was taken and burnt to ashes, and we can't learn here as there is one man escaped. I am in some doubt that there are some that are taken captive and gone to Canada, and so I ain't altogether without hopes of seeing some of them again.

The speed made by the scalping party from Deerfield Meadow to Crown Point, one hundred and twenty miles in just six days, was much better than the speed of the news of the capture of the fort, thirty miles in just ten days.

Sept. 1–3. — We tarried still at Crown Point. The weather was something lowry, but warm. I lived with the General and about half a dozen more officers, who lodged in the same house. Our diet was very good, it being chiefly fresh meat and broth, which was a great benefit to me. We had also plenty of Bordeaux wine, which being of an astringent nature, was a great kindness to me (having at that time something of the griping and bloody flux). While we lay here, we wrote a letter to the Hon. John Stoddard, Esq., at Northampton, to give him a particular account of our fight and surrender; as also some other private letters; the French gentlemen giving us encouragement that they would send them down by some of their scouts to some part of our frontiers, and leave them so that they should be found; but I have not heard of them since, and conclude that they destroyed them.

It is not certain whether any of these letters ever reached the English "frontiers" or not; Deacon Wright saw a letter the 11th of September following, written by Mr. Norton, about the siege and surrender of the fort; but it is more likely to have been the letter nailed by the Chaplain "on the west post" the morning after the surrender. Our readers shall see the entry in Wright's journal, *verbatim*, and then they may decide for themselves. It is but fair to premise that Mr. Drake considered the letter referred to, to be the one written from Crown Point to Colonel Stoddard.

Sept. 11, 1746. — I saw a letter wrote by Mr. Norton at Hoosick after the fort was taken, and he says that they were besieged by several hundred French and Indians, and they being brought to a great strait, the enemy prepared a vast quantity of faggots in order to burn down the fort by force, but the French General came to them for capitulation, and told them if they would resign up the fort he would treat them all well and carry them to Canada; that they should be redeemed as soon as there was any opportunity, and if not he would kill them all. And so they resigned up the fort, and lost but one man, named Knowlton; and had two wounded, and so all the rest are gone to Canada. He says they are all well used by the enemy.

We shall now no longer follow, in order and in detail, the copious diary of the Chaplain's journey to Quebec, and of what happened to him and his fellow-captives on the way thither, and after they arrived there; not because the entries are not interesting and instructive, but because comparatively few of them bear directly on Fort Massachusetts and the straight course of our story. The captives embarked with their victors at Crown Point, for Canada, on Thursday, the 4th of September, which was the sixteenth day from their capture. They encamped the first night on the New York side of the lake, in a cave so clearly described, that it might, doubtless, be easily identified at this day; and the next time on the Vermont side, at a place afterwards called Windmill Point by the English, a few miles below Burlington. In this voyage down the lake, they did not see an inhabited house on either side, or meet a living person, till on Sunday they entered the Richelieu River, and met a boat with three men in it, who brought a packet of letters for the French officers, containing what the latter called "news," very favorable to the French cause in Europe, the accuracy of which, the bold Chap-

lain disputed to their faces, which led to a warm political debate
between them, over the battle of Culloden Moor the preceding
April, and over the House of Stuart and the Catholic religion in
general. It seems odd enough in our time, to think of Celt and
Briton hotly disputing in September, whether the Duke of Cumberland were killed at Culloden in April, and whether the House
of Hanover — "Cromwell's faction" — were about to yield to the
young Pretender. The place, too, of the debate in the uninhabited
wilds of Canada, and the uncertainty of both parties to it, as to the
facts alleged, in which both were afterwards proven to be largely
wrong and slightly right, add to the queerness of the scene.

Before night of this Sunday they reached the village and fort of
Chambly, which is thirty-seven miles below the present boundary
line of British America. The French officers were in high spirits.
M. Demuy told Norton the next day another piece of news, namely,
"that one of their men-of-war had taken an English man-of-war
near Louisburg, after a whole day's engagement; that the blood was
midleg deep upon the Englishman's deck when he surrendered."
"They fought courageously," retorted Norton. "True, but they
were taken notwithstanding." "Moreover, they have taken three
hundred and twenty men out of her, who are coming up to Quebec,
where you shall see them." They got to Montreal two days later,
where the Town Major and many former captives from New
England came to visit the Chaplain. He was courteously entertained
while there at the house of M. Demuy, who took him to see the
Governor. The Governor said little to him, but told him that after a
few days, he must send him with the rest of the prisoners to Quebec.
The "few days" proved to be but two, when they embarked in
boats, all but six men, who were yet with the Indians, and John
Perry's wife, who had already gone on to Three Rivers, for Quebec.

Saturday, 13. — This day we had a fair wind, and sailed down the river
twenty-five leagues, when we arrived at the Three Rivers. We went into an
inn. The General [Vaudreuil] and some others of the gentlemen which went
down with us presently went out to the Governor's, leaving only their soldiers
to guard us. And after a little time the Governor sent for Sergeant Hawks and
me to come and sup with him. Accordingly we went, and were courteously and
sumptuously entertained by him; and while we sat at supper the gentlemen fell
into discourse about the wars, and about the wounds they had received. The
General's wound was discoursed upon, and the Governor desired Sergeant Hawks
to show his scars, which he did. The Governor then informed us of a fight he
had been in at sea in former wars in which he received fifteen wounds, and he
showed us several scars. This I thought was a very remarkable thing, that
he should receive so many wounds, and yet have his life spared. This night
John Perry's wife was also brought to us, and added to our number.

Monday, 15. — This day we sailed seven leagues and came to Quebec. We were landed at the east point of the town where St. Lawrence meets with Loretto, and were conducted up by a number of soldiers through the lower town to the Governor-General's, where I was taken into his private room, and he desired me to tell what news we had in New England. I told him of considerable news we had from Europe concerning the Duke of Cumberland's victory over the rebels. He seemed to have a great mind to persuade me that the Duke was killed, but I told him he was alive and well. I told him of several other pieces of news, but none very good for the French. He told me he had heard that we designed an expedition against Canada. He asked what there was in it. I told him that I lived at a great distance from Boston, and could say but little about it. I had heard that his majesty had sent over to some of the governors in America, that he had thoughts of an expedition against Canada, and would have them in readiness to assist him, in case he should send a fleet over. He inquired what it was that had put it by. Something, he said, was the matter. I told him I could not tell ; so he seemed to be pretty easy.

Marquis de la Galissonière was the Governor-General of Canada, with whom this interesting conversation was had. He was a hump-back; but his deformed person was animated by a bold spirit and a penetrating intellect. He was a devoted student of natural science, and a very distinguished naval officer of France. He had but recently come to Quebec as Governor-General, and was only destined to remain less than three years; but he stayed long enough to give his King most excellent advice, as to the matter of increasing the population of Canada by new colonists, as to a plan of uniting Canada and Louisiana by chains of forts strong enough to hold back the British colonists, and as to the management and Christianization of the Indians. In short, he was one of the ablest and best of a long line of French governors of Canada, closed in 1759 by Pierre Vaudreuil, the best of all, son of Philippe de Vaudreuil, Governor from 1703 till his death in 1725, and brother of Rigaud de Vaudreuil, captor of Fort Massachusetts. The two brothers returned to France on the downfall of French Canada, the late Governor to be imprisoned in the Bastille on charges preferred by the friends of Montcalm, and stripped of most of his possessions, though exonerated and released, and the brave soldier was still living at St. Germaine in 1770.

After this I was conducted to the Lord Intendant's, who inquired also after news, both of me and Sergeant Hawks ; after which he gave us a glass of wine ; then we were conducted to the prisoners' house, which is a guard-house standing by a battery towards the southwest end of the town, about one hundred and fifty feet in length, and twenty in width, and two stories high ; and we made to the number of one hundred and five prisoners. Here we had the free liberty of the exercise of our religion together, which was matter of comfort to us in our affliction. Sergeant Hawks and myself were put into the Captain's room.

The Governor-General and the Intendant of Canada answered to those officials in a French province at home. The Governor was usually a military noble, and the Intendant drawn from the legal class. The Governor was superior in rank to the Intendant, since he commanded the troops, conducted relations with foreign colonies and Indian tribes, and took precedence on all occasions of ceremony. Unlike the provincial Governor in France, he had great and substantial power. As we have already seen, there were local governors at Montreal and Three Rivers; but their power was carefully curbed, and they were forbidden to fine or imprison any person, without authority from Quebec. The Intendant, on the other hand, was a sort of official spy on the Governor-General, of whose proceedings and of everything else that took place, he was required to make report to the home government. The Governor, too, wrote long letters to the Minister of State; and each of the two colleagues was jealous of the letters of the other. Indeed, the French Court did not desire the perfect accord of the two officials; nor, on the other hand, did it desire them to quarrel; while it aimed to keep them on such terms, as, without disturbing the machinery of administration, should make each of them a fair check on the other.[1]

Tuesday, 16. — This day there came some gentlemen to see me, among whom was Mr. Joseph Portois, who understands the English tongue, and Mr. Pais, who, Mr. Portois told me, was his kinsman, and that he was a Protestant, and came on purpose to see me, and to show me a kindness. He gave me twenty-four livres in cash. From this time to the 23d there was nothing remarkable happened only this, — that the Jesuits and some unknown gentlemen, understanding I was short on it for clothing, sent me several shirts, a good winter coat, some caps, a pair of stockings, and a few handkerchiefs, which were very acceptable.

About a week after this, David Warren and Phinehas Forbush, two of the captured garrison, who had been behind with the Indians, came into the prison at Quebec, and reported that John Aldrich was still in the hospital at Montreal. A few days later, Jacob Shepherd, of Westboro, another of the fort-captives who had been behind with the Indians, was brought into the common prison-house; and on Sunday, October 5, the remaining three of the enforced stragglers came in, namely, Nathaniel Hitchcock, Stephen Scott, and John Aldrich. The entire number captured at Fort Massachusetts were now together in the prison, except Josiah Reed, who had died at Dutch Hoosac (now Petersburg Junction) two days after the surrender; but his place had been taken, so to speak, by Captivity

---

[1] See at length Parkman's *Old Régime*, 265, *et seq.*

Smead, the infant born the same night that he died and at the same place, but the full ranks of the thirty were soon to be thinned by death, as we shall see.

Wednesday, 22. — I sent a petition to his lordship, the General of Canada or New France, to permit me to go home to New England, upon a parole of honor, setting me a suitable time, and I would return again to him; but I could not prevail.

The good Chaplain does not obtrude his private griefs even upon the pages of his private journal; but he was doubtless thinking, when he sent in his petition, of his young wife and two little girls left in the garrison at Fort Shirley two months before, when he expected to return to them from Fort Massachusetts in "about a month." One of the little girls he was never destined to see alive. Captain Ephraim Williams, the founder of the College, commanded Fort Shirley that autumn and winter, and doubtless ministered as best he could to the wants of this poor woman.

Friday, 31. — Here I shall speak of the sickness that prevailed among the prisoners. It had generally been very healthy in the prison before this fall; for though there had been some prisoners there sixteen months, and about fifty nine months, yet there had but two died. But our people who were taken at sea by the two French men-of-war, viz., the *Lazora* and *Le Castore*, found a very mortal epidemical fever raged among the French on board their ships, of which many of them died. The prisoners took the infection, and a greater part of them were sick while they lay in Jebucta [Chebucto] harbor; yet but one or two of them died of it. Some of them were taken with the distemper upon their passage to Canada, and so brought the infection into the prison; and the fever being epidemical, soon spread itself into the prisons, to our great distress. Those who brought it into the prison most recovered, and so there were many others that had it and recovered; but the recovery of some was but for a time, — many of them relapsed and died.

Nov. 17. — Died Nathan Eames. He belonged to Marlborough in the province of the Massachusetts Bay; was taken with me at Fort Massachusetts, August 20, 1746.

The sickness increasing and spreading itself so greatly, we sent a very humble petition to his lordship, the Governor-General, entreating that the sick might be removed out of the hospital, lest the whole prison should· be infected; but he refused to send our people to the hospital, for they told us that their hospital was full of their own sick; yet he did not wholly neglect our petition, but ordered that one of the most convenient rooms in the prison should be assigned for the sick, where they should all be carried, and have their attendance, and this was directly done, and the sick were all brought in.

Dec. 11. — Died Miriam, the wife of Moses Scott. She was taken with me at Fort Massachusetts. She got a cold in her journey, which proved fatal, her circumstances being peculiar. She was never well after our arrival at Canada, but wasted away to a mere skeleton, and lost the use of her limbs.

Dec. 23. — Died Rebecca, the wife of John Perry. She was taken with me at Fort Massachusetts, August 20th, 1746. Her illness was different from all the rest. She had little or no fever ; had a cold, and was exercised with wrecking pains until she died.

Dec. 24. — I was taken with the distemper ; was seized with a very grievous pain in the head and back and a fever ; but I let blood in the morning, and took a good potion of physic, and in a few days another ; so that I soon recovered again.

The sickness thus increasing, there were many taken sick [in the prison], which I don't pretend to mention. The sickness also got into the prison-keeper's family. He lost a daughter by it, the 4th instant [January]. Upon this the Governor ordered a house to be provided for the sick, where they were all carried the 12th instant, about twenty in number, with three men to attend them ; and after this when any were taken sick, they were carried out to this house.

The Chaplain did not forget, in the prison-house of his foes and amid personal sicknesses, that he was a minister of the glad tidings. On this 4th of January, the day the prison-keeper's daughter died, as we learn from another source than his own journal, he preached two discourses from Psalm 60 : 11, — "Give us help from trouble; for vain is the help of man." He had quoted, however, in his diary, when the sickness first began, several passages of Scripture from both the Testaments, of which these two may serve as samples: "My virgins and my young men are gone into captivity." "Abroad the sword devoureth, at home there is death."

Jan. 23. — Died Samuel Lovet, after near a month's sickness. He was taken with me. He was the son of Major Lovet of Mendon.

Feb. 11. — Died in the morning, Moses Scot, son to Moses Scot. He was a child of about two years old, and died with the consumption.

March 21. — This day died Samuel Goodman of South Hadley. He was taken with me at Fort Massachusetts, and died of the scurvy.

March 29. — Died Mary, the wife of John Smeed, after a tedious sickness of about eight weeks ; was taken with me.

This was the brave woman who was delivered of a child about thirty-six hours after the surrender of the fort, at the junction of the Little Hoosac with the Hoosac River.

April 7. — Died John Smeed Jun. He was taken with me at Fort Massachusetts. He was seized with the distemper in October last, and was bad for a time, and then recovered in some good measure, and after a little time relapsed, and as he did several times, till at last he fell into a consumption, of which he died.

April 12. — Died Amos Pratt. He was taken with me. He had a hard turn of the fever in November and December, but recovered ; was taken again the latter end of March, and so continued till he died.

The 28th of this instant, when the prisoners were all confined in their rooms, but one or two in the lower room cooking the pot, the prison-house took fire. It began on the ridge. We supposed that it catched by sparks lighting upon it. It being very dry, and something windy, it soon spread upon the house, and we could not come at it, having no ladder, to quench it. There were no lives lost, but many lost their bedding and clothing. We were conducted by a strong guard to the governor's yard, where we were kept till near night, when we were conducted to the back of the town to the old wall, in the bow of which they had set up some plank tents something like sheep's pens. We had boards flung down to lay our beds upon, but the tents generally leaked so much in wet weather, that none of us could lie dry, and had much wet weather this month. The gentlemen of our room sent in a petition the beginning of May, that they might be removed to some more convenient place. Upon which we had a house built for us in the prisoners' yard, about twenty feet square, into which we removed the 23d instant [May]. This was something more comfortable than the tents. In this yard we were confined, having the wall behind it and at each end, and the fort side picketed in, and a guard of about twenty men to keep us day and night.

May 13. — Died Daniel Smeed, a young man. He was taken with me, and was son to John Smeed. He was first taken sick in November, and by frequent relapses was worn out, and fell into a purging, by which he wasted away and died.

May 17. — Died Captivity Smeed, an infant about nine months old, daughter to John Smeed.

May 20. — I was taken ill with a grievous pain in my head, and a sore eye, that I was almost blind with it. The 21st I yielded to be sick. Capt. Roberts and Capt. Williams were also both of them very sick, being taken a few days before me. This day I was blooded, having something of the fever. The 23d I was blooded again; the doctor also gave me a bottle of eye-water, and advised me not to be concerned about the fever. I was sensible they did not apprehend how ill I was. I entreated of him to give me a potion of physic, which he did, the 25th, and it worked very well. In the night I fell into a sweat, and was in hopes it would go off, but I was sadly disappointed, for I grew worse the next day. My reason departed from me and returned not, until the 14th of June. Part of this time I was given over by every one that saw me. I had the nervous fever, and was very much convulsed. I was exceeding low and weak when I first came to myself, but I recovered strength as soon as could be expected; for, by the 24th of June, I got out and went into the chamber.

In this three weeks' interval of delirium, some one must have made brief entries in the Chaplain's journal for him, at least of the deaths occurring almost daily; or else he afterwards copied these from the synchronous diary of Sergeant Hawks, which may be still in existence, although this is not likely, since nothing has been publicly heard of it for three-quarters of a century, or since General Hoyt used it in the preparation of his "Antiquarian Researches," published in 1824. Hoyt died at Deerfield in 1850. Rumors have been current that this diary was brought into Berkshire County from Hampshire by the Pomeroy family, when they migrated to

Pittsfield, but nothing definite has ever been ascertained in relation to it. Its probable destruction makes all the more precious for preservation the Chaplain's entries, which he evidently recast and expanded somewhat after his return from captivity, and in preparation for the printing of it in Boston in 1748, where it "was sold opposite the prison." As the prison at that time was in Queen Street, where the court-house now is, and as Daniel Fowle is known to have kept in Queen Street at that time, he may probably be supposed to be the printer. Whoever he was, he did not perform his share of the work with much credit to himself, which may be the reason for withholding the printer's name from the pamphlet.

May 22. — Died Nathaniel Hitchcock of Brimfield. He was taken with me.

May 30. — Died Jacob Shepherd, a pious young man, well-beloved and much lamented. He was taken with me.

The same day (July 16) died Phinehas Forbush of Westboro', taken at Fort Massachusetts with me. He was a very likely man.

July 21. — Died Jonathan Bridgeman of Sunderland. He was taken with me at Fort Massachusetts.

July 25. — We came on board the ship *Vierge-de-Grace* [Handsome Virgin], which the governor of Canada sent with a flag of truce to Boston. The 27th we set sail for New England, at ten in the morning. August 1st we came in sight of Cape Breton Island.

August 16. — We arrived at Boston. The sick and infirm were taken to the hospital. Col. Winslow sent to me and desired me to come and tarry with him while I continued in Boston. I thankfully accepted it, and was courteously entertained. This was a day of great joy and gladness to me. May I never forget the many great and repeated mercies of God towards me.

END OF THE REDEEMED CAPTIVE.

This Colonel Winslow, who showed such hospitality to Mr. Norton on his arrival at Boston, was great-grandson of Governor Edward Winslow of the *Mayflower.* Like his grandfather, Josiah, the first native-born Governor of Plymouth, 1673–80, this John Winslow was every inch a soldier. He had been a captain in the unfortunate expedition to Cuba in 1740; he was the commander and principal actor in the tragedy of the expulsion from their homes of the hapless Acadians of Nova Scotia in 1755, a tragedy which Longfellow's "Evangeline" has made familiar to all the world; he was commander-in-chief at Albany of 7000 New Englanders designed for Fort William Henry on Lake George in the disastrous summer of 1756; and he was a major-general of courage and ability in the successful conquest of Canada in 1758–59. It is a singular and memorable fact that twenty years after Winslow had ruthlessly, but with no more than the necessary cruelty, harried out of their homes in Nova Scotia for political reasons the French peasants and papists, nearly every person of Winslow's lineage in New England was compelled, for political reasons (they were Tories in 1775), to transplant himself for a home to the very soil from which the Acadians were expelled.

It is by no means probable that Mr. Norton was "courteously entertained" for many days by Colonel Winslow at his house in Boston, because the heart of the good Chaplain must have been drawn with powerful attraction towards the mountain fort where he had parted with young wife and children just one year before. He had left Shirley for Massachusetts, Aug. 14, 1746, and landed in Boston, Aug. 16, 1747. The following epitaph upon a rude head-stone that stood nearly 140 years in Shirley field, a few rods to the west of the site of the fort, and that is now in the historical museum in Clark Hall, shows how nearly contemporaneous was his arrival in Boston and a sad burial in a bleak field enclosed by an unbroken forest. Probably some soldier in the fort, to comfort the stricken parents, chiselled upon the rough quartzite the inscription as follows : —

Here lys ye body of An^{na}
D: of ye Rev:
Mr. John Norton. She died
Aug: ye — aged — 1747.

This stone stood there in the open field, solitary so far as any existing evidence points, exposed to the suns of summer and the storms of winter, until the number of years she had lived and the day of August on which she died became illegible by exposure, — impossible to be now deciphered. The oral tradition is still lively in the town of Heath, and it may well be an historical fact, for it has been handed down by an aged citizen there whose life began with the nineteenth century, that there used to come up from Connecticut on an occasional pilgrimage to the site of Fort Shirley, and particularly to the grave of Anna Norton, some relative or relations of hers. This is very likely in itself; for John Norton became in 1748 a pastor in the parish of East Hampton, Middlesex County, Connecticut, where he died in 1778; and one may still read on his tombstone there the following inscription : —

In Memory of
The Rev. John Norton
Pastor of the 3d Church in Chatham
Who died with Small Pox
March 24th a.d. 1778
In the 63d year of his Age.

He contracted the disease, of which he died, while returning from Middletown, on the opposite bank of the Connecticut River, from some person or persons who engaged him in conversation respecting the way to some place in the immediate neighborhood. It was supposed that one of the parties had just been taken from some pesthouse. He was buried, consequently, not in the God's-acre of his own parish, but, with a few other victims of the same dreadful disease, in a cultivated field on Miller's Hill, a few rods east of the residence of Leverett D. Willey. There, on a red sandstone slab, ornamented with a winged head, may be read the epitaph just quoted.

He left several children. Among these an unmarried daughter, Eunice Norton, who lived till 1825. The records of the church of East Hampton, of which Norton was the pastor from its organization, are lost during the thirty years of his pastorate; and it is supposed that they, with other of her father's papers, were destroyed by fire when Eunice Norton's house was burned down. It is no mean touch and print of vital human sympathy that is left upon the now desolate sod beneath the great tree in Shirley field, by the evanishing figure of one lone woman, who came and came again from a distant place to catch, it may be, but a dreary note from the sad music of the distant past, and to drop a tear upon the grave of a sister, whom, perhaps, she never saw.

Norton found a transient home, after his return from captivity, in Springfield. He did not resume his chaplaincy to the line of forts, nor was any other one appointed during this war to minister in his place. His Memorial to the General Court of the Province of Massachusetts Bay, copied from the archives in the Secretary's office in Boston, tells its own tale as follows : —

To his Excellency William Shirley, Esq. Capt. Gen. and Gov'r in Chief of this Province, the Hon'ble his Majesty's Council & House of Representatives in Gen. Court assembled —

The Memorial of John Norton of Springfield in the County of Hampshire, Clerk, humbly showeth That in the month of February, 1746, he entered into the Service of the Province as a Chaplain for the Line of Forts on the Western Frontier and continued in that service until the Twentieth day of August following, when he was captivated at Fort Massachusetts and carried to Canada by the enemy, where he was detained a prisoner for the space of twelve months, during which time he constantly officiated as a chaplain among his fellow-prisoners in the best manner he was able under the great difficulties and suffering of his imprisonment, and your Humble Petit'r begs leave further to inform your Excell'c & Honors that besides the great Difficulties and Hardships that your Petit'r indured during his captivity abroad, he and his family by means thereof are reduced to great Straight and Difficulties at home. He therefore prays your Excell'c and Honors would take his distressed Circumstances into your wiser Consideration and grant him such Help and Relief as your Excell'c, and Honors in your Wisdom and Goodness shall deem meet, and your memorialist as in duty bound shall ever pray.

JOHN NORTON

Springfield, Jan. 25, 1748.

[ENDORSED]

In the House of Representatives, Feb. 23, 1748.

Read and Ordered that the sum of £37, 10s. be allowed the memorialist in consideration of this Officiating as Chaplain to the Prisoners whilst in captivity at Canada.

In council read & concurred   W. Hutchinson, Speaker
J. Willard
Sec'y

Consented to
W. SHIRLEY.

Mr. Norton's second settlement in the ministry at East Hampton in November, 1748, like his first one at Fall Town in November, 1741, was in troublous times and among a very poor people. His salary was to be 100 ounces of silver, or public bills of credit equivalent thereto, for the first three years after his settlement, and after that time an addition to that in proportion as they should add to their property-list, until it should amount to 130 ounces of silver, and that to be his standing salary. This, which amounted to near $170 of our own money, was never promptly paid, and but a small portion of it in cash, the rest being bartered for in country produce at variable rates. The universal interest in New England in the first campaign of the next French war, the campaign of 1755, led Mr. Norton's ministerial neighbors of the Hartford South Association, to which he belonged, to agree to supply his pulpit for him from October of that year till the following February, in order that he might again become a chaplain for a short time among the troops, gathering at the northward for the reduction of Crown Point. He went accordingly in that capacity with Colonel David Wooster's Connecticut regiment. They did not reach Lake George until after the battle there of the 8th of September, in which Colonel Ephraim Williams was killed. We shall learn later how that winter was spent by troops and Chaplain at the head of Lake George. One motive of the latter in going again to the front may have been to obtain for the use of his family a little ready money as salary for his services from the colony of Connecticut. While he had been in captivity at Quebec, his wife, then with the garrison under Captain

Williams at Fort Shirley, had applied to the colony of Massachu.
setts for the wages due him as chaplain, and had received at one
time, March 12, 1747, what was then due, £1 16s. 6d.

The ancestry of John Norton in the old country seems to be well
authenticated as distinguished. At any rate, it was of Norman origin.
Le Seur de Norville, the name afterwards changed to Norton, came to
England with William the Conqueror in 1066 as his constable. The
place to which the family ever traced its planting after crossing the
Channel is Sharpenhow, a hamlet of Bedfordshire. Richard Norton
of London was the thirteenth generation from the Norman constable.
John Norton, his son, with wife Dorothy, were the immigrant ancestors, who came to Brandford, Connecticut, from England in 1646.
Their son John, born in Brandford, Oct. 14, 1651, migrated with his
father to Farmington in 1661, and died there April 25, 1725. His
wife's name was Ruth Moore. They had a son John, born in 1684,
who married Anna Thompson, and our Rev. John Norton was one of
their thirteen children. He was born in Farmington, Nov. 15, 1715,
was graduated from Yale College in 1737, and was ordained Nov.
25, 1741.

On the same flag of truce from Quebec to Boston, on which the
good chaplain returned, came also Sergeant John Hawks, and all
the remnant of the garrison of Fort Massachusetts still alive straggled back in the course of the summer, some by way of the West
Indies and some through the wilderness, including John Aldrich of
Mendon and Benjamin Simonds of Ware River, both of whom were
left sick in the hospital at Quebec when Hawks and Norton left.
Simonds was sick at the taking of the fort, and Aldrich was
wounded in the foot, and both were unable to travel when the
captives started for the northward, and both were put into a canoe
with John Perry's wife at what is now the "River Bend Farm" in
Williamstown, the point farthest up the Hoosac to which any boats
were brought in this expedition. It does not positively appear
from any existing record that either of these men got well during
the year at Quebec; at any rate, they were both left there sick after
most of the remaining survivors had returned to Boston. Four of
the soldiers came in within a week, and one a full month, after the
two officers. As in duty bound, Sergeant Hawks made his report to
the government of the colony in respect to his command, but
tardily, and some time after the Treaty of Aix-la-Chapelle had been
formally proclaimed at Boston. This report is extant, and is interesting, and shall be given here in full.

An Account of the Company in his Majesty's Service under the command of Sergt. John Hawks who were taken with him at Fort Massachusetts Aug. 20, 1746.

			RETURNED	WEEKS & DAYS		PER MONTH
John Hawks	Sergt.	Deerfield	Aug. 23, 1747	52	5	33/8
John Norton	Chaplain	Line of Forts	" " "	"	"	"
Stephen Scott	Soldier	Sunderland	Aug. 26, 1747	53	1	25/8
David Warren,	Soldier	Sunderland	Aug. 26, 1747	53	1	25/8
John Smead Sen.	"	Pequaog	Aug. 31, 1747	53	6	"
John Smead Jun.	"	"	Deceased April 7, 1747	33	0	"
Daniel Smead		"	" May 13, 1747	33	1	"
John Perry	"	Fall Town	Aug. 26, 1747	53	1	"
Moses Scott	" "		" " "	53	1	"
Joseph Scott		Hatfield	Sept. 27, 1747	57	5	"
Nathaniel Ames	"	Marlborough	Died Nov. 17, 1747	12	6	"
Josiah Read		Rehoboth	" Aug. 21, 1746		2	
Samuel Lovat		Mendon	" Jan. 23, 1747	22	3	"
Samuel Goodman	"	Hadley	" March 21, 1747	30	4	"
Amos Pratt	"	Westborough	" April 12, 1747	33	5	"
Nathaniel Hitchcock	"	Springfield	" May 22, 1747	39	3	"
Jacob Sheppard	"	Westboro'	" May 30, 1747	40	4	"
Phineas Forbush	"	"	" July 16, 1747	47	2	"
Jonathan Bridgman	"	Sunderland	" July 21, 1747	48	0	"
John Aldrich } Pd. by the Treasurer } "		Mendon	" Left sick } Since returned but can't			
Benjamin Simonds Pd	"	Ware River	{ Left sick at { ye hospital } say the time.			

HAMPSHIRE SS. DEERFIELD, Sept. 19, 1749.

Then John Hawks personally appearing made oath that the preceding roll contains an account of the men taken with him at Fort Massachusetts Aug. 20, 1746, and also an account of their decease, and return to their several homes.

Before WILLIAM WILLIAMS *Just. Pacis.*

To the Hon.ble Spencer Phipps Esqr Lieut Govr and Commander in Chief, the Hon.ble his Majesty's Council and House of Representatives in General Court assembled Boston Novr 1749:

The Petition of John Hawks for himself and others named in the Acct annexed humbly sheweth —

That he together with sundry others named in said account were detained in the Service of this Province at Fort Massachusetts in Aug. 1746 when the same was attacked by an army of about a thousand French and Indians, that they defended the same to the utmost of their power, and whilst their ammunition lasted repulsed the enemy to their considerable loss, but that failing and no relief appearing, and near half that were in the Fort sick, — they were obliged to surrender themselves into the hands of their enemy, and were by them carried to Canada, and there retained the time set forth in said acct, till the death of some and return of the rest to their respective homes, — and also lost their arms.

Your Petr prays your Honors consideration of their services and sufferings.

and that you would in your great Goodness grant them such relief as to you in your Wisdom shall seem best, and as in duty bound shall ever pray —

JOHN HAWKS.

[Endorsed on the above]

In the House of Representatives Jan. 22, 1749, —

Read and Ordered that the following allowance be made to the several persons herein mentioned — viz. To each man or their representatives, the sum annexed to his name.

	£	s	d
To JOHN HAWKS	£21	15	1
STEPHEN SCOTT	16	12	2
JOHN SMEAD	16	16	7
JOHN SMEAD, Jun.	10	6	3
DANIEL SMEAD	11	18	5
JOHN PERRY	16	12	2
MOSES SCOTT	16	12	2
JOSEPH SCOTT	18	0	3

And that the Commissary General be directed to deliver to each of the above-named men a gun out of the Province Store, except John Hawks who has already rec^d one. — The above sums and guns to be delivered to Timothy Dwight Esq., for the use of the abovenamed persons. —

Ordered also that there be paid to Mr. Samuel Witt for the afternamed persons, or their representatives, the following sums, viz.

	£	s	d
To NATHANIEL AMES	£ 4	0	1
To DAVID WARREN	16	5	11
To JACOB SHEPHERD	12	13	7

And that the abovenamed Nathl Ames and Jacob Shepherd be allowed each a gun out of the Province Store.

It is also further Ordered that the following sums be paid to Capt. Samuel Chamberlayne for the use of the persons hereafter named, viz.

	£	s	d
To EBENEZER GOULD	£0	10	0
BENJ. FASSETT	0	15	0
NATH^L HUNT	0	12	6

in full for horse hire when they were carried from Fort Massachusetts sick.

Sent up for concurrence

THO. HUBBARD
Spt.^{r} pro tempore.

We must now take our final leave of the captives of Fort Massachusetts as such. When the fort was beleaguered, there were thirty persons within it; namely, twenty-two men, three women, and five children. One of the men, Thomas Knowlton, was killed the day the fort surrendered; another, Josiah Read, died the next day at what is now called "Petersburg Junction," where was born the same night "Captivity" Smead. None died on the way to Quebec, leaving twenty-nine captives to enter that city. The first death among them there, where all the circumstances being considered they were well treated, was that of Miriam, wife of Moses Scott, who had "catched a grievous cold" in "a very heavy shower of rain," that fell the day the captives crossed the Battenkill, the first Sunday after the surrender of the fort. She died December 11. Twelve days later died Rebecca, the wife of John Perry. February 11 died Moses Scott, Junior, a child two years old. On the 29th of March fell the first of a series of heavy blows on the soldier, John Smead, in the death of Mary, his wife. Just three weeks later died their daughter "Captivity," nine months old. Of the ten soldiers who died at Quebec, two of them, Daniel and John, Junior, were sons of John and Mary Smead. The father returned to his home in Athol (Pequoag) on the last day of August, and on the 19th of October was travelling from Northfield to Sunderland down the Connecticut River, when he fell into an Indian ambush and was killed and scalped. How many of the captives, then, ever got back to their homes? All three of the women died, and two of the six children, and twelve of the twenty-two soldiers, leaving but fourteen of the thirty-one; and of these fourteen, John Smead survived his return just seven weeks; four of the thirteen left were children; the Sergeant commanding and the Chaplain recording reduced the number to seven soldiers; namely, Stephen Scott, David Warren, John Perry, Joseph Scott, John Aldrich, Moses Scott, Benjamin Simonds. Of these, two only, Perry and Simonds, were any way conspicuous in later life. The place of residence of Thomas Knowlton, shot in the watch tower of the fort, is unknown; but he was a son of Joseph Knowlton, who some time after received from the colony the wages due his son when killed.

The curious petition of John Perry to the General Court, written out with his own hand, ostensibly not long after his return, though evidently and properly receiving no recognition at the hands of that body, while he was afterwards paid with the rest his full wages during his captivity, is well worth full quotation on several accounts:—

PETITION OF JOHN PERRY.

To the Honorable Representatives of the Great and General Court now in Boston, the Petition of John Perry humbly showeth—

Whereas your Honours Humble Petitioner Enlisted in the service of the Country under the Comand of Captain Ephraim Williams in the year 1745,

190 ORIGINS IN WILLIAMSTOWN.

and was posted at Fort Massachusetts in housuck, and upon ye encouragement
we had from ye late honorable Col. John Stoddard, which was that if we went
with our Families he did not doubt but ye Court would grant us land to settle
on, whereupon I your Honours Humble petitioner carried up my family there
with my household stuf and other effects and continued there till we was taken
when we was obliged to surrender — to the french and Indian Enemy August
the 20 1746. I would humbly lay before your Honours the losses I sustained,
which are as followeth, a house I built there for my family 80 pounds two
feather beds with their furniture 100 pounds two suits of apparel apiece for me
and my wife 150 pounds two Brass Kettles a pot and pewter with tramel tongs
fire slice and knives and forks to ye balance of 20 pounds one Cross cut saw 20
pounds and one new broad ax 6 pounds three new narrow axes 8 pounds and
one adds 2 pounds two steel traps 14 pounds two guns 32 pounds one pistol 5
pounds one 100 weight of suggar 20 pounds total 457 pounds with a great many
other things not named; the losses your Humble Petitioner hath met with
together with my captivity hath reduced me to low circumstances, and now
humbly prayeth your Honours of your goodness to grant him a grant of land to
settle up near ye fort where I fenced about a mile west of the fort, or elsewhere,
where your Honours pleaseth and that your Honours may have a full reward
hereafter for all your pious and Charitable Deeds your Honours Humble petitioner shall alwais pray.

JOHN PERRY.

Nov. 5, 1747.

John Perry was a carpenter, as the reader will remember. If his
estimate of the value of his tools and other "stuf" seem ridiculously
excessive to us, we must remember that Massachusetts was then
using "Colony bills," which were greatly depreciated as compared
with silver, and which the colony soon after (1749) redeemed in
silver at 11 : 1. "Ye late honorable Col. John Stoddard" died June
19, 1748, which makes quite suspicious the *date* of this petition;
then it is altogether too pious — "charitable deeds" are not in
order for a General Court in war-time, or peace either; and besides,
there had been a preliminary survey by the colony of two townships — East and West Hoosac — in 1739, covering the ground
"where I fenced," to be followed in 1749 by the ultimate survey
and allotment of lands, and of course the Court did not wish to tie
itself up by making any grants likely to prove inconvenient in the
sequel. It must be remembered, nevertheless, that perhaps Perry's
petition, whensoever sent in, had some influence as towards the pre-
emptions and privileges of the later soldiers of Fort Massachusetts
in the "House Lots" of West Hoosac, of which we shall hear more
by and by.

News travelled slowly in August, 1746, from the upper valley of
the Hoosac over the mountain by the old Indian path to the Connecticut River. In Deacon Noah Wright's journal this entry: —

Aug. 30, 1746. — A post returned this day to and from Fort Massachusetts, and brings us news that the fort was taken and burnt to ashes, and we can't learn here as there is one man escaped. I am in some hopes that there are some that are taken captive and gone to Canada, and so I ain't altogether without hopes of seeing some of them again.

As soon as the news came to Hatfield, a party under Captain Oliver Partridge went up to the site of the fort, as we learn from the following item of a bill sent to the authorities at Boston: "Also by Capt. Partridge for horse-keeping when he went to bury the dead at Fort Massachusetts after the Fort was taken — £10 0 0." They found but one body to be buried, and that the mutilated one of Thomas Knowlton. It is more than probable that it was Captain

"SADDLE MOUNTAIN,"

Early so-called, overlooking towards the north the Hoosac River and the site of Fort Massachusetts. The rounded peak to the left is the northern extremity of the middle lobe of Greylock, and has long been called "Mount Williams," and its lower decline towards the river and fort is now called "Slope Hawks"; the sharper peak to the right is the north end of "Prospect," and its decline to the meadow is "Slope Norton."

Partridge who took down from the well-post the letter which Chaplain Norton had nailed there on his departure as a captive; for we find this entry in Deacon Wright's journal, just about the time when Partridge may be supposed to have returned to Hatfield: —

Sept. 11, 1746. — I saw a letter wrote by Mr. Norton at Hoosick after the fort was taken, and he says the fort was besieged by seven hundred French and Indians, and they being brought to a great strait the enemy prepared a vast quantity of faggots in order to burn down the fort by force, but the French General came to them for capitulation, and told them if they would resign up the fort he would treat them all well, and carry them to Canada; that they should be redeemed as soon as there was any opportunity; if not, he would kill

them all.   And so they resigned up the fort, and lost but one man named
Knowlton, and had two wounded, and so all the rest are gone to Canada.   He
says they are all well used by the enemy.

When Partridge's men left the site of the first Fort Massachusetts
on this occasion, — we may suppose about the end of the first week in
September, 1746, — the spot itself and the whole valley of the Upper
Hoosac remained an utter solitude, so far as the presence of white
men goes, for seven or eight months.   The meadow was then only
partially cleared; the part cleared was cluttered with stumps; nothing was left of the fort but the well, on the "west post" of which
the letter had been nailed; the forest to the westward was unbroken
to Van der Verick's place at the junction of the Little Hoosac with
the main stream; the forest to the eastward over the Hoosac
Mountain was equally unbroken to the upper valley of the Deerfield in what is now Charlemont, where Captain Rice kept watch and
ward; and the wintry snows soon sifted down upon the shaggy
mountain and its flanking valleys, covering even the immemorial
Mohawk trail that traversed all three alike with impassable deeps of
whiteness.

On the 9th of May, 1748, Sergeant John Hawks started from
Deerfield in command of fourteen men, and went, so the record
states, "as far as the Dutch settlements at Hoosuck"; that is to
say, he revisited Van der Verick's place under circumstances doubtless more agreeable to himself than those of 1746.   The camping-
place there, where Captivity Smead was born, and whence the
Indians kindly took Benjamin Simonds (sick) down the Hoosac in
their canoe, must have awakened in his breast vivid recollections
and warm thankfulness, and may have stimulated him to write on
his return the memorial to the commander-in-chief at Boston, which
enriches our next paragraph.

One more original document must be quoted here, before we take
our final leave of the first Fort Massachusetts ; namely, the

Memorial of John Hawks of Deerfield, yeoman, dated June 2 1748, humbly
sheweth, That on the 9th of May 1746, when a soldier at Fort Massachusetts he
was fir^d upon by a Party of the Enemy and grievously wounded and considerably disabled for any further services ; and also on or about the 20th of Augt then
next when the said Fort was reduced and demolishe^d, he was captivated by the
Enemy and carried to Canada and there detained a prisoner almost a year during which time he underwent great Hardships and Difficulties in addition to the
Losses he sustained at the Reduction of said Fort ; and also on the Eighth Day
of February last he w^t John Taylor and Matthew Clesson set out (by your
Excellencies order) w^t Monsr Raimbault in order to recover some English Persons out of the Hands of the French and on the last day of April return^d again

from Canada to Deerfield w^t Nathan Blake and Saml Allen two English captives recovered from the French — For all which Services and Sufferings w^t others that might have been mentioned Your Petitioner has never had any consideration or allowance from the Government. Your Petitioner therefore prays Your Excellency and Hon^s Consideration of the Premises as well w^t regard to the said John and Matthew as himself and such Relief under his Difficulties in particular therefrom arising as your Excellency and Hon^s in your known Wisdom and Compassion shall seem meet, and your Petitioner as in Duty bound shall ever pray.

JOHN HAWKS.

To Wm SHIRLEY &c. &c. &c.

The old French and Indian War, sometimes called Governor Shirley's War, went vigorously forward in the way of preparations on both sides, during the winter of 1746–47. With the course and issue of it in general we have no present concern. Only as it stands related to events in the valley of the Upper Hoosac have we to do with it here. In the same sense we are interested in the character and activities of William Shirley at Boston. Of English birth and education, as a lawyer he had practised some years in Boston, when, in 1741, he was appointed by the Crown, governor of Massachusetts, — an office which he held to the striking profit of the colony, and with credit to himself, until 1757, when he was succeeded by Thomas Pownall. In military affairs he acted to the westward of his province, through Colonel John Stoddard of Northampton, till the latter's death in 1748, and then mainly through Colonel Israel Williams of Hatfield. The fall of Fort Massachusetts affected Shirley more deeply than any other man in the colony, and next to him, undoubtedly, Stoddard himself. The following letter, in Shirley's own hand, gives us a vivid idea of him as a man and a governor, and of his sense of the importance, at that time, to English interests in New England, of the site of that fort; and goes far to justify the later characterization of the spot, by Edward Everett, as a " Thermopylæ " : —

BOSTON, April 10, 1747.

GENTLEMEN, — You are hereby desired and directed to provide for the erecting, and then to erect and build a good commodious Blockhouse at or near the place where the Fort called Massachusetts late stood. — You must take effectual care that it be built in the best manner for defence and strength, and for the accommodating and lodging a Garrison of thirty men, with convenience for such other men as His Majesty's Service may occasionally require to be there quartered or entertained; and to build another Blockhouse at some convenient Place West of Fort Pelham; you must take care that each Blockhouse have a good Well within the Works. — You must use all needful Frugality in this Business, and particularly in employing some of the soldiers in this Work if anything may be saved this way without Prejudice to the Work. I shall order you a Guard for the Protection of those Persons that may be employed in cutting and hauling the Timber, building the House and other Services. You must send an account to the Commissary General of the Utinsils that may be necessary for the Use of the Garrison in each Blockhouse.

Your assured Friend and Servant

W. Shirley.

To John Stoddard
  Eleazar Porter } Esqrs
  Oliver Partridge

Governor Shirley had no local knowledge of the lay of the land west of Fort Pelham. The original design and order in 1744 when the war broke out was, and it is here reiterated, that there should be at least one fortified place between Pelham and Massachusetts; the old military road from Coleraine past Shirley, and past Pelham, was continued for a mile or more due west, as if expecting to reach such a place; and the writer has often traversed this piece of old road with curious eyes (it is not now used for travel), until its straight course suddenly ceases, and a narrower road strikes it on the left, running down southwest to the Deerfield River at the present "Hoosac Tunnel" station. The truth was and remains, that a range of steep mountain intervenes between Pelham Fort and the Deerfield River, which here has a due south course, only bending sharp east at the mouth of the tunnel, and from the west bank of which rises with equal precipitancy the Hoosac range, the western flanks of which reach almost to the site of Fort Massachusetts. There was no room for an intermediate fort, and consequently none was ever attempted.

Fifteen days after the above letter was written, namely, April 25, 1747, Governor Shirley writes again to Colonel Stoddard: —

I have written to the Govenor of Connecticut (at the Desire of the two Houses) to request that Government to send 500 men for the Defence of your County, and to be under your Direction ; and accordingly I desire and expect that if the said men or any other Number of men should be sent out of that Government into the County of Hampshire that you take effectual care that they be employed in the best manner for the Security of the Inhabitants and Annoyance of the Enemy.

The General Court having allowed a great Gun of four pounds shott and two swivel guns for the Fort of Number Four, and as the present violent assaults of the Enemy upon your Frontiers will necessarily oblige you to defer the Building of the new Blockhouses at present: you must deliver the great Gun and two of the swivel Guns out of the Guns I have ordered the Commissary General to send to you for the Use of the Blockhouses built or to be built in your County; and which he accordingly sent by sea about ten days ago. I have ordered the Commissary General to send you by the first conveyance the four pounder and swivel Guns first mentioned.

Fortunately there has been preserved in the Secretary's office, at Boston, a package of receipted bills, marked, "French War — Forts to Westward," among which is the following interesting item : —

To transporting three 4-pounders from Boston to New York	£2	
" " " " " New York to Albany	1	10
" " " " " Albany to Van Der Hiden's Ferry,	0	9
" " " " " thence 36 miles to Fort Mass	2	6

The "landing-place at Van Der Hiden's" is the present location of the city of Troy. These guns undoubtedly reached their destination on the desolated site of the first fort before any steps had been taken there to renovate and rebuild. But these steps were not long delayed. Shirley's apprehensions that "the present violent assaults of the enemy upon your frontiers will necessarily oblige you to defer the building of the new blockhouses," were not justified in fact, for Massachusetts had kept a considerable body of troops under pay throughout the preceding winter; and General Joseph Dwight of Brookfield, who had served with great credit at Louisburg, who afterwards became a distinguished citizen of Berkshire, had raised a regiment in the autumn, principally from the Connecticut valley, for the projected expedition against Canada; and, with his next in rank in the regiment, Lieutenant-Colonel William Williams, and the regiment itself of ten companies, had been employed during the winter in northwestern Hampshire in detached parties, scouting, garrisoning, and in every way guarding the endangered section. On the 21st of April, two of these companies and a part of a third were assigned to Colonel Williams for the purpose of rebuilding Fort Massachusetts. In giving this immediate order to his lieutenant, William Williams, General Dwight added, "I suppose Captain Ephraim Williams will send all or a part of his, if you desire it, who, I think, ought to do their part of this duty." Captain Ephraim Williams had undoubtedly spent the winter in Fort Shirley, and was still in command of the line of forts from Northfield to Fort Pelham in what is now the town of Rowe.

Just here another member of the Williams family comes prominently into our field of view for a short time, later to reappear upon these pages for a considerable stay. This is Ephraim Williams, Senior, the father of the Fort Shirley captain and founder of Williams College. He was born in Newton, near Boston, Aug. 21, 1691. He became a man of considerable repute in Newton, a captain of the militia, and a justice of the peace there. In the first part of June, 1739, he and Mr. Josiah Jones of Weston brought their families to

Stockbridge and settled there, being two of the four English families who, by the order of the General Court of Massachusetts, were to establish themselves there on lands granted to them for that purpose by the Court, for the moral support of John Sergeant the missionary, and Timothy Woodbridge the schoolmaster, to the Indians gathered there in a Christian mission under the auspices of the colony. The other two Christian families were those of Joseph Woodbridge of West Springfield and Deacon Samuel Brown of Spencer. Even as early as the original order of the Court, 30 Nov., 1743, to raise a committee to build garrison-houses and set defences to the westward, Blanford, Stockbridge, and Sheffield were mentioned as places to be defended in connection with the line of forts running westward from the Connecticut River at Northfield. Dec. 24, 1745, Governor Shirley wrote to Colonel Stoddard as follows : —

I have had application made to me by Capt. Ephraim Williams in behalf of Stockbridge, and by the proprietors of Blandford in behalf of that town, for soldiers to be sent to each of those places for their further defence ; and I desire you would consider their respective circumstances, and order out of the forces now in your parts what you shall judge necessary and what may be spared for their protection. — *P. S.* Capt. Williams desired me to give him an Order for eight Indians to scout, but I have referred him to yourself.

Governor Shirley writes again to Colonel Stoddard under date of Aug. 2, 1746, as follows : —

As to the difficulty respecting a Major of Col. Dwight's Regiment, altho I have a good esteem of Capt. Williams, and have considered his superior character in the same light you mention, yet Major Pomroy's serving in the late Expedition and with faithfulness and good courage (by all that I can learn) seems to give considerable advantage to his pretensions ; but (as I perceive by Col. Dwight's letter) Maj. Pomroy is not agreeable to him, nor like to be so to the Officers and Soldiers, I am determined in favor of Capt. Williams, and desire you would endeavor to make Maj. Pomroy content with a Capt^ns commission only, which he ought the rather to be, etc., etc.

The elder Williams was thus undoubtedly appointed Major of Colonel Dwight's regiment about the time of the fall of the first Fort Massachusetts ; and when the next spring opened, and the two companies and a part of the third of this regiment were set to rebuilding the fort on its old site under Lieutenant-Colonel William Williams, second in command in the regiment, Major Ephraim Williams accompanied them as next in command to his near kinsman, who had recently returned from Louisburg with a very considerable military reputation. We possess no details of the processes of the rebuilding. The pine trees were growing in abundance upon the meadow itself. They were felled and hewed and jointed and pinned together; doubtless as at Fort Shirley, two years before, the three four-pounders were doubtless on the ground, ready to be mounted as soon as the walls were up. There can be little question that numbers of those soldiers that had wrought on Fort Shirley, and on the first blockhouse here, were now employed also on the new fort of similar construction, for William Williams had had the charge of building both of those works, and he knew what men had shown aptness in such labors, and if any of them were in his regiment now, they would be altogether likely to be assigned again to the familiar tasks. Two to one, that our old friend, John Perry, "carpenter of Fall Town," though he did not get back from his captivity in Canada in time to build on the new structure, yet revisited later the scene of his earlier hazards and exploits, becoming familiar with the second fort; and Philip Alexander (who certainly toiled on Fort Shirley) and Michael Gilson, too (whose name is often on the muster-rolls of Fort Massachusetts), because we read expressly in the history of Putney, Vermont, that these three men, "emigrants from Massachusetts," located on the Great Meadow there, and built, in company with others, in 1755, a blockhouse on the meadow almost the exact counterpart of the second Fort Massachusetts. The Putney fort is described as follows in Thompson's "Vermont":—

This fort was 120 feet long by 80 wide, and was built of yellow pine timber, hewed six inches thick and laid up about 16 feet high,—the houses were built against the wall, with a roof slanting up, (called a salt-box roof,) to the top of the wall, the wall of the fort making the back wall of the house, and the houses all fronting the hollow square in the centre of the fort. It was garrisoned by troops from New Hampshire until about 1760.

Besides Colonel William Williams in command at the rebuilding of Fort Massachusetts, and Major Ephraim Williams his second in command there, Captain Ephraim Williams also then commanding in the line of forts westward from Connecticut River, was at Fort Massachusetts while the work was going on there in some connection with the Commissary department. His cousin, Major Israel Williams of Hatfield, was commissioned "Commissary to the Western Forces," Oct. 18, 1744, and continued in that capacity till the death of Colonel John Stoddard in 1748, when he succeeded Stoddard in the command of the western militia, and Major Elijah Williams of Deerfield became Commissary to the westward. The General Court had resolved to garrison 100 men in Fort Massachusetts so soon as it should be completed. Israel Williams was experienced enough to know that a very considerable base of supplies would be needed to maintain such a garrison in such a place, nothing short of Albany; accordingly, Captain Ephraim Williams was sent from the fort to Albany with an escort of 100 soldiers to guard provisions purchased there on their way thence to the fort, as he himself expressed it in a memorial dated November, 1747: "That in the month of May last I went from Fort Massachusetts to Albany to bring out stores for the use of the Government at that Fort," etc., etc. Before the return of this escort from Albany, and while the workmen were still employed on the construction of the fort, a body of the French and Indian enemy approached the fort with the double intent of interrupting the work upon it and cutting off the escort of the provisions, and lay concealed for some time in the circum-adjacent woods. On the 25th of May, the vanguard of the escort arrived near the fort, and was suddenly attacked by the enemy that had been in ambush. The workmen on the fort, who always had their arms close by, immediately advanced on the enemy, putting him between two fires in the sharp skirmish that ensued, which resulted in driving him into the woods for good, so that the escort came up with the loss of only one Stockbridge Indian and two men wounded.

Just a week later than this skirmish, the fort being now completed and provisioned, the command over it was transferred by the following written order, happily preserved to us among the papers of the writer, Colonel William Williams: —

FORT MASSACHUSETTS, June 2, 1747.

MAJOR EPHRAIM WILLIAMS

Sir, — Intending by the leave of Providence to depart this fort to-morrow, which, through the goodness of God towards us is now finished, I must desire you to take the charge of it; and shall, for the present, leave with you eighty men, which I would have you detain here till the barracks are erected, which I would have you build in the following manner, viz., seventy feet in length, thirty in breadth, seven-feet post, with a low roof. Let it be placed within five feet of the north side of the fort, and at equal distances from the east and west ends.

Let it be divided in the middle with a tier of timber; place a chimney in the centre of the east part, with two fire-places to accommodate those rooms. In the west part, place the chimney so as to accommodate the two rooms on that part, as if the house was but twenty feet wide from the south; making a partition of plank, ten feet distance from the north side of the barrack, for a store-room for the provisions, &c.

The timber, stone, clay, lath, and all materials, being under the command of your guns, I can't but look upon you safe in your business, and desire you to see everything finished workmanlike; and when you have so done, you'll be pleased to dismiss Capt. Ephraim Williams, with his men, and what of my company I leave. You'll not forget to keep a scout east and west, which the men of your company are so well adapted for, and can be of very little service to you in the works.

Sir, I shall not give you any particular directions about maintaining the strong fortress or governing your men, but, in general, advise you always to be on your guard, nor suffer any idle fellows to stroll about. Sir, I heartily wish you health, the protection and smiles of Heaven on all accounts, and am, with esteem and regard, sir

Your most humble servant,

W^M. WILLIAMS.

This is, on the whole, the most interesting contemporary document extant relating to the second Fort Massachusetts. The directions and descriptions in it are at once clear in terms, courteous to his subordinate, military in form; and withal a trifle grandiloquent, as befitted an officer left in command of the "grand fortress" of Louisburg only the year before. The contrast must have been great in his mind — although this order does not betray it — between that genuine "Gibraltar of America" and this rustic blockhouse of pine wood; but he makes the most of it, such as it was. It was indeed, in point of strength, a great gain over the first fort. The newly arrived cannon were already mounted upon its corner platforms. It was this feature, if any, that justifies his epithet of "strong fortress." The barracks soon to be built would furnish the garrison two rooms for eating and sleeping, thirty-five feet by fifteen, and two more thirty-five by ten feet, and one room on the northwest corner for provisions, thirty-five feet by ten.

The rations allowed the troops on these frontiers during this war were as follows : —

GARRISON FORCES.

1 lb. of Bread
½ pint of Peas or Beans } per day ;
2 lbs. of Pork for three days ;
1 gallon of Molasses a man for 42 days.

MARCHING FORCES.

1 lb. of Bread
1 lb. of Pork } per day.
1 gill of Rum

The length of the new blockhouse is nowhere mentioned in any of the papers remaining that relate to its construction; but it could not have been less than 100 feet, and there are some slight grounds for inferring that it was 120 feet. The barracks were to be placed "within five feet of the north side of the fort, and at equal distances from the east and west ends." As the barracks were to be seventy feet long, if the fort were 100 feet, there would have been fifteen feet free at both ends of the north side, and if 120 feet, twenty-five feet free. There was to be, some years later, a mount for observation over the northwest corner of the fort, as there was to the old one; and we may be sure that the cannon were mostly ranged to the west or north, because the enemy would surely approach and probably attack on those sides. The sole entrance to the fort (always on the north side) was flanked at five feet distance by the barracks. The alley-way between the two was convenient for the ingress and egress of officers and soldiers without going through the barracks. The officers' quarters were undoubtedly within the main enclosure, as was also the well, and there must have been at least one chimney within for the accommodation of those quarters, which would still leave an ample parade. And so William Williams doubtless left the fort June 3d in the hands of the two Ephraims, father and son, expecting that the father, so soon as the barracks were finished, would dismiss the son to the care and control of his mountain forts to the eastward.

The late President of the College, Mark Hopkins, was in the direct line of descent from Ephraim Williams, Senior, the officer thus left in command of the second Fort "Massachusetts"; and he more than once spoke to the present writer (although in general he had very little interest in such matters) of a tradition that had come down lively in his family, that the elder Williams once held for a time the command at Fort Massachusetts. That tradition is now and here historically verified for the first time. The confusion has always been great between father and son in this case, because both not only bore the same name, but also carried in pretty quick succession one after another the same military titles. Dr. Smith, the historian of Pittsfield, who has cleared up admirably the story of Colonel William Williams, falls here into the erroneous conjecture that "the Major to whom the command was thus transferred was the founder of Williams College," and that "Capt. Ephraim Williams was probably a Connecticut officer in command of one of the companies sent by his colony in aid of the common defence." Connecticut had sent as yet no soldiers into these parts, although she did so in the next war, as we shall afterwards have occasion to notice. The "Capt." here was the eldest son of the "Major." The former and not the latter became the founder of the College. And let it be just noticed in passing, that distinct tra-

ditions of the kind alluded to above are never to be lightly thrown
away in historical research, even though at any given time no contemporaneous written confirmation can be found for them. They
are never to be taken in themselves as authority, but they have
proven many times as guides to the written and certain word of
proof, and sometimes been fairly confirmatory of otherwise doubtful contemporary testimony.

The following memorial of Ephraim Williams, Senior, to Governor
Shirley, will give a glimpse of the nature of his brief activities in
connection with Fort Massachusetts. It was the son and not the
father who linked the name of "Williams" intimately and indissolubly with the fort and the towns around it, and the whole stretch
of country from Deerfield to Lake George : —

To his Excellency Wm. Shirley Esq Governor and his Majesties Council &
House of Representatives in Gen¹ Court assembled Novr. 1747.

The memorial of Eph^m Williams of Stockbridge, in the County of Hampshire
Humbly Sheweth

That in the month of May last, I went from Fort Massachusetts to Albany
to bring out ye Stores for the use of the Government at that Fort four B^bls of
Powder I was obliged to give my obligation too to the Commissary there 400
W^t of Lead I Borrowed of Lif^t. Coll Robberts which is not yet returned to him,
Six Iron Potts I Bo't for the use of the Fort, as also ten Skepple of Salt, and
three Cask to put it in, for which I am now D^r there, all which I did for the
Emediate bennefit of the Govern^t. the Commissary Gen^ll Informs he Cannot
Settle the account & discharge me without the Courts order, Woold therefore
Humbly move y^r Excellency & Hon^rs to give directions to the Commissary
Gen^ll to settle the said accounts with me, or otherwise provide for my discharge,
as in your Wisdom you shall see meet, & as in Duty Bound Shall Pray &c.

EPH^M. WILLIAMS

In the House of Representatives Dec. 10, 1747. Read and Ordered that the
Commissary Gen¹ be directed to allow the Commissary Emerson in the acc^t for
the four barrells of Powder. And that s^d Commissary Gen¹ return the four
hundred Weight of Lead for the Use of Col° Roberts in the Goverm^t of New
York. And that He allow the Memorialist in his Account for the Six Iron Potts
and Ten Skipple of Salt above mentioned.

Sent up for concurrence.

In Council Dec. 11, 1747.
        Read & Concurred.

            J. WILLARD Sec^y

Consented

        W. SHIRLEY.   T. HUTCHINSON Spk^r.

How long Major Ephraim Williams continued in the command of the second Fort Massachusetts from this assumption of it in June, 1747, there are no present means of determining, nor is it of much consequence, since the time was short at the longest, and since nothing of much importance occurred, during its continuance, in or around the fort. The war was carried on in a desultory way through that summer and autumn, in various parts of New England; Peter Bovee, one of the soldiers of Fort Massachusetts, of whom we shall hear more by and by, was captured near the fort on October 1; on the 19th of the same month, our old acquaintance, John Smead, one of the heroes of the capture of the first fort, and but recently returned from his captivity, was killed near the mouth of Miller's River between Northfield and Montague; and five days later, Oliver Avery, afterwards an officer in Fort Massachusetts, and a distinguished citizen of Charlemont, being one of a party of twelve soldiers passing down the Connecticut from No. 4, was wounded in an attack by Indians, in which two of his companions were killed, one captured, and the rest compelled to retreat to the fort. Major Williams was an ambitious, self-seeking, not over-scrupulous, frontiersman at that time. He had been for ten years a denizen of Stockbridge, ostensibly assisting John Sergeant, who married his daughter, to civilize and christianize the Indians there. His home was on the "Hill," where he possessed a broad estate, and he had, besides, both landed and mercantile interests on the "Plain" and elsewhere in the town. Nothing is more likely than the supposition that the Major soon wearied of the monotony of garrison life, to which he was not accustomed, and withdrew, in the course of the autumn, to more congenial pursuits and opportunities in Stockbridge.

The following letter from Colonel John Stoddard to Governor Shirley, dated "Northhampton, March 1, 1748," without mentioning Major Williams at all, gives glimpses of how things had been at the fort during the preceding winter and up to that date: —

Sir, — I rec^{ed} Your's of 25 Feb.ry with the votes of Assembly. There are fourty able souldiers posted at Fort Massachusetts, and I was in expectation that Capt. Ephraim would have taken the charge of that garrison, but home affairs have hitherto prevented him. We could at first get no better officer than a serg. nt, afterwards I gave a Lieut^{nts} commission to Mr. Elisha Hawley, who is the only officer there at present. And it is vain to expect that suitable persons can be obtained for that service so long as their wages is so contemptible, unless we can find some persons out of business. I think no man amongst us equal (for that service) to Col^{el} William Williams, but he has lately engaged in the Commissary business, and I can't think that he can afford to serve his country without some reasonable pay. Capt. Ephraim Williams must be thought the fittest man that is likely to be obtained. He is accounted a man of courage, has lived at Fort Massachusetts, and is well knowing in that country. It is generally talked that he maintains good government, and I know no man amongst us (except Col. Williams) that men would more cheerfully List under than he.

I know no others hereabout, that are any way equal to the business, that would think it worth the while to leave their own private affairs for the sake of that pittance they expect from the Government. . . .

JOHN STODDARD.

To Gov. SHIRLEY.

The "votes of Assembly" referred to in this letter of Colonel Stoddard are as follows, and are here verbally given from Stoddard's own copy, sent to him from Boston, as the commander of the western frontiers of Massachusetts, for his guidance in the campaign of 1748 : —

Voted, That his excellency, the captain general, [Gov. Shirley] be directed to cause, as soon as may be, so many men to be enlisted, by the encouragement voted by the Court, as, with the soldiers already posted at No. 4, and at Fort Massachusetts, will make the number at each, one hundred effective men (officers included) ; and to give orders to the commanding officers in said garrisons respectively, that a suitable number be constantly employed to intercept the French and Indian enemy in their marches from Wood Creek, and Otter Creek to our frontiers ; to continue in said service until the first day of October next ; and that the commanding officers keep fair journals of their marches from time to time, and return the same to this Court ; and that over and above the bounty above mentioned, and the pay and subsistence of the province, agreeable to the last establishment, there be, and hereby is granted, to be paid to the officers and soldiers, in equal parts, who shall be on any scouts that may kill or capture any enemy Indian, the sum of one hundred pounds ; the scalp of the Indian killed, to be produced to the governor and council as evidence thereof.

Accordingly, Captain Phineas Stevens was again appointed to the command of No. 4, now Charlestown, New Hampshire ; and Captain Humphrey Hobbs was ordered to the same post, to act as second in command. Everything indicates the determination of Massachusetts to make the campaign of 1748 a decisive one ; and to make Fort Massachusetts and No. 4 the principal points of military operation, perhaps to the relative neglect of forts Shirley and Pelham. This may account for the willingness of Captain Ephraim Williams to take the command at Fort Massachusetts, notwithstanding "home affairs have hitherto prevented him." At any rate, he came into the command there not long after Stevens went up the Connecticut ; but unforeseen and important events, both at home and abroad, prevented the expectations of Massachusetts from being realized either in that year, or even in that war. For one thing, the sudden death of Colonel John Stoddard in June, by all odds the most powerful man in the western end of Massachusetts, while attending the General Court at Boston, was a serious loss to the western frontiers in every civil and military aspect. Colonel Israel Williams, of Hatfield, who had acted as Commissary under Colonel Stoddard, was appointed to succeed him in the chief command, and immediately entered upon that difficult duty; and Major Elijah Williams, of Deerfield, was at the same time appointed to the commissary department on the western frontier, under John Wheelwright, Commissary-General at Boston.

For another thing, public affairs were so shaping themselves in Europe during that summer, as to indicate the present weariness of both parties with the war, and a disposition to postpone the final struggle between them for the possession of America, to a date in the still not distant future. The Peace of Aix la Chapelle, signed on the 18th of October, 1748, was a truce rather than a settlement. To the disgust of the New England colonists, who had conquered it by their own (almost) unaided resources in 1745, the fortress of Louisburg was surrendered back to France; and to soothe the ruffled feelings of Massachusetts in the matter, England shipped to that colony, in coin, as a sort of ransom for Louisburg, £138,649 sterling, which Massachusetts used at once to redeem her outstanding bills of credit, at the then ruling rate of eleven of paper to one of silver, and became thereby, for a time, the so-called "silver colony." But before the news of Aix la Chapelle reached the colonies, there was one warlike exploit in connection with No. 4, and another in connection with Fort Massachusetts, which are well worth narrating here; and even after the news of the Treaty had been received, Massachusetts showed her suspicions of its probable brevity, by maintaining reduced garrisons at forts Dummer and Massachusetts, and small posts at Deerfield, Northfield, Pontoosuck, and Stockbridge. By a vote of the General Court, passed Dec. 27, 1723, namely, "To build a blockhouse above Northfield," Lieutenant Timothy Dwight, the same who was concerned twenty years later in building forts Shirley and Pelham, left Northampton with sixteen men, Feb. 3, 1724, to go up the river and begin the works, which came to be called "Fort Dummer," and which was the first settlement of white men within the present state of Vermont.

As to the first exploit, in June, we cannot do better than to quote the vivid account given in Hoyt's "Indian Wars": —

Captain Humphrey Hobbs, with forty men, was ordered from Charlestown, through the woods to fort Shirley in Heath, one of the posts on the Massachusetts line. The march was made without interruption, until Hobbs arrived at what is now Marlboro in Vermont, about twelve miles northwest of Fort Dummer, where he halted on the twenty-sixth of June to give his men an opportunity to refresh themselves. A large body of Indians, under a resolute half-breed chief by the name of Sackett, discovered Hobbs' trail, and made a rapid march to cut him off. Without being apprised of the pursuit of the enemy, Hobbs had circumspectly posted a guard on his trail, and his men were regaling themselves at their packs, on a low piece of ground covered with alders, intermixed with large trees, and watered with a rivulet. The enemy soon came up and drove in the guard, which first apprised Hobbs of their proximity. Without the least knowledge of their strength, he instantly formed for action ; each man selecting his tree for a cover. Confident of victory from their superiority of numbers, the enemy rushed up and received Hobbs' well-directed fire, which cut down a number and checked their impetuosity. Covering themselves also with trees and brush, the action became warm, and a severe conflict ensued between sharpshooters. The two commanders had been known to each other in time of peace, and both bore the character of intrepidity. Sackett, who could speak English, in a stentorian voice frequently called on Hobbs to surrender, and threatened in case of refusal to rush in, and sacrifice his men with the tomahawk. Hobbs in a voice which shook the forest as often returned a defiance, and urged his enemy to put his threats in execution. The action continued with undaunted resolution, and not unfrequently the enemy approached Hobbs' line ; but were driven back to their first position by the fatal fire of his sharp-sighted marksmen ; and thus about four hours elapsed, without either side giving up an inch of their original ground. At length finding Hobbs determined on death or victory, and that his own men had suffered severely, Sackett ordered a retreat, carrying off his dead and wounded, and leaving his antagonist to continue his march without molestation.

This interesting struggle took place on the very upper waters of Green River, which drops into the Deerfield only a mile or two above the point where their united stream finds the Connecticut ; and from this " rivulet " it was not far in a southwest direction to the east branch, and thence on the same line to the west branch, of the North River, so-called, which falls into the Deerfield a few miles above Shelburne Falls ; and near this latter " rivulet " stood Fort Shirley. Fancy the scene at the gate of the fort when these thirty-three or thirty-four victors, for they lost but six men in the fight, greeted their garrison brothers twenty-four hours later ! There was more life, depend on it, in and around that sixty-foot square block-house at that moment, than there ever had been before, or has been since ! They raised Hobb there ! The monotony of garrison life had been terrible on that hilltop for four years ; but now it was broken for once ! The victors boasted that the Indians had been pretty certainly four to one of the English. They related how, often during the fight, they had seen the dead bodies of the Indians they had killed, sliding along the ground, as if by magic, when the comrade nearest to the killed, crawled up under cover of the trees and brush, and fixing a tump-line to the body, dragged it to the rear, after the Indian custom. Captain Ephraim Williams had left a little time before this his previous headquarters at Shirley, to take up the new command at Massachusetts; and so these jubilant soldiers from No. 4, coming we know not on what errand, and going, we know not when and whither, left behind them vivacious traditions of their exploit among the soldiers serving along the Massachusetts line, and left also the for once vivified Fort Shirley to its subsequent insignificance and ultimate desolation.

The other military exploit of the summer, happening on the 2d of August, concerns us much more nearly, inasmuch as it took place at Fort Massachusetts, and affords us also our very first chance to study in action the character of Captain Ephraim Williams, with the added privilege of studying his own careful account of the affair written on the very day it occurred.

It was from August to August two years between the first general attack upon and the consequent surrender of the first Fort Massachusetts in 1746, and the second and only other general assault upon the fort after its rebuilding. The second fort was much the stronger, as we have already seen; but the cannon were undoubtedly mounted so as to sweep the north and west, on which sides the French and Indians would naturally appear, both from the point of their general approach and especially from the lay of the land there, and on which sides in the main the attack of 1746 was made; while the attack of 1748 was very shrewdly planned on the part of the French, was made from the east and south sides, — on which the fort was less formidable, — and came very near being successful on account of what one cannot help regarding as rashness on the part of Captain Williams. We shall let him tell his own story in a moment, but an outline of the main facts will prepare us the better to judge of that and of him.

In the late afternoon of the 1st of August, the garrison (then full) had good reason to believe that an ambush of French and Indians had been laid in the woods that skirted the river on the side next the fort. The place where the old Mohawk trail crossed the Hoosac — a trail still used in these French wars — was due east of the fort about fifty rods. The place is perfectly plain to this day, — a broad shoal in the stream easily fordable, — and still used as a ford whenever anything happens to the highway bridge just a little above. Just a little below the fording-place, the stream, which here falls southerly, turns westerly, and keeps that course at about the same distance to the south of the fort as to the east of it. Dense woods skirted the stream on those sides of the fort. At six o'clock on the morning of the 2d, Captain Williams went out at the gate to observe the motions of the fort dogs, and satisfied himself that the ambush was about forty rods to the east of the fort, between it and the fording-place; and going back into the fort, where all was commotion, a few men were eager to go out and reconnoitre. He refused to let them go because they were too few, and, getting ready fifty men for a sally, he found that four men had gone out without his permission, and were standing their ground against twelve or fifteen who had come out into the open; whereupon, Williams hastily sallied with thirty men, and drove these back into the woods near the fording-place, when fifty Indians in ambuscade on his right (southeast of the fort) rose and gave him a general discharge of their guns and then tried to get in between him and the fort, that is, to cut off his communications; but by a quick movement in retreat, the Captain and his party regained the gate just in time to have it shut in the face of the enemy. Lieutenant Hawley and Ezekiel Wells were wounded (the last mortally) in the sally. A large body of the enemy, probably their whole force, estimated as between two and three hundred Indians and thirty Frenchmen, then came out from their cover and opened fire on the fort, which they continued nearly two hours under a spirited response from the fort. One of the garrison, Samuel Abbot, was killed. The enemy then drew off down the Hoosac by the old trail, carrying their killed and wounded.

The criticism has often been made on Captain Williams that he put everything to hazard by sallying when he was only half prepared for it, before he had ascertained at all the strength of his foe, and without entrusting his command to a subordinate. Had he fallen in the sally, his party would in all likelihood have been cut off, and the loss of the fort might have followed. Courage he had in plenty. Had he a due military caution? Under a proper soldierly discipline, would four men have gone out in the face of the enemy "unbeknown" to their commander? Certain events in the vicinity of Lake George, seven years later, throw back a melancholy light upon these questions, and deepen the impression produced on the mind by the history of war, that *circumspection* is one of the chief virtues of a military officer. The Captain's own letter addressed to Colonel Israel Williams, his immediate military superior, written on the day of the fight, is crowded with interest in every line, makes the best explanation of his conduct possible to be had, unfolds his own personal traits in several lines, and gives precious glimpses of the conditions and circumstances of the time.

FORT MASSACHUSETTS, Aug't 2, 1748.

Sir, — You may remember in my last I informed you y^t our scout to Scatticook was discovered July 23 by the enemy and followed in, and that they had observed the motion of the garrison night and day ever since — and that the guards I had sent to Deerfield to bring stores I feared would be ambusht by an army in yr. return. But to my great joy yesterday at 2 aclock post m. ye 2 Lieuts Severance and Hawley with 40 of the guard arrived safe at the fort. Had not made any discovery of an enemy in their march from Deerfield here. But in less than two hours after their arrival the dogs began to bark, run back on their track some distance — were exceeding fierce. We all then determined the enemy had followed them in. Kept a good look out, last night. This morning at 6 o'clock being out at ye gate and observing the motion of the dogs I determined their was an ambush laid about 40 rods from ye fort, between the fort and where we crost the River to go to Deerfield. Some of the men were desirous to go see if it were so. I told them they should not go out so few. But we would send out 50 men, (supposing we cou'd have given them a welcome reception) (by taking ye advantage of the ground, with the assistance of our cannon). I went into the fort to consult my Lieuts. ; ordered them to git ready. Had no sooner got into the fort but one of the enemy fir'd at our dogs, which I suppose would have seaisd him immediately had he not. Upon that there went of a volley of 12 or 15 guns at Severall men which had got out unbeknown to me, who returned their fire & stood their ground. Finding our scheme was at an end, we made a sally with about 35 men (in order to save those that were out, & must in a few minutes have fallen into their hands). Engaged the enemy about 10 minutes & drove them off the ground. Upon which, an ambush of 50 men about 10 rod off arose on our right wing, & partly between us and ye fort, & discharged a volley upon us, at which we were obliged to retreat. Fought upon a retreat untill we got into the fort, which they attackt immediately upon our shutting the gate. Upon this I ordered the men to their posts, (it being our turn now) & play'd away with our cannon and small arms, for the space of an hour and 3 quarters by the glass. They then retreated by degrees at a considerable distance, & so drew off. We had some fair shots in the fort. As to what number we killed & wounded of the enemy is uncertain. We saw them carry off but two, that was just as the fight was over. But this is certain a great many of the men fired 4, 5, or 6 round apiece in fair sight, & at no greater distance than 15 rods — a great many shots not above 7. On our side we had not one killed on the spot & but 3 wounded, though I fear 2 are mortally so. The men which are wounded are Lieut. Holley,. Sam^{ll} Abbot, Eze^{ll} Wells. Lt. Hawley is shot through the calf of his legg with a large buck shot. Not hurt the bone. Abbot is shot in below his navel. The bullet cut out at his buttock. Wells is shot in at his hipp. The bullet is lodged in his groin. (The reason I write so particular is on account of their friends.) One thing is very remarkable (never to be forgot by us) that we should receive 200 shot at least in the open field, not anything to git behind, and make a retreat of 40 rods, and but 2 men wounded (for Abbot was not out with us).

We have been out some distance [west] in order to judge better of their number. Ye army consisted of at least between two and 300 men, which was chiefly of Indians, though I believe there was 30 French with a Commander in Chief. Some of them talked good English, whether Indians or French I know not.

I conclude by ading one thing more (viz.) ye officers and men behaved like good soldiers. Not one man flincht in the wetting that was perceiv'd. Thus Sr. I have given you an account of the whole affair as near as I can.

Blessed be God we have cause to sing of mercy as well as judgment.

I am Sr. Your Most Obedient
Humble Servant,

EPH. WILLIAMS, JUNR.

MAJ. ISRAEL WILLIAMS, Esqr.

P.S. We have received one gun 2 hatchet & divers other small things. E.W.

At the time when this interesting letter was written from Fort Massachusetts, public affairs in Europe were converging towards the Peace of Aix la Chapelle, which was duly signed on the 18th of October, 1748, and which terminated for a time the war between England and France; but international news travelled but slowly in those days, and colonial hostilities were kept up more or less until the outbreak of the next war, partly on account of ignorance of the Peace, and partly in consequence of colonial dissatisfaction with the retrocession at Aix, of Louisburg to France. The garrisons, however, were gradually reduced, as the true state of things became better known; from Sept. 10, 1748, to December following, there were eighty men at Fort Massachusetts; from December to June, 1749, fifty men; and from June to Dec. 10, 1749, but twenty men. Williams continued in command there during the entire interval, though he was but rarely personally present. Shirley and Pelham soon fell into relative insignificance even as compared with the more western fort; and on July 15, 1749, Lieutenant-Governor Phips (Governor Shirley being then, and for a long time, in England) sent orders to Colonel Israel Williams, "that the forces within ye County of Hampshire be doomed to the number of fifteen men only, including officers, and them to be posted at the Fort called Massachusetts Fort, and to be continued in pay till the first of May next, the rest of the men to be forthwith discharged."

Let us now conclude the chapter designed to contain this first section of the history of Fort Massachusetts, with some account of the later activities of its early hero, Sergeant John Hawks. The Sergeant had returned from his captivity in Canada, as we have already seen, about the same time as the rest of the survivors of the fort-capture, the northward journey, and the prison hardships,

that is to say, in August, 1747.   He did his best to secure from the
General Court what was due to his fellow-soldiers returned, and to
the families of those who returned not, as appears from the following
minute of the House : —

> Aug. 17, 1747.   Voted, That the Treasurer be directed to pay what wages
> there shall be due to the several soldiers arrived from Canada, who were taken
> captive at Fort Massachusetts ; upon the certificate of Sergeant Hawks, that
> they were in the service as entered upon the Muster-Roll.

Hawks was a citizen of Deerfield, and highly esteemed there ;
and so was John Catlin, whose acquaintance we have pleasantly
made as arranging for the early supplies of the fort.   It will be
remembered also, that a part of the force coming to besiege Fort
Massachusetts in 1746, passed on to Deerfield, about forty miles
eastward, killed many persons there, and took young Samuel Allen
captive to Canada.   Though his father was killed in this fight, and
his sister Eunice had her skull fractured by a tomahawk, young
Allen's friends were desirous to recover him, if possible, from
Canada ; and so, in February, 1748, Hawks received a commission
from acting-Governor Phips to go to Canada, and obtain young Allen
in exchange for Pierre Rambout, a French officer recently captured
at Winchester.   Two Deerfield men, Lieutenant Matthew Clesson
and John Taylor, with the French captive, accompanied him.

The four men proceeded up the Connecticut to what is now Charlestown, New Hampshire, then called fort "Number Four."   On the
11th of February the party started for Crown Point, across the
Green Mountains ; the route was through an absolute wilderness,
there not being a solitary English settler within the present limits
of Vermont ; the season was inclement, the ground covered with
snow, the march made on snow-shoes, and all their stinted provisions
transported at their backs.   They camped at night upon the snow
after the Indian manner, sometimes with no covering but the bare
heavens ; and though they bore a flag of truce, they were not without well-founded apprehensions of meeting with hostile savages,
who might not understand nor respect their mission.   Hawks had a
compass, and what is better, a good topographical instinct ; he had
kept his eyes open to good purpose eighteen months before, when
he had gone with the captives down the Hoosac, and up Owl Kill,
and across to a tributary of Pawlet Creek to Whitehall ; there were
rudimentary Indian paths in summer-time through the wild forests
and over the watersheds, but these were mostly without a trace in
the winter snows, and the compass and the course of the streams

were the only guide; at first they followed up the Black River on the ice, as they thought, about twenty-two miles, to the present town of Ludlow; here they left the Black River, and crossing the crest of the Green Mountains in the modern town of Mount Holly, they struck an upper tributary of Otter Creek, which they followed to its junction; thence down Otter Creek, about twenty-four miles as they judged, passing two cataracts; and then they left the Creek, turning sharp to the left, and hit the head of a small stream, which fell into Lake Champlain opposite to Ticonderoga. The route was then continued on the ice to Crown Point, and thence, in the usual course on the lake, to Canada.

As this travelled route across Vermont, thus extemporized by John Hawks with three companions, in 1748, became ten years later the famous military road of General Amherst's campaign against Canada, a part of it laid out by Hawks himself as a result of his earlier experience gained along this way, as John Stark took his soldiers from New Hampshire to Bennington, in 1777, along a part of this very road, and as the present railroad across the Green Mountains, and so onward to Ticonderoga, follows in large part the route taken by Hawks in 1748, both outward and on his return; it may be useful to give here in order the names of the Vermont towns traversed by Hawks and his party, beginning at the mouth of Black River: Springfield, Weathersfield, Cavendish, Ludlow, Mount Holly, Shrewsbury, Clarenton, Rutland, Pittsford, Brandon, Sudbury, and Orwell on Lake Champlain.

When the party arrived at Montreal, Pierre Rambout was delivered over to the French commander there, and inquiries set on foot for Samuel Allen, who was a nephew of John Hawks, and the main object of the whole excursion. After a good deal of search, he was found among the Indians, and had become so much attached to their mode of life in the eighteen months he had lived among them, that he was unwilling even to see his uncle, and showed great aversion to returning home. When brought into Hawks's presence, he acknowledged with reluctance that he knew him, and refused to converse with him in English. Various means were used with him to win him back to his friends and country, all to no purpose, and he was only recovered by threats and force. When the party started to return with the lad in the early part of May, the Indians showed a strong disposition to follow after and rescue him; but they did not, and Samuel Allen lived in Deerfield to old age, and maintained his Indian attachments to the last, being heard often to declare that the Indian mode of life was the happiest.

On the 7th of June of this year, the following message was sent
by His Excellency, the Governor, to the Colonial House of Representatives, by Francis Foxcroft, Esq. (viz.) : —

Sergeant John Hawk having laid before me the Journal of his Travel to and
from Canada, and his Petition to this Court for some Allowance for his Services
and Sufferings in the War, I can not but think he is well entitled to the Favour
of the Court ; and that what Notice you may take of him in these Circumstances
may be of publick Benefit by encouraging others to behave well in the Service
of their Country ; and therefore I would recommend it to you to make some
proper allowance to the said Sergeant Hawk upon his Petition.

This message was signed by William Shirley, and was referred,
together with Hawks's journal and petition, to a committee consisting of Colonel Stoddard, Colonel Storer, and Major Cushing,
who reported, and the House thereupon ordered : —

That the following Allowances be made out of the publick Treasury, viz.
To Sergeant John Hawk, for his services in his Journey to Canada, thirty
pounds.
To Matthew Clesson and John Taylor, for their service, each twelve pounds
ten shillings.
To Sergeant Hawk, on account of his being wounded ; losing his gun and
diverse implements provided for the use of the Garrison [at Fort Massachusetts
two years before] ten pounds twelve shillings and six pence.

We must here take present leave of John Hawks, who was forty
years old when he made this successful and well-appreciated trip to
Canada, and who continued for thirty-six years longer to be a useful
and prominent citizen of Deerfield in both private and public relations.   The present writer copied, some years ago, from a headstone
in the old burying-ground at Deerfield, the following epitaph : —

IN MEMORY OF COL. JOHN HAWKS
WHO DIED JUNE 24, 1784
IN THE 77TH YEAR OF HIS AGE.

Before we take our final farewell of the first Fort Massachusetts,
and of the body of men who served within it and were carried into
captivity from it, some of us may be pleased to look over a list of
soldiers recruited for the fort during that summer of 1746, even up
to August 20, the day the fort surrendered to the French, especially
as nearly all of these enlisted men, although there was no fort for
them to serve in upon the Hoosac Meadow for more than nine
months, are nevertheless found as soldiers in the second fort, and

several of them continued in the service till they were discharged by reason of death, and still others of them continued in it till the close of the war.

Ephraim Williams, Jr., Capt.	Stockbridge.
Elisha Hawley, Lieut.	Northampton.
Daniel Severance, Lieut.	Fawl Town.
Caleb Chapin, Sergt.	Fawl Town.
Elisha Chapin, Sergt.	Springfield.
Nathaniel Eustis, Sergt.	Goare.
Adonijah Atherton, Sergt.	Deerfield.
Ebenezer Gould	Chelmsford.
Charles Parmeter, Sergt.	Sudbury.
Jonathan Stone, Sergt.	Leicester.
Abraham Bass, Sergt.	Worcester.
John Hooker, Gunner	Hatfield.
Richard Treat, Chaplain	Sheffield.
Phineas Nevers, Surg.	Deerfield.
Isaac Wyman, Clark	Woburn.
Ebenezer Reed, Cent.	Simsbury.
Barnard Wilds, Cent.	Rodetown.
Edmond Town, Cent.	Framingham.
John Harriss, Cent.	London.
Thomas Waubun, Cent.	Sherburn.
Micah Harrington, Cent.	Western.
Benjn Gould, Cent.	Woburn.
Esack Johnson, Cent.	Rehoboth.
William Williston, Cent.	Rehoboth.
Charles Wintor, Cent.	Oxbridge.
James Hathon, Cent.	Ireland.
Richard Staudley, Cent.	Loudon.
Abner Robarts, Cent.	Sutton.
Jonathan Barren, Cent.	Westfield.
Timothy Hollen, Cent.	Sutton.
Moses Attucks, Cent.	Leicester.
John Crofford, Cent.	Western.
Daniel Ward, Cent.	Upton.
William Sabin, Cent.	Brookfield.
Portu* Taylor, Cent.	Leicester.
Silas Pratt, Cent.	Shrewsbury.
Charles Coats, Cent.	Deerfield.
Seth Hudson, Cent.	Marlborough.
Samuel Abbot, Cent.	Hardwick.
Ithamar Healey, Cent.	Rehoboth.
John Barnard, Cent.	Waltham.
John Morison, Cent.	Colrain.
John Henry, Cent.	Colrain.
John Martin, Cent.	Sudbury.
Ezekiel Wells, Cent.	Rodetown.

Samuel Wells, Cent. . . . . Rodetown.
George Quaquagid, Cent. . . . . New London.
Thomas George, Cent. . . . . New London.
Ebenezer Graves, Cent. . . . . Deerfield.
John Bush, Cent. . . . . Summers.
John Taylor, Cent. . . . . Long Island.
Conawoca Delow, Cent. . . . . Deerfield.
John Harmon, Cent. . . . . Deerfield.
Nath. Brooks, Cent. . . . . Deerfield.
Stephen Collier, Cent. . . . . Oxford.
Jonathan Ennis, Cent. . . . . Summers.
John Perkins, Cent. . . . . Summers.
Aaron Denio, Cent. . . . . Deerfield.
Benj'n Hastings, Cent. . . . . ———
Benj'n Fassett, Cent. . . . . Westford.
Benj'n Robbarts, Cent. . . . . ———

CHAPTER III.

EPHRAIM WILLIAMS.

" How sleep the brave who sink to rest,
   By all their country's wishes blest !
   When Spring, with dewy fingers cold,
   Returns to deck their hallowed mould,
   She there shall dress a sweeter sod
   Than Fancy's feet have ever trod.

" By fairy hands their knell is rung,
   By forms unseen their dirge is sung ;
   There Honour comes, a pilgrim gray,
   To bless the turf that wraps their clay,
   And Freedom shall awhile repair,
   To dwell a weeping hermit there.''
                              — WILLIAM COLLINS, in 1746.

IT is difficult, from the scant and scattered materials now extant,
to gather a clear and certain notion of the private character and
public services of the founder of the College, and the godfather of
the town ; and it is impossible to do this without characterizing at
some length, and through several generations, a family which had
striking traits of its own, the members of which to an unusual
degree clung together for mutual interests and advancement, and
which intermarried from time to time, with other prominent and
influential families in New England, — the whole giving a sort of
historical setting, and throwing an illumination around the bachelor
life and soldierly career of our founder.   No other character in connection with the town and the College, has anything like the interest
and fascination for posterity that attaches to him ; an interest that
awakens and deepens at every gleam of light which falls upon his
name and story from the pen of others, and especially which is
engendered by the comparatively few words now possible to be
found, falling from his own pen.

Robert Williams sailed from the port of Norwich, England, and
settled in the town of Roxbury, Massachusetts, in or before the

year 1638; because it is a matter of record that he became a freeman of that town in 1638, and it is also a matter of record that his
son Isaac was born in Roxbury, Sept. 1, 1638. The common inference, however, is insecure, that, because he sailed from Norwich, he
was a Lincolnshire man, or even an Englishman. There has been a
strong tradition among his descendants for several generations, and
it was more than once expressed to the writer by the late Mark
Hopkins, who stood in the direct line, that Williams was a Welsh-
man; and leading traits of the man and his successors, of whom
Farmer writes, that he was " the common ancestor of the divines,
civilians, and warriors of this name, who have honored the country
of their birth," have often been appealed to as Welsh. Edward A.
Newton, of Pittsfield, who married into the family, wrote in 1847,
not only in testimony of the family tradition, but also of his own
observation, — "Besides, the prevailing traits of character in all the
family I have known are Welsh." Robert Williams's wife was Elizabeth Stratton. She died July 28, 1674, at the age of eighty. Her
gravestone is still extant in the Roxbury burying-ground. His last
will and testament was drawn up in full in 1685, and probated in
1693, the year of his death. His temporal estate was disposed of
mainly to his three sons, Samuel and Isaac and Stephen; and in
small part also to his brother, Nicolas Williams, and to three
grandchildren.

Robert's son, Isaac, born Sept. 1, 1638, married Martha Park,
daughter of Deacon William Park, of Roxbury. On reaching his
majority he purchased an estate of 500 acres on the Charles River,
in what is now the city of Newton, and settled upon it. Here his
first wife died, having borne him eight children; and, in accordance
with a usage then almost universal in New England, he took a
second wife, Judith Cowper, about 1680, and she bore him four
children, of whom the youngest was Ephraim, born Oct. 21, 1691.
The children of the first wife soon found that they were possessed
of a step-mother, and that she was possessed of a devil. She proved
to be a cold, selfish, grasping woman, having little or no sense of
what was fair and right as towards the older children, — qualities
which she certainly transmitted to her only son, and which seem
to have come down more or less to descendants in several generations. In March, 1704, three years before his death, he conveyed
by deed to his youngest son Ephraim (then twelve years old) " in
consideration of the love, good will, and endeared affection, my
present dwelling-house and barn, with the land and meadow adjacent,
being all the land under my improvement, and all the land on the

east end of my farm, called the ' new field,' and half the land in
the 'old field,' that is, all on the north side of the cart way, now
occupied by my son Eleazar, and all the wood land at the west end
of Eleazar's line, being the whole tract of land between the Fuller
line and the causeway over the meadow, leading to the Island, only
reserving half my said dwelling-house, and fire wood, for my dear
and loving wife Judith, during her life ; also a piece of meadow on
the south side of the land, called ' the Island,' containing about six
acres, and one acre of salt marsh in Cambridge." He also made a
will confirming this conveyance by deed. It is no wonder that
Jackson, in his "History of Newton," employs the following strong
language : —

It seems apparent from the record, that the influence of the second wife prevailed in this transaction, to secure most of the estate to her darling Ephraim ;
that, although he held a Captain's commission, she probably acted in this
instance in that capacity, with the assistance of some lawyer, who was willing
to take fees for helping enact injustice ; which will appear the more glaring when
we know that a large part of the estate came by the grandfather of the first
wife's children, whose portions were thus attempted to be wrested from them.
Of course the first wife's children remonstrated to the judge of Probate against
the will, as being " imperfect and insensible," stating that the lands of their
grandfather, William Park, in Newton, were never so alienated from him as to
cut off their descent to them ; and praying that the whole of those lands of
their grandfather Park, may be divided among the children of the first wife, as
is their right, and as the law directs. If not, they will proceed in their suit
before the Governor and Council.

As we might naturally suppose, the Judge of Probate set aside
this will as invalid, the attempted wrong signally failed of execution, and one year after the father's death the estate was finally settled by mutual agreement among all the children. The father,
Captain Isaac Williams, died Feb. 11, 1707, aged sixty-nine, and was
buried under arms by the company of foot which he had commanded. It is a comfort to be able to add, that the widow Judith
lived among her children and step-children for seventeen years
longer, and had ample leisure, at any rate, for reflection and repent-
ance. Captain Isaac Williams was a weaver by trade, a deacon of
the church, a captain of infantry, many times a selectman of his
town, and representing it in the General Court in 1692 and 1695
and 1697 and 1699 and 1701 and 1705.

Ephraim Williams, born in Newton Oct. 21, 1691, notwithstanding these untoward beginnings, which colored in spirit his entire
life, had a large career before him, and stood in such relations, both
before and after, that history can never pass him by without copi-

ous notice. He married Elisabeth Jackson, April 1, 1713, and took the ancient mansion and 100 acres of the homestead, that is to say, one-fifth of the landed estate; and his mother lived with him for eleven years, until 1724, with "her firewood free," when she died, aged seventy-six. Two sons were the fruit of this marriage with Elisabeth Jackson, namely, Ephraim, Junior, born March 7, 1714, and Thomas, born April 1, 1718. There was a second marriage with Abigail Jones one year after the death of Elisabeth in connection with childbirth. There were seven children by the later marriage, three of whom will figure more or less on the future pages of this book, while our chief interest will concentre, of course, upon the two sons of the first marriage, especially the elder. The father in due time became Justice of the Peace, and was seven times Selectman of Newton. The last year of this service was 1736. The next year he sold out the homestead and seventy acres of land to Jonathan Park, and removed his residence, in 1739, from Newton to Stockbridge, where he played a prominent part almost up to the time of his death in 1754. The occasion of his removal to Stockbridge was peculiar, and worth noting in this place. A successful Mission to the Housatonic Indians had been established in Stockbridge in May, 1736, under the patronage of Governor Belcher and the General Court of Massachusetts, which excited a deep interest throughout this country and the mother country as well. When the town was originally laid out, one-sixtieth part of the land was reserved for the use of Mr. John Sergeant, the missionary, and another sixtieth for Mr. Timothy Woodbridge, the missionary teacher; and four other white families were also to be "accommodated with such part as they should see fit," — a laudable provision for fellowship intended not only for the society of the missionary and the teacher, but also to afford practical models for the education of the natives in agriculture and housekeeping. Joseph Woodbridge from West Springfield, Ephraim Williams from Newton, Josiah Jones from Weston, and Samuel Brown from Spencer, constituted the heads of these four families, all of which became resident by 1739. Ephraim Williams was chosen moderator of the first town-meeting in Stockbridge, convened July 11, 1739. He was soon appointed a judge of the Court of Common Pleas of Hampshire County, in conjunction with Joseph Dwight of Great Barrington, the new county of Berkshire not being organized till 1761, their courts being mainly held in Springfield. In consequence of the long journey to his court by the old military road through Barrington and Westfield, and the personal inconvenience accruing by absence from his family and interruptions to his local business, Williams resigned his judgeship in 1749, and gave himself thereafter with unusual diligence to the buying and selling of lands in the western end of the state, to a mercantile business on what has since been called Stockbridge "Plain," and later to much supervision and actual or attempted control of the Indian Mission in Stockbridge, which led him into a large correspondence and to frequent visits to the so-called commissioners in Boston. His homestead was on the "Hill." His house there was afterwards occupied by Rev. Dr. West, his son-in-law, and the site (in general) is still pointed out by the dwellers on that charming elevation. For reasons which will be again referred to in another connection, Judge Williams, who was also a colonel of the militia, was bitterly opposed to the coming of Jonathan Edwards to Stockbridge as missionary and preacher, as successor to John Sergeant, Williams's son-in-law, who had died, beloved, in 1749; and this hostility to Edwards, sometimes open but more often underhanded, and to the real interests of the Mission and its schools, gradually led to an entire loss of confidence in him on the part of the people of Stockbridge, to a frank exposure of his cold and selfish character by Edwards himself in a letter to the commissioners, and to a consequent sale in 1752 of all his property in Stockbridge to his eldest son Ephraim, and to his abandonment of the town and a lonely life of two years in Deerfield, where in the old burying-ground (not far from the grave of John Hawks) one may still read his epitaph: —

> IN MEMORY OF COL° EPHRAIM WILLIAMS ESQ.
> OF STOCKBRIDGE, WHO DIED AUG⁸ᵀ YE 11ᵀᴴ
> 1754, IN YE 63ᴰ YEAR OF HIS AGE.
>
> Blest be that Hand divine which laid
> My Heart at rest beneath this humble shed.

The following letter from Rev. John Sergeant to Rev. Stephen Williams, never before printed, gives a pleasing idea of the man, — his sincerity and manliness. He did not belong to the goody-goody order of men. He showed his piety by his life-work, and not particularly by his words at any one point of his extraordinarily useful career. The most casual reader cannot fail to be struck with the contrast between this letter and the next one, which is a letter from Ephraim Williams, Sergeant's father-in-law, called out by the death of the latter, and written to the same party as the other. One would say, judging from this letter, that Williams was too pious by at least nine-tenths of the quantum; and by his actions afterwards towards Sergeant's successor, — for whom he bespeaks Stephen

Williams's prayers, — that he was too carnally-minded in at least the same proportion : —

STOCKBRIDGE Feb. 22, 1741½

Revd Sir, I have yours in answer to one by an anonumous writer of Jan.y 14 last. Tis certain a Gentleman of my acquaintance wrote to you about that time, but what business he had to write in answer to something you wrote to me without his name I cannot conceive ; if I find an opportunity I will give him the castigation he deserves. — I conclude you have seen Mr. Woodbridge before now, and that he has informed you, that two of Mr. Hollis's boys are willing to go abroad again — If you can take them or anybody else with you I will send them down immediately upon Mr. Woodbridge's return. I have received ye 5£ Bill you sent by Capt. Williams and will send you another by the first safe opportunity.

I design by the favor of Providence to be at the Association. But am sorry tis appointed to be at so great a distance as Sunderland. —

You find by the Publick Prints, that Count Zenzendorf is come into America, and that Mr. Tennant finds him guilty of holding no errors. For my part I much scruple the account Tennant gives of his doctrines, both because some of them appear too absurd and ridiculous to be held by any man of Learning and Sense, such as I suppose the Count is, and because one of his Missionaries near Hudson's River, with whom I have begun a Correspondence, does not appear to entertain such silly notions — for tho' he writes in a peculiar and enthusiastical manner, yet he seems to have right notions of the manner of Conversion in Adult sinners ; at least he plainly eno' supposes a deep conviction to be the antecedent of it.

To   I am Sir, your obedient
    the Rev^d ·   humble servant
        Mr. STEPHEN WILLIAMS   J. SERGEANT.
        at Springfield
            Longmeadow.

STOCKBRIDGE August 7th 1749.

Rev^d and Dear Sir : Conclude the Surprising and Sorrowful news of mr. Sergeants death, has reacht you before now : a most awful frown of Heaven on us in this place in perticular, and a more Public loss than some may think in Gen^{ll} he was an Example in life, of Hollyness, meekness, Self-denial, patience, diligence, and unweried application of body and mind, in the great and good work, his Lov^d Lord and master, in his Providence, called him too : was faithfull in it till death.   Suddenly called him from his toilsom painfull Labours to (no doubt) receive the wages and (of free grace) reward of a faithfull Stuard of the manifold Grace of God : — The Lord in mercy, Sanctify to us this heavy stroke of his holy hand. Support under it, and teach to proffit savingly by it : and now my kinsman and friend as I am sensible you will be nearly toucht with this stroke : so you will have a fellow feeling Simpathy, and mourn with us that mourn : bear us continually on your mind and heart before a compassionate Saviour, who is the refuge of the distressed, comforter of the afflicted, the God and Husband of the widdow, and father of the fatherless — and as you was Instrumentall in bringing and setling the Gosple of Christ here, desire the Continuance of your advice care concern and utmost endeavor that

we may have a resettlement here with all possible, Convenient speed, and such
a won as shall bring great Glory to God and true peace comfort and enlarge-
ment, to us and his Church hear. in particular ask your prayers for the
Bereaved, desolate family : that God would shine on them for the Lord's sake.
Sir, please to accept mine with my wives, Sincere Love and Respects, to
yourself consort and family : — from your Sorrowfull, afflicted Kinsman ; and
Hum^ble Servant

EPH^M WILLIAMS.

Ephraim Williams, born in Newton March 7, 1714, became the
father of this town and the founder of this College. The present
writer fortunately found among the papers of Israel Williams, of
Hatfield, who was the lifelong friend and near kinsman and co-
executor of the will of Ephraim, the following memorandum, which
sets at rest forever the long-disputed day and year of his birth: —

> Col° Ephraim [Williams]
> Born March 7 — 1714
> new stile - Feb. 24 — old
> Æ. say 41½
> I have the record I. W.

The confusion both as to the month and day as well as to the
year of Ephraim Williams's birth, all of which have been variously
stated, arose not only from the change from Old Style to New Style,
which England formally adopted only in 1752, but also from the
differing dates at which in different countries the New Year was
commenced, England also changing by the same Act of Parliament
in 1752 her old New Year's of the 25th of March to the 1st of January. Ephraim's own mother died when he was four years and one
month old, leaving his uterine brother Thomas scarcely two weeks
old ; and their grandfather, Abraham Jackson, took both these boys
to his own home and brought them up, and gave them a good education for that time. He died in June, 1740, when Ephraim was
twenty-five years old and Thomas twenty-one, and bequeathed the
two grandsons in his will £200, saying in that connection that he
had already spent considerable sums for their bringing up and
education. Abraham Jackson was son of the first settler of Cambridge Village (afterwards called Newton), Deacon John Jackson,
baptized in the parish of Stepney, London, June 6, 1602, and settling in Newton in 1639. Both father and son had a good estate
and bore an excellent reputation, and it goes without saying that the
future prominence of Ephraim and Thomas Williams was due far
more to the care and training of their maternal grandfather than to
any influence exerted upon their lives by their own father. These

simple facts are absolutely all that we know, or ever can know, of the childhood and youth of Ephraim Williams from contemporary testimony. All else, until he assumed command at Fort Shirley in 1745, — as was related in the last chapter, — when he was thirty-one years old, is either an inference or a tradition or the result of inquiries instituted long after his death. For instance, Ebenezer Fitch, the first president of the College, wrote a paper in January, 1802, for the Historical Society of Massachusetts, of which he was then a member, which is entitled, when published in the eighth volume of their Collections, "Historical Sketch of the Life and Character of Colonel Ephraim Williams." This was forty-seven years after his death. It is true there were then living in Williamstown and its vicinity several survivors of the old garrison of Fort Massachusetts as commanded by Williams, particularly Benjamin Simonds and Seth Hudson, and nothing is more likely than that the former of these furnished Fitch with the comparatively few details relating to the personal traits of Williams and to his early life. The following sentences are the most precious in the sketch : —

Colonel Ephraim, the son, for several years in early life, followed the seas ; but, by the persuasion of his father relinquished that business. In his several voyages to Europe, he visited England, Spain, and Holland; acquired graceful manners and a considerable stock of knowledge. In his person, he was large and fleshy. He had a taste for books ; and often lamented his want of a liberal education. His address was easy, and his manner pleasing and conciliating. Affable and facetious, he could make himself agreeable in all companies; and was very generally esteemed, respected, and beloved. His kind and obliging deportment, his generosity and condescension, greatly endeared him to his soldiers. By them he was uncommonly beloved while he lived, and lamented when he died.

The occasion of his " relinquishing " the seas may well have been the death of his grandfather and foster-father, Abraham Jackson, in 1740 ; possibly in some connection with the bequeathment to him, by the latter, of what was then considered a considerable sum of money. It is expressly said by Fitch that he left the seas at the persuasion of his father, who had become established in Stockbridge, in 1739, with every prospect of position and fortune. It is certain that the son became a resident and citizen of Stockbridge not very long after the father died ; for he bought lands there about that time, as the Deed Registries demonstrate ; and it is confidently stated by Dr. S. W. Williams, in his "Williams Family," — a book, by the way, whose otherwise unsupported statements are to be received with great caution, — that he even represented Stockbridge in the

General Court at Boston. This statement of his kinsman, derived undoubtedly by a lively tradition in the family, is strongly confirmed in two special ways, and becomes thereby entirely credible. First, the entire military history of Williams from its very beginning in 1745, to its ending in 1755, shows that he had a remarkable personal influence at Boston, both in the executive offices, and over the General Court, because his requisitions for supplies and recruits were, as a rule, complied with at a speed unusual in such matters with such bodies, his own promotions in military rank were more rapid than was then common, and all his existing correspondence with the officials at Boston indicates, as to both parties, a sense of equality and familiarity uncommon in corresponding letters of the time. Second, this statement that he was early a member of the General Court from Stockbridge, explains, among other things, the following significant sentence from Fitch's sketch : —

His politeness and address procured him a greater influence at the General Court than any other person at that day possessed. He was attentive and polite to all descriptions and classes of men, but especially to gentlemen of dignified characters ; and sought the company and conversation of men of letters.

As the news of the Peace of Aix la Chapelle, such as it was, slowly diffused itself over New England in the fall of 1748, the emphasis of the line of forts connecting the Hoosac with the Deerfield and the Connecticut, and of present military employments as compared with civil, naturally declined in the minds of prominent and ambitious men; and Ephraim Williams, not promoted to be Major until June 7, 1753, although he continued throughout most of the interval till the outbreak of the next war in the nominal command of Fort Massachusetts, yet his subordinates of lower rank were found mostly adequate to the actual command of the now diminishing garrisons, while the able and aspiring Captain naturally looked for openings to some congenial civil employment not incompatible with a general oversight and responsibility of his men in the fort. He continued to report their needs and their numbers at stated times to headquarters. The officers and men referred to him their jealousies and grievances. He made requisitions on the Government for their supplies. He had fifty-six men at Fort Massachusetts from Sept. 11, 1748, to March 11, 1749, and the original muster-roll is still complete and legible in the Secretary's office at Boston. From March 12 to Dec. 11, 1749, he had fifty-seven men under his command there. Seth Hudson, whom we shall learn to know better by and by, was one of the sentinels at 40s. a month.

and also Surgeon at £44 7s. 6d. a year. From Dec. 11, 1749, to June 3, 1750, there were only thirty-one men in that fort; and Hudson's salary as Surgeon was scaled down to £23 13s. 4d. a year. The Captain had 42s. 8d. per month. Isaac Wyman was Clerk at 28s. 2d. a month. Ever after the rebuilding of Fort Massachusetts in 1747, the line of forts to the eastward were under a separate command mostly, if not wholly; and Captain Israel Williams, of Hatfield, had fifty-three men at Shirley and Pelham and Coleraine, from Nov. 1, 1748, till April 3, 1749, having dismissed thirty-five men at the first-mentioned date. Lieutenant William Lyman, of Northampton, had only twenty-six men from June, 1749, to January, 1750, in the whole line from Shirley to Northfield, inclusive, mentioning in his return that a large part of the 100 men ordered thither by the General Court had been dismissed.

But his principal residence now for several years was at Hatfield, on the Connecticut. There resided Israel Williams, his half-cousin, five years older than himself, who had just become Colonel of the Hampshire Militia, in succession to Colonel John Stoddard, of Northampton, a very able and ambitious man, who afterwards became " ye monarch of Hampshire." Hatfield was rather the big hive of the Williams family at that time, on account of the settlement there as a minister of the Gospel, in 1685, of Rev. William Williams, who was graduated at Harvard College two years before, who died there in 1741 in the fifty-sixth year of his ministry, and who left distinguished sons, leaving in turn a distinguished posterity. Dr. Chauncy wrote of him in 1768, as follows: " I have read all of Mr. Stoddard's writings [Rev. Solomon, of Northampton], but have never been able to see in them that strength of genius some have attributed to him. Mr. Williams, of Hatfield, his son-in-law, I believe to have been the greater man, and I am ready to think greater than any of his own sons, though they were all men of more than common understanding. Rector Williams and Solomon, I give the preference to the other sons."

Stockbridge, with its Indian population, its dozen or so English families, and its half-cleared forests, was no such place for a rising young man of power as populous Hatfield, with its powerful family influences, closely connected as it was, by intermarriage and otherwise with Deerfield and Northampton above, and Springfield and Weathersfield below, on the river. Here were developing the men, like Joseph Hawley, of Northampton, and Israel Williams, of Hatfield, and John Worthington, of Springfield, who, not long afterwards, used to be denominated in Boston as "the river-gods." At

Deerfield dwelt then and ever after, Ephraim's only own brother, Dr. Thomas Williams, a notable physician; and the former appears to have alternated his bachelor home for some years between that of his cousin in Hatfield, and that of his brother in Deerfield. Another very prominent man in Hatfield was Oliver Partridge (Yale College, 1730), then High Sheriff of the county of Hampshire, who soon appointed him Deputy Sheriff. In this capacity, the principal courts of the county being then held in Springfield, Williams came into terms of great intimacy and friendship with Colonel John Worthington, who later became co-executor of his will. Indeed, his position and relations were such, his genial and facetious and aspiring qualities were such, that he easily found entrance and welcome in the best families of the entire region; including those of Major Elijah Williams, of Deerfield, then Commissary in the western department under John Wheelwright, of Boston, Commissary-General; this Élijah Williams was son to Rev. John Williams, of Deerfield, the famous "Redeemed Captive" of 1704, who was half-brother to Ephraim, Senior, so that the Commissary was half-cousin to Ephraim, Junior; and of Colonel John Stoddard, of Northampton, Colonel Oliver Partridge, of Hatfield, and Colonel John Chester (Harvard College, 1722), of Weathersfield.

Israel Williams stood in his generation in such constant and influential relations to causes and effects in the western end of Massachusetts, and in particular to his half-cousin, the founder of our town and College, being his chief counsellor while the latter lived, and the main administrator of his property afterwards, that it seems needful to our general purpose to give some details of the course of his life. He was born in Hatfield, Nov. 30, 1709. His mother was a daughter of Rev. Solomon Stoddard, for fifty-six years pastor of the church at Northampton; he was graduated at Harvard College in 1729; and he married Sarah Chester, of a Weathersfield family no less distinguished than his own. His father had been in the ministry at Hatfield for fifty-six years when he died in 1741, as his grandfather had been at Northampton the same length of time when he died in 1729. He was own cousin of Jonathan Edwards, whose mother was also a Stoddard, of Northampton. He was the only son of his father that remained in Hatfield as a home, and he naturally entered into his father's great influence there, which he came to supplement by military and organizing abilities of a high order. His brother, Solomon, D.D., became a notable clergyman and author at Lebanon, Connecticut, and was the father of William Williams, a signer of the Declaration of Independence. Another brother was Rev. William Williams, of Weston, Massachusetts, a graduate of Harvard in 1705, who married his step-mother's eldest sister, Miss Stoddard, of Northampton, before his father connected himself with that celebrated family of sisters. He was the father of Colonel William Williams, of Pittsfield, and of Anna, wife of Colonel Oliver Partridge, and of Esther, wife of Ephraim's own brother Thomas. Still another brother of Israel was Rev. Elisha Williams (Harvard College, 1711), who married Eunice Chester, of the Weathersfield family, and became President of Yale College in 1726, an office which he filled acceptably till 1739. Israel's own sister, Dorothy, married Rev. Jonathan Ashley (Yale College, 1730), long the minister of Deerfield, very intimate with our founder till the latter's death in 1755, and who lived long enough to manifest offensively to his own people and to all his neighbors up and down the valleys of the Deerfield and the Connecticut, those pronounced loyalist (Tory) views, which were characteristic of the whole Williams family living at the outbreak of the Revolution.

As Israel Williams was own nephew of Colonel John Stoddard, as he early showed signs of good military capacity, and as he was five years older than his half-cousin Ephraim, it was natural and proper that the former was pushed forward by the Colonel, as the French War progressed, more prominently than the latter. During the summer and autumn of 1748, while Ephraim was in command at Fort Massachusetts as Captain, Israel, with the same rank and with headquarters at Fort Shirley, held command over the entire line of forts to the eastward. He makes return in November of that year, of eighty-nine officers and men under his immediate orders. His pay as Captain was 80s. per month. John Catlin, his lieutenant, took 60s. 9d. per month. The sentinels had 40s. a month. At that date there were at Fort Shirley, thirty-six men; at Pelham, thirty men; at Morrison's Fort in Coleraine, twenty-five men; at Coleraine South Fort, sixteen; and at New Hampton and Blandford, twelve men. During the same summer and autumn, Captain William Williams, who was now Commissary at Hatfield, commanded also a company of fifty-seven men, enlisted for "the line of forts" or other service. In October, he was promoted to be Colonel.

It fell to Israel Williams, on the death of John Stoddard in 1748, to become Colonel of the militia of Hampshire County, then covering the entire western end of the state. In that capacity, he had the direct oversight of all the forts and military operations within the county; he made the general plan, on the basis of which the campaigns of the next French war were conducted in the west; his correspondence with the authorities at Boston and elsewhere was very voluminous, much of which is still extant among his papers preserved; the reports from the forts, and from the scouts, and from secret agents or spies, fell primarily into his hands; he was often called to Boston in council; he was looked up to everywhere, much as John Stoddard had been looked up to, but he had a personal vanity and a lofty pride, and a sort of scorn for men of low degree, to which Stoddard was a stranger. Civil emoluments accompanied and especially followed these military preferments, and ministered, perhaps, even more to his already profound sense of his personal and political importance. He became a member of the Governor's Council in Boston, and a judge of the Court of Common Pleas. Francis Bernard, who succeeded Thomas Pownal as Governor of Massachusetts in 1760, and held the office for nine years, came into great intimacy and mutual influence with Williams, which lasted after his recall to England and advancement to a baronetcy, as is seen in part by Williams's stiff loyalism, and his appointment in 1774 among the *mandamus* councillors, although he never took the oath. There is a long and most interesting letter in Volume XX. of the "Proceedings of the Massachusetts Historical Society," pages 46–48, from Oxenbridge Thacher, of Boston, to Benjamin Prat, Chief Justice of New York, and a former member of the bar of Massachusetts, written in 1762, which graphically depicts, without naming him, the traits and one of the characteristic schemes of Israel Williams : —

What occasions ye most gaping of late (we are not awake enough to speak), is a charter for a new college in ye county of Hampshire. The monarch of ye county, (you know it always was under regal governmᵗ) took great offence at his son's being placed some years ago something lower in a class at our college than befitted ye son of a King. He therefore, and his privy council came down ye last Sessions prepared with a petition to incorporate a college in yᵗ county, which they modestly said was all they desired. They wanted no money from ye government to support it. A bill passed in ye house for this purpose but was rejected at ye board. In ye situation the governor [Bernard] granted a charter himself by his own single authority. This alarmed both houses; they chose a committee to wait on ye governor, to desire he would recall ye charter. At last ye overseers of our college waked enough to have a meeting on ye subject. There it was yᵗ your old friend Summa [Thomas Hutchinson, then Chief Justice and Lt. Gov. — very intimate with Williams] was put to his trumps. You know he is ye idol of ye Clergy : you know also he is in strict alliance, offensive and defensive, with the monarch of Hampshire and his dominions. The only card he had to play was to delay ye question. This he played pretty dexterously. He magnified ye abilities and ye interest of ye Hampshire members, intimated that it would be dangerous to offend them, suggested that measures should be taken to quiet them and persuade them to give up.   In vain for at three o'clock (to which time from ten o'clock ye governm^t and Summa had prolonged ye debate) it was voted to choose a committee to prepare reasons against ye s^d college.   This was accordingly done, ye remonstrance prepared and preferred to ye governor, and he has given a gracious answer promising to vacate ye charter, and I believe he will keep his word; for your honest old friend Lyman [Gen. Phineas Lyman of Northampton] assures us y^t ye project is as much disliked in Hampshire as it is here.   Thus ye remonstranses of his proper subjects, may reach ye ear of the monarch, and he may give leave to ye gov^r to keep his word.

It would not be fair to "the monarch" to conclude from this pungent extract from Thacher's letter that he had no other motive in attempting to establish "Queen's College" on the Connecticut than to spite Harvard for an alleged ill-treatment of his son and himself "some years ago."   The facts were these: John Williams, the son referred to, was graduated at Harvard in 1751, and his name is placed in the Catalogue fourteenth in a class of thirty-five.   As at that time disposed, college names were not placed alphabetically as now, but according to the social rank of the members, as that was understood by the government of the College.   The Colonel was undoubtedly offended by the relatively low estimation in which his own pretensions were held at Cambridge, and one evidence of this is, that his next son, William, was graduated at Yale College in 1754, and was there placed fourth in a class of sixteen.   It is only a decent charity to suppose that Williams and the rest of the "river-gods" had a natural feeling of locality and a genuine conviction that the river was by this time entitled to a college of its own, all its leading towns from Northampton to Weathersfield having been established for more than a century; and Professor Tyler, in his "History of Amherst College," refers with satisfaction to this earliest effort to found a college in that neighborhood as a premonition and sort of justification of the sixty-years-later foundation of Amherst in the same stretch of the valley.   By whatever motives actuated, Williams's manuscript papers show his deep interest in the proposed Queen's College.   Among them is the draft of a charter issued by Governor Bernard, incorporating "Israel Williams, John Worthington, Oliver Partridge, Elijah Williams, Josiah Dwight, and Joseph Hawley, Esquires, and the Revs. Stephen Williams, David Parsons, Jonathan Ashley, Timothy Woodbridge, Samuel Hopkins, and John Hooker, ministers of the Gospel," as President and Fellows of Queen's College in New England.   The names designated in this act of incorporation demonstrate again for the hundredth time the thorough alliance in New England during the eighteenth century between bar and bench and clergy in all public action, especially in defence of the old-time methods in Church and State and Education. There was a ruling class in New England just as much as in Old England, and their grip was just as firm. In Massachusetts, Israel Williams stood at the head of the consolidation in the west as Thomas Hutchinson did on the seaboard.

There is a draft of a letter among his extant papers that also serves to exhibit Williams's motives in starting the new College in a better light than that thrown on them by Oxenbridge Thacher. It is directed to William Smith, of New York, who afterwards became Chief Justice of that Province, as did also Benjamin Prat, the correspondent of Thacher. From this letter it appears that Williams's first design was to obtain a charter from the King, — that is, through Governor Bernard, as representing the royal authority; but on learning Smith's legal opinion, that a charter through Bernard, under the Massachusetts Constitution, would not be valid, he determined to reach his end in the most open way possible, namely, by means of a petition to the whole Legislature, of which at that time the Governor and his Council formed the Upper House. Williams proceeds to say : —

Accordingly one was prepared. When I went to court, soon after, I waited upon Governor Bernard and let him know our design, your opinion, and that Mr. Gridley was of the same. He freely and fully went into the consideration of the affair [the founding of the new college], and expressed himself entirely pleased with the proposal; but as to the charter he was of opinion he had a right to give one as the King's representative, and that it was a royal right reserved in the crown which by the charter [to the Province] the King had never given away.

Accordingly, Bernard issued the charter for the College in due form and in the King's name, much as about the same time John Wentworth, of New Hampshire, chartered Dartmouth College and Jonathan Belcher the College of New Jersey. When Bernard yielded, however, to the remonstrances of Harvard, and invalidated the charter for the present, Williams was naturally much displeased, and went on in this letter to Smith to inveigh against what he regarded as the timidity of the Governor, who tried, nevertheless, to placate him by desiring the corporators to take a copy of the charter and to organize the body so far as to be in readiness to act in case the charter might receive the necessary future confirmation. The charter permitted the College to be in Northampton, Hatfield, or Hadley. There were two meetings of the corporators accordingly, — one in March, 1762, at the house of Rev. John Hooker in

Northampton, and one in May following at the house of Rev. Samuel Hopkins in Hadley. The project went so far as the erection of a building in Hatfield, or at least the designation of a building already erected, as "Queen's College," and students were certainly in preparation for entering it. Long into the present century an old gambrel-roofed schoolhouse stood on Hatfield Street, and persons were still living there in 1880 who had not only seen it but had heard it called "Queen's College." The present writer called about that date upon an old man there, born and bred in Hatfield, then about ninety years old but in good possession of mind and memory, who assured his incredulous caller with emphasis, — "There used to be a college here, and I have seen it myself!" The same narrator related to the same listener traditional stories of the haughtiness of Israel Williams and of his habitual contempt for the common people, and ending with the usual futile threat of those times on the part of one thus maltreated, — "I'll shoot him in battle in the next war, if there ever comes another war!" A clear tradition preserves the site of the Colonel's house on Hatfield Street, but the place of "Queen's College" — short-lived if not stillborn — can no longer be identified. The loyalism of Williams and of his special friends, also, intensified as the Revolution drew on and progressed; and in Sabine's "Loyalists" occurs the following passage relating to him : —

Though old and infirm, he was visited by a mob at night, taken from his house, carried several miles, and put into a room with a fire, when the doors and the top of the chimney were closed, and he was kept several hours in the smoke. On being released he was compelled to sign a paper dictated by his tormentors. The circumstance did not escape Trumbull's caustic pen, and he asks in "McFingal," —

> " Have you made Murray look less big,
> Or smoked old Williams to a Whig ? "

Colonel Williams died in 1788, in consequence of a fall down his own cellar-stairs. His age was seventy-nine. He outlived his cousin and intimate friend — the subject of this chapter — for thirty-three years. He served his active generation with more ability, more fidelity, more conspicuity, than did that other. His name, nevertheless, is growing dimmer and dimmer all the while in the minds of men; the name of that other is growing brighter and brighter as the decades and half-centuries go by. What is the reason for this ? It all turns on one act of that other, done in the last summer of his life, done as an alternative to another that hovered and almost prevailed over him, an act indeed carried into execution by the then foremost but now hindmost man, — an act of thought-fulness and of provision for the poor and for the future!

We return now to Captain Ephraim Williams in his connection with military affairs. Although he lived but little at Fort Massa-chusetts in the years 1749, 1750, and 1751, that was all the while his headquarters. He controlled as Commander the ongoing of things; he sent in from time to time the muster-rolls of the men at this post to the provincial government at Boston, and took oath to their general correctness; he ordered supplies for the sick soldiers under his care directly, and indicated to Elijah Williams at Deerfield, the Commissary, the present and prospective needs of common supplies; and while his chief residence during these years was on the Connecticut River, he was often in Boston on military and other business, and often at the forts, not only on his way back and forth but also as the agent of the Government in subsisting enlisted men, and certain French Protestants also, who had become a charge to the authorities at Boston.

June 3, 1750, Paid to Eph. Williams for subsisting 11 men at Shirley and Pelham £16., 5., 10. Ditto ye remainder at Fort Massachusetts, £198., 0., 8.

FORT MASSACHUSETTS (for the sick)

30 gallons of Rum	£14., 5
50 Butter	3., 15
100 lbs Sugar	6..
60 candles	4., 10
100 lbs Rice	3..
5 Bush. Indian Meal	2..
2 Bush. Oat Meal	1., 10
4 Wood Axes	3..
1 Grindstone	2., 10

EPH. WILLIAMS, Capt. (own hand).

Many such bills as these are scattered through the records, indi-cating a large activity on the part of the officer, and unusual confi-dence in his integrity on the part of the authorities above him.

A MUSTER ROLL OF THE COMPANY IN HIS MAJESTY'S SERVICE UNDER THE COMMAND OF EPHRAIM WILLIAMS, JUNR. AT FORT MASSACHUSETTS, FROM MARCH TO DEC. 11, 1749. [Sworn to Dec. 11, 1749]

Ephraim Williams, Capt.	Jonathan Stone, Corp!
Elisha Hawley, Lieut.	Abraham Bass, Corp!
Caleb Chapin, Sergt.	Isaac Wyman, Clerk.
Nathaniel Eustis, Sergt.	John Hooker, Gunr.
Charles Parmetor, Corp!	Elisha Chapin, Serjᵉ

Phineas Nevers, Surge.

Seth Hudson, Surge.

Seth Hudson, Cent.

Oliver Avery, Cent.

Lemuel Avery, Cent.

Moses Peter Attucks, Cent.

Jonathan Barron, Cent.

John Bush, Cent.

Nathan¹ Brooks, Cent.

John Croffard [Crawford], Cent.

Charles Coats, Cent.

William Sanderson, Cent.

Charles Denio, Cent.

Jonathan Evans, Cent.

Ebenezer Graves, Cent.

Micah Harrington, Cent.

James Hathorn, Cent.

Timothy Holton, Cent.

Ithemer Healy, Cent.

John Henry, Cent.

John Harmon, Cent.

Benja. Hastings, Cent.

John Morrison, Cent.

Silas Pratt, Cent.

Benja. Roberts, Cent.

Abner Roberts, Cent.

Ebenezer Reed, Cent.

James Smith, Cent.

Edmond Town, Cent.

Fortunatus Taylor, Cent.

John Taylor, Cent.

Daniel Ward, Cent.

William Williston, Cent.

Samuel Wells, Cent.

Ezekiel Wells, Cent.

Simeon Wells, Cent.

Samuel Calhoun, Cent.

Daniel Graves, Cent.

Nath. Harvey, Cent.

Barnard Wiles [Willis], Cent.

Samuel Taylor, Cent.

Lem! Avery, Cent.

Sam! Calhoun, Cent.

Cesar, Negro, Cent.

Zacha. Hicks, Cent.

Benja. Tilton, Cent.

Moses Tinney, Cent.

Here are fifty-seven names; but one of them, Seth Hudson, is repeated, and two others, Lemuel Avery and Samuel Calhoun, *seem* to be repeated. Seth Hudson, afterwards a prominent settler in Williamstown, was "Centinel" at 40s. per month, and at the same time "Surgeon" at £44 7s. 6d. per annum. Silas Pratt was from Worcester, Micah Harrington from Upton, Edmond Town from Framingham, — all later settlers in Williamstown. Calhoun, Willis, Morrison, Denio, and Crawford were certainly Scotch-Irish, and probably two or three more. Charles Coats, who could not write his own name, was a trusty scout, who had been in the service from the opening of the war. "March 3, 1746. Received of Maj. Is. Williams ten pairs Indian Shoes, which I promise to deliver to Capt. Elijah Williams of Deerfield. Charles _{his mark} Coats." A severe sickness had prevailed at Fort Massachusetts during the autumn of 1748, which may go far to account for the presence of two surgeons there during the next year, as by the above muster-roll. The roll sworn to Nov. 3, 1748, contains the names of but forty-three men, while another roll, made out some months earlier, holds the names of eighty-four men. There lies now before the writer a copy of a list of thirty "dismissed men," sworn to April 10, 1749.

Whether these were sick men, dismissed on account of inability the previous autumn, or were men dismissed on account of the news of the Peace of Aix la Chapelle, cannot now be certainly known. It is certain, however, that Lieutenant Daniel Severance, of Falltown, and Corporal Ebenezer Gould, of Chelmsford, were already dead when this list was sworn to at Boston. Two Indians are among the number dismissed, — Thomas Waubun and George Quahquaquid.

A previous roll of the garrison at Fort Massachusetts, extending from December, 1747, to March, 1748, covering time before Captain Williams had reassumed the command at that end of the line, is interesting as giving the *residence* of the men so far as was known.

A MUSTER ROLL OF THE COMPANY IN HIS MAJESTY'S SERVICE UNDER THE COMMAND OF ELISHA HAWLEY.

Elisha Hawley, Lieut.	Northampton.
John Foster, Sergt.	Deerfield.
Ebenezer Gould, Corp'l	Chelmsford.
Oliver Avery, Cent.	Deerfield.
Oliver Barret, Cent.	Dracut.
Jesse Heath, Cent.	Woodstock.
Jonathan Barron, Cent.	———
Abraham Bass, Cent.	Worcester.
Thomas Hooper, Cent.	Mendon.
Daniel Ward, Cent.	Shrewsbury.
Zachariah Hicks, Cent.	Sutton.
Richard Burt, Cent.	Kingston.
John Crooks, Cent.	Marlborough.
Richard Staudley, Cent.	Woburn.
Nathaniel Smith, Cent.	Marlborough.
David Thomson, Cent.	Bilerica.
Daniel Kinney, Cent.	Sutton.
Thomas Blodget, Cent.	Chelmsford.
Isaac Wyman, Cent.	Woburn.
Nathaniel Hunt, Cent.	Dracut.
Eliseus Barron, Cent.	Dracut.
Joseph Wilson, Cent.	Bilerica.
John Cory, Cent.	———
James Smith, Cent.	Leicester.
Jonathan Dutton, Cent.	Bilerica.
Joseph Washburn, Cent.	———
Edward Brooks, Cent.	Western.
Fortunatus Taylor, Cent.	Shrewsbury.
Amasa Cranson, Cent.	Shrewsbury
Benjamin Fairbank, Cent.	Dudley.
William McClallan, Cent.	Worcester.
Silas Prat, Cent.	Worcester.

Abner Robards, Cent. . . . . ——
Moses Peter Attucks, Cent. . . . . Leicester.
John Crafford, Cent. . . . . Worcester.
Samuel Bowman, Cent. . . . . Worcester.
Abraham Peck, Cent. . . . . ——
Hezekiah Wood, Cent. . . . . ——
William Sabins, Cent. . . . . Brookfield.
John Morse, Cent. . . . . Woodstock.
Cesar Negro, Cent. . . . . ——
Thomas Walkup, Cent. . . . . ——
Joseph Bates, Cent. . . . . Dracut.

Cesar Negro was a servant or slave of Hezekiah Ward, and doubtless did military service in behalf of his master; Moses Peter Attucks stood in a similar relation to John White: the names of the masters stand in the margin of the muster-rolls over against the names of the servants. It will be remembered that slavery was not legally abolished in Massachusetts till 1780, and then only indirectly, as the result of phrases in the state constitution of that year.

The next roll in the order of time extends from Dec. 11, 1749, to June 3, 1750, and gives twenty-one men to Fort Massachusetts, five expressly to Fort Shirley, and five, apparently, to Fort Pelham, although the official indorsement mentions only "Eph^m Williams and Co. at Fort Massachusetts." As most of these men gained a certain prominence afterwards in civil life, and some of them even distinction, no one will begrudge the space here taken up by their names.

Ephraim Williams, Captain
Elisha Hawley, Lieut.
Isaac Wyman, Clerk.
Seth Hutson, Surgeon.
Oliver Avery, Cent.[1]
Samuel Avery, Cent.[1]
Abraham Bass, Cent.[1]
Ebenezer Graves, Cent.[1]
John Hooker, Cent.[1]
Micah Harrington, Cent.[1]
John Harmon, Cent.[1]
Silas Pratt, Cent.[1]

Abner Robbarts, Cent.[1]
Ebenezer Reed, Cent.[1]
John Taylor, Cent.[1]
William Williston, Cent.[1]
Samuel Taylor, Cent.[1]
Samuel Calhoun, Cent.[1]
Nathaniel Harvey, Cent.[1]
Ezekiel Foster, Cent.[1]
Moses Tenny, Cent.[1]

[Foster was "omitted in my last"
Tenny do. "on Col. Williams Roll"]

William Lyman, Lieut.
Peter Bovee, Cent.
Gershom Hawks, Cent.
John Pannell, Cent.
Samuel Stebbins, Cent.
} Fort Shirley

Joseph Allen, Sergant.
Joshua Hawks, Cent.
Joshua Wells, Cent.
Daniel Donnilson, Cent.
William Stevens, Cent.
} [Fort Pelham]

The next roll in order of time covers but seventeen men, and extends from June 4, 1750, to Jan. 13, 1751.

In connection with this roll, Williams sends in a bill for sundries necessary at Fort Massachusetts. The bill, the note appended, as well as the signature, are in Williams's own handwriting.

1 Flagg and haliards 5 yards Fly
4 Water Buckits
1 Box Candles   30/
4 Wood Axes

SUNDRIES FOR THE SICK

1 Firkin Butter   20/
½ bl. N. E. Rum
1 Peck Oatmeal
½ lb Rice ½ Sugar

These certifies yo' honours y^t none of the above articles have been supplyed Capt. Williams since Dec. 1749, and has had noe Flagg and Halliards for Massachusetts Fort since it has been built.

EPH. WILLIAMS JR.

Peace was thinning out the ranks of the garrisons; but there were numbers of men in Western Massachusetts and elsewhere, and Israel Williams was among them, who already clearly perceived that the "Peace" was to be only a "Truce," and that preparations were only in order for what was felt would be a decisive struggle between England and France for the possession of North America. It was planned during this winter to build a "mount" upon one of the corners of the Fort Massachusetts, which should be forty feet high, and also to strengthen the fort on the outside by a strong line of high pickets, similar to those that constituted the fort called "Pelham" to the eastward; both of which plans were accomplished in the sequel by the agency of Ephraim Williams, as we shall shortly see. Israel Williams was already studying on that detailed plan of offence and defence for the next war, which he communicated in form, not very long afterwards, to his superiors at Boston, parts of which were ultimately adopted by Governor Shirley and the officers summoned into council with him. Forts Shirley and Pelham, upon their distant hilltops, had proven themselves to be nearly useless in the late war, and Colonel Williams advised their abandonment, and the fortifying of Fort Massachusetts, and the using of the Hoosac Route as the way of offence against the French. In the meantime it is rather pleasant to run over the names of the men who spent that long winter on the Hoosac Meadow, Deerfield being their nearest place of supplies, meditating, as men must under those circumstances, "What shall be on the morrow?"

Ephraim Williams, Capt.
Elisha Hawley, Lieut.
Oliver Avery, Cent.
Lemuel Avery, Cent.
Abraham Bass, Cent.
Samuel Calhoun, Cent.
Ezekiel Foster, Cent.
Ebenezer Graves, Cent.
Micah Harrington, Cent.

Nathaniel Harvey, Cent.
Seth Hudson, Cent.
Elisha Chapin, Cent.
Abner Roberts, Cent.
Samuel Taylor, Cent.
Isaac Wyman, Cent.
Paul Langdon, Cent.
Aaron Vanhorn } omitted on my Roll end-ing 1746. } Cent. .

BOSTON, Jan. 13, 1751.   Errors Excepted.
Per Ephraim Williams.

The blacksmith work for the fort itself and also for the soldiers garrisoned there was done in all these years by Seth Pomroy, of Northampton.   There is an extant bill, written out as follows in the blacksmith's own hand, and sent in a letter sealed and addressed to

MAJ. EPHRAIM
WILLIAMS att
Hatfield.

CAPT. EPHRAIM WILLIAMS DR. TO S. POMROY

July 1750 { To mending your Soldiers guns at sundry times in lawfull money }	0	14	0
July 1751 { More to mending guns and Locks at sundry times }	0	10	4
	£1	4	4

Seth Pomroy.

To 38 Indian Shoes for the Scouts at Fort Massachusetts, & the line of forts per order	8	4	8
To one deer skin to mend the Shoes		8	10
Law¹ money	£8	13	6

Sworn to before Elijah Williams   Israel Williams
          Just. Pacis   Ephraim Williams.

Bill allowed to Eph. Williams for furnishing provisions at Hatfield, Deerfield, Charlemont and Fort Massachusetts to French Protestants, £6 0 0.

PROV. MASSACHUSETTS TO EPHRAIM WILLIAMS DR.

To 72 Butter @ 1/ 2d.	£4	4	·
85 Sugar @ 1/ 10d.	7	15	10
10 galls Rum ye Doctor expended in dressing the wounded at 10/		5	
New Tenor	£16	19	10

Nov. 4, 1748

Eph. Williams Jr.

1751   PROV. MASSACHUSETTS TO EPH^{M.} WILLIAMS DR.

June   To Erecting a Watch Box 40 Foot high and 8 Foot square
          To cash p^d a Carpenter for 10 days Work @ 4/   £2   0   0
          To cash p^d 2 Labourers 20 days @ 2/   2   0   0
          To 15 sacks   @ 3/   2   5   0
          To cash p^d Freight of 3:4 pounders with Carriages from
              Boston to New York   2   0   0
          To ditto from New York to Albany   1   10   0
          To ditto from Albany to the Landing place at Van-
              derhidens [now Troy]   0   9   0
          To Transporting them 36 Miles to Fort Massachusetts   2   0   6
                                        Lawfull Money   £12   4   6

     Exa. & Alow'd by the
            Com^{tee} J. Osborne
        Boston January 8th 1752
     Suffolk ss. January 20th 1752
        Sworne to before the Committee
           Jacob Wendell Just. Pacis
                                              Errors Excepted
                                              p Eph. Williams junr.

              PROVINCE MASSA^{TTS} TO EPHRAIM WILLIAMS DR.

   1751   To sundry Goods for the Mohawks delivered To Col^o Joseph Pinchon
   Augt 21   Capt. Josiah Dwight and Capt. John Ashley the General Courts
            Committee.   Viz^t
              To 4 Ells Garlick a 3/ 4^d ½ per Ell   13   6
              To 2 yards of Callico a   4   3½
              To 1 Piece Callico   3   7   6
                                           L. M.   £4   5   3½
        Alow'd by the Com^{tee}
              J. Osborne.

              PROVINCE MASS^A TO EPHRAIM WILLIAMS DR.

   1751   To Cash paid Major Pomroy for mending the Soldiers
   July   Guns posted at Fort Massach^{tts}   £1
   1754   To an Express sent by Col^o Israel Williams to
   Sept. 17th   Goven^r Shirley vizt
            4 days Travel & Expenses a 6/   1   4   0
            To my Time in Wating upon His Excell^y 5 days a 3/   15   0
            To my Expences 5 days a 4/   1   0   0
            To Cash paid Horse Hire for the above Express   12   0
                                                       £4   15   4

                        Boston November 16, 1754
     Alow'd by the Com^{tee}   Errors Excepted
              J. Osborne   Eph. Williams.

1751   PROVINCE OF YE MASSACHUSETTS BAY DR.
         To ANTHONY GLAZIER

To going to Fort Massachusetts & back at 20s old Ten*r*
    Provisions per day for 28 days   28   0
                        Supra C*r*
By 12 days Provisions of ye Comiss*rs* at 20/

                        Old Ten*r* per day   12   0   0

                        Due in Old Tener   16   0   0

                        Balance L M   £2   2   8
    Alow'd by the Com*tee* J. Osborne
        going Interpreter w*th* ye Palatines.

1751   PROV*ll* MASSACHUSETTS TO EPHRAIM WILLIAMS DR.

        For Provisions and other subsistance supply'd the French Protestants
        after the Provisions was Expended that the Commissary General
        supply'd them with —
Decemb*r*
        To Cash p*d* for Provisions for them at Hatfield   £0   7   2
        To Ditto at Deerfield   .   1   15   0
        To Ditto at Charlamont   0   10   6
        To Billeting them at the Fort and Provisions till their
            Return to Boston 76 days for 1 man   4   13   8

                        Lawfull Money   £7   6   4
    Boston Jan*ry* 7*th* 1752
            .
                        Errors Excepted

                                Alowed by the Com*tee*
                                    J. Osborne
    Suffolk ss. Jan*ry* 20*th* 1752
        Sworne to before the Committee   Per Eph*m* Williams jun
            Jacob Wendell
                Just. Pea:

        INDENT OF SUNDRYS NECESSARY AT FORT MASSACHUSETTS

4 Water Bucketts — 1 Box Candles 30 *lb* — 4 Wood Axes

                Sundrys for the Sick Viz*t*

1 Firkin Butter 30*lb* — ½ bb. New England Rum — 1 peck Oatmeal ½ b*l* Rice
    — 10 *lb* Currents, 10 *lb* Reasins
January 10*th* 1750, The above Articles were supply'd Capt. Williams, and
    none Since
                        Attest
                            J. Wheelwright
                Boston January 8*th* 1752
Endorsed   Errors Excepted
    Capt. Ephraim Williams jun*r*   Per Eph Williams juner
        Fort Massachusetts
        His Indent for sundries
            to January 1753.

The above bills and receipts were taken almost at random from a miscellaneous package in the archives at Boston, endorsed "French War." They serve to illustrate the varied activities and responsibilities of Captain Williams during all the years of his command on the western frontiers. By his own direct agency, and through his kinsman and confidant, Israel Williams, of Hatfield, his superior in military rank and in political position, he became the factotum of the government at Boston, in matters both military and civil. Many cares were constantly coming upon that government. Exiles from the Old World for conscience' sake were crowding into Boston in these decades of the old French War, poor and persecuted, and had to be provided for by the public authorities; Palatines from both banks of the Rhine, French Protestants from the home-land as well as the Catholic exiles from Acadie, tested about this time the hospitalities of Massachusetts; and the line of forts to the westward were opening up fresh lands and new townships, that might serve as homes for the new-comers. Dec. 23, 1749, was read to the Great and General Court the Report of their Committee appointed in the April preceding "to repair to the Province Lands near Hoosuck, to lay out two townships of the contents of six miles square," etc.; and the detailed plan of the said two townships was presented at the same time. Just a month later, there is recorded a vote of the House, granting four townships to foreign Protestants, — two in the eastern and two in the western part of the province, — the two western to be "the easternmost township lately laid out at or near Fort Massachusetts [afterwards called Adams]; and the other to the eastward thereof" [probably Savoy].

Spencer Phips, who was Lieutenant-Governor of Massachusetts in 1731–57, and who administered the government from September, 1749, for four years, while Governor Shirley was in Europe, wrote the following letter from Boston to Captain Williams at Fort Massachusetts, dated Nov. 26, 1751. The letter explains itself, and gives also a glimpse of the friendly and intimate relations between the Captain and the government of Boston.

SIR: This comes to you by two or three French Protestants, that are come over with expectation of settling upon the Province Land voted by the General Court for foreign Protestants. These persons have desired to view the said land, that they might know the soil and situation for the incouragement of themselves and their friends in Europe to settle thereon, if they like it.

You are therefore directed to give them necessary provisions out of the publick stores while they are with you, and on their return to Boston. You are likewise directed to show them the lands in the western parts, being in your neighborhood destined by the General Court for foreign Protestants; and for your further direction in finding the said land, I herewith enclose you the vote of the General Court on that affair.

I am, Sir,
Your Friend and Servant,

CAPTAIN EPHRAIM WILLIAMS.   S. PHIPS.

For the general reasons implied in the foregoing, and for other reasons of a military character implied in the increasing expectation that the "Peace" would prove short-lived, Fort Massachusetts filled a larger space in the public eye from year to year, and made Captain Williams more vigilant in respect to its prospective defences. The fort was kept well stocked with provisions. The following bill of 1749 indicates commissariat operations there on a much grander scale than Catlin's "whete" contracts with the "Duch" in 1745: —

Capt⁹ Ephraim Williams
  bo't of Wm. Williams   Vizᵗ Sundry Provisions at
                                   Fort Massachusetts.

103 Bushells Flower at 42/	£216	6	
Transport from Sheffield to sᵈ Fort £14.10 for every 10 Bushell	£149	16	8
2324 lb Pork at 2/	£232	8	
5 Bushells Salt at 112/	£28		
To Scalding and packing 10 Bbls of Pork at 11/	£5	10	
To Driving the above Pork to the Fort	£23	10	
72 Gallons Rum at 60/	£216		
13 Bushells of Peas at 40/	£26		
To Transporting yᵉ same	£13	10	
	£911	0	8

To my Trouble and Expenses in and hiring ye Transport of the
  above articles, with the risque &c.   89

£1000   0   8

Another thing that indicates on the part of Massachusetts a growing sense of insecurity as to the provisions of the Peace of Aix la Chapelle, is the proposal by the General Court, in the summer of 1751, that Fort Massachusetts should be surrounded by a line of pickets at some considerable distance from the walls of the blockhouse, after the general manner of Fort Pelham, on the hilltop to the eastward. Captain Williams had been drawn towards his fort and its defences that year by new personal interests in its neighborhood. In January he had petitioned the General Court for a grant of lands in the vicinity, in consideration for which he agreed to build a gristmill and a sawmill on one of the branches of the Hoosac River, in what is now the village of North Adams. In February a committee of the Court, having personally viewed the lands, recommended the grant of 190 acres, reserving "ten acres of the land adjoyning to the land already reserved round said fort for the use of the Province." He was obligated to build the mills on the north branch of the Hoosac, a stream the Indians called *Mayunsook;* and he must keep the mills in good repair for the space of twenty years, casualties excepted. The committee afterwards recommended, when the grant was under discussion in the House of Representatives, an additional grant of ten acres, to make up for the ten acres reserved around the fort; and the bill was so passed.

This was the first grant of land in fee simple to a private party by the province in the valley of the Hoosac. John Perry, as we have seen, did not obtain his picturesque desire and petition of five years before. For some reason not down in the record, Williams actually built his mill, or mills, on the south branch of the Hoosac, the *Ashuwillticook*, near its junction with the Mayunsook; and the site of his dam across the stream is well known to this day. It is the same "privilege" as that of the century later Phenix mill, but the present dam is about a dozen rods nearer the junction of the two branches. *Ash-a-wog*, or *Nash-a-wog*, an Indian word, which means "a place between two rivers," was common in New England in various combinations, and seems to be the radical element in Ashuwillticook, as it certainly is in Ashuelot and Nashua, in New Hampshire. It will be plain enough to any one, however, who even at this day examines the lay of the land there, why the fall on the south branch near the junction was preferred to that on the north branch for the mill privilege, because it lay on higher ground and was considerably nigher the old Mohawk trail, which was then the only road to the fort. The present Main Street in North Adams, and the road west over Furnace Hill, between the public bridge over the south branch and that over the Hoosac near the site of the fort, follow the course of the old trail, although the old ford over the Hoosac, by which the fort was reached, was three or four rods below the present highway bridge. It is perhaps half a mile between these two bridges.

Captain Williams congratulated himself, and was congratulated by others, on the acquisition of this fine piece of real estate, which, with the reserve, now the centre of the meadow, encircled the fort on every side. It was then densely wooded, except the field immediately around the fort, from which the stumps were slowly disappearing under the cultivation of the remarkably rich soil. The

southern bend of the river just east of the meadow, in consequence
of its striking a quartzite ledge, makes a large ox-bow at that point,
which has always constituted a fertile and famous farm. After it
passed out from province control, it was owned and cultivated for
sixty years by Israel Jones till about 1830, since which time it has
been owned and cultivated for an equal number of years by the
Harrison family. It showed the popularity of the Captain with
the General Court that he obtained this grant without difficulty or
delay. It showed also, indirectly, the influence, in Boston, of his
cousin, Israel Williams, and of his other cousin, William Williams.
His father, Ephraim Williams, of Stockbridge, had had for several
years a large influence over the political and missionary movements
in Boston, but this personal influence was now decidedly on the
wane there and elsewhere, although this was about the time when
the phrase " *Williams family*" came to be employed a good deal
(sometimes in a sinister sense) in the political, and especially in
the religious, correspondence of the period. " Ye monarch of Hampshire " was Colonel Israel Williams, of Hatfield. The Captain, also,
who had become wonderfully popular the last few years on the
Connecticut River, was now owner of an estate of large possibilities
on the Hoosac, and was shortly to purchase the fine landed interests
of his father on the Housatonic ; and it is no wonder that such
letters as the following came to be addressed to him by persons of
position and influence, who sought to cultivate his friendship and
even to promote his spiritual welfare.

This letter, which is well worth printing in this connection, is
neither dated nor signed, but the original is among the Israel Williams papers, and it was certainly written during the season of 1751
by either Rev. Jonathan Ashley, of Deerfield, or Rev. Timothy Woodbridge, of Hatfield, both of whom are known, on other grounds, to
have been friends and intimates of the Captain. The latter sent a
note dated " Hatfield, May 10, 1751," addressed " To Cap'n Ephraim
Williams at Fort Massachusetts," and signed " Timo. Woodbridge,"
to this tenor : "I have drawn at Hoosuck No. 3," — meaning the
original house lot so numbered on the present main street in
Williamstown.

SIR: I wish you a great deal of ease and contentment in your scituation at
the fort. Perhaps the progress you make in the improvement of your new
grant adds to the pleasure of your scituation there. I was pleased when con-
versing with the Col° upon it to hear him observe that it was more valuable
than ever I imagined, for I can assure you that it affords me a particular pleasure
when I hear of the prosperity of the generous and the kind, and you may easily

think its an addition to the pleasure when I see a kind Providence smile upon those of this character I can number among my very good friends. I wish your scituation in the world may be allways pleasant and prosperous, and my wishes rise still higher that the beneficence of your Heavenly Father may be allways gratefully resented by you, and that His care and smiles may be constant incentives of every generous and gratefull passion, and lead you to adopt the language of the sacred penman, and say What shall I render unto the Lord for all his benefits? You will ever consider, Sir, all temporal advantages but an inferior and subordinate good, and infinitely unworthy your supreme affection and chief pursuit. But I hope, Sir, your own meditations upon such a topick will furnish you with better sentiments than any I can suggest. I shall be glad if I can get an opportunity this summer coming to visit you at the fort, for I am sure it would be to me a very agreeable amusement.

I have no news very material to write you. The Col° since his return from *Boston* tells me that he conjectures from the scituation of affairs that the peace will not continue long. The Col° has another pritty daughter added to his family. Daughters they say are an indication of peace. I wish the old proverb may be verified.

I have snatched a moment to write to you the Association being at my house, and can only ad that

I am, Sir, your affectionate friend and Very Humble Serv't,

[TIMOTHY WOODBRIDGE.]

There is a letter from Captain Williams in his own handwriting, which comes in at this point, and which illustrates in several ways how the tedium of garrison life was broken up during this peace year of 1751. The direction of the letter is as follows :—

To the Honrable
Spencer Phips Esqr
Lieut Govenour and
Comander in Chief of
His Majesty's Province of the
Massachusetts Bay &c. &c.
at Cambridge.

FORT MASSACHUSETTS, Sept. 3, 1751.

May it plese your Honour

Last week came to ye fort 8 Scattecook Indians, who told me the land was theirs, and that the English had no Buisness to Settle it Untill such times as they had purchased of them. They further said yt when we began to Built the first Fort, they told the English they must not Build the Fort Except they would pay them for the land, and that the Commandr had promist them pay, but the English had not been as good as their word. In answer I told them as to what promises they had had, I was not Accountable, but be they what they would, I did not Suppose they were binding Upon Us now, for it was wellknown that their tribe was in the French Interest the last war, and that a number of them assisted in taking the Fort and that we now held the land by Right of Conquest.

They said it was true a number of ye tribe was gone to Canada but they were not the proper owners of the land. I told them if those Indians were here they would challenge the land as they now did, and denie that ever they were in the French interest, that if the English were disposed to purchase the land it was Impossable to know who were the right owners, notwithstanding I would inform the goveᵘ and Doubted not but he would lay the matter before the Court. but then I must know how much land they called theirs, and what their price was ; they told me it was theirs as far South as the head of all streams that Emtied into Hoosuck River, [the watershed is in Hancock and Lanesboro] and their price was £800 ye york money, I told them I thought the price was anough, and that the Province would not give it. there is no doubt with me but yt the French are at the bottom of all this, a part of this tribe is now at Canada, and in order to git the Rest they have set a price for the land they know we never will comply with. Last night came to the Fort 2 French men and one English Captive whose name is John Carter he was taken when Deerfield was Destroyed [1704] he is now maried in Canada and has a family there: the French mens mother is an English Captive taken at the same time she was old Mʳ Thomas french's Daughter. they had a pass from the goveᵘ of Canada, and are agoing to see yʳ Relations as they say ; but if the truth was known I believe they are Sent for Spies.

plese Sir to turn over

I askt them what news ; they said there was 14 ships from France several of which were men of war, but they had not brought any news remarkable I then Inquired whether the Indians want gone to war Upon our frontiers in the Eastern Country they said No, they had done now.   .

Concerning the Deer your Honʳ spoke to me about. I have done all that has been in my power to serve you though to little purpose. I have been 20 miles west of Albany but cou'd not git any.

I should have Informed you Sooner but had not an opportunity except I should have sent your Honour an Express which I dont Remember was your Desire.

I am Sʳ your Honʳ most obedient Humble Servᵗ

EPH. WILLIAMS JUNR

GOVENEROR PHIPS

[Endorsed]

In the House of Representatives Jan. 23, 1752. Read and Voted that Col. Lydius of the City of Albany together with the within named Capt. Ephraim Williams be desired to make thorough Enquiry respecting the Indian Title to said lands, whether they belong to said Scauticook Indians or other Indians living near the Hudson's River, or at Stockbridge — And report thereon to this Court as soon as may be.

There is every reason for believing that Captain Williams was assiduous in his attendance upon his duties at the fort, and upon his personal interests in that vicinity, during the entire year 1751 and well into the next also. We are not possessed of many details of his activity in that interval of time, but there is a muster-roll extant, endorsed "muster-roll of Capt. Ephraim Williams at Fort Massachusetts from June 3, 1751 to Jan'y 5, 1752." There are also proposals in his own handwriting, as intimated above, in behalf of himself and seven other soldiers at the fort, to picket that blockhouse by contract with the General Court. These proposals are dated Aug. 18, 1751. Nine days earlier than that, Secretary Willard, of the Provincial Government at Boston, wrote the appended letter to Colonel Israel Williams at Hatfield : —

Sir, I am directed by the Lieut.' Gov-r and Council to inform you, that after all the solemn professions of the Penobscot Indians to maintain the peace, and their great desires to meet the Lieut.'t Govenor at St. Georges, and attend the proposed treaty there, for confirming the same ; this morning we have certain advices from Capt. Bradbury that a considerable number of the Penobscot Indians had joined with those of the St. Francois, and that in a day or two they would set upon the English inhabiting on St. George's River. This advice I am ordered to send you, and to desire that you would in the most suitable manner apprize the inhabitants above you, and other places about you that may be exposed to an enemy, of this state of affairs, that so they may provide for their defence ; and particularly that you would give intelligence of these matters to the several garrisons at Number Four, Fort Dummer, and Fort Massachusetts, or elsewhere in your neighborhood where there may be any soldiers in the pay of the Province.

I am, Sir,

Your very humble Servant,

Colo. Israel Williams.　　　　　　　　　　　　　　　　J. Willard.

There was time for this warning to reach Fort Massachusetts in season to hurry forward the following proposals to picket the fort. There were hardy riders as well as swift runners round the headquarters on the Connecticut, either of whom could compass the fort within forty-eight hours.

Fort Massachusetts, Aug: 18, 1751.

Whereas it has been proposed by the General Court yt ye fort shou'd be pycetted we the subscribers engage for ourselves yt we will git 3000 picketts which shall be 6 Inches diameter, 9 feet and 1 half long and that we will see them all Burnt 2 feet from the bottom untill the sap is all drawn out, and we further promise yt we will see a trench dug one foot and 1 half deep and all of them [set in] and [then ribbed together] from one end of them to the other end : and a good pin drove through each pickett and Ribb : at such distance from the ground as shall be thought best. And when the whole is completed the Commander of the fort shall have the improvement ——————— and it is further agreed that we ye subscribers shall have one Half of what shall be allow'd by the Genll Court : and the Command'r to have the other half, and in case nothing shall be obtained, then we will be at half of the charge and he shall be at the other half of the charge : and it is further agreed by the Com'r and we the above subscribers that an Exact account of ye labour shall be kept by every man in particular, and after a reasonable charge which shall be taken by the whole which shall be sett by the major vote, it is further agreed that what the province shant allow, if anything, shall ——————— that when any of them are dismist by order of government with in ——— years, then a soldier yt may come in his room shall ——— have the refusal of his part, and if he who comes in wont take it and pay him the charge yt has been out that the Com'r obliges himself to pay it, and where as Ephᵗ Williams, Jr., has the command of it at present he engages yᵗ the subscribers shall have the bene-fit of 15 rods beginning at the aboves'd mount and running to the aboves'd stump and then Northedly 30 rods, then Westardly 30 rods, then Southardly 15 rods, and then Easterly 15 rods, untill they come to the north corner of the northwest mount: for [as long a time] as he shall have the command of sᵈ fort: and we the subscribers promise that if we fall back before the hole is completed that we will each of us forfit the sum of ten pounds in witness whereof we have set our hand

Eph. Williams   Seth Hudson
Isaac Wyman   Silas Pratt
Samuel Calhoon   Elisha Chapin.
Ezekᴸᴸ Foster

Those proposed pickets were set not very long afterwards, it is to be presumed, of the size and in the general manner herein set forth, and by the men in general who hereby offered to put them in place. This stockade long survived the blockhouse it enclosed. Two acres and three-quarters of beautiful meadow land were thus fenced in; they were cultivated by the garrison and others for many years before the bulk of the surrounding meadow was cleared up, and while the timbers of the fort were slowly rotting down; they seem to have been the perquisite of the successive commanders as such, of the fort itself, without reference to the ownership of Cap-tain Williams's farm surrounding them; it is altogether probable, one might almost say proved, that they were esteemed a part of the ten acres reserved from Williams's original grant "for the use of the fort"; and the last glimpse that we gain of the enclosure and of what it enclosed, reveals one of the signers of the above pro-posals, Isaac Wyman, the final commander of the fort, as living in a house within the pickets and as cultivating the ground covered in by them.[1] His rank was then Captain. The year was not far from 1761.

These proposals throw considerable light upon the way in which Fort Pelham was undoubtedly constructed six years before; that, however, was a mere stockade twelve rods by twenty-four, probably enclosing nothing but a well and a small magazine, and a covered lodging-place for the garrison in one or more of the interior angles. There was certainly a mount at Pelham, in all likelihood upon the northwest corner, and under this would naturally and cheaply be

[1] Field's *History of Berkshire County*, page 425.

the quarters for the soldiers. We have already learned in an earlier chapter that the outline of the Fort Pelham can be distinctly traced to this day by the pillow of earth originally thrown out to make a trench for the pickets to stand in, and then thrown back on both sides to help hold them in place, and that the author, with his friend Haynes, found in this pillow a gnarled and knotted remnant of one red-oak picket that had stood in its place more than 130 years, the ground of the fort having apparently never been ploughed; while no such memorials of the stockade at Fort Massachusetts could, of course, be expected long to survive the constant ploughings of that fertile meadow both within and without the line of pickets, which ploughings began under Israel Jones in 1766, and continued, with the proper agricultural intervals, for sixty years under his direction as owner of the meadow.

The seven names appended to these proposals for "pycetting" around Fort Massachusetts will never cease to be interesting names to the dwellers in the valley of the upper Hoosac. All of them were then soldiers at the fort, had been soldiers there for some years, and continued to be soldiers there some years longer; all but one of them became, that very year, with thirty-nine others, *original* proprietors of the entire township of West Hoosac, now Williamstown; and at the house of one of them, built on house lot No. 9 and still standing, the first legally warned meeting of the proprietors of the said township was called in due form by William Williams, of Pontoosuck, "to assemble at the House of Mr. Seth Hudson in said township on Wednesday the Fifth day of December next [1753] at Nine of the Clock in the forenoon"; and all seven of these subscribers left their permanent mark on the civil as well as military course of things in this region of the fort.

The first name in this list of seven is, and always will be, the greatest name in the annals of Northern Berkshire. He was the first landed proprietor in that section of the province. He built the very first mills in a locality since become extraordinary for mill manufacturing. He became the first public benefactor of his neighborhood. He chose a method for his public benefaction (not large in amount of money) that has proven itself, during a whole century, to be vital and fructifying. Public interest in the life and death of Ephraim Williams is increasing, and in ever-widening circles; and the present pages find their chief significance in a painstaking attempt to gather up every scrap of contemporary testimony that may help serve to depict, as distinctly and truthfully as possible, a character and a life-work appealing to the thoughtful interest of mankind. According to the terms of these proposals to picket the fort, the prospective lion's share of the reward to come from the province as a whole, was to be holden by the then present Commander; and at least two reasons will occur to the reader towards justifying this: (1) the hard-wood staddles of the right size to serve for pickets would probably have to come, in large measure, from Williams's own private woods around the fort, for most of the timber on the meadow was certainly soft wood, — pine and spruce and hemlock, and the ten acres reserved for the use of the fort would not furnish proper staddles enough; and (2) it would be the influence of the combined Williams family, if anybody's, that could carry such an appropriation for such a purpose through the General Court at that time. The Williams family always acted together for their own interests, and for those of the public. At that time their influence was decidedly predominant in the western third of the province. William Williams was the patriarch of Pontoosuck, now Pittsfield; Ephraim Williams, Senior, then held a like position in Stockbridge; and Israel Williams was the Colonel of the Hampshire Regiment, the highest military official in this end of the province, and on various grounds very influential in the General Court at Boston.

Our story, in some of the following pages, will concern itself considerably with Captain Elisha Chapin, — another of the seven subscribers, — who next succeeded Captain Ephraim Williams in the command of Fort Massachusetts, who, about the same time of this promotion, bought, in conjunction with Moses Graves, of Hatfield, for £350 (both giving bonds therefor), Williams's land-grant around the fort, and who was characterized, four years later, by Williams in his will, as "the poor, distressed, and imprudent Captain Elisha Chapin," in the same clause that remitted to him £100 out of his part of the debt. Chapin was of "Chickobee," now Springfield, of a family since very distinguished along that stretch of the Connecticut River. His original house lot in Williamstown was No. 41, the front of which is now occupied by the fine house of the Chi Psi fraternity, and down the centre of which south runs the lately named "Hoxie Street."[1] Chapin was brave, courteous, and obedient to his military superiors, and loyal to the service as he conceived of its objects and interests; but he sadly lacked caution and moral control over men, and all the indirect evidence points to a free personal use of liquors

---

[1] In the spring of 1891, in legal town-meeting, the town formally named its streets and roads and bridges and hilltops in accordance with a report of a committee consisting of A. L. Perry, John Bascom, and A. E. Hall.

and a too free distribution of them among the men under his command. In the piping times of peace he would make a fair commander of the Fort Massachusetts, and was given a captain's commission for that purpose in the spring of 1752, while for various reasons the interest of Captain Williams waned in the affairs of the Hoosac and waxed as towards those of the Housatonic. Ephraim Williams, Senior, whose home had been in Stockbridge since 1739, was getting to be an old man. He had large property interests there, while he had greatly compromised his moral standing there, and he needed much the advice and support of his eldest son. The latter was given a commission as major in the *southern* regiment of Hampshire County, commanded by Colonel John Worthington, of Springfield, on June 7, 1753, and his principal residence was in Stockbridge from the close of 1751 till September, 1754, when he returned to Fort Massachusetts as commander, with a much enlarged military authority to the southward. In the interval Chapin commanded there. His first muster-roll, extending from June, 1752, to June, 1753, runs as follows: —

A MUSTER ROLL OF THE COMPANY IN HIS MAJESTY'S SERVICE UNDER THE COMMAND OF ELISHA CHAPIN.

Elisha Chapin, Capt.		John Adams,	Centl.
Isaac Wyman, Serg't.		Elijah Brown,	do.
Abraham Bass, Centl.		John Chamberlin,	do.
Samuel Taylor,	do.	Christopher Tyler,	do.
Peter Boovee,	do.	Thomas Train,	do.
Silas Pratt,	do.	Archibal Panil,	} do.
Gad Chapin,	do.	of Fort Shirley	
Ezekiel Foster,	do.	George Hall,	} do.
John Crawford,	do.	of Pelham Fort	
Samuel Calhoun,	do.		

Chapin's second roll, under precisely the same heading, sworn to by him before William Williams at Pontoosuck, Dec. 13, 1753, contains the same number of men and names the same men, except that Elkanah Parris and Elisha Higgins and Benjamin Fairbanks take the places of Brown and Tyler and Calhoun. Panil and Hall each keeps his solitary watch and ward at Shirley and Pelham respectively.

The third roll, from December, 1753, to May, 1754, sworn to before Jacob Wendell, June 1, 1754, presents no differences from the preceding except that Edmund Town and Enoch Chapin and Nath. Harvey take the places of three of the former sentinels.

Chapin's fourth and last roll, covering the time till Williams. resumed the command in September, 1754, holds twenty-four names, of which Oliver Avery and John Bourn and George Willson and Tyras Pratt and Isaac Soldan and Jeremiah Chapin and John Roshet and John Wells and Benjamin King (afterwards killed) are new to his lists.

The two following letters from Captain Chapin to Colonel Israel Williams from Fort Massachusetts, dated respectively Aug. 3 and Aug. 25, 1754, furnish some idea of him as a man and a commander : —

Sir Last Sunday morning I sent a scout to Sencoick [St. Croix] and returned this minit. They find where the Indians marched off and burnt all afore them. They think there was about 400 of the enemy. They see a man come out of Albany yesterday. The Gent. of Albany was very desirous that he should come to the fort and acquaint me that there is 44 Indian cannoes come out 9 days sence and desine for our scatereing frontteers in New England.

From Sir

yrs

to com :

ELISHA CHAPIN.

Sir, This day there came a man from the Dutch and informs me that 4 days past there came 5 Indians from Crownpint and informs them that there is eight hundred Indians desine to destroy Hosuck and oare new town and this fort and desine to be upon us this night. I sent a man right down to Hosuck to here farther about the iffair, but the people was all moved of but 2 or 3 that was a coming to the fort and they tell him the same account. The Indians that brought the account was sent in order to have some parsons move from Sencoick that they had a regard for, but if they come I hope we are well fixt for them.

In hast from

Sr

Your's &c

COMMAND ELISHA CHAPIN.

In the course of this summer of 1754, when the war clouds were darkening and beginning to mutter, Israel Williams wrote as follows to the governor at Boston : —

Capt. E. C. [Elisha Chapin] has now ye com'and of Fort Massachusetts. I can't think it prudence he should have the com'and of a place of such importance in time of war. I know not of a Gent'n in ye County that will be easy to have him trusted with it. He is a bold and venturesome man, but fails in conduct and gov't. If Maj'r Williams would return to that com'and, it would give universal content, und'r whom Chapin I believe would be glad of a L'cy [lieutenantcy]. Y'r Ex'cy influence may probably prevail with ye Maj'r to accept ye com'and of that garrison. If he should, it would be best he should have ye com'and of the men that are or may be posted at Pontoosuck also.

As Ephraim Williams is properly denominated "Major" in the above letter, and as the date and circumstances of his promotion from captain to major have long been a matter of doubt and dispute, it is better to quote here *verbatim* his commission: —

PROVINCE OF THE MASSACHUSETTS BAY } Spencer Phipps Esq., Lieutenant Govenour and Commander in Chief in and over His Majesty's Province of the Massachusetts Bay in New England, &c.

TO EPHRAIM WILLIAMS, JUN'R, ESQ'R, GREETING:

By virtue of the Power and Authority, in and by His Majesty's Commission to me granted to be Lieutenant Govenour over this His Majesty's Province of the Massachusetts Bay, aforesaid, and Commander in Chief during the absence of the Captain General [Shirley was still in Europe]; I do (by these presents) reposing especial Trust and Confidence in your Loyalty, Courage and good Conduct constitute and appoint you the said Ephraim Williams to be Major of the Southern Regiment of Militia in the County of Hampshire in said Province whereof John Worthington Esq'r is Colonel, and Captain of the third foot Company in s'd Regiment.

You are therefore carefully and diligently to discharge the Duty of a Major and Captain in leading ordering and exercising said Regiment and Company in Arms, both inferior Officers and Soldiers, and to keep them in good Order and Discipline; hereby commanding them to obey you as their Major and Captain and yourself to observe and follow such Orders and Instructions, as you shall from Time to Time receive from me, or the Commander in Chief for the Time being, or other your superiour Officers for His Majesty's Service, according to military Rules and Discipline, pursuant to the Trust reposed in you:

Given under my Hand and Seal at Arms at Boston, the Seventh Day of June, In the twenty sixth Year of the Reign of His Majesty King GEORGE the SECOND, Anno Domini, 1753.

S. PHIPS.

By Order the Honorable
the Lieutenant Govenour,

J. WILLARD, Sec'r'y.

Suffolk SS. June 16, 1753.

Ephraim Williams Esq'r Subscribed the Test and Declaration and took the Oaths appointed by Act of Parliament to be taken instead of the Oaths of Allegiance and Supremacy, and the Oath prescribed by a late Law of this Province for calling in the Bills of Publick Credit on this Province and ascertaining the rate of Coin'd Silver &c.

S. DANFORTH } Of the Council and
SAML WATTS } Justices of the Peace.

The tenor of this commission took Major Williams from the northern to the southern parts of the county of Hampshire, and to a pretty steady residence, for more than two years, in Stockbridge, the home of his father and of most of his half-brothers and sisters, his only own brother Thomas being already settled in Deerfield as a physician. The father and his immediate family had long been in a bitter controversy in Stockbridge with Jonathan Edwards, the celebrated preacher and Indian missionary there, just as all the Williams family along the Connecticut River had long previously been in a similar controversy with him during his pastorate at Northampton. The merits of this controversy lie wholly beyond the scope of the present book; like all theological and ecclesiastical, and even moral, strifes, there were two sides to it; it is enough to say here, that the father does not shine (quite the reverse) in the records of it, and that the son apparently kept himself out of the worst heats of it, so far as possible. Twice in the course of his will the son refers to Colonel John Stoddard, who died in 1748, as " my great benefactor," and he was own uncle to Jonathan Edwards, and Edwards himself was own cousin to Israel Williams, the head and front of the opposition to the preacher both in Northampton and Stockbridge, so that something of a family feud mixed itself in with strong religious antipathies, as towards the great theologian, on the part of almost the entire Williams family ; while Major Ephraim, after he went to Stockbridge, where his father and brother-in-law (General Joseph Dwight) were losing moral ground daily in their general machinations against the Indian missionary, seems to have personally kept out of the strife and to have attended pretty strictly to his military and business matters, although he had certainly used his influence previously, at Boston, with officials and dignitaries there, in behalf of his own family interests and prejudgments, in matters relative to the Indian schools and other strifes in Stockbridge. After all these conflicts had died down, on the abandonment of the town by the elder Williams, and the consequent personal triumph of the missionary and his spiritual adherents, the younger Williams continued to be the principal man perhaps in Stockbridge, having the direct command of all the soldiers there and in Pittsfield, and of all the forts in the present county of Berkshire.

There is a deeply interesting note extant from Jonathan Edwards to Ephraim Williams, written six months after the death of the latter's father in Deerfield, which the reader will be glad to see in this place, the contents of which reflect equal credit upon the writer and the recipient, and which implies a state of things in Stockbridge, during the autumn and winter of 1754, very similar to that in Pittsfield and Lanesboro and West Hoosac at that time. The last French War had broken out in earnest. The frontier settlements in New England, and in particular those of Western Massachusetts, were exposed to unceasing anxiety and alarm from their constant liability to attack from the French, and their more savage allies. In the autumn of 1754 several of the inhabitants of Stockbridge were killed by these marauders; in consequence of which it became a garrisoned town, and every considerable family had quartered upon it its own quota of the soldiers necessary for the defence of the place. Much may be learned in many ways from the letter but just now referred to. It was only five months to the death of Williams, and three years to that of Edwards.

STOCKBRIDGE, Feb. 20, 1755.

Sir, We have not lodgings and provisions, so as to board and lodge more than four soldiers; and being in a low state as to my health, and not able to go much abroad, and upon that and other accounts, under much greater disadvantages than others to get provisions, it is for this reason, and not because I have a disposition to make difficulty, that I told the soldiers of this Province, who have hitherto been provided for here, that we could not board them any longer. I have often been told that you had intimated, that you have other business for them in a short time. Captain Hosmer has sent three of his men to lodge at my house, whom I am willing to entertain, as I choose to board such as are likely to be continued for our defence in times of danger. Stebbins has manifested to us a desire to continue here. Him, therefore, I am willing to entertain, with your consent. Requesting your candid construction of that, which is not intended in any inconsistence with my having all proper honour and respect,

I am

Your humble servant,

JONATHAN EDWARDS.

We have gotten a little ahead of our story in point of time, through a desire of completing the relations of Ephraim Williams with Stockbridge, the place, which, more than any other, was his home to the last. A single extract from another letter of Jonathan Edwards, however, written to Rev. Mr. Erskine, of Scotland, six weeks after the above, illuminates so fully the general matters we are dealing with, and justifies so completely the opinion of Colonel Israel Williams of the unfitness of Captain Elisha Chapin to command at Fort Massachusetts under the circumstances of the time, a point to which we shall return in a moment, that we quote it, believing that readers will pardon it, even if they do not approve of it.

I have nothing very comfortable to write, respecting my own success in this place. The business of the Indian mission, since I have been here, has been attended with strange embarrassments such as I could never have expected, or so much as once dreamed of: of such a nature, and coming from such a quarter, that I take no delight in being very particular and explicit upon it. But, besides what I especially refer to, some things have lately happened, that have occasioned great disturbance among the Indians, and have tended to alienate them from the English. As particularly, the killing of one of them in the woods, by a couple of travellers, white men, who met him, and contended with him. And though the men were apprehended and imprisoned, yet, on their trial, they escaped the punishment of death : one of them only receiving a lighter punishment, as guilty of manslaughter: by which these Indians, and also the Indians of some other tribes, were greatly displeased, and disaffected towards the English. Since the last fall, some Indians from Canada, doubtless instigated by the French, broke in upon us, on the Sabbath, between meetings, and fell upon an English family, and killed three of them ; and about an hour after, killed another man, coming into the town from some distant houses ; which occasioned a great alarm in the town, and in the country. Multitudes came from various parts, for our defence, that night, and the next day ; and many of these conducted very foolishly towards our Indians, on this occasion, suspecting them of doing the mischief, charging them with it, and threatening to kill them, and the like. After this, a reward being offered by some private gentlemen, to some that came this way as soldiers, if they would bring them the scalp of a Canada Indian ; that they, in the night, dug up one of our Indians, that had then lately died, out of his grave, to take off his scalp ; that, by pretending that to be the scalp of a Canada Indian, whom they had met and killed in the woods, they might get the promised reward. When this was discovered, the men were punished. But this did not hinder, but that such an act greatly increased the jealousy and disaffection of the Indians, towards the English. Added to these things, we have many white people, that will, at all times, without any restraint, give them ardent spirits, which is a constant temptation to their most predominant lust.

Going back now to Captain Elisha Chapin at Fort Massachusetts, and to the prospect of his being superseded there by Major Ephraim Williams, as war became more imminent in the summer of 1754, it is pleasant to note the record of a modest memorial of his to the General Court, "praying that there may be allowed an Augmentation of the forces at said fort," and the action of the House thereon June 11, 1754, " That the Captain-General be desired to make an addition of Five Men to the forces already ordered at Fort Massachusetts"; together with the answer thereto in the message of Governor Shirley, two days later, who had now returned to his post after seven years' absence in Europe, which message ran as follows : —

Gentlemen of the House of Representatives, — According to your Desire to me expressed on the Memorial of Capt. Elisha Chapin, I shall give orders for the reinforcement of Fort Massachusetts with five men ; and considering the importance, and its great Distance from any of our Settlements, it would have pleased me if you had made provision for a few more men there.

Upon this Occasion I must put you in mind of the hazardous Condition Fort Pelham and Fort Shirley are now in, if there should be any sudden Assault from the Indians on that Frontier ; we must expect that the thing they will do would be to burn those forts, which they might easily do in their present Circumstances.

Therefore I must recommend it to you, that provision be made that some better care may be taken for preserving them.

W. SHIRLEY.

Governor Shirley also gave immediate attention, as was his wont, to the letter (already quoted) of Colonel Israel Williams to him respecting a change in the command at the chief fort in the line. His letter in reply is significant in several respects, especially in his evident leaning towards Chapin as a man and an officer; and we shall discover in the next chapter that he held similar prepossessions towards him as a householder in West Hoosac, and the leader of a knot of householders there in decided discontent with Fort Massachusetts and the whole authority emanating thence.

BOSTON, September 26, 1754.

Sir, Maj. Williams will accept of a new Commission for Fort Massachusetts, which I design shall be enlarged by a Superiour command over the soldiers posted at Pontoosuck — in special cases; I should be sorry to do anything which may look like a slight upon the present commander Capt. Chapin, of whose courage I have a good opinion ; But as the command, which the King's Service now requires the Captain of that Fort to have given him, must be enlarged, and Major Williams beside being an officer whom I look upon to be well qualified for it, hath those farther pretensions to it, that it was upon his resignation of the command of that Fort, that Capt.ⁿ Chapin was commissioned for it, I hope he will not think a slight upon him, if when I add another charge to the Captain's Commission for that Fort, I give it Maj. Williams ; I shall be very glad if he will serve as a Lieutenant under Major Williams, and will give him the first proper promotion which shall happen in my power; you will be pleased to let Capt. Chapin know this ; and I leave to your discretion to act in the manner you shall think proper, with the inclos'd *blank* Commissions concerning the Captain and Lieut! of Fort Massachusetts as well as the others.

W. SHIRLEY.

Colonel Williams was " pleased to let Capt. Chapin know this " at once, and in a note dated Hatfield, October, 1754, he writes: —

Sir, His Excel'cy has given the Com'and of Fort Massachusetts with the forces posted at Pontoosuck to Maj'r Williams, whereby you will see ye Captain's of that Forts Com'and is enlarged. The Gov'r directs me to let you know he shall be very glad if you will serve as a Lieutenant under Maj'r Williams, and he will give you the first proper promotion in his power. He has also sent me a blank Commission to fill up for you, if you will undertake that service.

It appears, also, that Major Williams himself addressed one or more communications to Chapin after the former reassumed the command of the fort. These have perished. Happily there survives a letter from Chapin to Williams, which, though badly mis-spelled, is evidently a pretty honest document, although it is colored by the semi-hostility already existing between the first settlers of West Hoosac — among whom Chapin was a leader, and in whose behalf he made the journey to Boston referred to by him in the letter — and the authorities at the fort. It seems, from this letter, that Chapin was appointed a sort of sub-commissary at the fort, and that there had been dissatisfaction with him in that capacity, and a dismissal from his post in connection with some mutinous move-ments of the garrison, all which will be plainer when we come to quote in the next following chapter a copious narration of events at the fort and at the inchoate settlements in "the west town," — as West Hoosac was commonly called in current correspondence, — written by Colonel Israel Williams in justification of his own con-duct in the premises. Otherwise, Chapin's letter to Major Williams requires no commentary.

FORT MASSACHUSETTS, Jan. 29, 1755.

Sir, I received your's dated Jan. 14, and am very much surprised that you should have such hard thoughts of me to think I slighted your offers which you no I readely accepted and had desired to wait on the Col. for the Commission when I come from Boston. But a great way back on the road I head the news that the Col. had given the Commition to Wyman. So I thought it in vain to go there for it. And I offen hear that the Col. seams to be insenced against me and what it is for I cannot tell, for I never spoke a hard word of him in my life, and you no I allways set high by him, and· allways was willing to serve and obay him, and as to the Commissary business, his Excelency told me ore and ore that no man should take it from me. He frealy spoke about it again and again and nobody pretend to do that. I was obliged to do it till I new of another, and I never have been without a good stock, onely when the snow was deep, the weather cold, and the mill got out of order, and I could not grind in some days, and was near out of meat, but had a good stock of wheat of my own. Whoever reports these things against me do no better than lie.

Sir, you seame to speak as if I had a hand in the late disturbaince. Had I not been hear it would have been carried to a far greater length than it was. I got the men together and asunder pacified them, or else it would not be over till this day. Some ill minded person hath done all they can to hurt me. I have been informed that the most of it comes from Graves. They mite say a great deal against me and speak true, but what you writ to me your authors imposed upon you very much, and now Sir if you can look upon me to be a man of common truth you can easily be satisfied, for wear I upon oath I could not tell straiter. I should inlarge and mention some more things, but I can never send a letter in the county but that it is brook open, so I shall conclude,

Your very friend and humble
Servant to Command,
ELISHA CHAPIN.

MAJ. E. WILLIAMS.

The strife continued between the east and west forts, and between the scattered settlers on the house lots of the west town and the Williams family influence, both military and civil. The details are not worth preserving. Chapin was the champion of the Chidesters and of the so-called West Hoosac Fort. He was countenanced more or less by Governor Shirley, and made more than one journey to Boston to obtain and maintain that favor. But his star was going down. Under date of May 17, 1756, Isaac Wyman, his second successor in the command of Fort Massachusetts, wrote to his superior, Colonel Israel Williams: "I understand by Serg^t Taylor that Chidester hath taken Capt. Chapin into the service at the west town. He is to do the duty for the billeting. He hath taken one of the Horsford's place, and John Vanarnum the other Horsford's place, and they are both gon home." In less than two months thereafter, the Colonel sends out this news from Hatfield: "This morning by an express from Fort Massachusetts, I am informed that on the 11th instant, near sunsetting, Serg't Chidester, his son James Chidester, and Capt. Elisha Chapin, went from ye block-house at West Hoosack to seek their cows, were soon fir'd upon and all killed or captivated." Three days later, Wyman sent to the Colonel the following detailed account: —

FORT MASSACHUSETTS, July 16, 1756.

Hono^d Sir, The three men that ware shot upon by the enemy are all found. Two of them were kill^d upon the spot where the enemy first fired upon them. They took Capt. Chapin about eighty rods, where they kill^d him. I sent out Ens^n Barnard with nineteen men from the fort to bury these men. They found where the Enemy had laid an ambush between this Fort and the Town. They judge to be not less than one hundred of them. Hudson saith that the bigest part that he saw ware French. I believe it will not be longue before the enemy will be upon us again. I am persuaded that there is a large body of them lieth watchin our army find that they doant move, and so drive down upon us.

The two swivels guns that Serjt Chidester petitioned for are placed in the best maner upon Carageses for the defence of the House where all our stoars of provision are keept. One of them is placed at the South West corner of the Fort which clears of the South side of the House — the other placed at the north east corner of the Fort clears the east side of the House. These guns are as grait defence to us as any of the artillery we have at the fort.

I find that the Colo. was afraid we ware short on't for amonition. I have not less than three hundred weight of powder and lead anserable. About three weeks ago I sent thirty weight of powder and lead anserable to the Town and one month's provision. The people of the town have a grait desire to git of with their famaleys, if they could have a strong guard, provided they can't have any more men allowed them.

If they can't have a better fort built and more men I believe it is the best thing they can do is to pull their fort down, and come of, provided that the war continues. The Monday before last came in Capt. Buterfield from the camps with one hundred and forty men. Found eight of there men kill'd upon Hoosuck — the other five I suppose are taken. I enclose Chidester's patition also a Journal of our Scouting.

This from, Sir,
Your verry Humble Serv⊥
ISAAC WYMAN.

Four days after this letter was penned, Colonel Williams wrote to Governor Shirley from Hatfield : —

Lieut. Barnard and a number of soldiers from Fort Massachusetts have been over since I wrote last. Find Chapin and the two Chidesters kill'd and scalp'd. He judges by ye signs there was one hundred or more of the enemy. Its highly probable, considering who had ye care of ye garrison, their carelessness, and ye insufficiency of ye fort, had not those three imprudent unhappy men accidentally come upon ye enemy, and thereby obliged them to discover themselves sooner than they intended, by morning they would have surprised ye garrison and destroyed it.

So falls the curtain forever on " the poor, distressed, and imprudent Captain Elisha Chapin." His widow and administrator of estate, Miriam Chapin, sold to Ephraim Seelye, in March, 1767, his house lot 41 and its after-drafts for £25, " for the payment of his debts." He himself sold his lands in " Chickobee " in April, 1755. He then denominated himself " of Fort Massachusetts."

As we have already learned, and shall have occasion to note hereafter again and again, the large immigration into New England in 1718 of the Scotch-Irish people from Londonderry, and the region round about, colored in various ways its thoughts and its growths, — a series of influences that have not ceased to this day ; and the third of the seven signers to the joint enterprise of setting the pickets around Fort Massachusetts 30 × 15 rods, " square timber or pickets or both," on the 18th of August, 1751, belonged to a family of that race ; and, though never distinguished himself, was connected by name and blood with those who became so. This was Samuel Calhoun, who enlisted from the same stretch of the Connecticut River as Elisha Chapin, and who was almost constantly a " centinel " in the western line of forts during both " King George's " and the " last French war." He was always a quiet man, but enterprising and persistent, just such a man as Ephraim Williams would like to associate with himself in a practical, and perhaps profitable, enterprise in the slack of the strain of war. In the original drawing of house lots in West Hoosac, Calhoun happened on No. 5, one of the best lots on the main street, and he sold it not long after to Josiah Dean, Junior, of Canaan, Connecticut, and Dean sold it in March, 1759, to Benjamin Simonds; and it has continued ever since to be a part of the fine homestead now owned and occupied by the Sabin family. Simeon H. Calhoun (Williams College, 1829), tutor here for two years, and ever after a remarkably useful and prominent missionary in the Levant till his death in December, 1876, was a member of the same general family in New England, and connected as well in traits, as in name and race, with the distinguished statesman of South Carolina. It is significant that the parents of S. H. Calhoun were among the original members of Park Street Church in Boston, where the son was born in August, 1804; and when his age was ten years, he removed to Rindge, New Hampshire, into the same racial and theological influences then presided over by the elder and fervent Dr. Payson. The name of another Simeon H. Calhoun, a nephew, is borne on our triennial catalogue under date of 1857, and he has been a prominent citizen of Nebraska till the present time (1891); and one other Calhoun is on our graduated list, the only son of the Mt. Lebanon missionary, Charles William Calhoun, under the date of 1873. He died in 1883; living and dying a faithful missionary within the shadows of the same great mountain.

A fourth signer of these proposals to picket the fort came out of the loins of a very different set of ancestors, and gave birth to remarkably different lines of descendants from those related to Simeon H. Calhoun. This was Silas Pratt, who enlisted into the line of forts from Worcester, sometimes stated to be Shrewsbury, who had near relatives (Noah Pratt and Tyras Pratt) as fellow-soldiers from the same localities, who was very active both as soldier and citizen in the earliest settlement of Williamstown, although not an original proprietor of any of the house lots, who was a blacksmith by trade, who was long of the garrison in the blockhouse at West Hoosac, who lived and died on the first farm in Pownal as one goes over North West Hill from this side, whose son "William" may be first male child born in West Hoosac, whose name is commemorated in the rapid "Pratt Brook" which tumbles down from the Taconics through his old farm to the Hoosac, and who has left more descendants (largely clinging to the old neighborhood) than any other one of the primeval settlers of Williamstown down to the present time. There was much energy in that man, and in his immediate family, both in peace and war. He and his son Silas were in the battle of Bennington. His son William, as a Revolutionary soldier, witnessed the execution of Major André, Oct. 2, 1780; lived to receive a pension from the United States as a three-years drummer in the army, 1777 to 1780; died Jan. 16, 1846, in the eighty-sixth year of his age; and his epitaph states that he was a member of the Methodist Episcopal Church for forty-three years. Lively traditions have come down in his family in respect to the brave conduct of old Silas Pratt in the battle of Bennington, operating behind his staddle, Indian fashion; and the present writer has been told more than once by his grandson, William Pratt, son of William, the first-born, that he himself had heard from his own father (the drummer whose arm being stiff could not carry a gun), and from his uncle Silas, many a story of the Revolutionary War. Old Silas Pratt could set pickets as well as the next man, and fight behind them or in front of them when necessary; he could clear up with his own hands and those of his growing boys, a large and rugged farm, stretching up into one of the gorges of the Taconics, where now stands the stone marking a corner point of Massachusetts and Vermont, and also a point in the eastern line of New York nearly midway north and south; and he could, apparently, transmit to descendants of the fifth generation a story-telling faculty, which, in the mouths of "Steve" Pratt and "Jerry," his brother, was the wonder of the idlers in this vicinity during the last quarter of the nineteenth century.

Ezekiel Foster, the fifth of the picket-signers, was from Fall Town, now Bernardston, and quite constantly a sentinel in the line of forts from the beginning to the end. He drew house lot No. 13 in the original "lotting" of West Hoosac. He called himself of "Fall Town" a little later, when he sold one-half of the after-drafts of 13 and the whole house lot 59 to Stephen Davis and Thomas Dunton, both of Western; but, nevertheless, he was the head of one of the first "eleaven families of us," already domiciled in West Hoosac, who petitioned Governor Shirley from Fort Massachusetts, to which these families "ran for shelter upon the late alarm" in October, 1754, for aid and military encouragement to "return to our settlements" at the west town. Foster became a considerable landowner and a prominent citizen of Williamstown, and we are likely to learn more about him before we are through with the task now in hand. Captain Ebenezer Foster, with his brother, Dan Foster, who came into South Williamstown from Hancock quite early in this century, and lived useful lives as farmers, — the one on the Hancock and the other on the Ashford road, — may have been his sons.

The sixth signer of the picket-proposals and the last survivor of them, and of all his active contemporaries in this valley, was Seth

Hudson. The Hudson family was a roving one, and its connection was as locally fixed in Lexington and in Marlboro as anywhere. Charles Hudson, perhaps the most distinguished representative of a name considerably distinguished in this country, said of them: "All who have borne the name have been rather migratory in their character. It may, however, be said of them with truth, that they have manifested a natural affinity for military adventures. The whole Hudson family appear to have been men of *arms* rather than of *letters*." Our Seth Hudson was son of Seth, and was born in Marlboro, April 13, 1728, the eldest of eight children. He must have received some sort of medical training in his youth, for he was employed by the year, or otherwise, as surgeon in Fort Massachusetts at the same time he was "centinel" there, and acted in both capacities from about the time of the rebuilding of the fort in 1747. Perhaps he was not paid as "surgeon" for a couple of years or so thereafter. He was two years younger than Benjamin Simonds, with whom he was closely associated nearly all the time, till the latter's death in 1807, as a fellow-soldier in Fort Massachusetts; as a co-laborer in the very outset of the subjugation each of his own house lot in West Hoosac (these two house lots being in plain sight of each other); in the building and manning of the blockhouse in West Hoosac, of which Seth Hudson became the commanding officer on the death of Captain Elisha Chapin in 1756, with the rank of Captain; in all the early troubles of the little hamlet, both military and civil; in all the burdens and hazards and privations of the Revolutionary War, either here or elsewhere, during the course of which Simonds outstripped the other in rank and influence as he far outstripped him also afterwards in civil position and property; and, finally, in a part, at least, of the strifes incident to a struggling and impoverished township just before and just after the opening of the present century.

To "Dr. Seth Hudson" fell lot No. 9 in the original drawing of the West Hoosac house lots in 1751. Fifteen of these lots fell thus by bargain to soldiers in garrison at the east fort. One of the prescribed conditions for holding the lots was, — "That he shall within the space of two years from the time of his being admitted build a house eighteen feet long, fifteen feet wide, and seven foot studd." That Hudson fulfilled this condition on lot 9 is proven by the fact that the first proprietors' meeting in the precinct was legally warned to be holden within it on the 5th of December, 1753. That house is still standing, the interior substantially unchanged during the 140 years from the primal gathering of the "rude forefathers" within its bare walls, although it has been twice moved in this extended interval of time, — first about seventy years ago, half a mile due north, to the west bank of Hemlock Brook in Charityville, to be used as a wheelwright's shop by Abel Cowdin, and second to higher land, more secure from the brook's overflow, three or four rods due west, to be repaired. and enlarged for a dwelling by Ned Reagan, an Irishman, who long owned and occupied it.

A daughter of Mr. Cowdin, Mrs. Thomas Mole, has more than once expressed to the writer her perfect recollection of the putting this house in place for her father's use on its first removal. She remembered pairs of the oxen and the drivers of some of them. John R. Bulkley, the elder, was present with his team of oxen, and she was astonished at hearing him *stutter*, — a new experience for the girl of ten years; and she remembered especially Coey Danforth, both busy with his oxen and talkative with the crowd, already much the worse for liquor at that the final stage of the "bee." They were then unhitching the oxen. She remembered, also, playing afterwards around the original cellar of the house on Main Street. The stones of the old foundation were loose, and she was chided by her father for fooling with them. This was in or about 1827. The shop was placed too near the brink of the brook, for she remembered an overflow, not long after, that did damage, and later overflows caused the removal of the building to its present location. The first moving was undoubtedly across the Buxton bridge, or through the brook near to that, and then adown on the west bank to its stopping-place.

Hudson was enterprising and restless. He bought and sold lands a good deal in West Hoosac and elsewhere. In nearly all instances the deeds display a certain pride and dignity. He has himself set down in them as " Gent.," in contrast to the " cordwainer " or " yeoman " with whom he deals. Isaac Searle, for example, originally from Northampton, who became his fellow-soldier here and co-malcontent, under the domination of " ye monarch of Hampshire " and his minions at Fort Massachusetts, and who was, in 1765, the largest taxpayer in Williamstown, is set down as " cordwainer " in one of Hudson's deeds to him, while the grantor is nothing less than " Gent." In 1764, Seth Hudson is a " resident of Great Barrington," and sells out, under that designation, a part of his lands in West Hoosac. He does not appear to have remained a great while in Barrington, nor to have made much of a mark there. He certainly played no part to speak of in Williamstown during the Revolution, and it is quite improbable that he lived here then; but, at any rate, he returned hither in his old age, poor, and James Smedley remembers him distinctly about the years 1811–14 as coming to his father's house more than once as a veterinary, to treat sick cows and horses. He lived then in an old house on house lot 58, — a site soon to be occupied by the new and fine house of Daniel Noble, — from which Joseph White, another treasurer of the College, was borne to his grave in 1890. Hudson, at that time an old man, was living with a second wife, who had borne to his old age two sons, Ward and Polydore. The mother was intemperate. In accordance with the slang of those days, she was said to be capable of "getting drunk on cider emptyings." She not only had a stomach that craved, but also a tongue that wagged. The boy James, the deacon's son, then being religiously brought up just over the Green River, was over-persuaded by another boy, named Horace Brown, that the latter's father was in some way in business company with Dr. Hudson, and consequently that Brown, Junior, had a perfect right to some of the cherries growing on a big tree in the rear of Hudson's old house, the two boys approached cautiously, in a manner that betrayed and belied their alleged rights; and the tree was scarcely reached before the shrill voice of old Mrs. Hudson, the termagant, standing in the back door, caused both boys to scud through the corn-rows for dear life and the Green River!

There is no direct evidence known to the writer as to the localities where Captain and Dr. Hudson put in his work during the Revolutionary War; but nothing is more likely than that he returned to the eastward, perhaps to his native town, Marlborough or Lexington, both of them then full of his kin, and sufficient researches in that direction might disclose him as bustling and efficient as ever. At any rate, he came back to Williamstown in his old age, and was the last survivor by some years of the soldiers in garrison at the block-house in West Hoosac. It was deliberately voted by town-meeting of Williamstown, in the spring of 1891, that the second of the four swells on the summit of East Mountain, reckoning southward from "Mount Hazen," be named "Hudson's Height," in memory of the old soldier and surgeon.

The seventh and last of the co-signers to the proposals to picket the main fortress on the Hoosac River was Isaac Wyman, of Woburn. He was in the second Fort Massachusetts, in some capacity, almost all the time from its erection, in 1747, till its final abandonment in 1760. He had crept up, step by step, from sentinel to Captain. He always possessed the confidence of Ephraim Williams. Some years after the death of the latter, and the consequent outbreak of a violent quarrel, as between Colonel Israel Williams and his subordinates at Fort Massachusetts and Captain Seth Hudson and his men in and around the block-house at West Hoosac, there was a formal investigation, by a committee of the General Court, of the whole matter and of all the parties concerned; and, after a full examination, including the memorials of all the officers, and numerous depositions in support of, and in opposition to, the complaints of the petitioners at West Hoosac, the committee made a formal report that the complaints (with one or two exceptions) as to the conduct of Captain Wyman were not proved. After a final end was put to the French wars by Wolfe's great victory on the Heights of Abraham in 1759, Captain Wyman continued for some time to cultivate his farm within and without the pickets which he helped contract to set up. He removed to Keene, New Hampshire, whence, at the outbreak of the Revolution, he was appointed Lieutenant-Colonel of the First New Hampshire Regiment, commanded by Colonel John Stark, — a position which he did not hold long, and from which he passes out of our sight utterly.

Before giving the details of Wyman's life and services as commander of the fort, we must now go back a bit and pick up the thread that interlinks Ephraim Williams once more with the fort and connects him, also, indirectly with the Expedition to Lake George in 1755, during the course of which he lost his life, but gained his fame.

The encroachments of the French along the Ohio River in 1754, in steady opposition to which George Washington became the forceful agent of the Province of Virginia; the hostile conduct of the Indians on all the frontiers of New England under the influence of the Canadian French, such as the ravage of Dutch Hoosac (Petersburg Junction), about ten miles west of Fort Massachusetts, in May, and the burning, next day, of all the settlements at St. Croix, from both which places the people had fled for safety mostly to the fort; the fright of the people at Pontoosuck and Stockbridge at the bold Indian depredations and murders committed there in the early summer, and similar outrages in Maine a little later, — so convinced the government of England and the local governments of all the provinces on this side that a new and great war with France and her allies was on the carpet, that special orders were sent from England to her colonies to repel force by force, accompanied with a recommendation to them to form a solid union for mutual defence. Thus was summoned, under the personal lead of Governor Shirley, the first American Congress. Delegates from the four New England colonies, and from New York, Pennsylvania, and Maryland, met at Albany, June 14, 1754. Benjamin Franklin was the leading spirit of this gathering. An elaborate Plan of Union was framed, and a copy was sent for approbation to the King in council and to each of the provincial governments. The scheme met with the singular fate of being rejected by each and every one of the proposed parties to it; by the King, because it was thought to grant too much power to the colonial assemblies, and by each colony because it was supposed to give too much authority to the King. And the shrewd Franklin wrote afterwards, that the contradictory reasons of dislike to the Albany Plan of confederation made him think that it must have been just about the golden mean.

This plan of union having failed, the colonies were left to prosecute the war under their former disjected system. Colonel Israel Williams, of Hatfield, commanding the northern regiment of militia in the county of Hampshire, as Colonel John Worthington, of Springfield, commanded the southern, was again entrusted with the defence of the western frontier. He had gained valuable experience during the former war and a practical knowledge of the geography of the country bordering the limits of Massachusetts and New Hampshire (then including Vermont), which enabled him to draw a rough sketch of the lay of the land and water, and this he communicated to Governor Shirley, with a detailed plan of defence to be adopted. He proposed to abandon forts Shirley and Pelham, as having afforded but little protection in the preceding war; to strengthen forts Dummer and Massachusetts, furnishing them larger garrisons and more light artillery, and to connect the two by a line of smaller works erected on the north side of Deerfield River; and to abandon the fort at Charlestown, New Hampshire, as being out of the jurisdiction of Massachusetts and difficult to supply. The General Court adopted bodily the Colonel's system of defence, excepting the abandonment of Charlestown, and new bodies of troops were ordered to be raised for the western frontiers, and to be stationed at the discretion of Colonel Williams. It was under these auspices and prospects, as has been seen incidentally already, that Major Ephraim Williams was willing to leave Colonel Worthington as his superior officer, and Stockbridge as his principal place of residence, and to resume the command at Fort Massachusetts, with authority added over small garrisons posted or proposed to be posted to the south and to the west of it.

Dropping the rank of Major, which he had borne in the southern regiment, and reassuming that of Captain, which he had carried now

for ten years, Ephraim Williams went back to Fort Massachusetts
about the first of September, 1754, for his third and last command
there.   His last muster-roll from there, to whose correctness he took
oath at Boston, June 13, 1755, probably one of his very last acts
before leaving for Albany and Crown Point, contains the names of
forty-one men whose service covered the interval from September to
March, 1754–55, a list that will be here given at length for several
reasons.   It holds the names of five of Williams's co-signers to the
picketing proposals of 1751 ; the name of one of the Canada captives taken from the first fort Aug. 20, 1746, honors this final roll
of his old Captain ; and fifteen of the names are of men who took
the risks of the earliest settlement of West Hoosac.

A MUSTER-ROLL OF THE COMPANY IN HIS MAJESTY'S SERVICE UNDER THE
      COMMAND EPHRAIM WILLIAMS CAPTAIN, VIZ.

Ephraim Williams, Capt.	John Crofford, Cent.
Isaac Wyman, Lieut.	John Bowin, Cent.
Samuel Taylor, Serjt.	Tho's Trail [Train?] Cent.
Edmond Town, Serjt.	John Herrold, Cent.
Gad Chapin, Serjt.	Micha. Harrington, Cent.
Oliver Avery, Corp'l.	Ezra Parker, Cent.
Sam'll Calhoun, Corp'l.	John Balsh, Cent.
Sam'll Catlin, Cent.	Josiah Goodwish, Cent.
John Taylor, Cent.	Nath. Nickells, Cent.
Elisha Higgins, Cent.	John Gray, Cent.
Benja. King, Cent.	Seth Hudson, Cent.
George Willson, Cent.	Mayhew Daggitt, Cent.
John Rosher, Cent.	Gideon Warren, Cent.
Tyrus Pratt, Cent.	Elisha Sheldon, Cent.
Noah Pratt, Cent.	Simeon Crawford, Cent.
Abraham Bass, Cent.	John Meacham, Cent.
Jeremi'h Chapin, Cent.	Derrick Webb, Cent.
John Mills, Cent.	Benja. Simonds, Cent.
Enoch Chapin, Cent.	Gad Corss, Cent.
Silas Pratt, Cent.	Henry Stiles, Cent.
Ezekiel Foster, Cent.	

John Gray and John Crofford and Simeon Crawford of this list
were certainly Scotch-Irishmen, and possibly others, doubtless enlisted from Worcester or its vicinity.   Micah Harrington and Benjamin King and the Captain himself were killed in the fast-coming-on
battle of Lake George.

In the meantime, as was natural, there was developing in several
quarters a good deal of jealousy towards Colonel Israel Williams,
on account of his imperious manners and subtle ways of compassing

his ends in the General Court and elsewhere. This jealousy intensified itself later into a many-sided quarrel, involving on one side prominent relatives and previous coadjutors of his along the Connecticut River, and on another side the subaltern officers and some of the soldiers of Fort Massachusetts interested in the original layout of West Hoosac. Neither duty nor inclination draws us into these disputes, except so far as is needful to illuminate the pathway in which both duty and inclination compel us to walk at present. Some of the roots of this controversy ran back into the ecclesiastical persecution, and apparently unfortunate dismissal of Jonathan Edwards from his church in Northampton. Others of them ran still farther back into the personal qualities ingrained in the members of the Williams family, and the consequent nepotism and consolidated (though often secret) influence of the family as such.

Joseph Hawley, of Northampton, was own cousin to Jonathan Edwards. So was Israel Williams, who was fifteen years older than Hawley. Under the guidance of the older man, Hawley, who himself had begun life as a preacher, became a violent opposer of the ecclesiastical measures of Edwards, and very active in effecting his removal from Northampton. He afterwards saw reasons for radically changing his views as to that whole matter, and gradually became a warm advocate of his old pastor, then resident in Stockbridge, and in 1760 wrote a letter of regret and penitence for his own previous action in the premises that will ever be remarkable, and that was for half a century famous. The following letter from Hawley to Williams, dated Northampton, Oct. 3, 1754, though bearing not the least reference to the Edwards affair, will interpret itself to the penetrating reader. Williams was at the time in Hatfield, his home. Hawley was then thirty years old, already distinguished for legal attainments and political knowledge and stern integrity, and destined to become, perhaps, the most influential member of the House of Representatives of Massachusetts from 1764 to 1776.

S'r I unerstand from my brother y'^{t} ye present scheme is to have two places fortified at Pontoosuck — y'^{t} there shall be 15 men posted at each — and y't at Hoosuck there be 50 men. It is not of importance that I know of for me to say how disagreeable such a settlement to the westward is to me. But I humbly apprehend y't it would conduce much to ye concerting of a good scheme for ye defence of our people on ye west of Connecticut river y't yourself, Col. Partridge, Maj'^{r} Ephraim and I should have a free conference together before ye next session of ye Gen^{ll} Court, and y'^{t} we labour to agree in some gen^{ll} plan y't we shall labour at least to effect.

Otherwise it seems to me all our separate designs and projections will be

likely to prove abortive. From my observation the case stands thus (if I may
be permitted to speak it) you, S'r, and Maj'r Ephraim concert what you think
proper, and labour it with ye Govenour, and he also with ye whole Court. Col
Partridge schemes something different perhaps, which he will labour with ye
Govenour and House. I am privy to neither scheme, and perhaps ye first of my
hearing thereof should be in ye House. Neither may appear perfectly agreeable, and altho' I am a person of but small consideration, yet if Providence
should so order it that I should be in ye House when those matters should be
considered, if there appears sinister designs interwoven in ye plans, it will be no
difficult matter to prevent their taking. I don't think y' in my private capacity
I am of much importance in such matters, but as a member of ye House it is
possible I may be, for I have always spoke my mind in ye House and sometimes
have been heard.

And if Providence should give me opportunity probably I shall be as free as
usual respecting affairs this way especially. A man of little influence can
obstruct disburstment of money.

I am, S'r, with all due respects,
Your's

COL. WILLIAMS.   JOSEPH HAWLEY.

A yawning breach as between the cousins is visible enough in this
epistle, — not only an unuttered protest against "ye monarch of
Hampshire" personally, but also against the long-ago observed
tendency of the "Williams family" to pull together, and that
secretly. But Joe Hawley was sturdy and patriotic and cou-
rageous. Two years later, when he heard the news from the West
Hoosac fort of the killing of Captain Elisha Chapin and the two
Chidesters, almost within the very sweep of their mounted guns, he
wrote to the Colonel the annexed letter, under date of July 18,
1756, seven days after the disaster on Hemlock Brook: —

COL. WILLIAMS S'r Mr. Barnard has given me a sketch of the news from
Hoosuck. If they are sure y'¹ they saw French in [the crowd of Indians] I
think we may be pretty certain y'¹ there is an army there. Should it prove
y'¹ there is an army there, and either one or both of the forts should be taken,
you, S'r, never will be pardoned if you don't send the militia. Were it not for
two reasons I would readily offer my service to go — the one is that the weather
is so extream hot that it would instantly bring ye disorder to which I am incident in hot weather — the other is that it is a hurrying time in ye business of
my profession, and some other affairs which claim my particular attention at
this time.

Perhaps you have some good man in y'r eye. I should think Capt. Willm Lyman was ye best with us. Pardon my officiousness.

I am Sir y'r's
JOSEPH HAWLEY.

The "officiousness," if any, consisted in his commending his
neighbor, Lyman, to the now vacant headship (such as it was) of

the West Hoosac fort. We shall see in detail in the next chapter how that troublesome post came to be occupied, if not filled, by Captain Seth Hudson. It is difficult for a writer, himself deeply interested in all the details of his task, justly to estimate how far his readers also may take pleasure in the same; yet one may scarcely question the prospective interest with which a future reader of these pages will con a statement from the pen of Governor Shirley himself, as to the success with which " You, S'r, and Maj' Ephraim concert what you think proper and labour in it with ye Govenour."

BOSTON, Sept. 26, 1754.

Sir, I have received a packet from you by Major Williams, containing a plan of the western parts of the Province, a list of the officers and centinells in your Regiment, and three letters, one dated the 12th and two the 17th of September instant.

I am extremely well satisfied with the great care and vigilance you have already show'd for the protection and safety of the people upon the Western Frontier, and have great confidence in your abilities and fidelity in the discharge of your military trust, upon any future emergency, at this dangerous conjuncture.

As to the difficulty you mention in your letter of the 12th instant to arise from the appearance which my second orders to you have of abridging the power given you in my first orders, and confining it to the limits of your own Regiment, I think my remark upon the enclosed copys of the orders I sent to Col. Worthington, and my second orders to yourself, will best clear that up, and explain both of them, so as to make them consistent with each other.

I am glad you found your Regiment and the towns within the limits of it, so well provided with arms and ammunition as they appear to be by your return upon those articles ; exact care should be taken that all failures and deficiencies should be fully and speedily made up : the refusal of the select men of the town of Northamptown to give any account of their town stock shall be inquired into.

It is necessary that the limits of yours and Col. Worthington's respective Regiments should be settled. I don't apprehend any better rule for doing that than the former settlement under Col. Stoddard, vizt. the northern line of Springfield, which is the southern line of Northampton and Hadley, to be the dividing line ; and so I state it ; at least for the present ; if there should be any good reason for altering it, that may be done hereafter.

I enclose a Major's commission for Capt. Elijah Williams, dated the day after Major Hawley's commission. Be pleased to let him know that it is my clear opinion he may accept it quite consistently with his honour, considering the circumstances of Major Hawley's appointment, notwithstanding Major Hawley is a junior Captain to him. I shall likewise appoint Captn Williams Commissary, as desired in your letter. I approve very well of the command you propose for Lieuten't Hawkes, whom I have a good knowledge and opinion of, and enclose a blank commission for him, to be filled by yourself accordingly. The plan you sent hath been of great service for my information in the state of the Western Frontier, and I much approve of the line of Forts proposed by you for the defence and protection of it, by marching parties or scouts.

So far as I could go in the Execution of it before the meeting of the General Court, I have gone, and propos'd to his Maj'ty's Council the augmentation of the garrison of Fort Massachusetts with 25 men, and 30 men to be posted and employed in Scouting as you shall think meet for the protection of the Frontier under your Care, which you will find they have advised to, and you will raise the men accordingly.

When the General Court meets I shall endeavor to carry the remainder of your scheme into Execution, and shall make the protection and defence of that part of the Province, in the most effective manner in every respect, one of the principal objects of my attention. Major Williams put me in mind of a special commission which I gave the late Col. Stoddard, which he held during the late war, for the defence of the Western parts of the Province; I should be glad if you or Major Williams could by any means recover a copy of that commission for me. I shall be glad to give you a mark of the regard I have for you, in that way or any other which may happen in my power, and am,

Sir, your most assur'd Friend and Servant,

W. SHIRLEY.

COL. ISRAEL WILLIAMS.

We must now return for a little to Isaac Wyman, and finish the record relating to him. Although Ephraim Williams was appointed to command at Fort Massachusetts, and took his station there about the 1st of September, 1754, under the expectation that a large body of French and Indians were about to repeat the operations of 1746, and under the current impression that Elisha Chapin was unequal to the emergency impending, it is plain, that, as the autumn wore on and no such army appeared, all expectancy of its coming that year disappeared, and the fort, as a place to be defended against an assault, lost its interest for the present; and, in the meantime, as important councils were being taken at Boston and elsewhere in relation to three great offensive expeditions against the French so soon as the next spring opened, that Major Williams found himself more useful and influential in connection with these councils at Boston, in which even George Washington participated in person, than at his own fort, and left consequently the direction of affairs there to his second in command, Lieutenant Wyman. The appended minute shows this, and also especially a letter soon to be quoted from Israel Williams to Wyman direct.

These certify that the soldiers belonging to Fort Massachusetts have been absent on furlows since Sept. 22d, 1754, to March ye 28th, 1755, in the whole one hundred twenty one weeks one day — for myself and negro 14 weeks.

ISAAC WYMAN, Lieut.

HATFIELD, Dec'r 31, 1754.

Sir, The accounts I had bro't [to me] from your Fort not long since of good order and regularity subsisting there gave me singular pleasure. And therefore the information I now have of the clamorous, mutinous behavior of many if not most of the men under your com'and was the more unexpected and surprising. The reason pretended for so much disorder is a very poor one and altogether insufficient to justify it. The men have a right to the allowance granted 'em by the Government, and if detain'd or deny'd unreasonably have a right to seek it in a proper and suitable manner, and may expect relief and justice, and whilst the care and government of the garrison is devolved upon you, in case of the Com'issarys failing to supply it will be expected you inform your superior officer that the grievance be redress'd. Lt. Graves tells me he has supply'd the garrison with a sufficient quantity of rum for ye men posted there, since Maj'r Williams has had ye Com'and of ye garrison ; but it seems it has been disposed of, I fear unnecessarily, whereby a failure has happened — and perhaps its chiefly owing to those persons imprudent use of it who now make ye greatest Complaint and Clamour. However those matters are or have been conducted, the late mutinous behaviour of the men is to be condemned, and in such a way instead of obtaining relief they must expect to loose all, and suffer a much greater punishment, and that they may know what I mean, I incert the following paragraph of a law now in force, viz. : that any person that shall be in his Majesty's service being mustered and in pay as an officer or soldier who shall at any time during the continuance of this act excite cause or join in any mutiny or sedition in the army, Company, Fortress or garrison whereto such officer or soldier belongs, or shall desert his Majesty's service in the Army, Company, Fortress, or garrison shall suffer death, or such other punishment as by a Court Marshal shall be inflicted.

And for your further encouragement I hereby let you know that so far as I have been informed I highly approve your conduct, and you may depend upon being effectually supported, and as it does not belong to you to settle but keep ye acct^s of the Fort, and distribute the allowance from day to day, as you receive it, during the absence of the Capt, so I expect you proceed and see to it the duty asign'd the garrison be punctually performed.

As soon as you receive this muster the soldiers belonging to the garrison and communicate it to them, and unless those who have been seditious and mutinous, give you ample and full satisfaction for their great offence, and proper assurance of better behavior for the future, I hereby direct you forthwith to transmit to me the names of such delinquents, with a full acc^t of their crimes, that there may be a full inquiry, and they proceeded with as to law and justice appertains — and in case any shall offend in like manner hereafter, whilst the com'and is devolv'd upon you, you are directed to give information imediately to your superiour officer. I hereby direct you further to send me a list of the names of the soldiers belonging to your garrison — and also a list of those that belonged to it when Capt. Chapin was dismissed.

I am y^r friend and serv't,

Isr. Williams.

[Filed " Let^r to Lt. Wyman."]

The above letter was dated on the last day of 1754. The opening months of 1755 were busy as never before along the Atlantic shore, from Alexandria in Virginia to Falmouth in what is now Maine, in fitting out three formidable military expeditions against the French posts fronting the English settlements. These expeditions were highly pleasing to the English frontiersmen, because they flattered themselves that such conspicuous offensive operations would relieve them from further incursions of the Indians from the north. They enlisted with alacrity in all three of the campaigns, — that from Virginia, to be commanded by General Braddock, with British regulars as well as volunteers, directed against Fort Du Quesne at the forks of the Ohio; that to be led by Governor Shirley in person against the French posts on the Niagara River; and the one headed by Sir William Johnson, with the rendezvous at Albany, against the fortress at Crown Point. But the hopes of the settlers proved fallacious in this respect. Under this new impulse, however, in part, Massachusetts promptly raised one entire regiment for Crown Point, principally in the old county of Hampshire, largely from soldiers who had served in the cordon of forts; and, after a good deal of management and something of finesse on the part of the "Williams" influence, Major Ephraim was appointed the Colonel, and his personal popularity soon filled the ranks up to the full. He resigned his command at Fort Massachusetts on the 28th of March, 1755, and Isaac Wyman was at once appointed to succeed him, being promoted for the purpose from Lieutenant to Captain. A little further on in this chapter we shall carefully follow the fortunes of the Johnson expedition, — in order to elucidate the story of Colonel Williams to the end, — although it never reached Crown Point and never reflected any credit on its commander-in-chief, while the results, on the whole, were much less disastrous than those of the other two marches.

Additional forces were soon after raised by Massachusetts, the garrisons strengthened on all the frontiers, and the people were required to go armed when attending public worship, it being made the duty of the militia officers to see that the order was strictly enforced. Corps of rangers were now ordered to be raised to traverse the woods to the northward of the cordon of forts; and, to induce them to turn out more readily, bounties were offered for Indian scalps. As Governor and General Shirley was now occupied in the military organization of his central column, designed to strike Niagara, Lieutenant-Governor Phipps resumed the cares of the local government of the province, which he had borne before for several years while Shirley was in Europe, and issued the following instructions to Captain Lyman, of Northampton, who had been appointed to command one of these ranging parties : —

BOSTON, June 19, 1755.

Sir, Having appointed you to be captain of such volunteers as have enlisted or may enlist under you (not to consist of less than thirty men) upon the encouragement offered by the government, to such companies as shall penetrate into the Indian country, in order to captivate or kill any of the tribes, this government hath declared war against. You must take care to enlist none but able bodied men, and see that they be well armed, and furnished with proper ammunition. You are allowed to take thirty days' provisions for your company, out of the commissary's office, before you march.

You must perform a scout of at least thirty days upon every march, unless some special reason for the good of the service shall appear for your returning before that time. And in such case you must account for your company's provisions not expended.

You may march in a whole body or in two or three divisions, and upon several routes as you and your commissioned officers shall judge most expedient, and most likely to answer your design.

You, and each of your commissioned officers, must keep as exact journals as you can, in each of your marches, to which you must be sworn before me, or one of his Majesty's justices of the peace, and exhibit the same to me, or to the commander-in-chief. And before you receive the bounty for any Indian killed or captured, you must deliver up the person captivated, or scalps of those you kill, at Boston, to such person as I shall order to receive the same.

I am your friend and servant

PHIPPS.

To CAPT. LYMAN.

Eight days before these instructions were given, — that is, on the 11th of June, — a party of six Indians swooped down upon the Deerfield valley in what is now Charlemont, while Captain Moses Rice, the first proprietor and settler there, with his son Artemas Rice and grandson Asa Rice, and several others, were hoeing corn in his meadow, just south of the present village road, one man acting as sentinel and the firearms of the rest being placed against a pile of logs, and suddenly fired upon the party at work. Phineas Arms fell instantly dead in the cornfield, while Captain Rice received a severe wound in the thigh, and was taken prisoner with his grandson and one other. The three captives were taken to the high plain in the rear of the present public house in Charlemont village, where the old man, after a fearful struggle with the single savage to whom he was given over, fell beneath the tomahawk, was scalped, and left bleeding, to die after some hours. The other two prisoners were led to Crown Point, and thence to Canada, whence the grandson was ransomed after a captivity of six years; and Titus King, the other, being carried to France and then to England, at length returned to Northampton, his native place. Captain Rice was a great-great-grandfather of Joseph White (Williams College, '36), and treasurer of the College from 1859 to 1886.

.. The very day of this tragedy at Charlemont, the government of
Massachusetts established by law the monthly pay of the officers
and men employed on these frontiers. For the Ranging Forces, as
involving more arduous and hazardous duty: Captain, £4 16s.;
Lieutenant, £3 4s.; Sergeant, £1 14s.; Corporal or private, £1 6s.
8d. And for the Garrison Forces: Captain, £4; Lieutenant, £3;
Sergeant, £1 10s.; Corporal, £1 8s.; Drummer, £1 8s.; Sentinel,
£1 4s.; Armorer at the westward, £3.

The Ranging Corps required men of great strength, inured to
fatigue and danger. They must start with thirty days' provisions
on their backs, and in addition carry their muskets and equipments,
with the requisite ammunition. At night their camp was upon the
bare ground, with no cover unless it were brush huts. In winter the
march was made upon snow-shoes, to the use of which they were
sometimes trained before the campaign began, and their lodging was
generally in the open air, Indian fashion. If a man became sick, or
was wounded, he was either sent back or carried on by his companions. There was little room for medicine or surgery, and consequently little chance for recovery. In forest stratagem these
rangers of the last French war showed themselves little, if any,
inferior to the Indians, and in sustained fighting on equal terms
generally superior. They knew nothing of regular military tactics,
and if they had known, it would have been a constant impediment
to them in the woods, as was demonstrated in the case of the British regulars in Braddock's march and battle and retreat. Provided
they were brave and hardy and good marksmen, — and these were
their general characteristics, — nothing more was supposed needful
to qualify them for this partisan service. The celebrated partisan,
Major Robert Rogers, a Scotch-Irishman of Southern New Hampshire, introduced into his corps something a little more elaborate
than prevailed in this region, which proved itself to be excellent in
his numerous marches and countermarches to the northward; namely,
a simple order of advance for the centre column, with flankers on
each side, and a rule for forming on sudden emergencies by file
movements and by signals. John Stark, the subsequent hero of
Bennington, was a Captain in Major Rogers's corps of rangers in
the course of this war.

The bounties offered on Indian prisoners and on Indian scalps, to
which Governor Phipps refers in his instructions above quoted,
were an inducement by which scouting parties turned out from the
militia not at the time in active service, as well as an incitement to
vigilance and bravery on the part of those specially enlisted for the

garrison or partisan service. The bounty on Indian captives was generally the same as that on scalps. In New York it was higher on the living prisoner; but, in any case, the temptation was strong to put their prisoners to death and carry the evidence to head-quarters for a reward, rather than to take the constant risk of their escape and even of losing their own scalps, to be exhibited for a corresponding reward in Canada. The bounty, when obtained, was to be divided equally, without distinction, between officers and men, — among all who constituted the scouting party or the garrison. In February, 1748, the House of Representatives of Massachusetts had voted, — "and that over and above the bounty above mentioned, and the pay and subsistence of the Province, there be, and hereby is, granted, to be paid to the officers and soldiers, in equal parts, who shall on any scouts that may kill or capture any Indian enemy, the sum of one hundred pounds; the scalp of the Indian killed, to be produced to the governor and council as evidence thereof." The following letter throws light upon the manner of obtaining the reward offered : —

FORT MASSACHUSETTS, August ye 12, 1755.

These few lines are to inform your Honour [Col. Israel Williams] that we have been down with a scalp. Your Honour not being at home, we went to Major Elijah Williams, and had his advice concerning it, and we left the scalp at Lieutenant Graves. We heard that the Assembly was to set pritty soon, therefore we desire your Honour would send us word whether we must come down or not, and trust your Honour would be so good as to send us word if your Honour would think proper for us to carry it down to the Assembly or not. We rely on your Honour to see us satisfied concerning it. So we rest and remain your Honour most Dutiful and Obedient Servants,

JOHN CRAWFORD
and
GIDEON WARREN.

This particular scalp was paid for before the month was out, and the money distributed among the forty-five men then composing the garrison of Fort Massachusetts, under the command of Captain Isaac Wyman. We shall meet with Crawford and Warren again, perhaps, when they will be engaged in something better worth the doing than carrying one scalp between them from the fort to "old Hatfield." Both had a hand in laying some of the early foundations of the "new town," now Williamstown. The same month and the same day on which the two soldiers wrote to Colonel Williams about the scalp, Captain Wyman gave account to the same party, as follows, of a scout that he had accompanied from the fort to the northward : —

Honou'd Sir, According to your directions I took 20 men with 2 fortenits provision. We went to the head of Melomscook [Walloomsac] River the first day, and there we camped [near Center Pownal]. We saw a grate many signs of Indians but none verry new. From there we steared north [into Bennington], and then we turned our coars down the River for Saincoyck [St. Croix]. The 3 day of our march about 12 a clock we got to the mouth of the River [Hoosac Junction]. From there we set out and steared north, but we got but a little ways that night. Georg Willson was taken verry ill and continued so all that night and the next day, so that he was unfit to go forard. We maid no new discovery of Indians, and we turned back and got into the fort the fifth day. S'r, there is Daniel Miller which I have sent down, he hath bin verry ill this some time, and is verry unfit for the service. He is willing to give 2 months wages if there be ceason for it to hire a man to supply his place. I told him that I did not dout but that the Colo. would be willing to change him. I have no nuse to acquaint the Colo. of. I shall send a scout up to the Carring Place [Fort Edward] the next week. There is 2 or 3 hundred of Hampshire forceses gon alongue this week to Albany [Crown Point Expedition].

These from, Sr,
Your verry Humble Serv't
Isaac Wyman.

Disheartening in the last degree, both to the British and the colonial governments, were the issues of the entire campaign of 1755. No one of the three warlike expeditions of the year had even reached their objective point: General Braddock's advanced column had been wofully defeated, and the General mortally wounded, seven miles at least from the site of Fort Du Quesne, now Pittsburg, Pennsylvania; Governor Shirley, whose son William, a British officer, was killed with Braddock, commanded in person the central expedition directed against the Niagara frontier, but neither he nor any part of his column got beyond Oswego, scarcely more than half-way from Albany to Niagara; and the Crown Point expedition, under the command of Sir William Johnson, a rival and personal enemy of Shirley, though it did the best fighting of the year in the battle with Dieskan at the head of Lake George, Sept. 8, stopped short there about midway between Albany and Crown Point, and wasted the autumn in building what Bancroft calls a "useless fort of wood." Johnson called his new fort "William Henry," and the fort at the carrying-place on the Hudson below, "Edward," from members of the royal family, while the lake itself he very properly named "George," in order to honor his king and "to ascertain his undoubted dominion here." Things looked no better for the English throughout the year 1756, when the formal declaration of war was had between England and France, though the war had then been going on two years; and, in some respects, they looked worse still in 1757, when Montcalm swooped down from Canada and took and burnt Fort William Henry, and exposed its surrendering garrison to the horrors of Indian massacre.

In the meantime, Isaac Wyman was faithfully performing in a small way the functions falling to him at Fort Massachusetts. He kept a journal, as required, of his scouts sent out, and of all other noteworthy events at his fort, from which some quotations will be made pretty soon. He had a chaplain there, Rev. Mr. Strong, during the summer of 1756; and, so far as now appears, this was the first stated service of the kind at the fort after the "captivation" of Rev. John Norton there in the summer of 1746. Besides these two, we only know of one other stated chaplain at the fort, and that was Rev. Stephen West, who served during the summer of 1758. Wyman wrote the following letter, dated May 17, 1756, to his superior, Colonel Williams : —

Honoured Sir, I have finished the south side of the Fort that was fallen down, all but the picket in the top of the single work — and have secured the west and north side of the duble work so that I believe there is no danger of its falling verry soon. The top of the Fort wants picketin all round. There was forty six feet in length of the walls was fallen, which I have built all of new timber as high as the double work was before, and fill'd up with gravell. The top timbers ware almost as sound as ever. I began to repair the Fort on Monday the 10 day May, and Fryde the 15 day about noon I finished it. There is Bass and Meacham I have consented should come in Simeon Morgan and Sam¹ Southrick's, if the Col° be willen, for a while. They are to return back any time if they are call'd for.

I keep the scouts constant east and west. They have maid no discovery of Indians all this spring. I send the Col°. the accompt of the scouts I have sent out this Spring. I understand by Serg.ᵗ Taylor that Chidester hath taken Capt. Chapin into the service at the west town. He is to do the duty for the bileting. He hath taken one of the Horsfords' place, and John Vanarnum the other Hosford's place, and they are both gon Home [to Canaan Ct.].

These with my due regards to the Col°.

I remain S'r

Your verry Humble Servᵗ ISAAC WYMAN.

There was found among the papers of Captain John Williams, of Conway, son of Colonel Israel Williams, by General E. Hoyt, the antiquarian, Aug. 31, 1820, a document entitled "Capt. Isaac Wyman's Journal of operations at Fort Massachusetts, in 1756." The first entry on the journal is under the date of May 17, the date of the letter but just now quoted. The "accompt of the scouts I have sent out this Spring," which was obviously sent at the same time with the letter, has not come to light ; furthermore, it is not of much consequence, for the scouts "have maid no discovery of Indians all this spring." But the supplemental journal, recovered by General Hoyt sixty-four years after it was written, covering the time from May 17 till July 10, is invaluable. We quote a few of the more significant entries : —

May 19th. Sent a scout — 4 men guarding men aplowing.

20th. Sent 2 men to guard plowmen.

23d. Sent a scout up the North Branch [of the Hoosac-towards Stamford]. 2 sermons preach^d by Mr. Strong — one man in from Town [West Hoosac].

24th. Sent a scout west — the scout return^d. Discov'r'd the signs of 2 or 3 Indians about four miles distance from the Fort. Brought the nuse that Vanarnum's boys [first " boys " on record here !] saw 2 Indians running up the River to head them.

25th. Sent 2 scouts one East one West — the west scout found the yesterday's nuse to be nothing but some of the Town's people out a fishing.

27th. This day stormy and wet — no scout.

28th. Sent 2 scouts one East one West. Dismiss'd John Herult from the service.

30th. Sent a scout west — Sunday — 2 [religious] Exercises.

31st. Sent 2 scouts one east one up the South Branch to Rush Medow [between North Adams and Adams].

June 1st. Sent 2 scouts — one west one to the Dutch Setlments [Dutch Hoosac]. Muster'd the men to punish one man being found unfaithful on his duty.

6th. Sent a scout East — 2 Exercises by Mr. Strong.

7th. Sent a scout west — Benj^a King William Meacham — the scout ret^d about 3 a clock. Within ¾ of a mile from the fort [east end of Blackinton near where John Perry "fenced" and built in 1746] ware shot upon by a scout of Indians and boarth killed and scalp'd. I sent Ensign Barnard with Eight men to pursue them — they followed them — found they could not overtake them — ret^d to the fort — I sent of a scout to the Town — brought home the dead men — sent of a post to Deerfield in the night — came in the scout from Town [West Hoosac] with some men that came from Albany Aron Denio — they saw fore Indians about 6 miles from the fort — likely to be the same Indians that killed our men.

8th. Sent Ensign Barnard with 7 men with Aron Denio and Cors in serch after the [word illegible] and lading that they left yesterday in there surprise — found them bag and bageg — ret^d to the fort — sent 4 men to garde Denio and company to Charlemont — buried the 2 men kill'd by the Indians [King and Meacham].

9th. The four men that went to guard Denioh and others ret'^{d} from Charlemont

11th. This day our scout ret^d from Deerfield — sent over some stoars to the Town.

13th. Sent a scout west — 2 Exercises by Mr. Strong.

15th. Sent a scout up the North Branch [Mayunsook] — I with 5 men went to the top of Sadel Mountain [first record of an ascent of Mt. Williams] — at night came in Maj'r Thaxter from the camp at the Half Moon with 160 men — brought in 2 men on bears, one wounded by a shot of a pistol from one of there own men, the other sick of the fever — they saw 3 Frenchmen one Indian at Melomscot [Walloomsac] and fired at them.

16th. This morning the wounded man died was buried — sent a scout west — at seven a clock Maj'ᵣ Thaxter marched of for the camp at Half Moon with all his men but six three of them not well.

17th. Our scout east heard guns supposed to be fired by the Indians — one Frenchman or Indian was seen within fifty rods of the Fort, running to git around one of our men — I emediately went out with twenty men in pursuit of them — found where a small scout of them ran acros't the River — I retᵈ to the fort — took twenty one men with me and 2 days provision — set out for the loare End of Hoosuck — found where the Indians had crosᵈ the River stearing towards Melomscook.

20th. Sent no scout — 2 Exercises this Sunday by Mr. Strong.

22d. Sent no scout it being stormy weather.

23d. Sent 2 scouts one east one west — the east scout saw signs of a scout of Indians stearing towards the Fort — Sent a scout to pilot three men to the army at the Half Moon.

24th. The men retᵈ that I sent out to go to the army — saw the signs of twenty or more Indians about ten mils distance from the Fort.

25th. Sent out Ensign Barnard with Eighteen men to range the woods all round the Fort — retᵈ — maid no discovery of Indians. Sent a post to Colo. Williams of Hatfield.

26th. At night came in an Indian fellow from the Camps — brought the nuse that there ware 14 of them in company together within about thirteen miles of this fort ware fired upon by a large body of Indians — he maid his escape to the top of a large mountain where he saw the enemy march alonge thrue a large field — he thought there ware better than two hundred of them. Lieut. Grout was head of our scout coming from the Army.

27th. Sent Ensⁿ Barnard with 2 men to see what he could discover of the enemy and to find whether they ware gone of or coming up this way — sent a scout west — the scout upon there return come so near a scout of Indians that they heard them run down a hill — they followed them — found they steared towards the Fort — 2 meatins as usual being Sunday.

28th. Ensⁿ Barnard retᵈ — he discovered the signs of a small scout of Indians stearing towards the Fort — he and the two men with him went down within ten rods of the place where the Indians fired upon our men — coming from the camps saw three lie dead in the path — they heard the cracking of sticks like men walking alongue a little beyond where the dead men lay — they thought it not prudence to go any farther for fear the enemy ware lying in ambush to catch them — so maid of and retᵈ to the fort.

29th. Sent a post of 2 men to Colo. Williams of Hatfield — Serj'ᵗ Elisha [illegible] with 2 men belongin to the army to acquaint the General of the Indians falling upon a scout of his men that ware coming up to our fort — at three of the clock come in the post that was sent last Fryday morning Serjᵗ Chidester with them.

30th. Sent a scout west — discover'd signs of Indians up Green River [earliest record of that name] — 2 scouts of them six in each scout — saw the signs of them west of pine hill [Dea. Foot's hill] just gon alongue — saw other signs of them in another place where they had just crossed the River towards the Town.

July 1st. Sent a scout east — the scout retᵈ — discovered new signs of Indians — cleared the well in the paraid.

2d. Sent a scout west — saw the signs of ten or twelve Indians stearing towards the fort.

4th. Sunday — sent no scout — 2 sermons by Mr. Strong.

5th. Sent Ensⁿ Barnard with Eighteen to guard provision to the West Town — at night came in Capt. Buterfield from the Camps at the Half Moon with one hundred and forty men — found eight of there men killed by the Indians the 26 day of June — coming to the Fort they buried them.

6th. Sent a guard of 12 men to guard eight men howing corn about three quarters of a mile from the Fort [probably the patch John Perry "fenced" in 1746].

10th. Sent a scout East.

The next day after this last entry in Wyman's journal, Captain Chapin and the two Chidesters were killed and scalped on Hemlock Brook in the West Town, as already related. There is a letter from Colonel Williams to the Governor at Boston, enclosing an "Express" from Captain Wyman in relation to the killing of King and Meacham the month before. The enclosure is as follows: —

FORT MASSACHUSETTS, June 7, 1756.

Sir, Our scout I sent west this day upon their return was shot upon by the Indians, about half a mile distance from the Fort, and are booth killed and scalp'd. Benjⁿ King Wᵐ Meacham was the scout. I sent Ens. Barnard with a number of men after them. They returned in a short time. Thought they could not overtake them. The Enˢ thinks there was about Seven or Eight of the Indians.

I. WYMAN.

William Meacham was from New Salem, in the present county of Franklin, the first settler of which town, in 1737, was Jeremiah Meacham, of Salem by the sea. The first of the name in this country was Jeremiah, of Salem, 1660, a fuller. The fate of their brother (or cousin) William did not deter James and Jonathan Meacham, who were cousins, from coming a few years after from New Salem as permanent settlers in the "new town," where both became prominent landowners and useful citizens; and where James, who became one of the two original deacons here, left a large landed estate, which is still in the hands of his great-grandson of the same name, James B. Meacham (Williams College, 1854).   Deacon James Meacham died in 1813, aged 79.   His youngest son, Israel, was a graduate of the College in its third class, 1797, who became a physician in Richfield, New York, and died there in 1824.   Both James and Jonathan Meacham will cross our path many times in many relations; and members of the family, intermarried with the Warners, immigrated early into western Vermont, and have been prominent and excellent people there.   James Meacham, clergyman and college professor, was member of Congress from the Middlebury district from 1849 till 1855.

The last of June of this discouraging year, 1756, Captain Wyman wrote the letter that follows to Colonel Williams, which is worth quoting entire for many reasons, especially as indicating a better state of feeling than always existed between the garrisons at Fort Massachusetts and at West Hoosac.   The last sentence of the letter, namely, "Serj." Chidester is not ret⁴ yet," may perhaps go far to explain this.

Hono⁴ Sir, The seventeenth of this month one of our men saw an Indian about sixty rods from the Fort. I went out with eighteen men. Found where five or six of them run acrost the River. Stearing west, I ret⁴ to the Fort. Called the men together and enlisted sixteen of em to go out with me two day scout. We went to the Town. They join'd us, maid our number twenty one with the Duch that went with us. I went down the River 10 mils that night. The next morning I set out to go to the loar eand of Hoosuck Town. Found where some of the enemy had got before us. We went down a little further — found a place where we thought they would come along, if we ware before any of them there. We laid an ambush, but did not see much above half a day. Our men seem to be as uneasy as tho they lay on nettels. We ret⁴ within about ten miles of the Fort — there lodg⁴. The next day we ret⁴ to the Fort. Our scouts have discovered signs of the enemy booth east and west. I sent of one man yesterday to pilot three men acrost to the army, at the Half Mon. They came upon a number of Indian tracks about ten miles Norwest from the Fort. · They say they believe there is upwards of twenty by there signs. The enemy's tracks seem to be as new as thers they tell me.

General Winslow sent last week Maj. Thaxter with one hundred fifty men acrost to our Fort at the loar Eand of the Melomscot. They saw three Frenchmen and one Indian, and shot at them. They run up the mountains. The Maj⁵ told me he thought it not worth a while to follow them. They wounded one of there men by the way with a pistail going of so that he died the next morning at the Fort. They left one man sick and 2 lame at the Fort, and three to tend them. The General rote me word that the enemy ware verry thick about them.

Serj![*] Taylor is very desirous of being put into the service somewhere if it could be. He hath no way to supoart his famole under his circumstances. He liveth there at the Town waiting for some releaf. It is a general time of helth amonst us. I have bin not well this two or three days. I am got some better. Serj![*] Chidester is not ret![d] yet.

From, Sir,

Your verry Humble Serv![t]

ISAAC WYMAN.

The only direct evidence known to the writer, that there was a fort during this war near the junction of the Walloomsac and the Hoosac, what is called now in railroad phrase "Hoosac Junction," is the incidental expression in the above letter, "our Fort at the loar Eand of the Melomscot." This fort was doubtless built and maintained by the province of New York, within whose assumed jurisdiction it stood, although the boundary line between New York and Massachusetts was not settled till 1787, and still later the line between Vermont and New York. It was a strategical point, at any rate, for much the same reason as the site of Fort Massachusetts was at the junction of the north and south branches of the Hoosac, twenty miles up that stream. The Walloomsac gave easy access by its three main head streams (though small) from the Green Mountains to the central valley of the lakes and the Hudson, up and down which, of geographical necessity, all the chief operations of all the French wars had to be conducted. There was then, and remains to this day, a ford across the Walloomsac about twenty rods from its mouth, the stream below the ford being deep and swift, and above it a series of stony rapids and steep banks. Across this ford passed our captives of 1746, on their way to Canada, and all the soldiers of Massachusetts to and from Ticonderoga and Crown Point; for the path lay on the north bank of the Hoosac all the way, and another path ran up from the ford on the north bank of the Walloomsac to the north end of Bennington Hill, and it was not an unreasonable matter (as happened once in a notable case) for soldiers coming from the north to mistake the path leading to Bennington for the one leading to Fort Massachusetts. It was along this very path up the Walloomsac, later widened into a rude road, that the so-called battle of Bennington was fought in 1777.

Captain Wyman mentions more than once in these dispatches "the loar Eand of Hoosuck Town." This was at the junction of the "Little Hoosac" with the Hoosac River proper, about six miles south of the Walloomsac ford, termed now in railroad parlance "Petersburg Junction." The extended hamlet along the lower Little

Hoosac and on the broad meadows around its mouth was called in those days "Dutch Hoosac," from the nationality of its first settlers, —Van der Vericks, Bratts, Breeses, Van Vosburghs, and others,—and included the present village of North Petersburg and the scattered farm-houses on both the Hoosacs near their junction. The next hamlet north is what was long denominated "Hoosac Corners," because the turnpike from Bennington to Troy here crosses the old Hoosac road. Next below is "Hoosac Falls," the origin of which designation is obvious. Then follows at the mouth of the Walloomsac the "Hoosac Junction," of which we have been speaking; and up the Walloomsac itself, where the "Little White Creek" drops into it from the north at right angles, is the straggling village of "North Hoosac," where the battle of Bennington began and ended. All five of these present railroad stations, and indeed a sixth, called "Buskirk's Bridge," where Owl Kill tumbles in also from the north into the Hoosac below the junction, are within the large township of Hoosac, Rennsalaer County, New York. All these places are of lasting interest and significance, (1) because they were points and camping-places on immemorial Indian paths; (2) because most of them played a figure and came of record during the old French wars; and (3) because many of them were either a rendezvous or a fighting-place in the war of the Revolution.

The appended letter from Colonel Williams to the governor at Boston bears indeed no date, while its contents demonstrate that it must have been written in July, 1756. It was about the darkest period for all the English colonies in America during the whole course of the Seven Years' War. In no other letter of Israel Williams extant is there seen so pervading a spirit of despondency as in this. There was jealousy and bickering between Sir William Johnson and Governor Shirley, the commander-in-chief; and a cabal instituted by the former against the latter made head with the home government, and sent over in succession three Incompetents, Webb and Abercrombie and Loudon, to supersede Shirley, and to botch the whole business. While General John Winslow, of Massachusetts, was pushing his men and supplies forward from Albany to Half Moon and beyond to Fort William Henry, French and Indian scouting parties constantly harassed him; although the colonial rangers became after a little as active as the French, and Captain Robert Rogers particularly distinguished himself in this and the following year, both years however proving in general disastrous to the English.

Sir, This acquaints you that at Capt. Bridgman's Farm about Eight miles above Northfield a week since 3 women 11 children were captivated by the Indians — 1 man kill'd, and one Endeavoring to make his escape supposed to be drown'd in Con't River.   The buildings burnt — and Tuesday last one man killed or (?) captivated at ye Ashuelots.   The enemy are discovered dayly, and within these few days — in almost every part of our Frontiers, 150 are said to be come down with design to murther and destroy our people.   We have full evidence of their being very numerous.   This Morning by express from Capt. Wyman of Fort Massachusetts I am inform'd that the scouts from that garrison this week discovered the tracks of 30 or 40 Indians steering towards pontoosook, besides diverse other small partys — their course southward — Two men present in order to inform ye people at pontoosook saw five, fir'd upon 'em & probably kill'd one.

The people in the new places above keep close — business is at an end, and they will be impoverished and ruin'd.   And if our enemys continue to press us at this rate, we must quit our husbandry and other business and take to our arms.   I can't think the people at Southampton Blondford No. 1 — New Marl-borough &c, &c, and the other places between Westfield and Sheffield will be safe & secure any longer.   I sent 8 men yesterday to Wings garrison at No. 4 — and expect 8 men more from below, which I design for Southampton.   It is not in my power to grant relief to any other at present.   Several places before men-tion'd are a cover to your people, and unless protected, they tell me they must & will leave their habitations.   Notwithstanding the gloomy prospect our people support with the hopes of being soon delivered from ye cruelty & inhumanity of our inveterate as well as savage foes.

To have our people women & children butcher'd and captivated by such miscreants is very provoking, but not wholly to be prevented.   The murdhers & deaths of so many innocents, & the Cruel oppressions we now groan under, Cry aloud to Heaven for vengeance.   If our iniquities don't prevent may we not hope to have an Almighty arm engaged for our help.   Pray God turn to flight the armys of the aliens, & crown all our enterprizes with success.

I have directed ye bearer to wait y'r answer.

I am w.h sincere respects to y'r Hou'ble Council of war, Sir,

Your Most Ob.t Hum'e Serv't,

I. W. [ISRAEL WILLIAMS].

Meanwhile things were going badly at the West Hoosac fort. Aug. 9, 1756, two days less than one month after the surprise and massacre there of Chapin and the two Chidesters, Captain Wyman writes from Fort Massachusetts to his Colonel at Hatfield as follows: —

Hono.d Sir, The men at the west Fort live in continual confusion together. Serj't Taylor was over at our fort last Satoday with fore men with him for stoars.   They tell me that Seth Hudson, Jabez Worren, John Horsford, Will'm Horsford, and Will'm Chidester are set upon it that they will obey no orders but what cometh amediatly from the Governour to them.   Hudson and those with him ensist upon it that they are an endependant Company.   The way that they go in I am afraid will not only be a means of there losing there own lives but the lives of those that are posted there with them. Taylor tells me they go as carles about there work as tho there never had bin any Indians there, and will do no scouting at all, but seam to trye to destroy themselves and others withe them as fast as they can. My having to many men at this fort I have dismissed Tyras Pratt and Noah Pratt I have sent over to fill up the vacancy there. I have neglected sending a scout to the army by reason of a scouts coming from there last week. Our scout have of late discov'd the tracks of Indians boorth east and west of us Small scouts of them.

These from, S'r,

Your Verry Humble Serv't,

ISAAC WYMAN.

For some reason not known to the writer, Captain Wyman was absent from his fort in October of this year (and perhaps for a longer period), and Ensign Salah Barnard, of Deerfield, afterwards Captain in Colonel William Williams's regiment, who seems to have been for some time second in command to Wyman, became for a little the chief officer at the fort, and consequently the superior officer over the one having for the time being the command over the blockhouse in the West Town; and, in this capacity, Barnard wrote a letter to Colonel Israel Williams, describing a visit which he made to the blockhouse, and letting us into the secrets of that establishment as they were slowly revealing themselves in the early days of October, 1756. We dwell with the more interest and in the more detail upon these rude contemporary documents because they give up glimpses — not always flattering to the men themselves — of those who commenced "to replenish and subdue" the original fields and homesteads of a town now dear to multitudes of hearts. Most, if not all, of the men mentioned by name in this letter were among the early proprietors of Williamstown.

FORT MASSACHUSETTS, Oct. 3, 1756.

Hon'r'd Sir, The paper y! you d⁴ to me at y' Hon's is enclose⁴ herein. When
(delivered)
I was at the West Fort I let the men know that I had it by me and if they own⁴ it as theirs ait (?) they might have an opportunity to put their hands to it. At first the two Horsfords, Warren, and Noah Pratt made answer that they intended to have done it before it was carried down, but when it was read to them they refused to do it, but said since it was to be laid before His Excellency they chose to have one written in another form and send it themselves, fearing that might turn to their disadvantage.

Serj't Taylor requests that he may carry his family from the Fort, the which I let the men know, which seam'd to pleas them quite well. But at the same time I let them know y! I should not consent to it untill I could see a better spirit in them towards him, and that since they had try⁴ to impose upon him in every respect he should still continue to have the command of that garrison. Taylor has all along taken his turn in the Box with the rest of the men, but

I have let them know that I think that by their misdemeniours they give him
quite trouble enough without assisting them in that shape, and therefore have
freed him from that part of duty. Warren has got liberty to be absent from the
garrason ten days. Suppose he intends to ask a dismission from the service
when he comes to see yᵣ Hon'ᵣ. Should be glad you wᵈ grant him his request if
you can think proper. It may be a means of making peace at the garrison.
Serjt Taylors intend to carry off his family to Northfield as soon as he can get
liberty. Sends his duty and prays that yᵣ Honᵣ wᵈ give him a birth as near his
family as may be.

          I am Sir,
                    Yᵣ very Humble Serv'ᵗ,
Colᵒ Israel Williams.   Salah Barnard.

This Samuel Taylor referred to in the above letter as commanding
at the blockhouse at West Hoosac, and as being very desirous to be
dismissed from that service, was a Northfield man, born in 1716;
was older than most of his fellow-soldiers in Fort Massachusetts and
at West Hoosac, but was constantly in the service with them from
1746 to 1757; his wife was with him much of the time in the garrisons; their daughter, Susanna, was born in Fort Massachusetts,
June 27, 1754, and their son, Elias, exactly two years later to a day
in the West Hoosac Fort; and so far as appears at present, this
"Elias Taylor" was the first male white child born in Williamstown.
Rachel Simonds was born here, April 8, 1753, and this Taylor boy
was apparently next in order, and the first of his kind. The father
soon obtained the dismission from West Hoosac that he desired, for
we find him the next March in the service at Charlemont, and a year
later at his home in Northfield. He and his wife were dismissed
from the church in Northfield in March, 1780, to be gathered into a
church in Hartford, Vermont.[1]

We must now go back a little in point of time to the expedition
against Crown Point of 1755, under the command of Sir William
Johnson. Our long story of Williamstown and of Williams College
turns radically upon this expedition, and upon some of its issues,
and particularly upon Ephraim Williams, who commanded one of its
regiments, who had had a peculiar personal training for ten years
in connection with a line of small forts and their garrisons stretching from the Connecticut River to the upper water of the Hoosac,
who had had also an unusual opportunity during these years to
acquire influence with each branch of the Provincial Government at
Boston, whose popularity in the West had been availed of by the
government to raise a new regiment for the expedition, who had
started upon his march from Fort Massachusetts to Albany with

[1] See Family Genealogies in Temple and Sheldon's *Northfield*, pp. 555, 556.

unwonted trains of thought stirring in his brain, — trains of thought that discriminated him sharply from all the rest of his own able, and ambitious, and self-compacted coterie; trains of thought which not the trials nor the turmoils of the rendezvous, nor even the desperate news soon arrived from the Monongahela, could drive away. There is a plenty of indirect proof that premonitions of coming death hovered over his mind. He was forty-one years old. He had neither wife nor child. A very few children had already been born to his trusted comrades, subalterns, and centinels, in, or in connection with, each of the rude forts of his line; there would certainly be more, and especially at West Hoosac, where the centrifugal force of the numbered house lots, several of them with their "regulation" houses already erected and individually owned by the garrison, made against the common blockhouse on No. 6 as a centre, which came to be regarded rather as a place of refuge in times of alarm than as a residence for their families; and Colonel Williams that summer through all its delays, first in Albany itself, and later camped with his regiment "On the Flats" to the northward, kept thinking of those children present and prospective, and could not rest at ease in mind in the "Dutch" country till the stranger lawyer was sought out, the scheme of the school for his comrades' children unfolded, the will drafted and signed and witnessed and sent back to his executors upon the Connecticut. There were picturesque incidents, a great number of them, that late summer and early autumn along the upper Hudson and across the "Great Carrying-Place," in the "Bloody Morning-Scout," and in Dieskau's deadly battle on the lake; but looked back upon from the vantage-point of three half-centuries of development, nothing seems to the present onlooker so pregnant of consequences and so potent of good-will to men, as the bluff questions put and the legal queries raised, the tentative dictation of items on the one hand and the awful legalization of terms on the other, the solemn and soldierly signature and seal-affixing with the witnessing of the three other Yankees (one of whom signed twenty years later the Declaration of Independence), in that lawyer's office in Albany on the twenty-second day of July, 1755.

About a month before this memorable date all the forces destined for the reduction of Crown Point had assembled at Albany. They were composed chiefly of provincial militia from the colonies of Massachusetts and Connecticut. New York had contributed one regiment to the expedition, mainly in recognition of Braddock's courtesy at the council at Alexandria in the spring, in making their fellow-citizen, William Johnson, a Major-General and Commander-in-

Chief of this one of the four campaigns of the season; and New Hampshire had raised for the same object 500 sturdy mountaineers, and had placed them under the command of Colonel Joshua Blanchard, and John Stark (later to become famous) was one of Blanchard's Lieutenants. Boston had been, during the preceding winter, the head-centre of counsel and intrigue. Massachusetts was loyal towards the crown, and bitter towards the French Catholics and the wily savages of Canada. There was no proposal to invade Canada in the present campaign, but only to repel encroachments along the frontiers from the Ohio to the Gulf of St. Lawrence. Massachusetts cheerfully levied about 7900 men, or nearly one-fifth of the able-bodied men in the colony. Of these, one detachment under Winslow took part in the scandalous deportation of the Acadians from Nova Scotia, and the rest mustered under Johnson at Albany. The towns on the Connecticut River, on both banks, and pretty well back from the stream east and west, which was the realm of the Williamses, shared to the full the military spirit of the colony in general, and this, as well as the natural push of these leaders, gave them a right to expect and courage to demand from Governor Shirley both influence and promotion. Letters passed back and forth with rapidity, and journeys were frequent. As always happens under such circumstances, there were envies and jealousies a plenty. Colonel Israel Williams, of Hatfield, very properly and very strongly considered that he should have the direction of affairs at the west; also that it was time his cousin, Major Ephraim Williams, should have the command of a regiment of his own; had he not been for ten years pretty constantly in the service on the frontiers in subordinate positions? and that Major Joseph Hawley, of Northampton (though then fully in the ring), and Major Seth Pomeroy (distinguished at Louisburg in 1745) ought not to claim precedence over the bachelor and popular and aspiring man of Fort Massachusetts. The writer may be mistaken in his judgment, but he believes that some at least of his future readers would like to take a look into some of the letters of that time and that crisis, both as illustrating colonial character and manners, and as forecasting a light on the great revolution even then drawing on.

The following extended letter from Colonel Israel Williams to Governor Shirley at Boston, which is dated Hatfield, Sept. 12, 1754, will well repay an attentive perusal in every line of it, both for the light that it casts on the temper and position of the Colonel and the governor respectively, and for that cast also on the circumstances (trying enough) under which each was acting at the time: —

Sir, I conclude you have before this time been fully informed of ye hostile attempts of ye Indians, and the mischiefs done by them in our own Frontiers, & also in ye Frontiers of ye neighbouring Gov<u>ts</u> — in one of which they have made most terrible wast — and the universal terror and surprize the people are in. It's now open War, and a very dark & distressing scene opening. A merciless, miscreant enemy invading us in every quarter, push'd on by our invet- crate enemy as if their savage nature and blood-thirsty temper needed excite- ments to perpetrate their cruel and barbarous & designs. The designs of ye French in all this are very visible — to prevent our making any new sett<u>lmts</u> to ye North — ye Northern Gov<u>rs</u> sending any assistance of men to Ohio — impov- erishing even as much as possible, preventing y<u>br</u> Indians trading to Albany, opening the way for ye reduction of that city, and finally, if attended like suc- cess, ye securing ye Six Nations in their interest — which when effected farewell peace & prosperity to New England, yea to North America.

It gives me no small satisfaction that under God we have y<u>r</u> Ex'cy still whose enterprizes ag't our common enemy have heretofore been attended with great success to apply to for relief in our distresses, of whose wisdom, care, and com- passion we have had so large experience, and in assurance of y<u>r</u> tender care, ability, and readiness to afford succour & help to us under our pressures, we shall as to our Com'on Father make our application.

My situation & circumstances makes ye Western Frontiers of the County of Hampshire ye imediate object of my attention, and the violent attacks of ye enemy in this quarter calls for the publick more than any other part of the province. I begg leave therefore to represent the state of this Frontier, and to lay before y<u>r</u> Ex'<u>cy</u> what I judge woud most conduce to its safety, & ye security of His Majes<u>ts</u> subjects here & ye neighbourig Gov'<u>ts</u>. Herewith I send a plan of the Western Frontiers, by which y<u>r</u> Ex'<u>cy</u> will be able to form a judgment of our situation, and whether what I am about to propose will serve ye good of ye whole — which is that there be a garrison at Fall Town, another at Coldrain, at Morrisons, two at Charlemont, Massachusets Fort — & a garrison at Pontoosook. At the two first places there are Forts, which the Gov'<u>ts</u> have been at some expense in building heretofore. At Charlemont & Pontoosook the people are preparing for their defence, and the charge in makeing those places sufficient will not as I apprehend be great to y<u>e</u> Gov'<u>t</u>.

I propose that there be at least fifty men posted at Fort Massachusets — thirty at Pontoosook, they to maintain a constant scout from Stockbridge thro' the Westerly part of Framingham [Lanesboro], and the west Township at Hooseck [Williamstown], to ye fort, & from thence to ye top of Hooseck Mountain. That there be 12 at each garrison at Charlemont, 20 at Morrisons & 12 or 14 at Fall Town, who shall perform a constant scout from Con'<u>t</u> river against Northf'd to ye top of Hooseck Mountain.

These scouts thus perform'd will cross all ye roads ye enemy ever travail to come within ye afore<u>sd</u> line of Forts. The'd also afford ye people a guard where they can be spar'd for that purpose. There will doubtless be more men wanted for ye protection of ye inhabitants at Coldrain and some other places. However I apprehend the aforemention'd garrisons will be a great security to ye old towns and new places within ye line aforesaid — and if the scouts are faithfully perform'd there can't any considerable body of ye enemy come within ye line aforesaid undiscov'd, and they will be a great restraint upon small parties, who

will be afraid of being ensnar'd.   The reasons why I propose such a large number of men at Fort Massachusets and Pontoosook are, because it's most likely
the approach of ye enemy within ye line will be chiefly thro' ye line of scouting
from Stockbridge to ye top of Hooseck Mountain, and if they make a discovery
there ought to be a sufficient number of men imediately to pursue within ye line
and out — and also to give intelligence & defend ye garrisons at ye same time,
and also that parties might be sent from Fort Massachusets to way lay ye roads
from Crown Point, & we not be altogether upon ye defensive.   The enemy generally when they leave Crown Point come to ye south side of ye Lake or
Drowned Lands, leave their canoes, and come down to Hooseck, or turn off to
ye East.   Let which will be ye case that fort is best scituate to send out parties
from to gain advantages.   The reason why I woud neglect Shirley & Pelham is
because the Indians were scarce ever known the last war to come down Deerfield river, and that road is almost impassable.   Shirley is rotten, and if main-
taind must be rebuilt — and I think that at Morrison's will answer all intents
full as well, & be much easier supply'd.   As to ye forts above ye line, if ye
Gov'! of New-Hampshire will support 'em it will be well.   But as for ye advantages that will arise to this Gov'! should they maintain & defend 'em, they
will never countervail ye charge and expence.   Notwithstand'g a garrison at
No. 4 the Indians can & will come down Black River, Williams River, or West
River, turn down South, pass over Connecticut River to ye Eastern Towns, without the least hazard, and, when they have done mischief, return with like security,
or pass up above.   The last war the French were with ye Indians, and the Forts
were often attack'd, & ye enemy in some measure diverted.   But Indians alone
will never fight forts much, and indeed we lost more men above ye line ye last
war than in all parts of ye frontiers, those taken at Massachusets Fort included.

   The grand design Colº Stoddard proposed in having a garrison at No. 4
was that parties might be sent from thence to way lay ye roads from Crown
point, and said there ought to be 100 hundred men posted there, one half
to be out at a time.   But his scheme was intirely frustrated.   The Gov'! never
did afford a sufficient number of men for that purpose, and they were scarcely
able to obtain a supply of provisions for those that were there, and many there
were lost in going thither without doing any good.   I expect ye like shoud that
place be again detain'd, and it appears to me to be much best that those distant
places should be broke up, as it never'was prudence to attempt ye settlement of
'em, whilst there was such a wilderness between them & ye old towns, & the
charge of defending 'em will be very great   protection being granted
other places within our own Jurisdiction, which will want it every whit as
much, whether those places above ye line are protected or deserted.   The
·charge to ye Gov't in supporting men at Northfield and other places East will
be much cheaper to ye Gov't, and with suitable guards provisions may be rais'd
for ye men necessary to be sent there.   It appears most likely this will be a
scalping war till ye French openly enter into it, and affect all parts of ye
frontiers, and therefore our interest to be as compact as possible.

   I would further propose that two forts be built between Massachusets &
Hudson's River as laid down in ye plan between which places there is a large
opening where the enemy can come down to ye Dutch settlements or to Stockbridge & Sheffield & whe' they are gone to Connt without difficulty — That one
Fort be built and garrison'd by Con't, ye other by New York.   This line of

Forts will shut up all between Con'! & Hudsons River, & be ye best defence & security to all within, if well supply'd wi'ʰ men of anything I can think of, and if y'ᵣ Excy approves of it & should press it upon those Gov'ᵗˢ, it is so reasonable & necessary for their safety, I can't but think they will at once comply with it.

I submit ye whole, and ask y'ᵣ Exᶜy'ˢ patience for ye tediousness of my lettᵣ.

[ISRAEL WILLIAMS.]

This document demonstrates Israel Williams to have had a good military eye, and a sterling regard for the welfare of the new settlers who had been crowding in upon the exposed frontiers over which he had been in faithful charge ever since the death of Colonel Stoddard in 1748. More than on anybody else a good deal, military affairs in the west of New England turned on the vigilance and activity of this patriotic and competent officer, until the great battle of Wolfe in 1759 settled that whole set of questions. For the most part he stuck steadily to his headquarters at Hatfield. Expresses were all the time coming in to him from the forts and the scouts, and couriers as constantly going out bearing orders and conveying counsels to non-combatants; and consequently it was necessary for him to keep confidential agents more or less constantly both at Boston, whence his own authority emanated at once from the General Court and Governor Shirley, and later at Albany, where the Crown Point expeditions concentred. It was undoubtedly this felt need for authentic news and for influence as direct as possible on affairs, that led him to find Major Ephraim Williams more useful to the cause by attending on the governor and Court during the fall and winter of 1754–55 than he could be presiding over the routine of the line of forts. There were also ulterior reasons, of course. Both of these gentlemen were ambitious of personal and family preferment. They all clung together as towards these ends with remarkable skill and persistence. The now to be quoted letter from the Major to the Colonel reflects abundant light upon the character of each, and also upon the general state of colonial activities as the great crisis was now drawing on.

BOSTON, Novᵣ 21ˢᵗ, 1754.

Sir, I have recv'ᵈ yours & [one from] Capt. Steven. Have inclos'd the directions from Moffet. Shall bring Mr. Sales Capashun [capuchin-cloak] with me. Sᵣ William [Johnson] has not been in town. I sent yᵣ letter [to] Colo. Williams of Weathersfield. Have received no answer. They have agreed to raise in the County of Hampshire 40 men to be posted at Stockbridge & elsewhere.

Lt. Brown is desirous to have 5 men put into the service Bilonging to Stockbridge, which are drove of their lands, which I can't but think will be very servisible for heds of scouts, since they are all smart able-bodied men.

As to Capt. Chapin gitting the Comⁿ from me I bleve there is nothing in that. But the Gover^r has promist to restore him to the Chief command of the Fort as soon as a fort is built west of that, which is to be erected imediately, which I conclude I shall have the command of, if I please. They have noted 530 pound to be laid out to the west, part of which is to be laid out for the above mentioned fort. The Com^{tte} is Capt. Ruggles, Maj. Hawley and Mj. Williams. They have not made any supply as yet. Last evening the Board nonconcur'd the Bill for laying the excise upon the Still Head. Chapin will be along very soon, I conclude, but has not got his money as yet. Can't git out of town without it. I bleve it will be most likely to keep things easy to let him have his Lt. Comⁿ.

The last time I dined with the Govr. he told me he would git your Com^s ready & send it up by me. I shall return as soon as I can have his leave.

I am S^r your Honr'^s Most Humble

Serv't, EPH. WILLIAMS.

COLO. ISRAEL WILLIAMS.

About three weeks after the above letter was written, the Colonel despatched to the Major an apparent reply from Hatfield, which indicates the extremely confidential relations between the two men, and illustrates at many points the condition of society at that critical time. The Colonel's wife was Sarah Chester, sister of Colonel Chester, of Weathersfield, Connecticut.

HATFIELD, Dec'^r 16, 1754.

Sir, I rec'd y'^{rs}. Maj^r [Elijah] W^{ms}. forgot in his hurry to leave any money.

I am sorry ye publick affairs are so many of 'em retarded, and am very much dissatisfied with ye conduct of his Majest'^s Wise Council in some particulars. I hope you are satisfied as to the necessity & prudence of your remaining at Boston, and that you do good ef others dont — if not I think you ought in duty to return to y^r family. The great schemes on foot we are not inform'd. I wish well to my country, & hope others will be directed right, and a foundation laid for our future tranquility & well being. I mentioned to you ye advantage that woud arise from ye intelligence that might be obtain'd from a certain quarter with some cash. I am certain of a greater necessity now than ever. The Scanticook Indians have been to Hooseck & and tell ye Dutch they must not stay longer than March, when the river must be open. They are gathering their stuffs & preparing for a remove.

Chapin return'd across lots — Tells the Soldiers he has got no money, and that he has ye comisary business. The man has undone himself and Graves is in great horror least he undo him, and beggs your help. He has deliv'd into ye fort under ye care of Lt. Wyman, to whom I have given a Commission, ab^t 12000 ^{lb} of meat, and is purchasing what wheat he can, but complains there is no convenient place for ye stores.

If you dont interpose in Graves's behalf and secure ye Comisary business to him he will be soon ruin'd ; and as it's probable he must pay all if you ever get y'r money, I think you ought in justice. He desires you to send him 1 doz. of lemons by ye first opportunity, which are wanted to make a medicine for his poor wife. I hear nothing from S'^r W^m. Conclude he will be at Boston, & desire you would press him on my behalf. I rec'd a Comission from ye

Gov'r. I don't write him because he is so extremely press'd, but if you are permitted at any time to see him, return him my thanks, and tell him I wish my service may be acceptable to him. If we are to have a Vice-president, use all your interest in engaging those who can do any good by writing to ye other side of the water for Gov'r Shirley. He is certainly best acquainted by far of any Gen'l's with the state of ye Colony & North America that we can expect, and I dont doubt but he will vigirously pursue their several interests and exert himself as much as any man for ye ruin of ye comon enemy. God can and I know will raise up instruments to do his own work. What is in ye womb of Providence, or what ye event of ye present projections may be I desire humbly to refer to ye wise Governour of ye world, who can save His people and advance ye Redeemer's Kingdom in ways unthought of by us. May Zion's peace be prolong'd and establish'd. I desire you would get me 2 quire of Blanks & a box of wafers, & other things wrote for heretofore. Remember ye blank musterolls, and be able to let me know ye Establishment wages of officers & men, how many Subalterns etc. Get me 2 ^{lb} of good tea — we have drank wishwash till we are tir'd. Inclos'd is ye pattern of ye cloth I chuse for a coat unless he has a better. Let there be a collar, & mettle buttons — not too bigg — no shapes.

There will be occasion for a considerable number of magasons ; if Mr. Wheel-wright will give order, our leathr will do for that purpose. There are but a few left that are good, they are now wanted for ye scouts. If you can find at ye leathr-dressers a good fine oil dress'd skin that is clean & white I desire you to get me one large eno for a p'r breeches. I send no money — Col. Chester pays all. I have put down things as they come to mind in my hurry — & you will think it well crouded wh. errands. Salles is afraid ye winter will be over before ye Capashun [the cloak] arrives. The news you will write me if you shoud not return soon yrself. The men ordered to Stockbridge Sheffield Brewers Kings Glasgow &c. are not needed, and ye main of them at present are a needless expense to ye Gov't. I hope unless they are needed for some service ye Gov't will give orders for their discharge, which may be of advantage hereafter. Those in ye line for scouts, and some at Pontoosook are necessary, & at present ye Cont soldiers are at ye last place. I fear ye great schemes afoot will prevent due care of ye frontiers, and also prevent ye building of Forts, & before we put our schemes into execution the French will theirs, surprize us in ye spring, & very much distress us. But as I dont expect to turn ye tide, shall make myself easy. I have wrote the Gov'r my fix'd opinion, respect'g Stockbridge Indians, and if a neutrality be never discovered, I shall notwithstanding firmly believe it. I am determined never to restore Capt. C——n [Chapin] to his butlership. He has almost ruin'd ye garrison as I am sufficiently inform'd — the soldiers were debauch'd &c. Wyman behaves well — has restored good order & government and things are now to satisfaction. I hear yt Carpenter is   & I fear Hall is who was dismiss'd from Pelham, and if so Cofferan. See how long. Keep this letter. Write without order to yourself.

I am y'r aff'te Hum'l Ser't,

ISR. WILLIAMS.

Maj'r Elijah just now sent ye money — I know not how much.

Sarah desires you would get her a white Twitcher — they know ye thing at ye shops.

MAJ's EPH's WILLIAMS.

There is a significant letter from Governor Shirley to Colonel Israel Williams, dated Boston, Feb. 7, 1755, which shows, among other things, that Major Ephraim did not fling up his general command over the forts and squads in the west, when he left Fort Massachusetts in the autumn under the direct command of Captain Wyman, but retained his position and pay as was proper, while residing mainly in Boston during the fall and winter, in close consultation with Governor Shirley and others in authority, as to the pressing matters of the impending campaign. Wyman's command was, and continued to be, merely local; and, as the offensive against Canada was already determined on in the projected Crown Point expedition, the soldiers posted at Blandford and Stockbridge and Pontoosuck, and relatively even those in Fort Massachusetts, — all to be soon in the rear of a large force advancing up the North River and down Lake Champlain, would be of little or no use where they were, and might well be drawn upon for the new regiments to be impelled northwards. The popularity of the Major with the scattered soldiers, who had been more or less under his command for ten years, is another thing very visible in this letter: it was evidently relied upon at Boston as a good resource for gathering in the new levies. That the Major had come to have a strong personal hold upon the governor, as well as upon the members of the General Court, who must pass all the legislation required for the campaign, — in short, that he was a very influential person in Massachusetts, during the last winter of his life, — may be read in every line, and between every two lines, of this brief letter.

> Sir, As Maj. Ephraim Williams will engage in my Regiment, it may be necessary to appoint an officer to his Command, which I must leave with you. The soldiers in the Several Forts he may enlist their places you must see supply'd by a new detachment or by a removal of the forty men sent to Stockbridge and places adjacent if you have not already dismist them.
>
> I am with great Truth, Sir,
> Your most assured Friend
> and Servant,
> COL. ISRAEL WILLIAMS.   W. SHIRLEY.

Four days after this letter was written to Israel Williams, in which Ephraim Williams is spoken of by Shirley as "Major," general orders for the guidance of his conduct in enlisting men were forwarded to him, which orders in full follow hereby, in which the title of "Colonel" is accorded to him in form, although in the body of the paper itself he is still denominated "Major," and although at that time (as we shall shortly perceive), he was only expecting a first lieutenancy in the "company" to be called Shirley's in the "regiment" to be so named also, which position involved certain precedencies and contingent promotions in the service, all which we shall understand better when we come to the battle of Lake George.

By his Excellency WILLIAM SHIRLEY, Esq., *Colonel of a Regiment of foot to be rais'd for the defence of his majestys Colonies in North America.*

To Maj^r Ephraim Williams,

Sir; As you have received Beating Orders from me to inlist men into his majesty's Service in the Regiment under my Command, for your management in that affair I give you the following directions.

1. You are to enlist no person below the age of eighteen years, nor above thirty five years.

2. You are to inlist none but able bodied, Effective men, such as be free from all bodily ails & of perfect limbs.

3. You are to inlist no Roman Catholic, nor any that are under five feet four inches high without their shoes.

4. You are to assure the persons inlisted that they shall enter into his majesty's pay from the day of their inlistm't to be paid them at their arrival at the headquarters, which is Boston.

5. You are also to assure 'Em that they are to have his Majesty's Cloaths deliver'd them before they enter on actual duty.

6. Such persons as shall not choose to inlist at large you are to engage for three, five, or seven years, & for those who inlist for three years, I will allow twenty shillings sterl'g a bounty, for five years thirty shillings, & for seven years forty shillings, & for those who shall inlist at large fifty shillings apiece, one quarter part to be paid at the time of inlistment & the other three parts at their arrival at the Head quarters.

7. You are to inlist no persons but such as you can be answerable for the money you advance, as well for their being fit for the service as for their desertion before their arrival at Boston.

8. You are before paying any part of the bounty to cause the 2^d & 6th Sections of the Articles of War to be read to them & have them also sworn & attested before a justice of the peace.

Given under my hand at Boston

By order of Gov'r Shirley,

E^M. HUTCHINSON.

Fortunately, we possess over his own sign manual the evidence that Williams (whatever his military title at the time) proceeded to carry out, at once, the desires of the governor in respect to the enlistment of men for what was to be called "Shirley's own Regiment," and in the exercise of that function ran across obstacles, which he himself describes in a letter to the governor dated "Hatfield, March 7, 1755." The "Phinehas Stephens," who signs the letter in conjunction with "Eph. Williams," was a man whose acquaintance we have already made, was a character which grows more interesting by lapse of time, had been a comrade with Williams many years before as well as at the present time ; while Williams was commanding at Fort Massachusetts in the last war, Stevens was a volunteer in an expedition against Canada, whither he had been carried a prisoner, at the age of sixteen, from Rutland, New Hampshire; he was after-wards ordered to the frontiers, and at "No. 4" made a memorable defence against the French and Indians in March, 1741; for his bravery on this occasion he was presented with a valuable sword by Commodore Charles Knowles, from which circumstance the name of No. 4 was changed to "Charlestown," where Stevens was in command till 1750; and Governor Shirley sent him on a confidential mission to Canada in 1749, of which he kept a copious journal published in the "New Hampshire Historical Collections." He died at Charlestown in 1756, surviving his old comrade and coadjutor but about one year, and leaving a name cherished on much the same grounds as his.

Sir, We have in pursuance of y'r Excel,cy's orders endeavor'd to enlist some effective men & have engaged between 40 & 50, and assured them upon what Colo. Partridge wrote their service would be to the northward, and we were to go with them, which we supposed we might safely do. But as the projections are still a secret, and fearing we may incur blame if we proceed & make such declarations, upon consideration, we think that it is our duty to acquaint your Excel,cy with what we have done, & further inform that unless the great obsta-cle, ye uncertainty of the service can in some measure be removed there is but little prospect of success, but if it can we have good assurances of raising a con-siderable number of likely, effective men, who act upon principle, and have the interest and security of their country at heart, and wou'd with courage and resolution engage the com'on enemy. The enlisting for three years is a difficulty with many, and that the bounty is no more for three years than for one, which occasions our losing some likely men, who engage in the other regiments. And yet after all if y' Excel,cy will give leave to enlist conditionally that if they should not be destined to the northward upon their returning ye bounty they be discharged, if they desire it, the bounty being increased withall, we hope to sur-mount the other objections, and engage some good men that we shan't be afraid to trust our lives with. People begin to guess that their is something projecting by the gover'² that will demand men, tho' they no not what, and imagine that their will be as much gain, & more freedom than in ye regiments now raising, however it may fare with those that now inlist if called to action, they shall be discharged and allowed to return to their respective homes.

We submit the whole to your Excel,cy's wisdom & direction, and beg leave to assure your Excel,cy we shall cherfully contribute everything in our power to serve our king and country, and to our utmost approve our selves, your Excelcy's

Obedient Humble Serv'ts

EPH. WILLIAMS
PHINEHAS STEPHENS.

GOV² SHIRLEY.

The same day on which this joint letter was penned by Williams, he wrote to Shirley another letter strictly personal, which we are happy to quote here in full, because it does great credit at once to the modesty and to the penetration of the writer. In no other extant letter of the founder so much as in this, perhaps, do the man's personal and radical qualities become so transparent. Every line in it is precious, because it emphasizes some line in the character of a man all too little known under the closest scrutiny of the far too scant records of the times.

HATFIELD, March 7, 1755.

Sir, I received a letter from Colo. Partridge at Fort Massachusetts by express, in which he assur'd me that your Excel,cy was pleased to signify to him it was your desire I should inlist some good Effective men to go in your regiment, with a prospect of having ye first Lieu,cy in your Exce,lcy's own Company with some other advantages — of all which I took a very gratefull notice and now return your Excel,cy my sincerest thanks — having maturely consider'd the proposal, I determined to quit my com'and & engage in the affair, yet with apprehensions of those difficulties, which Capt. Stephens with myself in our's to your Excel,cy of this date have mentioned — I have inlisted a few, but not with out engagements, and if the obstacles, we have suggested can't in some considerable measure be removed I shall not be able to raise any great number of such men as your Excel,cy expects — which if taken out of the way I have the vanity to think I could do, and of such with whom I shou'd not be affraid to venture my life. Some may probably drop in without conditions. By Colo. Partridge I am further informed, that your Excel,cy has some expectation of ye first Lieut's coming over, which may prevent my obtaining ye proposed commission — which has put me very much to a stand. I desire to be excused engaging in any shape inferiour, to what was propos'd, and am not over anxious about that, yet if it is your Excel,cy's pleasure I should engage in that form I will do what I can. The men I have engaged expect to go to the northward, and that I go with them, otherwise they declared they would not inlist. And if there be any difficulty like to arrise, whereby your Excel'y will meet with trouble, I chuse now to desist, upon that acco't, and also because of ye uneasiness I foresee will arise in the minds of the men that will inlist. I have no disposition to deceive or disapoint them or others, and shall not be forgiven by them or their friends if I shou'd, which nothing will tempt me to do. If your Excel,cy pleases to direct me to enlist men to go to the northward without any regard to my going with them (as was the case when I joined with Mr. Ingersol) I will endeavor it to my utmost, but without they are assured of that service, or to be discharged in case they are not destined that way, it will be I fear spending time to little purpose to attempt the inlisting likely men for 3 years. I shall wait your Excel,cy's answer & further orders, and if it be your Excel,cy's pleasure, I desist & return to the com'and of Fort Massachusetts, shall cheerfully obey, and am
Y'r Excel,cys Most Obe,dt Oblig'd Humble Serv,t,

E. WILLIAMS.

GOV'R SHIRLEY.

Both the last two quoted letters, dated March 7, were despatched from Hatfield to Boston by express, as urgent; and on the third day thereafter, Governor Shirley replied to them both, sending his answer also by express, which answer serves to show up Shirley also as an open and honorable dealer, even in the matter of offices. Shirley has been much maligned in New England for a century and a half. All the later and fuller researches, however, tend to exonerate and uplift him. This letter speaks well for him.

BOSTON, March 10th, 1755.

Sir, I am sorry you meet with the difficulties in raising men for my Regiment, w<u>ch</u> you mention in your letter of the 7th instant by express. I am persuaded that my Regiment will be continually employed to the Northward and Eastward of Philadelphia. But such conditional inlistments, as you mention in your letter, are not allowed in his Majesty's Service.

As there is this obstacle in the way of your coming into my Regiment, I shall think no more of it. But you may depend upon my providing for you in the other service to the northward, w<u>ch</u> you hint at in your letter (if it goes on as I hope it will) in the best manner I can.

I was very much disposed to have given you the Lieutenancy in my Regiment, as I told Colonel Partridge, I designed to do. But a letter, I have receiv'd since that from England, hath put it out of my power. It would have given me pleasure to have done you that piece of service, if it would have been very agreeable to you, and as things have happen'd, I am glad you are not over anxious about it.

You will greatly oblige me, if you can raise me some men for my own Regiment, and to make it more practicable I will allow fifteen pounds, old tenor, per man, for three years, twenty for five, thirty for seven, and thirty five for such, as shall enlist at large.

The more you 'shall enlist the better. But I desire there may be none, but right good men enlisted, and not under five feet five inches without their shoes, unless they are young enough to grow to that height, and none above forty years old.

I desire, you would pay the express and charge it to me.

I am, Sir, Your most assur'd
Friend and Servant,

MAJOR EPHRAIM WILLIAMS.   W. SHIRLEY.

When he received the above letter, Ephraim Williams was just turned of forty-one years. At this distance of time, and in the present ignorance of persons and circumstances then, one cannot see how Shirley could have written differently from what he did in this letter. He had been receiving constant instructions from England. He was a man under authority, as well as having soldiers under *him*, though Commander-in-Chief of His Majesty's forces in America, until superseded by Braddock, who arrived in Virginia only a few days before this letter to Williams was penned. What the British War

Office thought* of colonial officers in the pending war against the French, may be seen in Braddock's own constantly expressed contempt for them. Notwithstanding all this, Williams felt himself wronged by the present action of Shirley. Both were very ambitious men. Up to the present time, both had had remarkably successful careers, though that of Williams had been relatively obscure. As always happens under such circumstances, each had cliques of enemies, and also emphatically friends in cliques. The Williams family up and down the Connecticut, reinforced by the Chesters of Weathersfield, with whom they had intermarried, formed a clique of their own of strong consistency and great influence; and they had, consequently, what is called in modern corrupt parlance a "pull" on the General Court in both these colonies. Colonel William Williams, alluded to in the following letter, had already come to be by much the most important person in Pittsfield; and he never failed to strike in upon occasion in behalf of his relations to the eastward, as they, too, for him, when anything was to be gained in the way of profit or preferment. Under all these circumstances this letter from Major Ephraim to Colonel James Otis, the elder, then a very influential man in Boston, becomes unusually significant. It runs as follows: —

HATFIELD, March 28, 1755.

Sr, In my letter of yesterday's date, I forgot to inform you that Colo. Wm Williams has wrote to Sr Wm Pepperrel by Colo. Partridge to give me his Capt. Lieut,cy. It was what he did without my desire or knowledge. I knew nothing of it untill I heard him read his letter. I told him it was now too late for me to do any great feats in raising recruits, that I had not above 30 men engaged, the County now being full of recruiting officers, to raise men into his Majesty's service for the term of one year, and as the recruits for his Regiment must be raised for the term of three years, it would be imposable to raise many effective men for that term. I further told him that had I engaged to have gone in the Gov'rs Regiment when at Boston, and had then gone upon the business, had it been in my power to have made promises to the men, I could with ease have raised 200 good, effective men by this time, but as that was over I should not. think any more about it. I further told him when I spent some time in Sheffield, and in the uper parts of Connecticut in raising recruits for the Gov'rs Regiment, in company with Mr. Ingersoll, that in the time I spent with him in raising 25 men, if I should have told them I would have gone with them I could have raised 70. I conclude Sr the Government will raise a number of men to join the King's troops to go to Crownpoint, & I believe the gov'r means by the service to the northward that he will serve me in that service, which if it should I beg he will give his commissions to his friends, for I sha'n't thank him, nor will I take one in that service. If the Army should proceed for Crownpoint, & should meet with opposition & stand in need of more men, I will go with the greatest cheerfulness, with a number of men, but then it shall be without pay from the govern't. But if the Gov.r shall raise some more Regiments at the charge of the Crown, & should give Brig.r Dwight a Lt. Colo. commission, I shall look upon myself under oblagations if his Excel,cy wou'd give me a Majority in that Regiment. I have a great desire Canada should be demolished, and am willing to go personally, provided I could have had an equal chance in raising men, in order to entitle me to a commission. But when you with some other friends offer'd a handsom sum, & promist I should over and above raise a good number of men for a C——cy, which if I had obtained would have set me above some of mine & his enemies & have put me into a condition to have served him & myself, both at Court and in the Regiment, I say when this could not be obtained, & that a Lieut,cy shou'd be promised me one day & the next be out of his power to give, I assure you S.r sinks my spirits. The conciquence of this conduct is I am insulted by his and my enimies. You are sensible S.r I look to you as a Father, therefore intreet you would inquire into the affair I mentioned in my last letter, & let me know by a line, and if anything should open to the northward I have mentioned, you wou'd take some care of me. I further beg no person may know the contents of this or my other letter.

I am S.r with great Respect your Ho.nr most
obliged & most obe'dt Hum.bl Serv't,

EPH. WILLIAMS.

COLO. JAMES OTIS.

The very next day after Williams had penned the not unnatural, but yet ill-natured, epistle just quoted, Shirley wrote the appended courteous and kindly letter to Colonel Israel Williams; which shows him disposed to do what was fair and right in the premises, and which brings in again Major Joseph Hawley, of Northampton, who was one of the ablest and best of the "river-gods,"'into the circle of the well-wishers of the Williams family. We have already seen that he was at times more or less alienated.

BOSTON, 29th March, 1755.

Sir, I am now setting out on my journey to meet with General Braddock [at Alexandria]. Must entreat your favour and assistance in setling the Officers for a Regiment to go ag'st Crownpoint, the Regiment to consist of 500 men with ten Captains ten Lieutenants & ten Ensigns, including field Officers: it will be a great pleasure to me to have Maj'r Ephraim Williams engage as one. I can't be content without having the Officers of one Regiment from your parts. Major Hawley is coming up to settle the affair with you, who will bring all necessary papers with him.

I am with Truth & Esteem, Sir,
Your Most assur'd Friend and Servant,

W. SHIRLEY.

COL. ISRAEL WILLIAMS, Hatfield.

Within less than ten days from the date of this letter, Ephraim Williams was commissioned Colonel of the new regiment referred to in the letter itself. Shirley, by inference, fairly justifies this action, though he does not expressly authorize it in the letter. " It will be a great pleasure to me to have Maj'r Ephraim Williams engage " (as one of the field officers). He may have been more explicit with " Major Hawley [who] is coming up to settle the affair with you [and Colonel Partridge], who will bring all necessary papers with him." The whole matter was thus left in hands very friendly to Williams. Colonel Oliver Partridge, next to Colonel Israel Williams, was the most influential man in Hatfield. He was a Yale graduate of 1730. Traditions concerning him, who became more loyal to the colonies as the Revolution drew on than Israel Williams did, are only less lively in Hatfield to this day than those relating to Williams himself. At this time, and previously, Partridge harmonized fairly well with the Williams family, and is often reckoned in among the " river-gods," though never coming into rank with the "first three." That Joseph Hawley had been in some way personally efficient in the bringing about the colonelcy of Ephraim Williams, becomes plain enough in the tone of his letter written a few days after to the Hatfield parties, strongly commending Major Seth Pomeroy for the lieutenant-colonelcy of the same regiment. He was at once commissioned. He succeeded Williams in the colonelcy on the death of the latter at Lake George, the 8th of September, and buried him the next day under the pine tree. It is believed the reader will like to run over Hawley's letter entire, and it is consequently here quoted *verbatim.*

COL. ISRAEL WILLIAMS   }
COL. PARTRIDGE   } Gentlemen :   NORTHAMPTON, Ap'l 9th, 1755.
COL. Epʜ WILLIAMS   }

With great Submission I am still of the opinion as when at South Hadley y'ᵗ on all things considered Maj'ʳ Pomroy is ye best man to go second in ye regiment. It is ye general vogue & opinion of our people y'ᵗ he not only has meritted it, but y'ᵗ he will in most respects perform ye service and duty of that place well. He is much disposed to go as is pretty easily perceived by his conversation, and is very well satisfied with ye field officers already appointed, as he has fully declared to me, so that it will not probably be his fault if there should not be harmony among ye field officers in case of his appointmᵗ. There is not one man among us who will probably go in officers whom I have heard converse on ye affair but think that he ought to have ye aboveʳᵈ birth. And I am sure that if he is neglected, it will give uneasiness among us, and will very much prejudice ye service here, for it is generally thought by our people that he is free to go and has by his former services merited it. And it is said by sensible persons among us that altho' he was strait handed to his company in ye Canada service, yet he was just and honest to his soldiers, particularly my brother says y'ᵗ he is knowing to it y'ᵗ he never took any furlow money, which he says was generally by other officers taken to themselves. And it appears to me y'ᵗ it is of as much importance to promote and encourage ye service here as at Deerfield where Maj'r Elij'ʰ said it would discourage it, and even in that I believe he was mistaken. I don't doubt at all but L'ᵗ Hawks woud be well pleased with him if others should not disaffect him.

Gentlemen, I have this day heard y'ᵗ it is very probable y'ᵗ Capt. Nath'ᴸ Dwight would accept a Captaincy if he could have it seasonably, and it is thought there would be no difficulty in his raising a company spedily in his own parts, and for my own part I don't think there will be a better Capᵗ. in ye regiment y'ₙ he would make.

Please to pardon me if I am too officious. I think it of a good deal of importance be sure with us y'ᵗ the enlistment begins forthwith, for people are now full of ye affair. Ye spring business is now coming on, which will determine ye business of ye year, and if ye men are not taken before they engage in y'ʳ Spring business it will be vastly more difficult to obtain them. I think ye aff'ʳ ought not to suffer a moment's delay — and I am also sensible that with us the suspension of ye appointm'ᵗ of ye L'ᵗ. Col. injure ye aff'ʳ

I am, Gent'ₙ, with humble respects,

Y'ʳ Most Ob'ᵗ Humble Ser'ᵗ,

JOSEPH HAWLEY.

At the time when Williams received his long-coveted commission of Colonel, which may have been, say, the 4th of April, 1755, there was not, probably, a single one of the ten companies of which the regiment was to consist completely enlisted for the Crown Point expedition. That work was still largely to be done by the various captains, under the difficulty that the spring's work was now opening on the farms, from which alone the men were to be drawn. In accordance with a custom of that time, the Colonel of each regiment was also Captain of one of its companies, and had the emoluments of that position, so that we shall read pretty soon of Williams's company as well as of Williams's regiment. Undoubtedly, the "30 or 40 men," which he had just previously enlisted under other considerations, formed the body of his new "company," of which, as of all the companies, the normal number was fifty. The interesting reference in Hawley's letter, just quoted, to Captain Nathaniel Dwight, of Belchertown, as being probably able, in case he received a captaincy "seasonably" in the new regiment, "to raise a company spedily in his own parts," illustrates the way in which regiments were raised in those days. As a matter of fact, Captain Dwight did not go with Colonel Williams, but on the first news of the battle of Lake George, in September, he took a commission dated two days after the battle, and went to reinforce the army there, keeping a valuable diary, still extant, of the events of the autumn, from which we shall quote hereafter; and Colonel Williams and his captains, for the next two months after his commission was received, were busy in recruiting men and in getting ready generally for the "Marching Orders," which he received as follows, from Governor Shirley, on the last day of May : —

PROVINCE OF THE MASSACHUSETTS BAY.

By his excellency the Governour.

To Ephraim Williams, Esqʳ, greeting :

You are hereby required and directed to issue your Orders to the several Captains in the Regiment under your Command, requiring and directing them to march their several Companies, as they are able to compleat the same, without delay, to the General Rendezvous at Albany, and on their arrival there to follow such orders and directions as they shall receive from Major General William Johnson, Commander in Chief of the Forces raised within the several Provinces and Colonies, for the intended expedition to erect a Fort or Forts on his Majesty's lands near Crown point, and for the removal of such encroachments as have already been made there by the French.

Given under my hand at Boston, the thirty first day of May 1755, in the twenty eighth year of his Majesty's Reign.

W. SHIRLEY.

The road by which Colonel Williams was thus ordered to take his companies to Albany, and did take them, was a rude road laid out as such by the colony of Massachusetts in 1735, from Westfield through Blandford and Otis and Sandisfield and Monterey and Barrington to the New York line in North Egremont. This came very shortly to be commonly called the "Albany road." Like all the other oldest roads in New England of any considerable stretch, this was undoubtedly an Indian trail from immemorial time. It was the probable route of Major John Talcot, of Hartford, to his successful battle with the Indians on the Housatonic River in 1676; for Hubbard says in his "Indian Wars," that about 200 fugitive Indians were observed to pass by Westfield, going on westward; and "news thereof being brought to Major Talcot, he with the soldiers of Connecticut colony under his command, both Indians and English, pursued after them as far as Housatonic river (in the middle way betwixt Westfield and the Dutch river and Fort Albany), where he overtook them and fought with them, killing and taking 45 prisoners, 25 of whom were fighting men, without the loss of any one of his company save a Mohegan Indian."

In connection with the laying out of this road, and during the same year, a committee of the General Court reported, that they were "of opinion that there be four new townships opened upon the road between Westfield and Sheffield, and that they be contiguous to one another, and either joined to Sheffield or to the township lately granted to the proprietors of Suffield," which was the present Blandford, at first called New Glasgow by its Scotch-Irish settlers. These townships were, at first, numbered, and afterwards named in order, Tyringham, New Marlborough, Sandisfield, Becket. The new road led to the settlement of these townships, and especially of the more important townships on the Housatonic, Stockbridge and Barrington, in one or the other of which occurred Talcot's fight in King Philip's War. For some years the new road was passable only on horseback; but in the winter of 1738-39, ten of the principal dwellers on the Housatonic, two of them, John Sargeant and Timothy Woodbridge, missionaries to the Stockbridge Indians, —

did undertake and with great fatigue and difficulty upon our own cost and charge make a good and feasible sleigh-road from New Glasgow, being according to common estimation thirty five miles, by which means a much more safe and convenient way of transportation is now oppened from said Sheffield and the several settlements upon the Housatonic river to Westfield and the neighboring towns, and whereas, before it was very difficult for anybody, and for strangers almost impossible, in a snow of any considerable depth, without a track, which often happens in the winter season, to find the way, now by our having marked a sufficient number of trees on each hand, an entire stranger cannot easily miss it, and the people living in these parts are now able, and in the winter past actually did pass and repass to and from Westfield, with more than twenty sleighs, well laden, through a wilderness which before that was almost impassable on horseback, which by reason of the badness and length of the way, it was almost if not utterly impossible, for his Majesties' subjects living in these parts of the Province, to supply themselves with foreign commodities, the never so necessary in life from any town within this section.

If the reader be interested in early roads through this region of country, he will find in "Berkshire Book," Vol. 1, a paper on this topic of good interest and authority by H. F. Keith, from which the following excerpt relating to the old Albany road is taken.

After passing through Blandford, the road entered Berkshire County at East Otis, and formerly made a detour to the north of the East Otis hotel, thence in or near the present travelled way for a short distance ; thence by a direct westterly course it crossed the Farmington River a little over a mile south of Otis Centre, thence continuing westerly over a steep hill, through the northerly part of Sandisfield, between the two Spectacle Ponds, to a junction with the present road from Cold Spring to West Otis, about one mile south-east of West Otis. Within the distance just described of about six miles, and which is now almost entirely abandoned, there were in the time of the Revolution four hotels, at one or more of which Burgoyne and portions of his troupe and captors, en route for Boston, were fed and lodged. From West Otis the road followed in or near the present travelled way through Monterey, past Three Mile Hill, through the village of Great Barrington, across Green River, through North Egremont, and thence into New York State. With the exception of about a mile and a half of new road in the westerly part of Monterey, laid north of the old road, it can be readily traced as one drives over the present road.

It is almost certain, when Williams's ten companies, one after another, averaging perhaps forty men each, made their way over it as best they could in obedience to his marching orders received, that no organized military companies had ever before straggled and struggled over this Albany road; but four years later, and earlier in the season, Major-General Amherst took a large army of British regulars and American militia over this road to the Hudson, and from the Hudson to Ticonderoga and Crown Point; and in less than twenty years after Amherst's final overthrow of French America, Major-General Burgoyne, with a part of his captured army, traversed the same in the reverse direction; while many a regiment of New England soldiers, in the War of 1812, passed and repassed that way in both directions. After a full century's use as the main thoroughfare between New England and Albany, it was still a doubt and a debate whether the Boston and Albany Railroad, which was laid out alongside the eastern end of the old road from Westfield west, should continue to the Housatonic in Barrington, or should turn to the right up the west branch of the Westfield River over the watershed in Washington to the main Housatonic in Pittsfield. The latter course was preferred; as was also a more northern route through Worcester, and the Brookfields to the Connecticut at Springfield preferred to the old "Bay Path" through Grafton, and Sutton, and Oxford to Hartford.

It is evident in many ways, that Colonel Williams's enlistments for his new regiment drew heavily from the garrison at Fort Massachusetts, and from the men who had formerly served as soldiers in the line of forts under his command. He was always personally popular with the men under him. He joined in their recreations, whenever it was proper for him to do so. The discipline was doubtless lax as compared with that in all regular services then and now; for the volunteer was in most cases an independent farmer or artisan, who felt himself the equal in nearly all respects with his superior officer. The following resolve, passed at this time, shows the difficulty of keeping men in garrison, when active and offensive service under an officer known and liked was optional.

In the Hous of Rep^{ts}, June 12, 1755.

Resolved that in order to prevent an impress of men there be a bounty of three dollars per man allowed to fifteen men who shall inlist for Fort Massachusets and find their own gun, the s'^{d} fifteen men being part of the forces allredy allowed on the Western Frontiers, the money to be put into the hands of Israel Williams, Esqr for that servis, he to be accountable.

Sent up Concurrance,   T. Hubbard, $Sp^{\prime t}$

Rev. Stephen Williams, of Longmeadow, was appointed Chaplain to his cousin's regiment, as he had been Chaplain also ten years before, under Pepperell, at Louisburg. He was son of Rev. John Williams, of Deerfield, the famous "Redeemed Captive," and shared the captivity of his family in Canada during his twelfth year, and wrote at the time a full diary of its incidents, which was published a century and a third afterward by Dr. S. W. Williams, of Deerfield. These two chaplaincies scarcely interrupted a continuous ministry at Longmeadow from 1716 to 1782, — sixty-six years. His receipt for his first month's salary as Chaplain in the Crown Point expedition is annexed: —

June 24, 1755.

Rec'd of Col. Ephraim Williams by hands of John Worthington, Esqr six pounds eight shillings, being in full for one month's advance pay from the Province as Chaplain in his Majesty's service for the Expedition to Crown Point &c.

STEPHEN WILLIAMS.

The following letter from Captain Isaac Wyman, now commanding at Fort Massachusetts, to Colonel Ephraim Williams, illustrates at once the eagerness to get men to enlist for Crown Point, the looseness of military discipline on the western frontiers at that time, and, more obscurely (at the end), some difficulties that had arisen between Fort Massachusetts and the West Hoosac in Williamstown, which will be illuminated in the course of our next chapter: —

FORT MASSACHUSETTS, June 28, 1755.

Hono^d Sir, I have one man deserted from the Fort, Joseph Bigelow, and Capt. Joseph Whitcome hath inlisted and taken him to Albany, and I was acquainted of it before they got verry far from the Fort and sent Serj^t Taylor with 5 men with orders to bring him back to the Fort. The Serj^t overtook them and got the man, and bringin him of Capt. Whitcome ordered two Serj^ts with two files of men to take him from them, which they did and are gone of with him. I weight your Honours pleasure to know what to doe in the afair. My scouts are constant east or west, and have not maid any late descovery of an enemy.

From Sr Your Most Humble Servt,

ISAAC WYMAN.

Sir there is a famoley of the Duch that have maid there escape to the Fort when the Indians fell upon them at Hoosuck. Serj^t Taylor and Silas Pratt will moove there wives out of the Fort as soon as the Duch can git away with safty.

I. W.

Here should come in a precious bit of officialism in a letter from Governor Shirley to Colonel Williams, in relation to the oaths to be exacted from all the officers in the latter's regiment. The history of all these oaths would involve pretty much the whole political history of England after the great revolution of 1688. It is pleasant to reflect that the then present war against the French, in America, was the last one in which such ponderous and multifarious swearing could be demanded of American officers of any sort.

PROVINCE OF THE }
MASSACHUSETTS BAY. }

By His Excellency the Governour.

WHEREAS Commissions are issued to the several officers of a Regiment of Foot, whereof Ephraim Williams is Colonel, being part of the Forces raised within this province for the expedition against Crown point, of which Forces William Johnson, Esqr, is Commander in Chief.

THESE are to authorize and impower Ephraim Williams, Seth Pomroy, and Noah Ashley, Esq'^{rs}, or either of them, to administer to the said officers respectively the Oaths appointed by Act of Parliament to be taken instead of the Oaths of Allegiance and Supremacy ; and to cause him to repeat and subscribe the test or declaration in said Act contained together with the Oath of Abjuration, and also the Oath appointed by Law to be taken respecting the Bills of Credit of the neighboring Governments ; Return to be made of this Warrant with the Doings thereon into the Secretary's Office in *Boston*.

Given under my Hand and Seal at Boston the twelfth Day of June, 1755.
In the twenty eighth year of His Majesty's Reign.

W. SHIRLEY.

Posterity is fortunate in possessing an all too brief, but sufficiently ill-spelled, letter from Ephraim to Israel Williams, relating to his journey from Stockbridge to Albany, and also to what he found at that rendezvous at first. Stockbridge was all the home he had had for some years, and the chief seat of his landed property, which was not considerable in amount. He seems to have had a sort of premonition of coming death before he started, which showed itself in a desire to put into manageable shape his private affairs of all kinds, and which was further illustrated in the making of his will almost as soon as he reached Albany. Two or three sentences of this letter are quite obscure in meaning, but the general drift is plain enough. To share "bed and board" with a trained engineer of the British regulars, was no small privilege for a colonial Colonel, whose active military life had been confined to the routine of Fort Massachusetts.

ALBANY, July 8th, 1755.

Sir, I wrote St Williams of my disapointment in not gitting to Blanford on Wednesday, which was no small damage to my private affairs, as I was obliged to go of from Stockbridge and settle y^m in part. We got to Stockbridge a Thursday night, altho we had 30 horse in company, Friday to Kenderhook, Satterday about 2 of the clock we arrived safe at the Green Bush, where I found the biger part of my Regiment, in as good health as cou'd be expected.   I hear nothing of Gov. Shirley, nor Gen.^{ll} Johnson is not come to the city, tho' expected every hour.   I hope some of the troops will march for the carying place [Fort Edward] this week.   I look upon it necessary ye men should march very soon, or else they will be sickly.   The battoes are in a good way, tho' very little care has been taken about them untill about 15 days ago, and by a genⁿ one Capt. Smith Ayrs whom Gen^{rll} Braddock has sent for our engineer.   He is a genⁿ of smart powers, understands his business well it's said by those y^t know what belongs to it.   In a word we bed and bord together.   Appears a good companion.   As yet I feel bravely.   Should have felt much better, had it not been for some imprudences which happin'd among us a little before our coming, of, which I fear has laid a foundation for a grait deal of trouble this campaign, tho' at present nothing appears.

I am S^r y^r Hon^{rs} most ob^t Humble Serv't,

EPH. WILLIAMS.

P.S. I return thanks for ye two bottles of wine.   Send proper salutations to your family and all inquiring friends.   I desire you wou'd allow Capt. Sheldon what is proper, for bringing back my horses from Stockbridge, and desire Colo. Partridge to pay it out of the money he stopt of Daggit's (or Doggit's) wagis.

E. W.

I hear S^r Wm. Pepperall is sick at New York.

What is fairly suggested by the letter of Captain Isaac Wyman, now commander at Fort Massachusetts, to Colonel Ephraim Williams, quoted in full a little way back, is pretty certainly made out by a second letter from same to same, dated July 11, and sent to Albany; namely, that Colonel Williams still retained a nominal superior command over that fort; for Wyman virtually writes to him in both letters for instructions and orders; and although in the second letter, Wyman refers to Colonel Israel Williams as his undoubted military superior in the matter of the Indian shoes, he also in the same makes a full return of his men, as well as asks for orders, to Colonel Ephraim.   It is to be presumed that Colonel Ephraim held on to his nominal command at the fort, and perhaps also to its current emoluments, with reference to returning to them both when the Crown Point expedition was over.   All this would be in accordance with the usual precedents of the British army, and especially with the prevailing methods of the unusually consolidated Williams family.

Hono^d Sir, I rece'd your letter by Serj'^t Town, and according to your orders and instruction I shall improve the first opportunity of persuing the Enemy that is likely for success.   Ensin Barnard with the men are ret^d with the scalp which they found the Indian about one mile distance from where he was shot down. I hope your Honour will direct them what to do with the scalp so that they may return as soon as posable they can. I should be glad of some Indian shues for these marches, if the Col⁰ could send me them. The old ones are allmost all woar out. I send you the names of the men.

From Sir your Humble Serv⁴,

ISAAC WYMAN.

Ensin Barnard	Clerk Chapin
Serj⁴ Taylor	John Crawfourd
Serj⁴ Town	John [illegible]
Eben'z⁴ Graves	Jabiz Warren
John Wells	Derick Webb
Tyras Pratt	Benj⁰ Simonds
Thom⁸ Train	Seth Hudson
Gad Cors [Corse]	Gidan Worren
John Vanornum	Joseph Brush
Elijah Sheldin	John Holdbroock
Benj⁰ King	Daniel Miller
George Willson	Joseph Richards
Noah Pratt	Sam⁴⁵ Hudson
Abra⁵ Bass	Isaac Sarls [Searle]
Enoch Chapin	Willi⁵ Barron
Silas Pratt	Simon Morgan
Adington Gardner	Ezek¹ Day
Isaac Bond	Isaac Morgan
Joseph Lovell	Levi Eley
Josiah Sodwick	Joseph Bigelow — deserted.
Pall Rice	

Of these forty names (skipping the deserter), almost exactly one-half will meet us again in the next chapter, among the earliest proprietors and landowners of Williamstown. Of several of them, we have made partial acquaintance already; particularly, of Benjamin Simonds, Seth Hudson, "Clerk Chapin," and Captain Wyman himself. At the time this return was made, about a dozen of these men were clearing up and cultivating in the summer their little homesteads in West Hoosac, where they had troubles enough, as we shall see, both as among themselves relating to their two rival forts, and as from their constant enemies, the French and Indians. Two of them, Simonds and Wyman, lived to distinguish themselves, the former especially, in the Revolutionary War.

The troops that had been straggling into Albany as a rendezvous, preparatory to marching up the North River to "ye great carrying-place," later named by Johnson "Fort Edward," and the town there still so named, were mostly New Englanders, some of them led by officers who knew better what French and Indian war was, than did Johnson himself, who was a young Irishman of no military experience, sent over in 1738 by his uncle, Admiral Sir Peter

Warren, to care for some lands of his iu the Mohawk valley. He was then twenty-three years old. About seven years later he built a massive stone house on some land purchased for himself, which he called Mount Johnson, which became the seat of numerous conferences with the Indians, the Six Nations, and others, over whom Johnson gradually acquired a great influence and even ascendency, which he continually turned to the advantage of the English; and on this account Shirley had early named him as a proper person to command the Crown Point expedition, and he had been confirmed for this post by the council at Alexandria. But he was unfit for the place. He gained no military reputation that was permanent, either then or afterwards, although the Parliament voted him £5000 in money and made him Sir William Johnson, Baronet, on account of a partial victory at Lake George gained wholly by the brave conduct of the New Englanders.

Among those Yankee officers gathered at Albany to be under his command, who surpassed him in knowledge and experience of war, were General Phineas Lyman, a Connecticut man, a graduate of Yale College in 1738, and thereafter a tutor there for three years, a lawyer in Suffield, a conspicuous civil magistrate, Commander-in-Chief of the Connecticut militia, placed now second in command to Johnson; Colonel Moses Titcomb, of eastern Massachusetts, who had been a Major in Hale's Essex Regiment at the siege of Louisburg in 1745, and had rendered distinguished services for its reduction, who came now to Albany at the head of a Massachusetts regiment; Lieutenant Colonel Seth Pomeroy, of Northampton, who had been engaged in militia matters from a boy, became Captain of his company in 1744, was an efficient Major in his regiment at the capture of Louisburg the next year, and now for ten years had been an interested student and counsellor of every phase of military affairs in western Massachusetts; and even Colonel Williams himself, for whom military eminence cannot justly be claimed on any ground, though now superior in rank to Pomeroy, may fairly be said to have seen more and known more of war, as well as to have more stomach for it, than Johnson. Another Massachusetts Colonel was at Albany with his regiment, Timothy Ruggles, of Hardwick, a graduate of Harvard in 1732, a lawyer and an inn-keeper, who, though he was scarcely more used to arms than Johnson, was in several respects the most remarkable man in the camp, rude in speech and manner though a scholar and a wit, destined to become president of the Stamp-Act Congress ten years later, and destined thirty years later than that to end his days as a self-exiled Tory in

Nova Scotia. The later famous John Stark was a Lieutenant in the New Hampshire forces present, as was also present the afterwards not less famous Israel Putnam, born in Massachusetts, though now a Connecticut private.

While New England energetically and patriotically sent her officers and men to fight the French, in the loose organization of the colonial governments, and over the wretched roads between the Connecticut and the Hudson, it was difficult or impossible to supply them at Albany with prompt and sufficient commissary stores. The following letter from Ephraim to Israel Williams discloses the pitiable situation of the men under the deplorable weakness of their commissariat.

ALBANY, July 15th, 1755.

Sir, I received your's per Smith. Have sent you 2 since my arrival at this place, but as they were wrote in such hurry & confusion, I bleave you could not read them. I have yet to inform you that our kittles are not arriv'd, nor any necessarys for the sick, nor is the doct's chest, nor do I hear of any fresh provitions upon the road. Our men begin to be sickly. Some Company's are a great part of them ailing, & had not the people been kind in lending their kittles, I make no doubt ½ of the men would have been sick, but then, Sir, you can easily perceive y't they are not able to supply them with half kittles enough, so that great part of ye men are oblig'd to eat the victuals almost as salt as brine. The Doct. tells me by the best observation he can make that in a very little time (except fresh provitions can be had) the men will be so sickly y! the expedition will be at an end. You must know, S!, our being long in camp must be fatal, and can't but know it's impossable to march the whole, untill the above mentioned difficultys with the addition of one more is removed, which is that the ordenence stores are not yet arrived. Now, S!, how must you feel, and every honest man, when he sees a number of brave [men] who have engaged cheerfully in a most glorious cause, where everything sacred is [at stake] should be murdered by those persons from whome they might justly expect to be supply'd with everything necessary for their comfort. This minute Colo. Ruggles is ordered to march & join Gen:!! Lyman, with his Regiment, 1400 troops in the whole. Is to march for the carying place [Fort Edward]. I hope to have orders to march part of my own Regiment with them. I have deliver'd your letters to ye Gov!, but can't get an opportunity to say a word to him in private. Have dined with him today as all the rest of the field officers from this Gover't. He appears cheerfull but something lies heavy on his mind may be easily discovered by those of his acquaintance. Yesterday we passed ye 2 Revew, which was pleasing to him, to see so many of his children as he was pleased to call them. The Review was at 2 places, Conn.', Road Island & New York, with 2 of my Company's was at the Green Bush — the province troops of Colo. Scyler's at the Flats. I beg you would take care to send us fresh provitions, it being the life of the army. I pray God bless you & your's with all friends in ye county, & send proper salutations to all y! inquire after me.

I am your Hon'r's most oblig'd Humble Serv't,

COLO. ISRAEL WILLIAMS. EPH. WILLIAMS.

Leaving for a moment only the destitutions and distresses of the soldiers in the camps near Albany, the jealousies and counterworkings usual in such circumstances among the officers of all grades in the town itself, and the forebodings produced by the news that now began to trickle in of a great disaster to Braddock and his troops on the Monongahela, let us give our attention to a letter written six days after the preceding one, and between the same parties, relating to a matter that will engage us with some deviations increasingly from now on to the end of our self-imposed task, — relating, in short, to Colonel Ephraim's will. His premonitions of approaching death, of which mention was made a little way back, were not likely to be weakened by the confusions and sicknesses of the camp, and especially by the rumors of Braddock's defeat and mortal wound on the 9th of July instant. At any rate, he had his last will and testament drawn in Albany, signed and sealed it on the 22d of July, and sent it with the accompanying letter to the two executors in order named within it. The writer has studied carefully the original of this letter, — now in the possession of Captain Ephraim Williams, U. S. A., a descendant and heir of Dr. Thomas Williams, the Colonel's only own brother, — and has satisfied himself that the erasures near the middle of it were made after the writer's death by the recipient or his representatives, on account of one or two expressions deemed disrespectful to the memory of Ephraim Williams, Senior, the writer's father, probably on the principle that no evil should be spoken of the dead. It may be added, that the alleged copy of this letter, printed in the appendix of Durfee's "History of Williams College," is a mere mangling and caricature of the letter itself. The contents of the will will not be studied in this place, but considerably further on ; but it is relevant to remark here, as perhaps partially explanatory of the letter, that a tradition came down in the Williams family and was more than once mentioned to the writer by the late Mark Hopkins, a lineal descendant of the elder Ephraim Williams, that Ephraim Williams had contemplated marriage at one time (it may be guessed to a daughter of Israel Williams), and that the money donated in the will to found a free school in Williamstown might readily have taken another direction. "The lady Colonel Williams didn't marry !" was toasted with applause under Mark Hopkins's auspices and impulse at the "Jackson Festival" of 1859.

ALBANY July 21, 1755

Sir Inclosed I send you my last will and Testament, & desire you together to consult with Mr. Worthington whether it be legal — if it is not plese to write one that is — send it up and I will execute it — I have altered my mind since I left your house for reasons as to what I designed to give (which should have been handsome) to one being near to you — have given a small matter to others, as near to you — whose conduct to me has [proved] themselves most amiable. Also since I left your house for reasons I have altered my mind as to what I designed to give to ye children of my great Benefactor; have given but a small matter to two of y^m only — you will perceive I have given something for the benefit of those unborn — and for the sake of those poor creatures I am mostly concerned for fear my will should be broke. I believe, Sir, it would have been more agreeable to you if I had gave it for an Accadamme at Hadley. I turned the affair over and over in my mind, found some difficulties, & thought it was best to give it in another shape. I desire that you and Mr. Worthington would inquire into the affair of Stockbridge Indians, which my Hon^d [Father] left in charge by no means [satisfactory to me ?] I desire you to pay at a venture [£20 to the ?] widow of Jonathan. [I do not know as we owe ?] 1 quarter of it, but for fear, you do, I will put enough in. Also plese to pay the following persons whose names are hereafter mentioned, if they are to be found, being soldiers under my command. I received the money out of the Treasury, but never could find the men. Have paid all but these — Danl Wood £4, 10s 8d. Jonathan Conolly £1, 13s. 6d. Nathl Ranger £2, 10s 0d. Wm Williston £1, 16s — lives near Rehoboth. These things above mentioned are most material. I shall conclude by recommending myself to your prayers & you & your dear family to the Divine Protection.

I am, Sir, with great esteem
Yr honored & most humble & most obliged servant
EPH. WILLIAMS.

To ISRAEL WILLIAMS ESQ.

P.S. In my will you find provided some money for the benefit of ye East town, I dont know there will be enough for the west, but so far as it goes, very well, and then some good will come of it.

E. W.

P.S. Let no one but your whole self and John Worthington know what my will contains.

The next day after the letter transmitting his will, Colonel Williams wrote again to the same correspondent, announcing the important news that had now reached Albany in two or three different ways, — the entire defeat of General Braddock before Fort Du Quesne, with all that that involved to the prospects of the two remaining expeditions that *were* to act simultaneously with Braddock's, and that still lay almost helplessly at Albany. The good plan, devised at Alexandria, was, that Braddock, the Commander-in-Chief, should strike the French line at the head of the Ohio River; Shirley, the next in command, the central point in that line at Niagara; and Johnson, the vital outpost of Canada at Crown Point. The first was intended to be the main expedition, composed mostly of British regulars, though Washington was there as Braddock's aide-de-camp, and many backwoodsmen of Virginia and Maryland, whom Braddock despised as militia. Now, word comes to Albany that makes, indeed, Shirley Commander-in-Chief of His Majesty's forces in America, by reason of General Braddock's death, but greatly discourages the officers of both expeditions still lying there, which ill news the officers strive in vain to keep from their own rank and file. There was an increasing jealousy between Shirley and Johnson, although the latter owed his undeserved appointment to the former. Shirley, doubtless, heard of Braddock's death before anybody else did at Albany. The news brought him promotion indeed, but also vastly augmented responsibilities. In the letter appended, Williams could not understand why Shirley still tarried at Albany. He tarried because he was now responsible for Johnson's expedition to the northward, as well as for his own to the westward. Johnson intrigued against Shirley, and the latter's heart was heavy. There were direful premonitions of disaster in both directions, which actually followed in due course of time. Neither Niagara nor Crown Point was reached in this campaign. All the papers of General Braddock fell into the hands of the French at the Monongahela, and these unfolded to them the entire plan of the campaign, and halved the chances of any English success at the northward. Williams's letter that follows does credit to his mind and heart. It is sad reading, but it lets us into the man more than any other document he left behind him, except his will: —

ALBANY, July 22th, 1755.

Sir, In my last I let you know that Genᵣˡˡ Lyman had orders to march for ye Carrying place, with a Detachment of 1000 men, &c. He marcht last Wednesday with his own Regiment. Colo. Ruggles was to join him with his & 4 Companys out of mine. But insted of joining we are not marcht from the Flats yet. What with the quarrel about Com,gs [Comissaries? Companies?], and what for want of stores from Boston, we have been retarded ever since. Gov'ᵣ Shirley has given orders y't Mr. Emerson should not give out but 10 weeks' allowance. Emerson in obedience to ye Gov'ʳˢ orders will in his computation allow nothing for wastige nor leakige. So y't as to ye Rum it will not hold out nine weeks. I am suppris'd to see how things are conducted. Hear Gov'r S——y lies [yet], for what no person knows, except its said to pus—e [puzzle?] the Ex—n to C—n P—t. Things appear most melloncolly to me. Their is no provition to pay the waggoners, I am told. How the stores will be got along leave you to judge. Last evening an express arrived from Meriland with advice y't Genᵣˡ Braddock has been attaced, & has lost many men, with part of the artilery. Is himself wounded. It's to be feared he is cut to pieces and great part of the army, if not the whole. I have seen Capt. Shirley he tells me he can't let me know what he knows. He is under oath. Expect to hear the next news of a total over through.

I have this minute something more perticular — the acco't comes from Fort Cumberland — Colo. Eanas (?) — he received it from one who made his escape, who says they had got within 20 or 25 mile of the Fort. The General had sent 600 some small distance before. He then marcht himself with the baggige and artillery. The French and Indians let the 600 pass them, and fell upon the General, cut him to pieces, and the party with him, before those in the rear got up — that they took all the artillery. He farther says the whole army is lost. 'Tis certain this is the acco't y't is come, for I have had from two y't heard the letters read. Now L!̇ all the hope y't we have left is, y't a man coming of in that manner, is such a supprise, may in many things be mistakein. We expect a post very soon, which will give us a more perticular acco't. I have not to ad, save this, The Lord have mercy upon poor New England.

I am your Hon'ᵣ Most Humble Serv't,

EPH. WILLIAMS.

COLO. ISRAEL WILLIAMS.

P.S. I salute all your famely with all friends.

E. W.

COL. ISRAEL WILLIAMS.

The forces destined for the reduction of Crown Point had mostly, if not wholly, assembled at Albany by the 1st of July. They were in camp at two places: partly at Green Bush, on the east of the Hudson, and partly at "The Flats," so-called, on the Mohawk near its mouth, a few miles above Albany to the west of the main river. They were composed chiefly of provincial militia from the colonies of Massachusetts and Connecticut. New Hampshire sent 500 men, largely Scotch-Irishmen, under the command of Colonel Joshua Blanchard, John Stark being one of Blanchard's lieutenants. Both of these officers, as well as many of their men, were out of the immigration to Londonderry of 1719. Governor Wentworth sent Blanchard first to build a fort on the Coös meadows of the upper Connecticut, being under the impression that that was the true route to Crown Point. Shirley, however, sent Blanchard advices to hasten to Albany; and he retraced his steps to "No. 4," and marched through the woods, it is likely, by substantially the same route Stark took twenty-two years later from No. 4 to Bennington. New York contributed one regiment to the expedition. Hendrik, the Mohawk chieftain, who had been much in Stockbridge, bringing the youth of his tribe to the Indian school there, who was well acquainted with Colonel Williams and always faithful to the English, brought 250 braves of the Six Nations to the camp on the Mohawk. Johnson had expected many more, and referred the failure of his Indians to rally at his call, to mischief wrought among them by Shirley and his agents.

Shirley, as was natural and proper, had become fully conscious on Braddock's death, that he was Commander-in-Chief of all the English forces in North America. Johnson, apparently, never recognized the difference between those broad functions, and those of a royal governor of Massachusetts, and a second in general command. This was the fountain and origin of all the quarrel between the two men; which became bitter at the time, and lasted long afterwards; which, in its results, wrecked, as Shirley believed, his own, the central expedition to the Niagara frontier; which prevented, as Johnson thought, the coming of as many more Iroquois to his standard as those that actually followed Hendrik to Lake George; and which made Johnson regardless of Shirley's orders to push on the offensive to Crown Point after the battle there, with the men who had not been in that fight, on the boats which were already launched on the lake. We have no call to enter into these disputed, and no longer important matters; but as Hendrik's name will be forever strongly associated with that of Colonel Williams, since they fell in the same ambush, if not by the same volley, it is proper that we should place here one of Hendrik's speeches, the last formal one he ever uttered, made in council at the lake only four days before his death, explaining to Johnson and the other officers why so few warriors had joined their standard: —

Some time ago, we of the two Mohawk castles were greatly alarmed, and much concerned, and we take this opportunity of speaking our minds in the presence of many gentlemen concerning our brother, Governor Shirley, who is gone to Oswego; he told us, that though we thought you, our brother Warraghiyahgey [Johnson], had the sole management of Indian affairs, yet that he was over all; that he could pull down and set up. He further told us, that he had always been this great man, and that you, our brother, was but an upstart of yesterday. These kind of discourses from him caused a great uneasiness and confusion amongst us, and he confirmed these things by a large belt of wampum.

I just now said, these matters made our hearts ache and caused a great deal of confusion in our castles. Governor Shirley further told us : "You think your brother Warraghiyaghey has his commission for managing your affairs from the King our father, but you are mistaken, he has his commission and all the moneys for carrying on your affairs from me, and when I please I can take all his powers from him; it was I gave him all the presents and goods to fit out the Indians with."

He further told us when he came to our fort: "This is my fort; it was built by my order and directions; I am ruler and master here, and now brethren, I desire twenty of your young warriors from this castle to join me as your brother Warraghiyaghey promised me you would do, and be ready at a whistle. Brethren, you may see I have the chief command; here is money for you, my pockets are full; you shan't want; besides I have goods and arms for all that will go with me." He said a great more of the like kind, which time will not permit us to repeat at present.

He was two days pressing and working upon my brother Abraham to go with him as a minister for the Indians, he said to him : " Warraghiyaghey gives you no wages, why should you go to Crown Point, you can do nothing there ; but with me there will be something to do worth while." Those speeches made us quite ashamed, and the Six Nations hung down their heads and would make no answer.

But brother, notwithstanding all these temptations and speeches, we that are come and now here, were determined to remain steadfast to you, and had it not been for Governor Shirley's money and speeches you would have seen all the Six Nations here. Brother, we have taken this opportunity to give you this relation, that the gentlemen here present may know and testify what we have said, and hear the reasons why no more Indians have joined the army.

In the meantime, on the 2d of August, as we shall see in the next following letter of Colonel Williams, orders came to march all the Massachusetts and Connecticut troops from their camps near Albany to the "Great Carrying-Place," whither General Lyman had gone a short time before with a considerable detachment in order to build a fort, on or near the site of the old Fort Nicholson; that is, the point where the North River turns pretty sharply to the south from its previously southeast course out of the Adirondacks; a point midway between the head of Lake George to the left, and the navigable part of Wood Creek flowing north to Lake Champlain on the right. In Queen Anne's War, well-nigh forgotten in 1755, Fort Nicholson had been built on the Hudson, and Fort Anne on Wood Creek, the one to command the old Indian Carrying-place to Lake George, and the other the equally old (both immemorial) route to Lake Champlain. Over these portages the Indians had carried their canoes, and the French their bateaux, along Indian trails from water to water, nobody knows for how long a time. It was fourteen miles from river to lake on the left hand, and more or less than that on the right hand, according to the place of embarking on Wood Creek. General Johnson had not made up his mind by which of these routes he would strive to reach Crown Point; and General Lyman worked away at his fort on the east bank of the upper Hudson, for a year or two justly named Fort Lyman, until Johnson, after directly complimenting his king by naming what had hitherto been a French lake, " Lake George," indirectly complimented him further by christening his own fort at the head of the lake "William Henry," and rechristening Lyman's fort "Edward," in memory of the king's grandsons.

CAMP AT THE FLATS, August 2d, 1755.

Sir Enclosed is a list of the officers killed and wounded on the Banks of Monongahela — if this should arrive before you have it in the public prints I shall be glad. — I received it of the Gen[ll] with a charge not to let any one see it

in the camp.   Notwithstanding I have suffered Lt. Col. Whiting & Doctor Marsh
to take a coppys of it for his friends in New England.   Gen[ll] Shirley & Johnson
both keep it as private as they possibly can, for fear it should intimadate the men
— and as we have had various accounts — and know not what to depend upon,
it has in a very great measure answered their intention.   It appears at present
the Gen[ll] was not so much to blame as was expected by the first accounts.   It
seems when he had got within about 10 miles of the Fort with the first Devition,
He sent S[r] John S[t] Clear with a detachment of 300 men to Reconnoytoire the
country & cross the revir ; to support him he sent 200 at a small distance and
brought up the rear with 100 men, being at about five miles distance from Col[o] Dun-
bar, who brought up the rear of ye whole body, and who had with him ye heavy
artillery.   S[r] John crost the river without any opposition, but had not march far
before their rise up a number of Indians, about (as it is said) 300, with some
few French, and fired upon him, & gave a horrible shout.   It being a large
medow and the breacks [brakes] being high, they all fell flat, so that the men
could not see their enemy, if they had had a mind to fight.   It seems the shout
set them into a pannick (and they in spite of all their officers could do) turnd &
run back to the 200 yt was to support them which put them into disorder, so that
the whole run back to the main body, which put them into such a disorder yt
they could not be prevailed, upon to make the least stand.   The Gen[ll] did all in
his power to make them face about, but to no purpose.   During the engagement
he had four horses shot under him, at last was shot through his arm, & the
bullet lodgd in his vitals.   In this confused manner, he retreated back to Dun-
bar, and notwithstanding they had when they were joined, 1500 men, they could
not prevail upon them to make a stand, but were obliged to blow up Maggazien
and leave all the artillery and baggige to fall into the enemy's hands.   The
Gen[ll] died of his wound on the forth day after the battle.   It appers the officers
behaved exceeding well, for after their men left them, they fought untill almost
all of them were killed and wounded.   This acco't was wrote by order of Mr.
Orn? aid de camp to the Gen[ll], but was not able to sign it by reason of his
wounds.

No doubt we shall have a more particular acco't very soon in the prints.
S[r] we have orders to march this day for the great Carrying Place with part of
the artillery.   The whole of the troops belonging to the Massachusetts and
Connecticut, — the Gen[ll] with the rest will march next week !   We are as heathy
here as can be expected — much better for having bran kittles.   How they be
above us can't tell.   Ensign Barnerd informs me you will send a scout to the
Carrying place, which I like much.   I send proper salutations to your family &
Enquiring friends.

I am your Hon[rs] most obed[t] Humble Servt.

EPH. WILLIAMS.

To COL[o] ISRAEL WILLIAMS.

Inadequate as was Williams's conception of the true character of
Braddock's defeat in a French and Indian ambush, as appears at
length in the above letter, it was still correct enough to have put
him thoroughly on his own guard against anything similar as likely
to occur in his career as a commanding officer.   Before this letter

was commonly known, the excuse was often raised in Williams's behalf in view of a like disaster happening to himself and his command just a month after, that he did not know of the details of the rout and ruin of Braddock. But he did know them. He knew also in general, from his long experience of French and Indian warfare, its wiles and stratagems, as commander at Fort Massachusetts what should be the caution and prevision of one taking the offensive against them, exposing his own and the lives of other brave men in such circumstances. Ephraim Williams had many amiable, and some great, qualities; but a high military capacity was not among them. His good name and never-to-be-forgotten memory rest on other foundations.

His regiment, when reunited at Fort Lyman, appears to have consisted of about 420 privates, and about thirty officers of all grades. There were ten companies. The Colonel, Lieutenant-Colonel, and Major had each a company; and Captain Burt, Captain Hawley, Captain House, Captain Porter, Captain Ingersoll, Captain Hitchcock, Captain Doolittle, were each at the head of the other seven companies. There were many old soldiers of Fort Massachusetts among the rank and file. Better and braver men never marched along a river's brink, or plunged into the stream to haul boats up over its falls, or in camp gathered more reverently to daily prayers and sermons twice a week, and joined in frequent Psalm-singing that alternated with the military drill, than the Connecticut and Massachusetts men who marched up the Hudson to a temporary camp at old Fort Nicholson. "Prayers," wrote Johnson at the time, " have a good effect, especially among the New England men." "Not a chicken has been stolen," wrote William Smith, of New York. "Prayers among us night and morning," wrote Jonathan Caswell, a private of Massachusetts, to his father: "Here we lie, knowing not when we shall march for Crown Point; but I hope not long to tarry. Desiring your prayers for me as I am agoing to war, I am your ever dutiful Son." On the other hand, Colonel Williams wrote in the letter about to be copied in full: "We are a wicked, profane army, especially the New York and Rhode Island troops: nothing to be heard among a great part of them but the language of hell. If Crown Point is taken it will not be for our sakes, but for those good people left behind."

The army, marching up the west side of the Hudson, crossed the river where it had been crossed also in both the two preceding wars; namely, at the point where Fish Creek drops rapidly into the main river on the west side, and where the village of Schuylerville now

lies.   Old Fort Saratoga, built by the English and burned down by
them in 1747, stood on the opposite bank.   The present writer has
traced the old road up this bank (now much depressed and over-
grown with trees) from the brink of the river to the site of the
fort.   From this point one old trail, already in 1755 developed into
a road, ran up the river due north to old Fort Nicholson; and
another ran southeast, crossing the Batten Kill twice, through what
is now Union Village and Cambridge, to North Hoosac on the
Walloomsac River.   Over the latter trail, since become a highway,
passed both detachments from Burgoyne's army to the battle of
Bennington, while at the crossing-place at Schuylerville Burgoyne
himself surrendered his army the 16th of October, 1777.   Colonel
Williams's letter from the "Great Carrying-Place" will be found
illuminating.

Camp at the Fort Nicolson,
August 16, 1755.

Sir, I received your favour yesterday per Colo. Willard.   Have to inform y't
we arriv'd here on the 14 instant, with the remaining part of Connecti'ct troops.
Road Island and New York we expect will join us tomorrow.   Expect to proceed as far as Wood Crick, if we should go that way, also expect the several
Governments reinforce us as soon as possable.   I don't expect at pressent we
shall succeed without greater numbers.   Colo. Gilbord is sent Express.   Beg if
you have any regard for your friends, you send us fresh provitions, which will
be much the cheapest.   It's not in our power to purchase y^m here.   The men
have been extremely beat out in haling the battoes over the several falls, being
obliged to waid up to their middles near $\frac{1}{2}$ day at a time.   Our heavy artillery
& magazine are arrived safe.   The rest comes in the last Divition.   Ye Gen$^{r\underline{ll}}$
arrived the same day we did, with about 20 Indians fit for war.   We expect a
large number soon, but the defeat of Braddock has shaggrined them very much,
& Gov. Shirley has took too many indirect methods to git them with him, has
offered them large sums of money, has done everything in his power to disaffect
them to the General, and its said has counterfitted Letters, too many things to
mention at this time, the consequence of which no doubt will be y't they won't go
to war at all, I mean not $\frac{1}{2}$ the number which otherwise might have been expected.
I am sorry we did not go by the way of your town & so Fort Massachu,ts, &
carried our 18 & 32 pounder.   I am sure it would not have cost the Gov'r'nt
$\frac{1}{2}$ it has now done, & would have been terrible to the Enemy.   Our great difficulty now is to know which way to go.   It's agreed on all hands yt Wood Crick
is best, if there was water, but by several scouts it seems y^r is not.   But we
shall be able I hope with the help of the Indians to go forward in a few days.
What you propose in your's as to the Mohawks, I will lay before the Gen,$^{r\underline{ll}}$.
I believe we have not one man of any consideration at all but is determined at
all adventures to conquer or die, but then if it should appear y'^{r} numbers vastly
exceed our's, you must expect we shall not proceed to lose the whole.   Therefore I hope the people in gen'l^{ll} as one man will be ready at a minute's warning,
(if the reinforcements are not sufficient) to come for our relief, & their security.

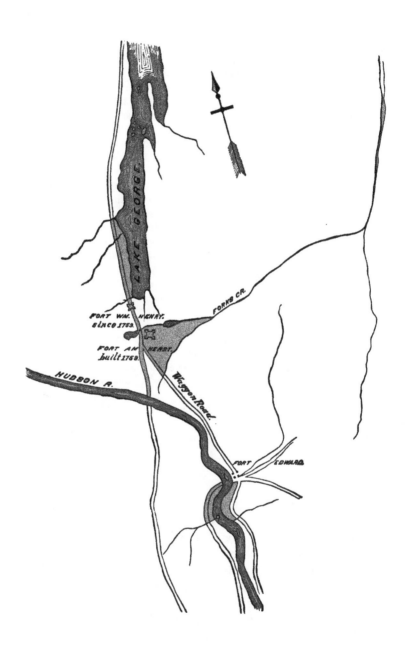

THE OLD "CARRYING-PLACE," FROM THE HUDSON TO LAKE GEORGE.

The Locality of the "Bloody Morning Scout" and of the "Battle of Lake George,"
Sept. 8, 1755.

321

I don't know what Admiral Boscawen is about. If he would proceed up the River of St. Larence, it would be of infinite service to us. Whether their has been proper care taken, or not, I can't say. I had the misforten to have one of my men (big) Winchell have one of the waggon wheels of a 32 pounder run over him, which however only broke his thigh. Another man in a Connectic't regiment shot his arm to pieces and has had it cut of. You mention in y'r letter sent by Ashley, you would look into my will, and give your opinion. I should be glad that you would, & that Colo. Worthington does also, & let it be drawn over again, if it won't answer, by you both, as near as you can to what it is now, & send it up by an express. I will be at ye charge of it. I assure you, Sir, y't affair lies much on my mind. Am sorry you did not give me your advise at least, in your last but one, although you then had not seen Colo. Worthington. I hertily mourn with you, in the loss of y'r Brother. Pray God to sanctify it to all of us, & fit us for our own turns which will soon arrive — how soon God only knows. I beg your prayers for us all, & me in perticular. We are a wicked profane army, more especially New York troops & Road Island, nothing to be heard among a great part of them but the language of hell. I assure you, S:, if ever the place is taken, it will not be for our sakes, but for those good people left behind. I salute your family, with Mr. Woodbridge's, & all inquiring friends.

Colo. Ruggles sends his compliments to you. We have a very good understanding — line in harmony. I understand by Capt. Porter, y't he expected to have his part with all ye rest of the Com'n officers of what ye Gov't allowed for our table, y't he had his acco't from Colo. Porter & Capt. Marsh. I told him I should make no divition [with him] nor no one else. It seems there has a number sent down a petition to the Court, which I am not sorry for. You won't forgit to send your scout.

I am, S:, with great Respect, your Hon'r's Most Obed't Humble Serv't,

EPH. WILLIAMS.

COLO. ISRAEL WILLIAMS, ESQ.

The above letter was written on August 16, and it is a pleasant coincidence that we happen to possess the military "orders" for that day, given out by Peter Wraxall, aide-de-camp, to the army at old Fort Nicholson, then called Fort Lyman, and a little later christened by General Johnson Fort Edward. Owing in part to this superabundance of names, the place continued to be called for some time the "Great Carrying-Place," it being nearly equidistant from the head of Lake George to the northwest, and from the navigable point on Wood Creek to the northeast, over both which intervals boats and luggage had to be borne by hand. Wood Creek drops into Lake Champlain at what is now Whitehall. Doubt as to which of these routes it were best to take for Crown Point delayed the army a long time at this Carrying-place, and so jeopardized the success of the expedition. The Orders of the Day throw some light on the situation.

HEAD QUARTERS AT THE CAMP AT THE GREAT CARRYING PLACE,
FRYDAY the 15th August, 1755.

PAROLE LYMAN — ORDERS.

Colo'l Titcomb Field Officer of the Day for tomorrow.

That Colo'l Ruggles and such other officers as he shall pitch on do imediately look out for proper places to erect a sufficient maggazine for powder, and also a proper place to build an Hospital on, and make a reports of the same at Head Quarters.

That publick proclamation be forthwith made by the Maj'r of each Regim! that whosoever presumes to fire off his piece without leave first obtained from the field officer of the Day be immediately put in confinem! to be tryed by a Court Martial for the same.

That publick proclamation be also made by the Maj'r of each Regim't that no person whatsoever does presume to sell or give to any Indian either rum or any other strong liquor, and that no soldiers come over to the Ilsland where the General is encampt, without being sent or ordered by their proper officers, when they are first to come to Head Quarters.

That these two foregoing orders be wrote out in a large, legible hand, and fixed up at the Head of each Regim't.

That a Serjt from each Regiment be appointed weekly, to take care that their respective encampm'ts be kept clean, & all filth removed as soon as discovered.

PETER WRAXALL
A. D. Camp.

AUGUST ye 16, 1755.

These was the within orders publickly read unto the Ridgment under the command of Colo'l Ephraim Williams, Esq, per me

NOAH ASHLEY,
Major of sd Regiment.

It may well have been that very day also, when Ephraim Williams received at the Carrying-place the subjoined letter from Solomon Williams, a distant cousin, which emphasizes a point we have already learned; namely, that the Colonel was desirous to settle up his pecuniary affairs and to collect his debts, before exposing his life to the French. His will indicates directly the same anxiety that is implied indirectly through this letter of his lawyer: —

SALISBURY, [CONN.], August 4th, 1755.

Sir, Tis a common observation that let men care never so little about their agents, they have always a special regard for their *acts*, as they sensibly affect their constituents. Taking this for truth, I make bold to trouble you by acquainting you that ye Execut'n vs. Kent is paid up — that against Fitch is put into ye officer's hand, tho' nothing as yet done upon it. Am at a loss within myself what directions to give ye off'r which will be most expeditious in procuring ye money tho' have told ye aff'r that provided F—h could not turn out estate, that would speedily command ye cash to commit *him*, for their is no other way as yet opens whereby I can come at *it*, unless ye execut'ᵃ is extended upon his land, & that dare not do without first having y'ʳ approbation. There is so much of his estate already parted by means of other execut'ⁿˢ that half enough personal estate is not, now, left him, to satisfie your's, so that *Neck* or *land* seem to be ye case, & which impatiently wait your resolve. Have nothing worthey notice to communicate, saving that this Colony, understand, have resolved to raise a body of reserve to ye town of 500 men, to be in half pay till by ye General call'd for. Should be glad to know ye true reason of General Pepperell's return home, for see *one* in a news print a few days since which I take to be a very salim sarcasm, viz⁺: that he was to take ye Command of 5000 men, provided with a fine train of artillery, to rendezvous at Fort Hallifax, & thence to proceed immediately towards Quebuck, &c. Should be glad to hear of y'ʳ welfare, as well as of ye whole army — how far you have proceeded on y'ʳ march, & of any remarkable occurrent during ye same.

With proper compliments to all Friends, wishing you in constant readiness every heroic virtue that can render man illustrous, is all at present from y'ʳ poor tho' sincere Friend & very humble Servant,

SOL'ᴺ WILLIAMS.

Colᵒ. Eph: Williams — marching to Crown point.

The New England. men, whose hearts were thoroughly in this expedition against Crown Point, some more on one account and some on another, but nearly all in dead earnest, were restive enough under this long delay through August at the Carrying-place. Protestant zeal in a war against Catholics influenced some of the men. To them it seemed as if they were engaged in a crusade against the myrmidons of Rome. Seth Pomeroy, of Northampton, second in command of Williams's regiment, wrote to his friend, Israel Williams: "As you have at heart the Protestant cause, so I ask an interest in your prayers that the Lord of Hosts would go forth with us, and give us victory over our unreasonable, encroaching, barbarous, murdering enemies." Others were more touched by a remembrance of the sufferings of New England under former inroads of the French and Indians, — of the sack of Deerfield in 1704, for example, — and there was at least one man in the army, Captain Joseph Kellogg, who was a child-captive to Canada on that occasion; and Colonel Williams could not but be reminded of the burning of Fort Massachusetts in 1746, and the massacre on Deerfield meadow following upon that, and he wrote from the camp, "The Lord have mercy on poor New England!"

Dr. Thomas Williams, only own brother of the Colonel and Surgeon of his regiment, was chafed at the incessant delays, and especially at the unaccountable slowness in determining by which of the two possible routes to proceed from the present camp northwards. Letters are preserved from the Surgeon to his wife, and from the Colonel to his cousin Israel, both written on the 17th of August, and both breathing a spirit of impatience. The Surgeon writes:—

It seems if we drive on (not Alexander like) we may possibly see Crown Point this time twelve months. It is a fortnight this day since I came to this place, and was in hopes that ere this time we should have advanced to the other side of the Carrying Place, but the old proverb is, great "wheels move slow." I wish it may be sure ; am pretty certain of a long expedition, and I can't say I dont fear a fruitless one. We know not yet which way we are like to proceed, as the country has not yet been sufficiently recconnoitred, at least so as to give us satisfactory intelligence, notwithstanding we had about eight days ago 300 men at work cutting the road to Fort Ann, supposing we should go by Wood Creek, and in two days they cleared a road thirty feet wide, about eight miles, or two thirds of the way to Wood Creek, but now that is stopped, and forty picked white men, with three of the General's Indians are gone to view that whole country, in order to find out the best way for us to proceed. Captain Taylor of Hartford, a vigilant, active, good officer, goes ahead. Captain Burke is also this day going with ten picked men, and three of the General's Indians to Lake St. Sacrament to view that road. With submission to the General officers, I must think it a very grand mistake that the business was not done two months agone, but so it is, and impatience will only add to difficulty. I endeavor to keep myself calm and quiet under our slow progress, and wait God's time who orders all events, trusting he will yet appear for our help, and his own time favor this our cause which I believe to be just and good.

Colonel Ephraim's letter, written the same day, must now be quoted in full, as it is the last but one that we have from him. The things concerning him have an end. This letter is significant, in that it proves, that he had at length the full particulars of Braddock's defeat and death; that he was coming to have, in common with most of the New England officers, a high opinion of General Johnson; that his feelings ran strongly against Governor Shirley, Commander-in-Chief, then on his military way to Oswego; and that, like his brother, he was full of forebodings over the issue of their own expedition.

CAMP AT THE GREAT CARRY-PLACE,
Aug'st 17, 1755.

Sr, My other letter I was sending by the way of Springfield, but that minute I finished it, the scout arrived from yr Fort. This day we have sent off the Capt's person [Capt. Taylor of Hartford] with 40 whites and 3 Indians, in order to find out a road to Broad Bay [commonly called "South Bay"]. My Capt. Lt. [Capt John Burke] is ordered to go to Lake St. Sacrement, with 12 whites & 3 Indians. We are sensible what is like to be the consequence of Braddock's defeat. Begin to feel it in the Five Nations, as the Gen'r'll has let us know at Council.

No doubt Sr you are quite wright when you say you can't think our men, upon hearing of Braddock's defeate, will be intimidated, but on the contrary will be inspired with more courrage & resolution, but I assure you I wont be bound for many who have the most true account of that defeat. Must think it will [be] for the best to have it remain at uncertainties.

As for Gov'r Shirley, I wish him well. Don't think but he will return again, however the battle goes with the rest. Must think if Braddock was alive he soon wood feel the resentment of his sovereign, for being so slow in his march. The old fellow went of with a heavy heart. Was hertily sorry it was not in his power to order the whole y't way. I long to see the worst of it. Don't find but ye Gen.ʳˡ considering he has not had experience, behaves extremely well — longs to be upon action. I doubt not but he will turn out a man of courage & prudence. I take it for granted you will continue your scout to Wood Crick, or where ever we may make the next place for our retreat. I heartily wish you & your's the Divine protection.

I am, Sᵗ your Hon.ʳˢ Most Humble Serv't,

EPH. WILLIAMS.

COLO. ISRAEL WILLIAMS.

While the Crown Point army lay at Fort Edward, and afterwards, while Fort William Henry was abuilding and garrisoned at the head of Lake George, Fort Massachusetts was the chief half-way house between the army and the Connecticut River and Boston, — a sort of rest and rendezvous for soldiers going both ways, and the principal point of communication, both west and east, for letters and expresses and scouts. The only other way was by Albany and the old road thence through Blandford to Springfield. Captain Wyman kept faithful and efficient watch and ward at the old fort. The first sentence of Colonel Williams's letter, just quoted, shows how the way homewards looked to the Massachusetts officers at the Carrying-place: "My other letter I was sending by the way of Springfield, but that minute I finished it, the scout arrived from your fort" (that is, the fort under your military authority). The letters of Surgeon Williams to his wife show the same thing: "I having an opportunity to send to Fort Massachusetts, improve it to let you hear from me, as also the rest of my friends there, if I have any, which I might rationally suspect I·have not, by not receiving any tokens thereof for above a month past, excepting a line from the Rev. Mr. Ashley, which favor I have a few days since returned him my thanks." And again, later: "I wrote a line by Dr. Mattoon to Dr. Field, desiring him to send two horses by the first opportunity to Fort Massachusetts, in order to Capt. Wyman's sending them to Albany." Surgeon Williams's letters, of which a large number are extant, indicate that he had a much better education than his uterine brother, the Colonel. He acquired a high professional reputation both in the army in several campaigns, and in Deerfield and vicinity, where he practised till his death, in 1775; and, unlike his brother, who died unmarried, he has had, in successive generations, a very large posterity, both direct (bearing his name) and in collateral branches, many of whom have been distinguished physicians. Dr. Edward Jenner Williams, who died at Charles City, Iowa, about 1880, born in Deerfield in 1823; his father, Dr. Stephen W. Williams, born in 1790, and living his whole life in Deerfield (1790–1855); and his father, Dr. William Stoddard Williams (1762–1828), son of Dr. Thomas Williams, and practising in Deerfield till his death, illustrate the heredity in the direct line. Dr. Stephen W. is reported to have said: "My father was a doctor, my grandfather was a doctor, I am a doctor, and, I swow, Jenner shall be a doctor!" Three of Dr. Thomas's daughters married physicians; and Dr. Timothy Childs, of Pittsfield, and his more distinguished son, Dr. Henry W. Childs, long head of the Berkshire Medical Institution, were physicians in collateral lines.

Excepting that we shall quote in full, a little later, Dr. Thomas Williams's account of the battle of Lake George, as an eye-witness and participant, we here take final leave of him with the remark, and the proof of it, that he seems to have been much too favorably impressed with the military abilities and resolution of his General, the later Sir William Johnson. This impression was indeed shared, more or less, by most of the New England officers in this expedition. His brother had it, and tough old Seth Pomeroy had it, and others; but the verdict of history, which has the marked advantage of hindsight, does not corroborate it. The Surgeon writes to his wife, just one month after the battle, in reference to General Johnson : —

I must say he is a complete gentleman, & willing to oblige & please all men, familiar & free of access to the lowest Centinel, a gentleman of uncommon smart sense & even temper ; never yet saw him in a ruffle, or use any bad language, — in short I never was so disappointed in a person in the idea of him I had before I came from home, in my life ; to sum up he is almost universally beloved & esteemed by officers & soldiers as a second Marlborough for coolness of head & warmness of heart. We are now building a strong fortress, expecting to go no further considering the advanced season [Oct. 8] & difficulty of provisions being brought us, which is extremly great.

On August 22 a serious and extended council of war was holden at Fort Edward. Johnson had sent four Mohawk scouts to Canada, and they had returned on the 21st with the report that the French were alive to the situation, and that 8000 men (French and Indians) were coming to defend Crown Point. The council came to two main conclusions : (1) To send back to the colonies for strong reinforcements; and (2) to advance by way of Lake George, and not by way of Wood Creek. The vigor of the call for reinforcements appears best in the letter of Governor Phips, of Massachusetts, in response, Governor Shirley being now in the field as General-in-Chief. The letter was written to Colonel Israel Williams at Hatfield, who was and had been doing his duty manfully as the general commander in the western part of the province. We will furnish the reader this letter in full: —

BOSTON, Aug. 30, 1755.

Sir, Last night I received by express a letter from General Johnson, and a result of a Council of War begun & held at the Great Carrying place the 22^d instant, by all which it appears absolutely necessary there should be a strong and speedy reinforcement of our Army against Crown Point; and as your County is so much concerned in the event of that expedition, & so well spirited in promoting the same, I have enclosed you beating Orders and blank Commissions for you to fill up, confiding in your wisdom and great fidelity, not doubting but that you will exert yourself in so critical a conjuncture. The bounty money shall be paid with punctuality, & the officers and soldiers be put upon the same footing with the rest of our Forces.

I shall depend upon hearing from you touching the premises, as often as the importance of these affairs shall demand.

I am extreamly pleased with the Scouting Party you have destined for the recovery of intelligence from the army by w'^{ch} I hope to hear from them much oftener than I could have done any other way.

I am, Sir,
Your Humble Servant,
S. PHIPS.

The decision of the council as to the route of advance was no less definite. They would turn to the left and go by Lake George, although a military road had already been cut two-thirds of the way to Wood Creek, for this best of all reasons, that a boat-journey down the southern end of Lake Champlain through what were then, and are still, called the "drowned lands," would expose both their flanks without the possibility of resistance to the cannon of the French army at this moment advancing up the lake. Gangs of axemen were sent at once to hew out the new road; four days after the council 2000 soldiers were ordered to the lake; while Colonel Blanchard of New Hampshire with 500 men remained to finish and defend the new fort at the Carrying-place. The farmers of the province of New York had furnished a train of Dutch wagons to bear the stores and artillery; and while these jogged slowly over the stumps and roots of the new road, guarded by small bands of soldiers, the regiments followed on at their convenience. Although there are two small islands in the Hudson directly west of Fort Edward, on the larger of which Johnson had his headquarters while at the Carrying-place, and over which the Saratoga and Whitehall Railroad now crosses the river, the army did not cross there, which would involve another crossing further up at Glen's Falls, but preferred to go straight north on the east side of the river to its great bend where the village of Sandy Hill now lies, and then to turn sharp west to Glen's Falls, thus avoiding any crossing at all. From Glen's Falls to the head of the lake the route was a straight line bending a little west of due north. This road, then opened, has never been abandoned. A plank road followed it with scarcely any variations during the last half of the nineteenth century.

Seth Pomeroy, Lieutenant-Colonel in Williams's regiment, in his ill-spelled journal, gives a pleasing picture of the way the chief officers jogged along from the fort to the lake. "We went on about four or five miles [to the sharp bend of the Hudson south], then stopped, ate pieces of broken bread and cheese, and drank some fresh lemon-punch and the best of wine with General Johnson and some of the field-officers." Also the next day: "Stopped about noon and dined with General Johnson by a small brook under a tree; ate a good dinner of cold boiled and roast venison; drank good lemon-punch and wine." That afternoon they reached the head of Lake George, fourteen miles distant from Fort Edward. The axemen had preceded the little army, and had cut down the pine trees on a strip of rough ground reaching down to the water's edge, considerably longer north and south, — that is, alongside the new road, — than east and west, that is, at right angles to it. The tents were pitched, and a considerable number of wooden storehouses were built among the stumps of the newly felled trees. The camp fronted south, towards ground gently rising up from the lake, and covered with a pitch-pine forest; on their right was a marsh, choked with alders and swamp-maples; on their left lay the low, rocky hill, on which Fort George was afterwards constructed; and in their rear was the peaceful lake.

We will now leave the army in this their well-chosen position for a little, in order to bring up some subsidiary matters needful to the comprehension of our story as a whole. The New England men were far from home. Supplies were forwarded from Albany with great difficulty. If the army were to reach Crown Point by the lake, vast numbers of boats must be brought up the river from Albany to Fort Edward, and then carted across the Carrying-place to the camp. Boats began to arrive in this way almost as soon as the camp was laid out. Some were thrust out into the edge of the lake and fastened to the shore, and some were dumped down almost at random, to be used a little afterwards in strengthening the breast-works. Strong words had gone back to New England for reinforce-ments, and a deep interest was felt in the situation throughout the towns of the four provinces. The interest in the expedition had been large throughout the summer; but the last Sunday in August, and the first Sunday in September (the day before the battle at Lake George), had been rallying days at home, as well as solemn days in camp. Rev. Stephen Williams, of Longmeadow, himself one of the "redeemed captives" of 1704, now a gray-haired veteran, Chaplain of his cousin Ephraim's regiment, preached in camp on both these Sundays to the gathered Mohawks the first day, — but how New England Calvinism lent itself through an interpreter to Mohawk terms hath not come down to us, — and on the second day (September 7), to the white soldiers from a text in the prophet Isaiah. On the first of these Sundays, young Chaplain Newell of the Rhode Island troops expounded in the afternoon, to the New England men, a text apparently untimely, — "Love your enemies."

No one can fairly estimate what a significant day in the history of New England the 8th of September, 1755, proved in the sequel to be, who does not glance at some of the contemporary proofs of interest in the expedition extending through the later summer months. There is a letter, for instance, from Dr. Perez Marsh, sur-geon's mate to Dr. Thomas Williams, the Surgeon of his brother's regiment, who married a daughter of Colonel Israel Williams, — a letter written to William Williams, of Hatfield, destined a little later to become, with Dr. Marsh himself, the two foremost founders and settlers of Dalton in this county.

ALBANY, July 7, 1755.

Honest Friend, You remember I set out on Wednesday. I lodged at West-field that night. Joyn'd in Company about 30. A Thursday to Stockbridge. A Fryday after dinner to Canterhook. A Saturday about noon to Albany. All the Connect! & Rhode Island Forces are arrived, and the most of the Companys under Col's Williams, Ruggles, & Titcomb. The Govenour [Shirley] is not arrived, nor any of our stores, medicines &c. The Commissary's obliged to borrow all the provisions. Connecticut Forces are allready to march, and Generall Lyman is determin'd they shall set out this weak at all adventures. About five hundred of the Six Nations have taken up the hatchet under General Johnson, the most of them determined for Crown Point. The Catnowagoes they appear to be very friendly, and the Generall is confident we shall meet with no oppositions from them. By reason of the tents not being come, the soldiers lodge in barns at all corners of the city. They at present are healthy, but I fear they will not continue so, for I see no prospect of our marching this month. No Governour, no stores, no medicines, no battoes, at least there is not one ready — there are a number made but not corked nor tared. They tell me the reason of their being so slow in their motion is because nobody hurrys them. There are men enough in the city understand the business, and one of the carpenters told me this morning he was certain he could have them allready in five days if they could say the word. I very much fear the consequences of thus delaying Doct'ʳ Williams and myself. Lodge at the house of one Mrs. Wendell, a widow woman whose husband was brother to Col. Wendell of Boston. They are quite friendly & obliging old & yong. I like the city & the people in generall much better than I expected, and believe them to be as hearty in the present Expedition as any of us. They seem all engaged to expedite matters as much as possible. This is contrary to common fame, but I must at present believe it (excepting two or three Gentlemen) General Johnson is to be here this day. What determinations will he come into after his arrival I know not. Would delay wrighting, but the bearer sets out immediately. Thus, Sʳ, without form or connection, in a hurry, I have given you an imperfect sketch of my journey, safe arrival, and the most material things worthy of notice.

I am, Sʳ, in good health and spirits, after proper salutations to your Hon'ᵈ Father and Mother, To the Rev'ᵈ Mr. Woodbridge, Mrs. Sally &c, Your Sincere Friend & Most Obliged Hum'ˡ Serv'ᵗ,

PEREZ MARSH.

To Mr. WILL'ᵐ WILLIAMS.

Then there is a letter written about the same time by Colonel John Worthington, of Springfield, to Colonel Ephraim Williams, which presents both of them in a pleasing light, and which serves in part to unfold the reason why Williams, in drawing his will in Albany at just about this time, made Worthington one of his two executors. The other was his cousin, Israel Williams. These two were his most intimate friends; and they were also, in secular matters, the two most influential dwellers in the valley of the Connecticut within the limits of Massachusetts at the middle of the last century. It was characteristic of the founder of the College, as it was of the individuals of his tribe generally, to select "the best" that offered as friends and companions: they came under the sweep of the saying, then and still current up and down the Connecticut, "Tell me who your company are and I will tell you who you are"; and there was something good personally and socially, as well as something evil socially and politically, in the general habits thus engendered. The Williamses and their special confederates became what were termed at the time "aristocrats"; and, lacking a true fellowship with the masses, when the struggle with the mother country broke out, they took the side of the crown almost without exception. John Worthington writes: —

Sir, I rec'd yours by L'u't Taylor. Am very much oblig'd to you for your care in the favours I ask'd of you.

Leut Taylor informs the officers here that the present design respecting the soldiers is that they march to Westfield on their tour to Albany & be muster'd & receive the residue of bounty, wages, &c there at Westfield. This S'ᴿ gives them uneasiness, very considerable, & if orders peremptory are given for it I am very sorry, & I may S'ᴿ say it to you tho not to them that tho I am all submission to the wisdom of our Fathers (if their Wisdom is in it) yet that this must needs be misjudged. The soldiers ought in all reason to have been muster'd ten days ago, & to have known certainly who would be accepted & who not, that such as were accepted might have had their money to have furnished themselves wʰ necessary cloathing &c for their march, & to have provided to have left their families (such as have them) provided for at home, for many such there are who depended on their money to do those things, & will be reduced to great difficulties without they receive it in season, & where they can dispose of it to these purposes. This sh'ᵈ have been done also that such as are so unhappy as not to be admitted to risque their lives for us, may be saved as much trouble as might be, & be denied the favour on the cheapest terms. It would have been easy I conceive for the Gent'ⁿ commission'd to muster the men to have muster'd them near home seasonably for their being allowed to return home after muster for the purposes I have mention'd, & for others y'ᵗ might be suggested. I am sure it could make them but little trouble, nor the Province but a trifling expense. The contrary I am as sure will subject the soldiers to difficulties very great and very needless, & I am very sorry to find that any of the men of this respectable character (I mean soldiers S'ᴿ) who deserve esteem & acknowledgmᵗˢ from everybody where they have out of regard to the public good voluntarily offered themselves to risque their lives & encounter fatigues & hardship in a thousand various shapes, that we might some of us rest in ease & quiet at home, should in any instance imagine they have the least colour to suspect they are subjected to any one additional inconvenience that is not necessary for the publick service.

If this matter can be otherwise I am certain it will be a great favour to the men, but if it cannot they must bear it as it comes, & we will endeavor to relieve & quiet them under it as well as may be.

I am, Sir, with great respect for you in every charact'r, but especially now in that of a soldier,

Your very humble Servant and Sincere Friend,

J. WORTHINGTON.

COL. EPHᴿ WILLIAMS.
SPRINGF'ᴰ, June 15, 1755.

It is no inconvenience to the men to have their blankets & knapsacks [kept back], but the contrary, but as to their money it is much otherwise.

There is also an illuminating letter, that belongs here, from Israel Williams, co-executor with John Worthington of Ephraim's will, a will not yet a month old, but already hastening towards its probate, a letter that lets us more deeply into the personal and patriotic affections of "ye monarch of Hampshire" than perhaps any other one of a long series. The details of Braddock's defeat, and its points of application to the Crown Point expedition, had not then been ascertained on the Connecticut, as they were by this time thoroughly known at the Great Carrying-place; and yet the present reader will observe how prompt Colonel Israel was to draw the lesson of the Monongahela, and to exhort the parties immediately concerned on the upper Hudson to apply to themselves the fore-thrusting precautions. " I am extremely concerned for you and the forces with you, and beg you to take all necessary precautions, and if you want help let us know it. If Braddock is lost, it will be ye greatest folly for Maj'r Gen! Shirley to proceed, and hope you will join and be joined with a greater number of troops and proceed directly for Canada." The following letter, taken as a whole, presents the Hatfield Colonel to us in such a natural and favorable light, that we are glad to take formal leave of him while dwelling on the traits presented here, as a vigilant commander of men, a wise military counsellor, a warm personal friend, and a loving father of a family. Five years before this we have seen him intriguing persistently, almost malignantly, against his great cousin, Jonathan Edwards, his neighbor in Northampton; fifteen years after this, we might find him taking strong sides for King and Parliament against another great cousin, Joseph Hawley, who was slowly organizing the patriotic forces of the valley to co-operate with similar forces on the seaboard under the lead of Samuel Adams; but we choose to take historical leave of him, though we shall casually cross his path again, penning this friendly letter of caution and counsel to still another cousin, five years his junior, constantly cared for by him as a son.

HATFIELD, Aug'! 7, 1755.

Sir, The enemy are still very thick in ye frontiers, destroying our people and their substance. A particular acc'! you will have by Col. Willard or others. And if Gen'! Braddock is disappointed I expect ye French will take courage, and by their Indians press us much harder, as ye forces belonging to New Hampshire are come away from their Frontiers. The Inhabitants above ye line will be imprison'd in their garrisons, and ye Indians will come lower for game I expect very soon. I should be glad to hear you are mov'd from Albany and like to do business. I am extreemly concern'd for you & the Forces with you, & begg you to take all necessary precautions, and if you want help let us know it. If Braddock is lost it will be ye greatest folly for Maj'r Gen! Shirley to proceed, and hope you will join and be joined with a greater number of troops & proceed directly for Canada. We hear the Regency upon ye rec't of Admiral Boscawen's Express imediately ordered 20 more ships of ye line to Nova Scotia. What is doing or what orders may be sent I dont know. Hope for ye best, and if possible some past mistakes will be rectified.

Our Gen'! Court sits this week — for what, I dont know. I tho't it was more duty for me to take care of ye Frontiers. Give my service to Gen'! Johnson, and tell him that if he woud send out some of his Mohawks with directions to speak with ye French Indians, & tell 'em our designs, and that unless they return'd, & left off harassing us, they might possibly be oblig'd to pay part of ye reckoning, they might bethink themselves & not pursue us so violently, and much bloodshed be prevented — this way they might do much good for New England. The French doubtless secrete things from 'em. We at home are thro mercy well. Biller & Sister gone to Boston.

I am your Aff^{te} Hum^l Ser^t,

COL. EP. WILLIAMS.   ISR. WILLIAMS.

"Posterity delights in details," said John Quincy Adams, presumably in relation to his own minute diary, kept throughout an exceedingly busy life, and since published as if to test and verify the dictum. A firm persuasion that there will always be those in every generation who will be glad to see all accessible data throwing light upon the life and service of the founder of this town and College, has colored the construction of the present chapter throughout; authentic details have been given wherever they have been found, and illustrative documents have been copied at length and arranged in historic order; and the same considerations now determine the quotation in full of the last pecuniary account passing between Ephraim Williams and his native province of Massachusetts, which he served in a public capacity almost uninterruptedly from 1744 to 1755. The final account, as here presented, relates solely to the raising and equipping and marching and paying his new regiment, recruited expressly for the Crown Point expedition, and led by him to Albany, there to unite with other forces from New England and New York, all under the immediate command of General William Johnson, soon to be knighted; himself, however, subordinate after Braddock's death to Governor and General William Shirley.

It is plain by all the papers left behind him by Colonel Williams, and especially from the details of his last will and testament, that he " was fond of money," as that phrase has long been current in New England, to express at once power and zeal in acquisition, and some ostentation in expenditure. In these and nearly all other traits of character, he belonged emphatically to the Williams family. There was no such other family in New England during the eighteenth century as that constituted by the descendants of Robert Williams, of Roxbury, who died Sept. 1, 1693. This Robert left a very considerable estate by will, mainly to his three sons. The same is true of one of these sons, Isaac, who died in 1708. The elder Ephraim Williams, son of Isaac, was a man of large property for the times, acquired by assiduity and enterprise. Quite a number of associated lines of descent under the Williams name exhibited the same traits : inheriting and acquiring wealth, they displayed it freely in the fashions of the times; they were quite select in their associations and intermarriages; they were fond, as a rule, of public office, — of its emoluments and display; they esteemed themselves to be " of the best," and were regarded by their neighbors as "aristocratical" in their tastes and tendencies; they were almost all of them professedly religious men, perhaps as prominent in church as in state; and several of them, for whom Elisha Williams, Rector of Yale College (1726–39), may stand sponsor, were remarkable for preaching power and for long pastorates in the best places. As a family, though widely scattered locally, each branch and individual stood up for the personal and political preferment of other branches and individuals in a manner unparalleled in the history of New England. As a single instance of this, in a small way, let us see how Colonel Ephraim Williams organized his own personal staff in the Crown Point expedition. He had raised his own regiment for the occasion, in virtue of his great popularity in Hampshire, and by an appeal to his old soldiers in the line of forts, who had served under him, more or less, for ten years past. He appointed his own brother, Thomas, just three years younger, *Surgeon;* Perez Marsh, who married Sarah Williams, Colonel Israel's eldest daughter, *Surgeon's Mate;* William Williams, called in all the letters of the time "Billy," eldest son of Colonel William Williams, of Pittsfield, *Surgeon's Mate's Assistant;* Rev. Stephen Williams, of Longmeadow, *Chaplain;* another William Williams, son of Rev. Dr. Solomon, of Lebanon, Connecticut, — twenty-one years afterwards a signer of the Declaration of Independence, — was Colonel Ephraim's *Adjutant,* or *Quartermaster;* and his half-brother, Josiah, was *Ensign* in one of the ten companies, and was fearfully wounded in the battle.

Dr. The Province of the Massachusetts Bay to Col? Ephraim Williams.

To raising 406 private men a 4 dollars p'r man	£487	4
To cash del? Col? Clapp to raise a Company as pr his receipt will appear.	163	4
To cash del? Col? Partridge Muster-Master for the County of Hampsh? for 420 private men — 2 dollars bounty for each man's finding his gun & £1 6 8 pr man for his month's adv?? pay	812	0
To marching Capt. Doolittle's, Capt. Ingersoll's and my own Company from their respective homes to the place of muster in the County of Hampsh?	30	0
To marching Col?. Pomeroy's, Capt. Hawley's, Capt. Porter's, Capt. Doolittle's & my own Company from Northampton, Hatf?, Deerf? to Albany each man being allowed 6 days for his march	85	0

To marching Capt. Hitchcock's Comp^a ad 6 days allowance — pard pd the Capt. and part pd Lieutenant Taylor	£ 17	0	
To march'g Capt. Burt's Comp. to Albany — part pd the Capt. and part Lieut. Taylor a 7 days allowance.	20	0	
To mustering eight men & paying them £1 18 8 pr man for finding their own arms and for their advance pay	15	9	4
To powder for their march to Albany 8/4	8	4	
To inlisting 406 men a 1/6 p man	30	9	
To marching Maj. Ashley's Company a 3 days allowance . . .	8	10	
To supplying with blankets in ye whole fifteen	8	0	
To a Month's advance pay to officers	184	1	1
Harrison Gray, Esqr, Dr. to a mistake in ye money sent to Col. Pomeroy	3	5	
To two Inlistments more a 62/8 p 1 a 50/8	5	12	4
To pd Lieut. Rolf for the inlistment of one man 1/6 and for his travel to Albany after ye settlement of ye above acco^t 11/4,		12	10
	£1870	3	1
To pd. Ensⁿ Pixley for his march to Albany 3 days 3/5 and also for finding his own blanket 12/ after ye settlem^t as afores^d,		15	5
	£1871	11	4

CRED^E.

By Cash to inlist 500 men	£600	0	0
By warrant for Bounty & adv^e pay	937	17	10
By a warrant to march my men and advance pay	200	0	0
By a warrant for advance pay for officers	184	1	1
By a warrant for pay for 23 Blankets	12	5	0
	£1934	3	11
	1870	3	1
Ball^{ce} due to the Provin^{ce}	64	0	10
	1	8	3
[Some errors in the figures] Due	£62	12	7

The above Acc^t I Certifie to be a true account according to the best of my knowledge.

         EPH. WILLIAMS.

ALBANY, July 16, 1755.

It has already been mentioned that an important council of war, held at Fort Edward on the 22d of August, decided on the future route of the expedition, and also to request instant reinforcements of the several governments represented in the army. This was by much the most important council of war ever attended by Colonel Ephraim Williams, or ever held at any stage of the Crown Point expedition. The proofs are strong that Williams possessed the complete confidence of General Johnson. For reasons never fully cleared up, there was some lack of harmony and co-operation between

Johnson and Lyman of Connecticut, who was the second in command : the renovated fort at the Carrying-place was named, at first, " Fort Lyman," and very properly so, for the renovation was made under his own direction; and the reason for the continuance of the name was emphasized by Lyman's great skill and courage at the battle of Lake George, where he was the real commander on the English side, Johnson having been wounded at the outset of the fight, and kept thereafter in his tent; but in Johnson's official and extended account of the battle to the respective provincial governors, Lyman's name is not even mentioned, and Johnson soon after gave to the fort the name which the locality still bears, " Fort Edward," from one of the boys of the royal family of England.

We are now to quote in full the last letter, apparently, that Ephraim Williams ever wrote. The original is endorsed to this effect by its recipient, Colonel Israel Williams, of Hatfield. It was written from what is now Fort Edward, on the 23d of August, 1755, just sixteen days before the death of the writer. It carries a serious and earnest and patriotic and comprehensive and disinterested tone. The letter is worthy of the man, the cause, the environment. There is in it much of the soldier, something of the statesman, and a great deal of the neighbor and counsellor and friend. Let us read the lines and between them.

FROM THE CAMP AT YE GREAT CARRYING PLACE,
Aug't 23, 1755.

Sir, By the information Gen'll Johnson has obtained from Canada, the whole body of the Indians, and all the strength that [they] can raise, will undoubtedly meet us. I suppose that the Indians in the French interest, as well as the English, will be very much affected by the success of this army. The defeat of Braddock has had such effect on them that their has not yet above sixty joined us, tho' more are expected, & all tho' they say they are our Brothers and will live and die with us, I should not choose to venture my life with much dependence on them, for anything but intelligence, unless we could raise in them some confidence of success. I can't but think to lie still will have a bad effect on ym, and give great advantage to the French. We have therefore resolved, at a council of all the field officers, to march by the way of Lake St. Saccrement, and to immediately open a road there, and build a very strong fort, sufficient to stand a regular siege, which will doubtless be done soon enough to take Crown Point, before winter, if sufficient reinforcements should join us without loss of time, and from there we can have constant intelligence of the state of ye French army, and shall march against ym from thence, as soon as we shall judge it safe, considering the vast importance of success. The reason of chusing that road rather than Wood Creek, is because the way down the Drawned Land is such y't a few French, with a battery of Cannon, might stave us to pieces, when we could not get to shore to attack them.

By the Lake it's said the road is good both by water and land, on the west side of the Lake, but we must land 20 miles on this side the Narrows called Tenondorogo [literal], and draw the cannon by land. There is 400 men at work to open the road, and on Sat,day next we expect to set out with 2000 to finish the road to said Lake, and shall build as above, and also shall take along half the artillery. The Council of War are fully of opinion that we must take them winter or summer, and are unanimously willing to venter on and continue, till the work is done, viewing our all to be at stake. And we think there is time enough if the recruits are sent quick, for it will probably take but a short time, when we march from the next stage. We are all willing to venture our lines as far as the good of our country calls us, and have no fears of success, if we are soon joined by a sufficient number of men, which may be supported here till provition may be sent after the army. We have agreed to support the N. Hamp'se troops untill they can be provided for, not being able to march without ym.

The several Governments are to be at their proportionable part. Whether the [Court] Sets or not am not able to say. But beg when it does set y't you have Colo. Partridge to take care of the Frontiers, & go to Boston. I refer you to Genr.l Johnson's letter to Gov.r Phips for a more perticular information. As ye Council did not think it proper to fix upon any number of men, yet it was agreed we might wright to our friends our opinion, which is y't the jobs will not be done short of 10000 or 12000 men. We have not above 3000 effective men in the whole, including New Hampshire troops. You must remember we have often said it would take as many men to take Crown point as Canada, without their strength could be devided. Had Braddock, Shirley and we struck at same time, it might have answered to have proceeded with our number. But y't is over, and if we should be beat, our country is lost. Therefore suffer me once for all to beg of you to exert you self for your country — it's upon the brink of ruin. It's who shall remember Sr what King William said, when the case of the Dutch was prity much the same with our's — I pray God unite your Councils, and show the world you are true patriots of your Country, and give to us to behave as becomes Englishmen.

I am, Sr, your Hon'r's most obed't Humble Serv't,

Colo. Israel Williams.   Eph. Williams.

P.S. I should of wrote to my good friends Worthington and Partridge, but as you are all together at Springfield, this would answer. Being also desired by the Genll to wright to several members of the House, I had but little time to spare. E. W. I send my best compliments to all inquiring friends.

The same day this letter was written by Colonel Ephraim Williams, Dr. Thomas Williams, his own brother and Surgeon of the regiment, wrote a letter from the same place to his wife in Deerfield, as follows : —

FROM THE CAMP AT THE CARRYING PLACE,
Aug. 23, 1755.

My Dear: I having an opportunity to send to Fort Massachusetts, improve it to let you hear from me, as also the rest of my friends there, if I have any which I might rationally expect I have not, by not receiving any tokens thereof for above a month past, excepting a line from the Rev. Mr. Ashley, which favor I have a few days since returned him my thanks. I am now at the same place I was 20 days agone. The Expedition goes on very slowly, in some expectation of marching two days hence to Lake St. Sacrament [Lake George], as they have this day begun to open a road that way, not being to find one any other. I suppose the several governments are sent to, to reinforce us with more men, which I hope will be cheerfully complied with, if they desire we shall be successful against Crownt Point. My compliments to Major Williams, let him know I expect he will, agreeable to his promise, be here with some of his first recruits. Saving a too great laxness of my bowels, which is common in the army, I am in considerable health. Want very much to hear from you and the dear children, who are often in my mind. Our army in general pretty healthy, not having more than 20 of the Province forces in the Hospital, & but one or two dangerous. have lost three of our troops, who died at the flats, ere they [sic] reached this place. Capt. Kellogg died at Schenectady last Monday, after an illness of 15 days. Fever and Dysentery.

Your affectionate Husband

THO^S WILLIAMS.

This Captain Joseph Kellogg, referred to here by the surgeon, was one of the Deerfield children carried captive to Canada in 1704, a sack and capture made doubly famous by the "Redeemed Captive," written by the Rev. John Williams, then pastor and principal man in Deerfield, and another account written by his son, Stephen Williams, a boy not quite eleven years old, when he began to share his father's captivity, Feb. 29, 1704. In this Crown Point expedition, Stephen Williams, then pastor at Longmeadow, was the Chaplain of Colonel Ephraim Williams's regiment, sixty-two years old. Besides his pastoral labors at Longmeadow, which continued from 1716 to 1782, he was much in the public service, for example, Interpreter for Governor Belcher in the Indian treaty at Deerfield in 1735; Chaplain under Pepperell in the Louisburg expedition in 1746; and again Chaplain under General Winslow to the northward in 1756.

There were two immemorial Indian trails leading from what is now Fort Edward to Ticonderoga: the first, running nearly due north soon struck Wood Creek, which drops into the head of Lake Champlain at Whitehall; the second, turning sharp west at what is now Sandy Hill, and at Glen's Falls (now so-called), leaving the Hudson for a straight course northward to the head of Lake George. It is thirteen miles from Fort Edward to the head of this lake; and just about the same distance to a point on Wood Creek navigable for that sort of boats with which the expedition of 1755 was provided. Johnson and his officers had been quite too slow in deciding which of these routes to take. A road was first begun to Wood Creek;

then it was countermanded for the excellent reason that both shores
that way were low and marshy, and that the French, known to be
coming up the lake to defend Crown Point, and who might well
come further south (as actually happened), could easily, with a few
cannon placed on some rising ground, blow the expedition out of the
stream, and they be helpless to land and defend themselves; and so
they began to open a road in the other direction on the 23d of August,
over a dry and sandy country covered for the most part with dwarf
pines. The reason why the locality at Fort Edward was so long
called the "Great Carrying-Place," is, that boats and their belong-
ings had to be carried by one or other of these two ways over the
watershed dividing the Hudson and its tributaries from the two
narrow lakes and their tributaries, flowing northward to their union
at Ticonderoga. Gangs of axemen were sent forward to cut down
the pines close to the ground, and remove such other obstructions
as they could; and the road thus made has continued for the most
part till this day to be the travelled way from Glen's Falls to Caldwell, at the head of the lake. When the plank road was laid over
the sand not far from 1850, it was found better to abandon that
stretch of the old military road that ran through the rocky ambush-
ground in which Colonel Williams and his comrades were killed, for
a more level lay of land a little to the eastward.

Accordingly, on the 26th of August, 2000 men were ordered over
the new road to the lake, while Colonel Blanchard, of New Hampshire, was left with 500 to complete and maintain Fort Lyman.
Parts of two days were occupied to reach their camp on the lake-
shore. On the march they had fronted north; but as the lake was
the best possible defence for their rear, their camp was laid looking
to the south, and the tents were pitched among the stumps along
the edge of the lake, on a piece of rough and rising and partly
swampy ground. In their front were the pine woods, through
which they had just come over their newly made road; on their
right was a considerable marsh, making a good defence on that
flank; and on their left was higher and better ground, over much of
which the native rock comes to the surface. The present writer has
studied carefully, at several different times, the lay of this ground,
the location of the original and later roads leading to it, and
especially the so-called "bloody pond" and the seat of the Indian
ambush of 1755, about three miles to the south of the lake. Nothing in the whole region has been changed much in the long interval
of time since 1755, except the camp-ground on the rim of the lake.
There the building of Fort William Henry in the autumn of that

year; still more the building of Hotel Fort William Henry, more than a century afterwards, on the same site; and, most of all, the building of a railroad and its appurtenances, about 1880, right across the old camp-ground and battle-field, have hopelessly disfigured (except to one skilled to pick the old out of the new) this most interesting stretch of ground.

Notwithstanding the Crown Point expedition was wholly an offensive one, in which everything depended on celerity and vigilance, — designed to assault and capture a fort on the Point that the French first built in 1731, — everything moved forward in a leisurely, happy-go-lucky manner, because General Johnson knew nothing of civilized warfare, and had received his command solely on account of his great influence over the Six Nations, of whom, nevertheless, fewer than 300 rallied to the expedition; while the French, under Baron Dieskau, who had learned war under the famous Marshal Saxe, were alert and swift and brave and skilled. Dieskau reached Crown Point at the head of 3573 men — regulars and Canadians and Indians — about the time that Johnson's camp was laid at the lake; but he had no thought of waiting there to be attacked. With short delay he moved on with nearly all his force, light-weighted, to Ticonderoga, a promontory at the junction of lakes George and Champlain, commanding perfectly both of the two routes, by one of which Johnson must strike at Crown Point, if at all. Dieskau did not know precisely where Johnson's army was, but he was led to believe that it still lay (at least a part of it, which was true) at Fort Lyman. At noon of the 4th of September, leaving a part of his force at Ticonderoga, he embarked 216 French regulars, 684 Canadians, and about 600 Indians, in canoes, and, taking the easterly water, he pushed up the narrow prolongation of Lake Champlain, through what are called the "drowned lands," towards the spot where Whitehall now stands. Just a little way above that point, he turned to his right into deeper water, then, as now, called South Bay. This led them southwest, in an almost direct line, towards the head of Lake George. They landed at the head of South Bay, left their canoes under a guard in a brook that drops into it, and started their march southward through the forest, just about midway between Wood Creek and Lake George. Two days more brought them athwart the new road leading from Fort Lyman to the head of Lake George, only three miles from the former post. Here Dieskau learned from a captured wagoner that a large English force lay encamped at the lake. His wish and will was still to strike and capture Fort Lyman, and thus put himself directly in the

rear of the entire expedition, trusting to his force left at Ticonderoga to keep the English between two fires, to their military
destruction. But his Indians now held a council after their manner, and soon announced, as the result of it, that they would not
attack the fort, which they supposed was well mounted with cannon,
but were willing to help attack the open camp at the lake. Dieskau
remonstrated in vain, and then yielded with the best grace he could.
This was Sunday, the 7th of September.

That Sunday was kept at the lake after the New England manner, except that 200 wagons came up from Fort Lyman loaded
with boats. The already venerable Stephen Williams, Chaplain of
Colonel Williams's regiment, preached to the assembled soldiers from
a text in the prophet Isaiah. The Sunday before, he had preached
to the Mohawks in camp through an interpreter. About sunset an
Indian scout came in, and reported the important news, that he
had found the trail of a body of soldiers moving from South Bay
towards Fort Lyman. General Johnson called for a volunteer to
carry a warning to Colonel Blanchard. A brave wagoner named
Adams galloped off with the letter, but he never reached Fort Lyman. Sentries were posted, and the soldiers went quietly to sleep.

A good idea of the ground, and of the way their tents were
pitched that night and on the eventful morrow, may be gained from
the annexed woodcut, taken from the original "Prospective Plan,"
made at the time by Samuel Blodget, an eye-witness of all that he
carefully describes as well as pictorially illustrates. If the reader
will imagine himself standing at the lower right-hand corner of this
picture, all will be easy to him. He fronts the west, with the edge
of the lake, in which the boats are represented to lie, on his right
towards the north; on his left, towards the south is a low rise of
ground, with smooth rock coming to the surface for the most part,
and so nearly destitute of trees; on his front lies the camp, irregular and inconvenient on account of gullies and swampy ground
near the rim of the lake, into which they drain, and marked "19"
on the plan; the collection of tents nearest to him in front marked
"33," is Colonel Harris's regiment, and directly behind his tent
stands the tent of General Johnson, marked "31," both tents sur-
mounted by the British flag; the next collection of tents beyond,
marked "32," were those of General Lyman and his Connecticut
men, both of whom did extraordinary service in the battle of the
morrow; in the rear of these towards the lake, marked "34," was
the regiment of Colonel Cockroft, and behind these tents, under
numbers "20," "21," "22," "23," "24," were "cannon pointed all

THE "ENCAMPMENT" AT THE HEAD OF LAKE GEORGE.

343

the ways in which the enemy could attack us with a number of men to make use of them," "wagons placed so as to be a kind of battery to the Guard," "our Magazine of Powder," "our Store of shot of various sizes," "our Shells of various Sizes"; the next regiment encamped towards the west, marked "38," was that of Colonel Gutridge, occupying nearly the centre of the camp east and west; then beyond the central gully, which really divided the camp in two, marked "35" on the cut, were the tents of Colonel Williams and his subordinate officers and men; behind these, and marked "36," lay Colonel Timothy Ruggles and his men; and still further on, at the extreme right of the camp, designated as "37," were the tents of the brave Colonel Titcomb and his no less brave men. Titcomb had done splendid service at the capture of Louisburg ten years before this; and Ruggles was one of the great men of Massachusetts, and was president of the Stamp Act Congress ten years later than this.

Thus things stood at the lake during Sunday night, the 7th of September. At midnight, however, some wagoners came into the camp and reported at headquarters that a war party of French and Indians were on the road, not far from Fort Lyman. Johnson called a council of war in the morning. Instead of sending out scouts (he had a plenty of skilled ones, both whites and Indians), and finding out all about this "war party," how many they were and whither they were bound, he began to act in needless ignorance, and, therefore, in criminal folly. The council came to the strange resolution of sending out immediately two detachments of 500 men each, in order, as Johnson explained the next day in his "Letter to the Governors of the several Colonies," "to catch the enemy in their retreat." But Dieskau had not the least thought of any retreat. Baffled by his Indians in his original plan to attack Fort Lyman, he accepted with vehemence and enthusiasm all the risks of an attack on the main army at the lake. He knew that they greatly outnumbered him. But did not Braddock, also, greatly outnumber the French and Indians at the forks of the Ohio, just two months before? He hoped to take the camp unawares, as Braddock was surprised on the Monongahela. He was already on the march while the council were debating. The new military road, just cut by the English a few days before, served his regulars well in their advance, while his Canadians and Indians pushed their way along through the trees on either flank.

When the decision of the war council at the lake — to send out at once two detachments, one towards Fort Lyman and the other towards the head of South Bay, where Dieskau had left his boats — was interpreted to Hendrik, king of the Mohawks, who himself knew a little English, in consequence of his having spent considerable time at the Indian Mission in Stockbridge, he gave his opinion significantly by picking up a stick, which he broke easily, and then by putting several sticks together, which he could not break. The officers were wise enough to learn from a better strategist than themselves, though a savage, and the two detachments were joined in one, to be under the command of Colonel Ephraim Williams. But the Mohawk chieftain was still unsatisfied. He shook his head: "If they are to be killed, too many; if they are to fight, too few." Nevertheless, he was too brave and faithful not to share in the risks he disapproved of. He had known the Colonel in Stockbridge, and the Colonel's father very well there. Mounted on a gun-carriage, he eloquently harangued his Mohawks, for he was the greatest Indian orator of his time; and then, bestriding a small horse lent him by General Johnson, he trotted to the head of the column, followed by about 200 of his Mohawks.

A little after eight o'clock, Colonel Williams led out his regiment a short distance from the camp, on the road towards Fort Lyman, and then waited a little while for the rest of the detachment, under Lieutenant-Colonel Whiting, to come up. Whiting was a Connecticut officer, and led Connecticut men, and both did excellent service on this memorable day. Going on about two miles further, there was another wait to allow Hendrik's Indians, who had fallen into the rear, to come up and take the head of the column again; and the march was resumed without any apprehension that the enemy were near, and without the precaution of throwing out flankers, or even a vanguard, in Hendrik's front. Possibly Colonel Williams entrusted this service to the Mohawks. Certainly his commanding General had set him a very poor example in respect to scouts and runners all the morning; but nothing can ever relieve the military memory of Colonel Williams of culpable negligence at this most essential point of vigilance, considering who his enemy were. *He* commanded this detachment of 1200 men. He knew even down to the details, and so did all the higher officers, of Braddock's terrible defeat in July, in rough and wooded ground, like parts of that through which he was leading some of the best men in New England.

On the other hand, Dieskau knew very well what was going on above him. His own mind worked like lightning, and he had nimble servitors on both his flanks and far in front, reporting to him constantly the lay of the land and the posture of the foe. Fortune favors the active and the provident. There was one piece of broken and rocky ground, full of bushes, with a few pines, through which the old road ran (not the present plank road), forming a sort of defile, and very suitable for an ambuscade in war. On the western side of the road the ground rises considerably, and is in places quite abrupt, extending about half a mile parallel with the road; while on the east side, for about half that distance, there is a ravine, through which ran and runs a small brook. This narrow and not long defile was entered from the south from tolerably open ground, and debouched on the north again into the open. Dieskau, commonly called the "Baron" by the New Englanders, who reported these events as eye-witnesses, had just time to deposit his packs under a small guard, and to plant his regulars (say 200) across the road near the southern debouche of the defile, and to post his Canadians and Indians (say 1200 in all), the greater part on the higher ground on the western side of the road, behind the trees and rocks and bushes, and the rest in the ravine sloping down to the east from the road. This was called at the time placing troops in *double potence;* that is, throwing forward both flanks at an angle from the base, thus making three sides of a rough parallelogram. It is like what is called in London streets a "close." In this case the nature. of the ground did not allow of right angles, but the whole position was curved like a sickle, the handle-flank being on the west side of the road and about twice as long as the other, and the soldiers pretty equally concealed around the whole curve by rocks and trees and bushes. The Baron's orders to both his flanks were to keep concealed and reserve their fire till the head of the English column should strike his regulars in front, where the battle should begin.

Continuing their march till about half-past ten without suspicions, the advanced Mohawks had gotten wholly within this ambush, and Williams's regiment partially so, when Hendrik, jogging along by Colonel Williams's side, between the two columns, said to him: "I smell Indians!" and, pressing on a short distance further, he was suddenly hailed by one of Dieskau's Indians, — "Whence come you?" — "From the Mohawks!" — "Whence came you?" rejoined Hendrik, who was dressed after the English manner. "Montreal!" was the answer. Just then a gun was fired from the bushes, whether by accident or design will never be known. It has been said that some of Dieskau's "Six Nations," who were kinsmen of the Mohawks, wished to give them warning before it was too late. At any rate, it was too late. After a momentary pause, the terrible Indian yell rose on both sides of the road, followed by heavy firing, especially from the ravine on the left, which cut down the Mohawks in front in large numbers, and the head of the English column on that side. King Hendrik's horse was shot down, and the brave chief bayoneted as he tried to rise. He was both old and corpulent. Colonel Williams, seeing rising ground upon his right, ordered his men, then extended in files along the road, to mount it, and gain a more defensible position. They obeyed, but had made only a short advance when they came within range of the main ambush on that (western) side, and a deadly fire showered down upon them, which killed the commander, threw the whole line into confusion, and strewed the ground with dead and wounded.

Then naturally enough there was a panic among the raw troops; considerable numbers abandoned the field in headlong flight; the vanguard suddenly became the rear; the Baron quickly brought up his regulars, and the men in ambush on both sides crowded after the confused retreat of English and Mohawks intermixed, and both fell in large numbers at this point; some of both, however, falling back fought bravely against their pursuers from tree to tree and rock to rock; and many of these pursuers never saw the English camp at the lake, nor their own men in the rear guarding the packs. Dieskau himself described a little later this part of the struggle, by saying, that the head of the English column was "doubled up like a pack of cards."

The annexed woodcut, also taken from Blodget's "Prospective Plan," though Blodget himself was not an eye-witness here, gives a correct outline of the ambush-field, and of the beginning of the fight. His accompanying descriptions, however, are not so vivid as those of the scenes at the lake in the afternoon, which he saw himself; nevertheless, we will give them in full because they are contemporary and illustrated.

1. The Road from the Camp to Lyman's Fort, in which Road a detachment of 1000 English and about 150 Indians, with Hendrik the Mohawk Sachem among them, were marching in order to annoy the enemy, who it was supposed were attacking the Fort, or retreating from it.

2. The Form in which the French and Indians appeared, being like that of a Hook; for so they had placed themselves, extending a curve line from their Front on each side of the Road, near half a mile on the Right, and about one half that space on the Left. They had Opportunity to do this, as they had received intelligence from a Scout they had sent out that a considerable Body of our Men were marching in order to oppose them. The Reason of their thus forming themselves was this ; — on the left of the Road all along the Line they had placed themselves in, they had the advantage of being covered with a thick

growth of Brush and Trees, such as is common to Swampy Land as this was: On the right they were all along defended, as with a Breastwork by a continued Eminence filled with Rocks, and Trees, and Shrubs as high as a Man's Breast. Our Men while marching in the Road, were within 150 yards of the Enemy, who lay invisible on either side. They had posted themselves in the most advantageous Place there was between the Camp and the Fort for an Ambuscade. And considering this, together with their great Superiority in numbers, being upwards of 2000, 'tis a wonder they had not entirely routed and destroyed this Detachment. Our men must have behaved with the utmost Bravery, and Wisdom too, or they could not have made so honorable a Retreat, killing even more of the Enemy than they lost themselves; as the French General owned after he was taken: Tho' in this Fight, which began about two miles and a half from the Camp, our loss both of Officers and private Men, was much greater than in the other Battle.

3. Hendrik, the Indian Chief or King of the Six Nations, who was dressed after the English Manner. He only was on horseback, because he could not well travel on Foot, being somewhat corpulent as well as old. He fell in this fight, to the great Enragement of the Indians, and our Loss, as he was a very good Friend to the English, and had most influence to keep the Mohawks so.

4. Our men represented as breaking their order, and hastily running. Their Design herein was to gain the Advantage of the Eminence on the Right; but the Enemy having unhappily got the Possession of it, rose up from the Rocks and Shrubs, and from behind the Trees, when our Men came within sure Reach of their Guns, and made a considerable Slaughter among them. The Trees were thinly scattered where our Men were thus fired upon, and the Shrubs but low: However they made the best use of them they could, and continued Fighting here for some time with the greatest Resolution. The greater part that were killed in this Fight, whether of the Enemy, or of our People, were found the next day at this Ambuscade, or not far distant from it; tho' they lay scattered more or less all the Way to the Camp.

5. An advanced Party of Indians, who first discovered the Enemy, and fired upon them; which gave the Alarm to our Men, began a very furious and desperate Fight and led the Enemy, by our Retreating from them, into the Engagement they afterwards had with the Army at the Camp.

Several eye-witnesses or participants give us more exactly what happened between the first panic and retreat of the Williams men, and the arrival of the broken detachment as a whole at the camp. A part of Williams's regiment rallied under the command of Lieutenant-Colonel Whiting at a small pond near the road, since called "Bloody Pond," and some degree of order was restored there, and good fighting done, when Lieutenant-Colonel Cole with 300 men from the camp, arrived at a point a little north of the pond, ordered by Johnson, so soon as he heard the firing below, to hurry to sustain Williams or to cover his retreat. Whiting and Cole united here, and maintained their ground for some little time with resolution and effect; for the tradition has been strong for a century that

"THE BLOODY MORNING SCOUT."

349

many dead bodies of Frenchmen and Canadians falling near by were thrown the next day into the pond, — hence called "Bloody Pond"; but they were soon compelled to retire from the position, overpowered by superior numbers, while that retreat was bravely made, continuing to fire for a mile or more from behind trees and logs and other covers, which checked the pursuit of the enemy and allowed the stragglers to get into the camp, and also many of the English who had been wounded in the running fight were carried by their comrades back into the camp. The Mohawks of the detachment, angry at the fall of Hendrik, did brave service in this retreat, and lost during the morning about forty of their warriors; but they did scarcely anything more after they reached the camp. Of course the fugitives and non-fighters of Williams's detachment, who arrived first at the camp, spread exaggerated stories of the numbers and ferocity of the enemy. The fighting men gave the French their last fire when within about three-quarters of a mile of the camp at the lake.

Thus ended what was long called in New England " The Bloody Morning Scout." Its details, with their inevitable exaggerations, and subsequent mixings and crossings with other war horrors in the same neighborhood during the three following campaigns in which New England again took large part, were talked over and over around New England firesides, until the American Revolution, which some of these very officers and soldiers lived to take part in, pushed back into a misty limbo the incidents of what they still fondly called the "Old French War." Strictly speaking, the column and the errand of Colonel Williams that morning was not a "Scout" at all; it might perhaps be called a " reconnaissance in force"; but old Hendrik was right in his judgment about it in the war-council of the early morning; it was a nondescript, unmilitary, and careless proceeding from beginning to end; it cost many very precious English lives; and it came near costing the destruction of the army encamped at the lake. For Dieskau, having repulsed the column, and sent the survivors *helter-skelter* within the camp, along the front of which, in the meantime, after the firing began to be heard to the south, a slight barricade of army wagons and turned-over boats and trunks of trees laid end to end in a single row had been hastily thrown up, ordered a halt of his men when he reached the eminence in the road, since called " Gage's Hill," in plain sight of the camp and the lake, and sounded his trumpets to call in his scattered Canadians and Indians; it has been thought by many, that if he had pressed right on down the little slope, and entered the camp

with the last of the fugitives, for the obstructións were low and
broken, the appearance of his regulars with their shining bayonets
(then a new thing in the colonies) formidable, the fugitives and the
wounded brought in had spread a sort of panic through the camp,
he might have borne down all before him, — making a path for his
Canadians and Indians, — and killed or taken prisoners or scattered
through the woods the whole little army.

This was certainly Dieskau's plan, and it might have prospered
in his hand, could he have controlled his allies. He saw that these
were inclined to scatter right and left from his regulars, who kept
the road in splendid order, and that he must halt for a parley with
them. His trumpets called them in. Parleying in battle-time is
always demoralizing. His Indians looked downcast and unmanage-
able; they had lost heavily in the encounters of the morning; they
knew also there were some cannon in the English camp, and probably they could see at that instant three or four of them mounted,
and pointing south: the Canadians, too, showed signs of discourage-
ment, for they had just lost their veteran commander, St. Pierre,
the same who had negotiated with Washington at Fort le Bœuf in
1753, and who, in this campaign, commanded both the Indians and
the Canadians. Nevertheless, the magnetic and imperturbable Baron
persuaded them all to move on with him again, — the regulars in
front and the rest on his left in straggling order, making their way
northwest and designing to operate on Johnson's extreme right;
and a little before noon, what Blodget calls "the second engagement"
began. The regulars advanced down the road to the edge of the
woods, deployed in front of Johnson's left-centre, and opened a
platoon-fire at a distance of about 140 yards, which kept up for some
time but without great effect; until Captain Eyre, who commanded
the camp artillery, trained three heavy cannon upon them (shown
in the cut of the fight under the numoral "11"), but these were
aimed too high, as is usual with inexperienced gunners, and the
balls crashed into the trees over the heads of the French some
twenty feet; and Blodget says, they were not "discharged more
than four or five times"; because the regulars, finding their platoon-
fire ineffectual, broke their ranks and took to cover Indian fashion.
Then it was that the second battle really began. The fusillade on
both sides soon became furious, and was kept up for about four
hours without intermission. The day was fair, but the wind was
southerly and drove the smoke into the eyes of the English. The
bullets flew all over the camp, even round the heads of the surgeons
dressing the wounded in the rear.

After the initial trepidation common to raw troops was over, encouraged and at first threatened by their officers with drawn swords, the New England men became cool and remained so, "our people took sight and were all good marksmen" (Blodget). The Baron, unable to make any impression on the English, left and centre, where the Connecticut people were, and a few Mohawks, seeing his regulars falling around him unsupported by his Canadians and Indians who had gone mostly round to a knoll on Johnson's right, changed his special point of attack towards the English right, and opened a heavy fire on the three Massachusetts regiments, — Titcomb's, Ruggles's, and Williams's, — the last now under the command of Lieutenant-Colonel Pomeroy. Apparently, one motive of Dieskau's in moving to his own left, was to knit connection with his allies already operating on that side. If so, he was disappointed. "Are these the so much vaunted troops?" he cried bitterly, as he saw some of them disinclined to fight at all, and some of the rest inclined to fight as safely as possible. Yet for all this, a galling fire was thrown into the camp, by a considerable party of French and Indians from the high ground beyond the swamp directly west of the Massachusetts regiments; until a field-piece, marked "12" on Blodget's Plan, was discharged, and two mortars marked "25" threw a few shells among them, and scattered them, weakening the whole attack on that flank.

Dieskau maintained a hot fire for about an hour opposite to the Massachusetts men. All fear was now gone from the latter, and they gave as good as they got. Johnson had received a slight flesh wound near the beginning of the fight, and had retired at once to his tent, leaving the sole command to Lyman, who was everywhere in the heat of action, directing and animating his men for four hours, and marvellously escaped without a wound. "16· Colonel Titcomb and Lieutenant Barron, that they might fire at the enemy at greater advantage, got behind this tree, tho' at a rod's distance from the breastwork; and here it was they both unhappily fell, being insensibly flanked by some of the enemy" (Blodget). Dieskau, exposing himself near the English line, was twice severely wounded; his Adjutant, himself wounded, was trying with a Canadian to carry their helpless commander to the rear, when the latter refused to be moved, and ordered the Adjutant to lead the regulars in a last effort against the English line.

But it was now too late. One by one, or in little knots, the New England men were already jumping over their row of logs; even the wagoners about the camp took guns and powder-horns from the wounded, and prepared to join in the fray; and in a few moments the whole line, with a great shout, dashed over the slight barricade, and fell upon the French, with hatchets and the butts of their guns. It was now near five o'clock. The French and their allies fled from all sides of the field unpursued, and had not rejoined a large body of Indians and Canadians who had retreated early in the afternoon, back to the place of the morning ambush, and a little further to the place where the French packs had been left as preparatory to that, when the latter body were suddenly attacked not far from Bloody Pond, and then and there took place what Blodget called "the third or last engagement":—and we will let him tell the story of this in his own words.

They heard at Fort Lyman, between 9 and 10 o'clock, the Noise of a Multitude of Guns; and as it continued without Interruption, they judged that our Army at the Camp [it was the Ambush-Fight] was attacked by a large Body of French and Indians: upon which it was tho't proper to detach between 200 and 300 men to their Assistance. This detachment consisted partly of Yorkers but mostly of New Hampshire troops [made up largely of Scotch-Irish], and was put under the Command of Capt. McGinnis and Capt. Folsom. They arrived between 4 and 5 o'clock, at the place where the French encamped the Night before, which was near the place where the Fight began in the Morning; and here they discovered about 500 of the enemy (chiefly Indians) who had fled from the Battle at the Camp; upon which they fell upon them, drove them from the Encampment, and pursued them till Evening came on, making a considerable slaughter among them. Our loss was small; but by all accounts, an Hundred of the enemy were killed. Our men loaded themselves with their Packs, and left great Numbers behind that they could not carry away; which were brought in the next Day, with as much Ammunition, Provisions, and other Plunder, as filled 4 or 5 Wagons. Their Flight was so hasty, that they dropped some of the Scalps of our Men, which we recovered.

The brave McGinnis was mortally wounded in this fight, in which the attacking party was greatly outnumbered. He continued, however, to give orders till the firing was all over, when he fainted, and was carried dying into the camp by the lake. The several bands of Dieskau's fugitives, from the several fields of fight, reunited themselves in the forest in the course of the evening, encamped there for the night, and reached their canoes, at the head of South Bay, the next evening, "spent," as Parkman[1] says, "with fatigue and famine." Dieskau himself had a hard fate. He was thrice severely wounded, the last time after his regulars had fled, and he lay helpless in his blood. He was carried into General Johnson's tent, where his wounds were dressed, though they proved to be incurable, and

[1] *Montcalm and Wolfe*, Vol. I., p. 309.

where he was defended by Johnson and other officers, and put under
a guard, against the bitter revenge of some of the Mohawks, who
tried repeatedly to kill him outright on account of the fall of their
Sachem, Hendrik. So soon as his desperate wounds would allow
it, he was carried on a litter, strongly escorted, from the lake to Fort
Lyman, and thence to Albany, and afterwards to New York. He
was an object of universal interest and curiosity wherever he went.
In the spring of 1757 he sailed for England, and was for some time
in Falmouth, and longer in Bath for the benefit of the waters. In
1760 the famous Diderot met him in Paris, and the latter's Memoirs,
published in 1830, give extremely interesting conversations as
between the two men at that time on this Crown Point expedition.
There is another paper in the French archives, purporting to be a dialogue between Marshal Saxe and the Baron Dieskau from the Elysian
Fields, in which the same expedition figures largely and truthfully.
Both these papers are translated in the New York Col. Documents,
X., pp. 340–343. Dieskau died in 1762. Interest will forever gather
on both the continents around the name and deeds of this gallant,
intellectual, vivacious, truth-loving, and grateful Frenchman, immortalized by one fateful day of intercourse with rustics and savages in
the wilds of northern New York.

The same day and the same field immortalized another man of
greatly inferior genius and prominence and opportunities, whose
grip, nevertheless, upon posterity, is even firmer than the Frenchman's, because on his way to the battle-field he turned aside to do a
conscious act of lasting benefit to those then unborn, and went forward to seal the contract in his own blood. Ephraim Williams's
niche of fame will be high and safe, so long as there remain citizens
of Williamstown and students of Williams College. The night
after the battle was dolorous in the camp at the lake, and the morning scarcely less so. The burial of the dead seems to have fallen
into the care of Lieutenant-Colonel Pomeroy, who had now succeeded
to the command of Williams's regiment. "At least forty biers,
cross-poles to carry the dead upon," were sent out; and sepulture
was accorded (for the most part) to the bodies of friend and foe
alike. When this fact was reported throughout New England, the
military authorities at the lake were harshly chidden; Dr. Chauncy
relates that the opinion in Boston was, that the officers were "too
polite by half to Dieskau, and all the French"; and attention was
widely called to the contrast between this and the treatment of the
bodies of English and Virginians on Braddock's Field two months
before.

Colonel Williams's body was found where it fell twenty-four hours before, — a little to the west of the old military road, on ground still rising to the west. The body had not been rifled or disturbed. His watch and sword, a small ivory memorandum-book, and several other trinkets were taken charge of by his brother the Surgeon, taken by him to Deerfield, where they were carefully preserved, together with the Doctor's own sword and other equipments, until the centennial celebration at the College of the battle of Lake George, when the watch and sword were presented to Williams College; and later the Doctor's own sword and other memorials of the two brothers were given to the College by Captain Ephraim Williams, U. S. A., and Bishop John Williams, of Connecticut, both of them lineal descendants of Dr. Thomas Williams. These relics are now (1892) in Clark Hall, forming a small, but valuable, part of a collection of local antiquities gathered by the present writer mainly in the decade of 1880–1890.

Colonel Williams was buried that day under a pine tree larger and taller than most of those then growing over considerable portions of the battle-field. Tradition naturally preserved the spot, for armies from New England annually, or oftener, passed it, till the final conquest of Canada; and very soon thereafter permanent settlers crept into that neighborhood, and kept alive the local word. Dr. W. S. Williams, a grandson of the Surgeon, found no difficulty in exhuming the skeleton in or about the year 1837. The skull was taken away at that time; and, it is said, was carried to North Carolina, where two members of the family, both physicians, resided about that time. When a committee of the alumni of the College. of which E. W. B. Canning (1834) was chairman, visited the place in some reference to the centennial of 1855, they found an old man living near who had helped in the exhumation just referred to, and had filled up the grave. He pointed out to this committee the precise spot of the burial, who caused to be drawn over it a rock of considerable size, into which the " E. W." initials were cut. About twenty-five years later, David Dudley Field authorized A. L. Perry, of the College, to purchase the ground holding this grave, and then to surround it with a heavy stone and iron fence. The land was accordingly bought, and stands now in the name of the President and Trustees of Williams College; and Robert R. Clark, for a whole generation the skilled and worthy carpenter of the College, was of much assistance in placing the granite posts, and fixing the iron rods which, in that sandy soil, will probably stand for a century in the true. The rock above the grave was left where it was placed in

1855, while the initial letters of the brave Colonel's name were more deeply and indelibly sunk into it. At the same time, Perry trimmed up carefully a young pine growing near, doubtless, in some sense, a representative of the old one of 1755.

Besides Blodget's very good descriptions of the battle, and his pretty fair pictorial representations of it, a large part of which he saw, and the Boston Dr. Chauncy's "First and Second Letter to a Friend," whose informants were a "Major Hore," a participant in the fight, and especially Blodget himself so soon as he returned to Boston, there are several other connected accounts of the scenes of the day, by those who were eye-witnesses and participators; and of these accounts, the readers of the future time will pretty surely approve the judgment of the present writer if he give in full General Johnson's official report, written the day after the battle, the letter of Colonel Pomeroy to Israel Williams, also written the next day, and the letter of Dr. Thomas Williams, the Surgeon, written two days later than these to his wife at Deerfield. We must remember while reading the official account, that General Johnson was inexperienced in civilized war, that he overestimated his own function in the fights, and that he does not even mention the name of his second in command.

Justin Winsor, Librarian of Harvard University, kindly sent to the present writer, with the word, "Professor Perry may like to see this," his own note on one of the contemporary pictorial representations of the battle of Lake George. The note is appended in full.

The sketch on the other side of this leaf follows an engraving, unique so far as the editor knows, which is preserved in the library of the American Antiquarian Society. It is too defective to give good photographic results. The print was "engraved and printed by Thomas Johnston, Boston, New England, April, 1756."

The key at the top reads thus: " (1.) The place where the brave Coll. Williams was ambush'd & killed, his men fighting in a retreat to the main body of our army. Also where Capt. McGennes of York, and Capt. Fulsom of New Hampshire bravely attack'd ye enemy, killing many. The rest fled, leaving their packs and prisoners, and also (2.) shews the place where the valiant Col. Titcomb was killed, it being the westerly corner of the land defended in ye general engagement, which is circumscribed with a double line, westerly and southerly; (3.) with the sd double line, in ye form of our army's entrenchments, which shows the Gen. and each Col. apartment. (4.) A Hill from which the enemy did us much harm and during the engagement the enemy had great advantage, they laying behind trees we had felled within gun-shot of our front. (W.) The place where the waggoners were killed."

On the lower map is: "The prick'd line from South Bay shews where Gen. Dieskau landed & ye way he march'd to attack our forces."

The two forts are described: "Fort Edward was built, 1755, of timber and earth, 16 feet high and 22 feet thick & has six cannon on its rampart."

"This fort [William Henry] is built of timber and earth, 22 feet high and 25 feet thick and part of it 32.   Mounts 14 cannon, 33 & 18 pounders."

The dedication in the upper left-hand corner reads: "To his Excellency William Shirley, esq., Captain general and Govr-in-chief in and over his Majesty's Province of the Massachusetts Bay in New England, Major General and Commander-in-chief of all his Majesty's land forces in North America ; and to the legislators of the several provinces concerned in the expeditions to Crown Point, — this plan of Hudson River from Albany to Fort Edward (and the road from thence to Lake George as surveyed), Lake George, the Narrows, Crown Point, part of Lake Champlain, with its South bay and Wood Creek, according to the best accounts from the French general's plan and other observations (by scale No. 1) & an exact plan of Fort Edward & William Henry (by scale No. 2) and the west end of Lake George and of the land defended on the 8th of Sept. last, and of the Army's Intrenchments afterward (by Scale 3) and sundry particulars respecting yᵉ late Engagement with the distance and bearing of Crown Point and Wood Creek from No. 4, by your most devoted, humble servant, Timᵒ Clement, *Survr*   Haveᴸ Feb. 10, 1756."

CAMP AT LAKE GEORGE, 9 Septbr 1755.

To the Governors of the Several Colonies who raised Troops on the present Expedition.

Gentlemen, Sunday Evening the 7th Inst I received Intelligence from some Indian Scouts I had sent out that they had discovered three large Roads about the South Bay and were confident a very considerable Number of the Enemy were Marched or on their March towards our Encampment at the Carrying Place where were posted about 250 of the New Hampshire Troops and five Company's of the New York Regiment.   I got one Adams a Waggoner who voluntarily and bravely consented to ride Express with my Orders to Col. Blanchard of the New Hampshire Regiment Commanding Officer there.   I acquainted him with my Intelligence and directed him to withdraw all the Troops there within the Works thrown off.   About half an hour or near an hour after this I got two Indians and two soldiers to go on Foot with another Letter to the same purpose.

About 12 o Clock that Night the Indians and Soldiers returned with a Waggoner who had stole from the Camp with about 18 others their Waggoners and Forces without order.   This Waggoner says they heard and saw the Enemy about four Miles from this side the Carrying Place, they heard a Gun Fire and a Man call upon Heaven for Mercy which he judged to be Adams.   The next Morning I called a Council of War who gave it as their Opinion and in which the Indians were extremely urgent that 1000 Men should be detached and a Number of their People would go with them in order to Catch the Enemy in their Retreat from the other Camp either as Victors or defeated in their design — the 1000 Men were detached under the Command of Collᵒ Williams of one of the Boston Regiments with upwards of 200 Indians — they Marched between 8 and 9 o'clock — in about an hour and a half afterwards We heard a heavy firing and all the Marks of a Warm Engagement which we judged was about 3 or 4 miles from us.   We beat to Arms and got our Men all in readiness — the Fire approached nearer upon which I Judged our People were retreating and detached Lieut. Col⁰. Cole with about 300 Men to cover their Retreat — about 10 o Clock some of our Men in the Rear and some Indians of the said Party came running into Camp and acquainted us that our Men were retreating, that the Enemy were too strong for them. The whole party that escaped returned to us in large Bodies.

As we had thrown up a Breast Work of Trees round our Encampment and planted field pieces to defend the same we imediately hauld some heavy cannon up there to strengthen our Front took possession of some Eminences on our left Flank and got one Field piece there in a very advantageous Situation. The Breast Work was manned throughout by our People and the best disposition made thro' our whole Encampment which time and Circumstances would permit. About half an hour after 11 the Enemy appeared in sight and marched along the Road in a very regular Order directly upon our Center. They made a small halt about 150 yards from our Breast Work, when the Regular Troops (whom we judged to be such by their Bright and fixt Bayonetts) made the grand and Center Attack, the Cannadians and Indians squatted and dispersed on our Flanks — the Enemys Fire we received first from their Regulars in Platoons but it did no great Execution being at too great a distance and our Men defended by the Breast Work. Our Artillery then began to play on them and was served under the direction of Capt Eyre during the whole Engagement in a manner very advantageous to his Character and those concerned in the Management of it. The engagement now became general on both sides — the French Regulars kept their Ground and order for some time with great Resolution and good Conduct, but the Warm and constant Fire from our Artillery and Troops put them into disorder, their Fire became more scattered and unequal and the Enemys Fire on our left grew very faint. They moved then to the right of our Encampment and Attacked Col. Ruggles, Col. Williams and Col. Titcombs Regiments where they maintained a very warm fire for near an hour, still keeping up their Fire in the other parts of our Line tho' not very strong, the three Regiments on the right supported the Attack very resolutely and kept a constant and strong fire upon the Enemy. This Attack failing and the Artillery still playing along the Line. We found their fire very Weak with considerable Intervals, this was about 4 o'clock when our Men and the Indians jumped over the Breast Work, pursued the Enemy Slaughtered Numbers and took several prisoners amongst whom was the Baron Dieskau the french General of all the Regular Forces lately arrived from Europe who was broᵗ to my Tent about 6 o'Clock just as a Wound I had received was dressed the whole Engagement and pursuit ended about 7 o'Clock.

I dont know whether I can get the returns of the slain and wounded on our side to transmit herewith, but more of that by and by.

The Greatest Loss we have sustained was in the Party commanded by Coll⁰ Williams in the Morning, who was Attacked and the Men gave way before Col. Whiting who brought up the Rear could come to his Assistance, the Enemy who were more Numerous endeavoured to surround them, upon which the Officers found they had no way to save the troops but by retreating which they did as fast as they could.

In this Engagement we suffered our greatest Loss. Col. Williams Major Ashley Capt Ingersal and Capt Cuter of the same Regiment. Capt Furrall Brother in law to the General who Commanded a party of Indians, Capᵗ Stod-

dert, Capt MaGinnis Capt Stevens all Indian Officers and the Indians say near
40 of their People who fought like Lions were all slain. Old Hendricks the great
Mohawk Sachem we fear is killed. We have abundant reason to think we killed
a great Number of the Enemy amongst whom is Mon^r St Piere who commanded
all the Indians the Each Number on either Side, I cannot obtain for tho' I sent
a party to bury our dead this Afternoon, it being a running Scattered Engagement we can neither find all our dead nor give an exact acc^t as fast as these
Troops joined us they formed with the rest in the main Battle of the Day, so
that the killed and wounded in both Engagements Officers excepted, must stand
upon my Return.

About 8 o clock last night a party of 120 of the New Hampshire Regm^t and 90
of the New York Regm^t who were detached to our Assistance under the Command of Capt McGinnes from the Camp at the Carrying Place to reinforce us,
were attacked by a party of Indians and Cannadians at the place where Coll^o
Williams was attacked in the Morning. Their engagement began between 4 & 5
o Clock. This party who our People say were between 3 and 400 had fled from
the Engagement here and gone to scalp our People killed in the Morning. Our
brave men fought them for near two hours and made a considerable Slaughter
amongst them. Of this brave party 2 are killed 11 wounded and 5 Missing.
Capt. MaGinnis who behaved with the utmost Calmness and Resolution was
brought on a Horse here and I fear his wounds will prove mortal. Ensign Fal-
sam of New Hampshire Regiment wounded thro' the Shoulder.

I this Morning called a Council of War a copy of the Minutes of which I send
you herewith.

Mon^sr Le Baron de Dushau [Dieskau] the French General is badly wounded
in the leg and thro' both his Hips and the Surgeon very much fears his Life he
is an Elderly Gentleman an experienced Officer and a Man of high consideration
in France. From his papers I find he brought under his Command to Canada
in the Men of War lately arrived at Quebec 3171 Regular Troops who are partly
in Garrison at Crown Point and encampt at Ticonderoga and other Advantageous passes between this and Crown Point. He tells me he had with him yesterday Morning 200 Grenadiers 800 Canadians and 700 Indians of defferent Nations.
His Aid de Camp says (they being separately asked) their whole Force was
about 2000 — severall of the Prisoners say about 2300. The Baron says his
Major General was killed and His Aid de Camp says the greater part of their
Chief Officers also he thinks by the Morning and Afternoon Actions they have
lost near 1000 Men, but I can get no regular Accounts, most of our People think
from 5 to 600. We have about 30 Prisoners most of them badly wounded the
Indians Scalped of their Dead already near 70 and were employed after the
Battle last night and all this Afternoon in bringing in Scalps and great Number
of French and Indians yet left unscalped. They carried of Number of their
Dead and secreted them. Our Men have Suffered so much fatigue for 3 days
past, and are constantly standing upon their Arms by day half the whole upon
Guard every Night and the rest lay down Armed and Accoutred, that both
Officers and Men are almost wore out. The Enemy may rally and we judge they
have considerable Reinforcements near at hand, so that I think it necessary we
be upon our Guard and be watchful to maintain the Advantages we have gained.
For these Reasons I dont think it either prudent or safe to be sending out
Parties in search of the Dead.

I dont hear of any Officers killed at our Camp but Col. Titcomb and none wounded but myself and Major Nicolls of Col. Titcombs. I cannot yet get certain returns of our dead and Wounded but from the best Accounts I can obtain We have lost about 130 who are killed about 60 Wounded and severall missing from the Morning and Afternoons Engagement.

I think we may expect very shortly another and more formidable Attack and that the Enemy will then come with Artillery. The late Col. Williams had the Ground cleared for Building a Stockaded Fort. Our Men are so harassed and obliged to be so constantly upon Watchful Duty that I think it would be both unreasonable and I fear in vain to set them at work upon the designed Fort.

I design to order the New Hampshire Regiment up here to Reinforce us and I hope some of the designed Reinforcements will be with us in a few days when these fresh Troops arrive I shall immediately set about building a Fort.

My wound which is in my thigh is very painful. The ball is lodged and cannot be got out, by which means I am to my mortification confined to my Tent.

10th This letter was begun and should have been dispatched yesterday, but we have had two Alarms and neither time nor Prudence would permit it. I hope Gentlemen you will place the incorrectness hereof to the Account of our Situation. I am most respectfully.

Gentⁿ Your most obedt servt

WM. JOHNSON.

If General Johnson in the comparative quiet and comfort of his tent during these two days, looking over at his leisure the papers of his distinguished captive, Dieskau, and holding pleasant conversations with him and his aide at sundry times, felt called upon to apologize for any incorrectness in his prompt report to the governors, what shall we say in the way of excuse for mistakes in his letter to Israel Williams of Colonel Seth Pomeroy, who, on the same day, was evidently in military charge of the camp, certainly of the Massachusetts end of it, giving orders of all sorts, receiving reports of the numbers of the dead and wounded and missing, superintending in some sense the burial of the dead, and the care of the stores and the spoils ? This letter will speak for itself in every way. It is among the most precious of the colonial documents during the old French War.

LAKE GEORGE Septm 9th 1755.

HONOR'ᴰ & DEAR Sᴿ

[TO COL. ISRAEL WILLIAMS.]

Yesterday a Memorable day. I Being the only Field officer In Colᵒ Ephreham Williams Rigement Suppos'd to be now Living think It my Duty to let you know what happen'd yᵉ 8th of this Instant which was yesterday — the forenoon & till near 2 of yᵉ Clock Spent In Council this Day & now So many to write too must be Excused for my Shortness & Imperfections — news as follows viz — Sabbath day Just night we had news yᵗ a Large body of men March'd up wood Creek Southwardly — we Suposing yᵗ they Intend to Cut of our wagons or atack

MONUMENT ERECTED BY THE WILLIAMS ALUMNI IN 1855 UPON A ROCK
WHICH BECAME THE TRADITIONAL, BUT WAS NOT THE ACTUAL, PLACE
WHERE COLONEL EPHRAIM WILLIAMS WAS KILLED.

yᵉ Fort at yᵉ Carrying Place but wanted better Information Sent monday morning about 1200 Men near 200 of them Indians Commanded By Colᵒ. Williams Colᵒ Whiting & Colᵒ Cole of Rhode Island Whiting In yᵉ Middle Cole brought up yᵉ rear old Hendreck king of yᵉ Six nations before with Colᵒ. Williams the Indians Some afore some in yᵉ middle & Some in yᵉ rear & so Intermix'd Through; as they got ready to March — got about 3 Mile off our Camp yᵉ guns begun to Fire It was then between 10 & 11 of yᵉ Clock we Put our Selves Into as good a Posture of Defence as we Cou'd not knowing but our men wou'd retreet & bring yᵉ army upon us, & not Long before (to our grate Surprise) they retreeted but numbers yᵗ Came furst Bringing wounded Men & Soon flock'd In by hundreds all yᵉ Time a Perpetual Fire & Drawing nearer and nearer & between 11 & 12 of yᵉ Clock yᵉ Enemy Came In Sight the Regulars March'd as near as I Cou'd Tell about 6 Deep & as I Judg'd about 20 rods In Length Close order, yᵉ Indians & Regulars at yᵉ Last wing hilter Scilter yᵉ woods full of them — they Came with In about 20 rods & fir'd Regular Plattoons but we Soon brook there order[1] yᵉ Indians & Cannadians Directly took tree with In handy gun Shot — Such a Battle It is Judg'd by all yᵗ I have heard was never known In America the Enemy Fau't with undanted Corage & the gratest Part of yᵉ English with Heroick Bravery till about 5 of yᵉ Clock aftarnon then we got yᵉ grown'd Having Lost at this place (I have not had time to get a Certin acct but going over yᵗ ground) about 12 Men. Colᵒ Titcomb was one — what yᵉ Enemy Lost I never took much Pain to know not having time only Just to run out upon yᵉ ground; before a party yᵗ Lay & stood along near ware I stood to fight; there I found ten Dead & 3 wounded all Frenchmen, them I ordered to be Carried In Immediately, one a Gentleman; yᵉ number In all taken (I have not Counted 'em) but I think it about twenty — amongst yᵉ rest the general of yᵉ French army & the A D Camp & by there Papars we know there numbers & what He brought with him the numbers at Crown Point . . . about 4000 brought with him about 1800 — the whole Plan of there opporration & Design, a map of our Fort at yᵉ Carrying Place & our Camp: an acct of Marches our number & 2000 more yᵗ they heard ware to joyne us: Came with full asureance to Lodge In our Tents that night which to his grat surprise Did (But Blessed Be God as a wound Captive) & It is thought not Like to live the French General Saith that our People made such a regular Retreet & gave them such Close shots yᵗ Dampen'd his Indians & Canadians; having there Principle Indian Officer Kill'd & a grate number of French Gentlemen Officers there was not above 100 of our men yᵗ Fired at all: But they Did with undanted Bravary & well answer'd yᵉ Caractter of Englishmen; kill'd Taken or Lost In that Battle In our Rigement I have Inclosed which was vastly yᵉ gratest Part; they being foremost & stood for a Considerable time the fire of there whole army till they ware lik'd to be surrounded which oblig'd 'em to retreat Colᵒ Williams was Shot Dead In a Moment & before he had Time to Fire his Gun Capt Hawley Shot I Fear Mortal before he had time to fire his gun: My Brother Lieut Pomeroy I have had an acct his being well till the army retreated & ask'd what are they a going to run; Yes It was said well said he I will give 'em one Shot more before I run any further I hant heard, since I have heard he is ded & scalpt. Our People are out Burying yᵉ Dead now when they return I may give a More Particular acct — we Design to Make a Stand here till we have

---

[1] Firing our Field Peaces among 'em not one Indian Found any ware there about.

a sufficient Reinforcement what number y^t must be I Cant tell but they Determine to stop us before we get to Crown Point the French General saith If we give them one more such a Dressing Crown Point & all there Country will be ours But they Design to Put a Stop to y^t — But I hope in God they will be Disapointed for I Judge humanly speeking our all Depends on ye success of this Expedition Therefore I Pray God wou'd Fire the Brests of His People with a True Zeal & a Noble Generous spirit to Come to the help of ye Lord to ye help of ye Lord against ye Mighty & I trust all those y^t value our Holy Religion & our Liberties will spare nothing Eaven to ye one half of there Estate General Johnson shot In the Thigh not Brook Maj^r General Lyman well both behaved with stediness & resolution.

I Desire ye Prayers of God's People for us, y^t we may not turn our backs upon our Enemies but stand & make a victorious Defence for our selves & our Country Crown us with victory to the Glory of God & return us in Safty.

From Your Most Obedient Humble Servt

SETH POMEROY.

P.S. ther is Someting I have omitted now han't room. Shall mention In one to my wife or Maj^r Hawley.

Probably as a sort of postscript of this letter, and almost certainly by the same messenger and on the same day, Colonel Pomeroy sent to Israel Williams at Hatfield the following official list of casualties in the Hampshire regiment. It will be remembered, that while there were then as now ten companies in a full regiment, there were but seven of these commanded by Captains, the Colonel and Lieutenant-Colonel and Major each having a technical company of his own. There were casualties in every company. The regiment was not full by any means.

A TRUE ACC^t OF THOSE KILLED WOUNDED AND MISSING OF COLO. WILLIAMS'S REGIMENT IN ACTION Sept. 8, 1755.

Colonel Williams's Company.

Colo. Eph. Williams Ensⁿ Stratton Serj't Welles Corp^l Graves Rob't Royn John Taylor.	Dead.
Corp^l Bourn Thos Serjeant Lemuel Stoddard Sol^o Stone.	Supposed Dead.
Micah Harrington Silas Graves.	Wounded.

Colo. Pomeroy's Company.

Serj't Caleb Chapin
Corp! Eben! Wright   } Supposed Dead.
Daniel Hinkley.

Capt. Simon Davis
Serj't Gen'll Thomas } Wounded.
Daniel Grainger.

Maj. Ashley's Company.

Maj'r Noah Ashley } Dead.
Israel Shaw.

Gideon Stiles } Wounded.
Gordon Symson.

Capt. House's Company.

Lieut. Cobb and Son
Serj't Kendal
Benj'n Bosberg (?)   } Dead.
——— Wertherley (?)
——— Fours (?).

Rob! Craige } Wounded.
Jon͇ Dracke (?).

Capt. Burt's Company.

Sam! Livermore } Dead.
Eben'r Ames.

Capt. Hawley's Company.

Capt. Elisha Hawley
Corp!. ——— Sternes } Wounded.
Lemuel Lyman
Sam! Fairfield.

Lieut. Dan! Pomroy
Serj't ——— Wright
Thomas Wait
Dan! Kentfield (?)
Sam! Marshal   } Supposed to be Dead.
Elnath͏ Phelps
Jon͇. Harmon
Eben'r Kinsley
Dan'! Wells.

Capt. Porter's Company.

Capt. Moses Porter
Ens'n. Reuben Wait } Dead.
Henry Bartlet.

Asa Stratton } Supposed Dead.
Zebediah Williams.

Zebediah Williams } Wounded.
James Hubbard

Capt. Ingersoll's Company.

Capt. Jon⁴. Ingersoll
Serj't —— Ball
Aaron Bagg
Abraʰ Picket
Richard Campbell.
} Dead.

Ensⁿ. Josiah Williams
Thoˢ Welcher
Jnᵒ French
Josiah Barker
Jnᵒ Aulkam
Hebert Miller
Samˡ Ponder.
} Wounded.

Capt. Hitchcock's Company.

Lieut. Burt
Wᵐ Hitchcock
Solom : Chandler.
} Dead.

Capt. Doolittle's Company.

Pelatiah Bugbe
Samˡ Southwark
Elijah Balcom
John Warrin
Charles Cuiso (?).
} Dead.

50 Dead — 21 Wounded.
French Captives 27, of which 20 Wounded.

The above accᵗ was drew in haste & I have had but a minute's time to peruse it. but I think it is a just account.

SETH POMEROY.

In a letter to his friends in Northampton, written a little later, Colonel Pomeroy gives the losses of the several corps as follows: In the Massachusetts regiments, the killed were, in Titcomb's, 35; in Williams's, 50; in Ruggles's, 37; — in the Connecticut troops, 39; in the Rhode Island troops, 20; in the New York troops, 10; and among the Mohawks, 40. This list aggregates 231 killed, and probably includes the missing. Dr. Perez Marsh, Surgeon's Mate in Colonel Williams's regiment, and ever after closely connected with the Williams family, making on the spot a two weeks' later calculation than Pomeroy's, concluded that there were 216 killed, 96 wounded, and a few missing. It will not escape the observing reader, that the proportion of killed to wounded was vastly greater in that battle than in any of the battles anywhere in the present century.

Herewith follows the deeply interesting letter of Dr. Thomas
Williams, the Surgeon, written from the camp to his wife in Deerfield the third day after the battle : —

LAKE GEORGE, Sept. 11, 1755.

My Dear Spouse : Last Monday, the 8th instant, was the most awful day that
my eyes ever beheld, & may I not say that ever was seen in New England, considering the transactions of it.   Having intelligence that an army of French &
Indians were discovered by our Indian scouts, part of our army were detached
to intercept their retreat, as it was supposed they were designed for Fort Lyman,
[*now Fort Edward*] at the south end of the Carrying-place ; about 1000 whites
under the command of my dear brother Ephraim who led the van, & Lt. Col.
Whiting who brought up the rear & about 150 Mohawks under the Command of
King Hendrick, their principal speaker, were attacked by the French Army consisting of 1200 regulars, & about 900 Canadians & Savages, about 3 miles from
our encampment.   & the main of our detachment it is said, put to a precipitate
flight, but the certainty is not yet known, besure those brave men who stood
fighting for our dear country perished in the field of battle.   The attack began
about half an hour after ten in the morning, & continued till about four in the
afternoon before the enemy began their retreat.   The enemy were about an
hour & a half driving our people before them, before they reached the camp,
where to give them due credit they fought like brave fellows on both sides for
near four hours, disputing every inch of ground, in the whole of which time
there seemed to be nothing but thunder & lightning & perpetual pillars of smoke.
Our Cannon (which under God it appears to me) saved us were heard down as
low as near Saratoga, notwithstanding the wind was in the south, & something
considerable, & which by the way was a great disadvantage to our troops, as the
smoke was drove in our faces.   The wounded were brought in very fast, & it
was with the utmost difficulty that their wounds could be dressed fast enough,
even in the most superficial manner, having in about three hours near forty men
to be dressed, & Dr. Pynchon, his mate & Billy (one of his students) & myself
were all to do it, my mate being at Fort Lyman attending upon divers sick men
there.   The bullets flew like hail-stones about our ears all the time of dressing,
as we had not a place prepared of safety, to dress the wounded in, but through
God's goodness we received no hurt any more than the bark of the trees & chips
flying in our faces by accidental shots, which were something frequent.   Our
Tent was shot through in divers places, which we thought best to leave & retire
a few rods behind a shelter of a log house, which so loose laid as to let the balls
through very often.   I have not time to give a list of the dead which are many,
by reason I have not time to attend the wounded as they ought to be.   My necessary food & sleep are almost strangers to me since the fatal day ; fatal indeed to
my dear brother Ephraim, who was killed in the beginning of the action, by a
ball through his head.   Great numbers of brave men, & some of the flower of
our army died with him on the spot, a list of which I refer you to Capt. Burke's
letter to Lt. Hoit, having not time to get a copy of one myself.   Twenty odd
wounded in our regiment, amongst whom some, I fear will prove mortal, & poor
brother Josiah makes one of the number, having a ball lodged in his intestines,
which entered towards the upper part of his thigh & pased through his groin.
Poor Capt. Hawley is yet alive, though I did not think he would live two hours

after bringing him in being shot in at the left pap (& the ball cut out near his shoulder blade) cutting his pleura, & piercing through the left lobe of his lungs. As the violence of his symptoms are this day somewhat abated, I have some small hopes he may recover. Our Mohawks suffered considerable in the action, having thirty three killed, with the brave King Hendrick, which has exasperated them much, so that it is with a great deal of difficulty that we can keep them from sacrificing the French General & Aid-de-camp, & the rest of the French prisoners, about 21 in number, which we have taken. The French General is much wounded, whose name & title is as follows : (as appears by his papers) *M. Le Baron des Dieskau, Marshall de Camp et Armies Envoye in Canada pour Commander Tout les Troupes.* It seems he was a Lt. Col° under Count Saxe last war in Flanders ; & was sent over with the same power & command from that country that the late Gen. Braddock was from England ; but must conclude, being interrupted every moment by my patients wanting something or other.

Our recruits begin to come up, which if the remainder soon join, hope we shall yet see Crown Point in a few weeks, & by God Almighty's assistance make it our own. The remainder of the French army were attacked by 250 of the New Hampshire troops after they left us ; & put to a precipitate flight, as they were not apprised of those troops, they left their baggage & most of their provisions, packs, & some guns, & many dead bodies on the spot where the attack began in the morning, when our troops came upon them, as they were sitting down to rest after their fatigue with us. The French General says he lost 600 of his men, & the Aid-de-camp says more, & that they have lost 1000. It is certain they were smartly paid, for they left their garments & weapons of war for miles together after the brush with the Hampshire troops like the Assyrians in their flight. If we had had 5 or 600 fresh troops to have followed them it is thought very few would have gone back to Crown Point to tell what had become of their brethren. It is now 11 oclock at night & I have had scarce any sleep since the action, must therefore wish you a good night, looking to a merciful & gracious God to keep & preserve you with all my dear relatives & friends & in his own due time return me home to you in safety laden with the experience of his salvation, & a grateful sense of his divine mercies to us all. With love to my dear children & proper regards to all, as due, I subscribe myself

Your affectionate Husband till Death.

THO⁸ WILLIAMS.

MRS. ESTHER WILLIAMS.

The official and original return of the losses of the day, as given by Peter Wraxall, who signs himself " A. De Camp to Gen! Johnson," now lies before the writer, and is one of several valuable originals loaned to him for the purpose to which this is now put by his friend and former pupil, Fisher Howe, of Boston. Only the losses in Colonel Williams's regiment are given in detail here from that invaluable paper, and then a summary of the losses in the other regiments, and then the aggregate of them all.

	KILLED	WOUNDED	MISSING
Col. Eph. Williams	1	..	..
Major Noah Ashley	1	..	..
Capt. Moses Porter	1	..	..
Capt. Ingersole	1	..	..
Lt. Simon Cobb	1	..	..
Lt. Dan! Pomroy	1	..	..
Lt. Nath! Burt	1	..	..
Ensign John Stratton ·	1	..	..
Ensign Reuben Wait	1	..	..
Serg?? Corp?? and Privates	32	..	..
Capt? Simon Davis and Elisha Hawley	..	2	
Ensign Josiah Williams	..	1	
Sergts. Corp?? and Privates	..	23	..
Missing	..	..	3
	41	26	3
Col. Titcomb's Reg.	9	27	25
Col. Ruggles' Reg.	5	1	28
Lyman's (Conn.) Reg.	9	3	2
Goodrich's (Conn.) Reg.	29	16	..
Rhode Island Reg.	20	6	1
Three (Conn.) Comp. with N. Y. Reg.	7	1	3
Total N. England	120	80	62

Capt. Stoddart, Capt. Magin and Capt. Stevens, Indian officers, all killed in the Morning Engagement.

There are several good reasons that make it seem proper that this chapter on Ephraim Williams should be brought to a close by quoting *verbatim* a letter written from Lake George less than three weeks after the battle, by Dr. Perez Marsh, Surgeon's Mate there, to "William Williams at Hatfield." Both the writer and the recipient of the letter became afterwards prominent people in Dalton. Marsh was graduated at Yale College in 1748, became a physician, married a daughter of Colonel Israel Williams, was appointed Justice of the Peace at Dalton in 1761, and a Judge of the Court of Common Pleas in 1765, — retiring from public life in 1774, because he sympathized strongly (like the Williams family in general) with the royal cause. The recipient of the letter, William Williams, was son of Colonel Israel Williams, removed from Hatfield to Dalton not far from 1761, became deacon of the church and a father of the town, was an original member of the Board of Trustees of the Williamstown Free School and later of the College, and was chosen the first President of the Board. This letter shows, as no other contemporaneous document shows, the strong colonial strifes and jealousies, felt if not manifested, even on the battle-field, as between Yorkers and New England men in general, and more minutely as between the men of the separate eastern colonies one against another. The letter shows also the kind of stories current in the camp in those days, and under those circumstances, both in regard to allies and enemies. The damaging reference to Lieutenant-Colonel Whiting, of the Connecticut troops, had probably not a particle of foundation in fact. That a commander should wish to pull his men back out of a local ambuscade is natural enough, and would seem to be good tactics. Indeed, the military criticisms of Dr. Marsh, including the fling (if it be one) at Colonel Pomeroy, are very light weight. Let the surgeon stick to his scalpel.

In reference to the poisoned bullets alleged by Marsh and many others to have been used in the battle of Lake George, it is certain, if that were done at all, that it was not done with the knowledge and approval of the government of France, or of the Baron General Dieskau. It was done secretly by the savages, if it were done at all. If actually used by the Indians in that battle, it would have been just as likely beforehand to characterize the Mohawks on the English side, as the Canada Indians on the French side. In truth, the charge, though stoutly raised by the New England men against their enemies in general, was never *proved* in any proper sense of the word. The surgeons strongly suspected it in certain wounds proving mortal; they allowed the accusations to go forth; they even specified the names of certain supposed victims, particularly Micah Harrington, of Fort Massachusetts; but lapse of time and the nature of the proof gradually made the surgeons less confident, and the public less credulous about the whole matter.

LAKE GEORGE 26th Sept'r/55

D'r S'r, I this instant received yours of ye 12th. Colº· Pomroy rec'd another. The letters I imagine have been at Albany about a weak. Col'º. Pomroy has wrote several times since the date of these & Withal has given you a truer representation of the Battle & all its circumstances than I can amidst sick & wounded who take up the most of my time & tho'ts — so Much that I have hardly realiz'd ye death of our dear friend who fell gloriously in the defence of y'r Country & priviledges. The victory be sure is great & noble, but the loss of so many good men — the best in ye regim't, the best in ye army — the loss itself especially considered in its circumstances, eclipses all the glory & darkens every prospect. In the first place that the army should be here a fortnight in the enemies country without the least fortification is to me very surprizing, but that they should still continue in this defenceless posture, even after they had heard of an army not far off, is more surprizing. But the most astonishing thing that happened was that Colº. Williams should go three miles from the Camp, with 12 hundred men, expecting an attack every minute, or at least that it was quite probable, & yet keep no [advanced] scouts. I have often heard him speak of this very thing, & the danger of marching without it. That the Colo'll should neglect this & give ye enemy the best advantage you can conceive of is very remarkable. The enemy could not have had a more advantageous place, nor our Forces a worse. One thing more, which is your desire to know, & most shocking & surprizing to us was the shamefull retreat of a certain Gent'n in the Army who brought up the rear, Notwithstanding ye express orders of our dear friend Colo. Williams that no man retreat upon pain of death. This Gent'n, upon the first fire of the enemy, gave express Command retreat! retreat! — left their friends (who fought valiantly while they lived) to fall a prey into ye hands of an enemy whose orders were ye most shocking that ever were heard — neither to give nor take any quarters. Agreeable to ye same we found Capt. Porter & others butcher'd alive who were captivated by 'em without any wound.

The Gent'n whose conduct has been thus surprizing you have doubtless been acquainted with at N. Haven. The Col. & he were peculiar good friends, which aggravates ye thing & makes ye sin unpardonable, for had they stood ye ground, tho' they were under such disadvantages, I doubt not they could easily have drove 'em, & had not those in ye camps perceived their fire to draw nearer they would soon have issued forth to their assistance, but on ye contrary hearing by ye report they came nearer to ye camps every minute all they had to do was to put 'em [themselves] into a [readiness] to engage 'em. The enemy 'tis true were confident of success, & behaved with all the courage & resolution possable. I suppose one half of the 1200 who were first attack'd never fired a gun till they came within ye camps, their fright was so great they disheartened many soldiers in ye camps, & they & many others would have gon clear, had not it been for the Gen'rl & other officers who drew their swords & declar'd they would run em thro. After they were once ingaged they fough[t] well. The Gen'rl's observation who [Dieskau] we took prisoner was that our men "in ye morning fought like good boys, about noon like men, but in the afternoon like the Devil." The numbers of the enemy slain is not known. An account of ours you have doubtless heard in our report — 45 dead — 24 wounded. In the army, 216 dead, 96 wounded.

The cruel treatment of our regiment, who, without any disparagement, was the best in the army, you have doubtless heard. Envy & mallace seems to be ye occasion. I hope for ye honour of ye County, without bringing into consideration the reflection upon Col. Pomroy, your honour'd father will exert himself in this affair, for if possible we have actually jumped out of the frying-pan into the fire.

Capt. Hawley is dead you will hear by the bearer. Ens'n Williams is not out of danger, but vastly better. His wounds work exceeding well, & 'tis probable he may recover. You have heard the acc'ts of poison bullets &c. I would be more particular, but Mr. Clarke [the messenger] was ready to set out when I receiv'd your letter. His Company is gone and he impatient. I hope to see you shortly, & converse freely.

Please to make my compliments acceptable to all friends.

Your sincere friend & Hum'bl Servant,

PEREZ MARSH.

P.S. Whether we proceed this fall is now debated, & what will be determined I know not, but tis generally tho't in ye negative.

A little side light is thrown in conclusion upon the futile Crown Point expedition by the following bill for services rendered the returning soldiers at the close of the season. Dr. Samuel Lee, who had come into what is now Berkshire County, from Lyme, Connecticut, and was practising medicine at the time in the Upper Housatonic township (Great Barrington), sent in a bill to the General Court as a "Practitioner in Physick," of which the following is the heading: —

THE PROVINCE OF THE MASSACHUSETTS BAY DR.
FOR WHAT I HAVE DONE FOR THE SOLDIERS ON THEIR RETURN FROM THE CAMP AT LAKE GEORGE.

These services extended throughout the month of December, 1755. At that time the principal road from Albany to Westfield and Boston ran through the Upper Housatonic township, and had been called since 1735 the "Albany road." Over this road passed, both ways, most of the military companies between the Connecticut and the Hudson during the two last French wars and the Revolutionary War that followed.[1] Dr. Lee had many patients among the Massachusetts soldiers, sick and scattered along this road. He speaks of an Aaron Smith, belonging to Captain John Phay's company, who "was sick 8 or 9 miles from me," and whom he visited repeatedly. He speaks also of "Eben: Hide 2d Belonging to Capt. Elisha Noble's Company in ye Reg: of Col: Ephraim Williams Esq. Deceased. The Above Said Hide was sick about Nine or Ten miles Distant from me." He also treated Ensign Caleb Wright, of Captain Elisha Noble's company.

Dr. Lee took oath to this bill (before sending it) in Canaan, Litchfield County, Connecticut, before David Whitney, Justice of the Peace. The aggregate charges were £3 1s. 9d.

The charges in the above account I apprehend to be reasonable.

W. BRATTLE.

[1] See *Berkshire Historical Collections*, v. 1, pp. 118 *et seq.*

CHAPTER IV.

" — Holding the care
Of home and children, and the hope to die,
Remembered 'mong the mossy names that haunt
The pine-hid churchyard; happy in the toil
That seeks night's peaceful couch with lamps unlit."

UNTIL the building of Fort Massachusetts in 1745, very little was known in the settled parts of the state about its extreme northwest corner. It was cut off on the east by the high mountain wall of the Hoosacs, over which there ran at that time only a very narrow and pretty straight Indian trail. The only other practical access to it was from the south, over the rough and rocky watershed that divides the head streams of the Housatonic from those dropping down into the Hoosac. Much interest was felt, however, in this strip of land and in those streams, by the people of the "Bay," and perhaps even more by the dwellers along the Connecticut; for New Hampshire had long claimed a strip off the northern boundary of Massachusetts, and New York quite as persistently another strip over the Taconics to the eastward. The former controversy was finally settled in 1741, and the latter only in 1787.

Access was really had into the valley of the Hoosac for purposes of settlement and civilization from the south, namely, from the Indian town of Stockbridge, incorporated in 1739. The first English family to join the missionary station in Stockbridge, started in 1734 by John Sergeant and Timothy Woodbridge, was that of Ephraim Williams, Senior. He had been a man of affairs in Newton, Justice of the Peace and Captain; and when the General Court made grant to the Housatonic Indians of the town of Stockbridge, they made reservation of certain portions of the land to Sergeant and Woodbridge, and also certain other portions to four gentlemen whom they might appoint as companions and exemplars to assist the missionary and school-teacher in civilizing and Christianizing the

372

Indians. The first named of these four, and the first to arrive in the early part of the year 1739, was Ephraim Williams. It is just about forty-five miles from the Connecticut River through Westfield to Stockbridge. A horse-road had just been laid out over the hills following in general an old Indian trail; and Williams is said, by tradition, to have brought his young children to Stockbridge in panniers on a horse. Williams brought also with him to Stockbridge a commission to lay out at his earliest convenience two townships on the Hoosac River; and apparently as soon as he had gotten his family housed on Stockbridge Hill, and their most pressing exigencies provided for, with proper assistants he carried out this commission according to his best judgment, and reported results to the court in Boston in the month of June. This is called the survey of 1739. The report of it is interesting reading, as it is preserved in the archives of the state; and especially interesting is the rude map of the townships accompanying the report.

In the wood-cut annexed the reader will see the reproduction of that map, and the earliest local construction of these two townships on the Hoosac, by the first white men known to have ever traversed the banks of our river and those of its two forks. They made the main river the centre of the west township, and as far as possible the two forks the middle of the east township. The courses of the two forks are, in general, almost continuous north and south, and they come together at a very large angle in the present town of North Adams; the course of the united stream for five or six miles is nearly west, so that the plan of Williams required a lay-out of the two townships nearly at right angles with each other: the east town lying in general north and south, and the west town bearing an east and west course.

For some reasons (we do not know what they were) this first survey, doubtless made in haste, for all the lines of it were not fully brought together on the map, though the wood-cut represents them as completed, did not please the parties most interested in the locality. After Fort Massachusetts was built in 1745, and rebuilt in 1747, quite a number of the "river-gods" clambered over the Hoosac Mountain to take a look at the main valley, and the subordinate valleys. Colonel Oliver Partridge came over in 1746, to superintend burying the dead around the fort, and Major Ephraim Williams doubtless made himself very familiar with the lay of the land throughout; at any rate, after the representations of somebody, the General Court ordered, in April of 1749, a new survey and plan of the two townships, then first distinctly designated as "East Hoosac"

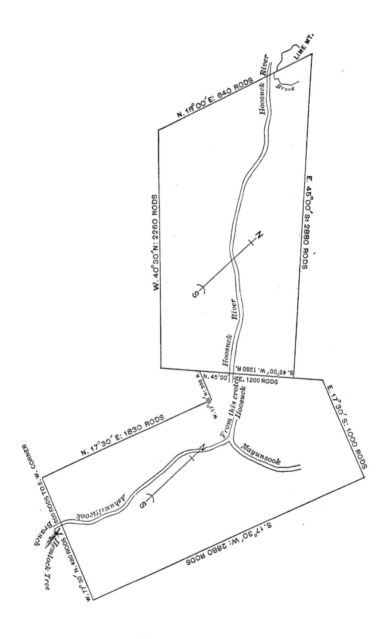

"A Plan of 23,040 acres of Land lying on the East Side of Ashuwilticook River and South Branch of Hoosuck River, beg'ing at a Hemlock Tree mark'd O+.

"Surveyed May 1739, by the Needle of the surveying Instrument,

"By Mr. NATH. KELLOGG,

Surveyor."

and "West Hoosac." The reader will be doubtless pleased to see the order of the court in their own language : —

IN HOUSE REPS. APR 18, 1749.

Ordered, That Col. Dwight & Col. Choate with such as the Hon. Board shall join be a committee to repair to the Province Lands near Hoosuck, as soon as may be, with a skilful surveyor and chainmen under oath, and lay out two Townships of the contents of six miles square, in the best of the land and in as regular form as may be, joining them together, and return a correct plat of said Townships to this court for their further order thereon. And also to return the course and distance said Towns bear from Fort Massachusetts, and as near as they can the quantity of Intervale Land contained in each Township and what the quality of the soil adjoining to the said Township is.

This order was concurred in by the Council, and Oliver Partridge, Esq., was joined to the committee on the part of that body.

The new survey discarded the former one. It set down the new towns parallel with each other, rectangular in form, intended to be equal in area, although the most cursory observation showed the west town to be much the better for agriculture, because it held much more intervale and the upland was more level. Partially to equalize this difference, the north line of the east town (later Adams) was not carried north over the mountain to Hazen's line run eight years before, and its south line was carried south (where there was better land) a corresponding distance below the south line of the west town. The north line of the west town was Hazen's line for the distance, and its south line, of course, so much above the south line of the other. The committee had been instructed by the court to lay out both townships six miles square; but the lay and the quality of the land alike forbade this; twelve miles from the assumed east line of New York (not finally settled until 1787) would have carried the east line of East Hoosac well up the precipitous sides of the Hoosac Mountain ; and so the actual survey made the townships about five miles wide, and something more than seven miles long. The division line between the two has never been altered to this day, and the same is true of the eastern line of East Hoosac, although that township was divided a few years ago into "North Adams" and "Adams" by an east and west line near the middle.

The official report of the committee for the new survey makes interesting reading. It was made on the 10th of November following the appointment of the committee in April, 1749, by Oliver Partridge, of Hatfield, their chairman : —

The com. appt'd by the Great & Gen Court in April last to repair to the Province lands near Hoosuck to lay out two Townships of the contents of six miles square &c Report —

That on the 26 day of October the com. went from Hatfield, and the next day came to Fort Mass — (having obtained Mr Nathaniel Dwight a skilfull Surveyor to survey the Townships) The next day we went out to view the lands, ordered the surveyor to measure the distance from the fort to the line that is run between this Government & New Hampshire (which was run some years since by Mr. Hazzen) and on Monday & Tuesday following we proceeded to view the lands. In the meantime directed the Survr to take the courses & distances of ye adjacent mountains, and when we had sufficiently satisfied ourselves in what form the Townships be laid out, we directed the Survr to lay them out agreeable to the plan herewith presented (Having caused the Surv & chainmen to be sworn.)

As to the quantity of intervale contained in the townships, we made no particular measure thereof by the survey, but carefully viewed the townships and would inform that the land on the river, running through the centre of the East Township for more than 4 miles northerly and southerly about half a mile East & West appears rich & good, a considerable part thereof is intervale.

In the West Township there is no so great quantity of Intervale, but a very valuable and rich tract of land in the middle of the Township, insomuch that the com. do deem the West Township the most valuable.

Great part of the land in both townships is considerably loaded with timber.

As to the quality of lands adjoining sd townships the Com. would inform that on the East of sd Townships lie the Great Hoosuck Mountain (so-called) which is about 7 miles from side, on which mountain there is a sufficient quantity of land for a township or two — a great part of it is valuable — On the West side of the West town lays a range of mountains, and between the two townships lays another range of mountains over which the dividing line runs — Between the North line of the East town and the Province line the land is mountainous and broken — and the land on the south of sd town is — some very poor and some of it good and accommodable for settlement.

All which is humbly submitted in the name and by the order of the Committee.

Ov. Partridge.

Nov. 10. 1749.

The north line of West Hoosac was shortened a few rods at its western extremity, in 1787, by the final New York line, which shaved off an elongated corner at that point of no great consequence; while the establishment of the same New York line created an elongated gore, 446 rods long at its base, which was continuous with the original south line of West Hoosac, which came to a point at the point of the little triangle just referred to as cut off at the north, which gore was added to Williamstown in 1837; so that only the east line of West Hoosac remains now the east line of Williamstown, just as it was platted in 1749.

At the next session, January, 1750, the settlement of the township thus laid out was under the consideration of the Legislature, and the result was the adoption by both branches of the following orders: —

Voted, That Col. Miller and Capt. Livermore with such as the Hon. Council shall appoint be a com. to lay out 63 house lots in the Westernmost Township (Each house lot to draw one sixty third part of sd. Township) one for the first settled minister, one for the ministry, and one for the school, as near the centre of the Township as may be with convenience, the said lots to contain 10 or 12 acres each as the Com. shall best judge — said house lots to be adjoining — and also that said Com. be directed to lay out such Highways, streets and lanes to and amongst the house lots as shall be necessary and convenient, and that said Committee have power to admit sixty settlers or inhabitants into said Township — each of them shall be entitled to one sixty third part of said Township upon the conditions following viz. — That each settler pay the Com. upon his being admitted, £6. 13. 6 Lawful money for the use of the Government, and that he shall within the space of Two years from the time of his being admitted build a house 18 feet long, 15 feet wide and seven foot studd, and shall fence five acres of his said house lot and bring the same to English grass, or fit it for plowing and raising of wheat or other corn, and shall actually by themselves or assigns reside on said house lot five years in seven from the time of their being admitted — and that they do settle a learned Orthodox minister in said Town within the term of five years from the time of their being admitted — And in case the aforesaid conditions are not fulfilled, according to the true intent and meaning thereof — that then such settler or settlers' right shall be forfeit and revert back to the Province to be disposed as the Gen. Court shall and may hereafter order and determine — any thing in their grant to the contrary notwithstanding.

And that the sd Com. be further directed to take a bond of each person by them admitted as a settler of the penal sum of fifty pounds money payable to the Province Treasurer or his succesors in sd office for the faithful performance of the conditions of sd grant — the sd Com to make report of their doings — and due return of sd bonds to the Province Treasurer as soon as may be — who shall be paid for their service out of monies received of the settlers — And as to the Easternmost Township to be settled as the Gen Court shall order. Sent up for Concurrence.

THOS. HUBBARD, Speakr Pro Tempore.

In council Apr 6. 1750

Read and Concurred and James Ninatt Esq is joined in the affair. Saml Holbrook Depy Secretary

Consented to S. Phipps.

The normal scheme on which these lots were to be laid as a village centre is plain enough both from what was actually done, and from the later testimony of some of the original proprietors; namely, to lay out on both sides of a main street fifteen rods wide, extending from Green River at the east, one and three-eighths miles to Buxton Brook at the west, sixty-three house lots, each lot thirteen and one-third rods wide on the street, and running back from it 120 rods, thus making each lot contain just ten acres.   The odd number of the lots (63) made a strict rectangle of them impossible; and the actual encroachment of the Green River on the southeast corner of the general plot, as that was then located, threw five lots more on to the north side of the street than on the south side.   Sixty-three lots were laid out on the prescribed street, but they are both wider and deeper than the normal plan allowed for.   Instead of a uniform depth on both sides of 120 rods, Alexander Walker, a Scotch surveyor of some attainments and reputation, for a long time now (1892) a citizen of Williamstown, after repeated and variously diversified measurements, finds the thirty-four lots on the north side of Main Street each 125 rods deep, and the corresponding twenty-nine lots on the south side, each 129.5 rods deep.   The normal plat would have been 255 rods north and south, and 420 rods east and west. The actual plat is irregular for two probable reasons : (1) The Green River cuts off a considerable corner on the south side towards the east, and (2) The surveyors of that time are known to have made large allowances in their measurements for "slag" or slack; that is, the chain could not be carried straight and held taut on account of trees and other impediments in the line being measured, and accordingly the chain was reckoned short, and more land given to the rod. The actual *width* of the lots, according to Walker, is very nearly 13.75 rods each, instead of the normal 13.33 rods each; which is an increase very nearly in proportion to the increase in the *depth* of the lots from 120 rods to 125 on the north side of the street. Nothing known to the present writer accounts for the still greater depth beyond the normal of the fewer house lots on the south side of the Main Street.   In those days lands were abundant, and consequently cheap; and all of the after lots surveyed in West Hoosac now overrun in the same way, and probably for the same reason, their original and prescribed dimensions.

Mr. Walker makes the bearing of the Main Street N. 61° 55' W. In this direction, accordingly, the actual plat was extended, as between the two streams mentioned a moment ago, over four eminences, the summits of each of which are very nearly 100 feet above the Hoosac River, flowing north of the village plat at an average distance of perhaps three-quarters of a mile from its northerly line. The Main Street bisects the plat the longer way, and is itself bisected the other way by a continuous North and South Street, whose bearing is S. 29° 30' W. or N. 29° 30' E.   The broad space at the intersection of these streets was originally called "The Square," and is now called "The Field Park."   It constitutes the third of the eminences but just now referred to, and was occupied for a century by two Congregational meeting-houses in succession. The first two " Inns " of the village adjoined upon it, as do also the two present hotels. It was designed to be, it has always been, and is likely perhaps ever to continue, the technical centre of the village; but a strong competitor for this position, certainly in point of business and places of assembly and residence, have latterly become the two more easterly eminences and the shallow valley between them. Into this valley came the new meeting-house in 1869, after its immediate predecessor was burned on the old site in 1866; and about the same time was built, in the same valley, the principal school building for the village, accommodating also the High School of the town.

On the north side of the Main Street were laid down thirty-four settling lots, — seventeen on each side of the North Street; on the south side of Main were plotted twenty-nine of these lots, — seventeen on the west side of the South Street and twelve on its east side. The Green River tumbles down over natural falls and through precipitous places, just where five of these lots would naturally have been located, although Water Street finds a way from Main Street, down a steep hill and then up alongside Green River, and, although one house lot, No. 57, was laid out àt right angles to all the rest, parallel with and alongside of the Main Street to its east end. This lot, 57, is not as long as the rest, and is in several ways anomalous. The contents of each of the rest of the lots on the south side of Main Street are eleven acres and thirteen one-hundredths, while the area of each of the lots on the north side is ten acres and three-quarters. The aggregate area of all the house lots, exclusive of the streets, and reckoning No. 57 as a full lot on the southern tier, is 687 acres and a quarter. The average contents of the sixty-three lots is, as nearly as possible, eleven acres.

The original house lots of the town having been thus surveyed and mapped out for exhibition to would-be purchasers, the next thing in order was to dispose of them to actual settlers. There were two main obstacles in the way of this. Almost everybody expected a speedy resumption of hostilities in a renewed war with the French and Indians; and, in that case, West Hoosac would lie right on the path of all the main war parties from Canada, and any scattered dwellings built on these lots would be wholly exposed to the merciless savages. In the second place, similar lands and homes were then being offered by agents of the General Court in perhaps a score of new towns scattered through the western part of the colony. Ephraim Williams, Senior, had, some time before this, opened up the four "Housatonic townships," so-called, and invited into them his old neighbors of Newton and Watertown, and welcomed new-comers from any quarter.   Stockbridge itself and Pittsfield were then bidding for English inhabitants.   Good lands were then very cheap, in any quantity, on every hand.

The committee in charge of selling the West Hoosac lots could, nevertheless, make a pretty fair show.   The original scheme of the village contemplated two roads, each parallel with the Main Street, along the ends of the lots the entire distance, both north and south. A part of this north road was actually built very early, is still in use at the northwest corner of the plat, but was there intermitted as to the rest of the circuit, and has never been resumed.   These roads looked well on a parchment plot of the proposed homesteads, in connection with the central streets in both directions, which latter formed a perfect Greek cross.   Then, the purchaser of any one of these house lots bought thereby and at the same time the fee simple of one sixty-third of the whole township, as the proprietors might conclude afterwards to divide up the lands among themselves, as into meadow lots, oak lots, fifty-acre lots, and so on, until all the land was thus distributed.   Moreover, the committee could say and did say to buyers, "Fort Massachusetts is only about four miles from 'The Square' of the new village, and will serve as some sort of defence — at the least, of a refuge — to the pioneer settlers." So they offered the lots for sale, under the certain prescribed condi-tions already quoted, which were considerably complicated, to the officers and soldiers in Fort Massachusetts, in the chief towns along the Connecticut, in Concord and Boston, and in Canaan and Litch-field, Connecticut.   It took a good while to dispose of them all.

In the meantime, at the beginning of February, 1751 (new style, 1750 old style), the following petition was presented to the General Court by Captain Ephraim Williams, in behalf of himself and some of the soldiers under him in Fort Massachusetts : —

Feb. 1750 — Petition of Ephm Williams Commander of Fort Massachusetts :
Most Humbly showeth that your petitioner hath been detained in Boston ever since ye last of Nov. past waiting for money due to him and Company out of the Province Treasury for which he hath his warrants duly executed.   But there being no money in the Treasury for the payments of them, he must either wait longer (which is very expensive) or return home without ; ye later of which will be very Detrimental (as also the former hath been) by reason that fifteen of the Lotts in ye land to the westward of sd Fort Massachusetts, and (by the Committee appointed for the sale of them) virtually Bargained to some of his soldiers upon conditions they speedily pay what they bargained to give, which they (foremost of their money due aforesd) are unable to do and so consequently

must lose them, and as that would be a great disappointment, therefore your petitr Humbly prays Your Honr and Hours would direct the Comee aforesd to take ye warrants above mentioned into their own hands, they advancing the Contents of them to your Petitr, which will not only enable sd soldiers to pay for sd Lotts, but Save your Petitr a vast charge, which he humbly hopes your Honor and Honors in your known wisdom will do and as in duty bound will ever pray — signed E. Williams Jr — (own hand).

This petition appealed to the sense of fair and right in the minds of the legislators, and was acted upon at once and favorably, as appears by the following vote : —

HOUSE REPS. Feb. 7, 1750.

Recd and Ordered that the Comee for admitting settlers in the West New Township at Hoosuck, be and they hereby are directed and impowered out of the monys which they shall receive from the said Settlers to pay the within named Williams the money due on said warrants — He delivering the sd committee with proper orders on the Treasurer to discount the same with them.

And the said committee are also allowed to admit as many of the Soldiers at Fort Massachusetts, as Settlers as they shall judge proper. Sent up for concurrence. T. HUBBARD Spkr.
Concurred — Consented. T. Phipps.

As an inducement to buyers and settlers, the committee were able to urge the fact, that, in 1750, a grant of 200 acres of land had been made to Captain Ephraim Williams, Junior, in East Hoosac, by the General Court, on condition that he should reserve ten acres of the meadow around Fort Massachusetts for the use of that fort, and also build a grist-mill and a saw-mill on one of the branches of Hoosac River near their junction, and keep the same in repair for twenty years for the use of the settlers in the two townships. The mills were built accordingly on the south branch (Ashuwillticook) at a natural fall, still utilized for a water-power, a couple of rods above the bridge, by which one enters the present village of North Adams from the west. The mills were the first resource of the first settlers of both townships.

The committee were required, by law, to reserve three house lots in West Hoosac, " one for the first-settled minister, one for the ministry, and one for the school, as near the centre of the township as may be with convenience." They reserved, accordingly, for these purposes in their order, near the square, Nos. 36, 38, and 35, the first two out of the north tier, and the third from the south tier alongside the South Street. The remaining sixty lots were put upon the market substantially in the following manner: The price was uniform for all the lots, namely, £6 13s. 4d., although there were very considerable differences in the value of the same for homesteads.

Chance determined by the *number* drawn the location of each man's purchase. One could buy just as well in Concord or Litchfield as in West Hoosac itself; and the process could go on without confusion till the last number was drawn from the box. The name of the man and the number of the lot went together; there was no opportunity of choice as between the lots themselves.

In September, 1752, the committee reported to the province of Massachusetts Bay in the following words: —

We the Subscribers appointed by this Honored Court to lay out 63 Houselotts in the Westernmost Township at Hoosuck — sixty of which to be disposed of by us — We have completed that service as directed by the order of the court herewith exhibited.

Com. { JAMES MINOT
SAM^L MILLER
SAMUEL LIVERMORE. }

The committee then present their account for services, horse-hire, and subsistence, — fourteen days in "lotting": —

3 days at Concord to sell lots at 6/ per day —
3 " " Worcester " " " 2/ horsehire —
1 " " Watertown " " "

Total	£ 34	10
To surveyor & chainmen	9 18	10
Paid Prov. Treasurer	239 15	
	£284 3	10
Balance to be paid Treas.	115 16	2
	£400	

The committee charge themselves for several lots of land, to wit: —

60 Lotts of land sold to several persons as per particular list herewith annexed at £6 13 4.

3 Lotts to ye minister, ministry, and school. —

In Council Jany 3, 1753. Voted, that the within account be allowed, and that the Com. to pay the ballance thereof being £115 16 2 into the Province Treasury.

S. PHIPPS.

Thus the house lots were all disposed of in the first instance, — about one quarter of them to officers and men at Fort Massachusetts; some to land speculators of the time; some to men whose motives appear to have been patriotic merely, to help on the settlement as a good mode of defence against Canada; and some to men whose residence and character cannot be ascertained at this late day. There were forty-six buyers in all. Lieutenant Samuel Brown, of Stockbridge, took three lots, and there were twelve others who took two lots each. The remaining thirty-three subscribed for one lot only. It is probably best to make a permanent record here of all the names of these forty-six persons, their residences at the time so far as these are known, and the numbers of the house lots originally drawn by them; although a brisk trade in the lots sprang up almost immediately, and only a small part of these first drawers ever became resident settlers upon them. Before doing this, however, we will give the original scale as each man drew his lot, or lots, and the place of each lot upon the rectangle.

ORIGINAL DRAWINGS OF HOUSELOTS.

Reuben Bilding	33	34	John Moffat
Micah Harrington	31	32	Elisha Williams Jr
Nath'l Russell	29	30	Tho' Train
George Willis Esq	27	28	Isaac Wyman
Lemuel Avery	25	26	Josiah Dean
Tho' Moffat	23	24	W'' Chidester
Elizur Dickinson	21	22	Beng. Simonds
John Chamberlain	19	20	Aeneas Mackey
Lieut Moses Graves	17	18	Joel Dickinson
Thos Moffat	15	16	Josiah Williams
Ezekiel Foster	13	14	Abner Roberts
Joseph Smith	11	12	Sam'l Wells
Dr. Seth Hudson	9	10	Eph'm Williams Jr
Josiah Williams	7	8	" " "
Sam'l Calhoon	5	6	W'm Chidester
Timo Woodbridge	3	4	Col. Oliver Partridge
Sam'l Brown Jr.	1	2	Lieut Isaac Wyman

S. STREET — SQUARE — N. STREET

School	35	36	Ministers
Sam'l Calhoon	37	38	Ministry
Lieut Sam'l Brown	39	40	Lieut Elisha Hawley
Capt. Elisha Chapin	41	42	John Buch
Elijah Brown	43	44	Josiah Dean
Lieut Obadiah Dickinson	45	46	John Moffat
Joseph Hawley Esq	47	48	Moses Graves
Daniel Haws	49	50	Sam'l Taylor
Elisha Allis	51	52	Saml Smith
Eben'r Graves	53	54	Saml Brown
Olivur Avery	55	56	Eben'r Graves
		58	Saml Brown
		59	John Crawford
		60	Aaron Denio
		61	Obadiah Dickinson
		62	Aeneas Mackey
		63	Dan'l Donillson

Green River — 57 Nath'l Harvey

LOTS AND PURCHASERS GROUPED.

Capt. Ephraim Williams, Jr.	Fort Mass.	8 10
Lieut. Isaac Wyman	" "	2 28
William Chidester	" "	6 24
Dr. Seth Hudson		9
Samuel Calhoun		5 37
Ezekiel Foster		13
Benjamin Simonds		22
Abner Roberts		14
Thomas Train		30
Micah Harrington		31
Elisha Chapin		41
John Bush		42
John Chamberlin	.. ..	19
Lieut. Samuel Brown	Stockbridge	39 54 58
Samuel Brown, Jr.	"	1
Josiah Williams	"	7 16
Col. Oliver Partridge	Hatfield	4
Timothy Woodbridge	"	3
Lieut. Moses Graves	"	17 48
Reuben Belding		33
Lieut. Obadiah Dickinson		61 45
Elisha Allis		51
Joseph Smith		11
Samuel Wells		12
Joel Dickenson		18
Joseph Hawley, Esq.	Northampton	47
Lieut. Elisha Hawley	"	40
Josiah Dean	Canaan, Ct.	26 44
Elisha Williams, Jr.	Weathersfield, Ct.	32
Oliver Avery	Charlemont	55
Serg. Samuel Taylor	"	50
Thomas Moffat	New London, Ct.	15 23
Ebenezer Graves	North Reading	53 56
John Moffat	Boston	34 46
Daniel Donalson	Coleraine	63
Aaron Denio	"	60
Nathaniel Harvey	"	57
Samuel Smith		52
Daniel Hawes	"	49
John Crofoot (Crawford)	Worcester	59
Aeneas Mackay	Unknown	20 62
Lemuel Avery	"	25
Elisha Brown	"	43
George Willis, Esq.		27
Nathaniel Russell		29

These forty-six were the "first proprietors" of Williamstown. By much the most distinguished name among them is that of Joseph Hawley, of Northampton, who played a great part in the history of Massachusetts for thirty years after he became proprietor here of house lot 47. Some account of this man's activity and influence in church and state has been given on a preceding page. The writer has now in his possession the manuscript deed of Joseph Hawley, wholly written out with his own hand, conveying to Nehemiah Smedley, in April, 1760, this original house lot 47, alongside of which, and partly through which, runs the present Spring Street of our village. Two of these first proprietors were killed in the battle of Lake George with Colonel Ephraim Williams in 1755; namely, Lieutenant Elisha Hawley, brother of the statesman; Micah Harrington, supposed to have been killed by a poisoned musket-ball; and a third, Ensign Josiah Williams, half brother of the commander, was severely wounded. Two others of these proprietors were killed July 11, 1756, near the West Hoosac fort, as we shall learn more particularly later, namely, Captain Elisha Chapin and William Chidester, both long in Fort Massachusetts, and in West Hoosac fort also.

The first actual settlers upon any of these lots, who were also original proprietors of the same, seem all to have been soldiers at Fort Massachusetts. Isaac Wyman, second in command there, commenced pretty soon on his lot, No. 2, which stretched along flanking North Street on the west side, and the front of which is now graced by the Lodge of Kappa Alpha; Seth Hudson, sometimes surgeon at the fort, and sometimes commander of West Hoosac fort, very influential in the settlement, and by much the last survivor of the original proprietors, built his house on his lot No. 9, which lay on the west declivity of the third eminence, south side of Main Street near Hemlock Brook, which house is still standing, much transformed, about half a mile down the brook from its first site; Benjamin Simonds, the same who was carried captive to Canada from Fort Massachusetts in 1746, began to clear up and to build on his drawn lot No. 22, situated on the east slope of the fourth eminence north side, where the underpinning of the house is still (1892) visible, two or three rods southwest of the Danforth monuments in the old cemetery, in which house was born the first child of the hamlet, Rachel Simonds, April 8, 1753, and near which are still living and growing less four or five old apple-trees probably set in that year or the next, which house is yet standing, substantially unchanged across the Main Street nearly opposite where

it first stood; Thomas Train, who drew No. 30, which was the
fourth lot west of Simonds's, in the same tier of lots, and who married long afterwards this same Rachel Simonds, whose posterity
both from this marriage, and a second with Deacon Benjamin Skinner, have been numerous and prominent in Williamstown; Ezekiel
Foster, who was of Fall Town (Bernardston), began on his drawn
lot No. 13, which was the second west of Seth Hudson's in the same
tier, and lay a good deal in the valley of Hemlock Brook; and Ebenezer Graves, who was from North Reading, and who drew Nos. 53
and 56 near the east end of the plat, 53 being on the south side,

SETH HUDSON'S ORIGINAL HOUSE ON LOT 9.
First Proprietors' Meeting held in it.

and 56 on the north, the front of the latter being now occupied by
the premises of James M. Waterman.

Besides these six, there were seven others, who may fairly and by
way of precedence be termed the *original settlers* of West Hoosac,
that is to say, who actually occupied their lots before the renewal
of the French War in 1754, and who united in a petition soon to be
quoted entire to the General Court in September, 1753; namely,
Elisha Higgins from Fort Massachusetts, Silas Pratt from Worcester,
Allin Curtiss from Canaan, Connecticut, Gideon Warren from Brimfield, Darius Mead from Dutchess County, New York, Tyras Pratt
from Shrewsbury, and Elihu Curtiss from Canaan, Connecticut.

In response to this petition, William Williams, Esq., of Pittsfield, "oue of his Majesty's Justices of the Peace for the County of Hampshire," was authorized by the governor and Council to issue his warrant for the first proprietors' meeting in West Hoosac, and it was issued accordingly, directing Isaac Wyman to "Notifye and warne the said proprietors to assemble at the house of Mr. Seth Hudson on Wednesday the fifth day of December next, at Nine of the clock in the forenoon," to act upon articles specified in the warrant. Thus began the civic life and government of West Hoosac, and it has never been intermitted from that day to this. Allin Curtiss was chosen the moderator of this first meeting, and Isaac Wyman proprietors' clerk. To choose committees to lay out new

BENJAMIN SIMONDS'S ORIGINAL HOUSE ON LOT 22.
Moved, but otherwise unchanged in 1894.

divisions of land, to lay out roads, and to lay and collect suitable taxes, was the principal business of this meeting. Its date was Dec. 5, 1753. There is no proof that Ephraim Williams, although he constantly kept the earliest settlers in mind until he fell, ever took any practical steps to have either of his two lots cleared up and built upon, in accordance with the terms of the legislative grant; he was extremely busy elsewhere during those four years. Colonel Oliver Partridge, of Hatfield, gave his house lot No. 4, the second lot west of North Street, and next to Captain Wyman's, to Thomas Train, whose own lot 30 was less eligible, on condition "that he completely fulfill the conditions enjoined by the General Court." Partridge, however, reserved to himself a part of the afterdrafts of the house lot, which Train subdued, and cultivated till 1768, when he sold it to Dr. Jacob Meack for £40. Meack, who was the first physician in the place, if we except Seth Hudson, later made his homestead just over Hemlock Brook, on No. 12 north tier, in a house still standing, but many times built over. Partridge's lot, then Train's, then Meack's, is the lot next west of the Kap lot, and the highest and easternmost portion of the fine estate of Mr. Proctor. Timothy Woodbridge, of Hatfield, kept his lot No. 3 for twelve years, and paid his annual dues for the same, and then sold the house lot, and the meadow lot, and the second-division fifty-acre lot drawn by No. 3 to Benjamin Simonds for £25, Aug. 15, 1764. This lot is exactly opposite across Main Street to the Partridge lot No. 4. This became the home and the tavern-stand of Simonds for many years.

But the larger part of the first proprietors began at once to sell off their rights to other parties, oftentimes without ever having seen them. As a sample of many more, we will just trace the fortunes for a few years of house lot No. 1, whose front is now covered by the beautiful stone building of the Delta Psi Society, and ran along South Street, as far as the present land of Deacon James Smedley. In the original drawing this lot fell to Samuel Brown, Junior, of Stockbridge, who belonged to one of those four English families first brought thither by the action of the General Court for the encouragement and support of the Indian Mission. Brown held the lot but a short time, and then sold it to Ezekiel Hinds, a resident of Stockbridge and a soldier at Fort Massachusetts, who sold the same to Samuel Smedley, of Litchfield, Connecticut, Oct. 31, 1752, for £27. Consequences important to Williamstown in the sequel followed upon this sale of No. 1 from Hinds to Smedley, "husbandman" to "husbandman"; [1] for one result of it was, that three young men from Litchfield, Nehemiah Smedley and William Horsford and Josiah Horsford, the first the son and the two others later the sons-in-law of Samuel Smedley, came up here probably in 1753 to look the ground over. They liked it, but they did not like the increasing signs of a renewed French and Indian war. They returned to Connecticut, and not very long after enlisted in a military company raised by that colony to protect itself from Indian incursions, by helping Massachusetts garrison, the "West Hoosac fort," so-called. Afterwards all three of these young men became very prominent in the settlement. It was believed and reported by his eldest son,

[1] The deed now lies open before me. It is one item among the "Smedley Papers."

Levi, in his old age, that Nehemiah Smedley set out the first orchard in town on No. 1 in 1754; it was, at any rate, in full bearing in 1765. After the death of the father, Samuel Smedley, No. 1 was deeded to Nehemiah by the widow and the eldest son, John, March 21, 1758. Precisely when Nehemiah Smedley built the house on No. 1, whether it were before or after he became the sole possessor, cannot now be told; it was a "regulation" house, and its sills were of white oak; it had been incorporated early in this century into a larger gambrel-roofed house, which had become old itself and was taken down in 1884 to make room for the Delta Psi Lodge; the present writer found then and there pieces of two of the old oaken sills, and bits of them are preserved in the historical museum in Clark Hall; and he hazards little by the opinion that those sills had lain there at least one century and a quarter undisturbed.

No. 1 continued to be the homestead of Nehemiah Smedley till after 1765, when the next stage of our story will begin, since that is the date of the incorporation of West Hoosac under the name of "Williamstown"; and in the mean time five brothers and four sisters of Nehemiah came up from Litchfield to become dwellers in West Hoosac, all sons and daughters of that Samuel Smedley who bought No. 1 of Ezekiel Hinds in 1752, whose own genealogy is so significant and relevant to the after history of Williamstown, that it may as well be given here as anywhere.

When the Rev. Peter Bulkley, of the parish of Odell, Bedfordshire, in the diocese of the Bishop of Lincoln, emigrated to this country with a considerable number of his English congregation, and settled with them in Concord in 1636, there were two brothers in his church, both admitted freeman in Concord in 1644, namely, John and Baptist Smedley. John was the elder, and became the more prominent in church and state. He was representative to the General Court in 1667 and 1670, and was senior selectman in 1680. A colony went early from Concord to Fairfield, Connecticut; and Samuel Smedley, undoubtedly a son of John, appears in Fairfield in 1690. The name soon became extinct in Concord, so that the historian of that town knew nothing of any Smedleys anywhere; but this Samuel, of Fairfield, preserved the seed of a large family in Connecticut. His son, Samuel 2d, was born in 1702, married Esther Kilborn Feb. 1, 1729, and died Feb. 16, 1756. He had moved from Fairfield to Woodbury, and from Woodbury to Litchfield, and bought a farm in 1741, "at ye south End of ye Great Pond" (now Bantam Lake in Morris), of fifty-four acres, from which all of his eleven children with one exception, Joshua, the youngest, became sooner or later residents of Williamstown: the sons, John, Nehemiah, Jedidiah, Samuel 3d, Moses, and Aaron; and the daughters, Esther, Jemima, Ann, and Lucina.

Samuel 1st, of Fairfield, had certainly one other son, Ephraim, and Ephraim had Ephraim, Junior, who was born in 1746, and married Ann Gibbs Jan. 28, 1767, and died May 20, 1821. He was the ancestor of the New Haven Smedleys, expressmen there, some of whom have strikingly resembled in physiognomy the Williamstown Smedleys. The Gibbs family, with which the Smedleys much intermarried, were neighbors of theirs on Bantam Lake. The most distinguished scion of the Smedley name in America was Captain Samuel Smedley, of Fairfield, perhaps another son of Ephraim 1st, who was a fighting sea-captain during the Revolutionary War. Major Hincks, in some sketches of the men of the Revolution, says of him: "Capt. Samuel Smedley sailed upon the Atlantic as commander of the brig *Defense*, perhaps the most successful vessel in the Colonial Navy. He captured many prizes, among them the British ship *Cyrus*, mounting eighteen guns and laden with a cargo that sold for about £20,000, one of the most valuable captures made during the Revolution. After the war Capt. Smedley was for many years collector of Customs for this district, residing and having his office at Fairfield." He was a Democrat in politics. President Jefferson appointed him to this office in 1801. He left some valuable papers, now in possession of the city of Bridgeport. In England, too, the Smedley family have continued to be somewhat notable in the eastern and northern countries. Frank E. Smedley, author of the "Colville Family," and other tales, is a writer of reputation at the present time; and we are told that the family circle in the sanctuary at Westminster Abbey have been Smedleys for several generations.

We return now to some others of the earliest actual settlers upon the house lots, besides those already characterized, who obtained their lots by purchase, or otherwise, from the original drawers of them. Speculation in the lots was rife almost from the beginning. Elisha Higgins, long a soldier in Fort Massachusetts, bought of Reuben Belding, of Hatfield, house lot 12, with all its afterdrafts, for £20, the 12th of October, 1753. This is the first lot over Hemlock Brook on the north side, to one going west on Main Street. He sold this the next spring for £27 13s., to Nathan Mead, "gentleman," of Oblong, Dutchess County, New York. Darius Mead, of the same locality, was a settler here in 1753, and both continued to buy and sell land here for several years, though it is not certain that Nathan Mead ever permanently resided here. Elisha Higgins, however, after selling No. 12, bought No. 17, the third lot west of 12 and on the southern tier of lots. Here he built his house and lived for many years, buying, in 1762, for £10, the next lot west, namely, No. 19; and still further west, along this tier, may be seen to this day the stones of cellar-walls and bits of brick of the chimneys of . two or three other houses. The southwest quarter of the plat, except the easternmost and the four westernmost lots, were not so eligible for building as most of the fronts of the lots in the other three quarters of the plat taken as a whole, on account of an irregular and rocky bluff that begins to rise on that side almost as soon as one crosses the Hemlock Brook. One such rocky protuberance from this base juts over across Main Street, and covers the street front of No. 22 on the north side, which was the reason why Benjamin Simonds placed his original house quite to the north of the street, over a little run of water (which was, doubtless, another inducement to the location of the house), near the top of a fine slope, giving a splendid view over the entire plat; so that Simonds, and, later, his son-in-law, Putnam (the lot is still called the " Putnam lot" by old inhabitants), reached the street by a road running down by the little water-course that flanked the bluff in front. Higgins's house was on the east declivity of the fourth eminence, just middle way between Nos. 1 and 33, which constitute (seventeen lots) the southwest quarter of the plat.

Silas Pratt, originally from Worcester or Shrewsbury, a good soldier in Fort Massachusetts for several years, a soldier also in the West Hoosac Fort, a man of courage and enterprise, who ultimately settled on Northwest Hill, on the first farm over the line in Vermont, who took part in the battle of Bennington with at least one of his sons, may perhaps be reckoned as the eighth positive settler in West Hoosac; and his son William, born in 1760 within the lines of the West Hoosac fort, may be the first male child born in town. Two girls had preceded William Pratt, namely, Rachel Simonds and Esther Horsford. All three were born within a stone's throw of Hemlock Brook; and the reader may have noticed that all the first homesteads thus far delineated were upon the third and fourth eminences, and most of them on the declivities sloping down to the brook between these. It is not entirely certain which house lot Silas Pratt first pitched upon, for he owned several of them first and last; but it is, on several grounds, probable that 19 was the number, because he certainly sold that to Elisha Higgins in 1762, and because John Chamberlin, who originally drew it, was a soldier in Fort Massachusetts with Pratt and Higgins. We shall learn more about Silas Pratt — and most of it to his credit — before we have done with him ; but we pass now to Tyras Pratt, many times closely associated with Silas, and probably closely related to him, who was a settler in West Hoosac in 1753, a soldier previously in Fort Massachusetts, and who made his home before 1757 in Roadtown, now Shutesbury, whence he went out soldier again in Captain Samuel Taylor's company, Sept. 17, 1776. We may call, if we choose, Tyras Pratt the ninth of our actual beginners on the purchased house lots, and may be pretty sure that he began on No. 53, at the other end of the plat from the rest, near the east end of the southeast quarter. At any rate, he sold that lot, in 1756, to William Horsford, with one-half of the afterdrafts, exclusive of the meadow lot.

Our tenth man, according to the loose reckoning followed at present, was Gideon Warren. We have already found David Warren a soldier in Fort Massachusetts at the time of its capture in 1746, and he was of Marlboro. Jabez Warren was a corporal in the fort at Coleraine in 1748, and he was from Brimfield. Gideon Warren was also a soldier in the line of forts, but we hear little of him till he made a settlement in West Hoosac in 1753, where for some years he was prominent. It is likely that he bought No. 50, on whose then rocky front Griffin Hall has stood since 1828, because he afterwards sold different parts of the first-division fifty-acre lot 30, which was drawn by house lot 50. Reference has already been made to the course of Green River as cutting off five house lots at the east end of the southeast quarter, leaving in that but twelve lots. There are two considerable falls in that stretch of the river running north that occupied what would otherwise have doubtless been a house lot, and another considerable fall at no great distance below, after the river turns sharply to the east — almost at right angles. It was early perceived that these falls would be useful for mills, and might make it needless for the settlers to frequent longer Colonel Williams's grist-mill, more than four miles away, in East Hoosac. The two first-mentioned falls came in the fifty-acre lot 30 and the last one in the corresponding lot 29.

Gideon Warren, yeoman, sold Samuel Payn, of Dutchess County, New York, for £6, two acres on Green River (part of a lot known as No. 30) with privilege of flowing the river bank "as hie up as ye top of ye upper falls "; " and also a strip of land two rods wide by the west side of said river, beginning at the north side of said land I sold to said Payn, and running north by the river to the mouth of the brook, and up the hill to the lot now enclosed, and so out to the main road or Highway, to be a highway for the use of the town." This important sale was made June 1, 1761. It opened into Main

Street at right angles to what has always been called Water Street, and paved the way for the first grist-mill in town, whose stones, and those of its several successors till this day, have been whirled by water stored up at the lower of the two falls.　The language of this old deed — "mouth of the brook" — gives the first mention of what has long been called "Phebe's Brook," from Phebe Holmes, an old colored woman, whose cabin stood near the head of the little stream, which, reinforced by the overflow of the "College Spring," drops into the Green River just at its own sudden bend to the eastward.

Samuel Payn bought also the next year, the meadow lot 56, eleven acres, about a mile above his mill privilege, on both sides of Green River, of Joseph Ballard, then of New Salem, but afterwards of West Hoosac.　Ballard also sold in August, 1761, to James Meacham, of New Salem, Nos. 7 and 8 of the first-division fifty-acre lots, which have been in active possession of his direct descendants from that day to this.　James B. Meacham owned in August, 1892, what lands his great-grandfather, James Meacham, first occupied in August, 1762, just 130 years.　The lots were bought just one year before that, for £73 8s. 8d.　Mrs. Meacham brought with her, through the almost unbroken wilderness, two little girls, one not quite four, and the other not quite two; and a third, Lucy, was born just six weeks after the father put up his temporary shelter on one side of an isolated big rock near the middle of fifty-acre lot No. 7.　The birth is recorded as falling on Sept. 26, 1762.　The mother also brought with her a root or two of a hop-vine, and planted it on the other side of the same rock.　That vine has leaved out, blossomed, and borne fruit for 130 years, and seems likely to do the same for a century longer.　A grandson of hers, Captain James Meacham, pointed out to the writer, about twenty years ago, the rock and the growing hop-vine; and the latter has taken occasion many times since to make the short pilgrimage thither (the rock is in plain sight from his south windows), to be sure that the hops were still growing.　The tall Captain died in his eightieth year, May 20, 1883.　Soon after their arriving, the first James Meacham was fortunate enough to kill a bear, which furnished the family what they quaintly called "pork"; and once, at least, they found a deposit of wild honey to be a welcome addition to their slender commissariat.

But the rock and its hop-vine, and the log-cabin lean-to, was a considerable distance from Samuel Payn's authorized road along the west side of Green River, to and past his mill-privilege; and so, our tenth settler, Gideon Warren, sold to James Meacham, both "husbandmen," another piece of eleven acres from his fifty-acre lot No. 30, drawn by house lot 50, which brought the Meachams snug up to Green River road, where they built their second house in 1764, which is still standing as a shed, in connection with their third house, a commodious brick one, to which the second one was drawn an eighth of a mile further north on the same street. Later on, we shall hear more about the Meachams. The Revolutionary War, and even Shays's Rebellion brought them into notice. Gideon Warren, too, will at least make his bow on our stage once or twice more.

The eleventh and last, but one, principal settler in West Hoosac before the renewal of the French and Indian war, was Captain Allin Curtiss, of Canaan, Connecticut. He bought the house lot originally drawn by Ezekiel Foster, of Falltown and Fort Massachusetts, namely, No. 13, already characterized in connection with Foster, who continued a settler and citizen for many years, but bought lands, and had a home in different parts of the town. Curtiss's dwelling-house stood just beyond the bridge over Hemlock Brook on the left-hand side to one going west. It is more than probable, that the present house of Mark Gamet occupies the site of Captain Curtiss's dwelling, in which was held the second meeting of the West Hoosac proprietors, in April, 1754. Captain Curtiss was then chosen "Moderator" in his own house. But he was also chosen Moderator of the first proprietors' meeting in the fall before, which was held in Seth Hudson's house just across the brook to the eastward, on No. 9. Curtiss was a very capable man. He returned after a little to Canaan, and the town books there show his activity and prominence for many years. There are still families of his name in Canaan, as there are also Deans and Horsfords, who represent, in a certain way, Josiah Dean, who drew, originally, house lot 26, and Josiah and William and John Horsford, who came from Canaan a little later, and stayed very much longer. Elihu Curtiss was presumably a brother of Captain Allin. Elnathan Curtiss, whose name we shall meet with pretty soon, was from Kent, a little way from Canaan, south, both on the Housatonic River.

The following petition to the General Court presented in September, 1753, by these first proprietors, shows that no provision had yet been made for their legal organization as a "Propriety" then so-called.

To His Exclly William Shirley Esqr Captain General &c., the Honble his Majisty's Council, and House of Representatives in General Court assembled Sept. 1753.

The Petition of us the Subscribers in behalf of ourselves and Others, Proprietors of the West Hoosuck Township at Hoosuck, Lately sold by the General Court Humbly Sheweth

That the General Court was pleased to open the sd Township and lay out the House lots under the Direction of the Courts Comtee, and the Proprietors owners of said lots are divers of them at work upon them and bringing forward Settlements; but upon advisement find they are incapable of Calling and Holding meetings, without the Aid of yr Excelcy and Honours which we exceedingly want in order to agree upon the building a Meeting House, Setling a Minister, Making Division of other Lands and to do and Transact all such matters and things as may be necessary and proper for proprietors of New Townships to do. We therefore Humbly pray yr Exclcy and Honurs to appoint some proper person to call a Meeting of said proprietors for such purposes as may be necessary and direct a method of calling meetings of said proprs in the future, and as in duty bound shall Ever pray &c.

	ISAAC WYMAN
ELISHA HIGGINS	ALLIN CURTISS
SILAS PRATT	DARIUS MEAD
TYRAS PRATT	SETH HUDSON
GIDEON WARRIN	THOMAS TRAIN
EZEKL FOSTER	EBENR GRAVES
	ELIHU CURTISS

IN THE HOUSE OF REPRESENTATIVES Septr 10. 1753

Read and Voted that William Williams Esqr one of his Majs Justices of the Peace for the County of Hampshire Issue his Warrant for calling a meeting of the proprietors of the West Township at Hoosuck so called Directed to one of the principal proprietors of sd Township, Requiring him to set up a Notification in some public place in sd Township Setting forth the time, place and Occasion of sd Meeting fourteen days beforehand, which Meeting shall be holden in sd Township, and such of the proprietors as shall be present at sd Meeting are hereby authorized and impowered by a Maj. vote to Determine upon a Division of all or a part of the Lands in said Township not already allotted, also Chuse a Comtee or Comtees to lay out the same, also to raise moneys to defray the Charges that may arise by means of laying out sd Lands, also for Clearing Highways, as also to Chuse a proprietors' Clerk, Treasurer, Assessors and Collectors and also to agree and determine upon a method of calling meetings of said proprietors for the future.

Sent up for Concurrence

T. HUBBARD Sp'k'r

In Council Sept. 10. 1753 — Read and Concurred

THOS CLARK Dep. Sec'y

Consented to   W. SHIRLEY.

In response to this order of the court, William Williams, of Pontoosuck, now Pittsfield, the real father and founder of that town,
issued his legal call to the West Hoosac proprietors, as follows : —

PROVINCE OF THE MASSACHUSETTS BAY.

Whereas I have Rec.d special Direction from the great and Gen¹ Court of this
province at there Sessions in September last to issue my warrant for calling a
meeting of the proprietors of the west township of Hoosuck so called Directed
to one of the Principal proprietors of s'd Township requiring him to set up a
Notification in some publick place in s'd Township seting forth the time place
and occasion of s'd meeting fourteen Days beforehand, s'd meeting to be held
in s'd Township and such of the proprietors as shall be present at s'd meeting
are by Said order of Court authorised and impowered by a major Voate to act
and Determine upon the following articles.

Vizt. To agree upon a Division of part or all the lands in said township Not
   allready allotted = to Choose a Committee or Committees to lay out the
   same = to Choose a Committee to lay out high ways = to raise money to
   Defray the Charges of laying out the Lands and highways and Clearing the
   same = or any other Necessary Charges.

   To Choose a proprietors Clerk.

   To Choose a proprietors Treasurer.

   To Choose proprietors assessors.

   To Choose a proprietors Colector or Colectors.

   To agree upon a method for Calling meetings for the future.

      In observance of which Direction

      Hampshire SS. To Isaac Wyman one of the proprietors of the
said west Township at Hoosuck Gentⁿ Greeting. You are hereby Required to
Notifye and warne the proprietors of s'd Township that they assemble at the
House of Mr. Seth Hudsons in s'd Township on Wensday the Fifth Day of
December next at Nine of the Clock in the four noon to act upon the fouregoing
Articles as they shall think proper by Setting up in some publick place in said
Township an attested Coppy of the foregoing order of Court and this warrant
by you Sygned fourteen Days before the time of said meeting.

Poontoonsuck

November 15 : 1753.   Wᴹ Williams
Just. Peace.

"Some publick place in said Township." Where was there such
a "place" in West Hoosac in November, 1753? There were probably eight or ten small houses of the prescribed pattern then built, or
begun, along the broad Main Street, which was then full of trees and
rocks from end to end; but nearly all of these houses were towards
the west end, either on the plateaus of the third and fourth eminences, or in the valley between them of Hemlock Brook. The
house in which the proprietors were to meet was on the east side of
the brook, and near it; the house of the man who was to be chosen
moderator was on the west side of the brook, and near it; so that

the supposition seems rational that Captain Wyman posted his "Notifycation" somewhere on the rude, log-built bridge over the brook, which was then the only bridge, and apparently the most "publick place" in the precinct. Accordingly, the proprietors present came together for their first meeting (a notable one) in the house of Seth Hudson. The room in which they met has been but very little altered since. The following is the official record: —

At a Proprietors meeting lawfully warned in the west township at hoosuck ss Called December the fifth 1753 — Voted by the major part of the proprietors at s'd meetin the fouregoing articles Vizt.

First. Voted and Chose Allen Curtice moderator for s'd meetin.

Second Voted and Chose Isaac Wyman Proprietors Clerk

Thirdly Voted by the proprietors to lay out all the medow land lying upon the Main River [Hoosac] and all the medow land lying upon green River as far as the first Brook or Creek in Equal proportion to each Right in Said Township and one hundred acres of upland to each Right adjoyning to the medow land or as Near as they Can to lay out the best land.

Fourthly. Voted to leave it to the Commite to Lay out the land in one Division or two as they shall Judge best.

5ly Voted and Chose Allen Curtice Seth Hudson Jonathan mechom Ezekiel Foster Jabiz Worren the Commite to lay out the land in s'd Township

6ly Voted and Chose Samuel Taylor Giden Worrin Jonathan mechom the Commite to lay out high Ways in s'd Township that shall be Necessary.

7ly Voted and Chose Allen Curtice sevayer to Clear the Roads in s'd Township

8ly Voted at s'd meeting to Lay the Roads at the Eand of each main street foure rods wide in said Township

9ly Voted that the Roads to accommidate the medow land shall be but two Rods wide. and all the Rods to accomidate the other Divisions two Rods wide allso

Voted to raise a rate of Eight Shillings upon Each Proprietors Right in s'd Town to pay the Charges that may arise by Laying out s'd Land

Voted to Rase ten shillings to pay for a Proprietors Book

Voted and Chose Isaac Wyman Proprietors Treasurer.

Voted and Chose Thomas Train Josiah Deean Colectors for said Proprietors

Voted and Chose Ebenezer Graves Allen Curtice and Ezekiel Foster assessors for said Proprietors

Voted at said meetin that five or seven of the proprietors of said Town makin application to the Clerk of Said Proprietors for Calling meetings for the future

Voted at s'd meetin to Lay out the Land in said Town as soon as may be convenant

at a meeting held at West Hoosuck pursuant to the Court order on the fifth Day of December 1753 the above said votes paist in a legial manor

Test = Allen Curtice moderator for said meetin

ISAAC WYMAN
Prop�tᵘ Clerk.

Then and there, and thus, began the self-government of this town. Further to the east in Massachusetts, what has been called the "New England Townmeeting," had been the governing agent in numerous little republics for a century; this was the first upon the Hoosac, or in its immediate vicinity. Of course, the royal governor at Boston, in this case a man of wide renown, William Shirley, as representing directly the crown of England, was the highest political authority in the province; but in all personal interests of the settlers, and in all local matters, the town-meeting was as sovereign then as it is now, and we look back with a fond curiosity, if not with affection, upon every man recorded as having a part in that primal assemblage of citizens. All but two of them had been soldiers in Fort Massachusetts; Isaac Wyman, the clerk, was then commanding officer there, and Seth Hudson had been surgeon there; Captain Allen Curtiss brought his military title from Connecticut, and after a couple of years carried it back there, where he honored it by a life of usefulness; and Jonathan Meacham, who was appointed on two important committees at that first meeting, was long a citizen and church member here. He was own cousin to James Meacham, who was lately characterized, and they both came here from New Salem, where their ancestor, Jeremiah Meacham from old Salem, was the first settler in 1737, receiving £10 from his fellow-proprietors, residents of Old Salem, for assuming the hardships of the pioneer in their new town. Jonathan Meacham was with Ephraim Williams in the battle of Lake George, nearly two years after this town-meeting.

Just four months after the first proprietors' meeting, a second was called by the clerk at the instance of "five or seven" of the local proprietors, as provided for in the first meeting: —

Whereas application hath bin maid to me the subscriber hearof by a number of the Proprietors of the west Township of Hoosuck so called to Issue out a warrant for Calling of a Proprietors meeting in s'd Township setting forth the time Place and ocasion of s'd meeting which meeting is to be held at the Dwelling house of Capt. Allen Curtiss then and there to act on the articles as follows: Vizt.

1   To choose a moderator for s'd meeting
2ly To se if the Proprietors will Except the Return of the Commite Chosen to lay out the Division or Divisions of land and the Return of the Commite Chosen to lay out the high ways
3ly To se if the Prop? will Draw for there medow Lots and there first 50-acre Division as they are now laid out.
4ly To se if the Proprietors will hear and Except the accompts of any if they be offered
5ly To se if the Prop⁸ will agree upon some place for a buring place or apoint a Commite to do the same and allso for Clearing some part of it.

6ly To see if the Propr? will have the Gospel Preach in this town this summer or some part of it and if so to Chose a Commite to bring in some authodox min. to preach the gospel.

7ly To se if the Propr? will raise money to Defray the necessary Charges arising in s'd Town

8ly To se if the Propr* will agree upon some man or men to buld a grist mill and a saw mill and what bounty they will give for the incouragement of the building the same

Which meeting is to be on Thirsday the Eightenth of this Instant at Nine of the Clock in the fournoon and such of the Propr? as shall asemble and meat at s'd time and place are hearby Impowered to act on all or part of the foregoing articles.

FORT MASSACHUSETTS April 5, 1754.

ISAAC WYMAN Propr? Clerk.

At a Proprietors meeting lawfull warned in the west Township at Hoosuck April the Eighteenth 1754

Voted and agreed upon at s'd meeting as follows Vizt.

1. Voted and Choose Capt Allen Curtiss moderator for s'd meeting

2ly Voted and Excepted the Return of the Commite Chosen to lay out the Divisions of lands in s'd Township and allso the Return of the Commite Choosen to lay out highways to accomidate said Town.

3ly Voted and agreed to Draw the medow Lots and the first fifty acre Division as follows: Choose Mr. David King Surveyor to Draw for the Divisions to Each Right in s'd Town s'd meeting adjourned untill one a Clock in the afternoon and then meet.

4ly Voted and Granted to Mr. David King, Surveyor his acompt for Laying out the Divisions of Land in s'd Township and Granted the whole of all the accompts Delivered to the Clerk of said Proprietors. Adjourned Said meeting untill the Nineteenth of this instant at 12 a Clock and then meet.

5ly Voted to Leve two accres and a half for a burial Place in said Town at the North East Eand of the Lot No. 2 on the west side of the street Leving a two Rod road at the cand of s'd Lot and allso to Clear half an acre at the South East Corner of s'd Land the Proprietors Cost.

6ly Voted and Granted to raise 12 Shillings upon Each Proprietors Right in s'd Town to Defray the necessary Charges arising at a meeting of the Proprietors regularly worned and met on the 18th of April 1754 the above written vots voted and mineted in a regular form. test ALLEN CURTISS moderator

ISAAC WYMAN Propr? Clerk.

So far, matters had gone smoothly in the settlement of West Hoosac. About a dozen house lots had been roughly occupied. A meadow lot of ten or eleven acres on one of the main streams had been drawn to each house lot, and one fifty-acre lot also. As the spring of 1754 was drawing on, there was a desire on the part of the settlers, who seem to have been contented with their home, to have some roads laid out by which they could reach their new lots, and also to draw their second-division fifty-acre lots, which, it was understood, would be located on the more level lands in the south part of the town.   Accordingly, about ten days after the adjournment of the second proprietors' meeting, application was made to Captain Wyman, at Fort Massachusetts, their clerk, to issue a call for a third meeting of the proprietors.   This proved to be the last meeting for more than six years and a half.   The French and Indian war was about to break out again with more violence than ever; and the almost universal law, that such an enterprise as settling and civilizing the beautiful Hoosac valley can only be compassed, in the nature of things, through contentions and difficulties, was soon to be illustrated for the thousandth time.   The following are the summons and the doings of that meeting: —

Whereas application hath been maid to me the Subscriber hear of by a Sufficient number of the Proprietors of the west Town at Hoosuck for to call a meeting of the Propr? of s'd town Setting forth the time Place and ocashon of s'd meeting Which meeting is to be held at the Dwelling house of Capt. Allen Curtiss on wensday the fifteenth Day of May at ten of the Clock in the fore-Noon then and there to act on the following articles : Vizt.

1.   To choose a moderator for s'd meeting
2ly   To see if the Proprietors will draw for there Second Fifty acre Division and after what manner they will do the same
3ly   To see if the Propr? will Clear Some part or all the highways that are Laid out to convene the fifty acre Division and the medow Land.
4ly   To see if they will Raise money to Defray the Charges of the same or any other Necessary Charges that may arise in said Town or to make any other proper votes as they shall think best.

These are therefore to Notifye and worn the said Proprietors that they assemble and meat at s'd time and place to act and Determine on all or part of the fourgoin articles as they shall Think Fit.

Isaac Wyman Prop Clerk

Fort Massachusetts April 29 1754.

At a Proprietors meeting lawfull worned in the West Township at hoosuck and the following articles acted upon as follows : vizt.

1.   Voted and Choose Capt. Elisha Chapin moderator for s'd meeting.
2ly   Voted by the Propr? to Draw for the Second fifty acres Division in the following manner Choose Capt. Allen Curtiss to Draw a ticket to Each Right for s'd Propr?
3ly   Voted at s'd meeting to Clear the Road from the North Eand of the Cross Streeat in s'd Town to hampshear line [Vt. line] one rod wide and for the Propr? to work for two shillings and Eight pence a Day.
4ly   Voted and granted Oliver Avery's and John Crawfoord's accompt for Clearing part of the burial Place
5ly   Voted and Choose Capt. Allen Curtiss surveyor to Clear the fore mentioned Road

6ly Voted and granted to Raise Six Shillings upon Each Propr Right in s'd
Town to Defray the necessary Charges of the Same.

Test. ELISHA CHAPIN moderator

ISAAC WYMAN Propr Clerk

War burst upon the valley just one month after this meeting,
May 28, 1754; about one hundred Indians assaulted "Dutch Hoosac,"
now Hoosac Falls, about twelve miles down the river. Their first
attack was made on a few men at a mill, where they killed Samuel
Bowen, and wounded John Barnard; they then rushed into the
little settlement, burned the houses and barns and a large quantity
of wheat in the stack, and killed most of the cattle. The next day,
they burned the little settlement at St. Croix, now Hoosac Junction,
so-called, at the mouth of the Walloomsac, and up its fertile valley;
but as most of the people had previously fled from both places, but
few lives were lost. The garrison at Fort Massachusetts was too
weak to afford effectual aid even to the West Hoosac homesteads,
still less to those lower down the river. Captain Elisha Chapin,
who commanded the fort at that time, the same who was the last
moderator at West Hoosac, stated the loss at Dutch Hoosac at seven
dwelling-houses, fourteen barns, and fourteen *barracks* of wheat;
and very nearly the same at St Croix; amounting, as he estimated,
to £4000 York currency. These depredations were attributed principally to the Schaghticoke Indians, many of whom were descendants of the New England Indians, who had left the region of the
Connecticut River in King Philip's war. Of course, these were
set on by the Canada Indians, and were soon followed by their
principals.

All the settlers at West Hoosac immediately abandoned the
place on news of the approaching ravages below them; those who
had families betook themselves to Fort Massachusetts, where they
were not very welcome, and others returned to their homes over the
mountain or into Connecticut. The second Indian party, more distinctly announcing the renewal of the French war from the north,
shrewdly avoided Fort Massachusetts, flanking it on the west, following up the Green River to the south, from its junction with the
Hoosac, and so over the low water-shed to the upper Housatonic,
which they followed down through Lanesboro and Pontoosuck as
far as Stockbridge. A scout was sent after them from the fort.
In following their tracks in what is now Lanesboro, two Indian
chiefs were discovered stooping down and tying on their moccasins.
Each of the two scouts selected one, and both the chiefs were killed

on the spot. The scout safely escaped to the fort, though closely followed for some distance. A larger party from the fort set out at once to find the bodies of the slain chiefs, and found them buried in all the bravery of their war-costume. The Indians proceeded through Pittsfield, driving off several families from there and Lenox, and penetrated to Stockbridge, where they attacked the house of Joshua Chamberlain, who lived on the "Hill," on ground well known to this day. It was Sunday, and most of the people of Stockbridge were at church. Chamberlain had a brave hired man whose name was Owen, who kept the Indians at bay while Chamberlain and his wife escaped, but who himself fell under mortal wounds, and died very soon. The Indians scalped him, and killed and scalped one child, and carried away another, which they soon killed and scalped, in consequence of discovering that a party was forming, or formed, to pursue them.

This bold incursion taught two important lessons. It taught the people of Connecticut that they were much exposed to Canada by way of the Housatonic, and that they ought to help the "Bay" to defend the gateway of the Upper Hoosac. They raised a small body of troops immediately, some of which were soon posted at Pontoosuck, and others, later, helped to garrison the West Hoosac fort as soon as that was ready to receive them. For the other lesson taught by the incursion of the summer of 1754 was, that Fort Massachusetts was not well placed to defend the frontier towns in what is now Berkshire from the French and Indians. It stood to one side of the hostile route. This item of experience doubled the confidence of the West Hoosac settlers, who were at the same time soldiers, to demand of the General Court a fort of their own, to be manned by themselves.

The following petition to the General Court gives an interesting account, written by themselves, of the condition of our pioneers during the summer of 1754, and probably discloses the names of all those who had made a beginning on their house lots and had not gone back to their original homes. Indeed, of the eleven precious names appended to this petition, there are only two with which we have not already become familiar; namely, Oliver Avery and William Chidester. Avery was from Charlemont, and Chidester was from Cornwall, Connecticut. The latter was an original proprietor in West Hoosac, drawing house lot 6, and in June, 1752, buying, by bond, house lot 18 (£20), which was the breadth of one lot east of Benjamin Simonds's lot; while in April, 1754, he sold to his son, of the same name, William Chidester, house lot 24, which was the

lot next west of Simonds's, — all, except No. 6, on the fourth eminence, northwest quarter.

To His Excellency Wm Shirley Esqr Captn Genl and Governor in Chief in and
over his Majesty's Province of the Massachusetts Bay and &c.

To the Honble his Majestys Council and The House of Representatives in
Genl Court Assembled — Oct. 17. 1754.

The Petition of the inhabitants of West Hoosuck — Humbly Sheweth

That upon Survey of the Plan of sd Township and from the information of
the Gentn of this Honourable Court that sold us our Respective Lotts we are
abundantly Satisfied that the Government designed it for a Barrier Town into
which Succour upon any rupture would be thrown, which induced us to take up
with Narrow Lotts less than fourteen Rods wide and thereby subject ourselves
to the inconveniences of living in a Huddle, also to give moneys for our Land
(which the Government has had the Benefit of) which used to be given upon the
promise of selling and Large Bonds to the Province Treasurer for Settleing which
now lie against us &c. But may it please your Excellency and Hours Such is
our case upon the late Alarm we for Shelter ran to fort Massachusetts and are
there with our familys who Clutter the Fort, and make our lives and that of the
Soldiers very uncomfortable — in this poor Situation your Pettnrs are waiting your Excellencies and Honours Directions how to Bestow ourselves, and
would let your Excellency know there is about ELEAVEN FAMILIES OF US that
would gladly Return to our Settlements, and a considerable number more, could
we receive proper incouragemt from this Honable Court, Whose Determination
we all Humbly wait

And as in Duty bound shall ever pray &c

Signed by

JONA MEACHM	SETH HUDSON
GIDEON WARRIN	WILLIAM CHIDESTER
BENJ. SIMONDS	EZEKL FOSTER
OLIVER AVERY	ALLIN CURTISS
THOMAS TRAIN	JABEZ WARRIN Junr
	JABEZ WARRIN

This petition for aid does not seem to have impressed the Legislature favorably, under the circumstances; and it was certainly
contrary to the views of Colonel Israel Williams, of Hatfield, the
military commander of the "western frontier" throughout the
impending war. He had advised the abandonment of forts Pelham
and Shirley upon the hilltops, and the concentration of all defences
into the valley of the Deerfield River, keeping up in full vigor, however, the one chief fort over the mountain, — dear to all the Williams
family, — Fort Massachusetts. He advised these petitioners to remove their gathered crops of wheat and their other effects to some
place of safety, and to abandon their little homes till after the next
year's campaign against Crown Point, which was already being coun-

selled over on both sides of the Atlantic. Jonathan Meacham and his brother William enlisted, the next spring, with several others at the fort, under Colonel Ephraim Williams, and shared in the perils of the battle of Lake George; and when the news of that drawn battle, as it were, reached Hampshire County, with a call for re-inforcements, James Meacham and others, of New Salem, enlisted in the company of Captain Nathaniel Dwight, the same who ran out the lines of our two towns in 1749, and his Diary notes the passage of his company through West Hoosac, on Sunday, September 28, on his way to Lake George. Not much, if anything, was done here in the way of improvements during that summer and autumn of 1755; but many an active young fellow from the eastward and southward had his eyes open as he trudged along the old military paths by the Hoosac, Owl Kill, the Battenkill, and the upper Hudson, prepared to take advantage of what he had seen when Peace and Canada had been conquered.

Besides the company of Captain Dwight, there were a good many other companies, and parts of companies, that pressed through West Hoosac in the fall of 1755, to reinforce Johnson's army at the lake, and to work on the great wooden fort that he was building on the northwest corner of his battle-field of September. He named this fort William Henry, after another of the grandsons of King George, and it was completed about the middle of November; and then the New England men, who had not already been sent home, turned their faces towards Fort Massachusetts. There were certainly some four or five hearth-fires kept burning in West Hoosac during that winter of 1755–56; and there is good reason for believing that the little hamlet on Hemlock Brook was not wholly deserted, except, perhaps, for a few days, even while the Indians were burning and ravaging on the Hoosac, a few miles below, in the summer of 1754. The women and children were taken over to the fort, while the men passed more or less back and forth. The evidence points to a prac-tically continuous occupation, on the part of a very few, of their little homes near the brook, from 1752. The conviction was deepen-ing on the part of all the actual settlers, and doubtless as well on the part of all the military bands passing through the place, back and forth, that Fort Massachusetts had been misplaced, and that the third eminence in West Hoosac could be more easily defended, and could much more easily defend the settlers. Especially would this be the view of the Connecticut men, having found out by expe-rience that the Green River made an easy path for the Indians to the Housatonic. Very interesting and significant, accordingly, is the following petition of William Chidester, a Connecticut man, to the General Court of Massachusetts, for aid to erect a blockhouse in West Hoosac. The petition was sent and answered in the depth of winter: —

	To his Honour Spencer Phipps Esq Commander in Chief in and over His Majesty's province of the Massachusetts Bay in New England, To the Honourable His Majesty's Council, and House of Representatives in General Court assembled the 18 Day of Jany 1756
Province of the Massachusetts Bay	

The Petition of William Chidester of the Place called Hoosuck in the County of Hampshire in said Province Humbly Shews:

That your petitioner purchased several lotts of land in the Westerly Town-ship called Hoosuck Townships, which lays about four miles to the westward of fort Massachusetts, and had Removed his family on to said lots In order to Per-form the Duties Injoined the several Purchasers of lotts in the said Township, with an expectation that the other purchasers would have followed him to fulfill their obligations on their Respective lotts, and so strengthen the Town, that they might not only Defend ourselves against the common Enimy, but be a Barrier to Province, But so it is that Your Petitioner and Some Others, TO THE AMOUNT OF FIVE FAMILYS are left alone in the said Westerly Township as he apprehends in Emmenant Danger of being Murthered, and their substance destroyed by the Common Enimy, as there is but about five familys between his habitation, and the place Coled Scotohook (Schaghticoke) in the Dutch County which the Indians and French burnt and distroyed the last fall, Notwithstanding our forces were at lake George at the same time. Your Petitioner therefore humbly Prays your Honour and Honours would be Graciously pleased to take his Distrest Condition into your wise Consideration and grant such Releife as in Your great Wisdom you shall see meet. And as in Duty bound shall ever pray.

WILLIAM CHIDESTER

This petition was acted upon in the Popular Assembly in ten days, and by the Council and governor in five days more. Their reply was as follows: —

IN HOUSE OF REPRESENTATIVES, Jany 28 1756

Read and Ordered, That the prayer of this Petn be so far granted as that the Commander in Chief be disired to give orderr, That if the Proprietors of said Township or any part of them shall at their own cost and charge erect a suffi-cient Block house in said Town, IN THE PLACE CALLED THE SQUARE by the tenth day of March next, that then there be allowed Ten Soldiers, either out of the number now Stationed at FORT MASSACHUSETTS, or otherwise by a new Levy as this Court shall judge best: and that the sd proprietors or such of them as shall appear and labour in the Erecting of sd FORT be allowed their Subsistence out of the province stores for the space of two MONTHS; and that if the Propri-etors shall not appear by the tenth of March next to erect a Block-house on the place called the square, that then the Petitioner with such as shall appear spirited with him, and shall erect a Block-house ROUND HIS HOUSE AND THE TWO OTHER HOUSES CONVENIENT TO BE TAKEN IN, shall be entitled to the same subsistence above sd while building said Block-house, and that when sd Block-house is finished Ten of the Inhabitants which shall have Erected said Block-house be put into pay and subsistence during ye Courts pleasure, and that the Commander in Chief be disired to give orders that there be a Guard of Ten men taken from Fort Massachusetts to guard the Labourers while they are at work on sd Block-house

                                     Sent up for Concurrence
                                                T. HUBBARD Spkr
    In Council Feb 2.   Read and Concurred
                   THOS CLARK Depty Sec'ry
        Consented to W. SHIRLEY.

    Governor Shirley issued an executive order on the 6th of February, in accordance with Chidester's request, authorizing him to build a blockhouse on the "Square," — that is, in the Main Street on the third eminence, — if he could induce a sufficient number of the proprietors to join him so as to complete the work by the 10th of March; otherwise to build the blockhouse on his own lot, house lot No. 6, and afterwards to picket the front part of that lot and of the lot next west, house lot No. 8.   Chidester only found encouragement to do the lesser thing.   Benjamin Simonds, Seth Hudson, and Jabez Warren, three of the oldest homesteaders whose lots were near Chidester's, chipped in to aid him in his work.   His own lot was the third west of North Street, or twenty-eight rods west of the present Kap House, east line.   These four men commenced at once to erect the blockhouse on the eastern line of No. 6, where it touched the Main Street; and several others, who had left on the alarm in 1754, and among them Nehemiah Smedley and Josiah Hosford and William Hosford, from Connecticut, returned and aided in the work.   Ten men from Fort Massachusetts served as a guard from February 29th to March 29th, when the blockhouse was finished.   We cannot tell exactly when it was done, but we know that pickets were set after the manner of Fort Pelham around the fronts of both of those lots, enclosing the two houses (built before), each on its own front lot next the street.   A good well was also within the enclosure.

    This rude work, not very well placed, and not meeting the views of a considerable number of the resident proprietors, was called "West Hoosac Fort," and it had a history, as we shall see.   It was accidental, but it is interesting nevertheless, that this local fort occupied the front of one of the two original lots drawn by Ephraim Williams, the founder.   It is claimed that William Pratt, son of Silas Pratt, born in this fort, was the first male child born in town.   He died in Pownal in 1846, and transmitted to his children many credible traditions of " ye olden time." The old well of the fort has had a somewhat peculiar history. After the tooth of time had gnawed into utter disappearance Chidester's house and the blockhouse, their site remained unoccupied and the well unused until about 1825, when the nucleus of the present house was built on the old site, and the well came again into family requisition. Arad Horsford, William Bridges, James Smedley, and Robert Noble lived in it successively, and usually found the well ample for their purposes. The last-named extended his kitchen northwards over the well, arranged a chain pump to draw up the water, when an animal of the genus not commonly mentioned in polite society (*Mephitis americana*) fell into the well, with such disagreeable consequences that Mr. Noble filled it in "for good." Its position, however, can be precisely pointed out at the present.

It was inevitable, in the nature of things, that jealousy should spring up between the newer and the older forts in one small valley. Before the blockhouse was finished, March 9, 1756, the General Court

Ordered, That there be Forty Men at Hoosuck and no more. Thirty whereof to be posted at Fort Massachusetts, and ten at the West Township, the said Ten at ye West Township to be inhabitants of sd Township, if there shall be so many inhabitants effective for the service, alwaies including the men that shall have been concerned in building the Block-house agreeable to the vote of this Court of the 28th of Jany last.

In obedience to this order Captain Wyman, March 23, detailed five men from Fort Massachusetts, under the command of Sergeant Samuel Taylor, to guard the new work, in connection with the men who had built it. This put the new fort under the control of a subaltern of the old one. Chidester went to Boston in April, and obtained from Governor Shirley a Sergeant's commission and authority to supersede Taylor in the command of the new fort. There seems to have been another jealousy stirring in the minds of these men, not exactly parallel to that as between the forts, but perhaps deeper than that, and, at any rate, working into the hands of that, — namely, the antipathy between the Connecticut men and the men of the Bay. Chidester and his chief friends were from the southern colony; most of the other leading men were from the eastward. This colonial bickering had certainly broken out at Lake George the fall before; and it seems difficult to account for the facts here without this further hypothesis. A portion of the settlers were not satisfied,

at any rate, with the proceedings of Chidester, his sons, and his
followers.

Thomas Train, who was originally from Weston (a part of Watertown), and who seems to have been a special friend of Colonel Partridge of Hatfield, which latter character married Anna Williams,
daughter of the Weston minister, and so came into favor beyond
his deserts with the Williams family as a whole, and who had given
to Train house lot 4 (next to the new blockhouse), presented the
following petition on the 27th of May, 1756, for public aid to build
another fort.

To His Honour Spencer Phipps Esq — Lieut Govr and Commander in Chief of
His Majisties Province of Massachusetts Bay &c

The Honble His Majisties Council and ye Honble House of Representatives
in General Court Assembled — May 26. 1756.

The memorial of Thomas Train of West Hoosuck in behalf of himself and
Divers others of the Proprietors of West Hoosuck, Humbly Sheweth:

That your Memorialist and others of the Proprietors of ye aforesaid Township, would with ye countenance and encouragement of ye General Court build
at their own proper cost and Charge a Block-house at said place upon the Square
so called which will be of special service in order to bring forward a settlement
of said place, and beg leave to Represent that ye Block-house (if it will bear ye
name) built by William Chidester and others answers no good purpose and was
erected contrary to the minds of ye Proprietors in general, and as we think
contrary to ye design and order of ye Genl Court ; therefore your memorialist
humbly begs leave to erect a Block-house at ye aforesaid place of ye following
Dimensions viz: Eighty feet square, two mounts twenty feet square, with a
sufficient Watch Box to ye same — all with Hewn Timber. And that your Honours in your wonted goodness would subsist your memorialists whilst erecting
said Block-house and grant them such a number of men to mantle ye same
(During their perilous season) as your Honours in your great wisdom shall see
best and as in Duty bound shall ever pray.

THOMAS TRAIN.

Attached to the above petition is the following subscription paper,
all the names upon which are men of the "Bay." Joseph Hawley
of this list, who then owned house lot 47, on which now stands the
Post-office and bank block of the town, was at that time the most
important man in Northampton; and John Moffat was a painter
in Boston, who sold in 1760 his house lot 46, on whose front the
Congregational Church now stands, to William Horsford for twenty
shillings. William Horsford also owned in 1765 the next lot west,
44, on which the president's house now stands; and Josiah Horsford
the next, still west, 42, on which the Whitmans lived for three-
fourths of the present century.

FORT MASSACHUSETTS, May ye 10, 1756.

We the subscribers do promise to pay unto Any Person or persons the several sums subscribed if they will undertake and finish a sufficient fort on the Square in the West Township at Husack so called at the compleat finishing said fort — the Dimentions are as followeth viz. said fort to be 80 feet square with two mounts each 20 feet square, the said Fort to be built of hewn timber and a sufficient Watch Box — and we the subscribers do promise to pay the several sums subscribed or to work till we have Compleated the Superscription, as witness our hands —

ISAAC WYMAN	6–0–0	THOMAS TRAIN	3–0–0
BEN SYMONDS	3–0–0	ELISHA HIGGINS	1–10–0
WILLIAM MEACHAM	3–0–0	WILLIAM TRAIN	1–10–0
TYRAS PRATT	1–6–8	JOSEPH HAWLEY	0–18–0
GAD CHAPIN	3–0–0	JONATHAN MEACHAM	2–0–0
JOHN WELLS	3–0–0	DERICK WEBB	0–1–10
NOAH PRATT	1–6–8	JOHN MOPPAT	3–0–0
SAML TAYLOR	3–0–0		

No response appears to have been made to this petition, with its liberal pecuniary offer of £35 12s. 4d. Meanwhile there were rumors here of an enemy approaching from the northwest. The blockhouse had no artillery at all, and had but ten men as a garrison. Early in June, Chidester went to Boston again, and took with him the two petitions that follow, whose contents and signatures, though they have a decided Connecticut flavor as over against Massachusetts, have also in both respects a spirit of compromise.

To his Excellency William Shirley Esq. Capt General, &c, and to the Houble his Majesty's Council, and the Honourable House of Representatives in General Court Assembled.

The Petition of the Proprietors of the West Hoosuck Humbly sheweth,

That whereas ten of the Proprietors of West Hoosuck have obtained Liberty from the Honble Court to build a Fort in sd township with the Incouragement of the Pay and Subsistence of the Province as Soldiers, and as there is allowed forty men for the Defence of the western fronteers at fort Massachusetts and West Hoosuck, fort Massachusetts is a Considerable Part of it fell down and it is Daly expected the rest will fall — and Concluding the Province will Either Rebuild that fort agin or Bild some other for the Defence of the fronteer, your Petitioners Humbly Prays that Massachusetts fort may not be Rebuilt but that we may Have the Liberty of Erecting a fort in our township that shall answer the (same) intent of the Government as that, and that we may have the artillery and the seame strength allowed as was there — and inasmuch as those ten of our Proprietors Have already ben at great cost in Erecting a block-house in town, and Have Don it in such a manner as with some addition will accomadate the whole propriety, your Petitioners Humbly Praieth that we may Have the Like Encouragement allowed us as those ten Have, and we will forthwith join those ten, and by adding other work to the fort allready Built make it a sufficient fort to answer the intent of the Government as a fort instead of Hoosuck fort,, which will at once Build up this town & will be as much Defence to the Government and for less Charge, the Determination of which your Pettrs shall wait and as in Duty bound shall ever Pray —

JOSIAH DEAN	ELISHA HIGGINS
SAMUEL KELLOGG	SETH KENT
NEHEMIAH SMEDLEY	JOSIAH HORSFORD
JONATHAN KYLBORNE	JESSE SAWYER
SOLOMON BUEL	ELNATHAN ASHMUN
ELISHA CHAPIN	TYRAS PRATT
NOAH PRATT	ENOS HUDSON
	GIDEON WARRIN

June 9th 1756 — presented.   Referred to ye next Sitting.

PETITION OF WILLIAM CHIDESTER.

BOSTON, June 10, 1756.

May it please your Honor,

Whereas there are now two small swivel Guns in Fort Massachusetts unimproved by said Garrison who are otherwise supplied with Artillery, and the same would be of Singular Service at the Block-house at Hoosuck where they are destitute of any artillery.   This is to pray the Favor of your Honours regard to our circumstances in Exigency as to give Orders that the same may be removed from thence to said Block-house at Hoosuck, with ammunition for the Improvement of said Swivel Guns in case of need.   Or otherwise supplyed as your Honour shall judge necessary at this time of Danger.   And your Petitioner as in duty bound shall ever pray &c   WILLIAM CHIDESTER

To the Honourable Spencer Phipps Esq. Lt Govr & Commander in Chiefe of the Province of Massachusetts Bay.

Chidester returned from Boston, without much, if any, encouragement from high quarters, to his blockhouse and few faithful companions at West Hoosac.   Before he arrived, perhaps the very day he started, at any rate on June 11, a series of hostile operations by French and Indians were begun on the Hoosac, which cost the lives of many of its brave defenders, and made the campaign of 1756 a gloomy one in New England, only surpassed by the deeper glooms of 1757.   It had long been the custom to keep small scouting parties in motion from fort to fort, from the Connecticut to the Hoosac, and down that river to the Hudson, and then back again. To the scattered garrisons, this was the main source of news from the eastward as well as from Canada.   Sometimes only two soldiers would make these reconnoissances, tramping and watching after the Indian fashion.   Benjamin King and William Meacham had been sent by Captain Wyman down the Hoosac on such an errand, and, returning, fell into an ambuscade only about three-quarters of a mile from the fort, and both were killed. This was June **11**. King was from Palmer; and his body lies in the old burying-ground there, with a still legible inscription on the slate-stone monument at his grave. Meacham was from New Salem, and was own brother to Jonathan, who played a pretty conspicuous rôle here for many years both in things civil and ecclesiastical. The brothers were own cousins to James Meacham, who was not, like them, in the battle of Lake George, but who became a soldier on that ground a few weeks later, and wrought in that capacity on Fort William Henry.

Fifteen days after this, a detachment of thirteen soldiers under Lieutenant Grant, from the main army of General Winslow, then encamped at Half Moon on the North River, were on their way to Fort Massachusetts, when they were surprised by the enemy in the present town of Hoosac, about thirteen miles below the fort; eight of their number were killed outright, and the remaining five captured. The next day, Ensign Barnard was sent from the fort by Captain Wyman, with a small party, to reconnoitre the ground, and, if possible, to bury the dead, when he found, on approaching the place where the dead bodies lay in the road, a large body of Indians in ambuscade ready to pounce upon the party. Barnard warily withdrew his men, and made good his retreat to the fort. Hearing of the circumstances, General Winslow detached Captain Butterfield with a strong body from Half Moon, who took possession of the ground and buried the slain.

July 11, as Chidester and his son James and Captain Elisha Chapin were looking for some strayed cows along Hemlock Brook at some little distance from their fort on the hillside above the brook, an Indian volley killed the two Chidesters, and wounded Chapin, who was seized, carried off about sixty rods, and killed and scalped. This was that Chapin of "Chickobee," who was characterized as follows in Colonel Ephraim Williams's will, drawn the year before: "I give and devise and remit to the poor, distressed, and improvident Captain Elisha Chapin, the sum of one hundred pounds, to be deducted out of the bond given jointly by Moses Graves, and said Elisha Chapin; the said hundred pounds to be remitted out of said Chapin's part." Chapin had some good and generous qualities. He had commanded Fort Massachusetts for a time in 1754, and had acquired the reputation of a brave officer. This surprise occurred about sunset. The Indians then pressed up the hill, opened fire upon the blockhouse, killed the cattle in the vicinity, and soon after retreated into the woods. Nobody dared, apparently, to carry the news at once to the other fort; and it was only on the second day from the attack, that "Captain Wyman sent twenty men to search for the body of Captain Chapin, who found him, and buried him in a decent manner, and returned with his family to Fort Massachusetts."

It was about this time, both before and after the death of Chapin and the Chidesters, nearly two years in all, that Seth Hudson was acting as surgeon at the two forts, as well as in other public capacities; and his original bill for medical services, presented to the General Court and approved by a committee of which J. Wendell was chairman, is now in possession of the excellent antiquarian, Fisher Howe, of Boston. He has kindly loaned it for use in the present instance. The heading of this bill entire, and some of the items in detail, the reader will certainly be glad to see. The whole bill would be here reproduced *verbatim et literatim*, were it not for the fact that the doctor deems it incumbent on him not only to specify the names of the soldiers treated, but also, in abbreviated medical terms, the general treatment followed, and the medicines administered. These are difficult to decipher, and, in the present state of medical science and of the apothecaries' art, are not important, especially as Hudson was always more soldier than surgeon. The heading is as follows: —

> Province of Massachusetts Bay to Seth Hudson Dr.
> for Medicines &c administered to the Souldiers
> at Fort Massachusetts, at the Blockhouse at
> West hoosuck, and others Souldiers in the Province
> Servince, from June 12, 1755 to April 1, 1757.

About one-half of the soldiers named in this bill as treated by him, were among the earliest proprietors of West Hoosac. The names are as follows: —

John Crosby	Edmond Townsend [Town?]
Gad Chapin	Joseph Bush
Noah Pratt	Adington Gardner
Samuel Calhoun	Derick Webb
Joseph Soodwick [Southwick]	James Butterfield
Jos. Birchard	Lemuel Lyman
Ebenezer Graves	Tyrus Pratt
Thomas Train	Elijah Shelding [Sheldon]
Job Spafford	Samuel Smith
Jacob Pattison	James Man
Abram Bass	Benj. Simonds
Jesse Graves	Joseph Lovel
Geo: Willson	William Horseford
Noah Brooks	John Horseford
Silas Pratt	

For "Bleeding" he seems always to have charged a sixpence. The largest single charge in this bill is on account of Benjamin Simonds: "Dressings and &c from 8th to 18th Nov. 1755, £1. 16. 6." The next June he treats Simonds again, bleeding him and administering spirits of nitre and (apparently) St. Croix rum and one other restorative, £0 14s. 6d. The entire bill amounts to £11 5s. 10d. It was allowed and certified in Boston, April 16, 1757. The bill bears, at the bottom, Hudson's own autograph, a handwriting much inferior to that in the bill itself, which is elegant. The Horsfords and Pratts and Derick Webb (twice) and Thomas Train and Ebenezer Graves, and other names familiar, all figure in this bill. To jot down the ailings of "Benj. Simonds," and the sums he cost the General Court for surgeon's service, gives the writer a queer sensation, while the Colonel's original portrait taken at seventy, in the flush and fulness of wholesome old age, looks down upon him from the wall of his study.

Seth Hudson succeeded to the command of the West Hoosac fort on Chidester's death, and considerable accessions of men were received there at various times during the next two years. Ammunition and subsistence were supplied from the older fort, and the settling of the town went forward somewhat; but the principal body of the settlers felt themselves aggrieved at what they considered the niggardly supplies of men and provisions received from the commander of Fort Massachusetts. The householders were evidently more or less divided into a party of the "Bay," and a party of Connecticut; and, what was much the same, into those who favored the pretensions of the eastern fort, and those who deemed the western the better place of defence. Of course, local pride and security entered, as elements, into the dissension. Jan. 11, 1757, twenty-one of the householders presented to the Legislature at Boston, through a device which they themselves explain, a petition for the redress of their grievances, as follows: —

To His Honour Spencer Phipps Esq Lieut Govr &c, The Honourable His Majesty's Council, and the Honble House of Representatives in Gen. Court Convened at Boston

Petition of a number of the Proprietors of West Hoosuck in behalf of ourselves and divers others of the Proprietors of West Hoosuck Humbly SheWeth:

That your Honours Petitioners Have Built a Sufficient Block-house in said township agreeable to the orders of the Government which will be of Special

Service in order to bring forward a Settlement in said place if we can but Support our Hold which we trust we Could Well Do, Had we but a little more Strength and a Sufficient Quantity of Stores within our walls. But since we are allowed but Ten men and all our stores to fitch from fort massachusetts or to subsist our Selves without any allowance from the Government the matter is somewhat Precarious — for during the Perilous Season the Sumer Past we with our teams was under a Necessity of taking one Part of them and to turn out and go to fort massachusetts once in 14 days for our Subsistence — Nor could we prevail with Capt Wyman to Let us Have any more than 14 Days allowance at a time and then stay until that was allmost gon before He would Let us Have any more — so that many times we had Had not a Days allowance in the fort at a time when we had Reason to think we should be attacked by the Enemy Daly by the frequent discoveries we made of them. — We have made application to Major Williams as we under Stood He was ordered by the Government to Subsist us, & likewise to Col Israel Williams and to the Comassary General, But all to no purpose as we apprehend, for the Last Stores we went for we Could not Get but 14 Days allowance, and a Number of us Have not Had any bread for three weeks past, only what we are forced to Provide for our Selves. Your Poor Petitioners Humbly Prays that your Honours in your great Wisdom & goodness would Consider our Distrest Circumstances, and if your Honrs in great wisdom can See fitt we Pray that we may be allowed twenty more men to be added to our Number, as we are the most remoat and most Exposed of any Place in the Government, and that we yr Honrs Petitioners that are not already in the pay and Subsistence of the government may be some of those that may be put in, and that we may be allowed the Liberty of Subsisting our Selves and be allowed therefor the Same Consideration that is allowed the Comasary for Hoosuck, for as there is a number of us Have our familys Hear we must Provide for them, and with a little more expense we could Subsist our Selves also, and could we but obtain leave therefor it woold Be a great Incouragement Settlers to come for it would Provide a sufficient Store of Provision in the Winter Season, so that we might not be layed under any obligation of turning out in the Perilous Season — furthermore our allowance is but Small and not Sufficient to live on, for we receive but five lbs and a half of flour for Seven Days allowance of Bread and six pounds and 2 ounces of pork pr week and six gills of rum for Seven days and half a pint of pease pr Day wine measure, which is the Whole that we get as allowance, and if any man is gon from the fort on what ocasion So Ever He Hires His Duty Done and looses His Subsistance, for notwithstanding a mans Doing His Duty Capt Wyman stops all his allowance so many Days as He is absent, and we By no means might be allowed to make Known our Circumstances to the Honourable Court but our officers Wholy refused us that Liberty, but now at Last we have obtained a furlofe [furlough] for one man, he not knowing our Design, but notwithstanding his furlo He must Hire his Duty Don at the fort and Loose His Subsistance. We furthermore Pray that we might Have an officer amongst our Selves one that would Do us Justice and lett us Have what is allowed by the government and not put it in to his own pocket, thus your Honrs petitioners Humbly beg that your Honours would do for us as in your great wisdom & goodness you see Best, and your petitioners as in Duty bound shall ever pray —

N B   All the assertions in the Bove written Petition Can and may be proved by able witness at the Desire or by order of the Honrble Court —

SAMUEL KELLOGG	SETH HUDSON
NEHEMIAH SMEDLY	WILLIAM HORSFORD
JONATHAN KILBORN	ISAAC VANARENEM
SOLOMON BUELL	JOSIAH HORSFORD
SETH KENT	JOHN HORSFORD
ELISHA HIGGINS	ISAAC SEARL
JOSIAH DEAN JR	TYRAS PRATT
ELNATHAN ASHMUN	GIDEON WARRIN
NOAH PRATT	WILLIAM CHIDESTER JUNR
JABEZ WARRIN	ARCHELAUS TEMPLE
JESSE SAWYER	

Fully one-half of these signatures are names new to the record up to this time. This proves that a considerable number of new settlers came in during 1756, and these mostly from Connecticut, notwithstanding the lack of all military successes to the westward that year. The next year, 1757, was destined to witness horrible military disasters at Lake George, which are only indirectly connected with our story. The Legislature received rather coolly the West Hoosac petition but just now quoted, as is shown by their answer to it, as follows : —

IN HOUSE REPS Jan'y 11, 1757 —

Read and Ordered, that Mr. Lyman and Capt Richardson with such as the Honble Board shall join be a Committee to consider this Petition, to repair to Hoosuck to examine ye state of ye forts there, and consider whether it be most expedient to Repair Fort Massachusetts & to Keep a Garrison there and at the Block-house, or to build anew elsewhere, & that the Comtee inquire into the Facts alleged in the Petition & hear ye parties, and are hereby impowered to take Evidences relative thereto on oath, and report.

Also Voted, That the Ten men stationed at West Hoosuck, as within mentioned, be allowed to Billet themselves at ye charge of the Province until the further order of this Court, provided they do not charge more than five shillings and four pence pr week for each man.

Sent up for Concurrence

T. HUBBARD Spkr

IN COUNCIL 11 JANV 1757.

Read & Concurred & James Minot Esq is joined in the affair.

A. OLIVER, Secy

Consented to S. PHIPPS —

For some unexplained reason, though it is easy enough to guess at it, the committee thus appointed failed to act in the premises, whereupon Seth Hudson, in behalf of the petitioners, presented the following on April 22 : —

Province of the   } To the Honble his majesty's Council and the Honble House
Massachusetts Bay } of Representatives.

The Petition of Seth Hudson, Humbly Sheweth

Whereas Josiah Horsford, and others, Proprietors and Inhabitants of West Hoosuck, on the 8th day of Jany last presented a memorial and Petition to this Honble Court, representing their grievances, and praying relief, and the Court was pleased, on the 11th of Jany, to grant us the liberty of Billeting ourselves, and also to appoint a Committee to repair to West Hoosuck, and examine the truth of our Complaint, but it hath so happened that the Committee hath not yet been there —

Your Petitioner humbly prays ; That the Committee appointed, or any other Committee, be directed to repair to West Hoosuck, and view our situation and circumstances, which when justly represented to your honours, will we doubt not, meet with due encouragement, as it is the most exposed of any upon the western Frontiers, and the properest place to make a stand against the Enemy —

Your Petitioner as in duty bound shall pray &c

SETH HUDSON
Commanding Officer at West Hoosuck

BOSTON 22d April 1757

IN COUNCIL April 25, 1757

Read and ordered that Timothy Woodbridge Esq, of Stockbridge with such as the Honble House shall joyn be a Comtee to take the Petition above referred to into Consideration, Repair to Hoosuck to Examine the state of the Forts there, and Consider whether it be most Expedient to Repair Fort Massachusetts, to keep a Garrison there and at the Block-house, or to build Elsewhere ; That the sd Comtee inquire into the Facts alledg'd, hear the Parties, and they are hereby Impowered to take Evidence relative thereto on oath,

Sent down for Concurrence

A. OLIVER Secy

IN THE HOUSE OF REPS April 25, 1757

Read and Concurred, and Coll. Morey & Capt. Livermore are Joined in the affair

T. HUBBARD S'k'r

The new legislative committee displayed the alacrity becoming to all the circumstances. Woodbridge, the chairman, had himself been a frontiersman for many years at Stockbridge, and knew how to construe the feelings and needs of the West Hoosac men. Woodbridge and his two associates at once " repaired " to the western frontier, and examined fully into the state of affairs there, studied the lay of the land in the whole region, talked with all parties and heard their complaints, and in little more than a month presented a full report to the General Court at Boston. In its general tenor, it was much more favorable to the West Hoosac settlers and their claims than anything before officially exhibited in their behalf. The court, however, took no action upon it for more than six months. Other matters were more pressing. Montcalm's capture of Fort William Henry at Lake George on August 9, and the massacre of large numbers of the garrison the next day, though prisoners of war, by Indians infuriated by rum and revenge, kept the thoughts of Massachusetts busy elsewhere for that summer and autumn.

The following deposition of the two Warren brothers explains itself, and gives a vivid picture of some of the privations and hardships and hazards incident to the settlement of West Hoosac.

The deposition of Jabez and Gideon Warren of full and lawfull age proprietors and settlers in the Township of West Hoosac. Testifie and say that in the Latter end of Augt 1754 when the Enemy fell upon and Destroyed what is called the Dutch Hoosuck. The Inhabitants of West Hoosuck Fled for shelter to the Fort Massachusetts when the said Inhabitants arrived at said fort with their families they found many of the Dutch who had Escaped the Enemy and fled there also. Which so cumbered the fort that it was with great difficulty that we subsisted.

But hearing that Capt. Ephraim Williams was Coming to the fort with orders to relieve the Inhabitants of West Hoosuck we patiently waited his arrival. But when he came he refused to give us any relief saying he had orders from Co^{ll} Williams [Col. Israel of Hatfield] not to take any of the Town Inhabitants into the service only Hudson Simonds and Meacham and not to take Hudson nor Simonds unless they would carry of [off] their families. The distressed proprietors earnestly intreated that they might be favored and put into the service alledging that they could reasonably expect the favour of the Goverment for they had spent all they had to Carry on a Settlement. Capt Curtis Mr. Chidester and others desired favour might be showed under our miserable Circumstances but was denied and ordered away with our families tho we desired the Liberty of building without the fort yet could not obtain the request altho many from the duch had it granted them and even allowed to live in the fort and in the very room where the Government stores were kept, and others was allowed to come to fort with their families soon afterward and altho the fort was not at that time supplied with its quoto of men yet the distressed proprietors could not be put into service when those who were no proprietors nor under such needy Circumstances were admitted and even one from another Government. Further your deponents say not. —

[Signed] JABEZ WORRIN.
GIDEON WORRIN.

March 30 1757 the above was solemnly sworn to before Tim^o Woodbridge Justice Peace.

On the same day, and at the same place, one of the above, namely, Jabez Warren, together with William Horsford, took "solemn oath" to the following.

The testimony of Jabez Warren and William Horsford of Hoosuck West Township of full and lawfull age who Testifie and say that in April 1756 when Serg^t William Chidester came from Boston with orders to take the Command of the fort west Hoosuck and for the Commissary for fort Massachusetts to supply said West fort with proper stores said Commissary directed Mr. Chidester to receive the same of Capt. Wyman at Fort Massachusetts. But we never have been able from that time to this to obtain more than fourteen days pr man allowed at a time Except twice we have been allowed one months provision for said fort. at all other times out of the few men we have we have been obliged to travil four miles once every fortnight at the peril of our lives to fetch our provisions which keeps us in perpetual danger and difficulty. And that the said Capt. Wyman has constantly kept back every mans allowance when absent altho the absent Soldier hires his duty done. And after Serg^t Chidester was killed the soldiers of said West fort being apprehensive from many reasons they should be ill used begged the favour of Lieut Barnard (who commanded at said fort) that they might lay the state of their Case before the Great and General Court and be directed by them but our request was perremtory refused and none of the soldiers could have Liberty to leave the fort but upon a promise that they would go no further than Hatfield.

And when the Government orders came for the Soldiers to billet themselves there was not stores in said fort for each mans allowance one week. Further one of the deponents says (viz) Jabez Warren that met with many discouragements in building said fort for the guard that was sent by Capt. Wyman would guard none but while the people were at labour at the fort and refused to do any other duty and would not put a hand to help up with a stick of timber tho we were few and our timber heavy and declared that to be their orders not to help us altho we offered them pay and sometimes the Guard left us entirely when greatly exposed. Further your deponents saith not. Stockbridge March 30th 1757. [Not like the preceding in Timothy Woodbridge's own hand.]

In the meantime, even before the committee reported in June, Seth Hudson, feeling his responsibility as the commanding officer at the fort, sent down a petition that some artillery might be allowed there, and also some services of a chaplain. One distinction of Seth Hudson is, that he was by several years the last survivor of those original property-holders at West Hoosac; interest attaches to him on many grounds; and we can perhaps gain a glimpse of some of his personal qualities from the words and arrangement of this petition.

Province of the }
   Mass. Bay   } To the Honble his Majesty's Council

The petition of Seth Hudson of West Hoosuck, in behalf of the Inhabitants there — Humbly Sheweth :

That the Block-house at W. Hoosuck is, by the continued labors of the Inhabitants made very strong, and greatly improved by additional works, so as to be the strongest Fort on the Western Frontier, well situated for a Barrier, and will probably save in a short time, great charge to the Government by its being in a Township of the finest land in the Province, which will soon fill with People, many of the Proprietors being in Connecticut, and others from that Colony being desirous of settling there; but we are wholly without artillery,

They therefore humbly pray your Honours would grant such a part of the artillery from Fort Massachusetts, with Powder, Shott, & Shells, with other necessarys, as may be suitable for defending the Block-house. And if a Chaplain should be appointed this summer for Fort Mass. we beg we may likewise have the privilege of his preaching with us, a favour we have not hitherto enjoyed, tho but four miles distant from Fort Massachusetts.

Your Petitioner as in Duty bound, shall ever Pray &c

SETH HUDSON
Commanding Officer of West Hoosuck

Presented. May 1757
The artillery in Fort Massa are ⎫
  3—4 Pounders   ⎪
  1—field piece   ⎬
  2—Swivels   ⎪
  2—Cohorn mortars —   ⎭

In official reply to this request, one of the three four-pounders, and the two swivels, named in the above memorandum, were sent over to the blockhouse. The following is the prompt report of the Woodbridge committee, so far as it relates to West Hoosac matters: —

The Comtee appointed to repair to Hoosuck to examine the state of the forts there and to consider the complaints contained in a petition Exhibited by Sundry persons of West Hoosuck,

Are of the opinion that the fort Called the Massachusetts being placed and built where it is was owing to the want of a better acquaintance of the state, Situation and Circumstances of that part of the province.

The Comtee Humbly conceive that the great ends and designs of the Government in being at the Expense of fortifying and maintaining a garrison there was to promote and bring forward settlements in that expos'd & unsettled part of the province, and to be a protection to such as would bring forward Settlements, and in some measure a defence to the Settlements below, by diverting discovouring annoying & giving intelligence of the approach of the Enemy. And if those things were the purpose of the Government the Comtee are of opinion that the said fort is not so Suitably and conveniently situated to answer those Ends as might be in some other place. For by the best information it appears that the enemies chief gangway to the western frontiers is about the west part of the west Township. The Comtee upon a carefull Examination of the Condition of the said fort find it much decayed, but still in such condition as may answer for a while the purposes of a garrison without cost to repair it

The Comtee upon a view of the Fort or block-house Erected in the west Township find it a place of considerable strength and tolerable situation, and with some additional building and properly man'd it would be in a condition of being maintained against a considerable force. And altho the fortress is not built on the Square yet it is so near that it will accommodate the Settlers almost as well, and with the addition of Barracks or Stockades from the block-house to the TOP OF THE HILL, ABOUT SEVEN RODS, with a mount at ye end of the said

Barracks or Stockades on said hill, the whole will be as well situated for defence as any place the Comtee could discover.

The Comtee having Examined into the grounds of the Complaints in the said petition committed to their Consideration are of the opinion that the complaints Exhibited in Said petition are well supported Excepting the charge of the Subsistence being withheld on all occasions when any soldier is absent from the fort. For it appeared to the Comtee that when any soldier is sent on an express his Subsistence is not withheld. The Comtee are also of opinion that the adding of twenty more men to the ten at the block-house or fort in the west Township would be of public service, as well as very beneficial to the settlers.

All which is Humbly submitted

Timo Woodbridge
Samuel Livermore
Moses Marcy

Stockbridge June 10. 1757

- In the House of Rep's January 10. 1758

Read, and Voted, That this report be accepted so far as it relates to Fort Massachusetts and the block-house at West Hoosuck

Sent up for concurrence

T. Hubbard Spkr

In Council Jany. 10. 1758

Read and Concurred

A. Oliver Secy

That part of the Woodbridge committee's report which related to the conduct of Captain Wyman in his capacity as commander at Fort Massachusetts, to Major Elijah Williams as commissary at the West, and to Colonel Israel Williams as commander of the entire western department, together with the copious memorials of each of these officers in the premises, was referred to a new committee to make further and more thorough examinations. A large mass of testimony was taken, including numerous depositions, in behalf of, and in opposition to, the complaints of the petitioners, which papers, in confusing abundance, are now in the secretary's office at Boston. Captain Wyman, on the whole, came out of the investigation unscathed.

In connection with the above action of the General Court, it was also voted there, —

Whereas the House are informed that there is a large Quantity of Provisions provided by private persons, and now deposited at the Block House at West Hoosuck which may be had for the Province use for billeting the Ninety men which by this court are destined for that place, which, if procured, will prevent a great Charge and Hazard to the Province in the transporting Provisions in this time of danger; therefore the Commissary-General be directed to contract with the proper owners for said Provisions, provided the cost shall not exceed five shillings and four pence for each man per week which is what the Inhabitants at that Block House have agreed to billet themselves for.

The reference in the foregoing vote to the "large quantity of provisions provided by private persons, and now deposited at the Block House at West Hoosac," is proof at once of the remarkable original fertility of the lands there, and of the industry of the comparatively few landholders there in clearing up and subduing their lots, all covered with heavy growths of timber, and of their courage also in holding their ground in war-time under the general protection of the two forts, and accomplishing so much with many interruptions in six years' time.

The military campaign of 1758, to the northward, participated in by a number of the settlers and soldiers at West Hoosac, and watched with deep anxiety by the rest, was hardly, if at all, less discouraging to them than that of the preceding year. Montcalm gained a complete victory over Abercrombie at Ticonderoga, July 8, in which Lord Howe, a great favorite in New England, to whose memory Massachusetts erected a monument in Westminster Abbey, was killed, when, as Major Mante says, "the soul of the army seemed to expire"; but the appointment of Jeffrey Amherst as Commander-in-Chief of the English forces in America, on September 30, two months after his reduction of the Fortress of Louisburg, gave a kind of presage that the tide of success was about to turn. Turn it did in the next campaign. The pivotal year in the history of America in the eighteenth century was 1759. The surrender of Crown Point and Ticonderoga to Amherst in person, and of Quebec to the army of Wolfe, September 13, ended the dream of French ambition in America, gave quiet and content to every English garrison and settlement on this continent, and opened up to peaceful immigration from the older colonies vast stretches of fertile lands both north and south.

From the moment that the military temper and resources of General Jeffrey Amherst were understood in New England, let us say from Sept. 30, 1758, the individual importance of the two forts on the Hoosac began steadily to decline, and of course also the bitterness and bickerings between them. It is pleasant to note, that the last official request of the commander of the West Hoosac Fort was, that his garrison and neighbors might share in the privilege of hearing the preaching of the chaplain at the older fort a part of the time. Since the captivity of Chaplain Norton in 1746, such an official had rarely visited Fort Massachusetts, and only one entry has been found of a money payment made to a chaplain there; during the season of 1757, the subject of a resident chaplain there was a good deal agitated, both locally and at Boston; and very early in 1758, Rev. Stephen West (Yale College, 1755) went there to reside, and stayed till November, when he was introduced to the church in Stockbridge, where he continued their pastor for sixty years. It is altogether probable, although the fact is not of record, that he preached occasionally, during that year of 1758, in the block-house, as Seth Hudson had requested.

Nobody in New England failed to appreciate the battle of Quebec, Sept. 13, 1759. Captain Wyman kept up the show of authority, and of garrison life at the eastern fort, for some time longer. He is known to have lived in the house within the pickets, and to have cultivated the land reserved for the use of the fort. There had been no proprietors' meeting called or held at West Hoosac for six years and six months, when Wyman was requested to call one Sept. 17, 1760, as still being nominally proprietors' clerk there. It is noticeable that he dated this call "East Hoosuck," and not any longer "Fort Massachusetts"; and the proprietors were summoned to meet "at West Hoosuck Fort." By this time, things were reversing themselves a little, along the river. Wyman could have had no heart in this meeting which he perfunctorily called and attended. He had not relished the charges so persistently made against him in his military capacity by his co-proprietors in civil life. He had indeed been exonerated for the most part of the charges preferred; but his personal interest in the little western hamlet had sensibly declined. He kept the record as clerk for the last time at this meeting of the proprietors in the fall of 1760, "at West Hoosuck Fort." William Horsford was then chosen clerk in his place; and we read in the Registry of Deeds, that "Isaac Wyman, Gentleman of Fort Massachusetts, sold to Benj. Kellogg of Canaan, Connecticut, for £140" all his lands in West Hoosac including his fine house lot No. 2, "November 13, 1761." Shortly after this, Isaac Wyman, who had played a large part here, disappears from the Hoosac records altogether. He comes into sight again for a little as a settler, in what is now Keene, New Hampshire, and on the organization of the 1st New Hampshire regiment in 1775, John Stark, Colonel, appears for the last time the name of "Isaac Wyman, Lt. Colonel."

A few of the otherwise homeless soldiers continued to linger around the old fort for some years. In 1762, the General Court sold at auction the entire township of East Hoosac, and Colonel Elisha Jones, of Weston, became one of the four proprietors, by an arrangement with Nathan Jones, who had bidden off the property in June for £3200. Weston was one of the seats of the Williams family, Rev. William Williams having been a minister there from 1709 till 1760. The Jones family were, doubtless, drawn towards East Hoosac by their relations with the Williams family. Ephraim Williams, the founder, was, it will be remembered, the first land-holder in the east township by grant of the General Court in 1750. The ten acres reserved out of his 200 acres enclosed Fort Massachusetts. Colonel William Williams, the father of Pittsfield, and Mr. Nathaniel Williams, almost equally the father of Lanesboro, were both sons of the Weston minister; and Israel Jones, son of Colonel Elisha Jones, of Weston, after a short residence in Pittsfield, became the proprietor, in 1766, of the farm, of which the main part was the broad and fertile meadow around Fort Massachusetts. By that time, the wooden fort had fallen into utter decay, and the exterior pickets had mostly rotted off at the ground, and Farmer Israel Jones began to plough over and around the rude lines, which process he kept up at intervals till his death in 1829. Clement Harrison, then of Williamstown, bought the farm of the Jones heirs, and continued to cultivate the meadow, and to plough down the little terrace, till few indications of the site of the old fort were left, but the print of a small cellar and some horse-radish that had been planted by the soldiers. In 1852, Mr. Harrison gave permission to the present writer to remove to the College the only remaining headstone from the little burying-ground of the fort, which had long been ploughed over, and the stone (lying on the ground) was in danger of becoming illegible. In 1858, the two men critically examined the ground together, with reference to the planting of an elm tree to mark the exact site of the fort. Mr. Harrison was confident that he could indicate very nearly what had been the centre of the parade; when the hole was dug to receive the tree, many bits of brick, and other fragments, were thrown out. A small party of college students assisted the writer to plant the tree, which, however, did not survive the following winter; with his own hands, in the spring of 1859, the writer set the elm which is now growing on the spot, and is represented by the accompanying cut as it was in 1888.

The decadence and final disappearance of West Hoosac Fort was similar in its course to that of the other. Besides the blockhouse, there were two other houses within the pickets, all standing on the front of lots 6 and 8, the blockhouse being on the eastern line of the third house lot (6) west of North Street, and the two other houses still further west, on the declivity towards Hemlock Brook. The picket line was twenty-eight rods along the Main Street. How far the picket lines extended northward, and consequently how much land was enclosed by them, there are no present means of determining; but the position of the blockhouse and the easterly line of pickets can be determined almost exactly. The writer has, this morning (April 25, 1892), carefully measured with a rod pole, made for the purpose, the front line of house lot 4,—fourteen rods,—begin-

PERRY'S ELM.

Planted in 1859.

ning at the southwest boundary stone of the Kappa Alpha lot, which is the front of house lot 2, and to the east line of house lot 6, which was the east line of the West Hoosac Fort, and found the southeast corner of Chidester's house lot exactly in line with a fine, large elm, standing on what is thought to be the original boundary line between Nos. 4 and 6. This elm is eight or ten rods north of that southeast corner of No. 6. The eastern line of the old blockhouse was in that line. That elm is likely to stand for a century longer. May it become as lasting a mark as "Endicott's Tree"! A magnificent house in Massachusetts colonial style has recently been built on the front of house lot 4, by H. T. Procter.

As the war-clouds gradually dispersed after the battle of Quebec, families continued to live in the houses within the pickets at West Hoosac, and particularly the family of Silas Pratt, originally of Worcester, and long a soldier at Fort Massachusetts, and afterwards one of the garrison at the west fort so long as it was used and desig-

nated as such.   His son William was born within the fort in 1760.
The following is the epitaph in the "Lovat burying-ground," just
over the line, in Pownal : —

IN MEMORY OF
WILLIAM PRATT
THE FIRST WHITE MALE CHILD BORN IN
WILLIAMSTOWN MASS. WHO DIED JAN. 16,
1846, IN THE 86TH YEAR OF HIS AGE. HE WAS A
MEMBER OF THE METHODIST EPISCOPAL CHURCH 43
YEARS ; HE WAS A REVOLUTIONARY PATRIOT ;
HE ENLISTED IN 1777, AND SERVED THREE YEARS.

This William Pratt was a drummer in the Revolution, and saw
the execution of Major André, Oct. 2, 1780.   He had a stiff arm and
could not well handle a musket.   He had an early pension from the
United States, and was always fond of telling stories of what he had
seen in the service.   He lived all his life on the northern slope of
Northwest Hill, on what was a part of his father's extended farm,
which is the first farm as one goes over the Hill and over the line
into Pownal.   Williamstown will always be proud of her first-born
son, and of his birthplace within the pickets of her only fort; for he
was a patriot in his boyhood, and served his country three full
years in the field before he reached his majority, and thereafter
served his heavenly Master during a long life.   He left his rude
house and small, rough lands to his son William, who also lived to
old age in and upon them, and from conversations with whom the
writer learned some of these facts.   For example, he said that he had
often heard his father, and his Uncle Silas, also, give incidents, by
the hour, of their personal experiences in the War of Independence.
      In the same burial-ground is extant and legible the epitaph of
this Silas Pratt, Junior, as follows : —

IN MEMORY OF SILAS PRATT,
WHO DIED APRIL 2, 1830, AGED 70 YEARS.
He was an honest unpretending man.
He has gone where decay or death may not come.

He, too, had a United States pension for revolutionary services,
always lived near his father on Northwest Hill, and the two were in
the battle of Bennington together.   The father used to say that
in the thick of the fighting, at the Tory breastwork, "I waited
behind a staddle for the smoke to clear away, when a bullet struck
the staddle, and then I let fly without waiting any longer!"   It will
be remembered that Pownal fell north of Hazen's Line, and couse-

quently under the jurisdiction of New Hampshire, which chartered
the township in 1760, and settlements commenced from this side in
1762, when there were four or five Dutch families there claiming
under the "Hoosac Patent," granted by the state of New York.
Under these circumstances, the first English families had close relations with Williamstown.   The town was named after Governor
Pownal, of Massachusetts.   In the Revolution the Pownal men
often enlisted in Williamstown companies, and served under Massachusetts officers.   Two of them certainly went up the Kennebec
with Arnold.   Charles Wright, originally from Amherst, an enlisted
man in Colonel Israel Williams's regiment for the northward in
1759, who had received a license from the Province of Massachusetts, a year or two later, to keep a tavern opposite Fort
Massachusetts, where Israel Jones afterwards lived and died (the
"Harrison place"), moved his family and his tavern down the river
to Pownal in 1762, after the migrations to Bennington had well commenced.   The Wrights, Pratts, Morgans, Dunhams, Nobles, Cards,
Gardners, and Seelyes, among the very first settlers of Pownal, were
almost equally at home in Williamstown.

Williamstown claims Silas Pratt, the elder, as one of her most
enterprising and persistent promoters.   He was a blacksmith by
trade.   He owned, first and last, several of our house lots, besides
making a home for some years in the old fort on No. 6; and he
seems to have sold out his lands here in time to migrate to Pownal
in 1762, and to be there among the very first settlers.   His nearest
neighbor in Pownal was Nehemiah Williams.   As early as 1767,
certainly, this neighbor, whose whole course in life was much like
his own, had bought a large farm next east to his, on the northern
declivity of the same hill, and built his house on the public road
(now discontinued) parallel with the western road on which the
Pratts lived.   The vestiges of this house are still to be seen two
rods west of a very big rock by the old roadside.   Here he brought
up a family whose descendants are still very numerous in the region
round about.   Our William Pratt married Rosanna Williams, who
saw from her father's house, in 1777, Burgoyne's men, as prisoners
of war, fill up with their shiny uniforms and equipments the road
on Pownal Hill opposite.   She lived to be very old in her husband's
house on the other road, and used to relate this incident of her girlhood to persons who lived to tell those still living.   A portion of
the surrendered army of Burgoyne certainly filed down Pownal Hill
that autumn, in plain sight of Nehemiah Williams's house.

Olive Williams married Silas Pratt, Junior; and Elsie Williams married John Smedley, 2d; and Stephen Williams, the eldest son, a shoemaker, lived in the corner west of the present schoolhouse where the present road turns north, and brought up a family, of which Electa married Amos Pratt, and Nehemiah married Sally Treadwell. Van Rennsalaer Williams, a good man, worthy of memory, son of these last, died here Jan. 15, 1887. The tradition is manifold and wholly credible, that while the first Nehemiah Williams was absent from home in Bennington Battle, one child lay dead in the house, and another dying; while the wretched mother, whose maiden name was Elsie Gallup, of Rhode Island, heard distinctly all day the booming of the cannon. The blood of old Silas Pratt and of old Nehemiah Williams has been greatly commingled, and, perhaps, somewhat degenerated, in the many generations since their time. Silas Pratt, Junior, and Olive Williams had, among many other children, Zadoc; and Zadoc's oldest son was Stephen, who married Margaret Green, daughter of Frederick Green, a family famous on "the Gore" in the olden time. Henry Green, of "Green Hollow" will probably step upon our stage in a later act. Stephen and Margaret were the parents of "Steve" and "Jerry," the noteworthy stage-drivers and story-tellers of our own time. Steve's best may serve as a sample of the good things of both: he had driven to the railroad station a not over-bright Williamstown boy and graduate, who was just starting to go to India as a missionary; as the train rolled off, "Steve" gravely informed the bystanders, "He has gone to teach ignorance to the heathen!"

To come back now to the West Hoosac Fort, — at least four proprietors' meetings were held within its rude walls of hewn timber in the years 1760 and 1761. At the first of these, held Oct. 1, 1760, it was

Voted as follers — Vizt — (1) Voted and Choose Jabez Worrin moderator for s'd meeting (2) Voted and Choose Willm Horsford proprietors Clerk (3) Voted and Choose Josiah Horsford Treasurer. (4) Voted and Choose Benj^a Simons Gideon Worrin and Seth Hudson a Commite to settel with the Colector and Treasurer (5) Voted to Clear the Streat East and West as far as the Town lots Extend and North and South from Stone Hill to the River — (6) Voted and Choose Jabez Worrin Sovare (7) Voted to hire preaching for Six months Beginning at the first of May next — the 8 artikel [which was "To bye a Law Book"] Dismist — (9) Voted to Rais 12 Shillings on Each Right to Defray the Chargeses.

Some comparatively new names greet us in this new record, — the first official record of the proprietors since 1754. William Horsford was chosen clerk in place of Isaac Wyman, towards whom there were already signs of decided hostility; and Josiah Horsford was chosen treasurer. These young men were from Canaan, Connecticut. The first connection of this family with West Hoosac dates from Nov. 1, 1752, when Daniel and William Horsford bought house lot 44, for £260 Connecticut money old tenor, of Josiah Dean, Junior. In the original drawing of lots, Josiah Dean, Senior, had chanced to get this choice lot, on whose front now stands the president's house, directly north of West College. The younger Dean sold it to the Horsfords, father and son, shortly after, and the son, William, bought out the father's share for £26, in February, 1761. Thenceforth William Horsford made this fine lot his home; built upon it early a good framed house, whose timbers are still standing in a two-story house on South Street; ten children were born here to William and Esther Smedley Horsford, of which the eldest, Esther, born May 19, 1760, was the second female child born in the hamlet; his mother, called in the record, "Elizabeth Horsford, the aged," died here in May, 1781; and his wife, Esther, died in March, 1791, aged fifty-four, not long after which the property passed over into the hands of General Samuel Sloan, who built upon it the present house, an extraordinarily fine one for the time. William Horsford served his generation well.

So did Josiah Horsford, his brother, whose wife, Jemima Smedley, was sister to William's wife. He settled down next to his brother on house lot 42, which he bought in October, 1759, of John Chamberlain, of Stockbridge, for £45. He, too, built a good house just west of his brother's, which is still the central part of what became long after the "Whitman house," and is now owned and occupied by Dr. L. D. Woodbridge. He had nine children born to him, 1762–84. Rev. Whitman Welch, the first minister of Williamstown, sold to Josiah Horsford, in October, 1767, "the minister's lot," so called, £25. This lot, house lot 36, was originally set apart to be given in fee simple to the first minister. This is the "Mansion House" lot, lying first east of North Street. Horsford also owned at different times, house lot 40, next west of his own, whose front has long been occupied by the house of the late B. F. Mather; and house lot 46, on which the Congregational Church now stands. There is extant an order of Josiah Horsford, per son Ambrose, for sling, on J. P. and T. Whitman, Aug. 3, 1803. As the Whitmans came here from Hartford in 1797, and bought Horsford's premises when they first came, there is a slight indication of decay in Horsford's circumstances in his old age. But his credit seems to have been good at "the store." John Horsford and Daniel, undoubtedly brothers of

William and Josiah, were settlers here very early, though they never became prominent. John and Daniel bought of Ephraim Williams, Junior, house lot 10, £30, April 14, 1753. John Horsford, "Bloomer," bought house lot 9, of Seth Hudson, "Gent." Indeed, all the Horsfords bought and sold land a good deal, as, indeed, did most of the early proprietors.

William and Josiah Horsford, by locating permanently on the second eminence, and by becoming influential men in the "Propriety," as it was then called, undoubtedly did something to draw actual settlements towards the east. The first centre of dwellings and of proprietary business was in the valley of Hemlock Brook, sometimes called in the records at that time "Hudson" Brook, from Seth Hudson, whose house, on No. 9 (pretty close down to the brook on the south tier of lots), held the first proprietors' meeting in 1753; when the proprietors met several times during 1760 and 1761 in the blockhouse, it was coming east nearly to the summit of the third eminence, but not quite upon the "Square," where at length the centre of business and of assembly rested for a century.

The most important vote in this meeting of 1760 was, "To clear the street east and west as far as the town lots extend, and north and south from Stone Hill to the River." The "river" means the Hoosac at what we call "Moody Bridge," and the term "Stone Hill" in this connection proves that designation to have been coeval with the laying out of the house lots in 1750. It has been the uniform designation ever since of that striking feature of our landscape. It is, perhaps, needless to write that a *vote* to clear the street was not equivalent to clearing it. To clear it with the then present means and numbers was a herculean, an impossible task. The street east and west was almost a mile and a half long, was laid out fifteen rods wide the entire length, ran over four quite considerable elevations with the intervening valleys; on at least two of these elevations (the first and second reckoning from the east) limestone rocks projected from the general surface from ten to twenty feet, the hollows between the heights were wet and Hemlock Brook ran low between precipitous banks, and first-growth forest trees of large size covered the greater part of this large space of rough ground. The street north and south, though longer, had been laid out much narrower, and ran, on the whole, over smoother ground. There were, however, three decided, though broad, elevations along this route, one on each side of the "Square," itself one of the eminences of the other street. The county of Berkshire, incorporated the next year, 1761, practically "cleared" this north and south street for its "County Road," which coincided for this distance with the West Hoosac lay-out of 1750. Roads were the great burden and expense of the little pro-priety until it became a town in 1765. It showed, however, great enterprise and persistency in this regard. "Water Street" was laid out and made passable in 1761; and it was voted on the 19th of April, 1762, "To clear a road to the East town for a cart to get along," and also (same day), "To clear a road through this town towards Framingham [Lanesboro] for comfortable carting."

Jabez Warren was chosen moderator of the first proprietors' meet-ing, after the close of the French War, marked by the surrender of Quebec, and also at the same time surveyor for the "Propriety." He was a husbandman from Brimfield, and sold land there in March, 1751; but he had been in the military service in the line of forts over the mountain, from Northfield to the Hoosac, during nearly the whole war. He was a corporal in Coleraine in 1748, and afterwards served both in Fort Massachusetts and in West Hoosac Fort. Gideon Warren, perhaps a brother of Jabez, and both, very likely, related to David Warren, who was carried captive to Canada from Massachusetts Fort in 1746, was chosen, at this first-renewed proprietors' meeting, one of a committee, Benjamin Simonds and Seth Hudson being the other members, " to settel with the Colector and Treasurer." These Warrens grant but scanty glimpses of them-selves to the modern investigator, but enough to excite his curios-ity to learn more. Gideon Warren owned, very early, first-division fifty-acre lot 30, which, with the windings of the lower Green River through it, occupied the southeast corner of the town plat, which space would otherwise have been laid out into five house lots like the rest. Warren, a yeoman, sold to Samuel Payn, of Dutchess County, New York, carpenter, "two acres of Green River, part of a lot known as No. 30," with the privilege of flowing the river bank " as hie up as ye top of ye upper falls," " and also a strip of land two rods wide by the west side of said river, beginning at the north side of land I sold to said Payn, and running north by the river to the mouth of the brook [Phebe's Brook], and up the hill to the lot now enclosed, and so out to the main road or Highway, to be a highway for the use of the town." Isaac Stratton and Daniel Stratton sign, as witnesses, this deed for the first opening of " Water St.," June 1, 1761.

Three years after this opening of Water Street into Main Street, Gideon Warren sold off eleven acres more from his fifty-acre lot No. 30, to James Meacham, who had recently established himself on fifty-acre lot No. 7, directly south of the southeast quarter of the house lots. This brought the Meachams into Payn's new road, along Green River and up the hill into Main Street, — a road the Meachams have been travelling ever since. James Meacham, a great-grandson of the original James, still owns the ancestral acres. Elkanah Parris and Josiah Horsford sign, as witnesses, this deed of alienation from Warren to Meacham. But Gideon Warren did not get rooted here, as did the Meachams and the Horsfords. He was swept on, with others, by a strong current, to the northward, into Vermont; and we find Warren proprietors' clerk in Pittsford, in March, 1771.

But both the Warrens had considerable more to do in West Hoosac before they should be suffered to pass on. In the second legal proprietors' meeting, after the French War was over, "att the Place Called the fort in West Hoosuck," Nov. 20, 1760, Jabez Warren was again chosen moderator and also one of the three assessors (the others being Thomas Dunton and Benjamin Simonds), the three being also authorized "to Sell the Land of those Proprietors who are Delinquit in Paying their Rates." Gideon Warren, too, and Thomas Train were chosen at this meeting "to Hier a Good orthodox Preacher for s'd Propriete." The chief purpose of the meeting was to settle for the work already done in the clearing of the Main Street, and to provide means for resuming that work in earnest the next spring. They voted to accept Jabez Warren's account, viz.: "Seventy Six Days works of men in s'd Highways in West Hoosuck at three Shillings a Day and fourteen Days Work of Oxen at one Shilling and Sixpence a Day in s'd Highways also a Plow one Shilling and Six Pence;" and they also voted "to Raise a tax of Eight Shilling on Each Proprietor's Right to defray the Necessari Charge in s'd Propriete."

The two proprietors' names encountered in the record of this meeting, with which we are not already somewhat familiar, are Thomas Train and Thomas Dunton. Train's story has the trail of mystery about it from beginning to end. If ever romancer to the manor born should seek for a theme amid the origins of his beautiful town, all the elements of a powerful story are found in the little that is known of Thomas Train. He was of Weston, which was a part of Watertown, right in the thick of the Williams family and influence. If the genealogical tables betray us not, he was a great-grandson of John Train, who came to Watertown in 1635, in the *Susan and Ellen*. Thomas Train, of Watertown, who died in 1739, aged eighty-six, may have been his grandfather. He was born in August, 1727. In 1751, when he was twenty-four years old, he was published

to be married with Abigail Viles, but for reasons unknown to us he
did not marry her, for she married a certain Jonas Barnard the next
year.   Thereafter, Train acted in certain respects like a disappointed
man bereft of hopes.   Before long, we find him an enlisted soldier
in the garrison of Fort Massachusetts.   When the house lots in the
west township were offered to that garrison, fifteen of them purchased the right to draw for choices at one time, and the state
accepted, at Ephraim Williams's instance, the evidences of their
soldiers' wages due, as payments made for their lots.   Train drew
house lot No. 30, which is the lot on which Judge Danforth now
lives, and on which his father lived before him.

Not long after, Train became possessed of house lot No. 4, which
was the lot next east of the fort, of which Train did not entertain
a good opinion, as we have already seen.   He sold house lot 4 to
Dr. Jacob Meack, in October, 1768, for £40.   He bought and sold
lots more or less, like the rest, but he does not seem to have settled
down in one place to try to find a home ; like many another, in
similar circumstances, he had, doubtless, resolved never to marry.
He seems to have been thrown in a good deal with Benjamin
Simonds, our old Canada captive of 1746–47, especially after the
latter was married in Northampton, to Mary Davis, April 23, 1752,
and brought his wife to West Hoosac, and settled down on house
lot 22.   Train's own original lot was house lot 30, the fourth to the
west in the same tier.   As Simonds has already been, and will continue to be a considerable figure in our story, it is, perhaps, worth
while to note in passing, that this marriage was performed by
Joseph Hawley, Esq., himself the original proprietor of house
lot 47, and that the celebration of the rite by the magistrate, rather
than the minister, was more or less related with the bitter quarrel
at that time going on between Jonathan Edwards and his late
parishioners in Northampton.

It is a strong tradition in the Meacham and Simonds families,
transmitted to present times by their children, that this husband
and wife were the eighteenth family to settle on the West Hoosac
house lots, and that, in the military troubles that soon came upon
the hamlet, this family often found a shelter or a temporary home
in the old fort or blockhouse on house lot No. 6, the ruins of which
remained *in situ* and in sight until the opening of the present
century.

April 8, 1753, a child was born to these parents, a daughter
named Rachel, the first child born in the propriety, nor was there a
second for seven years according to tradition, which must be wrong

in this particular, because the record of births in the old "Proprietors' Book" is distinct and unbroken, as follows: —

Benjamin Simonds and Mary his wife, —
> Rachel, born April 8, 1753.
> Justin, born Feb. 17, 1755.
> Sarah, born July 8, 1757.
> Marcy, born Dec. 2, 1759.

Then follows the record of the birth of six other children from 1762 to 1773, a stretch of time during which many other families in Williamstown were blessed with children, of which the first, according to the record, was that of William Horsford, whose first child, Esther, was born May 19, 1760. Then follows the birth of eight children in that family till 1779. The mother, Esther Horsford, died March 1, 1791; and this interesting item concludes that list, "Elizabeth Horsford the aged Died May 28th 1781." She was the mother of William and Josiah Horsford, of Canaan, Connecticut. Owing to the almost purely military origin of West Hoosac, very few parents of the first settlers accompanied or followed their children hither.

But Rachel Simonds, the first-born child in the place, — as such drawing the attention and exciting the interest of all the hardy settlers, especially as she in some sense belonged to the public, living in the people's own fort, at least a part of the time till 1760, — was growing up under circumstances of peculiar isolation from young men, and also probably of peculiar intimacy with Thomas Train, who was twenty-four years her senior. At any rate, when she was nineteen years old, early in January, 1772, they were married, and went to housekeeping on the south slope of Townsend Hill, in a small house whose cellar is perfectly visible to this day, and is marked by a rugged elm already of considerable size, and likely to endure for a century to come. This house stood on second-division fifty-acre lot 63, which was bought by Jonathan Train, probably a brother of Thomas Train, of Benjamin Simonds, whose house lot 3 drew this 63 in the regular order. Here, at all events, was born a daughter to Thomas Train and Rachel Simonds, Oct. 15, 1772. As Rachel Simonds was the first daughter of the town (1753), so, emphatically, was Sarah Train the first granddaughter of the town (1772).

But before this child was born, and before the mother was twenty years old, Thomas Train had gone off to Virginia, to secure a new home for himself and family. Why Williamstown did not satisfy him, what there was in Virginia to attract him, we shall never know; after obtaining a good title to some lands in this oldest of our commonwealths, and starting to return to the North, Train was seized with his mortal sickness, and lies buried no one knows where; the fact of the death, and probably the place of it, were communicated to his friends not very long afterwards; and after the Revolutionary War was over, and Virginia land-titles were settling into permanent record, there was an official communication from the South to his family here in relation to the land, but nothing further was ever done or known about it. Mrs. Thomas Train became, in a very few years, Mrs. Benjamin Skinner, — a very proper marriage in every respect to a man but three years older than herself, — and Sarah Train was brought up with Deacon Skinner's children, until she, too, at nineteen years of age, was married to William Blair in 1791. She had many children of her own, and died here June 26, 1864, in her ninety-second year; a mother in Israel.

Thomas Dunton was from Western, now Warren, Massachusetts. So far as can be known, his was the first family to settle directly on the bank of the Hoosac River, and his house was near the Noble Bridge, and he must have reached it from the Main Street, by a path corresponding, in general, with the present Cole Avenue. For a number of years, Dunton owned house lot 13, and sold to prominent parties the outlots drawn in succession by this house lot. For example, he sold to Daniel Burbank, also from Western, the second-division fifty-acre lot 56, October, 1763, which Burbank afterwards bravely defended in the battle of Bennington. Burbank's first house was a framed building of one room. He soon doubled his farm, by buying the adjoining fifty-acre lot 57, half a mile from South Williamstown on the road to New Ashford, and there his family resided well into the present century. Dr. Asa Burbank, his son, was a graduate of the College in 1797, a tutor, and a professor in the Berkshire Medical School; and the other son, Samuel, at the instance of his mother while Bennington battle was going forward, put his ear to the ground, and heard successive discharges of cannon. Daniel Burbank was then Lieutenant in the military company of South Williamstown; and to his neighbors, who crowded around on the return, and wanted to know if he felt afraid during the fight, he answered, "After they had fired once, and we had fired once, I was no more afraid on the battle-field than I am on the potato field!"

Thomas Dunton drew also in virtue of his house lot 13, 100-acre lot 23, which he sold to Hezekiah Brown, of Sharon, Connecticut, in

1767; two years later Brown sold the same to Joseph Deming, of Weathersfield, Connecticut, who, with his two sons, Aaron and Titus, purchased also the adjoining 100-acre lot 24, which two furnished a home to the Deming family for fully one hundred years. The tradition in the family was, that the 200 acres cost them at the rate of eight shillings an acre. The 100-acre lot 25, next south of 24 as that is south of 23, extends to the New Ashford line; and through all three flows down the Ashford Brook to its junction with the Hancock Brook at South Williamstown; and the public road to Pittsfield follows up the brook, and bisects all three of these lots. Joseph Deming, born in the year 1708, was about sixty-two years old when he came here, and died in 1783; his son, Aaron, born in February, 1744, died in March, 1837, aged ninety-three years. Aaron's son, Captain Joseph, with two unmarried sisters, lived till his eightieth year in the same house which his father had built, and Captain Joseph's son, Nelson, an excellent man, was the last of that name and line in Williamstown. Titus Deming, who left a posterity as numerous as did Aaron, though all of both lines are now gone from this town, established his homestead just where the two roads bifurcating at "Taylor's Crotch" come together again two miles and a half further south. He had four sons, of whom Francis inherited the farm, whose son, Richard Titus, was graduated at Williams in 1852; Moses, who is generally referred to as "Moses the Mormon," and who died in 1873; and Martin, born in 1792, whose son, Eli Rix, was adopted by the good Deacon Beers, otherwise childless, whose farm was 100-acre lot 26, which touched the other Deming lots on two sides, and which, when inherited by Rix Deming, brought all the Deming lands into contiguity. Rix Deming married Harty Johnson, a gifted daughter of one of the old families of South Williamstown; and they migrated about 1880 to Lawrence, Kansas, where they are living at the present writing.

Whereas Requist Hath Ben made to me the Subscriber by a Sofisient Number of Proprietors to Issue out a Warrant for Calling a Proprietors meeting to act on the articiles as follow (viz) 1ly To Chuse a moderator for s'd meeting. 2ly To Chuse a Surveyor for the Proprietors of West Hoosuck. 3ly To Chuse a Commetre to lay out a Common Rhoad or Private Way to Conveau the Intended Place of a mil or mils on Green River. 4ly To act on all the foremention articiles Which meeting is to be on tuesday ye fourteenth Day of July Next at the Place Called the fort att the House of David Robart in West Hoosuck att four o'Clock in the after Noon. West Hoosuck, June ye 30 Ad 1761 Test William Horsford Proprietors Clerk.

The term "the fort," as used in these minutes and in common talk at that time, included everything within the pickets or stockade; that is to say, the blockhouse that stood on the eastern line of house lot 6, and two houses, one on 6 and the other on 8, pretty near to each other. Soldiers lodged in any one of these, with or without their families, were said to live in "the fort." Silas Pratt was one of these dwellers, and here his son, William, was born in 1760; Benjamin Simonds lived here off and on according as the times were perilous, but whether any one of his four children born in West Hoosac before 1760 were born in the fort, or all were born in his own house on house lot 22, cannot now be determined; and according to this minute of June, 1761, David Roberts was one of the dwellers within the enclosure. Richard Stratton was chosen moderator of the meeting thus warned; Gideon Warren was chosen surveyor for the proprietors; and Richard Stratton, Thomas Dunton, and Josiah Horsford, were chosen a committee to lay out the road to the intended place for a mill, that is to say, Water Street. The return of this committee was rendered on the first day of August, 1761. This was the first road laid out by the proprietors. It was laid out two rods wide. The first half of it from the south, "Beginning at the North Side of Samuel Payen's land on the West side of the above s'd Rever," was near to and parallel with Green River, then it mounted "to the top of the Hill to the East Side of Gedion Warrin Land and by the s'd line upon s'd Warrin Land to the main Rhoad." Of ten trees marked by this survey for the line of this road, eight were hemlocks, showing the prevailing timber along the lower Green River.

The name of Richard Stratton appears for the first time officially in the minutes but just now quoted. He was moderator of that meeting, and chairman of its most important committee. His accession to the little settlement in the spring of 1760, bringing with him from Western (now Warren) a family of eight children, proved in the sequel to be a matter of great importance to the town. He was a man of probity and of property. He was a Baptist, and came to be called "Deacon," although there was hardly another person of that religious sect in West Hoosac for a number of years after he came; and although three of his sons and two of his daughters became prominent members of the Congregational church here. Ichabod Stratton came hither some time after his brother Richard, but presently went away again; and David Stratton, John Stratton, and Joel Stratton were fathers of families here in the last quarter of the last century, although not closely related to Richard. The latter bought of Moses Graves house lot 54 for £50, June 3, 1760. Unquestionably there was a "regulation" house upon that lot at that time, and Stratton moved his family into it upon his arrival; the price of the lot proves the presence of the house, because five months afterwards Stratton bought the adjoining house lot 56, which was every way as good *as land*, and on which Stratton proceeded shortly to build the first two-story house in the hamlet, which house is still standing substantially unchanged (1892), for only £12. Sixteen months after the second purchase, he bought the next adjoining house lot 58, together with thirteen acres of beautiful land to the north of that lot, for £34, the price showing that there could have been then no house on 58.

Now it is certain that, in April, 1762, Richard Stratton owned the three contiguous house lots just referred to, all of them as level as a barn floor, perhaps the best lots out of the seventeen constituting the northeast quarter of the entire house-lot plat. Directly across Main Street from the front of 58 was the then new opening into Water Street, and to its prospective and promised mills on Green River. What was it, then, that led Stratton to prefer the front of 56, on which to build a little later his own expensive residence? The reasons can only be guessed at at this late day; but even guesses on reasonable grounds, by and for the only parties legally entitled to that privilege, — namely, Yankees, — may prove not unacceptable. The present owner of 56, James M. Waterman, who has both owned and occupied the Stratton premises since 1860, and who, during much the larger part of this interval, has been the senior selectman of Williamstown, told the writer yesterday, that the natural site of the house, which is understood to be on the very line of Main Street, is considerably higher than the corresponding fronts of 54 and 58 Then the house already built on 54 could shelter the family, while the young men should be provided for with permanent homes, and the father could determine the most eligible place on which to build for himself. In 1765 the father had bought also house lot 52, the lot next west of 54, whose front came snug up to the foot of "Consumption Hill," afterwards so called.

In September, 1766, Richard Stratton both sells and gives to Isaac Stratton, "both husbandmen," for £7, "together with that parental love and affection which I have and do bair to him the said Isaac Stratton, my well-beloved son," the two fifty-acre lots 53 and 55 of the second division, and "the pine lot No. 30 in the north part of said Williamstown." Isaac was his eldest son, and was born Nov. 25, 1739. He was nearly twenty-one when the family came to

Williamstown, and fully twenty-six when he took title at South Williamstown. But he had been at work, the very first settler there, for three or four years before he took title, on the spot of 53 that has been a tavern almost ever since. He lived to play a great part in the civil history of the town, and in the hazards and successes of the Revolutionary War; and he died April 3, 1789, aged fifty years. He was alone in what is now the village at the south part for a considerable time; but Daniel Burbank, also from Western, became the second settler and his nearest neighbor about half a mile south on the New Ashford road. The way in which Burbank got hold of his farm illustrates a method of purchase more or less prevailing at that time. He bought of David Roberts, carpenter, one half of two fifty-acre lots drawn by house lot 14, No. 40 of the first division, and No. 57 of the second division, for £15, in December, 1761. Just two years later he bought of Benjamin Simonds the other half of 57, paying him for it *his* half of No. 40. In the mean time, Burbank had bought for £23 the entire lot 56 of the second division, adjoining Isaac Stratton's lot 55. So Burbank made up his farm at the south part. He was the first to clear up and plough those fertile acres. Let it be called the "Burbank farm" forever. Nine children, the eldest, Samuel, were born to Daniel and Mary Burbank, 1766–86.

Isaac Stratton's wife was Mary Fox. Their children were not so numerous as the Burbank children, but they were earlier born, 1762–75. A bridge over the Hancock Brook just before its junction with the Ashford Brook, the two constituting thenceforth the Green River, was built close by Stratton's first house, to accommodate him and Burbank before any bridge was put over Green River at the eastern end of the north-village plat. Stratton afterwards built another house across the brook on the right-hand side of the Ashford road, on which he left a lasting memorial of himself. The house is still standing in good repair. It is of two stories, and of large size. On the chimney any one may read to this day, "I. S. 1785." This house stands on lot No. 54, the middle part of his farm, and across the road a little further to the east, and near the junction of the two brooks, is the first and only "God's acre" for the south part, on his own land; and on a substantial tombstone there we may read, "Isaac Stratton Esq. died April 3, 1789, aged 50." We shall encounter this good man's name and deed in striking scenes before our task is done. His widow married Rev. Clark Rogers, and died March 20, 1812. She is buried by the side of her first husband.

It seems to be impossible to fix from extant data the exact year in

which Richard Stratton built the existing "Stratton house." It
cannot have been far from 1765. In a list of the holders of house
lots for that year, in reference to another drawing of outlots, his
original purchase, house lot 54, is put down to his son, Ebenezer
Stratton, then twenty years old; while in his own name stand
Nos. 52 and 7. In that year and the next, he seems to have been
dividing up his lands freely among his adult children. Isaac, the
eldest, had been already generously provided for at the south part,
although the legal title did not pass over to the son until September,

DEACON EBENEZER STRATTON'S HOUSE.

1766. In the same month and year, Richard Stratton sells and gives
to his son, Daniel Stratton, then twenty-three years old, for £5 and
for love, etc., the two meadow lots 26 and 27 so far as they lie "on
the north side of the stream of the river," and also the first-division
fifty-acre lot 51 (adjoining these meadow lots to the north), and also
the oak lots 14 and 27. Thus was laid out in a deed of gift from
Richard Stratton to Daniel, with just sufficient pecuniary consideration to make it legal, what has been known for more than a century,
and is still known, as the "Bridges farm," from Jonathan Bridges,
originally from Colchester, Connecticut, and from his son Samuel
Bridges, his grandson Edwin Bridges, his great-grandson Charles E.
Bridges, the present owner, in succession. The last-named has

lately sold parts of these lands to the Fitchburg Railroad for station and switching purposes.

The next February, Richard Stratton, " from parental affection," etc., sold his "well-beloved son, Ebenezer," the adjoining fifty-acre lots of the first division 54 and 33, except ten acres of the northeast corner of 33, also pine lot 45, and all that part of meadow lot 53 east of Green River. All these parcels were contiguous land not far from the eastern end of the village plat, and constituted what was commonly called the "Stratton lot"; and the town of Williamstown, in 1891, legally named the road that was laid out "to convean" this farm "Stratton road." Ebenezer Stratton was then twenty-two years old. He led an extremely useful life thereafter on that farm, till his death in 1814. We shall run across him later. One of the latter's sons, Rev. Ebenezer Harrison Stratton (Williams College, '28), was still living in 1892 in Branchport, New York.

In June, 1766, Richard Stratton sold to William Foster, blacksmith, 100-acre lot 15, drawn by house lot 7, "lying on or near Taylor's Crotch Brook," £20. That brook is what we call the "Hopper Brook," and its junction with Green River was long called Taylor's Crotch, from Samuel Taylor, of Charlemont, who first built mills there, where they have continued ever since. This William Foster married Richard Stratton's eldest daughter, Ruth, who was born in February, 1747. There are persons still living in town who remember "Aunt Ruth Foster," as she lived in her old age and poverty with her nephew, Cyrus Stratton, son of Deacon Ebenezer Stratton, and as at last she was assisted by the town. Richard Stratton's second daughter, Lucy, born July, 1753, married Seth Luce from Western, who bought 100-acre lot No. 3 in May, 1768, a rough lot well up on the side of Mount Prospect. Luce was a "joyner" by trade. His lot is still called the "Luce lot"; but it was sold to the Smedleys about 1812, and continued in their possession more than half a century. Ten children were born to these parents before they left the town, and were dismissed from the church, which both joined in 1780. Luce was often out as a private and also as a subordinate officer in the Revolutionary War, as the muster-rolls disclose to this day. He was born July 16, 1744, of Ebenezer and Sarah Luce, and had brothers Timothy and Ebenezer, and sister Sarah. Ebenezer Luce, whose wife was Sarah Stratton, lived for a time in Williamstown, and both united with the church here by letter in 1780, but they left no such impression on the town as did Seth and Lucy Luce. The sister, Sarah Luce, married Joseph Byam, of whom we shall hear more by and by.

The other children of Richard Stratton do not concern us particularly; but it may be worth the noting, that Abner was born Dec. 20, 1751, and Rachel and Phebe, twins, were born in August, 1756. It is more to the point to observe, that the three house lots, of which he first became possessed, and on the middle one of which he built his own fine house, were the only lots on either side of Main Street east of Chapel Hill to have houses built on them of much pretension either as to size or cost until the opening of the present century. Two possible exceptions to this statement might be made as to houses built in the last decade of the last century, namely, the brick house built on house lot 63 by Judah Williams, and so long occupied by the Nobles and the Coles; and the house on the opposite side of the Main Street built by Bissell Sherman. It is curious that that part of house lot 57, the only house lot that runs east and west, on which Bissell Sherman built this house, had been bought by Richard Stratton of Joseph Ballard, of New Salem, in March, 1762; one-eighth of this lot had been sold from off its western end in January, 1758, in some connection with the opening out of Water Street; and the remaining seven-eighths had passed through several hands, including Ballard's and Stratton's, when, in November, 1768, Jacob Meack sold to Ebenezer Cooley two acres from off the *east* end, reserving a roadway one rod wide "above the bank from the logway northward to accommodate the mill that is now standing, or mill hereafter to be built." This "one-rod road" is "Pork lane." Bissell Sherman, who was born in North Kingston, Rhode Island, Oct. 13, 1759, the very day the news of Wolfe's victory at Quebec reached North Kingston, came ultimately to own by much the most of house lot 57, and built his own two-story house (still standing) on about the middle point of it in 1796. The L part of this house is the old "regulation" house on 57, and is at least thirty years older than the main. It is characteristic of Bissell Sherman, who always seized the main chance, that when the carpenters then building the new meeting-house on the Square got short of lumber at one time in 1796, Sherman hired them off in a body to work on his new house. Under the circumstances he got them cheap.

But the two undoubtedly fine houses in this quarter of the town were the "Day" house built on house lot 54, and the "Noble" house built on house lot 58. Daniel Day came hither from Colchester not far from 1770, an enterprising farmer, and established himself on the fine lands on both sides of the line between Adams and Williamstown, just south of the Hoosac, and of the present village of Blackinton. He became very well-to-do, and raised a large family of nine children. He was generous, also, to his sister's children, a Mrs. Baker of Vermont, and Mary Baker was adopted by him. Some time before the close of the century, Day purchased house lot 54, and proceeded to build on it what was, for the times and circumstances, an elegant dwelling, so elegant, indeed, that it pecuniarily ruined him. Much of its ornamentation, both external and internal, was brought from Boston; and when his daughter Sophia was married in its parlor to James Sherman (Williams College, 1802), she was dressed, as she told her own girls in her old age, " Boston girls fashion" — white satin and all that. The father came naturally enough into financial straits, and sold his house and lot to Judge Daniel Dewey, and moved his family to Cazenovia, New York, where he kept a tavern for some time on the public square. Debts threw him again into difficulties, and James Sherman (his son-in-law) took the first mortgage on the public house, and temporarily relieved him. In his old age, he used to make journeys from "the West" to Williamstown and Colchester, in his own old-fashioned gig, and with his well-known sorrel horse. He died in Rome, New York, aged eighty-four. He was in the battle of Bennington. His house here became known as the "Dewey" house, and three generations of that prominent family dwelt in it; and it is now the home of one of the Greek-letter College Societies. Its entire interior was burnt in 1893, and elegantly rebuilt in 1894. Daniel Day's wife was Martha Isham; both united with the church here in 1806, and both were dismissed to the church in Cazenovia. Mrs. Day was sister of Mrs. Colonel Samuel Tyler.

The "Noble" house, on 58, was built in the early years of this century by Daniel Noble (Williams College, 1796), a son of David Noble, one of the early settlers. He was the first alumnus of the College to be placed on the Board of Trustees, and he was the treasurer of the College from 1814 till his death in 1830. He was a lawyer of ability, and commenced the practice of his profession in Adams, where he continued till 1811, when he returned to his native place. His house was not so fine as the Day house, nor so high between joints as the Sloan house; and tradition has it that his daughters cried with disappointment when they first saw the rooms, so inferior were they to what they had expected. But the house was a strikingly good one, and was occupied by the Noble family till past the middle of the century, when the estate was purchased by Joseph White, then treasurer of the College, was repaired and enlarged and beautified by him, and is still occupied by his family (1894). At the present time, there are two other noticeably fine residences on the plateau constituting the eastern end of our village ; namely, that built by the late Thomas Mole, and improved by its present owner, James White, who has been treasurer of the College since 1886; and the one of a quite novel pattern, long in process of construction, by Clarence M. Smith.

To return now to the struggling proprietors here during the autumn of 1761, we find from the minutes of a meeting, held at the place called " the Fort," September 24, of which Benjamin Simonds was moderator, and at which Richard Stratton was chosen clerk for the proprietors, that they had fallen into difficulties with Isaac Wyman, their former clerk; and that the main object of the meeting was to choose a committee " to sew [sue] the Proprietors Records Plan and Lift out of the Hands of Isaac Wyman the former Clerk." The committee chosen for this purpose were Gideon Warren, Benjamin Simonds, and Richard Stratton. Were ever the foundations of a New England village laid without a quarrel and a lawsuit ? Among other votes at this meeting, was one to pay Gideon Warren £2 5s., and Thomas Train 12s., "for Going after a minister," and another one, to appoint Josiah Horsford and Samuel Kellogg " to Hier a good orthodox Preachor."

One name of very considerable significance in the early history of this town, occurs, for the first time, in the Proprietors' Record just quoted, — that, namely, of Samuel Kellogg. From that date to this, the name has seldom been absent from the current records of the town and the church and the College. This Samuel Kellogg, son of Benjamin, was born in Old Hadley, June 9, 1734. He came to Williamstown from Canaan, Connecticut, where resided Benjamin Kellogg and Zebulon Robbins and others, who dabbled a great deal in real estate here, but never came to be permanent residents. Ebenezer Kellogg, a half-brother of this Samuel, and who, after the death of his wife without children, made Samuel's house his home to an extreme old age; Ebenezer Kellogg (Yale College, 1810), who was professor of ancient languages in the College from 1815 till 1844, and who had no children; and this Samuel, who left a large posterity, to say nothing at present of Charles and Nathaniel Kellogg, brothers, and those in the line of descent from them, — have made this name a notable one here in every generation, and in many relations.

It is noteworthy, that Samuel Kellogg received his first appointment at the hands of the proprietors, on a committee to hire a good Orthodox minister, because the New England Kelloggs, who believed themselves to be of Scotch descent, were certainly strict Puritans;

for Old Hadley, where this particular line of the Kelloggs in the person of their ancestor, Joseph, settled at the very outset, namely, in 1660, defended and concealed the English regicides, as all the world knows; and Benjamin Kellogg, father of our Samuel, born in Hadley, as was also his son, married into the family of Sedgwick, afterwards so distinguished in Berkshire, who were certainly in the line of Major-General Sedgwick, of Cromwell's army. Besides being Puritan Christians, they were usually prosperous farmers, and many of them were made deacons in their respective churches, selectmen, and minor military officers in His Majesty's colonial army. It is altogether probable from firm traditions in the family, although not provable, as in the case of Nehemiah Smedley and Josiah and William Horsford, that Samuel Kellogg was one of a party of quite young men from northwestern Connecticut, who came to the Hoosac to look out future homes for themselves during the lull between the last two French Wars, quite a number of whom, later, enlisted in a military company, and were sent by their colony to garrison West Hoosac Fort. At any rate, Kellogg came here to stay, and became a proprietor in 1761.

Although Kellogg bought and sold house lots and other lots in different parts of the town, particularly house lots 28 and 30, now, and long, a part of the Danforth estate, he selected for his farm and permanent home a section of lands in the eastern, and then wholly unoccupied part of the West Hoosac lay-out. The reason why that part had been so long neglected was, that the meadows along the Hoosac where it enters the town, and for some distance further, were low and swampy, and the higher lands sloping down to these from the base of Saddle Ball, were clayey and inclined to be wet. But the higher lands were naturally occupied first. Kellogg came to own, in a body, three of the fifty-acre lots of the first division, and several meadow lots, which here lie wholly on the south side of the stream. He paid Oliver Partridge, of Hatfield, £25 for No. 15, one of these three fifty-acre lots, in October, 1766. Benjamin Simonds and Oliver Partridge, Junior, signed this deed, as witnesses. His framed house of two stories, still standing *in situ*, and now owned, with the farm, by Fred. G. Smedley (Williams College, 1864), was built on No. 26, of the same division, which lay north of the road towards the river, while No. 15 and the rest of his uplands lay south of the road towards the mountain. There is no doubt that his first house was built on the higher ground south of the road, and that his clearings were first made there. His son, Samuel, born in 1766, used to say to persons still living, particularly to *his* son,

Giles B. Kellogg (Williams College, 1829), who is the unquestionable authority for many of these facts, that the forest was unbroken when his father began there, and that, when he himself was a lad, all that part of the farm lying between the house and the river was a spruce swamp, and the only way he could get through it was by jumping from one fallen tree to another.

The public roads in this part of the town, as they were early built and are still maintained, tell a striking tale to this day of the lowness of the land on the south of the Hoosac in this quarter, and of the difficulties in the way of anything like a straight road from the east end of our village to Fort Massachusetts. As soon as one crosses the bridge over Green River at that point, the road bends immediately to the right, in search of higher land for itself than any furnished by the Smedley meadows. After climbing the slight hill directly south of the Smedley house, the Stratton road continues due south a mile and a half, over high land, till it turns abruptly west, and strikes the Green River road at Blair's. But, pushing on from the Stratton road, still bending south in order to keep dry, the Adams road, when it comes opposite the Kellogg place, strikes the Luce road, another road straight south, parallel with Stratton road, "convening," like that, many of the fifty-acre lots of the first division, and, unlike that, in connection with the Paul road and its continuation, giving a southern and mainly upland way to North Adams. All these roads are old roads, going back nearly to the beginning of West Hoosac, formerly much traversed, now mostly abandoned, but destined, doubtless, to renovation and occupation.

Samuel Kellogg, after getting his home farm into some shape, possessed himself of another, a mile and a half to the southeast, reached by the Luce and Paul roads, and partly over the line in East Hoosac. It was afterwards called the "Loveland place," from a man of that name who lived on it and carried on a part of it on shares. Kellogg planted two apple-tree orchards on this place, and reserved on it a fine grove of sugar-maples, and used the rest, as did also his son after him, as pasturage for sheep and calves. The lot lay at the foot of Saddle Mountain. Shortly after locating his home lots, Samuel Kellogg found a wife in Chloe Bacon, daughter of Daniel Bacon, blacksmith, from Middletown, Connecticut, who, two years after this marriage (which took place on the 4th of March, 1764), located himself on Nos. 61 and 63 of the first fifty-acre division, which lay on the Blair road, and could be reached indifferently by the Luce road or by Green River road. A son of this Daniel Bacon, with the same name, was killed in the battle of Bennington, perhaps standing by the side of his brother-in-law, Samuel Kellogg, or by the side of his father's nearest neighbor, Absalom Blair; for they were all there in the same company, commanded by Captain Nehemiah Smedley. The information is direct and certain that Samuel Kellogg was an active patriot throughout the Revolution, and that he went to Boston several times as a member of the Committee of Safety, and on other business also pertaining to the colony. He was an enterprising and a leading man both in church and state. His name and that of his wife are on the earliest list of church members that has come down to us, — a list consisting of sixty-one members, twenty-four men and thirty-seven women, — who were members at the time of Rev. Mr. Swift's settlement in 1779.

Giles Bacon Kellogg, still living in extreme age and infirmity in Bennington, though his professional life was passed in Troy, a grandson of Samuel Kellogg, and one who enjoyed exceptional opportunities of learning about his grandfather, wrote as follows concerning him: "He was a Justice of the Peace prior to and during the Revolution. The mention of his being a Justice of the Peace reminds me that there was a tradition in the family that while he was Justice a gang of counterfeiters of money was arrested in the Hopper at the foot of Mount Saddle, on a process issued by him, who were betrayed by the smoke arising from their fires. I know there was a mysterious chest, kept locked or nailed up in the closet of the southeast chamber of our house, which was said to contain the tools taken from the counterfeiters and delivered to grandfather. I never heard what became of the counterfeiters, nor know what became of the tools." It may be added that this tradition of the counterfeiters has come down in other families, also, than the Kelloggs, particularly the Paul family. Alleged incidents connected with their trial and the testimony against them are repeated to this day. As Mr. Justice Kellogg died Sept. 2, 1788, when he was fifty-four years old, and as the first American silver coins were not issued till 1794, this story of the Hopper counterfeiters is considerably discredited by a comparison of dates, although it is possible they may have tried their hands to imitate the English shillings or the Pine-tree shillings of the Massachusetts colony.

Samuel Kellogg had a half-brother named Ebenezer, considerably younger than himself, who lived to a great age, who made his brother's house his home for many years, who outlived him, and who communicated to Giles B. Kellogg many facts of the earlier generations. He, too, was born in Hadley, married Filena Fuller, settled somewhere in the western part of Massachusetts; but, as he had no children, and his wife died early, he came, naturally enough, to lead the somewhat roving life that Giles B. Kellogg thus describes: "I remember him well. He continued at father's after grandfather died, and remained there as long as he lived. He was a man of no ordinary intelligence, in height above the common size, and well preserved in body and mind. He was a great hunter and fisherman, and claimed to be a skilful root-doctor. I have known him to leave father's house and be absent for a week at a time in the woods and mountains, hunting, fishing, and searching for roots." Further on in our task (if life be spared), we shall resume some account of the interesting and influential Kellogg family, and of the pioneers who settled beyond them on the eastern lines of Williamstown; but now we must go back to the strifes and struggles and physical difficulties of the first proprietors of West Hoosac.

March ye 11 — 1762 — whereas application is made unto me by five of ye proprietors of this township for calling a proprietors meeting they are therefore Notifyed & warnded to assembl themselves together at the dwelling house of Mr. Josiah Horsford in s'd town on monday ye 29 of this instant month at one of ye clock in ye afternoon then and there to act on or consider the following articles viz.

The action on these on that day was as follows: —

1. Voted & Chose Jonathan meachem moderator
2. Voted & Chose Nehemiah Smedley Surveyor of Highways
3. article of raising money to hire preaching tryed voted in ye Nagative
4. Chose for a commity to lay a road or renew ye road already allowed through this town towards fraimingham Richard Stratton Jonathan Meacham Asa Johnson commity
5. Voted to allow the following accounts

Mr. allin Curtises account	2£	5s	0d
thomas train	0	8	0
Ezekiel foster	0	2	8
micah Herienton	0	5	4
Isiah Horsford	1	2	8
gideon warrin	0	2	8
william Horsford	0	11	9
Jonathan meacham	0	4	0

The above s'd survaor & committy under oath

Test RICHARD STRATTON proprit Clark

The careful reader will note, at this point, how matters, public and private, in our incipient township, are working steadily towards the eastward in the local sense. No doubt, also, in the moral sense,

West Hoosac was striving to "orient itself." The first three or four proprietors' meetings were held in the very valley of the Hemlock Brook. The next three or four were held within the palisades of the fort, which stood considerably to the east, but still on the upper part of the slope leading down to the same brook; but now, by a long leap eastward, the proprietors are summoned to assemble at the house of "Mr. Josiah Horsford," that is, on house lot 42, that is, on the western slope of the second eminence, to crown which West College was built thirty years later. That house is still standing, — the small nucleus of a large house on the same site, — occupied by the Whitmans for three-quarters of a century, and now, after many alterations and additions, owned and dwelled in by Dr. L. D. Woodbridge.

The first action of the little propriety, in distinct and avowed reference to a neighboring one, is the vote of this meeting, in March, 1762, to lay or renew a road through this town "towards fraimingham." "Fraimingham" is Lanesboro. Its original proprietors in Framingham, Middlesex County, voted, in 1742, to call their township Richfield; but the earliest settlers, a dozen years later, called the place New Framingham, until in 1765, at the incorporation of the town, the General Court named it Lanesboro, undoubtedly at the instance of Francis Bernard, governor of Massachusetts 1760–69, out of compliment to the "lovely Lanesborough," as she was called, wife of the Earl of Lanesborough, who was extremely jealous of her, while both had much influence at the English Court. Looked at from one point of view, the change of name was a disadvantage to the little settlement on the uppermost Housatonic; for "Framingham" is a contraction, drawn in England, of the old Saxon words, *Fremdling Heim*, that is, Stranger's Home. There is still in the English county of Suffolk a town named Framlingham, in Norfolk another called Framingham, and in Northumberland a third denominated Framlington, — which is of the same derivation, except that the old German "ton" takes the place in the compound of the equally old German "heim"; and the good old English name, brought down through an early Massachusetts town, might have stimulated, had it been continued, some historical research on the part of some Lanesboro people, as well as have comforted new settlers there in the successive decades.

Two or three new names encounter us in the old record of the proprietors' meeting in March, 1762. Jonathan Meacham is one of these. He was cousin to James Meacham. Both were from New Salem. Both had been soldiers in the last French War, and had passed through this town, down the Hoosac, on their way to Lake George or Crown Point. James Meacham was a "centinel" in Captain Nathaniel Dwight's company, hastily mustered after the battle of Lake George, in September, 1755. Both were original members of the church in Williamstown, and James was one of the two original deacons; but there were these differences: except on account of his conspicuous sympathy and co-operation with Shays's men in 1787, James's character and conduct appear to have escaped serious animadversion on the part of his neighbors, while Jonathan came under the censure and public discipline of the church in a manner hereafter to be described. James left a large posterity, which has continued to be identified with the town until the present time, while, so far as the record goes, Jonathan left none. His wife, Thankful· Rugg, it is believed, was sister to James's wife, Lucy Rugg; and James continued all his life upon one farm, bought Aug. 5, 1761, and died lamented, in his own house, July 28, 1812. Jonathan lived in several different parts of the town, and finally removed to distant parts, it is not known whither, but undoubtedly into Vermont, which drew off many an old settler after the Revolution.

Both the Meachams bought lands here for new homes before they left New Salem, their old home. Jonathan's first purchase was house lot 43, bought of Dr. Seth Hudson, for £5, Oct. 2, 1760. It had been then several times bought and sold, but not yet builded on. Meacham's deed is witnessed by Noah Grant and Jedidiah Smedley, and it was acknowledged before William Brattle, of Boston. Meacham built his first house on the front of 43, and very near its western line, of which fact we should not have been so definitely informed, if it had not been for the construction of a tennis-court, in 1888, on the spot, which disclosed pieces of brick and other unmistakable signs of an old house. This tennis-court lay a little to the east of the present Chi Psi building, which itself occupies the front of house lot 41, close up to its eastern line. As the builders of West College, in 1790, found it impossible, on account of the underlying limestone, to dig a well in its near neighborhood, and as Meacham's house was only a dozen rods from West College, it is to be presumed that Meacham was obliged to bring his water from some distance, probably from the copious spring that still gushes out near the foot of Spring Street; and it is to be presumed further, that, as he soon came to own house lot 45 also, he built the house on 45 (quite near to this spring), the hearthstone of which was discovered in 1889, while digging the cellar of the house of Professor Bliss Perry. This hearthstone is now in Clark Hall.

Even if this original house on 45 were not builded by Jonathan
Meacham, it is evident enough that it was put up by somebody
there for the sake of easy access to this spring; because, so far,
every dwelling on the house lots had been placed on their fronts,
directly on Main Street, on the one side or the other; but this house
on 45 was located about seventy rods from Main Street, and as near
to the Walden Spring, which is on house lot 47, as it could be placed
on house lot 45.   But even this moderate proximity to the spring
did not ultimately satisfy Meacham, provided he was the builder of
that house; for he certainly erected afterwards, on house lot 49, at
a spot still further from Main Street, and almost on the very edge
of the College Spring, which is about fifteen rods east of the Wal-

AUTHOR'S HOUSE.
Built in 1872.

den Spring, another house, the cavity of whose cellar is still dis-
cernible just west of the big rock there, a present depression that
was a large open hole a few years ago, when it was filled in to
accommodate the students' ball-field.

Jonathan Meacham had evidently sterling qualities both for peace
and war, but was as evidently restless in relation to his home.
After living some time by the College Spring, he moved upon Bee
Hill, where the Hickocks now are, and have been for more than a
century.   He was often out during the Revolutionary War, — the
last date that has been noticed was in October, 1780, in Captain
Israel Harris's company of sixty-three officers and men, all from
Williamstown.   He mortgaged to Albany parties, in July, 1769, his

house lots 43 and 45, to secure a debt of £89, New York money, which was paid in 1772, — £102, principal and interest. Under date of Feb. 13, 1779, in the first entry made by Rev. Mr. Swift, in the church-record book, occur these words, "Voted that Sampson Howe and Nathaniel Sanford be a Committee to wait on Jonathan Meacham to inquire the reason of his absenting himself from Communion."

House lot 43, on which Meacham built his first house, is the lot on which the writer's own house has stood since 1872, which is fairly represented, when new, by the annexed wood-cut; the eastern line of 43 runs along by the lattice-work under the piazza of the house; consequently it bisects north and south the new chemical laboratory, which was finished for Professor Mears in the summer of 1892; and West College, while it stands wholly in Main Street, would be bisected in the same direction by the continuation of the line dividing 43 and 45. On the last-named lot, directly in front of the writer's house, was erected the same summer, by John B. Gale (Williams College, 1842), a dwelling for Professor Spring. The north front of that lot has been cumbered since 1847 by a small college dormitory, originally with two recitation-rooms on the lower floor, in one of which Professor I. N. Lincoln and in the other Professor A. L. Perry heard their first college recitations at the same hour in September, 1853. A tolerable picture of Kellogg Hall, with Mount Williams and Bald Mountain in the distance, will here be greeted, perhaps, with pleasure by many, especially as its speedy demolition is already projected. A physical laboratory to be used by Professor Lefavour, and to stand wholly on 45, and a biological laboratory to be occupied by Professor S. F. Clarke, and to stand wholly on 43, were projected and erected and completed by the bounty of Trustee Thompson.

Asa Johnson was another name first met with in the "Propriety" record of 1762. He came here, like many another young man, from Canaan, Connecticut; for we read that "Asa Johnson and Thankful, his wife, had Hannah born in Canaan, 29 Oct. 1760." We shall have to deal with many Johnsons in the course of this our task, but this Asa seems to be apart from the rest, with no signs of near relationship, and with some personal qualities discriminating him from them. He seems to have settled pretty soon after he came on first-division fifty-acre lot 37, its eastern end abutting on Green River, and its western running up on Stone Hill, about half-way between James Meacham's and Taylor's Crotch; for in March, 1764, he sold to Jacob Brown "one sartain fifty acre lot 37 that I now live on with the house and barn," etc. He sold, the year before, to " White David " Johnson, second-division fifty-acre lot No. 7, for £19, which White David cultivated as the house lot of " Stone Hill Farm " till after the opening of this century. He sold, also in 1764, meadow lot No. 1 for £5, " said meadow lot lyeth joining on the Township called East Hoosuck," to " Ephraim Selah." Notwithstanding these and other sales of property, including one to Benjamin Simonds for £37 10s., Asa Johnson could not get out of debt. Albany was then the chief market of the settlers for purchasing supplies. Robert

KELLOGG HALL.
Built in 1847.

Henry was then a merchant of Albany. Johnson was sued by Henry in September, 1766, and judgment found against him in £141 11s. 11d. debt, and £3 7s. costs. Samuel Kellogg and Richard Stratton and Jonathan Meacham took oath to appraise the real estate for satisfying this execution.

In the mean time Johnson had built a house and made a home on the county road, the extension of the North Street northward, between house lots 2 and 36, a six-rod road at right angles to Main Street, and from the northern end of the house lots (themselves bounded there by a two-rod road, which was never completed as intended) a four-rod road running north to the river and beyond. Just where the six-rod road contracted to the four-rod road, on the west side of the latter, and on the north side of the two-rod road, two acres and a half were laid out in October, 1762, as a burying-ground for the Propriety. It was three-eighths of a mile north of the Square, on the left hand of the road leading to Bennington, on the southern edge of first-division fifty-acre lot 35. It was used for some years as a burial-place, both before and after the formal bounding of the lot by a committee consisting of Samuel Kellogg and Thomas Dunton; in the warning for a meeting to be holden on the 19th of April, 1762, at the house of Mr. Josiah Horsford, the last article was, "To see if the propriators will clear any more of the burying place, or allow Mr. Johnson anything for the work he has done in the burying place," which article was voted to be "dropped" in the meeting itself; the place was difficult of access, on account of a very steep pitch in the clay road about one-eighth of a mile south of the lot 35, which obstacle to travel caused long after-wards the abandonment of that part of the county road in favor of another running down the Hemlock Brook, and coming back into the old road about fifty rods south of the bridge over the Hoosac; and how inaccessible the graveyard was from the west by the narrow road designed to flank the northern ends of the house lots, and actu-ally flanking them to this day about half of the way, any one may see by looking up the present rocks by the old poplars in the line of the Bulkley road east.

In the warrant for the next meeting is found the article, "To see if ye propriators will alter the burying yard"; and in the action on the same is found the clause, "Voted to alter the burying yard." Then comes the return of Kellogg and Dunton : —

Whereas We the Subscribers being chosen a commity to establish the bounds of the burying place and we have bounded the Same as follows beginning at a Stake at the North end of the Six Rods Highway where the four Rods Highway first Enters the first fifty acre Lot Nom^r 35 Runing thirteen rods and the third part of a rod North on the West side of S^d Highway from thence thirty rods West to a Stake & Stones from thence South thirteen rods and one third of a rod to a Stake Standing on the North Side of the two rod road that runs at the North end of House Lots from thence thirty rods east on the North Side of S^d Highway to the first bounds containing two acres and a half of Land bounded this 26 — day of October — 1762.

But nothing could make this yard for the dead — God's acre — accep-table to the majority of the proprietors. It was too inaccessible. Another was not long after selected, lying upon the Main Street, just west of Hemlock Brook, which has continued the principal cemetery of the town till the present time; and many of the bodies laid in the first ground were removed to this.

Asa Johnson evidently did not get on well pecuniarily. He was still in debt to Robert Henry. He sold off to William Horsford, for £9, in October, 1767, ten acres more of his fifty-acre lot 35, adjoining the burial-ground; and in 1770 he sold off the rest, and migrated to Vermont. He sold to Robert Henry, "merchant of Albany," for £45, twelve and one-half acres, including his dwelling-house and out-buildings. The plat is described in the deed as "bounded northerly on land of said Robert Henry, westerly on William Horsford's land, southerly on the burial yard, and easterly on the County Road." Going from here to what is now Rutland, Vermont, his family was one of the first four white families in that town. His daughter, Chloe, was born there, Oct. 3, 1770, the third white child born in Rutland, the two first having been born within the ten days preceding. His house here, which was well built, stood in its place by the old road for a century. The present writer remembers it well. It was occupied successively by Solomon Woolcot and Samuel Tyler. The old road, though long disused, can still be traced most of the way north to the spot where the new one joined it; and at the northern end of the part disused, a new road admirably constructed has lately been put in along the line of the old one, to his own elegant mansion crowning the height of the hill, by Eugene M. Jerome (Williams College, 1867).

The years 1762 and 1763 were pivotal in the history of West Hoosac. Not far from twenty-five young men were actually clearing up their lots, and fulfilling the other conditions prescribed by the General Court, under which the lots were to become their own in fee simple. They were stalwart young men, and they were looking forward. Those actual settlers even, who had had a past, like Isaac Wyman, for example, and still more those prominent men to the eastward, who had bought lots on speculation, or to encourage the settlement as a barrier against French and Indians, like Oliver Partridge, had, by this time, sold out and withdrawn from the field. Richard Stratton is almost the only instance of an elderly man, who had come and come to stay, — to cast in his lot for good or ill with the actual founders of a town. The proprietors' meetings during these two years were frequent and significant. The debates were earnest, and they concerned the future. They related mainly, (1) To clearing out and making passable the Main Street (especially towards its western end), and the two streets at right angles with this leading north and south from the Square, all which had been laid out in 1750; (2) To laying out new streets in the right places, so as "to convean" the purchasers of the outlots of the several classes; (3) To the raising of money by local taxation for these and other needful ends; (4) To the procuring and maintenance of "a good orthodox minister"; and (5) To getting into practicable communication with their neighbors both to the east and south.

We will now give a few votes, as specimens merely, under each of these heads, during those two years. We will also in this connection note the places of the meetings, and the names of any proprietors mentioned, who became prominent. Two of these meetings were held at the house of "Mr. Benjamin Simonds." As the meetings had been pretty constantly working their way to the eastward of Hemlock Brook, and as two or three of those just preceding these convened at the house of Josiah Horsford on the second eminence, this cannot mean that the proprietors were called on to cross that brook and climb up the steep pitch to the west of it to Simonds's house on No. 22, probably then the farthest house to the west on Main Street, and certainly further west than any meeting was held before; and when we come to look carefully, we find that Simonds had sold No. 22 to Joshua Simonds in 1760, and had begun the year before to buy up the house lots on the south side of Main Street, from Hemlock Brook up to the level of the Square, — buying No. 5 in 1759, 7 in 1762, 9 in 1762 also, and 3 in 1764. He ultimately placed his own-built house on No. 3, in which he kept an inn for several years, the site of the present elegant house of Henry Sabin; but 5 and 7 and 9 each had its house in 1762, and the proprietors had met more than once with Seth Hudson on his then No. 9; so that, these later meetings with Simonds were certainly east of the brook, and on one of his recent purchases. He is designated as an "innholder" in December, 1763, the first of that craft in West Hoosac, and prominent as such for many years, the necessity for the "landlord" being the current now beginning to set strongly from Connecticut into Vermont.

"Voted, to chuse a commity to remove all incumbrances out of the main street croos street or private Roads that obstruct common traveling." "Voted, to clear or dig to make comfortable passing on the west end of ye main street" [Danforth Hill]. "Voted, to clear a road through this town towards fraimingham for comfortable carting." "Voted, to clear a road to the east town for a cart to get along." "Voted, to clear a road from the east end of main street by weeb's [Derrick Webb's] to the mouth of green river." "Voted, to have preaching for the future." "Chose thomas dunton asa Jonson Samuel Kellogg commity to provide a minister." "Voted, to raise twelve shillings on each propriators rite to defray the charge of preaching." "Voted, asa Jonson's account of Nine days £3 12s. for going after a minister." "Voted Samuel Kelloggs account for going for a minister £3 14s." "Voted to give mr warner a call to preach on probation — 2 — chose Nehemiah Smedley Benjamin Simonds Derick weeb commity to treat with mr warner or provide another minister if need be." "Voted a tax of one pound on each rite" (19 April, 1762). "Voted twelve shillings on each rite" (10 March, 1763).

Several of the proprietors failed to respond to these lawful levies on their "rites," and the rights were accordingly sold at public auction; for example, Benjamin Simonds bought house lot 2, for £4, William Horsford bought house lot 4, for £4 12s., and Isaac Searle bought house lot 8, for £2. Samuel Kellogg and Zebulon Robbins were other purchasers at this "Publick Vandue," as Richard Stratton announced it, he continuing to be proprietors' clerk till 1765, when the town was incorporated. Lands were abundant in West Hoosac, and consequently cheap. Ever after the date last mentioned, and even somewhat before, the lands of Vermont came into competition with those on the upper Hoosac, and tended to make the latter cheaper still. All kinds of timber but pine were plenty in the town, and the proprietors voted themselves the "liberty to cut timber on the undivided land"; but the pines were more precious, and were zealously watched, — "voted and Chose Joseph ballard Josiah Horsford John Smedley commity to prosecute those men that have cut the pine timber in this township that have No rite in s⁴ township." The pines were localized on the northeastern boundaries of the town, and sixty-three pine lots were soon laid out, one for each owner of a house lot; most of these were on Broad Brook or near it, but eight of them may be said to have been on the Hoosac, Nos. 7 and 8 at the junction of the brook and river.

Whether it was as a member of the committee to prosecute trespasses on the pine lands, or in the exercise of native Connecticut sagacity as a private person, John Smedley, eldest of the five brothers, sons of Samuel, of Litchfield, early perceived the possibilities of both land and water at the junction of Broad Brook and Hoosac River. There were two pine lots, and parts of five meadow lots, the latter partially covered with pines also, in the north angle between the streams. He had noticed a considerable fall in Broad

Brook, just above the point where the bridge now crosses it, on the road to Bennington; and in June, 1763, he asked, in due and legal form, "If the proprietors will grant John Smedley liberty to Set up a Sawmill upon the brook called broad brook also to carry the water acrost the highway on his own cost to the common land Lying North of the meadow Lots nom^s thirty nine forty and forty one also to see if the proprietors will grant to the S^d John Smedley two acres and an half between S^d meadow Lots & the highway that goes to pownal to accommidate S^d Sawmill said land to be reducted out of his next draft or pitch of Land also to chuse a commity to Lay out S^d land on S^d Smedleys cost." A month later, the proprietors "voted John Smedley liberty to build a Sawmill on broad brook and to carry the water acrost the highway on his own cost also two acres and an half of land to acomidate s^d Sawmill S^d land to be Reducted out of his next draft or pitch of Land voted Richard Sutton derick weeb Jonathan Meacham commitee to Lay out the Land to accomidate S^d mill to be done on S^d Smedley's cost."

Here we have the interesting history of the second (even if not the first) sawmill in this township. Probably a dam had been thrown across the Green River by this time, at the lowest of the three falls, at the east end of the southeastern tier of house lots, where there has been a dam ever since, to which access was early given by "Pork lane," now dignified by the town as Bingham Street, and a sawmill located there. At any rate, Smedley soon had his mill agoing lively. It stood right on the bank of the Hoosac, into which his waste water fell easy, and its old timbers have been seen in place within fifty years by Ripley Cole, a reputable living citizen of the White Oaks; and the writer himself has seen immensely wide pine boards sawn at this mill, with which Smedley sheathed his own house, built on the bank above, along which now run the tracks of the Fitchburg Railroad. Those boards were then, doubtless, a century old, — probably more, — and were fastened to the studding by large, hand-wrought nails, both boards and nails wrenched and twisted by time and exposure. This house is figured on Coffin's map of Williamstown, 1843, as standing on pine lot No. 7, about equidistant from the Hoosac and the Broad. Smedley came to own both the pine lots there, parts of several meadow lots, and what he himself described as the "common land" north of the latter. He carried his water from brook to mill, about eighty rods, along a little channel dug by the north side of the "highway," still visible all the way, till it came near a steep rise then and now in the highway, when, as authorized, he "crost the highway," and took his water around the hill, on descending ground, to his primitive mill-race on the river. The sluiceway across the road is just where it was dug 130 years ago, and a little water still drizzles along the entire channel and across, under the tiny bridge, and disperses itself in the green meadow on the south of the road.

As it was with the pines, so also was it with the white oaks. They, too, were localized. They were wholly in the northeast cor-ner of the township, wholly north of the Hoosac, and almost wholly east of Broad Brook. There were almost literally none in the other parts of the town. The writer has heard an old woodsman declare that there was not a single white-oak tree within three miles of Greylock. Next after the pine lots, — which was the sixth division of lands among the proprietors of house lots, these constituting the first division, the meadow lots the second, the fifty-acre lots at the North Part being the third, at the South Part the fourth, and the 100-acre lots the fifth, — the sixty-three oak lots were laid out. There was a pretty strong desire to possess one or more of these, either by allotment or subsequent purchase, on account of the utility and durability of white-oak timber, especially for the sills of build-ings. There is good evidence, at least in one case, of such timbers being hauled, for such use, three miles or more into the Hopper. More than half of these oak lots abut on the western line of the present town of Clarksburg, and that entire line is covered by them; and the rest are scattered on or near Broad Brook, and between or among small groups of the pine lots. The oak lots were the seventh division. The eighth were sixty-acre lots. The ninth and last were "pitches," so-called, each owner of a house lot being authorized to lay out for himself, on any of the still undivided lands, thirty acres, in one or two or three pieces, as he chose. Even after these pitches were all located, there remained in the outskirts of the town, mostly on steep slopes of mountains in the south and west, considerable patches of undivided land. These were afterwards sold, if any one wished to purchase, by the Selectmen. A land-grabber of that period, named Ephraim Seelye, got most of these into his hands, and then peddled them out to a profit. He owned also, at one time and another, wide stretches of the best lands. It was said of him, by one of his quick-witted neighbors, that, had he been in the place of our Lord when Satan offered all the kingdoms of the world and the glory of them, he would have exclaimed, without a minute's hesitation, "I'll take it, I will!"

All that northeast corner of the town north of the Hoosac, and on both sides of the Broad, has been called, time out of mind, the

"White Oaks." It is a happy designation, and is to be presumed coeval with the settlement of the town. As "Broad Brook" is so named in the records the first time the stream is referred to, and as "Stone Hill" received that appellation officially as early as 1762, and as "Green River" was so called at least as early as that, it is pleasant to remember that the marked things here that needed naming, the things close at hand and striking, were well named at the very first; because

"The past will always win
A glory from its being far!"

The "Sand Spring," which is the jewel of the White Oaks, and which was naturally so called at the outset, because the warmish water gurgles up through innumerable little hemispheres of sand, and makes the bottom of the spring, to one gazing down through the depth of clear water, look like a gigantic ant-hill, itself a hemisphere made up of countless smaller ones. The first person known to live on the Sand Spring lot, which was a pine lot, was John Smedley, 2d, who married Hepzibah Philips in 1786; and the first person known to claim curative properties for the water, provision for bathing in which was very early made, and has never been intermitted, was old Aaron Smedley, his uncle, born March 9, 1750, who, though a land-owner at one time in Williamstown like all his brothers, became a sort of vagrant hunter in Vermont, and whose eczema (as he asserted) was always helped by a bath in the Sand Spring water.

The population in that part of the town was as respectable at first, and perhaps as independent, as that in the other parts, although much of the land there is stony, and more is sandy. Old John Smedley, born Jan. 4, 1731, did not borrow leave to dwell in plenty by his sawmill, where he reared a family of eight daughters; Ephraim Seelye, with a choice of lands of his own in every quarter of the town, fixed his permanent home at the junction of the "North Hoosac road" with the "Simonds road," as both were voted to be called by the town in 1891; Benjamin Simonds himself, before the outbreak of the Revolution, left his "inn" in the straggling village, which he had done more than any one else to build up, and built a much larger hostelry in the White Oaks on what is now named the River-Bend Farm, where he lived and died, rearing his seven daughters to match those of his neighbor to the north, John Smedley; and Jonathan Bridges from Colchester, Connecticut, early bought the fine farm on the North Hoosac road, still owned by his great-grandson, Charles E. Bridges, and, marrying Prudence Simonds, born Dec. 4, 1763, brought up a family that has brought credit to the White Oaks ever since. His youngest daughter, Lucy Bridges Smedley, is yet living in town, well on in her eighties, and well established in the respect and affection of her children and children's children.

But the fact is well known, and the reasons of it also, that a very different class of people gradually inserted themselves between the hills and into the dells of the White Oaks. Some lands were very cheap there, and others in the rougher districts could be squatted on with impunity. The line of Vermont borders the entire district on the north, and the line of New York is only a little way to the west; and it was easy for fugitives from debt, and from petty crimes too, to find a refuge in a bordering state, and in physical conditions so favorable to temporary concealment and permanent harborage. Negro slavery was not legally abolished in the state of New York until 1836. Considerable numbers of colored people from that state percolated into the White Oaks, and perpetuated themselves there. Indian-Dutch families, like the Orcombreits, came also. All sorts, and colors, and conditions crept in; low-downs from Massachusetts were not wanting: these all intermarried, or, at least, intermingled; and the result, in course of time, was a very curious and a morally obstinate state of society. Begging in the street, and thieving everywhere, became hereditary features in a number of families. The state of things over there rested, more or less, on the conscience of the churches over here in every generation ; various religious and educational efforts of a spasmodic nature were made from time to time for the benefit of the people. About 1865, Professor Albert Hopkins began on a systematic and persistent plan for the moral elevation of the White Oaks, by means of a local church and Sunday-school, in the execution of which, and in its continuation since his death, the brothers Woodbridge (Williams College, 1872 and 1873) and the family of the late B. F. Mather have been prominent and patiently efficient, and great good has been accomplished ; and, while during the last decade, the population of that section has rapidly increased, owing to the operations of the Fitchburg Railroad there, the current year has witnessed the hopeful beginning under Methodist auspices of vigorous religious efforts, of which the "Clarke Chapel" is the centre.

Before quitting the present topic, it will be proper to refer to the "Line House," so-called, the last house in the White Oaks, as one passes into Vermont by the river road. The division line between the states, which is Hazen's Line of 1741, passes directly through this house. It is a convenient site for a house, as Rattlesnake Brook flanks the place at short distance, furnishing both occupants and travellers abundant water. A certain Esquire Ware was the first known dweller and tavern-keeper there, after whom the brook was sometimes named " Ware's Brook "; Ephraim Seelye, Junior, whose wife was Ann Bridges, lived there a long time, and kept a tavern, as did also " Vane " Danforth, whose strange history may confront us later; and Charles D. Sabin, Jesse's son, died there, Dec. 27, 1841, aged thirty-four. On account of the house being situated in two states, and bearing, at least, a semi-public character, it was an early and frequent resort for clandestine marriages, — Mr. Justice-of-the-Peace Danforth (for one) being happy to *solemnize* that rite for Massachusetts parties in a room in the north end of the house, understood to be under the jurisdiction of the state of Vermont, whose commission as Justice he bore. Gradually, for this and other reasons, the house came to bear a questionable reputation. Since the liquor laws of Massachusetts have been stringent, and, of course, divergent from those of Vermont, the place has been noted for the illegal sale of intoxicants. The house, at present, carries a well-painted and sleek-repaired exterior, but passers-by, rarely, if ever, see the front door open, and those who prize character and good name most, are least likely to be seen at the back door by day or night.

It must be borne in mind as we study the present paragraph, that the committee of the General Court, laying out the limits of the town in 1749, prepared a rude plan of it, as did also the committee of 1739, and the proprietors, from the first, had a parchment copy stretched upon a bit of board, on which a few of the main roads were provisionally put down, but the proprietors had the right, practically, to build all the roads as and where they chose. Thus the plan contemplated two roads, each exactly parallel with the Main Street, along the northern and southern ends of the house lots; but the proprietors only built one-half of the proposed road on the north, and none at all on the south. There seems to have been sketched out on the plan, also, a road from Taylor's Crotch to the old Deming place, where the present Potter road joins the Ashford road. Richard Stratton and Jonathan Meacham and Asa Johnson were chosen, May 15, 1762,

a commity to renew the road towards fraimingham & to make alteration if we thought best We have therefore faithfully attended the business and we find according to the best of our Judement the Road must go on the West side of Stone Hill we begin at the South end of the cross Street & Keep the Road till we come to the Northwest corner of the lot Nom^b 9 fr' division then runing almost west acroos a corner of the Lot Nom^r 41 and then a little way near South in the Lot Nom^r 42 — the westerly side of the marked trees with one chop in the mark & on common Land till we come to the Northwest corner of the Lot Nom^r 46 — then keep the Road allowed on the plan by that Lot then Runing near Southeast the east side of the marked trees as afores^d acroos the Lots Nom^r 48 fr' division & nom^r 7 second di^v to the Northwest corner of the Lot Nom^r 8 second division. then runing the same course acroos the Lots Nom^r 30 & 28 — to a beach tree the Northwest corner of the Lot Nom^r 27, Standing on the former Road then Keep that Road as on the plan to the Southwest corner of the Lot Nom^r 53 where the Road comes in from the west [Sloan road] then runing South about one degree east acrost five Lots Nom^rs 54 — 55 — 56 — 57 — 58 and so by the marked trees on the lane of land that Lyeth along there till we come to the old Road and we think it not best to Lay it any farther at present.

Thus was early established the present Stone Hill road, and no change has been made in it for 130 years, except that a little part between the Woodcock road and the present Hemlock road was discontinued a few years ago, by town authority. It seems likely, however, to be reopened again shortly by the same authority. Two roads, in general parallel with this, now lead from the north village to a common junction in the centre of the south village; namely, the Green River road on the east, and the Hemlock road on the west. The latter was built about 1827, under the supervision of the elder Keyes Danforth. The former is but the gradual continuation up the Green River of the original Water Street, from Main Street to the mill privilege, whose story has been given already. When this committee made a point, in 1762, of "the southwest corner of the lot number 53, where the road comes in from the west," they marked the site, for all time, of the village of South Williamstown, a small spot of earth that has played its part well (as we shall see) from that time to this, in its varied relations.

In July, 1763, the proprietors are legally warned to "assemble themselves together at the place called the Schoolhouse in said township." This is the first reference to any such building. It is very doubtful whether any school of any kind had yet been opened in the town. There are votes a plenty in all these years in reference to getting a minister, or hiring preaching, or paying some committee or other for "going for" a minister; but no vote as yet about a school-teacher, or till now about a place for a school. The reason is obvious: the children to the first settlers, born in the hamlet itself, of which there were then seven or eight, five of whom were Benjamin Simonds's children, were not yet of school age; and while a few of these settlers brought older children with them, born elsewhere, most of them were young men bringing hither their brides. About this time, however, new proprietors came in, like John Newbre, for example, who lived just west of the second burying-ground, and very likely some of these had children requiring school privileges; and at any rate, we may fairly infer that the desire to procure a minister while there was no place for him to preach in, co-operated with the now-felt necessity for a school, to cause the erection of a building "called the Schoolhouse," which might serve (and did serve) both purposes. It is almost an accident that gives us certain knowledge of its location and character.

It was a log building of some size, and stood near the southwest corner of house lot 36, which had been originally reserved for the first minister, and which Whitman Welch sold, in 1767, to Josiah Horsford, for £25; and its location on the minister's lot, though back from its frontage on Main Street, where it might be supposed the minister would wish to place his own dwelling, indicates its purpose as a preaching-place, while it was also "called" the Schoolhouse. With one exception, when they met at the house of William Horsford, on house lot 44, where the president's house now stands, the proprietors uniformly held their meetings at this schoolhouse for several years; and public worship was held in it, whenever there was any, until the first rude meeting-house was built, 30 × 40, in 1768. The log building acquired a certain sort of sanctity thereby, which was never wholly lost as long as it remained standing. Its location was on North Street, a few rods back from Main Street, and in all probability it stood between the present "Laundry" of the Greylock Hotel, and the rear of the main structure. It may probably have been taken down on the erection in front of its site of the original "Mansion House," which was burned down in October, 1871; and its successor as a schoolhouse was certainly put up a little southwest across Main Street on the line between house lots 1 and 3, and quite on the edge of the street.

A circumstance that will commemorate forever the old log schoolhouse of West Hoosac was the assembling within it of the pious women of Williamstown on the afternoon of Aug. 16, 1777, to pray for the safety and victory of their fathers and brothers and kinsfolk in the battle of Bennington, then raging. The sharp and credible tradition is, that there were not men enough left in the entire town "to put out a fire." The boom of cannon to the northward was occasionally heard by the participants while the meeting was in progress; their fears were deepened by the sight of women and children in wagons and on foot, with their little valuables snatched up, hurrying past towards places of safety from Bennington and Pownal; and their hearts were filled to the full with gratitude when, in the edge of the Saturday evening, a swift horseman, said to have been sent by Major Isaac Stratton, of South Williamstown, from the field of fight, rode past the schoolhouse into the anxious hamlet, announcing a great victory, and so breaking up a unique prayer-meeting that had lasted for hours without intermission. These simple paragraphs are being written Aug. 16, 1892. It falls on a Tuesday, 115 years after the swift revulsion of feeling in the log schoolhouse.

The moderators of the various meetings of the proprietors, from the time they began to assemble in the schoolhouse, whence on one occasion they adjourned to the house of Nehemiah Smedley opposite across the "Square" on house lot No. 1, were William Horsford, John Newbre, Samuel Kellogg, Josiah Horsford, Titus Harrison, John Smedley, Ephraim Seelye, Samuel Payn, and Richard Stratton. The last-named continued to be "Proprietor's Clerk," and as such warned out all the meetings and authenticated their proceedings by his signature, until Dec. 3, 1763, when William Horsford was chosen clerk, and continued such till after West Hoosac became Williamstown in 1765. Some of the votes in this interval are of special interest: for example merely, April 16, 1764, "voted to build a bridge over green river by Isaac Stratton"; Sept. 27, 1764, "voted to build a bridge over green river at the east end of the town Street"; same day, "voted also taylor's crotch and ten acres of land for the privilege of a mill"; Dec. 3, 1764, "voted Nine Shillings on each rite to build the bridge over green river"; March 6, 1765, "votted there be Nine Shillings of money Raised on Eaich Proprietors Right to Soport the Gospel"; and April 12, 1765, "Votted that the Proprietors will Recawl the vote that Hath Ben Past to Sequester the Land on the North Side of the Greate River [Hoosac] and Lay out the Same in two Divisions and Left it to the Dischression of the Commetres to Lay out the Pine Lots as they Shall think Best Votted that the Second Division of Land on the North Side of the Greate River Shall be Sized both in Quantity and Quallity."

The enterprising proprietors were largely occupied during the two years preceding the incorporation of the town, (1) in laying out their roads "to conveau" the different parts of the town and the successive divisions of their lands; (2) in selecting and surveying and distributing the fifth, sixth, and seventh divisions, namely, the 100-acre lots, the pine lots, and the oak lots, each drawn in sixty-three parts; (3) in determining what portions (if any) of their territory "to sequestor" for the common use of the proprietors;

(4) in sending some one or more of their number on repeated, and for the most part futile, missions "to hier a minister," though they negatived a proposition to call "Mr. Strickland on probation"; and lastly, (5) in selling off at "publick vandue" for what they could get the lots on which the legally assessed "rates" had not been paid. For instance, March 10, 1763, Benjamin Simonds bought in this way house lot No. 2, for £4; William Horsford bought house lot 4, for £4 12s.; Isaac Searle bought house lot No. 8, for £2; same bid off second-division fifty-acre lot, "drew in favour of house lot No. 30," for £2 5s.; and Samuel Kellogg bought half of first-division fifty-acre lot No. 27, for £1 4s.

The money accounts passed upon at nearly every meeting of the proprietors, which were not otherwise valid for collection, are at this late day curious and instructive. Let us note those validated in public meeting May 21, 1765, remembering that the colonial pound was just three-fourths of the English pound, namely, $3.63.

	£	s	d
Richard Stratton to 10 Days Laying out Land	1	10	0
William Horsford to Billiting Mr. Hubbel one week	0	6	0
Ephraim Seelye 9 Days Laying out Land	1	7	0
Samuel Smedley Billiting the Surveyor [Hubbel] Six Days	0	5	2
Jonathan Meaicham Eight Days and a half Laying out Land	1	5	6
Jonathan Kilborn to 2 list of Assessment	0	4	0
Josiah Horsford to 8 Days Laying out Land	1	4	0
Asa Johnson to Laying out Land 2 Days and a Half	0	7	6
Samuel Kellogg 5 Days Laying out Land	1	15	0
John Newbre to Billitting the Surveyor 8 Days and a Half	0	7	6
Samuel Kellogg one Rate Bill and 2 Notifycations	0	4	0
Titus Harrison to keeping Mr. Hubbel's horse three weeks &c.	1	1	0
Nehemiah Smedley going after a Surveyor	0	7	8
Nehemiah Smedl'y Laying out Roads	0	4	6
John Newbre accompt for keeping a minister's horse one week also a Plough in the Highways	0	4	6

We will now leave the "Proprietors," technically so called, with their manly deeds and ill-spelled words, for a little time, premising, however, that the incorporation by the General Court at Boston, of the town of Williamstown, in due form, by no means submerged the proprietors as an organization keeping themselves especially in charge of the unsold and undivided lands of the town, and for a good while, also, of the places of public worship. Indeed, the proprietors, as a "Propriety," only went out with the century. They went out, little by little, as the town came, gradually, to assume the entire functions of government. James H. Meacham, son to James Meacham, was the last proprietors' clerk, and was sworn in as follows : —

Then personally appeared James H. Meacham who was duly chosen Proprietors Clerk of the Township of Williamstown by the proprietors of the same and made a solemn oath that in performing the duties of the said office he would do it faithfully and impartially, according to his best skill and abilities.

Before Wᴹ TOWNER, Just. Peace.

The last legal meeting of the proprietors was summoned at the house of Deacon James Meacham, on the 23d of December, 1800, and was wholly concerned with certain pitches and remnants of lands in various parts of the town; and adjourned, to meet at the same place, March 2, 1801, and then again to the second Monday in April, 1802; and then and there "Voted and desolved the meeting," — which never reconvened.

CHAPTER V.

> "He had observed the progress and decay
> Of many minds, of minds and bodies too ;
> The history of many families ;
> How they had prospered ; how they were o'erthrown
> By passion or mischance, or such misrule
> Among the unthinking masters of the earth
> As makes the nations groan."
>
> — WORDSWORTH.

BEFORE we quit for good our now familiar and significant and euphonious name of "West Hoosac," and accustom ourselves to the more commonplace, and yet most appropriate, and, in 1765, legalized designation of "Williamstown," it will be proper to quote, in reference to the earlier name, the unmatched authority of Mr. Secretary Trumbull, of Hartford : "*Hoosac* belongs to the *territory*, from which — as is the case with many Indian names in New England — it was transferred by the settlers to the *river*. It designates the place or region which, to the Mohicans of the valley of the Hudson, was 'far-off' or 'beyond' the mountains. In 'Housatonuc,' we have the term for 'mountain' expressed ; wauss'-auk ('beyond-place') and wauss'-atene-auk (the 'beyond-mountain-place') indicate nearly the composition and the relation of the two names."

It will be well also, before we proceed further on our quest, to remind ourselves that a committee of the General Court at Boston laid out the exterior lines of West Hoosac in the early autumn of 1749, and that another committee from the same authority, in the spring of 1750, laid out sixty-three house lots "of ten or twelve acres each," in the northerly part of the township between the Hoosac and Green rivers, and near to their junction. With one exception, these house lots *abutted* on a wide street one and three-eighths miles in length, whose bearing, by the solar meridian, is N. 50° 44' W. The exception is house lot 57, which *flanks* the Main Street at its eastern end, and is both shorter and wider than the others, whose normal length is 120 rods, and width thirteen and one-third rods, making an area of just ten acres ; but the actual average area of

467

the sixty-three lots is nearly eleven acres. These lots are divided in number, nearly equally, by a Cross Street at right angles to the Main Street, whose bearing, by the solar meridian, is N. 16° 46' E.

These lots, each one carrying with it a prospective valid title to one sixty-third part of the rest of the lands of the township, with a reservation of three of them for public purposes, had been sold, in the course of a couple of years or so, with some difficulty, by the commonwealth, to forty-six proprietors, only about one-third of whom became actual settlers. Before 1765, the rest, and even most

THE SMEDLEY HOUSE ON NO. I.

The Original "Regulation" House was built into the "Gambrel-Roofed" House, which was taken down about 1880.

of these, had sold out their rights to other parties. We have a complete list of the original purchasers, and a complete list of the legal owners in the year just named, and only two names are common in the two lists. These house lots, however, had aggregated, in the interval, into fewer hands. Eight persons now held thirty-seven of these lots. To take Nos. 1 and 2, both on the "Square," as specimens of the way in which nearly all of them rapidly changed hands in the land speculations of the time, we find that Samuel Brown, Junior, one of the principal founders of Stockbridge, bought No. 1 about as soon as the lots were exposed for sale ; he sold it to Ezekiel Hinds, then " resident " of Fort Massachusetts ; but soldier Hinds, apparently, bought to sell; for, on the 31st October, 1752, he sold the lot to Samuel Smedley, of Litchfield, Connecticut, for £27, Smedley appearing as "husbandman" in the deed, which was acknowledged "coram Joseph Dwight J. P.," in Stockbridge. Samuel Smedley having died in the interval, the lot was deeded over by Esther (his widow) and John (his eldest son), to Nehemiah Smedley, all of Litchfield, for £27 21s., March, 1758, the deed acknowledged the same day before Thomas Harrison, Justice of the Peace, of Litchfield. Benjamin Woodruff and Jedidiah Smedley sign as witnesses. All these Smedleys write a fair hand, and Nehemiah, who began to clear up the lot for his father in 1753, built the first house on it, and occupied the lot, in dead earnest, for more than twenty years. The young orchard that he planted on it was in full bearing in 1765.

Lieutenant Isaac Wyman, of Fort Massachusetts, was the original purchaser of No. 2. We have seen that he did his best to bring forward the settlement in its earliest days, apparently alternating his residence between Fort Massachusetts and his "regulation" house on No. 2; he was the last commander at that fort, and cultivated the land within the pickets even after the fort was dismantled; on grounds very imperfectly understood at this late day, he quarrelled with the other settlers and they with him, — the bone of contention was undoubtedly the West Hoosac Fort, the rival of the older establishment,—and he withdrew not without a mutual bitterness; and he sold his lot, with several other lots drawn by it, for £140, to Benjamin Kellogg, Nov. 13, 1761; and when the new holder failed to pay off the dues legally assessed on it, it was sold at public auction to Benjamin Simonds for £4, who held it (with six other house lots) in 1765.

The names of the holders of the house lots, when the town of Williamstown was incorporated, are as follows : —

NEHEMIAH SMEDLEY.	BENJAMIN SIMONDS.
MRS. DAVID ROBERTS.	RICHARD STRATTON.
BENJAMIN COWLES.	EPHRAIM SEELYE.
JOSIAH HORSFORD.	SAMUEL PAYN.
THOMAS DUNTON.	SAMUEL KELLOGG.
WILLIAM HORSFORD.	ASA JOHNSON.
ELISHA HIGGINS.	WILLIAM WELLS.
ELI COWLES.	SAMUEL SMEDLEY.
JOHN SMEDLEY.	JONATHAN KILBORN.
TITUS HARRISON.	DANIEL STRATTON.
JONATHAN MEACHAM.	JEDIDIAH SMEDLEY.
ICHABOD SOUTHWICK.	ISAAC WYMAN.
DERICK WEBB.	STEPHEN DAVIS.
ELKANAH PARIS.	EBENEZER STRATTON.

Besides these twenty-eight, who owned house lots in 1765, there were then just about as many more who had located on outlots in different parts of the town, as these had been successively divided off to the respective holders of house lots, in accordance with the original plan of the settlement. The following twenty-six names, together with those just given, comprise all the landowners and citizens of position at the organization of the town. These fifty-four men may be called, in strict justice, the actual FOUNDERS OF WILLIAMSTOWN. A few worthy names besides these, like Allen Curtiss for one, had labored faithfully in the very beginnings, and had retired from the grounds ; and a few of these, like Joseph Ballard and Seth Hudson, may not have been residents in 1765; but the first town-meeting was held July 15, 1765, and from the "List" of that year it appears that the taxable polls were only fifty-nine. Only about 578 acres were then under cultivation in the town, as appears from the listed tax of £426 at fifteen shillings per "improved" acre. Isaac Searle and Nehemiah Smedley were the only proprietors taxed for money at interest, the former for £700 and the latter for £126. These are the names : —

JAMES MEACHAM.	ISAAC STRATTON.
JOHN NEWBRE.	JAMES KELLOGG.
SAMUEL TAYLOR.	GIDEON WARREN.
ISAAC SEARLE.	JOSEPH TALLMADGE.
SAMUEL CLARKE.	NATHAN WHEELER.
JOSIAH WRIGHT.	DANIEL BURBANK.
ROBERT MCMASTER.	MOSES RICH.
SETH HUDSON.	JOHN MCMASTER.
BARTHOLOMEW WOODCOCK.	DAVID JOHNSON.
JESSE SOUTHWICK.	THOMAS ROE.
JOHN HORSFORD.	THOMAS TRAIN.
JOSEPH BALLARD.	ELISHA BAKER.
SAMUEL SLOAN.	EBENEZER COOLEY.

The town boasted at its inception of fifty-seven yoke of oxen, just about one yoke to each head of a family; of eighty-three sheep; two dairies possessed six cows each, and two others four; and the four largest flocks of sheep counted eighteen, fourteen, thirteen, eleven.

Now, it is to be noticed, that these men had not been at any time wholly absorbed in the pressing cares to provide a new home and maintenance for their families in what was then strictly a wilderness. Even after they heard the news in the late autumn of 1759 of General Wolfe's great victory at Quebec, they knew well enough there would be no more French and Indian wars. They knew that Fort Massachusetts and West Hoosac Fort had now lost their significance, though fully manned up to that time. With the feeling of security and stability thereby induced, and a consequent resolution to make a permanent home for themselves and their children in a beautiful and healthful and fertile spot, there recurred continually the desires and efforts to secure and maintain religious and educational opportunities. They built their log schoolhouse, which was to serve for the present for preaching also. May 21, 1765, they " votted and Chose Benjamin Simonds a Commetree to Geet a Coppy of Colonel Ephraim Williams sur-will out of the Probate Office in the County of Hamshier "; and a little later 3s. 4d. were paid to said Simonds for a copy of the will. In less than a month later, among the causes stated in the warrant for the next meeting of the proprietors was this, " To chuse a Commetree on the affair of Colonel Ephraim Williams Willing Land or money to ward a free school in West Hoosuck and said Commetree to prosecute the same." At the meeting, however, it was voted " to dismiss the articiel."

In truth, the question of a minister was the more pressing. They came up to it boldly again and again. They had had hard luck, and been at much expense, even to get a suitable man to try for a settlement. In two cases, where the candidate was willing, the constituency disapproved of him. At last a young man from New Milford, Connecticut, named Whitman Welch, a graduate of Yale College in 1762, seemed to meet the views of all parties concerned. In the legal call for a meeting " att the School House," on July 26, 1765, these points are stated : —

1st To See if the Proprietors will Give Mr. Whitman Welch a Call to the work of the ministry in this Town

2ly To See What Settlement they will Give Him

3ly To See What Sallary they will Give Him

4ly To Chuse a Commetree to give mr Welch a Call

To these queries the meeting in question promptly responded : —

1st Voted and a Greed to Give mr Whitman Welch a Call to the work of the ministry in this Town

2ly Voted to Give mr Welch Eighty Pound Settlement Lawfull money one Half to be paid the first year the other Half to be Paid Second year

3ly Voted to Give mr Welch for his Sallary Seventy Pounds a year forty Pounds the first year and forty Pounds the Second year then to rise three pounds yearly till it comes to Seventy Pounds and the use of the ministry House Lot Exclusive of the Remainder of the wright

4ly Voted and chose Samuel Kellogg Benjamin Simonds James Meacham Commetree men to treete with mr Welch Concerning His Settleing in this Town

Williams Town october 22ᵈ 1765 att a meeting of the Proprietors Lawfully Warned and Held att the House of Deacon Richard Stratton in Said township

1ˢᵗ Votted and chose Samuel Payen Moderator for Said meeting

2ˡʸ Votted and chose Richard Stratton Josiah Horsford and William Horsford a Commetree to Provide for the ordination

3ˡʸ Votted that they will Raise money to Defray the Charges of the ordination
Votted to Raise three Shillings on Eaich Proproprietors Right to Defray the charges of the ordination

4ˡʸ Votted Samuel Kellogg for going to the Association . . . . ˙. 9s 0
William Horsford for Keeping a horse for Mr. Welch 2s 0

The next meeting of the proprietors, on Jan. 14, 1766,

Voted Richard Stratton Expence of the ordination Vittels and Horse Keep-
. ing £5 2 8
Josiah Horsford to Providing for the ordination 13 0
William Horsford to Providing for the ordination 7 4

Thus came to Williamstown its first, and, all things considered, its most attractive, minister. His term of service was ten years, and was cut short by a series of romantic and patriotic incidents, which will draw our attention and sympathy in a subsequent chapter. He was a native of Milford, Connecticut; but, as his father died early, the care of his education devolved on an uncle, with whom he went to reside in New Milford. Not far from the time of his settlement here, he married Marvin Gaylord, daughter of Deacon Gaylord, of New Milford; and she, after the death of her husband, in 1776, returned thither with two or three children born here, and married there again, and lived to an extreme old age.

Professor Ebenezer Kellogg, writing, in 1829, for Field's *Berkshire County*, and deriving his information, in all probability, from Deacon Levi Smedley, born here in 1764, gave the following careful and vivid description of Rev. Whitman Welch: "He was a man of intelligence and activity, attentive to the duties of his office, and serious and earnest in the performance of them. His religious opinions seem to have agreed with those of the clergy of that day, that are now spoken of as approaching to Arminianism. He always wrote his sermons, and delivered them with animation and propriety of manner. He was social in his habits, fond of conversation, in which he was often sportive and shrewd, and sometimes, perhaps, too gay and jocose. In person he was rather short and light. He was fond of athletic exercises, and excelled in them whenever the manners of the day allowed him to join in them."

Unfortunately the records of the church during his ministry have not been preserved, nor is it certainly known when the church was formed, what persons first constituted it, how many belonged to it at the close of his ministry in 1775. The likelihood is, that the church was first gathered at the time of his ordination, for there is no hint of any such organization previous to that, all the motions towards getting a minister were made in the proprietors' meetings, and some of the men prominent in the entire quest are now known never to have been public professors of religion; and that the number of members was small at the outset is proven by the facts, (1) that fourteen years after the ordination of Mr. Welch, when Rev. Seth Swift was ordained, the members amounted to but sixty-one, — thirty-six of these women, — and (2) in 1768, when the ratable polls were 102, the "voters by law," that is, legal church-members, were only twenty. In truth, there is no historical basis for the claim, often made and reiterated, that Williamstown had a specially religious origin, and ever maintained a peculiarly religious character. This is neither true of the town, nor of the College. Though presumably and certainly Christian men, neither Benjamin Simonds nor Nehemiah Smedley, the two most prominent citizens of West Hoosac from its beginning, and of Williamstown for its first twenty years, were ever church-members. Next to these two, Richard Stratton, who was the most influential settler during the same interval of time, was a Baptist, and was usually called "Deacon." Though older than Smedley and Simonds, he was better educated than they, and was a long time clerk of the proprietors, and built the first two-story house in the hamlet, which is still standing intact; but he was not a "voter by law," because he did not belong to the "standing order." His two sons, nevertheless, Isaac and Ebenezer, were orthodox Congregationalists here, and the latter was chosen Deacon in 1784 and held the office till his death in 1814. As late as 1791, the town refused "to incorporate Matthew Dunning and fourteen others into a Baptist society," according to their petition; the next year, however, "Isaac Holmes was chosen tything-man for the Baptist society in this town." Without disparaging the religious motives or unanimity of the early settlers, it must yet be borne in mind, that worldly reasons conspired with the genuine religious impulse to settle a minister and build a meeting-house, because no new town in the commonwealth could successfully compete with other new towns for desirable inhabitants without offering the then usual and much-prized "privileges."

Doubtless the very considerable expenses connected with the ordination of Mr. Welch, and the difficulty in raising the money to meet them, led the proprietors to negative for the present the legal inquiry in January, 1766, "To See if the Proprietors will Come into Som measure to Build a meeting House and chuse a Commetree to do it and Determin How big and in what Shape s^d meeting House Shall be Built and How and by what means and When." The log schoolhouse was felt to be an unsuitable place for the young minister to preach in, or for the church and congregation to assemble in, but the proprietors did not feel able as yet to meet the cost of even a small edifice for public worship. In October, 1767, Whitman Welch sold house lot 36, the lot drawn for the first minister, and the lot on which the log schoolhouse stood, to Josiah Horsford for £25. Horsford was a strenuous supporter of Mr. Welch, and the latter bought back the lot when the former wished to leave town a few years later; the pastor had the use of the "Ministry lot" by the vote of the proprietors, but not of the outlots drawn by that, which was house lot 38, and contiguous to the "Minister's lot" east. After Mr. Welch's death, the ministry house lot was sold by the proprietors in 1777; and the school lot, which was house lot 35, and directly across the Main Street from the first minister's lot, and the outlots drawn by this and by the *ministry* lot, were sold in 1772 for £328, and the proceeds devoted to school and ministerial uses.

It is perhaps probable, at any rate, nothing to the contrary is certainly known, that Mr. Welch did not live during his ten years' pastorate either on the first minister's lot, which was his own in fee simple, or on the ministry lot next to it east, the use of which was given to him by vote of the proprietors. Such signs as are left point rather to his residence on the Green River, just outside the village plat to the eastward. He owned, at any rate, the meadow lot No. 14 drawn by house lot 49 very early, which lay alongside of the Green River on the east side of it — possibly on both sides of it — at the point where the road from Fort Massachusetts crossed the bridge built over that river in the early spring of 1765, and entered the Main Street of the village. Richard Stratton and Samuel Kellogg were the committee to build that bridge; and on the 6th of June, 1765, the proprietors voted "to accept the whole of the accounts of the committee to build the bridge over Green River, namely, —

For Bridge, ...	£2	8 0
For Railing, ...	1	4 9
	£3	12 9 "

A bridge had been built the fall before by the proprietors over Hancock Brook just before its junction with the Ashford Brook to form Green River, to accommodate Isaac Stratton; so that what is now the south village, had its bridge across its main stream before the north village had one; and what is always called in the records of the time the "Greate River," that is to say, the Hoosac, did not receive its first bridge till some time later, as we shall see. What evidence remains points to the residence of Mr. Welch on the south side of Main Street opposite the later "Smedley House." There was certainly a barn standing there, if not a house, when Nehemiah Smedley bought of Whitman Welch, May 4, 1775, the meadow lot No. 14. The original deed conveying this lot from Welch to Smedley now lies open before the writer. The consideration paid was £75 10s. The area of land conveyed was " Eighteen Acres and three Quarters with an allowance for the Highway." Smedley had then owned for ten years three other meadow lots, Nos. 10 and 12 and 13, in the immediate vicinity of this one; and he had owned for nine or ten years the two first-division fifty-acre lots, Nos. 28 and 29, which partly enclose these meadow lots; he had also in the mean time bought an oak lot or two on what we now call "Smedley Height," having evidently designed for at least ten years to aggregate a farm for himself at the junction of the Green and Hoosac rivers. It is almost certain that the present "Smedley house" was raised in October, 1772; that relatives of the family came to the "raising" from Bennington; that a cellar-kitchen was shortly after covered in, and a large stone-oven built in it, which remains intact till this day, and in which bread was baked for the soldiers in the battle of Bennington; and that the owner, having gone so far, and the Revolution already impending, said that he would wait the completion of his house till he could tell better who was going to own it! His eldest son, Levi Smedley, was born Oct. 8, 1764, and lived till May 13, 1849, and always said that the oak timbers of the house were lifted into their place the day he was eight years old, that is, Oct. 8, 1772; he always said that bread in large quantities was baked in the old oven on Saturday the 16th of August, 1777, and that he himself carried the bread to Bennington the next day after the battle, which was Sunday, to his father, who was certainly there both days as the Captain of the militia company of the north part of Williamstown; he was then thirteen years old, and might well have been trusted for such a purpose with the family horse and vehicle; and it may be added, that contemporary muster-rolls confirm his story in all its main particulars. Whether it were then completed or not.

the family had evidently moved into the new house before the battle
of Bennington. As it stands to-day, the house is figured below; but
as originally built, it had a flat roof, and the piazza, of course, is
modern, but the clapboards on the north end are still the thick and
rived clapboards of the Revolutionary time, fastened with the large
and hand-wrought nails of that time also.

· Pretty soon after selling this prominent meadow lot 14 to Smedley, which thus became incorporated with the Smedley farm, Rev.
Mr. Welch went to Washington's camp at Cambridge, where was
a company of minute-men, made up largely of his parishioners,

NEHEMIAH SMEDLEY'S HOUSE ON GREEN RIVER.

Its frame was lifted 8 Oct., 1772. He was born in Litchfield in 1732, and died in this house, 1789.

a number of whom were drafted a little later in the season, to
accompany Arnold through the then wilderness of Maine to a winter surprise of Quebec, with which the American Revolution offensively began. It is thoroughly characteristic of this pastor's
ignitable spirit and athletic body, that he felt an invincible impulse to accompany this expedition as a volunteer — not, as has
often been said, as a chaplain, but as a volunteer sentinel. After
the repulse from Quebec, he was seized ill of the small-pox, and
died in March, 1776, not far from Quebec. Samuel Spring, of Newburyport, was Chaplain to this extraordinarily hazardous expedition
in early winter up the Kennebec, and down the Chaudière, and

there is no hint of Welch being an assistant to him, or of his being anything else than a camp-follower and adventurer; but the fact that he went because he wanted to go, because he could not hide nor resist the inner bidding of his spirit, had its influence on Williamstown at the time, and has had its influence here ever since. The incident seems to be unique. The man stands by himself. His call was an inner call of the most constraining kind; he had a baptism to be baptized with, and was straitened till he had received it, — a baptism of blood; and Williamstown became a better town to live in, and to strive for, and Williams College became, long afterwards, a better and a broader and a more patriotic institution, because the first college-bred citizen here, the first Joshua on this ground, was a man who saw visions and dreamed dreams, was Whitman Welch, a young man aflame!

As both the Town and the College derived their permanent and legal designations under the last will and testament of Ephraim Williams, it is time now to furnish our readers that document entire, and, furthermore, to study it more or less in detail, with a view to gain any further characteristics of the Colonel accessible to us along this line of research, and also to trace back our Town and College to the germs of them as they lay in the mind of one, of whom it is possible to learn at this late day only a very little at the best.

It was not by any means a sudden impulse that led Colonel Williams to seek out a scrivener's office in Albany on that July day when his will was actually drafted at his own dictation. It had been on his mind all summer. More, perhaps, than is common in such cases, he had a premonition of approaching death from the outset of the campaign. His own brother Thomas, who was the surgeon of his regiment, related afterwards, that before they two left Deerfield for the rendezvous, Ephraim requested his help in drafting his will, although he gave no intimations as to the disposition of the property. As these two were the only children of the first mother, and as the property of each came in part from their own grandfather Jackson, Dr. Thomas, from motives of delicacy, declined his brother's request, and the matter was then dropped. A credible tradition has always maintained, that in some talk with his old soldiers at Fort Massachusetts, he intimated to them his purpose to do something for them in the way of a school for the children of the settlers, both at West and East Hoosac. Benjamin Simonds had certainly two children, both born in West Hoosac, when Colonel Williams was last at Fort Massachusetts.

Another entirely distinct tradition from this came down in the
family of Ephraim Williams, the father, to the effect that it was
expected in that family, that the younger Colonel would marry a
Miss Williams, of Hatfield, a daughter of Colonel Israel Williams;
and that his will would convey the bulk of his small property to her,
in case of his own decease. The late Mark Hopkins, of Williamstown, who was great-great-grandson of the elder Ephraim Williams,
repeatedly conversed with the writer in respect to this tradition in
his own family, which he trusted implicitly; and he once furnished,
accordingly, the following toast to one of the student-speakers at one
of the "Jackson Festivals" here in honor of the founder, namely:
"*The lady Colonel Williams did not marry!*" If the will had been
what the Hatfield Williamses had expected, there would have been
no free school at West Hoosac. In a letter from Albany to Israel
Williams, dated one day before the will is dated, Ephraim betrays in
three or four passages his sense that there would be disappointment
along the Connecticut River when the contents of his will became
known there. "I have altered my mind since I left your house, for
reasons, as to what I designed to give (which should have been handsome) to one very near to you." "You will perceive I have given
something for the benefit of those unborn, and for the sake of those
poor creatures I am mostly concerned for fear my will should be
broke." "P.S. In my Will you will find I ordered some money for
the benefit of the East town. I do not know that it will be enough
for the will, but as far as it goes it will pay well, and then some good
will come of it." "P.S. 2ⁿᵈ Let no one but yourself and John
Worthington know what my will contains."

While awaiting in Albany the gathering of the "new levies"
from New England for the Crown Point expedition, so-called, in
common with a number of other officers, Colonel Williams fell sick
in the July weather, and was reminded again of the uncertainty of
life in war time, and that his cherished purpose to bequeath something to the benefit of his old comrades at Fort Massachusetts was
still unfulfilled. He made no further delay. A competent scrivener
was looked up in some office, Dutch or other, along the street; and
it is pretty certain to have been a lonesome and homesicky function
to have gone over the numerous items one by one. It is evidently
his own work, item by item. His father had died the year before at
Deerfield, leaving some property matters dangling in a way quite
contrary to the son's sense of justice. His kinsman, William Williams, then a member of his staff, and afterwards to become a signer
of the Declaration of Independence from Connecticut, witnessed the

signature of the will, July 22, 1755, as did also Noah Belding, another of the Hampshire soldiers present, and Richard Cartwright, too, who may have been the drafter of the will.

The following letter, perhaps the last formal one ever written by Ephraim Williams, the founder, was sent down to Hatfield with the will itself, to Colonel Israel Williams, first of its two executors.

ALBANY, July 21, 1755.

Dear Sir: — Enclosed I send you my last Will and Testament, and desire you to consult with Mr. Worthington whether it be legal, — if it is not, please to write one that is, — send it up and I will execute it. I have altered my mind since I left your house, for reasons, as to what I designed to give (which should have been handsome) to one very near to you; have given a small matter to others, as near to you, whose conduct to me has rendered themselves most amiable. Also since I left your house, for reasons, I have altered my mind, as to what I designed to give to the children of my great benefactor [Col. John Stoddard of Northampton, who died in 1748]; have given but a small matter to two of them only. You will perceive I have given something for the benefit of those unborn, and for the sake of those poor creatures I am mostly concerned for fear my will should be broke. I believe, Sir, it would have been more agreeable to you if I had given it for an academy at Hadley. I turned the affair over and over in my mind, found so many difficulties, I thought it was better to give it in another shape. I desire that you and Mr. Worthington would inquire into the affair of the Stockbridge Indians, which my Honored [Father] left in charge; by no means let them be [wronged in any way]. I desire you to pay £20 to your nieces, at a venture upon [it. I do not] know that I owe them one quarter of it, but for fear I do, I will put enough in.

Also please to pay the following persons whose names are hereafter mentioned, if they are to be found, being soldiers under my command. I received the money out of the treasury, but could never find the men; have paid all but these: Daniel Wood, £4 10s 8d; Jonathan Conally, £1 13s 6d; Nathaniel Sawyer £2 12s 5d; William Williston £1 16s, lives near Rehoboth. These things above mentioned are the most material. I shall conclude by recommending myself to your prayers, and you and your dear family to the Divine protection.

I am, with great esteem, your honored,

Most humble, and most obliged servant

To ISRAEL WILLIAMS, Esquire.   EPHRAIM WILLIAMS.

In the Name of God Amen. I Ephraim Williams of Hatfield in the County of Hampshire in New England now at Albany in the Province of New York, on my march in the Expedition against Crown Point, being of sound and perfect mind and memory (blessed be God therefor) but not knowing how God in his providence may dispose of my life and remembering the uncertainty of it at all times, I do therefore make and publish this my last Will and Testament in the following manner.

First I give my soul into the hands of God that gave it and my body to the dust from whence it was taken humbly hoping for pardon acceptance and a resurrection to immortal Glory, thro' the merits & mediation of a Glorious Redeemer; and as touching such worldly estate wherewith it hath pleased God to bless me in this life, I give bequeath and dispose of the same in manner and form following that is to say.

Item It is my will and desire that my just debts and funeral charges be first paid and discharged by my Executors hereafter named out of my estate.

Item It is my will and desire that the Deed I gave my brother, Elijah Williams of my house and homestead at Stockbridge and my note hand payable for One Hundred pounds in twelve months after my parents decease, as also his mortgage Deed and his bond to me be destroyed and made of none effect. •

Item I give and bequeath unto my beloved brothers Josiah Williams and Elijah Williams and the heirs of their bodies my Homestead at Stockbridge with all the buildings and appurtenances thereunto belonging, with all the stock of Cattle and Negro Servants now upon the place to be equally divided between them upon the following conditions and not otherwise viz That they pay annually to my Honour'd Mother for her support Twenty six pounds thirteen shillings & four pence, and also provided they fulfill the obligations I laid myself under in a certain bond to my Hon^d Parents for their support and decent interment, exclusive of the money I there obliged myself annually to pay her, provided also that they pay unto my sister Judith Williams or the heirs of her body the sum of One Hundred pounds and to my sister Elizabeth Williams or the heirs of her body the sum of One Hundred pounds and to the heirs of my sister Abigail Dwight born of her body the sum of One Hundred pounds, to be paid them severally within twelve months after my hon^d mothers decease. In case my sisters Judith or Elizabeth should come to die without heirs then it is my will that her or their part or parts shall devolve to the heirs of my sister Abigail Dwight.

Item it is my will that in case of my aforesaid brothers die without issue then the whole of the above bequest revert to the survivor and the heirs of his body, provided he fulfill the above obligations laid on them both ; but in case my said brothers die without issue then my will is that the abovementioned estate be sold and the money be put out to interest, and that the said interest shall be used for some pious or charitable purposes, as the propagating Christianity, the support of the poor in the County of Hampshire, or for schools on the frontiers in the county aforesaid to be at the direction of my Executors hereinafter named, and after their decease to be at the direction of the Justices of the Sessions for the County aforesaid but in case my brother Elijah Williams should deny or refuse to destroy the above mentioned writings as above directed then it is my will to pay to my Hon^d Mother annually for her support Twenty six pounds thirteen shillings and four pence and also the sum of Thirteen pounds six shillings and eight pence to my brother Josiah Williams annually until my Hon^d Mothers decease after which to pay to my sisters and the heirs of my sister Abigail Dwight as above directed and that within one twelve month after my Hon^d Mothers decease, also to pay to my brother Josiah Williams or the heirs of his body the sum of Four Hundred pounds, and in case my said brother Josiah should die without issue then it is my will that my brother Elijah shall pay the said sum of Four Hundred pounds to my Executors to be appropriated by them to some or all the public uses above mentioned.

Item. I give and bequeath unto my beloved brother Thomas Williams One Hundred pounds to be paid him out of my bonds but in case of his decease in the present expedition to be equally divided amongst his five daughters viz. Elizabeth Anne Cynthia Mary and Martha.

Item   I give and bequeath unto my beloved cousin Thomas Williams son to my brother Thomas Williams Nine Hundred acres of Land known by the name of the Equivalent and joining upon the Township of Stockbridge, & in case he dies without issue, I give it to my beloved cousins Erastus Sergeant and John Sergeant to be equally divided between them but in case one die without issue the whole to go to the survivor if they both die without issue the whole to be appropriated to public uses as before mentioned.

Item   I give and bequeath unto my loving cousins Elijah Graves, Moses Graves, John Graves and Martha Graves children of Moses and Martha Graves the sum of One hundred pounds to be equally divided between them, in case any dies without issue, then the whole to go to the survivor or survivors, and in case they all should die without issue then the said hundred pounds to be appropriated to the publick uses as above directed, the said money to be taken out of Moses Graves and Elisha Chapin's joint bond and to be put on interest until the children come of age.

Item   I give and bequeath unto my beloved cousins James & John Gray sons of James and Sarah Gray Fifty acres of land lying north of the great pond in Stockbridge, so-called, bounded upon land of their father James Gray on the East by Josiah Jones' land on the West by the great pond on the South, & the Town line on the north to be equally divided between them, but in case they die without issue then the said land to be disposed of for publick uses as aforesaid.

Item   I give and bequeath unto loving cousins William Williams and Israel Williams sons of Israel Williams Esq? and Sarah his wife Two lots of Meadow land in Hatfield great Meadow, the contents of which & the bounds may be seen in a Deed given to me of the same by Moses Graves of Hatfield   The lot lying nearest to Pine Bridge I give to William and the other to Israel and in case one of them dies without issue then both lots to go to the Survivor if they both die without issue then the lots to be disposed of for the publick uses as above directed.

Item   I give and bequeath to my beloved Cousins Eunice Williams Jerusha Elizabeth and Lucretia Williams daughters of Israel Williams Esq? and Sarah his wife the sum of Twenty pounds each   in case any of them die without issue their part to be equally divided among the survivors, and in case they all should die without issue then the money to be disposed of for publick uses as aforesaid.

Item   I give and bequeath to my loving Cousin Elizabeth Williams over and above the Twenty pounds above mentioned my Silver Cream pot and Tea spoons.

Item   I give and bequeath unto my loving brother Thomas Williams all my Wearing apparel my Shoe buckles, but in case my said brother should die I then give them to my surviving brothers to be equally divided among them.

Item   I give to my beloved friend and kinsman Israel Williams Esq? of Hatfield my Sorrel mare now at Northampton and my bald Colt now at Sheffield.

Item   I give to my trusty and well beloved friend John Worthington Esq? of Springfield my Chambers Dictionary with the whole of Pope's works and some other books that came in the same box now in his hands and also my French Fire arm my case of Pistols and Hanger in case the French dont get them but if he dies without issue then the above articles to be given to the eldest male heir in Coll Israel Williams family.

Item   I give and bequeath to my beloved brother Thomas Williams my Fire arm now in his possession.

Item   I give the remaining part of my Library not yet disposed of (excepting my large Bible and Ridgley's Body of Divinity) to my beloved brother's, Thomas and Elijah Williams to be equally divided between them but in case my brother Thomas dies his part to go to his son Thomas and in case my brother Elijah dies without issue then his part to be given to my cousins William & Israel Williams to be equally divided between them, over and above the lots of land bequeathed them above, and it is my will and desire further that my cousin William Williams above mentioned shall have the perusal of the books hereby given to my brothers Thomas & Elijah, any reasonable time upon his desire.

Item I give and bequeath unto my brother Thomas Williams's two eldest Daughters Three Silver spoons now at Hatfield and a Silver Tankard now at Stockbridge and what Silver may be bequeathed me by my Aunt Cooke in Newton.

Item I give to my brother Josiah my large Bible and Ridgley's body of Divinity.

Item I give to Solomon & Israel Stoddard sons of my great benefactor John Stoddard Esq.[e] dec.[d] my two colts now at Northampton.

Item I give and devise and remit to the poor, distressed, and imprudent Captain Elisha Chapin the sum of One hundred pounds to be deducted out of the bond given jointly by Moses Graves and said Elisha Chapin the said Hundred Pounds to be remitted out of the said Chapin's part.

Item It is my will and pleasure and desire that the remaining part of Lands not yet disposed of shall be sold at the discretion of my Executors within five years after an established peace, and the interest of the money and also the interest of my money arising by my bonds and notes shall be appropriated towards the support and maintenance of a Free School (in a Township west of Fort. Massachusetts, commonly called the West. Township) forever, provided the s.[d] Township fall within the jurisdiction of the province of the Massachusetts Bay and provided also that the Governor and General Court give the s.[d] Township the name of Williamstown, and it is my further will and desire that if there should remain, any monies of the above donation, for the said School, It be given towards the support of a School in the East Township where the Fort now stands but in case the above provisos are not complied with then it is my will and desire that the interest of the above mentioned monies be appropriated to some pious and charitable uses in manner and form as directed in the former part of this my last Will and Testament.

Lastly I nominate and appoint my trusty and well beloved friends Israel Williams Esq.[e] of Hatfield and John Worthington Esq.[e] of Springfield in the County of Hampshire and Province of Massachusetts Bay of New England to be Executors of this my last Will and Testament and I hereby revoke disannul and make void all former wills and Testaments by me heretofore made done or executed and I do hereby confirm and allow this and no other to be my last will & Testament, and desire it may be observed as such.

In witness whereof I have hereunto set my hand and seal the twenty second day of July in the twenty ninth year of his Majesty's reign and in the year of our LORD one thousand seven hundred & fifty five.

Signed sealed published pronounced & declared by the s.[d] Ephraim Williams as his last Will and Testament (the erasure at the word Hatfield being first made) in the presence of us who were present at the signing. } EPH. WILLIAMS [SEAL]

W.[m] WILLIAMS Jun.[r]
NOAH BELDING
RICH.[D] CARTWRIGHT

At a Court of Probate holden at Northampton within and for the County of Hampshire on the second Tuesday of November being the 11ᵗʰ day of said month anno Dom. ˣ 1755 p. Timothy Dwight Esq. Judge of said Court The foregoing will was presented for probate by the Executors therein named and Noah Belding one of the witnesses to the same personally appearing made oath that Col.° Ephraim Williams Esqᵉ. the Testator, signed, sealed, pronounced & declared the above instrument as and for his last Will & Testament in his presence and in presence of William Williams Junʳ and Richard Cartwright the other witness to said will and that he the said Testator was of sound mind & memory when he did it and that he with the other witnesses above mentioned all signed as witnesses to the same in the said Testators presence, wherefore it is ratified approved & confirmed as the last Will and Testament of said deceased so far as to the conveyance of the personal estate of said deceased only according to the said Testators bequests of the same in the foregoing will

p. TIMOTHY DWIGHT

At a Court of Probate holden at Northampton within & for the County of Hampshire on the second Tuesday of December being the 10ᵗʰ day of said month Anᵉ Doˣ 1755. p. Timothy Dwight Esqʳ Judge of said Court William Williams Junʳ another of the witnesses to the foregoing will personally appearing made oath in every respect as the above said Noah Belding did as is above certified wherefore the said will is ratified approved & confirmed as the last Will & Testament of said deceased as to the conveyance of the Real as well as the personal estate agreeable to the Devises of the same in the foregoing will.

p. TIMOTHY DWIGHT.

HAMPSHIRE ss. PROBATE OFFICE Sept. 1, 1812.

I hereby certify that the foregoing is a true copy of the last will and testament of Ephraim Williams formerly of Hatfield in said County deceased as recorded with the probate thereof in said Office

Attest
SAMᴸ F. LYMAN Regʳ of Prob

Rev. Stephen Williams, pastor at Longmeadow, son of the famous "Redeemed Captive" John Williams, of Deerfield, at that time sixty-two years old, was in Albany when the will was drawn, as Chaplain to his kinsman's regiment, but he evidently was not consulted in reference to it, and it is plain that the relations of the two men were not any too cordial. An extant diary of the clergyman, as yet unpublished, for the year 1749–50 contains two or three memoranda[1] in relation to the officer : — "Dined with Col. Williams." "This night was hurt by discourse of Colonel Williams with Colonel Choate : I dislike ye conduct of my kinsman." Stephen Williams had been Chaplain under Pepperell at Louisburg, in 1745, and after this service at Lake George under Sir William Johnson ten years

[1] Communicated to me by my friend Fisher Howe, Williams College, 1872.

later, he served in the same capacity in the same region under
General Winslow in 1756. He was minister in Longmeadow for
sixty-six years, 1716–82. One of his deacons, Nathaniel Burt, was
killed in the battle of Lake George, alongside of Colonel Williams;
and his pastor published later an elaborate eulogy of him, and also
married his widow.

More is probably to be learned from this his will of the personal
characteristics of Ephraim Williams, than from all other sources
put together. If the kind reader please, we will study now this
document a little in detail, with a view to gain (if possible) a firm
possession of some of the founder's leading qualities.

(1) He was a man of more than common gratitude. "*Item.*
I give to Solomon and Israel Stoddard, sons of my great benefactor,
John Stoddard, deceased, my two colts now at Northampton."
When this will was drawn, Colonel John Stoddard had been dead
seven years. He was son to Solomon Stoddard, second minister of
Northampton, and own cousin to Jonathan Edwards, settled in
Northampton in 1727, as colleague with his grandfather Stoddard.
Thereafter, those two men, until the death of the Colonel in 1748,
were the most influential men in New England, at once in church
and state, as well in Boston as in Northampton. Edwards delivered
a commemorative discourse on the death of Stoddard, in which he
ascribed to him the highest native gifts of mind, a peculiar genius
for public affairs, a thorough political knowledge, great purity of
life, incorruptible principle, and sincere piety. "Upon the whole,
everything in him was great, and perhaps there was never a man in
New England to whom the denomination of a great man did more
properly belong." Governor Hutchinson says: "He shone only
in great affairs, while inferior matters were frequently carried
against his mind, by the little arts and crafts of minute politicians,
which he disdained to defeat by counter-working."

When Ephraim Williams came back from his foreign voyages to
stay, and his father had moved from Newton to Stockbridge, and the
thunder-heads of the old French War began to loom up around
the horizon of New England, John Stoddard stood at the head of
the political and military administration of western Massachusetts;
William Shirley was the able and excellent colonial governor at
Boston, whose estimation of Stoddard was so high, that he practically left the direction of affairs at the west in his hands; and it
was undoubtedly Stoddard's promotion of an untried man to the
command of the "line of forts" from the Connecticut River to the
Hoosac, and his steady support of him in that position, notwith-

standing some things that looked dubious in a military point of view, that constituted the "great benefaction" immortalized by Williams in his will. After so much lapse of time and change of circumstances, and after the benefactor had been seven years in his grave, many men, most men, would have regarded an incident of that sort as a by-gone, something, indeed, to be cherished in the personal memory, but not something to be formally and legally emphasized and thrust forward into another generation. Colonel Williams was a grateful man.

(2) He had more than the usual sense of what constitutes right and fair between man and man, without reference to the social position of the party of either part. This appears in numerous minute incidents in his career, and particularly in the letter which he wrote from Albany to Israel Williams, to accompany and explain the will. The writer has studied the original of that letter with care, and is certain that one passage in it is illegible, not in consequence of the gnawing of the tooth of time (the date is July 21, 1755), but in consequence of a purposed obliteration on the part of somebody (likely to have been Dr. Thomas Williams), in order to save his father's memory from a censure implied in the original phrases. Nobody in Stockbridge had been satisfied with the dealings, general and particular, of the elder Williams with the Indians there. He had left Stockbridge under the profound odium of a selfish and unchristian conduct towards them. In this letter the founder desires that the executors of his will " would inquire into the affair of the Stockbridge Indians, which my Honored . .. left in charge; by no means let them be . . . I desire you to pay £20 to your nieces at a venture upon . . . know that I owe them one quarter of it, but for fear I do, I will put enough in."

The Williams family, as such, were aristocratic in their tendencies, in their intermarriages with other families, in their political opinions strongly inclined to monarchy, and in their social instincts and practices haughty, even if not positively unjust towards the masses of men. The founder's father inherited from his own mother, Judith Cooper, a reckless acquisitiveness in relation to property, and a singular dulness of conscience in relation to the inherent rights of the poor and unbefriended; and it seems likely that he transmitted something of these traits to several generations of his descendants; but his eldest son appears to have been remarkably free from them; and wherever we can touch his points of contact with the common soldiers, and with others who had no champion, he shows the broad sympathies and that quick sense of justice that mark the true and great man. The obliterations made in this letter, probably long after it was written, do the writer much credit, and cannot but throw discredit back on the paternal stock.

(3) Considering his broken youth and imperfect education, and considering, too, that he never had a permanent home during his manhood, the thoughtful and religious traits of Colonel Williams strikingly appear in those phrases of his will that give the titles of some of his books, and make careful bequeathments of them all. "*Item.* I give to my trusty and well-beloved friend, John Worthington Esq., of Springfield, my Chambers's Dictionary, with the whole of Pope's works, and some other books that came in the same box, now in his hands; but if he dies without issue, then the above articles to be given to the eldest male heir in Colonel Israel Williams's family." This copy of the "Dictionary," or more properly Cyclopedia, of Ephraim Chambers, first published in London in two very large folio volumes, may, very likely, have belonged to the sixth and last edition, which appeared, with much new matter, in 1750, and became the basis of Dr. Rees's Cyclopedia in forty-five quarto volumes.

"*Item.* I give the remaining part of my library not yet disposed of (excepting my large Bible and Ridgley's Body of Divinity), to my beloved brothers, Thomas and Elijah Williams, to be equally divided between them; but in case my brother Thomas dies, his part to go to his son Thomas; and in case my brother Elijah dies without issue, then his part to be given to my cousins, William and Israel Williams [sons of Colonel Israel, of Hatfield], to be equally divided between them; and it is my will and desire, further, that my cousin William Williams, above mentioned, shall have the perusal of the books hereby given to my brothers, Thomas and Elijah, any reasonable time, upon his desire." This William Williams was just turned of twenty-one, and had just been graduated at Yale when these words were penned; and he lived to become, perhaps, the most efficient agent in the carrying out of another, the central, clause in Ephraim Williams's will, as one of the original trustees of the Free School and the College, and the first president of that incorporated Board. He will be hereafter designated in these pages as Deacon William Williams, to distinguish him from several others of the same name in the same general family.

"*Item.* I give to my brother Josiah, my large Bible and Ridgley's Body of Divinity." All these words taken in their connections, and taken in connection with the solemn commitment, at about the same time, of himself and others to the prayers of Israel Williams, "and you and your dear family to the Divine Protection," must be the words of a thoughtful and comprehensive and deeply religious spirit. Among the books that thus fell to his own brother Thomas, was "An Universal History from the Earliest Account of Time," in twenty large volumes, strongly and elegantly bound, published in London, in 1748, by "T. Osborne in Gray's Inn; A. Millar in the Strand; and J. Osborn in Paternoster Row." These volumes, complete, have recently been presented to the Williams College library by the heirs of Dr. Thomas Williams. They were kept, till well into this century, in the old Williams house in Deerfield. They passed through the hands, in regular descent, of Solomon and Henry and Henry. The last enters an interesting autograph account of them on the inner cover of volume first, in connection with their presentation to the College. Bishop John Williams, of Connecticut, an heir along this line of descent, has long been generous and intelligent in behalf of the College.

(4) A quick sense of humor, well known on other grounds to have been characteristic of the founder, comes out even in his will. He bequeaths to John Worthington "my French firearm, my case of pistols and hanger, *in case the French don't get them!*" Luckily, the French got nothing that belonged to him, except his life. His body was not rifled in consequence of the temporary retreat, nor his effects in his tent at the camp scattered. "My firearm, now in my possession," went, as he willed, to his brother Thomas; the sword and watch that he wore in the fight, and the sword that his brother Thomas wore at the same time, are the property of the College, and formed the nucleus of the small historical museum now in Clark Hall; and some other articles of utility and ornament on his person when he fell are in the hands of the descendants of his brother Thomas.

"*Item.* I give and devise and remit to the poor, distressed, and imprudent Captain Elisha Chapin, the sum of one hundred pounds, to be deducted out of the bond given jointly by Moses Graves and said Elisha Chapin; the said hundred pounds to be remitted out of said Chapin's part!"

(5) The magnanimity of Williams is shown in his will by his treatment of his half-brothers and half-sisters, as well as of some others. One would never know by the reading of this will, that the testator's relations were anywise different towards his uterine brother Thomas, with whom he had been brought up from infancy in the family of his grandfather Jackson, than those sustained towards his brothers Josiah and Elijah, and his sisters Abigail and Elizabeth and

Judith, who had been brought up in another family and under quite different auspices. "*Item.* I give and bequeath unto my beloved brothers, Josiah Williams and Elijah Williams, and the heirs of their bodies, my homestead at Stockbridge, with all the buildings and appurtenances thereunto belonging, with all the stock of cattle, and negro servants now upon the place, to be equally divided between them, upon the following conditions, and not otherwise, viz. : That they pay annually to my honored mother [step-mother], for her support, twenty-six pounds thirteen shillings and four pence, and also, provided they fulfil the obligations I laid myself under, in a certain bond to my honored parents, for their support, and decent interment, exclusive of the money I then obliged myself annually to pay her; provided also, that they pay unto my sister Judith Williams, or the heirs of her body, the sum of one hundred pounds, and to the heirs of my sister Abigail Dwight, born of her body, the sum of one hundred pounds, to be paid them severally, within twelve months after my honored mother's decease. In case my sisters Judith or Elizabeth should come to die without heirs, then it is my will that her, or their part or parts shall devolve to the heirs of my sister Abigail Dwight."

This sister Abigail, the first-born of Ephraim Williams's second marriage, born April 20, 1721, came to Stockbridge with her father's family in 1739, and was shortly after married to Rev. John Sergeant, the Indian missionary there, and became the mother of his three children, Electa, Erastus, and John. The latter are referred to in Colonel Williams's will, — "I give it to my beloved cousins, Erastus Sergeant and John Sergeant, to be equally divided between them." The missionary Sergeant died in 1749, and his widow not long after married Brigadier-General Joseph Dwight. The sister Elizabeth married Rev. Stephen West, who was, for a short time, Chaplain at Fort Massachusetts, and was settled pastor in Stockbridge from 1759 till 1818. She died in 1804. The third sister Judith married Rev. Ezra Thayer, of Ware, who was ordained there in 1759. The half-brother Josiah was an ensign in Ephraim's regiment in the battle of Lake George, and was desperately wounded. His half-brother Thomas, who was the surgeon there, wrote to his wife three days after the battle, — "Twenty odd wounded in our regiment, and poor brother Josiah makes one of the number, having a ball lodged in the intestines, which entered towards the upper part of his thigh and passed through his groin." Nevertheless, like Dieskau, Josiah Williams survived his wound for a number of years, though he ultimately died in consequence of it. The youngest half-brother, Elijah, born in 1732, lived an honored life in Stockbridge, and died there in 1815. The house is still standing in West Stockbridge, which he built and occupied for twenty-five years; and 'he was mainly instrumental in having that township set off in 1774 from the old "Indian Town."

(6) "*Item.* I give and bequeath to my beloved cousins, James and John Gray, sons of James and Sarah Gray, fifty acres of land lying north of the great pond, so-called, bounded upon land of their father, James Gray, on the east, by Josiah Jones's land on the west, by the great pond on the south [Stockbridge Bowl], and the town line on the north, to be equally divided between them." There are two reasons for referring now to this particular bequest; first, to discover the painstaking action of Williams's mind, to include in his benefactions all his relatives (even those by marriage), as well as to secure by means of other parts of his small fortune certain ends of public benevolence; second, to show how and how widely the Williams blood entered the leading families of western Massachusetts, particularly this Scotch-Irish family of Gray, with which the writer also is lineally connected. Sarah Williams, own sister of Ephraim Senior, and three years older, the two youngest children of Captain Isaac, himself son to the progenitor Robert of Roxbury, married John Marsh, of Hadley, in October, 1718. Her husband dying, she married James Gray, then of Hadley, a weaver, one of the Scotch-Irish immigrants of 1718 into Worcester. They were married in July, 1732, and had these two sons, James and John, mentioned by name in Colonel Williams's will, as above. They were thus his own cousins.

In February, 1749, James Gray, "Weaver," and Sarah, his wife, sold their lands in Hadley, and bought in the following October of Ephraim Williams Junior, "Gentleman," 200 acres of land in Stockbridge "on the north line of the town by the Great Pond," etc. In February, 1762, Sarah Marsh Gray having in the mean time died in Stockbridge, June 1, 1759, James Gray, "Weaver," and James Gray, Junior, "Gentleman," sold this land to Charles Stone, of Guildford, Connecticut, for £264. Notice that the father in his old age is still "weaver," and his son, by virtue of being the nephew of Ephraim Williams, Senior, is "gentleman." So it went in those days. Twelve days later the same two parties, under the same styles, bought fifty acres in the heart of Stockbridge village, for £264, "bounded by land of T. Woodbridge, and of the heirs of John Sergeant, and of land of Samuel Brown and James Wilson, with dwelling-house, orchard and growing grain."

The story of these youngsters of that time, James and John. Gray, and specially of the former and elder of them, may afford some instruction and more amusement. The Williams influence got James Gray appointed a sergeant in one of the companies of Colonel Pepperell's regiment, which accompanied Governor Shirley's central expedition against the French and Indians, in 1755. As General Braddock commanded at the southward, and Sir William Johnson to the northward, so Governor Shirley personally led the centre up the Mohawk River towards the Great Lakes. Shirley's own regiment, so-called, and Pepperell's, though paid by the king and counted as English regulars, were in fact raw provincials just raised in the colonies, and all hands wore their gay uniforms with an awkward air. Sergeant Gray wrote as follows to his brother John in Stockbridge of his status in the army: "I have two Holland shirts, found me by the king, and two pair of shoes and two pair of worsted stockings; a good silver-laced hat (the lace I could sell for four dollars); and my clothes is as good scarlet broadcloth as ever you did see. A sergeant in the king's regiment is counted as good as an ensign with you; and one day in every week we must have our hair or wigs powdered." More fortunate than young William Shirley, who went in a similar capacity with Braddock, and was killed, young Gray returned to Albany with the broken expedition, and kept some position in the army: for he writes a letter from Halifax, Nova Scotia, in 1757, "to Mr. William Williams at Hatfield." In this letter he sends his "duty to your honored parents," that is to say, to Colonel Israel Williams and his wife. His correspondent in this case became the Deacon William Williams, of Dalton, of whom much will be said in the sequel.

The name of this James Gray, Junior, appears in a ludicrously aristocratic light in the earliest records of the Court of Common Pleas of the county of Berkshire. This county was set off from the old county of Hampshire in 1761. The court followed closely the old common law forms, and insisted on great strictness in pleading, even in cases in which Parliament had by statute long before relaxed the formalities. At the September term, 1768, of the New Berkshire Court, a writ was brought by George Wilmot, of Hartford, "Gentleman," plaintiff against James Gray, Junior, of Stockbridge, "Gentleman," defendant. The defendant came into court and prayed that the writ might be abated for these reasons : —

1. For that he the said James long before the purchase of this writ, by a good and lawful commission from Francis Bernard Esq., Captain General of his Majesty's Province of Massachusetts Bay, was appointed, constituted and made

a Major of a Brigade to the forces raised by the said Francis Bernard, to be employed in his Majesty's service, in the year of our Lord 1762, under the command of His Excellency Gen. Amherst, *and therefore that he has not his proper addition given him in said writ*, for that he should therein have been called James Gray, Esquire, and not James Gray, Gentleman.

2. Because the plaintiff calls himself of Hartford in the County of Hartford, Colony of Connecticut, whereas before and at the time of the purchase of said writ, he lived at and belonged to Albany in the County of Albany, in the Province of New York, and ought to have been so called.

3. Because the plaintiff hath given himself the addition of Gentleman, whereas the said James says the plaintiff is not a Gentleman, and ought to have been called George Wilmot, Yeoman, and not George Wilmot, Gentleman.

The court after consideration and inquiry ordered, *that the writ abate, and the said James recover his costs.* The judges at that time were William Williams, of Pittsfield, a nephew of John Stoddard and of Colonel Israel Williams; Perez Marsh, of Dalton, a son-in-law of Colonel Israel Williams; John Ashley, of Sheffield, a descendant of John Pynchon, of Springfield; and Timothy Woodbridge, of Stockbridge, out of a long line of clergymen, and a great-grandson of the Apostle Eliot; the sheriff of the court was Elijah Williams, of Stockbridge, the youngest son of Ephraim Williams, Senior. James Gray was own cousin of Elijah Williams.

In January, 1768, James Gray, Junior, Esq., sold to Dr. Marshall Spring, of Watertown, Massachusetts, fifty-two acres of land in Stockbridge, on the road from the meeting-house to the Great Pond, for £100. His wife, Sarah Spring Gray, signs with him the deed of transfer; and she outlived him in Stockbridge nearly thirty years. The epitaph upon his tombstone there is as follows: —

COL. JAMES GRAY,
DIED AUG. 25, 1782,
IN THE 49TH YEAR OF HIS AGE.

One may read this, too, on a neighboring headstone: —

MRS. SARAH (SPRING) GRAY,
RELICT OF COL. JAMES GRAY,
DIED OCT. 26, 1809, IN HER 72D YEAR.
ERECTED BY HER GRANDSON JOHN HUNT.

(7) "*Item.* It is my will, that in case one of my aforesaid brothers die without issue, then the whole of the above bequest revert to the survivor, and the heirs of his body, provided he fulfil the above obligations laid on them both; but in case my said brothers die without issue, then my will is that the above-mentioned estate be sold, and

the money be put out to interest, and that the said interest shall be used for some pious or charitable purposes, as the propagating Christianity, the support of the poor in the County of Hampshire, or for schools on the frontier, in the county aforesaid, to be at the direction of my Executors, hereinafter named, and after their decease to be at the direction of the justices of the sessions for the county aforesaid."

This clause in the founder's will lets the penetrative reader deeper into his inmost character, and manifests forth better the real spirit and purposes of his life than any other clause of his writings, or than any other action of his life. He had not had the opportunity usually accorded to young men steadily to unfold, under the constant scrutiny of his contemporaries, the broad choices and best courses in life. His early manhood had been more or less perturbed, and more or less migratory by land and sea. Indeed, he had never had a true home of his own in his conscious life. His last ten years were spent in the military service of his native colony, — passing as an officer from pillar to post. Fort Massachusetts was as much his domicile as any other place. He had lived some time with his father in Stockbridge, and had even represented that town one or two years in the General Court. He had also dwelled, more or less, in Northampton, with the Stoddards and other relatives; he calls John Stoddard in his will "my great benefactor"; he also speaks in the same of "my sorrel mare now at Northampton," and of "my two colts now at Northampton."

Still, he was evidently drawn, in the later years, by somewhat different and stronger ties, to Hatfield as a transient home, — to the roof-tree of his kinsman and friend, Israel Williams; "my beloved friend and kinsman," he denominates him in the will. He bequeaths to him the sorrel mare just mentioned, "and my bald colt now at Sheffield." "*Item.* I give and bequeath to my beloved cousins, Eunice Williams, Jerusha, Elisabeth, and Lucretia Williams, daughters of Israel Williams, Esq. and Sarah his wife, the sum of twenty pounds each." "*Item.* I give and bequeath to my loving cousin, Elisabeth Williams, over and above the twenty pounds above mentioned, my silver creampot and teaspoons." Here it comes out. "The lady that Col. Williams did *not* marry," toasted at the Jackson Supper of 1859, was, in all human probability, Elisabeth Williams, of Hatfield. The reference is undoubtedly to her in the founder's last letter to Colonel Israel: "I have altered my mind since I left your house, for reasons, as to what I designed to give (which should have been handsome) to one very near to you." The reference of the strong tradition in the family that he intended to marry some one (which came down to the present writer direct, through the late Mark Hopkins, who belonged to the family by straight descent) was, beyond question, to Elisabeth Williams, of Hatfield. The tradition in *his* family, as it came down in Berkshire, is silent as to the "reasons" which led the Colonel to change his mind as to the amount of the bequest to her; the tradition in *her* family, as it has come down to the present in Hampshire, takes on the color that she rejected him in their last interview. She afterwards married, at any rate, Elisha Billings, Esq., of Conway, and Dwight Whitney Marsh (Williams College, 1842) is a descendant of that union, and publicly voiced, in a humorous way, the tradition of "rejection" at the Commencement dinner here in 1892. Her elder sister, Jerusha, also mentioned in the will, married William Billings, Esq., of Conway.

Now, for a man only forty-one years old, subjected to such strange and changing environments as his, having acquired a moderate fortune by his own exertions, to propose, of his own motion, on a not unlikely contingency, "that the above-mentioned estate be sold, and the money be put out to interest, and that the said interest shall be used for some pious or charitable purposes, as the propagating Christianity, the support of the poor in the County of Hampshire, or for schools on the frontier in the county aforesaid, to be at the direction of my Executors, hereinafter named, and after their decease to be at the direction of the justices of the sessions [Probate Court] for the county aforesaid," indicates a far-reaching benevolence and a Christian depth of purpose every way remarkable. Nor is it once only that he puts this general disposition of his estate upon a possible or probable contingency; he recurs to the same six times more in the course of the will, the last time as follows, after providing for the free school in the West Township, and contingently, also, for one in the East Township, he adds: "But in case the above provisos are not complied with, then it is my will and desire that the interest of the above-mentioned moneys be appropriated to some pious and charitable uses, in manner and form as directed in the former of this, my last Will and Testament."

(8) We come at last to that peculiar clause of the Colonel's will, which has immortalized his name in the name of a town and a college, and which has steadily altered and uplifted, for a century past, the entire development of the western end of Massachusetts. This clause is distinct in character and purpose from the general one quoted under the last head, and indicates a different phase of mind and heart from that as also characteristic of the personal

donor. That indeed refers, also, in a general way, to "schools on the frontier in the county aforesaid"; but this, on the other hand, is a specific appropriation of definite moneys for a single "free school," placed in a described locality, "forever," on two clean-cut conditions, both of which were actually met, "but in case the above provisos are not complied with," the moneys were to revert to the general and above-mentioned pious and charitable uses.

"*Item*. It is my will and pleasure and desire that the remaining part of lands not yet disposed of shall be sold at the direction of my Executors, within five years after an established peace, and the interest of the money, and also the interest of my money arising by my bonds and notes, shall be appropriated towards the support and maintenance of a free school (in a township west of Fort Massachusetts, commonly called the West Township), forever, provided the said township fall within the jurisdiction of the Province of the Massachusetts Bay, and, provided also, that the Govenor and General Court give the said township the name of WILLIAMSTOWN; and it is my further will and desire that if there should remain any moneys of the above donation, for the said school, it be given towards the support of a school in the East Township, where the fort now stands."

Ephraim Williams was, at any rate, a bachelor; it is possible, perhaps even quite probable, that he had then recently been disappointed in the expectation of a future marriage with Elisabeth Williams; he was already well forward in a military campaign that would certainly prove personally hazardous, and very likely to prove fatal; the natural coveting for personal remembrance after the inexorable has been confronted, which possesses, more or less, every man of culture and character, was without question felt by the lonely officer, as he saw around him at Albany, and more and more day by day, the instruments and agents of sudden death in the shock of battle; he had no child to perpetuate his memory, his relatives of the name were extremely numerous throughout New England, he himself had done and suffered nothing as yet, to give him a passport over more than one coming generation, and even his old sergeant (John Hawks), by an heroic defence of Fort Massachusetts against Vaudreuil, had attached his name to that locality more lastingly than its commander; to an elect and serious spirit like his own, it was, under all the circumstances, a God-given impulse to shape a sentence or two in his last will and testament, that might be likely in its results, not only to secure the lasting good-will and gratitude of some of his old comrades in arms along the Upper

Hoosac, but also to attach his name in a distinctive form, and for a definite reason, to a beautiful spot of earth sure to possess its loyal dalesmen till the end of time; and so, there came out of his human longings and aspirations the right and vital word, — "provided also, that the Governor and General Court give the said township the name of Williamstown."

They did. When the town was incorporated, ten years after this, that is to say, in July, 1765, the "West Township," dear to the Colonel's heart, became "Williamstown," never to be changed. While the Colonel's motive in the name was doubtless strictly personal, and appropriately so, and while any such end of personal remembrance as lay in his mind has already been reached a thousand-fold, and will be met in swelling volume till human memories shall fade out, the name of the Town and the College is also felicitous as helping worthily to perpetuate the memory of several other members of the Williams family who played well their part (though much subordinate to his), in the direct or indirect upbuilding of the Town and the College and the country. Let us briefly run over some of these services of the Williams family.

Ephraim Williams, Senior, father of the founder, was chairman of a committee appointed by the Legislature in January, 1739, "carefully to view the land situate on or near Hoosuck River; and if they find the land accommodable for inhabitants, that they survey and lay out one or more townships of the contents of six miles square and Return a Plat or Plats thereof to this Court at their next May session with an account of the Quantity and Quality of the said land, so that this Court may dispose thereof as they shall think proper." Thomas Wells was joined with Williams in this affair, and in May the committee repaired to the Hoosac, and with the aid of Timothy Dwight and Nathaniel Kellogg, surveyors, partially laid out three townships, and submitted their report in June following.

We the subscribers have carefully viewed the lands on and near the Hoosuck River and finding the same very accommodable for settlement have by the assistance of Timothy Dwight Esq., and Mr. Nath. Kellogg, survey's, laid out three townships each of the contents of six miles square. Two of which are adjoyning and lye on Hoosuck River the other on Mayoonsuck, being the northern branch thereof about three miles northward of the lowest of the two towns all which will fully appear by the plans herewith humbly presented. We have not perfected all the lines occasioned by the Great Opposition we met with from Sundry Gent'n from Albany a particular account of which we are ready to lay before y'r Excellency and Honours if thereto required, and are your Excellency's and Hon's most obedient and dutiful servants.

BOSTON June 6th, 1739.   EPH͟ᴹ WILLIAMS } Committee.
                                  THOMAS WELLS }

The " Gentlemen from Albany," referred to in this report, represented the government of the province of New York, between
which and the province of Massachusetts the boundary line was
not finally settled till 1787.   The report of Captain Williams excited a deal of interest in Boston, particularly on account of the
alleged encroachments and activities of New York along on the
Upper Hoosac; and a committee of the Council and House, to which
the report was referred, very speedily reported in turn in the following words: " The committee to whom was referred the Report
of Captain Williams and Wells and their doings with the platt of the
three townships lately surveyed and laid out at or on Hoosuck
River &c., Offer as their opinion that for the better securing the
undoubted rights this governm't have to those and other lands thereabout lying in this province, that the most northerly of the three
townships aforesaid of the contents of six miles square adjoyning
thereto and southward thereof, which. the said Williams and Wells
had not time to take a survey of tho' well assured of it and accommodable for a town and whereon some few people have already got
and inhabit; Bee granted to such of his Majesty subjects as will
effectually settle the same in the space of two years with fifty or sixty
familys on each tract and give sufficient bonds therefor," etc.

Something, we know not now what, quieted the fears of the authorities at Boston in relation to Dutch encroachments at the northwest
for several years, and then the breaking out of the old French War
made New York and Massachusetts allies as against a common enemy,
and the building of Fort Massachusetts in 1745 furnished a Yankee
garrison sufficient to protect eastern interests in the neighborhood
till the Peace of Aix-la-Chapelle; so that nothing was done in the
way of settlement until the new survey of the two townships in 1749,
which followed different lines throughout from that of 1739, and
which laid the western boundary of Williamstown (except at the
northwest corner) considerably to the east of the New York line as
finally adjusted forty years later.   It is to the credit of the Williams
family, and of the name officially given to the town in 1765, that the
founder's father made the first survey, and confronted for the first
time *in loco* the few Dutch inhabitants that had already straggled
up the Hoosac towards the junction of its two branches, and threw
bold protests into the face of the Albany "Gentlemen" who were
pushing these stragglers from behind.   The stragglers themselves
receded down the river.   Not a solitary Dutchman, or other squatter,
cumbered the ground in any direction when the house lots were surveyed out in the spring of 1750.

The claim of New York to extend over the Taconics to the east-ward, which had already been put forcefully forward in the southern part of the county of Hampshire, still hovered over the mind of Colonel Williams when he dictated his will in 1755; for he made it a proviso to his gift for the free school in the West Township, — "provided the said township fall within the jurisdiction of the Massa-chusetts Bay." It is a curious thing in this connection, that one of the most distinguished of the Williams family, Samuel Williams, a grandson of the original "Redeemed Captive," of Deerfield, surveyed and settled finally the boundary line between New York and Massa-chusetts in 1786–87, and so in the way of result added a very con-siderable area to the town of Williamstown, the southwest corner being thus placed 446 rods further west than the survey of 1749 made it. This Samuel Williams, who was a Harvard graduate and Professor of Mathematics, had a son, Charles K. Williams (Williams College, 1800), who became a governor and chief justice of Vermont; and the latter a son, Chauncey K. Williams (Williams College, 1852).

Colonel Israel Williams, of Hatfield, after the death of Colonel John Stoddard in 1748, had the direct military command of the western frontier till the end of the last French War. He planned the West Hoosac Fort, and controlled in the first instance all its relations with Fort Massachusetts. There was, indeed, a good deal of appealing on the part of the soldiers and settlers from him to the governor and Council at Boston; a good deal of fault-finding and general abuse of the Colonel, which called out from him at length, in the way of personal defence, a long statement of his action and policy through a number of years, — a paper which has never yet been printed, but which must needs be read, in order to understand fully his great services in critical times to this whole region round about. There are reasons multiform and manifold why West Hoosac should have been named Williamstown. The fact that Israel Williams developed into a Tory, and could not even be "smoked into a Whig," is no reason for belittling his long and stout services to Williams-town and its vicinity.

The issue of the battle of Lake George was the deliverance for the time being, and practically for always, of the Upper Hoosac from the French and Indian attacks. Besides the chief figure in that victory, commemorated in the name of our Town and College, there were five other men of the same name, all his near kinsmen, con-spicuous in the battle and its sequels. Williamstown might well have been so named even on account of the bearing on its history of these subordinate services alone.   There were Stephen Williams, Chaplain; Thomas Williams, Surgeon; William Williams, or "Billy," so called, Surgeon's Mate; William Williams, Quarter-Master; and Josiah Williams, an Ensign, fearfully wounded in the battle.   Besides these six members of the Williams family and bearing their name, there was present there, professionally, Dr. Perez Marsh, who married Sarah, eldest daughter of Colonel Israel Williams.

The reasons are not far to seek — that is to say, they are not hard to find — why Ephraim Williams in his will gave the west town precedence over the east as the certain seat of the free school for the benefit of the settlers.   So far as he himself held landed property in the two, it lay mostly in the east town.   In 1750, the General Court had given him, in fee simple, a fine estate of 200 acres on the great bend of the Hoosac, reserving to the province ten acres of the same, on which Fort Massachusetts then stood, on condition that he build and maintain, for twenty years, mills for the use of the soldiers and the settlers on one of the branches of the Hoosac above near their junction.   The mills were built.   We know their place on the Ashuwillticook in the heart of the village of North Adams.   On the other hand, he had drawn two house lots in the west town, Nos. 8 and 10, which would ultimately, if he held them, entitle him to two sixty-thirds of the entire township.   His farm (the present Harrison farm) and his mills were doubtless worth then four times as much as his house lots and their chances.

Still his mind was clear that the free school should be set up in the west town, and only the remnants of the bequest (if any) go to the benefit of the east town.   Why was this?   There were topographical reasons: the east town was relatively to the other a dell, a ravine, the two branches of the Hoosac rushing to their union between steep mountains and through very narrow valleys, the meadow on which Fort Massachusetts stood being the only broad and open space in the whole township; while the two main tributaries of the Hoosac in the west town, the Green River and the Hemlock Brook, had made in the course of ages comparatively wide valleys for themselves parallel to each other and at right angles to the chief·vale of the Hoosac, the spaces between which were beautiful uplands having knolls of every variety of shape rising up out of relative levels, the encompassing hills no longer steep and ragged barriers, but receding lifts of then warm woods and now fresh green fields.   The father had doubtless often told over to the son what his observant eye had caught on purpose to officially report, when he had rambled over these sunny hills and along these perpetual streams

with his surveyor, Nathaniel Kellogg, in 1739; and the Colonel himself, especially after another committee with their surveyor had
wisely laid out the house lots in 1750 at the northern centre of the
oblong concave, must more than once in the five years have personally scrutinized with the zeal of a landowner present and prospective,
and with the living interest in others of a proposed benefactor, these
varied slopes and hills and levels, already officially pronounced to
be so "accommodable for settlement."

There were agricultural reasons, — the soldiers at Fort Massachusetts, during the ten years past, had all been brought up on farms to
the eastward or southward, and were all looking forward, on their
discharge from military service, to farm life on lands of their own;
the heart of their commander had long been strongly drawn out
towards them and their future interests, as appears from letters and
arguments addressed by him in their behalf, to the General Court at
Boston. The testimony is abundant that he had drawn out towards
himself their respect and confidence to a remarkable degree. It was
to the interest of all parties that they should ultimately settle on
the best farming lands to be had in the province, and considerable
numbers of them had already purchased such lands in actuality and
prospective in West Hoosac; such lands as these were would be
pretty sure to be taken up pretty soon by actual occupants, while
this was more doubtful in respect to the less eligible lands in the
east town. The Colonel had noted well what almost everybody has
an opportunity to see, namely, that where folks are there will be
children; and, consequently, on this ground too, he made provision
for the school where it was most likely there would be scholars to
attend it and profit by it.

And there were historical reasons why the west town should have
the preference in this regard. As we have seen already, he himself
had assisted quite a number of his garrison to buy and pay for their
house lots in West Hoosac. One family there, well known to him,
had already two children, a boy and a girl, when this will was
drafted in Albany. It has been said and is credible, though the
authority for it is not distinct, that the Colonel had given some intimations to his men of his intention to do something for them, in a
general way, as settlers upon these fertile lots, of which he was a
co-purchaser with them. We have seen that the proprietors of West
Hoosac learned, in general terms, of this bequest not very long after
the will was probated in November, 1755. They do not seem to have
been surprised at all by its terms, and they took simple and natural
action in sending Benjamin Simonds, the father of the two children

but just referred to, down to Northampton to get a copy of the will. The charge for this service was extremely small.. It can scarcely be questioned that Simonds expected, in the person of his children, to become a speedy beneficiary of his commander's gift; but while he lived to see the free school open in 1791, and the College open in 1793, and twelve classes graduated in order from the latter, his youngest child was twenty years old when the school was opened. Very few, if any, of the children of actual settlers, prior to the incorporation of the town in 1765, ever received any direct advantage from the commander's charity, — so wisely and broadly did his executors construe their duties under the will in favor of a school of high grade, when once it might be established.

In quitting now for good the will of Colonel Williams, we quit also all further direct references to his motives and character. If we have not been able to reproduce so long after his death a living image of the man as he was, going in and out among men, it is because the data do not exist for such a vivid picture. Nearly every extant writing of the Colonel, whether epistolary or other, has been given and commented on in these pages at length. The reader may thus construct for himself, as well as the writer for others. The impression produced on the latter's mind by these long-continued studies is of a man attractive in person and manners, ambitious, scholarly beyond his opportunities, broad-minded in victory over strong temptation to be otherwise, democratic in the midst of a very aristocratic generation, Christian in and to the core even if not in form, influential in his life through obvious purity and strength of motives, able to receive from and impart to the very able men of his time, and through the divine blessing and happily concurring circumstances and obstacles overruled for good, powerful through a single clause in a simple will to maintain through many generations, not only his own name fragrant as ointment poured forth, but also the two causes dearest to his heart, — education and piety.

John Worthington, of Springfield, one of his executors and an intimate acquaintance, has left on record the following remarkable judgment: " Humanity made a most striking trait in his character, and universal benevolence was his ruling passion: his memory will always be dear."

The chief source of present knowledge of the slow developments of Williamstown as a self-governing body controlling all local affairs by the major part of votes in a legal assemblage, from the first meeting of the few proprietors, Dec. 5, 1753, till the end of that century, are the records in the old "Proprietors' Book," so called, of their duly warned meetings and votes from time to time. It is thus that we learn in detail, through a single example, the best lesson that New England has had the privilege of teaching to the world at large. The roots of all our civil politics, municipal and state and national, are uncovered and displayed at this point. In preceding sections and chapters we have often referred to, and quoted from, these precious records, with a view of exhibiting the individual and social condition of the primeval settlers in this loved valley; is it not our function, also, to remind the later generations of the way in which self-respecting and liberty-loving and rights-defending citizens of a great Republic made up of co-equal states were trained here from the very beginning?

In the fall of 1753, there were about sixteen proprietors of house lots living on their respective lots, and fulfilling the conditions prescribed by the General Court of the province of Massachusetts Bay requisite to their owning these lots, and the further rights coupled with such ownership. This province, or colony, was then living and acting politically under a formal charter, granted to it for that purpose by William III., king of England, in 1691. Most of these sixteen proprietors had been previously soldiers in Fort Massachusetts under the pay and direction of this province, which had built the fort, and maintained in subordination to the mother country a war against France. Isaac Wyman, then in nominal command of the fort in time of peace, and at the same time the most conspicuous of the West Hoosac proprietors, drew up a petition to the General Court at Boston in behalf of all the proprietors, himself and several others subscribing it, asking for formal organization as a "Propriety"; that is, to be authorized and empowered by a major vote, in regularly notified meetings, to divide and apportion the lands held common, to lay out and construct needed highways, to raise money by taxation of themselves to defray the charges of laying out lands and roads and any other necessary charges, and to agree upon a method of calling legal meetings in future.

In the House of Representatives, Sept. 10, 1753. Read [this petition of Wyman's] and voted that William Williams Esqr one of his Majesty's Justices of the Peace for the County of Hampshire Issue his warrant for Calling a meeting of proprietors of the West Township at Hoosuck so called Directed to one of the principal proprietors of said Township, Requiring him to set up a notification in some publick place in said Township setting Forth the time place and occasion of said meeting fourteen Days Beforehand which meeting shall be holden in said Township and such of the proprietors as shall be present at said meeting are hereby authorised and impowered by a major vote to Determine upon a Division of all or part of the Lands in said Township not already alloted also to Choose a Committee or Committees to lay out the same also to Raise monies to Defray the charges that may arise by means of laying out said land also for Clearing Highways as also to Choose proprietors Clerk Treasurer assessors and Collectors and also to agree and Determine upon a method for calling meetings of said proprietors for the future..

Sent up for Concurrence : T. Hubbard Spk?.

In Council Read and Concur.d Tho.s. Clerk Deputy Secry

Consented to W. Shirley

A True Copy per Thos. Clerk Dep'y Secry

William Shirley, one of the ablest and by far the most interesting of all the colonial governors of Massachusetts, had returned from England only just in time to sign, as governor, this bill for politically organizing the inhabitants of West Hoosac, some of whom had served as "centinels" in Fort Shirley, built in 1744, and named after him. Almost everybody of prominence in Massachusetts, during the last half of the last century, touched in some relation or other this remotest corner of the colony; and local students of its history may well feel a sort of gratulation that the governor's own autograph is appended to their humble *magna charta*, rather than that of Spencer Phips, who, during Shirley's long absence in England, had acted as governor, and had signed most of the papers relating to the line of forts, and to the surveys of the two townships. In 1755, Governor Shirley was appointed Commander-in-Chief of the British forces in America, and planned the expedition of that year against Niagara, which he led in person as far as Oswego, where his son John died in the service only about a month after his elder son, William, was mortally wounded with General Braddock at the forks of the Ohio.

Colonel William Williams, of Pittsfield, in some aspects of his remarkable career more potent than any other member of the family in that generation, took the next hand in helping to organize into a self-governing community the few determined settlers on the Upper Hoosac, his official mandate to them being worded as follows : —

Provance of the Massachusetts Bay. Whereas I have received special Directions from the great and General Court of this provance at their sessions in September last to Issue my Warrant for Calling a meeting of the proprietors of the west township at Hoosuck so called Directed to one of the Principle proprietors of the s'd Township requiring him to set up a Notyfication in some publick place in s'd Township seting forth the time place and occasion of s'd meeting fourteen Days beforehand, s'd meeting to be held in s'd Township and such of the proprietors as shall be present at s'd meeting are by Said order of Court authorized and Impowered by a major Voate to act and Determine upon the following articles, Vizt. To agree upon a Division of a part or all the lands in said township

Not allready allotted = to Choose a Committee or Commiteses to lay out the same = to Choose a Commite to lay out high ways = to Raise money to Defray the Charges of laying out the Lands and highways and Clearing the same or any other Necessary Charges = To Choose a proprietors Clerk. To Choose a proprietors Treasurer To Choose proprietors assesors. To Choose a proprietors Colector or Colectors. To agree upon a method for Calling meetings for the future.

In observance of which Direction

Hampshire ss. To Isaac Wyman one of the proprietors of the said west Township at Hoosuck Gentⁿ. Greeting you are hereby Required to Notifye and warne the proprietors of s'd Township that they assemble at the House of Mr. Seth Hudson in s'd Township on wensday the Fifth Day of December next at Nine of the Clock in the four noon to act upon the fouregoing Articles as they shall think proper by Setting up in some publick place in said township an attested Coppy of the foregoing order of Court and this warrant by you Sygned fourteen Days before the time of said meeting.

Poontoosuck

November 15: 1753.   Wm WILLIAMS Just. Peace

The two foregoing papers and the one to be appended to the present paragraph — namely, the record of the votes passed and of the persons present at the very first legal meeting of the proprietors — are the three most venerable political documents in the history of the town. It is reasonably certain that all the men chosen to offices and appointed as committees in this primal meeting were present and participators. There were eleven of them. Their names were these: Allen Curtiss, Isaac Wyman, Seth Hudson, Jonathan Meacham, Ezekiel Foster, Jabez Warren, Samuel Taylor, Josiah Dean, Thomas Train, Gideon Warren, Ebenezer Graves. Substantive political power passed over, then and there, into the hands of these men and their successors. Not so complete, indeed, was this jurisdiction as that conferred twelve years later, by the same body, in the act incorporating the town, but it was complete so far as it went; and even the town and the town-meeting under the Provincial General Court were not what these became twelve years later still, under an independent state Legislature. Power, in all its gradations, is agreeable to men, and it is to their credit as men that it is so. These eleven came together under the modest roof of Seth Hudson, and went out from it to perform, in due time, their several functions, with a decided accession of self-respect, with a new sense, the sense of citizenship, — a corporate sense of self-guidance as towards self-chosen ends. The room in which they met on that day has remained essentially unchanged until this day, — one hundred and forty years, — although the house has been removed down Hemlock Brook, about half a mile from its original location. Hudson drew house lot 9, and built his house near its northern end, on the eastern bank of the brook, called for some time, from this circumstance, Hudson's Brook. Captain Hudson, or Dr. Hudson, as he was indifferently called, because his medical and military education had been but indifferent, was a leading member and the last survivor of the original proprietors.

At a Proprietors meting lawfully warned in the west township at hoosuck ss called December the fifth 1753 = Voted by the major part of the proprietors at s'd meetin the fouregoing articles Vizt

First Voted and Chose Allen Curtice moderator for s'd meetin.

Second Voted and Chose Isaac Wyman Proprietors Clerk

Thirdly Voted by the proprietors to lay out all the medow land Lying upon the main River and the medow land lying upon green River as far as the first Brook or Creek in Equal proportion to Each Right in Said Township and one hundred accors of upland to Each Right ajoying to the medow land or as Near as they Can to Lay out the best land.

Forthly Voted to Leave it to the Commite to Lay out the Land in one Division or two as they shall Judge best.

5ly Voted and Chose Allen Curtice Seth Hudson Jonathan mechom Ezekiel Foster Jabez Worren the Commite to lay out the land in s'd Township.

6ly Voted and Chose Samuel Taylor Giden Worrin Jonathan mechom the Commite to lay out high Ways in s'd Township that shall be Necessary.

7ly Voted and Chose Allen Curtice sevayer to Clear the Roads in s'd Township

8ly Voted at s'd meeting to Lay the Roads at the Eand of Each main street foure Rods wide in said Township

9ly Voted that the Roads to accommidate the medow Land shall be But two rods wide and all the Roads to accomidate the other Divisions two Rods wide allso.

Voted to Raise a rate of Eight Shillings upon Each Proprietors Right in s'd Town to pay the Charges that may arise by Laying out s'd Land

Voted to Rase ten shillings to pay for a Proprietors Book

Voted and Chose Isaac Wyman Proprietors Treasurer

Voted and Chose Thomas Train Josiah Deean Colectors for said Proprietors

Voted and Chose Ebenezer Graves Allen Curtice and Ezekiel Foster assessors for said Proprietors

Voted at said meetin that five or seven of the proprietors of said Town makin application to the Clerk of said Proprietors for Calling meetings for the future

Voted at s'd meetin to Lay out the land in said Town as soon as may be Convenant

at a meeting Held at West Hoosuck Pursuant to the Court order on the fifth Day of December 1753 the above said votes paist in a legial manor

Test = Allen Curtice moderator for said meetin

ISAAC WYMAN
Prop⁸ Clerk

When these few proprietors of house lots then and thus entered upon the administration of affairs in West Hoosac, the only points that had been already settled for them by committees of the General Court at Boston were the boundary lines of the town as they were laid out in 1749 much as they are now, and the village plat or house lots as another committee from Boston determined them in the following spring. What we still call the "Main Street" had been then surveyed out fifteen rods wide from the Green River to Buxton Brook, that is, 467 rods east and west in general trend; and what we still call North and South streets was, at the same time, laid out six rods wide at right angles to the other, 265 rods north and south. The land covered by this extended Greek cross never became the property in any sense of the individual proprietors of the house lots that abutted upon it, and never came under the touch of the "Propriety" or the "Town" as a whole, except superficially for the purposes of a roadway. These two highways were surveyed and donated by the province as a condition precedent to the sale of the house lots. Each householder was to have the privilege of them as a roadway, and nothing more. There were no owners of adjoining lands, no "abutters" in the legal sense, when these roads were laid out. They were conveyed by the commonwealth as commons in perpetuity to a possible body corporate not yet created.

While these lines are being penned, a wordy and acrid controversy is going on in South Street as to the right of the selectmen of the town to treat that road solely in its interest as a highway, without reference to the wish or will of the parties owning the lands on either side of it. The selectmen have exercised this right with obvious legality and propriety. The ordinary claim of abutting owners to hold the land to the middle of the road, and to control it for all purposes except a free passing, only applies to roads built on lands owned by individuals, who do not part with the fee simple of their land in order that a road may be built, but only convey an easement to the authorities for roadway purposes. The same principle of commons to be controlled by representative officials only applied to any roads surveyed and set apart as such by the proprietors as a body, before any of the lands were parcelled out to individual owners. In their first meeting, months before there was any private division of the land, they voted "to lay the roads at the end of each main street four rods wide," and also, "that the roads to accommodate the meadow land shall be but two rods wide, and all the roads to accommodate the other Divisions two rods wide."

At their second meeting, April 18, 1754, they voted to accept the return of the committee chosen to lay out the divisions, and also the return of the committee to lay out the highways "to accommodate said Town." Such highways, so accepted, before there had been any (the least) actual division of the lands, were clearly not subject to any abutters' rights, because there were no abutters at that time.

The next thing at the second meeting was: "Voted and agreed to Draw the medow lots and the first fifty accre Division as follows: Vizt Choose m.ʳ David King Surveyor to Draw for the Divisions of Land to Each Right." At the same time, they voted and granted to Mr. King his accounts for laying out the first two divisions; namely, the meadow lots and the first-division fifty-acre lots.

The sixty-three meadow lots were surveyed out at an average of ten acres each — the modern measurements pretty uniformly overrunning the ancient — along the Hoosac and Green rivers, single lots more frequently than otherwise crossing the rivers. A half-dozen of the lots were located on both sides of the last stretch of Broad Brook also. Beginning very near the division line between the two towns of East and West Hoosac, on the river, with meadow lot No. 1, the lots are numbered regularly down the river, without any break, until, in No. 37, the river takes a sharp lurch to the north, striking there the stubborn roots of Northwest Hill, enclosing what is now called the River-Bend Farm, when, in consequence, the meadow lots jump across to Broad Brook, and, after the junction of that with the main river, the lots continue on the Hoosac to the Vermont line, ending there in No. 46. Then they commence again in No. 47, in what would have been a part of the village plat if the southeast quarter of that had been completed towards the east, on Green River, and, running regularly up that river to the south, complete their number — sixty-three — at what was then called (and long after) "Taylor's Crotch," or the junction of the Hopper Brook with the larger stream. Some of these meadow lots became afterwards the sites of important and permanent dwellings, in which the same family lived generation after generation. Such, for example, was No. 62, on which the Blairs lived for three long-lived generations, and No. 14, near which the Smedleys lived for four generations. As a rule, however, the meadow lots were low land, unfit at first for houses, and some of them were for a long time submerged. Samuel Kellogg, Senior, reported, in his old age, that the only way one could get over his own meadow lots along the river, at first, was by jumping from one prostrate log to another.

It was a much more important stroke towards the permanent

settlement of Williamstown, when, in this same spring, Mr. David King surveyed out and drew for each proprietor of an house lot a fifty-acre lot of the first division; for this was intended to be the out-farm, or the nucleus of it, of each village proprietor. The theory of the house lots was that the people must live close together and near the church, or meeting-house, as they called it, so as to be able to defend themselves and their dwellings from incursions of the hostile French and Indians. The theory of the other divisions, and especially of the two fifty-acre divisions, was apparently to furnish each villager with an upland farm, as much land as he would care to cultivate, with the due portions of pasture and forest, in addition to the home lot of ten acres and a meadow lot of the same area. This general plan, however, did not work well in practice. The fifty-acre lots, though they constituted the best lands in the town, were so scattered about all over the town as to be inconvenient of cultivation from the village. The village lot required a barn as well as a house, and the outlot would, in most cases, need another barn, or demand a far-carrying of crops and a tending of cattle at a distance from home. And so, even before the victories of Wolfe and Amherst dissipated the fear of the Indians, and more particularly after that time, the more thoughtful and enterprising villagers began to sell their house lots, and to make homes for themselves, as well as farms, on the outlots. For examples merely, Nehemiah Smedley sold his house lot No. 1, and slowly aggregated a fine farm for his family on Green River, near its junction with the Hoosac; and Benjamin Simonds sold his house lot No. 3, on which he had a home and tavern next west of Smedley's home, and bought the outlots on the Hoosac, constituting the River-Bend Farm, now owned and occupied by Sheriff George Prindle.

The lots of the first fifty-acre division were remarkably scattered over the town, and it is difficult to discover the principle of their numerical location. The first three numbers (1, 2, 3) and the last three (61, 62, 63) were laid out directly to the east of Taylor's Crotch, and this may probably indicate an expectation of a greater development around the mill privilege there than has ever been actually realized. There was a "mill lot" early laid out around the junction of the two brooks, of about seven acres, and Samuel Taylor became the first owner and improver of the privilege; it then went into the hands of Asa Douglas of "Jericho," now Hancock, who sold, in 1769, his "right in mill place called Taylor's Crotch" to William Krigger. The Kriggers, a Dutch family from down the Hoosac, — William, John, Peter, John George, — are characterized in old deeds as "Miller" or "Yeoman," and some of them carried on the sawmill and gristmill at the Crotch for two generations; some members of this family bought parts of No. 50 of this division, which lies to the west of the junction of the brooks, and these parts have remained in the mill-estate till the present time; and parties by the name of Sweet — whence the modern and transient designation "Sweets' Corners" — owned the lands around the mill till 1892, when the town bought them as a home for their poor.

Nos. 4, 5, and 6, of this division, were located north of the Hoosac River, as were also Nos. 51, 52, and 53, and these were the only fifty-acre lots of either division in the White Oaks. Five of these lots, beginning with No. 7, lie in order south of the southeast quarter of the village plat, and east of South Street and the Stone Hill road; while seven, commencing with No. 40, were laid out in order to the west of those highways and adjoining them, 46 and 49 lying to the east of the Stone Hill road towards the Crotch, while 48 is bisected by that road. Then four lots, 36–39, are located in order on the Green River road, from north to south, just about half way between the village plat and the Crotch, and made up some of the best farms in town. The seven lots, 28–34, were cut out of low and fine lands on both sides of the lower reach of Green River, east and southeast of the hamlet, 35 flanking the north ends of about half of the house lots of the northeast quarter of the plat. Beginning on the boundary line separating the two towns, Nos. 12–21 flank the main road connecting them; while 22 and 23 and 54–60 are all on the Stratton road towards its southern end.

As a sort of sample of the farms early constructed out of these first-division fifty-acre lots, though it be more favorable and permanent than the average of them, a sketch of the Meacham farm, comprising Nos. 7 and 8, whose west ends touch South Street, and east ends Green River road, may be rightly placed at this point. Jonathan Meacham, from New Salem, a soldier, who had been in the settlement from the very first, an influential though migratory body, never succeeded in fixing his name to a single local habitation, as did James Meacham, his cousin, from the same place, also a soldier in Captain Nathaniel Dwight's company, working on the construction of Fort William Henry in 1755, who bought of Joseph Ballard, both then of New Salem, these two lots for £73 8s. 8d. in August, 1761. Just a year later, he brought on his wife and family through the woods and over the Hoosac Mountain. His daughter Lucy was then six weeks old. She was the fourth child, and seven others were added here. Either on the way or soon after arriving, he was fortunate enough to kill a bear, which furnished the family what they quaintly called "pork" for a considerable time. Once, at least, they found a deposit of wild honey to be a welcome addition to their slender commissariat. Mrs. Meacham, whose maiden name was Lucy Rugg, brought along with her a root or two of a hop-vine. One hundred and thirty years has not yet exhausted the vitality of those roots, for the vine is growing yet by the side and in the crevices of the large rock on No. 7, near which they built their first log cabin. Their second house, which was framed and plastered, was built on a knoll to the southeast overlooking the Green River road and a spring near it, which was doubtless the motive for the new location. Their third house was of brick which were burnt near the site of the new house, which was placed much nearer the house lots than either of the others, and the second house was drawn down to the brick one to serve as an L or addition, and it is still standing in that relation in this year of Grace, 1892, though now used as a worn-out and topple-over shed.

The first James Meacham, besides being a prominent farmer and citizen here for fifty years, was one of the two original deacons of the church, which he served faithfully in that capacity nearly as long. He was a good and constant Revolutionary soldier and petty officer, though, like many another such, he sympathized with the movements of Captain Shays and his men in 1787, and left his home openly one Sunday morning (gun on shoulder) to join them. He died in July, 1812, in his eightieth year, leaving the farm to his eldest son, James H. Meacham, born here Christmas Day, 1769, who married Nabby Warner, a sister of the famous Colonel Seth Warner, and who became even more prominent than his father in the affairs of the town during a long and useful life. He died in March, 1837, in his sixty-eighth year. The farm descended to his only son, James Meacham (there were five daughters, of whom one, Emeline, is still living at the old homestead), born Feb. 3, 1805, and died May 20, 1883. This Captain James Meacham was an excellent man and a good citizen. He enlarged his already large house about 1840, to accommodate, for their meetings and festivities, the Kappa Alpha Society of the College. They continued to meet with him for many years, until they procured ample quarters of their own in the heart of the village. James B. Meacham (Williams College, 1854) and a younger brother, now a merchant in St. Louis, are the present owners of the farm, which has never been alienated from the family during the century and a third of unintermitted ownership and occupation. Israel Meacham, youngest son of the original James, was a graduate of the College of the year 1797, and became a physician; and Franklin Meacham, son of the late Captain James, born in 1833, was for many years a distinguished surgeon in the United States army.

The chief business of the third public meeting of the proprietors of West Hoosac, convened at the dwelling-house of Captain Allen Curtiss the 15th of May, 1754, was " To Draw for the Second fifty-acre Division in the following manner Choose Capt. Allen Curtiss to Draw a ticket to Each Right for s'd Propr.⁵ " Also it was then and there voted, " To Clear the Road from the North Eand of the Cross Streeat in s'd Town to hampshear line one Rod wide and for the Propr.ˢ to work for two Shillings and Eight pence a Day." At the same time and place it was, in addition, " Voted and granted Oliver Averys and John Crawfourds accompt for Clearing part of the buriel-Place." As no other and further proprietors' meeting than this was holden for six years and a half, on account of the acute reopening of the French War, viz., until October, 1760, and most, if not all, of the householders re-entered the military service, and the new West Hoosac Fort became the centre and support of the settlement much as Fort Massachusetts had been before, — this is the proper place to say what needs to be said about the fifty-acre lots of the second division.

The very best farming lands in the entire town were distributed in this third drawing. They were surveyed out in two groups: Nos. 1–6 lay together north of the north line of the village plat, and on its prolongation towards the west; and much of this land is now incorporated in the fine " Buxton Farms," of Colonel A. L. Hopkins; some of it surrounds the elegant summer home of Mr. S. P. Blagden (Williams College, 1862), and the rest is laved by the lower reaches of Hemlock Brook. Nos. 7–63 lie altogether in a rectangular body on the southern central plateau of our Williamstown valley, the straggling village of South Williamstown being somewhat to the south, and to the east also, of the centre of this parallelogram of good farms. The first-division fifty-acre lots were scattered, without much reference to their numerical order, pretty much all over the northeast quarter of the town. Not so the second division. The first six lots were all contiguous on the lower slope of Northwest Hill, the southern line of all of them resting upon the straight line but just now described. Most of the rest of these lots were very symmetrically arranged, abutting upon one or other of the two parallel east and west roads constructed on purpose " to conveau " them. For example, the north line of the lots, odd numbers 9–29 extending west to east across the plateau to Green River, abuts nearly at right angles upon the "Woodcock road"; while the south line of the corresponding even numbers 10–30, each odd opposite its even, juts down upon the same road.

Twenty-two of these lots were thus symmetrically disposed of, and made accessible by, the Woodcock road, Woodcock's own lot, still holding his cellar and the cellar a growing commemorative tree, being No. 27. John Torrey, of Middletown, Connecticut, bought No. 20 of Isaac Searle in 1766, and raised a very large family over a cellar still visible in a clump of bushes on the north side of the Woodcock road; and his brother, William Torrey, established himself, about the same time, on Nos. 14 and 16. William Torrey died Oct. 30, 1820, in his seventy-seventh year. His son William spent a long and useful life upon the same premises; his son Myron spent a life equally long and useful upon Nos. 10 and 12, parallel with, and just west of, his own. Myron's son, Homer Torrey, is present owner and cultivator of his father's farm; and all four of these men, in their three generations, have been much employed as town officers, particularly as selectmen and assessors and tax-collectors.

A similar lay-out of eighteen of these fifty-acre lots, Nos. 31–48, was made on either side of the "Sloan road," which stretches straight from the immemorial tavern in South Williamstown to "Oblong road." The south ends of the odd numbers, 31–47, running from east to west, abut on the Sloan road, while the north ends of the even numbers opposite, 32–48, strike the same road on its south side. By much the most remarkable family of those originally settling on these two tiers of lots was that of Samuel Sloan, of Canaan, Connecticut, blacksmith, whose original log house, built on the southern edge of No. 43, was standing well into the present century, and who opened the first tavern in what came to be the South Village, on another of these fifty-acre lots, No. 53, a site kept as a tavern ever since; while Sloan, rising up through all the grades of the militia service, became a General, and, rising up from the poverty of a journeyman artisan, with his kit of tools, through legitimate buying and selling, till he became the richest man in town, built for himself, at the very opening of the new century, by far the finest house in the town, now owned by the College and occupied by the president.

The rest of the lots of this important division, 49–63, with two unimportant exceptions, lay in a body at the South Part of the town and upon the most level area of land within the limits of the town. The junction of the Hancock Brook with the Ashford Brook to con.

stitute Green River falls upon No. 53, on the western edge of which is the tavern-stand so often referred to. The ten lots, 49–58, are contiguous with each other, run east and west, and the Green River, with its two tributary brooks, flowing for ages through that part of the valley, slowly flattened it almost to a dead level. The surveyor laid out these ten lots so that each of them is crossed by one of these streams. No wonder these lots took the eye of the very earliest proposed settlers at the "South Part," as this section of the town has always been called, and always will be. These lots were surveyed and distributed to the then owners of the house lots in 1754; but there is not a particle of proof that any one of them

GENERAL SLOAN'S HOUSE.
Built in 1801.

was built on prior to 1760. Renewed war rolled down the Upper Hoosac in that interval of time, until the English conquest of French Canada at Quebec and Montreal. Civil affairs were mostly at a standstill even within the village plat. Military exigencies controlled everything for six years. Lands, indeed, changed hands frequently. Speculators came and went. Richard Stratton and his two sons Isaac and Ebenezer, from Western, now Warren, all of them later among the most influential citizens of Williamstown, were among a very few others who came in that perturbed interval to cast in their lot, for better or for worse, with the soldier-men of West Hoosac. Richard Stratton bought, at different times, house lots 57 and 58, and at length built upon the latter the first two-story house erected in the borough, in which he died in an honored old age, and which is still standing substantially unchanged, having been the home for the past thirty years of James M. Waterman; about the same time, Richard Stratton, from "parental affection, etc.," sold his "well-beloved son Ebenezer Stratton," the first-division fifty-acre lots, 33 and 54, who occupied them as a farm during a long life, having his farm-house at first on a knoll near the southern limit of his farm, and afterwards, on account of winds and drifts, building another one near the northern limit of his land, much nearer to meetings for himself and to schools for his children, though both houses stood on the "Luce road," west side, the latter one, in which the good deacon died in 1814, standing till about 1880.

Isaac Stratton, born in Western in 1739, and coming here with his father and older brother on attaining his majority, preferred to pitch his tent alone at the South Part on the second-division fifty-acre lot No. 54. He was the first settler on any one of the lots of that division. It is nearly certain that he located his first cabin there in 1760; and it is certain that he had no neighbor at all upon that splendid level of fifty-acre lots for three full years. Then Daniel Burbank, from Western, located to the south of him on No. 57, his first house being a framed building of one room, erected on the east side of the "Ashford road," which runs here diagonally as straight as an arrow across the lots 53–58, Stratton's house being on the west side of the road, and just to the south of the brook, over which the town as soon as it was incorporated built a bridge for him and Burbank, even before they built a bridge over the Green River at the east end of the north village. Stratton built his second house, a large two-story one, on the same site in 1785, and the passer-by may still read on its chimney "I. S. 1785." Considering that he was the first settler in South Williamstown, and later proved attractive to valuable neighbors on every side of him, and considering the record he made for himself as a patriot Major in the battle of Bennington, the high mountain that rises up out of those farms (as it were) and overlooks them, and stands sentinel between the Ashford and the Hancock brooks, was deliberately christened by the town in 1891, for all time, "Stratton Mountain."

At this same proprietors' meeting, in May, 1754, it was voted, as the next most important matter, to lay out a road, one rod wide for the present, from the north end of the "Cross Street," which was laid out (on parchment) six rods wide, and at right angles to the "Main Street," which was to be fifteen rods wide, to the line of New Hampshire, so-called; that is to say, to "Hazen's Line," the present line separating Massachusetts from Vermont. West Hoosac was a very isolated spot in 1754. Hoosac Mountain, to the eastward, was high and broad, and had not then been tunnelled for a steam railroad. There was an old-time Mohawk path over it, and by much the larger part of all the soldiers and settlers had worked their way over that path from the valley of the Deerfield River. From a quarter to a third of the then soldiers and settlers on the Upper Hoosac had come up from Connecticut, following up the Housatonic to its main watershed at Pontoosuck, and then up the northern tributary of the lake to its head-springs in New Ashford, and striking, almost within a stone's throw, the source of the Ashford Brook, which finds its fellow at South Williamstown, coming down the Green River, that just laves the east end of the village plat of West Hoosac. The watershed is not high to the southward, but there was then no good market in that direction. Albany had been the best hold for supplies for Fort Massachusetts from the beginning, and it was the best hope, in 1754, of the dozen families or so clustered around the West Hoosac Fort; and the only way to reach Albany was to drop down the Hoosac to its junction with the North River. Hence this proposed road for two miles to the northward, to the New Hampshire line of 1741, had an energetic surveyor (Curtiss) to clear it, and fair pay per day (2s. 8d.), in lieu of rates to proprietors willing to work on it.

This very early sign of Albany as the place of supply for the pioneer farmers is followed, in due time, by signs in plenty of their uncomfortable indebtedness to Albany merchants for these supplies. For example, Jonathan Meacham mortgaged to Albany parties, for £89 (New York money) his two house lots, 43 and 45, — on the former of which he dwelt, and parts of both of which are owned by the present writer, — to repay a debt as it stood in July, 1769; it was repaid in January, 1772, — £102, principal and interest. Take another example, out of many: Isaac Stratton sold, by mortgage deed, to Robert Kinney and Robert Kinney, Junior, merchants of the state of New York, for £105, part of his original home lot 54, June 7, 1788. He did not live to repay this debt and release the mortgage. He died April 3, 1789, aged fifty years.

There was another pressing reason, however, aside from markets, for opening up that roadway to the north. Nearly one-third of the meadow lots, otherwise at that time inaccessible, could be reached pretty directly by that road of two miles. Not much, if anything, was practically done with any of the meadow lots for ten or fifteen years after this time. They lay low, as their name implies, and were heavily wooded with those kinds of trees that are not afraid of wetting their feet; but every householder owned one or more of them, and all were naturally desirous to be able to get at them to see them, and some, perhaps, to sell them. Moreover, although the pine lots were not yet surveyed out for distribution, this stretch of new road actually went through some of the finest pines in the township, — what furnished, at any rate, when they came to be set off, Nos. 1, 2, 3, 7, 8, 61, all nearer to the village than the rest of the pine lots, which lay, with two exceptions, on the extreme northern line of the town. Before many years had run their course, John Smedley had his sawmill built near this new road, on the bank of the Hoosac, near its exit from the town, though it was fed from Broad Brook, and the tall and huge pines from Nos. 7 and 8 — which lots became his property — soon felt the teeth of his steel.

One other vote of the last meeting before the six years' intermission will delay us but for a moment. Two householders, Oliver Avery and John Crawford, had, in virtue of a vote at an earlier meeting, expended labor and skill in clearing up a part of the burying-ground, which lay just at the junction of the proposed wide Cross Street with the now proposed narrow North Street. They brought in their bill. Their account was voted without delay or objection. Death had already visited the little settlement but two or three years old, and was sure to return on his never-to-be-intermitted rounds. The people were evidently then looking rather northward than southward from the Square, both for routes for the living and a resting-place for the dead. Many bodies slept in this first-chosen spot. For reasons not now capable of full explication, but springing perhaps in part from some want of faith as to whether the large scheme of the village and township would ever be fulfilled in such troublous times, and with so many such others bidding for the public favor, the resolve came very shortly to have another cemetery — that is, sleeping-place — within the house lots themselves, and nearer to the few homes already made. The short stretch of Hemlock Brook as it crosses the Main Street was just about the centre of the houses already built when the town was incorporated, and so the southern end of house lot 12, just over the brook and abutting on the street, was set apart for future burials. This choice of place was fortunate, and the location beautiful; a few bodies were removed from the earlier to the later ground; from time to time contiguous parts of house lots 14 and 16 and 18 and 20 have been added to the original plot; and it is much to be hoped that all of the land of these five lots west of the Hemlock and south of the

Buxton brooks, as far as to their junction, may ultimately be incorporated into this early and beautiful sleeping-place of our dead.

We have already given in preceding chapters, and in their proper places, the military events that make forever memorable this valley of the Upper Hoosac River in the interval of time between the proprietors' meeting in May, 1754, and the next following one in October, 1760. We gather up now in a few items and documents what remains of the most interest in the records of the French wars, having a bearing upon the growth and fortunes of Williamstown and its College.

The deposition of Jabez and Gideon Warren of full and lawfull age, proprietors and settlers in the Township of West Hoosuck. Testifie and say that in the Latter end of Augt 1754 when the Enemy fell upon and Destroyed what is called the Dutch Hoosuck [Hoosac Falls] the Inhabitants of West Hoosuck Fled for shelter to the Fort Massachusetts when the said inhabitants arrived at said fort with their families they found many of the Dutch who had Escaped the Enemy and fled there also. Which so cumbered the fort that it was with great difficulty we Subsisted.

But hearing that Capt. Ephraim Williams was Coming to the fort with orders to relieve the Inhabitants of West Hoosuck we patiently waited his arrival. But when he came he refused to give us any relief saying he had orders from Co^{ll} Williams [Colonel Israel Williams] not to take any of the Town Inhabitants into the Service only Hudson Simonds and Meacham and not to take Hudson nor Simonds unless they would carry of their families. The distressed proprietors earnestly intreated that they might be favored and put into the Service alledging that they could reasonably expect the favour of the Government for they had spent all they had to Carry on a Settlement. Capt. Curtis Mr. Chidester and others desired favour might be shewn under our miserable Circumstances but was denied and ordered away with our families tho we desired the Liberty of building without the fort yet could not obtain the request altho many from the duch had it granted them and even allowed to live in the fort and in the very room where the Government stores were kept. and others were allowed to come to fort soon afterward with their families and altho the fort was not at that Supplied with its Quoto of men yet the distressed proprietors could not be put into service when those who were no proprietors nor under such needy Circumstances were admitted and even one from another Government. Further your deponents say not.

[Signed]   JABEZ WORRIN
            GIDEON WORRIN.

March 30 1757 the above was solemnly sworn to before Timo. Woodbridge Justice Peace [Stockbridge]

Fellowship with the Dutch farmers further down the Hoosac had not yet come to be an achievement of the Yankee settlers above, as is evident from the tone of this deposition. Proofs as towards the same conclusion, not only for that time but also for times long subsequent, are abundant on all sides. The reasons also are very plain to be seen. For one, the boundary line between New York and Massachusetts was not finally established till just thirty years after this deposition was taken; and the feeling was strong on this side, that the other province was inclined to crowd, and had actually been crowding, its settlements too far to the eastward; as early as 1692, settlers under New York authority had occupied parts of what is now Mount Washington in Berkshire County, not without jealousy and protest on the part of Massachusetts; the slow pushing of the Dutch farmers up the Hoosac about fifty years later was one occasion of the erection of Fort Massachusetts, as we have seen; no love was lost as between Yankees and Dutchmen during the whole course of the French wars, so different were they in customs and costume; and even General Schuyler, substantial as were his merits, never drew during the Revolution the full confidence of the New England soldiers.

On the same day and at the same place of the above deposition, Jabez Warren, one of the deponents, and William Horsford, another of the original proprietors of West Hoosac, took solemn oath to the following: —

The Testimony of Jabez Warren and William Horsford of Hoosuck West Township of full and lawfull age who Testifie and say that in April 1756 When Serg^t William Chidester came from Boston with orders to take the Command of the fort west Hoosuck and for the Commissary for fort Massachusetts to supply Said West fort with proper stores said Commissary directed Mr. Chidester to receive the same of Capt. Wyman at Fort Massachusetts But we never have been able from that time to this to obtain more than fourteen days per man allowed at a time Excpt twice we have been allowed one months provision for said fort. at all other times out of the few men we have been obliged to travil four miles once every fortnight at the peril of our lives to fetch our provisions which keeps us in perpetual danger and difficulty. And that the said Capt. Wyman has constantly kept back every mans allowance when absent altho the absent Soldier hires his duty done.

And after Serg^t Chidester was killed the soldiers of said west fort being apprehensive from many reasons they should be ill used begged the favour of Lieu^t Barnard (who commanded at said fort) that they might lay the state of their case before the Great and General Court and be directed by them but our request was perremtory refused and none of the Soldiers could have Liberty to leave there but upon a promise that they would go no further than Hatfield.

And when the Government orders came for the soldiers to billet themselves there was not stores in said fort for each mans allowance one week. Further one of the deponents says (viz) Jabez Warren that met with many discouragements in building said fort for the guard that was sent by Capt. Wyman would guard none but while the people were at labor at the fort and refused to do any other duty and would not put a hand to help up a stick of timber tho we were few and our timber heavy and declared that to be their orders not to help us altho we offered them pay and sometimes the Guard left us entirely when greatly exposed. Furthermore your deponent saith not.

STOCKBRIDGE March 30th 1757.

In these papers the two Warrens and William Horsford do posterity a great favor, without foreseeing it at the time, or ever knowing it. They voice the inevitable jealousy between the garrisons and government of the older and larger, and the newer and more transient fort. They tell the truth undoubtedly, but not at all points the whole truth. Indeed, they were not in position to be able to see the whole truth. For instance, they represent as heartless and blameworthy their best friend, Captain Ephraim Williams, in insisting on the orders of his own superior officer, Colonel Israel Williams, requiring the West Hoosac men to go back to their cabins and defend and secure their crops, in August, 1756, while the Dutch farmers from below were allowed still to cumber Fort Massachusetts. The point was, that West Hoosac was an outpost very important to be defended against another raid of the French and Indians, and quite possible to be defended from Fort Massachusetts, provided the owners of the little properties there should go back and keep watch and ward over them, and be on the alert to send word to the fort of any approach of the enemy, who always came up the Hoosac, and had no other route; while Massachusetts, as such, had not the least interest in sending back and maintaining the Dutch farmers in their places below. The sooner those Dutchmen abandoned their farms as too hazardous, and gave up the job altogether, the better would like it the Great and General Court.

It is a curious thing, and yet explicable, that Captain Williams should then have brought over with him from the Connecticut permission to take three of the West Hoosac settlers, by name, into the province service at Fort Massachusetts and no more. These three were Seth Hudson, Benjamin Simonds, and Jonathan (?) Meacham. The condition was that Hudson and Simonds should carry off their families from the fort, implying that Meacham had, at least then and there, no family. We know that Simonds had then two children, both born in West Hoosac. It is implied that Hudson had also wife and children, but there is no record of it covering that time, and no probability of children born in West Hoosac at any time. Hudson was a man of merit on many grounds, as we have already seen; but he lacked the staying qualities of Simonds and Meacham; he came early and went often; of course, that involves that he returned from time to time. He came back in his old age, the last survivor of the first settlers, with young children of an undoubtedly second marriage, having been, in his comparative youth, both Captain and Surgeon in each of the forts; but Simonds came nearer than anybody else here to the full confidence of the Williams family, for he had begun early and suffered much; he had given hostages to society, and never failed at the sticking-point, and the contrast was great and painful in the opening years of this century (Colonel Simonds died in 1807) between the well-to-do and highly honored old age of the one, and the poverty-stricken and well-nigh forgotten status of the other.

"As the old birds have sung so the little birds will twitter." These very early jealousies and misunderstandings between the East Hoosac and the West, beginning in the forts and their administration, continuing more or less in all matters military and later civil, intensified by disputes over that clause of Colonel Williams's will, in which he seemed to make conditional provision for a school in the east town also, hinging in part, too, on the fact that nearly all of the first-rate land lay in the west town, which consequently drew nearly all of the soldiers of Fort Massachusetts thitherward as settlers, while a very different class of people, and many of them Quakers, came to be the inhabitants of the east town, have brought it about generation after generation that the neighborhood harmony, as between the two places, has never been striking; that the spirit and development of the two have been along quite different lines; that farming has always been the main industry of the one, and manufacturing of the other; and while both have proved in these latter days to be attractive to capitalists from other sections of the country, the beauty and variety and healthfulness of the hills and valleys of the one have proved inviting to retired and retiring capital, and the market opportunities of the other in banks and factories and all other kinds of trade have brought in rather the quick and still augmenting stores of capital.

The Petition of Thomas Williams
humbly shews

That Ephraim Williams of Stockbridge deceas[d] had the Honour to be Colonel of a Regiment in the Expedition against the French Fort at Crown Point A.D. 1755. And that in order to encourage the soldiers to engage in s[d] Service: It was by an Act of this Province of the 28 March, 1755 among other things provided that the Wages and Subsistence of the non-commissioned officers and soldiers should commence upon their Arrival at the Place of Rendezvous within this Province. That nine of the Companies in s[d] Regiment after their Arrival at the place of Rendezvous and before they march[d] on s[d] Service were subsisted according to the amount herewith produced. The Charge of which has never been paid by the Province. That s^d Ephraim relying on the Faith of the Province did in his life time defray part of the s^d amount and gave assurance in behalf of the Province for payment of the whole. Which engagements are not expected to be performed at the Expence of the Heirs of s^d Ephraim. And your Petitioner who had the honour of being appointed Lt. Col^o of s^d Regiment upon the Decease of s^d Ephraim humbly conceives the expence of s^d Subsistence is a just Debt on the Province to the Soldiers, and in behalf of said Companies prays the same may be allowed him for the use of s^d Ephraims Heirs so far as it was paid by him and the residue for the Use of the Soldiers as are yet unpaid. — and your Petitioner as in Duty Bound shall ever pray —

THOS. WILLIAMS.

[Endorsed]

April 16, 1757. Read and Ordered &c. &c. (except Major Ashley's Company already paid) at the rate of four shillings per week and so in proportion &c. And that the Sum be paid into the hand of the Petitioner Thos. Williams to be by him paid to the several persons &c.

T. HUBBARD Speaker
A. OLIVER Sec.

The whole action of the General Court of the province, the entire bearing of the several heirs of Colonel Williams as mentioned in his will, and especially the patience and assiduity of his executors, — Williams and Worthington, — were throughout favorable to the fulfilment of his desires in relation to a free school, and to the name of the town. The sums to be cared for by the executors were small and scattered and perplexing. The executors apparently never wearied for thirty years in giving thought to the dry details. So far as appears in the records examined by the writer, they did this as a labor of love and memory towards the testator, charging the estate nothing for their services. The relations, accordingly, of the Town and the College from the very first, and onwards to the commonwealth and its varied agencies of administration, have been special, and perhaps unique. Williamstown, with its school, is a "child of the state" in a sense in which Amherst is not, and possibly not even Cambridge.

Thomas Pownall, English Governor of Massachusetts in 1757–60, wrote to William Pitt, Prime Minister of England in 1757–61, that the whole cost to the province of the expedition to Crown Point of 1755, on whose issues so much of our local history for all subsequent time was depending, amounted to £87,058; the cost to Massachusetts of the next year's expedition to the northward, under General Winslow, was £101,613; and the expense to the same colony of the disgraceful campaign of 1757, under Lord Loudon, was £48,319.

The intimacy of the relations also between the settlement and development of Williamstown, and the friendly and masterful qualities of the man whose name it bears, is perhaps best made to appear in a comparison of the last muster-roll of the company of Captain Ephraim Williams, from Sept. 23, 1754, till March 28, 1755, with the names of the men now known to have been concerned in such settlement and development. The roll holds forty-one names. They had been subsisted at Fort Massachusetts, reckoned as one man, for 981 weeks and five days, at the public expense of £699 10s. 9d. lawful money at that time, which was silver debased twenty-five per cent as compared with the purity of the English shilling. Captain Williams took oath to the correctness of this muster-roll and subsistence June 12, 1755, before Samuel Watts, Justice of the Peace. In the mean time, he had been promoted to be Colonel in the current Crown Point expedition, and had been for weeks busy in enlisting men for his new regiment. In those days, and in that service, the Colonel was technical Captain of one of the ten companies in his own regiment; and a few soldiers from this last muster-roll in the fort service under Williams enlisted for Crown Point; not many, because the fort must be kept well garrisoned as a refuge and defence for the province in case of defeat to the northward.

Now, of these forty-one men, constituting Williams's last company at the fort, some of whom were killed with him at the lake, all whose names are worthy of this special and final record, more than half, or say twenty-four men, were personally engaged in the foundation and building up of Williamstown. This would never have happened under all the other circumstances, unless the captain had possessed remarkably attractive traits of character, unless he had enjoyed the respect and confidence of his soldiers to an unusual degree, unless they had actually found him by personal dealings with him to be a man of his word, and a man of solid power and strong influence to carry out his pledges.

Ephraim Williams Capt.	Isaac Wyman Lieut.
Samuel Taylor Serg!	Edmond Town Serg!
Gad Chapin Serg!	Oliver Avery Corp.
Samuel Calhoon Corp.	Samuel Catlin Cent.
John Taylor Cent.	Elisha Higgins "
Benjamin King "	George Wilson "
John Rosher "	Tyras Pratt "
Noah Pratt "	Abraham Bass "
Jeremy Chapin "	John Wells "
Enoch Chapin "	Silas Pratt

Ezekiel Foster	Cent.	*John Crofford	Cent.
John Brown	"	Thomas Train	"
John Herrold	"	Micah Harrington	"
Ezra Parker	"	Elisha Sheldon	"
John Bush	"	Simeon Crawford	"
Josiah Goodreesh	"	John Meecham	"
Nathaniel Nicholls	"	Derrick Webb	"
John Gray	"	Benjamin Simonds	"
Seth Hudson	"	Gad Corss	"
Mayhew Daggett	"	Gideon Warren	"

The incorporation of the propriety of West Hoosac into the town of Williamstown by the Great and General Court, under the usual terms and conditions, in July, 1765, made very little difference in the practical way of doing the public business until after the Revolutionary War. Whatever meetings may have been held by the "Town," technically so called, whatever business of any kind may have been transacted in them, no records have been preserved on the spot. The "Proprietors," technically so called, invested with their peculiar privileges of which they were jealous, and which were indefinite relatively to the privileges of the town as such, inasmuch as the proprietors and the citizens consisted for the most part of the same persons, continued to hold their meetings just as before, and to carry on the mass of public business just as before. Nearly the whole of this business came under the four following heads: (1) Gradually to distribute among themselves all the lands included within the limits of West Hoosac as laid out in 1749; (2) To construct highways to "conveau" as far as possible all the owners of these lands; (3) To provide both as to place and minister for religious worship, for schools, and burials; and (4) To lay and collect taxes among themselves for all these purposes. These were large matters for such men to handle in a wise and effective way. There were, as always in such cases, great obstacles. Differences of opinion were a matter of course. There were, for example, delinquent tax-payers: the only remedy as against such was to expose by special committee their lands for sale at public vendue; this was carrying coals to Newcastle, for the land-market was then overstocked everywhere. Proprietors, too, absorbed in the struggle for subsistence, and for other reasons as well, naturally became delinquent in attendance upon proprietors' meetings, — the only government among and over them, the one consequently whose strong maintenance was absolutely essential to their legal and prosperous continuance. Strange to say, as a remedy for this difficulty, they proposed, in November, 1766, what is sometimes practised by modern corporations to secure regular attendance of directors, namely, "To Se if the Proprietors will Pay those men that attend the meetings of Said Proprietors."

Probably there are, or may be some time, some persons who will not begrudge the attention of looking over a table compiled carefully from their own records — as testified to by their own clerk — of dates and places of meeting and moderators of these old, persistent, though often perplexed, proprietors, to whom the modern generations owe so much : —

DATES.	PLACES.	MODERATORS.
1753, Dec. 5	Seth Hudson's	Allen Curtiss
1754, April 18	Allen Curtiss's	Allen Curtiss
1754, May 15	Allen Curtiss's	Elisha Chapin
1760, Oct. 1		Jabez Warren
1760, Dec. 16	West Hoosac Fort	Jabez Warren
1761, July 14	West Hoosac Fort	Richard Stratton
1761, Sept. 24	West Hoosac Fort	Benjamin Simonds
1762, March 29	Josiah Horsford's	Jonathan Meacham
1762, April 19	Josiah Horsford's	Gideon Warren
1762, Oct. 21	Benjamin Simonds's	John Horsford
1763, March 10	Benjamin Simonds's	Josiah Horsford
1763, July 8	Schoolhouse	Josiah Horsford
1763, Nov. 16	Schoolhouse	William Horsford
1764, March 28	Schoolhouse	John Newbre
1764, July 16	Schoolhouse	John Horsford
1764, Sept. 27	Schoolhouse	Titus Harrison
1764, Dec. 3	Schoolhouse	Josiah Horsford
1765, March 26	Schoolhouse	Ephraim Seelye
1765, April 12	Schoolhouse	John Smedley
1765, May 21	Schoolhouse	Richard Stratton
1765, June 6	Schoolhouse	Richard Stratton
1765, July 2	Schoolhouse	Samuel Kellogg
1765, July 26	Schoolhouse	Ephraim Seelye
1765, Oct. 22	Richard Stratton's	Samuel Payen
1766, Jan. 14	Schoolhouse	Nehemiah Smedley
1766, March 17	Schoolhouse	Benjamin Simonds
1766, April 6	Schoolhouse	John Newbre
1766, May 15	Schoolhouse	Ebenezer Cooley
1766, Oct. 9	Schoolhouse	John Smedley
1766, Dec. 9	Schoolhouse	Richard Stratton
1767, May 8	Schoolhouse	Richard Stratton
1767, Oct. 13	Schoolhouse	John Smedley
1767, Dec. 25	Schoolhouse	Richard Stratton
1768, March 11	Schoolhouse	Richard Stratton
1768, April 18	Schoolhouse	Stephen Davis
1768, Nov. 7	Meetinghouse	Richard Stratton
1769, April 10	Meetinghouse	Richard Stratton
1769, Oct. 9	Meetinghouse	Jonathan Meacham

DATES.		PLACES.	MODERATORS.
1769, Oct.	30	Meetinghouse	Samuel Clark
1770, Jan.	1	Meetinghouse	Samuel Clark
1770, April	13	Meetinghouse	Elkanah Parris
1770, Nov.	1	Meetinghouse	John Newbre
1771, April	11	Meetinghouse	Josiah Horsford
1771, May	2	Meetinghouse	Isaac Stratton
1771, May	17	Meetinghouse	James Meacham
1771, June	20	Meetinghouse	Samuel Kellogg
1771, Aug.	22	Meetinghouse	Nathan Whetar
1771, Nov.	22	Meetinghouse	James Meacham
1771, Dec.	17	Meetinghouse	Elkanah Parris
1772, April	6	Meetinghouse	Samuel Kellogg
1772, Oct.	20	Meetinghouse	Josiah Horsford
1773, June	14	Meetinghouse	Samuel Clark
1774, Feb.	7	Meetinghouse	Jacob Meack
1792, Dec.	4	Meetinghouse	David Noble
1793, March	4	Meetinghouse	David Noble
1793, Sept.	2	Meetinghouse	David Noble
1794, June	16	Meetinghouse	Ephraim Seelye
1795, June	1	Meetinghouse	James Meacham
1800, Dec.	23	James Meacham's	Ephraim Seelye
1801, March	2	James Meacham's	James Meacham
1802, April	7	James Meacham's	James Meacham

The meetings and mutterings of the proprietors, as such, ceased
with the last distributions among themselves of the "common and
undivided" lands of the town.   These "leavings" lands were of
very little value, and excited little interest on the part of anybody,
and many of them were bought up for a song, or less, by Ephraim
Seelye, and afterwards peddled out by him, as woodland or mountain
pasture, to the neighboring farmers.   This was a legitimate transaction economically, but it made Seelye, who was much better off
than most of his neighbors, very unpopular among them, who called
him a land-grabber and a thief.   After the eighth division, — which
was into sixty-acre lots, — each owner of a house lot was authorized
to select and lay out for himself, from the still undivided land,
thirty acres, in one, two, or three pieces, as he chose.   These lots
were called "pitches."   When it came to such operations as these,
nothing could make the proprietors, as such, respectable, or their
meetings any longer significant.   They passed out of view, — that
is, out of existence.   The war and its results constantly brought the
"Town" forward as the unit of local government, subordinate to
the county, and the county as subordinate to the state, under its
new constitution of 1780, and the state, nine years later, as in some
sense subordinate to the United States.   We must still cling to the

acts of the proprietors, however, since all this is much later than the epoch we have reached in the unfoldings of Williamstown.

It will be noticed, from the table above, that every public meeting of the proprietors from November, 1768, till December, 1800, was holden in the "Meetinghouse." This meeting-house has an interesting history, and it may as well be given here as anywhere.

About eight months after the organization of the "Town," at a lawfully warned proprietors' meeting at the schoolhouse, March 17, 1766, which was organized by the choice of Richard Stratton as moderator, it was next voted to adjourn the meeting to the house of Lieutenant Benjamin Simonds. Simonds was then an "innholder" on house lot No. 3, the site of the present house of Mr. Henry Sabin. Why the meeting adjourned thither, immediately it was organized, can only be conjectured; one guess is perhaps as good as another; only a bold man would venture on two, namely, first, the schoolhouse was a public place compared with Lieutenant Simonds's, his bar-room, and the rights of the new town to build a meeting-house as compared with those of the proprietors, should that discussion arise, might be heard and reported by those unfriendly to the scheme of the latter; second, the services connected with the ordination of Mr. Welch were then only about a year old, the expenses of which had been paid by the proprietors, a considerable part of which expenses was for stimulants, and as the present question was about a meeting-house for Mr. Welch to preach in, it may have been thought that a more convenient proximity to the Lieutenant's bar might be a stimulus to some to liberality in votes for the meeting-house. At any rate and for *some* reason, they trudged across the "Square" to the tavern.

Voted to Build a meeting House also voted that said meeting House be forty feet in Length and thirty feet in Breadth Voted to finish Said House in two year Voted said House be Studed and Bracesed Voted to Plaster as far as is Needed Voted to Lay the uper floer on the top of the jice and Laith and Plarster on the under Side of the jice Voted and chose Nehemiah Smedley Samuel Sanford Richard Stratton Commetree to finish Said meeting House Voted to Raise three Pounds on each Right to Build Said meeting House Voted to Leave the Rest of Said work of ᵈ House to the Discrestion of Said Commetree.

William Horsford was the proprietors' clerk, who entered all these votes in his own hand and style. He was clerk for a great many years. He was one of the very earliest settlers in West Hoosac. His house lot was No. 44, and the frame of his house was removed therefrom to South Street to make room for General Sloan's fine house, still standing, as is also the other, moved by old Mr.

Bardwell for a long-time home, now owned and occupied by James Fitzgerald. William Horsford and his brother Josiah, both from the northwestern corner of Connecticut, both married Smedley sisters from Litchfield, and both raised large families here on adjacent house lots, Josiah's being No. 42, and his original house becoming the nucleus of the Whitman house, now owned and occupied by Dr. L. D. Woodbridge. William Horsford's eldest child, Esther, named from the mother, was born in May, 1760, and, next to Simonds's children (of which there were then four), was the first child born in the borough.

The committee to build the new meeting-house was well chosen, although we know but little of Samuel Sanford, except that he came here from Milford, Connecticut, which was also the home of Pastor Welch. Richard Stratton was then relatively an old man, but energetic for one of his age, and highly honored in the community. He was a Baptist, and was called "Deacon," though there was no Baptist society here till 1792; there was a small congregation of Baptists, however, much earlier, to which, doubtless, Deacon Stratton in some sense ministered. His capacity to serve on a building committee is demonstrated by the excellent state of preservation in which his own house is standing to this day, — the first two-story house built in the town. It is an odd coincidence that Nehemiah Smedley, the chairman of this church-building committee of 1766, built also for himself the second two-story house erected in the town, and that, too, is still firm and strong in this year of Grace, 1892.

The proprietors prescribed to their committee the dimensions of the building, 40 × 30, that there should be studs and braces, and that it should be lathed and plastered; and wisely left all else to their committee, in whom they felt full confidence. Their financial provision for the house would seem to have been meagre: "three pounds" tax to "each Right"; there were sixty taxable rights; three times sixty is £180, or $600, as the old colonial silver money would stand to the soon-to-be-adopted national silver standard. But then, the chief materials cost but little at that time. Lumber was exceedingly abundant. The sills and corner-posts were undoubtedly of white oak, perhaps, also, the rafters and studs and braces, and certainly all the pins that in those days fastened the timbers together; and white oaks were so plenty just north of the Hoosac as to give a permanent and beautiful designation to that entire locality. It is altogether probable that the white-oak timbers were sawed out at John Smedley's mill, which was two miles due north of the "Square" on which the meeting-house was to stand, and there was already a fair road passing near this mill to what is now the Vermont line. A bridge over the "Greate River" to connect the two parts of this north road had been ordered in 1765; a tax of fifteen shillings to each right was laid at the same time, in order to build it. Benjamin Simonds and Nehemiah Smedley and Josiah Horsford were appointed the same day a committee "to See the work is Don," so that there was no obstacle in fetching the logs to Smedley's mill from north of the river, even if it were necessary to go so far for the white oaks.

In respect to pine lumber for boards, pews, rived clapboards, cleft shingle, and finishing, there can be little doubt all these came from Smedley's mill; for pine lots Nos. 7 and 8 adjoined this mill, and became his own property, and the writer has himself seen immensely wide pine boards, used for external sheathing on Smedley's own house, which stood on No. 7, — lumber which, it is certain, whether in log or deal, was never many rods distant from John Smedley's sawmill.

At the same time it must be remembered that the meeting-house committee, whose chairman was Smedley's own brother, were not shut up to his mill. There was wholesome competition. Titus Harrison had come up here from Litchfield, in or near 1761, bringing with him a large family and much personal enterprise. Titus was a son of Thomas[3], who was the son of Thomas[2], who was a son of Thomas[1], the first settler of Branford, Connecticut. He and his children and grandchildren played a strong rôle in this valley, especially along the Green River, for a century. Titus is called, in the early deeds here, "husbandman," but later on "miller," because his first purchase seems to have been the middle water-privilege of the three on Green River, all coming in close succession in what would have been the southeast corner of the original village plat, if that had been carried out symmetrically. The fall of water at this privilege was so abrupt, and its volume then so ample, that it was only necessary to cut a conduit down the stream on its left bank for a few rods, to obtain head enough without any dam to run the sawmill and the grist-mill that Harrison soon had in operation upon a site that has never lacked a mill from that day to this. First the Harrisons, afterwards and now the Towns, have been the owners. Gradually, Titus Harrison increased his purchases of lands up the Green River from his mills until he became a large landholder. In 1765, he owned house lot 39. But as old age crept on, he practically gave away to his sons all of his real estate: first, to Noah, in December, 1785, thirty acres bounded on the west by

Green River road, on the south by land of Rev. Seth Swift, on the
east by Ebenezer Stratton's land, and on the north by land of Timothy Northam; and second, he deeded to his sons Almond and
Truman all his other lands on Green River, together with the
grist-mill, eighty-two acres in all, in consideration of their joint
bond for the fulfilling of certain purposes mentioned in the deed,
which was signed as a witness by Salmon Harrison, his fourth and
only other son.   This was in February, 1788.

To return to our tiny meeting-house on the Square.   The ridge-pole
ran north and south the longer way of the building, which was forty
feet.   The roof was plain, without belfry, or tower, or other protuberance whatever.   The only door was in the centre of the east
side; the only aisle led straight from the door to the pulpit, which
filled the centre of the west side within; the pews rose up at a
slight angle on both sides the aisle to the north and south ends,
which were thirty feet each; there were two galleries on these ends,
reached by stairways on either side of the pulpit; the pulpit was a
high one, as was universal in those days, and the preacher preached
at right angles to the people; that is to say, the audience on the
south side of the aisle below and above fronted exactly the audience
on the north side below and above; and it is no more than charity
allows us moderns to infer, that the young people certainly (perhaps
the old ones too) watched each other across the chasm more than
they watched the minister.   The windows were few, and there was
no chimney at all, consequently the room was relatively dark and
cold; the site was high, in the middle of the Main Street and at the
junction of that with the two cross streets, exposed to all winds in
all weathers, but somewhat protected, after all, in the fact that there
was no door or other opening on the west side, or either end.

As a place of worship, nevertheless, it was a large improvement
over the log schoolhouse, and also as a legal place of meeting for the
proprietors; and the Rev. Whitman Welch, after having preached in
the schoolhouse for more than three years, preached in it with animation and propriety for more than seven years, until the autumn
of 1775; and the proprietors did not await the conclusion of the
Revolution to settle a new minister, for the Rev. Seth Swift, a
graduate of Yale twelve years after Mr. Welch, was ordained in
May, 1779, and preached with power and success in the little building, which must have been sorely crowded at times, until 1797, when
a new church building was erected in its room.

Before that time the College had been founded, and there was no
place for the students to worship on Sundays except with the towns-

people, and that was already too strait for the latter, and so President Fitch interested himself in the project for a new church edifice, and wrote out and circulated personally a subscription-paper to that end. This paper is now in the possession of the writer, and will be referred to more at length on a later page. The scheme was successful. The money was raised largely under College influence and necessities. But the old building occupied the most conspicuous and central site in the village, and must accordingly be removed to make space for the new and larger edifice. In fact, it was turned half-way round, and hauled back a number of rods due west, so that the single door was now to the south, and what had been the north end was now the east end. Nothing was altered within, — the pulpit still towered, and the opposite galleries glared at each other. Gradually it became a scene of desolation. The regular meetings of the proprietors were held in it till 1795, and afterwards (and perhaps occasionally before) the regular town-meetings until 1828.

Schools were often held within it in summer until well into the present century; and it is from the living lips of one of these scholars, — an eye and ear witness, — that many points of this description have been carefully derived. William Townsend, a graduate of Yale in 1773, — always called here " Master Townsend," perhaps because he took his Master's degree there in 1778, — was one of those who taught in the old meeting-house. He taught also at the South Part and elsewhere. He had married a sister of the Skinners, two very prominent citizens here for many years, and was befriended by them in later life when he had become intemperate, and but for them homeless.. After General Skinner's death in 1809, Deacon Benjamin Skinner virtually provided for him till his death in 1822. Master Townsend's learning was ample, and his manners very courteous to everybody out of school; but he had made a substantial failure in life, and knew it, and became captious and cross to his scholars, who were crude and ignorant enough. In the dark and dismal den, to which the old meeting-house had degenerated, it would have been difficult for anybody to keep up uniform patience and courtesy. As a matter of conspicuous favor to the largest boys, he would sometimes allow them to study in the pulpit, but the concession did not always secure attention to study on their part. William Bridges and Albert Smith were boys once honored in that manner. " None of your pranks up there, William and Bill ! I will throw you over ! " Occasionally he would permit, if they desired it, some of the girls also to study in one of the galleries; but usually they were afraid to go up there : the whole place was peopled with spooks.

When my esteemed informant, who, as a school-girl, Mary Tallmadge, shared in the superstitions of the time and place, became
Mrs. Jeremiah Hosford, a name she still retains, she kept house and
boarders in a dwelling very near the old church, a dwelling that was
begun by Douglas Sloan, and has now been occupied, for more than a
whole generation, by the Noyes family.   One day in 1828, Mrs. Hosford expressed, in the presence of some of her student-boarders,
one of whom was Foster Thayer of that class, her disgust at the
proximity of the old shell, and her desire that some one would
burn it down.   In a few hours it lay in ashes.   General opinion
fastened upon Thayer as the torch-bearer; but as nobody regretted
the conflagration of what had become a public nuisance, he was
never seriously questioned or disturbed.   He was from North Carolina, became a clergyman, and, at the same time, a teacher at the
South.   " Bad habits brought him to a dishonorable death," says
Calvin Durfee, in his "Annals of Williams College."

The proprietors continued to experience difficulty in laying out
their own land in successive divisions.   The proximate reason for
most of this difficulty was, that they felt obliged to employ an
inferior surveyor, because they could get him cheap, who made gross
mistakes in his plotting, which gave rise to constant irritation and
interference and controversy.   Jedediah Hubbel was a common
farmer of Lanesboro, an excellent man, but a very indifferent surveyor, who possessed, nevertheless, such a good conscience in his
old age that he lived well into his 100th year, as one may read on
his headstone in the south cemetery of that town.

Anno Domini

1720

was born Jedidiah Hubbel

died Aug. 14, 1819.

In laying out the second division of fifty-acre lots, sixty-three in
all, most of which fell at the South Part, so many and so great errors
were committed by the surveyor and his helpers, that a resurvey
and attempted corrections were had, amid evidences of much dissatisfaction; but ultimately, through reiterated votes of the proprietors,
Hubbel's original lines were maintained just so far as they did not
clash with each other.   By sending to Northampton, or other Connecticut River town, or to what is now Belchertown, where Captain
Nathaniel Dwight lived, skilled surveyors could be had, and had
been had, but that would take much more money, and the only way
to raise it was by a tax levied upon each right; and when the tax

came to be collectible, it was found that many of the proprietors were non-residents, and their whereabouts unknown; and even when these delinquent rights, or portions of them, were exposed for sale at public vendue to meet these taxes, they fetched only a paltry sum, — such a drug, in the commercial sense, were lands here at that time. For example, at a public auction, Nov. 30, 1763, William Horsford bought one-quarter of the right, that is, the undivided land of house lot No. 9, for thirteen shillings; and Isaac Searle bought another quarter of the same, at the same time, for fifteen shillings.

At their meeting, March 26, 1765, the proprietors voted (1) " To Lay out another Division of Land to Eaich Right of one Hundred acres; (2) Chose Richard Stratton, Jonathan Meaicham, Josiah Horsford, Samuel Kellogg, Titus Harrison, Ephraim Seelye, and Asa Johnson, Commetree men to Lott out Said Division; (3) That there be Nine Shillings of money Raised on Eaich Proprietors Right to Pay for Laying out ʳᵈ Land." At a later meeting it was voted, (1) " That the Publick Rights Shall be Drawn out by a Common Lottery "; and (2) "That the Proprietors Will be Gin to chuse for their Hundred acre Lots the Seventh Day of June A D 1765."

Twenty-two of these 100-acre lots were located on Northwest Hill, Birch Hill, and Bee Hill, hills secondary to the Taconics, on pretty good upland, out of which came at length tolerable farms, though many of them are no longer ploughed and sowed, but are utilized as pasture and woodlands; beginning with No 1 on the North Adams boundary line near Paul's, the public road there towards Williamstown running through Nos. 1 and 2 and just grazing the upper corner of 3, twenty-two more of these 100-acre lots skirt round the base of Prospect, turn up into the Hopper to Bacon's and beyond, extending also south in a continuous line along the Potter road to the New Ashford line; and the remaining nineteen lots of this fifth division were placed pretty close together in the southwest corner of the town, nearly all of them on the Hancock Brook and its little tributaries. Numbers 45, 46, 47, and 51 of this division touch upon the Vermont line; No. 1 only, as has just been said, is coincident in its east line with the line of North Adams; Nos. 25, 36, and 37 rest on the southern line of the town; and Nos. 32, 33, 34, and 35 adjoin upon the original west line of the town, namely, the east line of the Gore.

These 100-acre lots proved attractive to a somewhat different class of settlers from those who had purchased the original house lots, those, namely, who had no objections to a sort of village life, and who looked to the after-drafts of their house lots to make up to themselves either *in situ* or by exchange, the requisites of an adequate farm. But 100 acres in one piece was enough in itself for an average farm. The village holder, who wanted an outlot or two, had, doubtless, in most cases, already supplied himself from the three previous divisions, — two of fifty-acre lots and one of meadow lots along the chief streams. Besides this, the new 100-acre lots of 1765 were mostly quite remote from the Square, and, moreover, had not in general been surveyed out from the more eligible patches of land. Clay predominated more than was meet (or meat) in most of the lots near the southern line of the town. For example, No. 25, which has always constituted the last farm in Williamstown on the Ashford road, and was very early cleared up by Andrew Young, from Western, now Warren; and Nos. 31–35 on the Hancock road, which have always constituted the so-called "Young neighborhood," and Nos. 29 and 30, on which the Corbens originally settled, and some of the fifty-acre lots opposite them, became noted as clay farms.

A scene once in town meeting will illustrate the reputation of some of these lands. The late Dudley White, who owned a farm in the Corben district, had occasion to appeal to the town for some legal alteration of a highway in his neighborhood. This was wittily and successfully opposed by a neighbor of his in South Williamstown, Thomas Smith, a blacksmith, on the ground of the difficulty of making a road on such clay, alleging that, "if anybody should stand on any one corner of Dudley White's farm in the springtime *and teeter, he could shake the whole farm.*" The Youngs, nevertheless, Moses and Andrew and William, all from Western, and the Corbens, Asa and Amasa and Joseph, from New Haven, Connecticut, and other early settlers on these 100-acre lots in the southwest, obtained a good living for themselves from off these lands, and transmitted to their heirs, fair farms and good houses.

Among the five shiploads of Scotch-Irish immigrants that landed at Boston in August, 1718, there were a very few Celtic-Irish families that had become attached to, and connected with, the Scotch people who had settled in Ulster a long time before. About one-third of those who thus entered New England at the invitation of Governor Shute, of Massachusetts, permanently tarried in Boston and Andover; another third proceeded to Worcester that autumn, and made a permanent settlement there; while the rest, wishing to look about more before they settled down, spent the winter and spring on the coast of Maine, and then sailed up the Merrimack

River and made their settlement in and around Londonderry, New Hampshire. Among those proceeding very shortly after their arrival, from Boston to Worcester, was a remarkable Irish family by the name of Young. The patriarch of this family was John Young, who is said to have been over ninety years old at the time of the immigration. He died, at any rate, June 30, 1730, and was buried on Worcester Common. His son David, who was thirty-six at the time of the coming-in, died in Worcester, Dec. 26, 1776, and was buried by the side of his father. David's son William was a stone-cutter, and put up the double stone on the common in memory of his father and grandfather, holding the following inscriptions:[1]—

Here lies interred the remains of
John Young, who was born
in the Isle of Bert, near Londonderry, in the Kingdom of Ireland.
He departed this life, June
30, 1730, aged 107 years.

Here lies interred the remains of
David Young, who was born in
the parish of Tahbeyn, County of
Donegal and Kingdom of Ireland.
He departed this life, December
26, aged 94 years.

The aged son and the more aged father
Beneath these stones,   Their mould'ring bones
Here rest together.

Besides William, the stone-cutter and rhymester, David Young had sons David, John, and Moses, all born in the old country; and Moses was the ancestor of the Williamstown Youngs. His wife's name was Rebeckah, and they were married in 1736. They migrated from Worcester, and made a home near the boundary line between Brimfield and Western, now Warren. He became a constable in Brimfield, and among his papers are receipts from Harrison Gray, Treasurer of the province of Massachusetts, for moneys thus paid in by him in 1764 and 1765. He never came to Williamstown, but three of his sons and two of his daughters had made permanent homes here before the father's death, which fell Sept. 25, 1781. His son Moses, born April 25, 1747, came first and "went to chopping" on 100-acre lot 34, which is still in the hands of his descendants. Before he had made much of a clearing, he went home to Western, and brought back with him, his younger brother Andrew, who bought the 100-acre lot 25, on the Ashford road. Andrew had no children, but was otherwise a prosperous man, and built the two-story house on that farm which was burned down about 1880. Not long after Andrew came William, the third brother, two years younger than Andrew, and seven years younger

[1] Lincoln's *Worcester*, p. 50.

than Moses. He settled in what is now the hamlet of South Williamstown, in a house that is still standing substantially as he occupied it, and as it had been built by Captain Samuel Clark, and came to play a conspicuous part in town affairs, and even in the politics of Massachusetts, as we shall see at length upon a later page. He was in the Legislature from Williamstown, in 1792, 1793, 1795, and in 1800–1808 inclusive. He was a Jeffersonian democrat, as have been most of the Youngs in Williamstown.

This William Young married first a daughter of Zebediah Sabin, who had established himself early on 100-acre lot 41, on which the west end of the Sloan road abuts directly, and which continued the

WILLIAM YOUNG'S HOUSE.

home lot of the Sabin family for much more than a century. This Mrs. Young died without children; when the husband married Currence Meack, a daughter of Dr. Jacob Meack, a German physician, the first of that profession to settle in Williamstown. His house is still standing much altered and enlarged on house lot No. 12, in the upper cemetery, just as one crosses the bridge over Hemlock Brook in the Main Street on the right hand going west. On account of his dwelling on its banks in the very early time, the brook itself was often designated the "Doctor Brook." Mrs. Currence Young had several children, and survived her husband many years. Her daughter, Zerviah, married Lorin Smith in 1833, and they spent their married life in the Young house, which is now owned and occupied by their son and heir, George Smith. The house has still a chamber in which the Freemasons are said to have met when there was a lodge at the South Part. Another daughter, Betsy Young, married Harry Johnson, who has descendants in Louisville, Kentucky. The only son of "Esq. William Young" went by the name of "Wicked Bill," and died in Canada. William Young went to Cambridge with the minute-men of Captain Samuel Sloan's company in 1775, and his powder-horn (still extant) bears date " ye 4th of May, 1775, Charleston." He carried the same powder-horn into the battle of Bennington, 1777. George Smith, his grandson, has a silhouette picture of him, hereby displayed in a woodcut, and valuable documents belonging to him. Also a silver shoebuckle, and other relics.

WILLIAM YOUNG.

When the first Moses Young died in Brimfield, Sept. 25, 1781, his three sons and two daughters in Williamstown, Mrs. Stephen Davis and Mrs. Robert Harrington, were not pleased with the disposition of his property made by will shortly before he died, and they sent the following letter from here there, which is interesting on many grounds. The original lies now before the writer, and is scrupulously transcribed.

WILLIAMSTOWN March 6 1782

friends and Brothers after servis and all due Regards we understand there is a will signed By father-young and commited to your Care which for sume important Reasons we object against first Becaus he was Not of A sound memory secondly Becaus Persons Born free are Not subject to Bondage By the will of any man 3d Becaus the persons are Coled Noncompus mentus that have been the instruments of Earning the Estate and for Ever ought to have the Benefit of it 4th Becaus we suppose it Not to Be the will of the Deceast as he inquired what thay was going to do when they asked him to sign the will and Persons then Present say that he was not himself — we Desire you to Omit the Execution of the will till you favour us with a Coppy — we Remain your Real friends

STEPHEN DAVIS
ROBERT HARRINGTON
MOSES YOUNG
ANDREW YOUNG
WILLIAM YOUNG

This letter was written and copied by Stephen Davis, the husband of Rebeckah Young, an elder sister of the three brothers here. He was an able and influential man. He had gone to Lake George from Western in Captain Nathaniel Dwight's company, — enlisted on the news reaching there of the battle of Lake George, in August, while Dwight's company passed Fort Massachusetts and down the Hoosac, in September, 1755. In the Captain's manuscript papers are receipts given by Davis, and others, who were afterwards settlers in Williamstown, for pay and arms. Davis's home lot was No. 11 of the first-division fifty-acre lots, which he bought of Eli Cowles, in October, 1763, for £30. He subsequently bought two other lots in close proximity to this, and thus aggregated a farm which has always been regarded as among the best in Williamstown. It now goes under the designation of "Farm B," and is owned by John B. Gale (Williams College, 1842), whose "Farm A" is next north of it, and separates it from the "Meacham Farm," — all three on Green River, to the west, and, in the reverse order, next and south to the house lots. Stephen Davis rose in the militia to be Captain, did excellent service in the Revolutionary War, and was a member of the Massachusetts Convention of 1779–80, called to frame the state Constitution. Elisha Baker was the other member from Williamstown. Jonathan Smith was their colleague from Lanesboro, and greatly distinguished himself in the councils and debates there.

Moses Young, the first of the name to settle here, and Susannah, his wife, brought up a very large family of children, all born between 1774 and the end of the century. He never left his original 100-acre lot as his own homestead, but settled his several sons on adjacent 100-acre lots, as they came to maturity, he holding the title to all the lands. He built for his own immediate family a large and strong two-story house, which is still owned and occupied by his grandson, Erastus Young, who pursues a policy with his sons, as to his own broad lands, similar to that of his grandfather; namely, giving them nominal ownership only to their farms during his life. This Moses Young died in 1819. Reuben, his firstborn, — which means in Hebrew "See! a son!" — became a prominent citizen at the South Part, and was commonly designated "Squire Young." He was a member of the Legislature in 1833. He lived and died near the east end of the Sloan road, north side, where the late Dr. Young lived. He once brought from Boston, in his satchel, some slips of willow, and a tree from one of these is still standing west of the house, and the little brook that crosses the road near by is often called "Willow Brook." Reuben Young married Sally Meack, a younger sister of Currence, his Uncle William's second wife. They had no children.

Reuben Young's brother, Moses, five years younger, lived and died on 100-acre lot 31, the lot next north of his father's old homestead, on the farm and in the house long afterwards owned by Augustus Hand, and carried on for him by a competent Irishman named Navin. This Moses, born in 1779, married on Stone Hill Lucy

REUBEN YOUNG.

Brewster, a daughter of Mrs. Mary Brewster, the second wife of "White" David Johnson, who came here from Middletown, Connecticut, about 1763, and began the Bulkley farm there, and built the house on it torn down in 1828 to make room for the present brick house occupied by the Bulkleys ever since. Mr. Johnson's first wife was Phebe Cole, from Canaan, Connecticut, and their marriage was the first one celebrated here by the Rev. Mr. Welch. Moses Young and Lucy Brewster were the parents of Horace H. Young, a distinguished dentist in Troy, New York; and of Betsey Ann Young, who became the wife of Dudley White, and later of

Titus Mitchell, of Ballston, New York; and of Eliza A. Young, who was first a Mrs. Bardwell, and afterwards Mrs. Bristol, of Utica. Mrs. Bristol's body was brought to South Williamstown for burial Nov. 11, 1892, accompanied by her only son, Henry Bristol, of Chicago.

The third son of Moses and Susannah Young, born on the old homestead in 1781, was John, who married Clarissa Crofoot, born Nov. 21, 1786, and the two passed a very long life together on land inherited from Father Young, and still owned and cultivated by their children. They were married in December, 1807. Their son, Seymour, has carried on the farm for nearly fifty years; and another son, Orange R., has long been a dentist in Troy, associated in business there with his cousin. The Crofoot family was more highly gifted intellectually than the Young family; both families probably came together from Ulster to Boston in 1718, in the very considerable migration of Scotch-Irish invited and facilitated by Governor Shute; the Crofoots, or Crawfords, however, were of the people who had previously migrated from Scotland to Ireland, while the Youngs were native Irish; the letter of the first Williamstown Youngs to their immediate kindred in Brimfield, quoted but a few pages back, resented the imputation put upon some of them by their own brethren, that they were "*non compos mentus*"; the records of Worcester, whither about a third of these immigrants passed in the autumn of 1718, make prominent among them both John and Robert Crawford; and there is probability, but no known proof, that the Crofoots of Williamstown were the progeny of these Crawfords working their way westward through the province gradually, with many other families of the same race, like the Blairs and the Duncans.

There were something like fifteen of the 100-acre lots located in a body towards the southeast corner of the town, and accommodated by what we now call the "Hopper road" and "Potter road" and "Burchard road." Joseph Crofoot, then of Weathersfield, Connecticut, bought in October, 1768, of Ichabod Southwick, of Williamstown, for £60, 100-acre lot No. 12 on the Hopper road. Isaac Stratton and Samuel Clark, then the two principal men in South Williamstown, sign the deed as witnesses. Crofoot's wife was Elizabeth Clark; and it is possible that she was related to Samuel Clark, who came here from Washington, Connecticut, in 1765. This farm, called for a century the "Crofoot farm," has been for a quarter of a century the farm of John Lamb, who, in conjunction with his excellent wife, kept the town's poor upon it for many years, until the town bought a small farm for that purpose at "Taylor's Crotch" in 1891.

Crofoot's family, which was large, lived for nearly twenty years in a log-house which stood a little back, that is, west, of the brick house which he proceeded to build in 1785, when he was sixty years old. He was a mason by trade, and he himself burnt the lime, and made the brick, and built the house. Limestone and clay lie contiguous upon a number of single farms in Williamstown. His granddaughter, Mrs. Anna Sherman, is competent authority for the statement, that on the very day he was sixty (June, 1785) he struck 3000 bricks with his own hand; and she remembered, in 1877, to have seen in her girlhood brick-molds, and trowels also of many shapes, in the garret of the brick house. He lived to occupy and enjoy his new house for nearly thirty years. In 1811, a cheese-press weight fell on his foot, as he was busy in making the cheese, and crushed the big toe. Dr. Porter was sent for, who was then at the height of his reputation as a country surgeon, and said the toe must be amputated. "Strike home when you do strike!" cried the old man, as he set his foot upon a block, and his son Joseph held him up, while the doctor with chisel and mallet excised the toe. He could not walk well after that, but would mount his horse on occasion and ride off like a boy. He had just entered his eighty-ninth year, when, being alone, he went, as he said, "to toggle the fire," and somehow fell upon it and was badly burned. He lingered, in great pain, from Monday till Friday, in July, 1813, when he died, and was buried in the Hemlock Brook ground at the North Part.

John Crofoot, eldest son of Joseph, reared here a family of ten children, all born between February, 1776, and April, 1792, one of them named Joseph and a twin brother with Benjamin, and all these moved as a family to Auburn, New York, after the death of the father. Joseph's second son was Mark Crofoot, who was in the battle of Bennington as one of a full company of sixty-five men from South Williamstown, and who seems to have been the wit of the family. His brother next younger, Joseph Crofoot, Junior, had a son named Joseph, and there were one or two more of the same name in the large circle before the patriarch died in 1813; and Mark used jocularly to designate the five Josephs — all here at one time — as "Old Joe, Young Joe, Young Joe's Joe, Cross-eyed Joe, and Toe-in Joe." Mark evidently thought, also, that there was scarcely room on the Hopper road for so many Crofoots as were accumulating there, for he moved from here with several other families about the same time to Granville, New York, where he died in 1818.

Joseph Crofoot, Junior, born March 6, 1768, and intermarried with Sarah Wilkinson, always lived with his father in the brick house.

He was lame in the hip for life from a cold caught after wading in the Green River in a chase of a deer near Deer Hill. He was the father of Clarissa Crofoot, who was the wife of John Young, and who died here as his widow April 4, 1876: John Young died May 12, 1857: he was the father also of Orange and of Joseph 3d. The latter married Ruth Williams here on Thanksgiving Day, 1811, and moved to Batavia, New York, where he died Thanksgiving Day, 1812, aged twenty-four. His brother, Orange, married his widow, and they continued on the brick homestead here until it was sold to another member of the same family.

This farm changed hands a number of times before it was bought by John Lamb, the present owner; and the brick house was constantly occupied by at least one family for a little over one hundred years, when Mr. Lamb took it down and built another commodious wood house in its place; and on one of the bricks, as they were taken from the old wall, was luckily noticed the word "Crofoot" neatly written upon the moist clay and perfectly preserved in every letter throughout the thorough burning and the century's service, — a pleasant and lasting memorial of a worthy family, whose name utterly disappeared from the town before 1830, and which does not appear at all in the church or College records.

William Young, still another son of the original Moses, was settled by his father on another 100-acre lot considerably south of the homestead on the same road. His wife was Lucy White, daughter of Peregrine White, who came to Williamstown from Hebron, Connecticut, about 1800, when Lucy was eight years old. They settled at first on Northwest Hill, and went thence to Westfield, New York, but returned after no great interval and located on Stone Hill, where the daughter was married in 1811. They spent their wedded life on this Young lot, but had no children. Mrs. Reed Mills once told the writer in her old age, that on her sleigh-ride to New Lebanon to be married, on a bitter cold day in the winter of 1816, they stopped to warm, both going and coming, with Mr. and Mrs. Young at their hospitable fire in this house where Hiram Smith has long lived at this end of the century. It is incredible in this more practical and comfortable generation, how thinly clad brides would then ride to their weddings in the depth of winter. Mrs. Young long outlived her husband. Her brother, Rev. Alfred White, was much with her in her later years, was much respected both as a man and a minister, and is buried beside her in the cemetery at the South Part.

James Young, still another son of the first-comer, Moses, was united in marriage with Narcissa Bliss, a distant relative, then of

Georgia, Vermont, June 4, 1818; and these, spending a long-continued married life on the original lot, and in the large house, transmitted both, under certain restrictions, to their sons Erastus and Justin, both of whom have reared families on the spot, and both are still tilling the ancestral acres. Harry Young, the last male scion of this long line to be mentioned here, led a highly respected life on another stretch of these broad Young lands; and two of his daughters, Mrs. Rand and Miss Sarah Young, are, at the present writing, in 1892, cultured people held in esteem in the city of Troy.

If we pass over now from the Hancock road and Young neighborhood located upon it, to the parallel Ashford road, a couple of miles to the eastward, we shall strike a number of 100-acre lots, that call for a brief notice at this point, and especially No. 24, next north of Andrew Young's lot on the Ashford boundary. Twenty-four became in a few years, and remained for a century, the most populous lot in its number of families, of any one in this fifth division. The land was fertile, the Ashford Brook flowed through it diagonally, it was well served with roads, and enterprising and excellent people first settled it. In August, 1766, Barnabas Woodcock, Junior, of Milford, Connecticut, seaman, bought this lot of Ephraim Seelye, landgrabber, for £30. It is evident that this Barnabas did not intend to abandon the sea, but that he did intend to assist his brothers Bartholomew and Nehemiah to keep comfortable, in his old age, their honored father. The following epitaph in the cemetery at the South Part is significant: "Here lies interred the body of Mr. Barnabas Woodcock, who was born in Dedham 25 Sept. 1710, and departed this life March 14, 1786, aged 76 years 5 months and 18 days." About the time his brother bought the lot 24, Bartholomew purchased lot 26 adjoining it to the west, and proceeded to settle upon it. The depression is yet visible of the cellar of the log-house which he put up on the east side of the road, just as one driving south is about to make the sharp turn to the left to cross the bridge and strike the south end of the Potter road. After some years of residence here, he built the substantial framed house still standing on the opposite side of the road near by, in which he spent his active life, selling this house and farm, in 1820, to his foster-son, Andrew Beers, for a consideration of $2000, and buying for himself, at about the same time, the Isaac Stratton place in the south village, where he died. Nathan Rossiter and Lyman Hubbell, both then prominent in that village, witnessed the deed from Woodcock to Beers.

Many stories with a point to them are still told of Thol. Wood-

cock, as he was always called by his neighbors, the Christian name
Bartholomew being quite too long for those busy times. He had
an agricultural maxim and practice which was probably more or less
current at that time, but has been supplanted by an opposite one, —
he would never sow grass-seed on his land to stock it down, saying,
"Land that will not seed itself is not good enough for me." The
common usage is now among farmers in Williamstown, to sow a
bushel of seed, for that purpose, to each acre. Any one passing
Woodcock's original farm, going south, will be likely to notice on
the broad meadow to his right, at some distance north of the house,
a very large elm tree. Woodcock himself used to relate when the
tree had become considerably grown, how he, while ploughing near
the spot, had bent the little sapling down to the ground to break it
off and be rid of it, when a chance suggestion of his own mind, or,
perhaps, of Andrew Beers, who lived with him, led him to spare it.
It has been the pride of the farm for three-quarters of a century.
Woodcock was in the battle of Bennington, with all his neighbors.
His name is borne on several other muster-rolls of the Revolutionary
time. He did not, like his brother Nehemiah, rise into influential
positions in the town and in the state. Neither name is to be found
on the records of the church. The epitaph of the one, however,
marks a difference between the two, — "Erected to the memory of
Nehemiah Woodcock he was one of the first settlers of Williamstown, a firm supporter of his Country's Rights and Independence."
He died March 10, 1816, in his seventy-ninth year.

Andrew Beers came with the Woodcocks from Milford, and passed
a long and honored life upon the same farm. He married Elisabeth
Deming, and they both lived to be very old, but they never had
children. Early in life he united with the church at the North Part,
and was chosen a deacon in it in 1828. Eight years later fifty-one
members of that church were dismissed in a body to constitute a new
church at the South Part; and Deacon Beers and Deacon William
Dickinson, who had been chosen a deacon in 1834, became the first,
and for a long time the only, deacons in South Williamstown. Elisabeth Deming united with the old church in 1806, and thirty years
later was dismissed with her husband and the rest to form the
new church. After 1820, they kept house by themselves in the
Woodcock house, and both died not far from 1870. As they had
no children, they adopted a nephew of Mrs. Beers, Eli Rix Deming,
whom they well brought up, to whom they transmitted the farm,
and who carried it on about fifteen years after their death and then
migrated to Lawrence, Kansas, with other members of his own

family. He united with the old church in 1831; and when he left town to go West about fifty years later, he was the only man in town bearing the name of Deming, which name had been very numerous here for a long time.

It was first brought here in a permanent way when Joseph Deming, of Weathersfield, Connecticut, bought 100-acre lot 23 in April, 1769, for £65. It was bought of Hezekiah Brown. Isaac Stratton and Daniel Burbank sign the deed as witnesses. Deming was sixty-two years old at that time; and his two sons, Titus and Aaron, came with him. Two other 100-acre lots to the west of this were soon bought, tradition says, at eight shillings an acre. The families localized themselves on these lots, and clung to them for three generations; and by and by required for their convenience the east and west road (long ago discontinued) connecting the Ashford and Hancock highways. This cross-road runs straight along the north line of lots 27 and 28 and 29, bridging the Hancock Brook at a point where there is a small mill-privilege, which was utilized by the Deming families for several manufacturing purposes at different times. The father, Joseph, built his house near the east end of this cross-road, — a good house that was burned down in 1876. There was another house a little further west on the same road, understood to have been built and occupied by the son, Aaron, and members of his family. The Demings were diligent and thrifty. The fathers cleared off the lands, and the sons widened and improved the clearings. They occupied altogether about as much land, and for nearly as long a time, as their neighbors, the Youngs.

Aaron Deming died March 12, 1837, lacking twenty-seven days of being ninety-three years old. Two unmarried daughters always lived with him, and his two sons, Joseph and Salmon, lived in the other part of the same house, which was a custom also with the Young families. The father, Joseph, had died in 1783, in his seventy-sixth year. Captain Joseph, the son of Aaron, died in December, 1870, seventy-nine years old. Nelson Deming, Captain Joseph's son, a man of admirable character, was the last of the name to operate the little mill on the brook, and the last of the name in town of the line of Aaron. His widow was the last person in Williamstown of either sex or of any age to bear the name of Deming. An easy lesson fell to the officiating clergyman to be given at Nelson Deming's funeral, namely, that the world is passing away and the lust thereof, to *families* as well as to individuals.

Titus Deming, the other incomer here with the father, Joseph, built his house on the southern line of lot No. 23, just at the point of junction of the two roads from the north, — the old road from Taylor's Crotch to the Ashford line, running wholly through 100-acre lots, and the road from the south hamlet to strike the other at right angles, running diagonally over a dead level of the second division of fifty-acre lots. Here Titus Deming reared his sons, David, Martin, Francis, and Moses the Mormon who died in 1873; and his daughters also, Betsey, Sally, Sybil, and Nancy. Their mother, Sybil, died in 1844, aged eighty-two years. This Martin was the father of Eli Rix, who was adopted and reared by Deacon Andrew Beers. Francis inherited the farm, and brought up in the ample and good-looking two-story house, two sons and one daughter. The eldest son was Richard Titus Deming, called from his grandfather Titus, a graduate of the College in 1852, and a classmate of the present writer. He was born in 1825, and was about three years older than the average age of his classmates, a tall and straight and fine-looking man, who assumed to say of the society of which he was a member, — " The Sigma Phi does not aim to exhibit scholarship, but to develop the practical man and the gentleman." He did not, accordingly, attain to a rounded education in his college course; and going afterwards to New York to study and practise law, the common belief and report was, that he was the means of bringing his father into severe pecuniary embarrassment, and that his own life was shortened and made useless by excesses and immoralities. He died, it was said, in the street, in 1868. At any rate, the home-farm was sold out of the family, and his younger brother, Dow Deming, an intelligent and estimable man, removed to Lanesboro, where he is successfully tilling a good farm.

Aaron Deming was in the battle of Bennington. He and his brother Titus were out repeatedly in the militia service during that war. The following list, compiled from the church records, contains the names of all the members of the Deming family who were members of the local churches : —

Dorcas Beckley Deming	Elisabeth Deming Beers
Sybil Jaffords Deming	Sarah Lewis Deming
Lydia Stoddard Deming	David Deming
Cynthia Deming	Sybil Deming Krigger
Sarah Chamberlain Deming	Salome Wright Deming
Martin Deming	Mary Utley Deming
Salmon Deming	Francis Deming
Nancy Deming	Mary Deming Mills
Moses Deming	Amos C. Deming
Ann White Deming	Titus Deming
Hester Whitman Deming	Eli R. Deming
Charlotte E. Deming	Harty Johnson Deming

The 100-acre lot that fell by chance to Rev. Whitman Welch, the first minister, was No. 7, situated on the east side of the Hopper road not far from the "Crotch"; and over this lot passes to this day the Burchard road to the centre of No. 16, where stands the Burchard house, which was built under extraordinary circumstances 115 years ago, and which is occupied at present by Chauncy Whitney. Samuel Burchard was from Danbury, Connecticut. He came early. In 1771 he owned five of the house lots, but it does not appear that he ever lived in the village. We run across him first as living on what is now called the Stratton road, east side, on No. 57 of the first-division fifty-acre lots, where William Hall lived for a long time, and after him George Ford, and now Abner Town. The house stands a little way back from the road. In all probability a farm was first cleared here by Burchard, who had a family largely grown when he came. They soon moved, however, to this 100-acre lot 16, reaching it through the Dominie's lot. Burchard and his wife, Elizabeth Hamilton, were members of the church. The father was several times out in the Revolutionary militia service, and one of his sons was so much afraid of being drafted for the war, that he wore round an overcoat in summer, pretending ague. The mother was a notable woman, and not afraid of anything. The late William Torrey used to tell from his father, a contemporary, that while the men folks were off in the war, Mrs. Burchard herself struck the brick for the present house, the clay being taken out from the cellar, and her girls carried out the moist forms from the moulds to dry. Exactly in what service the ague patient was then employed, tradition saith not. In their old age the Burchards bargained away their farm; the good lady, still active and economical, carried off and threw away a cartload of stuff from the house, old shoes and other such trumpery, and then when the bargain flew off, she went out and carefully gathered up the old things and brought them all back again.

This Burchard family must not be confounded with that of Joseph Birchard, who originally cleared up the Samuel Foster farm on Bee Hill, a sixty-acre lot of the eighth division, whose son Amos, after a considerable residence in Treadwell Hollow, went with his own children, and with at least four of his brothers and sisters, to Cattarangus County, New York, where, with other families from here, they helped to found another Williamstown.

The minister, Mr. Welch, sold off his lot No. 7, next north of the Burchards's lot, to two men of New Milford, — with which town he kept up close connection, — Ruggles and Hubbell, for £30, April 11, 1769. He had previously sold his house lot 36, which came to him, as the first settled minister, in gratuity, and which drew for him, in succession, meadow lot 51, fifty-acre lot (first division) 48, fifty-acre lot (second division) 51, pine lot 53, oak lot 5. He also bought and sold other lots upon occasion; for example, the meadow lots Nos. 24 and 25 in the "Great Meadow" on the Hoosac (£40), in June, 1766. He seems to have been an intermediary, or agent, in the good sense of those terms, between those of his former townspeople in Connecticut, who wished to buy lots up here, and those of his own people who wished to sell them. A good number of Milford and New Milford citizens settled here, first and last. He seems to have been very ready to help them in their selection of lots, and to sign their deeds for them as a witness. He also bought and sold lots on his own account, but not to any extent, or in any manner interfering with his duties and good name as a pastor. He was here as an ordained minister just ten years (1765–1775), the most critical decade in the history of Williamstown; and he probably did more than any other person, in that decade, to make the place attractive and the settlement permanent. He gathered a church of between seventy and eighty members in that brief time; for, while there is no list of them then, at the time of the settlement of his successor, Rev. Seth Swift, in 1779, there were seventy-nine members, and we fortunately know their names.

Some time during his pastorate, Mr. Welch bought lands on Green River, at the east end of the Main Street, and probably on both sides of the river. The only evidence as to the place of his residence while he was pastor here is the following: Chloe Bingham, who is now about eighty years old, and has always lived in one spot at the west end of the Green River bridge, has often repeated what she heard from her mother, — the eldest daughter of Theodore Boardman, whose home was near the same spot, and who was a contemporary of Mr. Welch, — namely, that the Welches lived directly opposite them, across Main Street, on ground just east of house lot 63, between that and the river. This was, indeed, outside of the house lots, and nearly a mile from his meeting-house; but then it was so much the nearer to Fort Massachusetts, and it was by much the safer end of the straggling village, for the French and Indians had always come on from the northwest, and it was on Hemlock Brook, and not on Green River, that Captain Chapin and the Chidesters had been killed, in 1756. At any rate, on the 4th of May, 1775, just fourteen days after the news of the battle of Lexington had reached Berkshire, and only thirteen days after Colonel John Patterson's regiment of minute-men had left Berkshire for Cambridge, and, beyond doubt, in some living relation with those stirring events to the eastward, Whitman Welch deeded to Nehemiah Smedley eighteen and three-fourths acres of land, directly east of Green River at that point, "with an allowance for the Highway" (the present main road to North Adams).

Those eighteen and three-fourths acres from Welch to Smedley were evidently adjacent to, and became easily a part of, lands previously bought by Smedley, namely, first-division fifty-acre lot 28, bought in June, 1765, and same division fifty-acre lot 29, bought in October, 1766. These Welch acres thus sold seem to include meadow lot No. 14; but it is remarkable that Coffin's map of 1843 puts an interrogation point, as indicating "some incongruity of the survey or other cause of doubt," after No. 14 of the meadow lots, as well as after Nos. 28 and 29 of the fifty-acre lots, which, with meadow lots 10 and 12 and 13, and oak lot 7, made up the noted Smedley farm. We cannot tell certainly on which of the lots the farmhouse (still standing) was put up in 1772. Smedley's oldest son, Levi, born Oct. 8, 1764, believed, in his old age, the house to have been built on the lot bought of Welch, which could not have been the case if the house were raised in 1772, for Welch did not sell till 1775. It is more probable that the house stands on fifty-acre lot 28, bought in June, 1765, of John Moffat, painter, of Boston, whither Smedley went personally to· make the purchase. Besides Levi's own statement in favor of 1772 as the date of the house, there is a strong tradition in the family that the house was raised the day Levi was eight years old, and that numbers of men came from Bennington to the "raising." That would be Oct. 8, 1772.

The deed of the eighteen and three-fourths acres is in Mr. Welch's own handwriting. The complicated surveyor's description — the plot had nine separate angles — looks as if he had also surveyed it, which, as a college graduate of that time, he was doubtless able to do. The deed was never recorded, and was never questioned. The land remained in the hands of the Smedleys for longer than a century's time. The consideration paid was £75 10s. This was undoubtedly the money on which Welch himself, shortly after, went to Cambridge, and late in the autumn went up the Kennebec to Canada, in Arnold's column, in volunteer company with several of his own parishioners. Nothing is said in this deed about any buildings on the land; but Levi Smedley said, in 1829, "One of the barns now standing there is much older than the house," which is pretty good, though not conclusive, additional proof that the Smedley house was not erected on the land sold by Welch to Smedley.

As Mr. Welch did not live to return from Quebec, Mrs. Welch, who was a daughter of Deacon Gaylord, of New Milford, went back to that town with two or three small children, was married again there, and lived to an extreme old age.   She left growing in her garden here (wherever it was) some roses of the simple red variety, from an original root or two brought with her when she came.   That she was highly esteemed here, and pitied in her strange widowhood, seems to be proven by the fact that Mrs. James Meacham and Mrs. Betty Cox transplanted the rose in memory of her, each to her own front yard, where they are still growing, much multiplied, with the present credible tradition attached to them, — a tradition that Bliss Perry has wrought out imaginatively, for publication, under the title, "The Colchester Rose."   The *Youth's Companion* of March 21, 1889, holds the story.

In the mean time, while these outlots of the fifth division were being slowly occupied, mostly by farmers from Connecticut who came up by the rude road over the watershed between the Housatonic and the Green rivers, a road since eulogized by Henry Ward Beecher, — "From Salisbury to Williamstown and thence to Bennington there stretches a country of valleys and lakes and mountains, that is to be as celebrated as the lake district of England or the hill country of Palestine," — matters were moving more briskly with the house lots and householders of the incipient village. Proprietors' meetings were held frequently, particularly during the year 1765, the birth-year of the town, and the first year of their ordained minister.   Every item of common expense must pass sharp muster in these popular gatherings, because every shilling of the money must come out of the individual pocket of the proprietors; roads were laid out in all directions, and each day's work of man or team must be passed upon and voted "pay for," in proprietors' meeting *viva voce;* the pine lots and the oak lots, all of both being located north of the "Greate River," were surveyed out by Jedediah Hubbell, and distributed by a "common lottery," in this year, 1765. The committee, under whom these surveys of the sixth and seventh divisions were made and reported, were Elisha Higgins and John Smedley and Thomas Dunton and Jonathan Kilborn; and William Horsford, whose house lot was 44, directly north across Main Street of the later West College, was the faithful proprietors' clerk from the beginning of 1765 till 1774.

Of course, the need of the common mechanic arts of all kinds was soon felt in the now growing hamlet; and a curious concession was made in the proprietors' meeting of Jan. 14, 1766, to Joseph

Tallmadge, a shoemaker who had recently come from Colchester; making shoes and tanning leather were trades, at that time, and long afterwards, in New England, closely allied, and often united, in the hands of one man; Tallmadge had evidently asked the proprietors for the privilege of having a tan-yard on the common land in the Main Street, near what has long been called Hemlock Brook, but which was then called "Hudson" Brook, from Seth Hudson, whose house stood on its eastern bank; and it was accordingly "Voted to Give Leave to Mr. Joseph Talmadge to Sett up a tan yeard on the North side of the Highway on Hudson Brook of one Quarter of an acre of Land to have the use of Said Land ten year Not obstruct or Hinder Passing Provided He the Said Joseph talmage can agree with Mr. Ebenezer Cooley & obtain Leave of Him." Ebenezer Cooley then owned house lot 12, just west of the brook, north side, in front of whose lot the tan-yard would be. It is not likely that his consent was secured, for he sold the lot in June following, to "Isaac Searle Esq.," for £20. Searle was, at this time, the most forehanded man in the borough, though he had come from Northampton as a "cordwainer" about ten years before, and it was not like him to buy encumbered property, or to agree to have his own encumbered in that way. Another thing that makes it improbable that Tallmadge actually gained the permission of the owner of No. 12, is the fact that he bought, himself, the next March, house lot 13, directly opposite No. 12, on the south side of the highway, and only the width of that way above on the same brook, described in the deed as "at the westernmost end of main street." He paid £15 for his house lot.

Whether Tallmadge actually started a tannery at the north end of his own house lot 13 cannot now be determined; there is no direct proof that he did; tan-bark is one of the most indestructible objects in nature, and none of this has been thrown up there by plough or spade in the memory of living men while the early existence of a tan-yard on the east side of the brook close by is proven by such casual manifestations there; and besides, Tallmadge only stayed on No. 13, with his newly married wife, Martha Marks, for three years, when he bought in April, 1770, his farm on Northwest Hill, on which he lived and died. This was fifty-acre lot No. 4. It was the ministry lot of the second division of fifty-acre lots, drawn by house lot 38. Tallmadge bought it of Samuel Smedley, and the deed was signed by Nehemiah and Aaron Smedley, as witnesses, all three of these brothers from Litchfield. This lot proved to be as productive as any parcel of ground in Williamstown, and has been

often called the best "grain-farm" in town. Its northern line just
grazes the Hoosac River, and its southern line is the straight highway bounding the ends of the house lots lying in the northwest
corner of the entire plat of house lots.

If Joseph Tallmadge had been content to confine himself to
ploughing his fields and raising his crops, he would have been a
prosperous and envied farmer. Indeed, he became and continued
such, until in an evil hour he concluded to utilize a fine spring to
the north of his house, whose clear waters drop down into a little
stream that drops into Hemlock Brook just before the junction of
that with the Hoosac, as a means of distilling brandy out of cider,
which had then become exceedingly abundant in the town. Public
opinion had not then turned against the distillation of brandy.
Deacon James Smedley told the writer, that he as a boy had helped
his father carry cider to this place to be distilled into brandy;
his father was Deacon Levi Smedley, the head of perhaps the most
precise and puritanic family in the town. Joseph Tallmadge did
not forfeit his good name among his neighbors by setting up this
still : there were at least three others put into operation not long
after in different parts of the town, all by reputable parties.
Nevertheless, the phrase above used, "in an evil hour," is well
considered and appropriate. There was a generation of drunkards
raised up in this town in direct connection with these four stills.
Not one of the four families escaped personal demoralization and
pecuniary losses. Tallmadge had four sons. Each of them became
compromised in turn, both in respect of the personal habit and of
the monetary ruin. The very locality, though naturally prospective and picturesque, became a by-word and a hissing.

The beautifully wooded little valley that runs across the farm
with its stream and its spring has been called now for a long time
"Flora's Glen," and A. L. Hopkins, who owns this and many
adjoining lots, has lately built two expensive dams on this stream
and thus made two lovely ponds, and also walled in the spring, that
bubbles out on the very marge of the lower pond, making the
whole region one of peculiar beauty and consequent attractiveness
both to natives and strangers ; but the late C. R. Taft, who was
more than twenty years postmaster, used to tell, that the whole
place was a "turkey-shoot" when he was a boy, and that he himself had witnessed the scenes of drunkenness and fighting, that
always in those days accompanied the cruelty and gambling of that
so-called "sport." Many persons still living remember Phebe
Holmes, an old colored woman, whether African or Indian was left

in doubt, who lived and died in an old cabin on the little brook that flows past the College spring. Her husband, Holmes, a well-authenticated Indian, was stabbed and nearly killed at one of these turkey-shoots near the "Still Spring." The name, "Phebe's Brook," commemorates in a pleasant way the poor and aged woman; the only memorial of her husband is the turning of a point in the description of a brutal. autumn festival, at once attracted by and affiliated with Joseph Tallmadge's cider-brandy.

After the public religious services of Thanksgiving Day, in 1892, the chief feature of which was a powerful sermon by John Bascom, on the nature and coming of the Kingdom of Heaven, the penman of these present lines visited alone the Still Spring and its neighborhood. Gratitude to God for the many favorable local contrasts as between the first and last decades of the century was tinged and intensified by a personal gratitude for a lifelong and stimulating friendship with the fearless and profound and eloquent preacher of that Thanksgiving Day.

Joseph Tallmadge had five children: Martha, the eldest, born in 1768, married shoemaker Stone, of Hoosac, both excellent people in all the relations of life; Joseph, the second, was born exactly two years after his sister, Feb. 27, 1770; the next son, Josiah, married Jan. 3, 1793, a Williamstown girl, Ada Hickox, and they became the parents of Mary Tallmadge Hosford, the oldest person now living in town, and one among those most highly esteemed by everybody; Ephraim, born in 1774, made his home elsewhere; and Asa, the youngest, born Oct. 1, 1776, who married Abigail Tyler, and reared a large family here, living on Northwest Hill, and in several other parts of the town, and manifesting in more directions than one (even to old age) the untoward influences of the cider-brandy still. His son, Edwin Tallmadge, and his daughter, Orcela Tallmadge Blakeslee, are the only persons now in town (besides Mrs. Hosford) perpetuating a respected name. Edwin Blakeslee, the husband, was born and bred in Rowe on the upper reaches of the Deerfield River, in plain sight of the vestiges of old Fort Pelham. His grandfather, Caleb Blakeslee, was the composer of the famous minor hymn-tune, "Windham," usually sung to the words, "Broad is the road that leads to death," etc., and very popular in New England for a century. He sold the copyright of the tune for thirty dollars, to his own and others' subsequent regret; for the tune should have borne his name. He was the son of Seth Blakeslee, of North Haven, Connecticut, whence the son came to Rowe.

Edwin Blakeslee built one of the first houses on the present Spring

Street in 1847; Thomas Mole had built the very first one the year previous, during which the street had been opened by S. V. R. Hoxsie; George Roberts, and Charles Spooner, and Edwin Sanderson, and Frederic Sanderson, the two last in company for a while with Edwin Blakeslee, all tailors, occupied houses on the same street within a twelvemonth. Blakeslee has practised his trade in this town and its immediate vicinity for more than fifty years. An eccentric and disagreeable character, Nathan Hoskins, who was graduated at Dartmouth College in 1820, a classmate and (as he always claimed) a room-mate, too, with Rufus Choate, was the seventh in order to build a house on Spring Street. All these houses were hastily and cheaply constructed, the ground was originally low, and otherwise seemed unsuitable for houses; Daniel N. Dewey, then treasurer of the College, opposed the opening of the new street, and Hoxsie was angrily compelled, owing to the situation of a corner of College ground, to make his lay-out narrow and inconvenient of entrance ; nevertheless, the new street was a necessity of the time in affording homes to many of the young artisans of the village; it has been pretty steadily lifted and improved as a place for residence, the town high-school building was erected upon it in 1866, and business of various kinds kept creeping in along its whole length until in 1892, by the removal into it of the post-office, and the bank, and several stores and places of recreation and amusement, it became, and will probably remain, the chief business street of the town.

The next public meeting of the proprietors to that which gave the concession to Joseph Tallmadge for a tan-yard, was occupied mainly with the vexed question of roads in the different parts of the town, — a point that made constant friction and open dissatisfaction for several years. The principal clause in the warrant for this meeting was as follows: "To See if the Proprietors will Chuse a new Commetee to Lay out Roads wheare they are Needed and give them Power to Prise Land that are and Shall be Laid out for Roads and to make Return to the Proprietors of the Sum or Sums and to Give the sd Commetee Power to Exchange Roads for Roads or Sett of Common or undivided Land to make Restitution for Land taken out of the Lots for Roads Belonging to any Person Whatsoever lying in this town." This article was voted bodily April 26, 1766, and a strong committee, consisting of Richard Stratton, and Benjamin Simonds, and Jonathan Meacham, and Samuel Kellogg, and Thomas Dunton, chosen to carry it out; but at the next meeting, May 15, a fortnight later, the vote was reconsidered, and it was agreed "to give the Road Commetee no Power only to Lay out Roads and to veu others Roads in order to Exchange and to veu Common Land in order to Pay for Land wheare it will sute and Bring their Doings to the Proprietors for Exchange." William Horsford had become obnoxious to some of the proprietors in connection with these road and land difficulties, and there was a clause in the April warrant, — " To See if the Proprietors will Chuse a New Clerk," — on which the May meeting " Voted in the Negative."

Civil government, under any and all circumstances, everywhere, is always an awkward instrument by means of which to reach the true ends for which government itself is instituted; the radical reason for this is, that the persons selected to administer the government, no matter on what plan, are always possessed of the same selfish tendencies, which, in the masses of men, make governments needful at all; all men esteem their own private interests higher than the interests of their fellows, and when these two seem to come into collision, are ready, unless restrained, to sacrifice the rights of others to their own apparent gains; this is the universal fact that makes governments necessary; but, unluckily, the governments are compelled to be administered by men of the same sort in this respect as all the rest, and political constitutions are framed with the express purpose of restraining this selfishness of the governors, as laws are enacted to restrain that of the governed; neither the one nor the other are ever wholly effective, and consequently the organization and continued administration of governments are always accompanied with frictions and difficulties and wrong-doings. This is just as true of local governments of small circumference, as of national governments of the widest, — just as true of West Hoosac and Williamstown, as of the state of Massachusetts in 1780, and of the United States in 1789.

The early roads here made endless trouble and contention, partly because individual proprietors cut roads to their outlying properties at their own cost, expecting to be reimbursed by their road becoming a public road, or by exemption from taxation for other roads ; and partly, because it was impossible to foresee in what directions population would ultimately become thickest, so as to demand public highways. At the next meeting of the proprietors, in chronological order, Oct. 9, 1766, another set of unavoidable difficulties confronted them ; namely, matters of taxes to meet current and past expenditures. " Voted to Raise Nine Shillings on Eaich Right to make up old Rearridges." " Voted and Chose Jonathan Meacham, Stephen Davis and Elkanah Parris a Commetree to sell the Land of the Proprietors that are Delinquent in paying their Rates." " Excepted the account of the Commetree of the Greate River Bridge which is £48 12 3." Then follow accounts of several publicly advertised "Vandues," "Published in the Boston Prints as the Law Directs," at which the lands delinquent went off, for the most part, pitifully low, many of them to Ephraim Seelye, the land-grabber. One oak lot, No. 12, was bidden off by Benjamin Simonds, for 1s. 4d. 3 farthings an acre. The only possible income for the propriety arose from lands, either the tax voted in the proprietors' meetings on each "Right," as it was called, or the small sums realized from the sales of the lots of those owners who refused, or were unable to pay, or had withdrawn from the settlement altogether, abandoning their lands. This aggregate income was always inadequate to the necessary expenditures. This led to frequent misunderstandings with the successive treasurers. The first treasurer, as we have learned already, was Isaac Wyman, long clerk and commander, both at Fort Massachusetts and West Hoosac Fort; but as treasurer of the proprietors of West Hoosac, he soon fell into distrust and troubles, and left the place entirely, and went to Keene, New Hampshire, where he was very prominent and much trusted, becoming Lieutenant-Colonel under Stark, in 1775, and appointed Colonel, in July, 1776. The second treasurer was Josiah Horsford, one of the early Connecticut soldiers here, whose wife was Jemima Smedley, and whose house is still standing as the kernel of the later Whitman house, now owned and occupied by Dr. Woodbridge; and he kept to the post patiently and uprightly till 1766, when Samuel Kellogg was chosen in his place. There were frequent "reasonings" and "reckonings" with the treasurer in all these years.

It may be easily gathered from all the foregoing that the stated proprietors' meetings were not specially attractive places to the proprietors themselves. The same is betrayed also by a clause in the warrant for such a meeting issued Nov. 24, 1766. "To Se if the Proprietors will Pay those men that attend the meetings of Said Proprietors." Though at the meeting thus called it was "Voted to Drop this articiel," its admittance into the public warrant reveals another large obstacle in the way of the practical administering of such a pure democracy as that was. All were on an equality of privilege within the government; but all, or nearly all, were poor; great sacrifices were required of all in order to build up and keep agoing the little rustic commonwealth, — roads and bridges and a meeting-house, and the ordination and salary of a minister, were to be provided out of their own slender gains or reserves; frictions between officers and non-officers, and between individuals as such, were certain to arise under such circumstances, and between the minority and the majority on many questions passed upon; an obvious way of manifesting those dissatisfactions was to stay away from the authorized and only legal gatherings for governmental purposes, and at the least it took time and trouble to attend them; and so, as the meetings grew thin, it occurred to somebody to try the experiment of a paid attendance. In their poverty, it is surprising that this should have been even proposed; more surprising, a great deal, than that bank directors and other members of corporations in our own day should be actually paid out of the common fund for participating in the common counsels of the body corporate.

Any five of the proprietors could, at any time, by request made to their clerk, secure the issuance of a public warrant by him, calling a legal meeting, the warrant stating in order the items of business to be acted on at that meeting, and no other business could then be legally transacted. The painstaking and fidelity manifested in general by the various committees raised to prepare the reports on which public and final action was to be taken, is proven and illustrated at length in the minutes of the proprietors, to which reference may be had. The original copy of these minutes is in the office of the town clerk of Williamstown; and the writer is possessed of a copy of that, made at his instance and expense, and sworn to as to its exactness before Keyes Danforth, justice of the peace, and Charles S. Cole, town clerk, Dec. 4, 1878.

We will give two specimens of these reports of committees, because we believe that the reader of the future will be pleased to see them just as they were rendered, bad spelling and all. The first is the report of Richard Stratton and Benjamin Simonds on a new burial-lot, the original lot for that purpose at the end of the North Cross Street having been proved unsatisfactory, presumably on account of the steep hill by which alone it could be reached.

October the 1 AD 1766 we the Subscribers being chosen a Commetee to Provide a better Place for a burying yard Have attended the Business and the Best Place we Can fiend is the frount of mr John Newbre Home Lot: No: 14 and Part of the Street Joyning to it we Suppose to Begin att the South East Corner of s^d Lot and runs Eight rods into the Lot Northward and 12 rods and an Half west and 5 rods into the Street we take of mr Newbre Land Half an acre and Half a Quarter we sopose to Give Him ·£2 10 0 for it what we take from the Street is a quarter and Half a quarter and 2 rod and an Half of Ground.

This is the origin and nucleus of the West Cemetery. It has been several times enlarged, more specially towards the west and north; and it is one of the current ideals of the town at present, that it be again much enlarged towards the north so as to have the shaded Hemlock Brook its eastern boundary for a considerable stretch, and be beautified throughout, as the lay of the land invites to ornamentation suitable to God's sown field and the burial-place of the fathers. Also this report is evidence enough of the little esteem had by the early settlers for the fifteen-rod Main Street west of the Hemlock Brook. It did not seem to them that so wide a street would ever be needed so far from the Square. This committee proposed a burial-lot of one acre, five-eighths off from one end of a house lot, and three-eighths out of the Main Street. The proprietors had granted leave conditionally only a few months before, to Joseph Tallmadge, to take one quarter of an acre for a tan-yard out of the street at almost the same spot, "not to obstruct or hinder passing." Passing was the main matter with them, and scarcely at all a broad and beautiful avenue for the future. The west end of the Main Street has never recovered from this levity of the original proprietors. It is nowhere of the full width, and much of the way quite narrow and neglected.

The second and only other specimen of early action that we will quote here, is in the form of a report from an important committee, consisting of Richard Stratton and Thomas Dunton and Samuel Kellogg.

Williams Town December the 8 1766 we the Subscribers being chosen to Lay out and Exchange Roads for the Propriete we Have Laid a road from green River Bridge a South East Coarse Eighty two Rods to a burch tree marked H then Running South theirty five rods to the old Road wheare the first two rod road goes of to the South to a maple tree marked H the road runs through Derick webbs meadow Lot No 14 and through Nehe Smedly fifty acre lot No 28 the Road to be four rods wide and said webbs and Smedly to have the old Road in Exchangue for this We Have also Laid a two rod road from the above Said Burch tree East forty eight rods through sd Smedly fifty acre lot to a maple tree marked H thence a little to the North East Eight rods a Crost a Little Corner of mr. Kellogg Land to the old Road by the meadow Lots sd Smedley to have the meadow Road through his land to Pay for this.

This was the beginning of the present road of egress from out the east end of our village, towards North Adams. It was a forked road, starting single from the bridge, and dividing at the foot of what used to be called the "Smedley Hill," and afterwards "Deacon Foote's Hill" (who married a Smedley and passed a long life there), avoiding the hill, and striking the old path to Fort Massachusetts at a point further east. This straightened, and, of course, shortened, the road to the East Town, besides avoiding a clay hill; but, for some reason (perhaps because the ground was wet as well as clayey), the new road was not long maintained, and there has been, of late years, much talk of reopening it, or one corresponding to it, across the meadow land nearer the Hoosac.

The Derick Webb referred to in the above report as the owner of meadow lot 14, which not long after became a part of Nehemiah Smedley's farm, had been a soldier in the line of forts ten years before, became a very early settler in West Hoosac, and made his home on the plateau west of Green River, and east of the northeast quarter of the village plat. This was on first-division fifty-acre lot 34, high ground, that skirted the meadow lots on lowest Green River, and on the Hoosac as far as the Noble Bridge. In all probability Rev. Whitman Welch had his home near to Mr. Webb's. The latter's meadow lot No. 14 joined his own home lot, though it lay mostly east of the river. Thomas Dunton, a man in whom apparently all the proprietors had confidence, a member of this very committee whose report we are considering, the father of five children, born 1762–1771, had pitched his place near the Noble Bridge on this same fifty-acre lot, where is now the hum of a huge cotton-factory and the bustle of a railway station. For some reason, partly, perhaps, because it was so sightly and defensible, this lot No. 34, which flanked the river on one side and the house-lot plat on the other, was early cut up into dwelling lots much more than any other fifty-acre lot of either division. A short time before the death of its late lamented owner, John M. Cole, he pointed out to the writer the remains of at least two cellars upon this plateau besides those of the three houses already referred to. It is quite possible that Derick Webb found his neighbors here too close; for we find him moving on into Vermont, after a fashion that was much followed later, and making himself a new home in Sunderland, Bennington · County, in the first company of settlers there in 1766. When he sold his Williamstown lands in July, 1768, he is described as of " Sunderland in the Province of New York so-called "; and the deed was acknowledged in " Hoosack before John Macomb one of His Majesty's Justices," etc., in December, 1769. Derick Webb was the holder in 1765 of house lot 58 here, and sold to Joel Simonds for £40, three years later, 100-acre lot 9, and oak lot 38, and pine lot 41, all drawn by house lot 58.

Just midway between the two villages in Williamstown, on the Green River road, is a fair mill privilege (formerly much better than now), called in all the old records " Taylor's Crotch," from

Samuel Taylor, the first proprietor of land at the junction of the Green River and the Hopper Brook, which constitutes the Crotch. Foreseeing that a mill would probably be needed there, the original proprietors sequestered ten acres of land, including the junction of the streams, for public purposes, and called it the "Mill Lot." It proves that population had already crept up the Green River beyond that point, when a proprietors' meeting on the 15th of October, 1767, "Voted to Give John Kriger Peter Kriger and William Kriger their heirs Liberty to Sett up a Grist mill att taylor's Crotch by the 1 Day of August Next on those Conditions that they have all the Land on the west Side of the West Branch except what is Necesery for Roads and as much of the East Side of the west Branch as is Nessery to Dam or flow for the use of the Corn mill With Liberty to Cutt any timber for the use of the Mill or Dam on the ten acre of Land theire Sequestered Provided they will keep sd mill in order Haveing a Sutable time to Repare said mill in when it is out of order they to Have the Privileges Solong as they keep a good mill and Nolonger." Under this public encouragement there came into town a family of Dutch millers, who were then living in Pownal below, and who became good citizens for a century, intermarrying with the Youngs and other old families, so that even the name has but recently died out here. "Krigers' Mills" is still the best established name of the locality; for a year and a half after the above concession on the part of the proprietors to the three "Krigers," they voted to the same parties by name "Liberty to Sett up a Sawmill at taylors Crotch on the East Branch Provided they will Sett up a Sawmill by the first Day of may Next on these Conditions that they Build Said mill and keep it in Good Repare So Long and No Longer they to Have it Haveing a Sutable time to Repare Said mill in."

A clause in the warrant for a proprietors' meeting, to be holden in the new meeting-house, Oct. 9, 1769, reads as follows: "To See if the Proprietors will a Low or for Bid milstones Being Carred out of Town that are found on the Proprietors Land with out a Reasonable Satisfaction." In the record of that meeting these words are found in relation to that item of business: "articiel Dismissed by a Vote." Mr. Dale, the United States geologist, who is familiar with every part of the surface of Williamstown, informs that those supposed millstones could have been no other than the quartzites, still found in limited quantities on Stone Hill and near the top of East Mountain. Quartzites, he says, are not well adapted to become mill-stones; nevertheless, they were sometimes used for that purpose, and the reference can be to no other.

Some proprietors continued to be delinquent in the payment of the rates assessed upon them from time to time, for certain public expenses, such as roads and bridges, and at length the meeting-housé; and public auctions were ordered, in order to sell off such portions of the lands delinquent as might satisfy these claims. Many lots became more or less divided up in this way, — titles disputable, and owners indifferent. Frequent parties from Connecticut, on their way through the town to new homes in Vermont, proved attractive to many families and individuals that had been less successful in their choices or less fortunate in their neighbors, and some of these dissatisfied ones passed on to the northward. The population, as a whole, was considerably unstable. The element that proved the steadiest, that had been the most successful, and that became, about 1770, in the good sense predominant, was decidedly the old garrison element ; that is to say, the young soldiers became settlers, who had done duty in the line of forts in the French war, specially in Fort Massschusetts and in the West Hoosac Fort. These men, as a rule, became the stand-bys and the leaders while peace lasted, and the strong defenders of colonial rights and liberties in the next decade.

The solidity of some of those old soldiers is illustrated in connection with the story of the first meeting-house. It was a good deal of an achievement to build that house, under all the circumstances. It was first occupied by the proprietors for one of their own meetings, Nov. 7, 1768. At that meeting it was " Voted to Give Instructtions to the meeting House Commetee Concerning the Pew Ground also Voted to Build Pews Voted that Said Commetee Go on and Build Pews according to their Dischression and then Sect Said House." At the same meeting, adjourned, — " Voted Excepted the Hole of the account of the meeting House Commetee in the Hole — £149 14s. 11d." Who were the persons entrusted with the delicate and much-disputed questions about the first meeting-house ? The original committee to build consisted of Richard Stratton, and Nehemiah Smedley, and Samuel Sanford. Sanford was from Milford, Connecticut, the birthplace of Whitman Welch, the minister, and was probably put on this committee as the special friend of the minister ; but, for some reason unknown to us, Sanford fell out before the work was done, and in March, 1768, the proprietors " Voted and chose Benjamin Simonds a Commete man in the Room of mr Samuel Sanford for Building the meeting House." Simonds's name is as indissolubly joined to the story of the Massachusetts Fort as that of any other man, unless it be Ephraim Williams ; and Smedley was a Connecticut soldier in the garrison at West Hoosac as early as anybody was, and his father had bought house lot No. 1, in October, 1752, which the son purchased in his own name, in March, 1758, and still held. There was great difficulty in determining the place of the new house of worship, as is shown by the clauses of the warrant for the meeting in April, 1768; namely, "to See if the Proprietors will appoint a Place wheare to Sett a meeting House or to Com into any measures for the Same"; "to See if the Proprietors will agree with the town to Chuse a Place for the meeting House or to chuse a Commete for the Same"; "to See if the Proprietors will forbid the Commetee to Raise the meeting House till such time as there is a Place legally appointed for the Same"; "to Give Instructions to the Commetee of the meeting House that they may know How to Proceed concerning the Charges for Raising Said House."

It will be remembered that the "Town," as such, was incorporated in 1765; but this came, very slowly, to be able to confront, as an organization, the older and naturally stronger "Proprietary," which held in its own hands the times and modes of dividing up the lands among the proprietors, and which owned absolutely all the common and undivided lands of the town. At the April meeting, 1768, the proprietors refused to let the "town" have any voice in fixing the site of the meeting-house. They refused, also, to forbid their committee to raise the house till a place were legally appointed. They voted, the same day, to appoint themselves a place "to Sett up a meeting House." They decided that each proprietor should have as many votes, for or against the "Square" as the place, as he was possessed of acres in the town. 9880 acres then voted for the location on the Square, and 5035 acres voted to the contrary, and finally (same day), "Voted to Leave it to the Discression of the Commetee to Provide for the Raising Sd House." In October, 1769, the proprietors "Voted to Raise one Pound on Eaich Proprietor Right to finish the meeting House and Some other old Rearriges." Also, "Voted Excepted accounts as follows to Benjamin Simonds and Nehemiah Smedley for finishing the meeting House: £4 8s. 3d." In March, 1770, it was "Voted to Build 2 Pews in the East End of the meeting House." Also, at the same time, it was "Voted not to Except the meeting House as finished." The records of the proprietors contain no further references to the erection and equipment of their meeting-house. It is plain that their building committee possessed their entire confidence both as men and as builders.

They had been instructed by vote of the proprietors as to the size of the building, 40 × 30 feet; as to its location on the Square, at the intersection of the Main Street by the two cross streets north and south, on nearly the highest ground in the entire stretch of the Main Street, which is one mile and three-eighths in length from Green River to the west branch of Hemlock Brook; also as to the pew-system and body pews, and two additional pews at the east end before the finishing; and the same committee was directed finally "to seat" the meeting-house, that is, to arrange the families in the pews for Sundays according to some imaginary order of rank or social worth. For the rest, the committee seems to have gone forward at its own discretion, and to have done everything to the satisfaction of their constituents. The house continued to be used for the worship of God for just thirty years, — the only one so used in the entire town. Towards the last, for some unknown reason, Stratton seems to have retired more or less from active direction in the building, and left it to his younger colleagues, Simonds and Smedley. Simonds was forty-two and Smedley thirty-six in 1768. It is a noteworthy fact, that, after building the meeting-house conjointly and thus demonstrating their capacity collectively, each of the three committee-men should have erected his own house not far from the same time, and that all three of these houses should be standing strong and in good repair and substantially unaltered in this year of Grace, 1893. All three are two-story houses, and 1773 may be fairly assumed as the average date of their erection.

Unluckily, the original seating of the meeting-house has not been preserved. There were certainly very few grounds of social distinction among the proprietors of West Hoosac in 1768. They were all farmers without exception; even the minister and the doctor bought and sold and cultivated lots more or less, like all the rest. The minister was the only college graduate in the place. The doctor was Jacob Meack, a German or Hollander, who had probably strolled up the Hoosac from Albany or its neighborhood. It is likely that he married his wife here, although her full maiden name has not been ascertained. "Betsey Meack, relict of Jacob Meack, physician: she departed this life 6 Nov. 1797, in her 57th year." They reared five daughters here, born 1768–76, and all were married here; Hannah to John Kilborn, Junior, Currence to William Young, Esq., and Sally to Reuben Young, Esq. Their home was on Main Street, house lot 12, just over the east branch of Hemlock Brook, which was often called from this circumstance the "Doctor Brook." The house is still standing, thoroughly repaired, after having been occupied for two generations by the Kilborn family. Nearly every other proprietor, besides being a farmer, had learned and could practise

some mechanical trade. One proprietor, doubtless, gained some little
precedence over others by length of time passed in the settlement
or its neighborhood, which tended so far forth to make prominent
those who had been soldiers in the two forts; the few who were
well-to-do had, of course, the usual advantage over those more straitened by the *res angusti domi;* and a greater age, a better education,
and any supposed superior personal merit, other things being equal,
would serve as principles of grading in seating a small meeting-
house. Any Yankee has the privilege of guessing as to the slight
precedence of 1768, after the minister and doctor.

1. Richard Stratton would be likely to come first. He was older
than the rest, came earlier than many, was well off, and he had
three or four promising sons who had nearly reached to man's estate
when he came hither to make his home, from Western, about 1760.
He was moderator of the proprietors' meeting in 1761, and served
in that capacity eight times more. There were sixty-three proprietors' meetings in all, from 1753 till 1802, and Stratton was moderator in one-seventh of them. No other citizen served so many
times. Josiah Horsford served five times, and James Meacham five
times, and all others a less number of times. The two most notable
purchases of lands that Stratton made, were house lot 58 and three-
fourths of house lot 57, which is the lot that runs at right angles to
all the rest of the house lots, on account of the lay of land and
water at the east end of the southeast quarter of the village plat.
He built his house on the front of 58 in such a masterly manner
that it is a good house to this day, and has had a remarkable succession of owners and tenants. Stratton himself died in it, although
we do not know the date; Dr. Remembrance Sheldon lived in it
many years at the beginning of this century; Gershom T. Bulkley,
the first postmaster of Williamstown, was long a tenant, if not an
owner; Captain Isaac Latham, also postmaster and a leading man,
owned and occupied it; and James M. Waterman, chairman of the
board of selectmen longer than any other citizen has been from the
beginning, is the present owner and occupant. The rear of this
house lot is just as it was surveyed out in 1750. Some time after
Richard Stratton came also his brother Ichabod, who presently went
away. Richard's sons, Isaac and Ebenezer, who came with him,
became leading men in the next generation. Isaac was the first settler at the south part, and continued the most prominent man there
so long as he lived. In February, 1767, the father sold his "well-beloved son, Ebenezer, from parental affection," for £5, the two fifty-acre
lots of the first division Nos. 54 and 33 (except ten acres, north-

east corner of 33), and pine lot 45, and part of meadow lot 53 adjoining the two larger lots. This virtual gift constituted Deacon Ebenezer Stratton's farm, on what we now call the "Stratton road," which he cultivated in whole, or in part, until his death in 1814. The father was commonly called "Deacon Stratton," and was a Baptist, but whether such when he came and when he helped to build and "seat" the meeting-house, is a point impossible now to clear up.

2. Captain Isaac Searle may well have ranked second on the meeting-house scale in 1768. He was a dweller in Northampton in 1749, and sold land there at that time. In 1759, and afterwards, he was a considerable buyer and seller of lands in West Hoosac, and is designated as "cordwainer" in all those deeds. He located early on house lot 55, which is the house lot that skirts Water Street on the west, as that street opens up on Main Street. The Methodist meeting-house and parsonage now occupy a part of the front of No. 55, as do also Sherman's hardware store, and the old and long two-story house just west of it. Searle lived on the site of this house; and it is more than probable that he built it in his old age. A little of the extreme west end of house lot 57, cut off to the west by Water Street striking Main at right angles, is now indistinguishable from the front of house lot 55; the old "Union House," so-called, long kept as a tavern by "Uncle Jerry Hosford" and others, stood where the church now stands, and probably wholly on No. 57; if so, the present lumber-yard and opera-house of Waterman and Moore in the rear, are mainly on 57, and partly on the side of 55. The Union House and the present hardware store are said to have been built by David Noble, a prominent character we shall have to study in the sequel; at any rate, Isaac Searle owned a good many lots of land on both sides of Water Street, all the after-drafts coming from house lot 55, other house lots too, and some of the after-drafts from them also. More than any one of his neighbors, Searle was getting rich under the circumstances. In the first year of the town government, 1765, he was taxed for £700 at interest. Only one other was taxed that year on interest money at all, and that was Nehemiah Smedley, for £126 in that form. Money makes the mare go; and his increasing stores made Searle of too much consideration to be longer characterized as "cordwainer" in the deeds, of which there were many; and he is "Gentleman" in this connection thereafter. He buys and sells lands, too, in other parts of the county, e.g., in New Marlboro; and in the *Vermont Gazette*, 10th July, 1795, Isaac Searle and sixty-two others were published

as delinquents in paying dues to the new town of "Stratton" on the Green Mountains, which derived its first settlers from Williamstown.

3. James Meacham is pretty sure to have been well rated in the meeting-house list the first time round. He was a subaltern in Captain Nathaniel Dwight's company, rallied to the relief of the camp at Lake George, after the battle there, Sept. 8, 1755, in which Colonel Williams was killed. Indeed, Meacham's commission is dated September 10, and the men were mustered for marching September 15. He was then twenty-two years old, having been born in Salem, March 19, 1733. When he was four years old, his father, Jeremiah Meacham, became the pioneer settler in New Salem, in what is now Franklin County. Dwight led his company up the Deerfield, and over the Hoosac Mountain by the old Indian trail, to Fort Massachusetts, and down the Hoosac, through what afterwards came to be Williamstown, and up to Lake George by the usual route, where he stayed through the autumn, working part of the time on the luckless Fort William Henry. Like many another soldier from the eastward, thus casually passing through the gateway of the west, James Meacham remembered, from the relatively barren hills of New Salem when he had gotten home at last from the wars, the fertile leagues of land on the sunset side of the mountain. A townsman of his in New Salem, by the name of Joseph Ballard, had already become possessed, in the usual ways, of several desirable lots in West Hoosac, and, on the 5th of August, 1761, sold to Meacham for £73 8s. 8d., Nos. 7 and 8 of the first fifty-acre lots, adjoining the village plat on the south. Meacham came over here to live in August, 1762, his family consisting of father and mother and three little girls, the youngest, Lucy, being only six weeks old. She never moved again, dying here, unmarried, May 6, 1842. Her mother was Lucy Rugg, one year older than her husband, who bore him eleven children. Both were original members of the church here, and he became its first deacon, serving till his death in his eightieth year. After he had been more than twenty years a deacon, he rode past the old Smedley place at the east end of the village, of a Sunday morning, with his gun on his shoulder, to take part with Shays's men in their famous insurrection of 1787. It is scarcely needful to add that many of his neighbors, and the Smedleys among them, did not sympathize with the good deacon in his political passions. But Berkshire was very much divided on the questions then at issue. Shays made his last stand in the immediate vicinity of Deacon Meacham's early home; and it is interest-

ing to conjecture that the man was thinking of New Salem that Sunday morning, as well as of democratic equalities, when he headed his horse to the eastward.

4. The second original deacon of the Williamstown church was a man of whom we know little, and would gladly know more, while he was sure to have a good seat — probably in a special deacon's seat — in the new meeting-house. His name was Nathan Wheeler. He came up here from New Milford about the time the young pastor did, and perhaps in some connection with him, as did certainly several others. He continued a deacon till 1784, when he went away. There is no record of children born to him here; but his son, Nathan Wheeler, Junior, came with him and probably went with him, and was an active church-member. His farm proved to be, and has continued to be, one of the best in town. Its original nucleus was fifty-acre lot No. 12, "lying on the east line of West Hoosuck," first occupied by Ephraim Seelye from "Amenia Precinct," Dutchess County, New York, "Gentleman," who soon passed on to Pownal, whence his sons, Ephraim and Reuben, returned after a few years, the whole Seelye family becoming a large factor (especially in relation to lands) for nearly a century of time. Ebenezer Stratton, son of Richard, became the successor in the deaconate to Nathan Wheeler in 1784, and Daniel Day his successor on the farm, much enlarged. The farm afterwards came into possession of old Bissell Sherman, and was inherited by one of his sons.

5. Jonathan Meacham, a cousin of the preceding Deacon James Meacham, who had also taken an active part in the French and Indian war, and was, in some respects, a more enterprising settler than the deacon himself, came also from New Salem before he did, and left lasting marks of his residence both in church and town records. He bought after some other and earlier purchases, which entitled him to a place in the first proprietors' meeting of 1753, first of Seth Hudson for £5 house lot No. 43, a lot a considerable part of which has long been owned by the writer, and on the eastern edge of which stands his present house. This purchase of Meacham's was made Oct. 2, 1760. He proceeded to set up his house on the north front of this lot on Main Street, very near where the West College was afterwards built. In 1886, one hundred and twenty-five years after, it may be presumed, that Meacham put up his house there, the College (now owning the land) gave permission to the Chi Psi fraternity, which had built its fine fraternity house a little to the west, to cut and use a tennis-court which happened to be laid out on the western edge of house lot 43. Here were then uncovered

the distinct remains of a house, some of the bricks being entire or
nearly so, and many more in fragments; and there can be very little
doubt that this was Jonathan Meacham's first house, although the
"oldest inhabitant" had no intimation that any house ever stood
there; and it is a matter of trustworthy record, that, in 1766,
Meacham lived in a house by the College Spring on house lot 49, a
lot which he certainly owned, and on which he had probably built
himself, and the cellar of this second house remained open till long
past the middle of the next century. It stood just to the west of a
big rock still reclining there. It is a fair conjecture that Meacham
found the same difficulty in finding water near his first house that
the builders of the West College experienced thirty years later; and
that what has been designated for a long time the "College Spring"
furnished the motive for his move from No. 43 to No. 49.   Somewhat later, he changed his residence again to Bee Hill, to the excellent farm on which four generations of the Hickox family have now
dwelt without a break.   Jonathan Meacham was an original member of the church, and so was Thankful Rugg, his wife; and the
first recorded instance of church discipline is stated in the following words, the church meeting being holden Feb. 13, 1779: "Voted
that Sampson How and Nathaniel Sanford be a committee to wait
on Jonathan Meacham to enquire the reason of his absenting himself from communion."   So far as existing church records extend,
this committee never made a formal report.   Meacham and his wife
were not dismissed from the church, but are designated among those
"removed to distant parts."

The second case of church discipline, which may be properly
enough conjoined with this, made pastor and people a vast deal more
of trouble, and issued rather in their humiliation than in that of the
offending brother disciplined.   Thomas Dunton, from Western or
its immediate neighborhood, had married there Mary Davis, a sister
of Stephen Davis, with whom we are already acquainted as the
husband of Rebecca Young.   The Duntons came to West Hoosac
very early as settlers, made their home on the Hoosac River near
to the present Noble Bridge, and took their full share in all the
forms of life within the narrow limits of the precinct.   Like the
rest, they bought and sold lands, the chief commodity at that time;
they reared at least five children, and he was in no wise remiss in
his duties as a citizen-soldier.   "This church think it their duty
to make known and declare to the world, That, whereas, Thomas
Dunton formerly a professing member of this church, having been
repeatedly guilty of excessive drinking or drunkenness was and has

been as this church trust dealt with according to Christ's rules and directions," — then follows a detailed account of the pastor's private interviews with the brother, in which the offence of absenting himself from the communion paved the way to a discussion of the more heinous sin of "excessive drinking"; and then an account of an interview between the pastor, accompanied by Captain Israel Harris and Mr. Nathan Wheeler and the member under discipline; and this, too, brought nothing to a head.   However, —

he said he would see and converse with the pastor in private within a few days. However the pastor did not have any opportunity to converse with him till sometime after, when Mr. Nathan Wheeler Jr. came to the pastor and informed him that Mr. Dunton was going to leave the Town in a short time and expressed an opinion that he should not leave the Town under these circumstances, therefore desired that there might be a meeting of the church as soon as might be: Accordingly one was appointed and the church met in the meeting house and a verbal complaint was exhibited to the church against Mr. Dunton for neglecting or absenting himself from the communion of the church and for being frequently guilty of excessive drinking or drunkenness and for persisting in these practices impenitent when dealt with by his brethren or in other words refusing to hear them. The church referred the matter and chose a Committee of three Capt. Israel Harris, Mr. Nathan Wheeler and Mr. Daniel Burbank who were to convey to him and ask him to answer to the above complaint. The Committee repaired immediately to Mr. Dunton and laid the result of the church before him. But he refused to come and appear before the church or give any satisfaction ; and even renounced all relation to or connection with the church and affirmed that he had never been a member of Mr. Swift's church, tho' it had not been known to any of the Brethren but that he was satisfied with Mr. Swift as to his pastoral character or with the conduct of the church at the time of his settling, for he made no objections but appeared pleased and spoke in favor of Mr. Swift's ministerial character repeatedly and did after his ordination apparently submit to brotherly discipline and reproof without pretending or intimating that he was not a member of the church. However at this time he refused all relation and connection to the church telling the church Committee that " he must answer for his conduct and they for theirs." This report the Committee brought to the church at another meeting. However after this upon Mr. Dunton intimating that he had something to say to them the church met. He appeared but said very little else than to renounce or repeat his renunciation of all connection and relation with the church alleging that they had gone and left him and he thought he had not left them, though it would not appear wherein unless every alteration and reformation of practice be a going away from him. These being the circumstances of the affair between Mr. Dunton and the church, Therefore: Voted and Resolved that this church do view and consider the said Mr. Thomas Dunton as unconnected with this church and not in the fellowship and communion of them.

Test. SETH SWIFT Pastor.

WILLIAMSTOWN the 2 of July A.D. 1780.

Thomas Dunton, of Williamstown, "Yeoman," sold to David Noble, of Williamstown, "Gentleman," two acres of land on Hoosac River "adjacent to my now dwelling house all the land lying on the easterly bank of said river which belonged to the meadow lot 19, and also a privilege to use and occupy the river on which said lot is bounded," etc. So vanisheth Thomas Dunton.

6. John Smedley, the eldest of a large family of brothers and sisters from Litchfield (now Morris), had become, by 1768, so prominent and prosperous a citizen as the proprietor of the chief sawmill of the place, and of the two best pine lots, and several meadow lots on the Lower Hoosac as well as of house lots Nos. 29 and 48, that he would naturally have been well seated in the new meeting-house. His brother Nehemiah, next younger, was of the building and seating committee, but that circumstance would hardly have postponed the claims of John Smedley, although very likely Smedley and Simonds, of that committee, would serve themselves later on that account, especially if they two had combined to give the other member of the committee the first seat, as has been supposed above. John Smedley was not a member of the church. Neither was any one of the building committee; but Richard Stratton's wife was an original member, and after his death (which occurred not far from 1779) the church repeatedly met at her house, which was then by much the best house in the hamlet. The meeting-house had been built and was always owned by the proprietors; undoubtedly, the seating proceeded on the basis of some real or fancied precedence among them. The concession has already been described by which the proprietors, in 1763, permitted John Smedley to take the water for his sawmill out of Broad Brook at the north end of the present bridge, and to carry it across the public road. In the warrant for a proprietors' meeting, issued in February, 1768, one of the items of business was, "To chuse a Committee to Sew John Smedley for Not making the Bridge when he turned the Brook." But at the meeting itself, in March, it was "Voted not to sew John Smedley." The Smedley family came with Rev. Peter Bulkley from England, and followed him from Boston to Concord, which he founded in 1636. They were John and Baptist. Both became freemen in Concord in 1644, and John prominent there later. John's son, Samuel, was in Fairfield, Connecticut, in 1690. His son, Samuel, born in 1702, married Esther Kilborn in 1729. Their eldest child, born Jan. 4, 1731, was our John Smedley. He married Deliverance Humphreys, and they had eight children, three born in Litchfield and five in Williamstown. One only was a son, John; the seven daughters all

lived to be married; Deliverance to Joel Baldwin, Amy to James
Fowler, Amelia to Samuel Hawkins, — these three continued to live
in Williamstown; Mary to John Boynton, who moved to Cornwall,
Vermont; Huldah to Warren Gibbs, who moved to Middlebury, Ver-
mont; and Tryphena to Richard Kinney, and Olive to Moses
McMaster, and both of these families removed to Georgia, Vermont.
Mrs. Baldwin lived here to old age, and went by the name of "Aunt
Dill" in the neighborhood where she dwelt, but finally migrated
with her grandnephew, Lemuel, to Great Bend, Pennsylvania, within
the memory of some now living.

John Smedley, Junior, married Elsie Williams, daughter of that
Nehemiah Williams whose acquaintance we have made as living by
the big rock near the Pownal line, on Northwest Hill, and as witnessing some of the surrendering soldiers of Burgoyne filing down
the opposite Pownal hills. Smedley's home was not far from his
father's, on fifty-acre lot No. 6, of the first division, which holds the
famous Sand Spring; and the second John Smedley was the first
known owner of that watering-place, which has had a vicissitudinous
history as such; and the tradition is still stirring, adown its appropriate lines, that old Aaron Smedley, born in 1750, who was a
vagrant hunter, living mostly in Vermont, used, on his visits to his
relatives in Williamstown, to frequent his nephew's rude bathing-
place, for the benefit of his eczema. A third John Smedley, son of
John, Junior, born April 21, 1780, married Mary Morse, moved
afterwards to Clinton County, New York, returned to Williamstown
in 1822, and then moved to Allen County, Ohio, where he died.
This Smedley is more interesting on account of his posterity than
from anything in his own biography. His daughter Lois, born
March 12, 1783, was married to Reuben Stetson at Cornwall, Vermont, in July, 1801, and thirteen children were the fruit of that
union. Mrs. Stetson died the last day of August, in 1866. One of
her sons, named Lemuel Stetson, after one of her brothers, Lemuel
Smedley, the same who took "Aunt Dill," in her old age, from
Williamstown to Great Bend, Pennsylvania, became the father of
Francis Lynde Stetson, born April 23, 1846 (Williams College,
1867), distinguished as a lawyer in New York, and particularly as
bringing into his law firm President Cleveland, at the close of his
first administration. F. L. Stetson's mother was Helen Hascall;
and his father was in political and judicial life in the state of New
York all the time (nearly) from 1835 to 1862.

7. Daniel Burbank, of Western, referred to in the above case of
church discipline against Thomas Dunton as a coadjutor with the

pastor, is written in old deeds as of "West Hoosuck," as early as 1761. He bought in that year, in company with Benjamin Simonds, one-half of two fifty-acre lots of the second division, — Nos. 56 and 57, — which, two years later, became wholly his own, and on the latter of which he built, shortly afterwards, the first *framed* house in the South Part. It consisted of one room. The next year another room was added, in which Aaron Deming was permitted to live until he could house himself upon his own 100-acre lot, as already described. Burbank's lots were level and fertile and heavily wooded. The Ashford Brook crossed them both not far from their eastern end and but a little before its junction with the Hancock Brook, and the road to the south crossed them diagonally just about their middle. He had at first but one neighbor, and that was Isaac Stratton, living then in a log-house on No. 53, just north of the Hancock Brook, where that hastens to unite with the Ashford, in the same lot, 53, on which is the present site of the Sabin House, in the centre of the little village, — a site that has been occupied as a tavern almost ever since. But Stratton soon crossed the brook upon No. 54, and built his house on the site occupied for life, a few rods south, on the west side of the road; and he shortly after owned and cultivated No. 55, also, which lay between himself and Burbank. The latter's own axe was the first to make clearings on 57 and 56, and his own plough was the first that ever stirred the rich intervale there. It was long called the Burbank farm. Let it be so called forever! His wife was Mary Marks, — likely to have come from Western, — and the eldest of their ten children was born in February, 1766. Both Burbank and his wife were original members of the one church, and their place of meeting was more than five miles from their home. The roads were rough, and over Stone Hill very steep both ways, but it is altogether likely that they were in their pew in the new meeting-house, after 1768, most of the Sundays of the year, and he was certainly often at the church meetings on week days. The same was true of Isaac Stratton, his next neighbor. Accordingly, we find the proprietors building a bridge for them over the Hancock Brook, in what is now the hamlet of South Williamstown, even before they built one over the Green River, at the eastern end of the north village, although there were many more settlers east of that stream than south of its tributary. The truth is, that Stratton and Burbank were pushing and prosperous young men, and soon became prominent.

The only reason why the writer presumes that Burbank may have been seated in precedence to Stratton is, that the latter was son to that one of the seating committee, Richard Stratton, who would naturally take the first seat, by the vote of his two colleagues, much younger than he. Burbank's life was uneventful, except as he went out repeatedly in the militia during the Revolutionary War. He was in the battle of Bennington as a private, though his rank in the militia at that time was Lieutenant. His eldest son, Samuel, between eleven and twelve years old at that time, lived to tell William Dickinson, who told the writer, that his mother directed him repeatedly, on the memorable day of the battle, to put his ear on the ground and listen, and that he did so, and heard the sound of the cannon distinctly and more than once. The distance is twenty miles. This son, also, transmitted the never-to-be-forgotten remark of the father, when he had returned from that battle, in which a bullet had grazed his ear: "After they had fired once and we had fired once, I'd just as soon be in the battle-field as in the potato field!"

8. Isaac Stratton had a much more intimate and influential connection with the battle of Bennington than his brave neighbor Burbank; but the story of that is best deferred until a later chapter may open up that whole subject. So far as appears at this late day, Isaac Stratton, more than any one else in the early times here, was under the dense shade of his father's good name and great activity. But they lived about five miles distant from each other, and the son easily held the first place at the South Part, as the father did more easily at the North Part. Richard Stratton's sons clung firmly to the old, established church order, as did also his wife, while he himself became a Baptist, and has no name on the Congregational church-record. This does not seem to have detracted at all from his influence and popularity. Isaac was his oldest child, and seven others followed, all born in Western. Isaac's birth fell in November, 1739, and he was consequently twenty-two years old, if, as is probable, the family moved hither in 1761. The father seems to have been a man of property when he came. He bought, in April, 1762, what ever after continued to be his homestead; namely, house lot 58, and a part of fifty-acre lot 34, directly north of the house lot, "and supposed to be about 13 acres." For this he paid Derick Webb £34, and Elkanah Parris and Isaac Stratton signed the deed as witnesses. It is reasonably certain that the older Stratton had bought, a year or two before this, the two fifty-acre lots at the south part, Nos. 53 and 54, which soon became the patrimony of Isaac, because the evidence is complete that Isaac built his cabin on No. 54 by the brookside in 1761, if not in 1760. Professor Kellogg, in "Field's Berkshire," wrote in 1829 from hearsay: "It was not till about 1760 that Isaac Stratton,

son of Richard, began on the spot ever since occupied by a tavern in the centre of the village. He was there alone about three or four years." In September, 1766, the father, in consideration of £7, "together with that parental love and affection which I have and do bear to him the said Isaac Stratton my well beloved son," deeded the lots, 53 and 55, to the son. In August, 1767, the latter sold No. 53 to Samuel Sloan, who soon built and opened a tavern on the site of Stratton's cabin, while the latter moved south of the brook and established himself for life on a pleasant knoll on No. 54.

Isaac Stratton and Mary Fox, his wife, had two children born to them while they still lived north of the brook, and at least three afterwards at their permanent home south of it. Both were original members of the church, and he died in its communion; while, after his decease in 1789, the widow married Rev. Clark Rogers and left the town with him; but when she died in 1812 her body was brought back, and lies buried by the side of her first husband in the burial-yard at the junction of the brooks. Besides military services of a high character under all the commissions in the militia up to Major, Isaac Stratton was early commissioned as a justice of the peace, and began to draw the simple legal writings needed in so primitive a community. He was town clerk also for a long time. He drew the entire confidence of the people in all parts of the town. He was pecuniarily prosperous in the then current usage of that term. After the definitive treaty of peace with Great Britain in 1783, he prepared to erect for himself a new house of two stories and ample dimensions. The materials, for the most part, were close at hand, growing upon his own land. The timbers are still in place and in good preservation to the present time. The rafters are long poles of quite uniform size, such as grew then luxuriantly on intervale land by the brooksides. A bit of white marble set in the chimney bears the legend legible yet : —

I. S.
1785

Stratton enjoyed his new house but four years, and passed on into a house not made with hands. His headstone in the cemetery nearly opposite the house to the eastward bears the simple epitaph: "Isaac Stratton Esq. died April 3, 1789, aged 50."

The precedence of Isaac Stratton at the South Part, both in point of time and general position over the other early and excellent settlers there, makes the appellation of "Stratton Mountain," appropriated to the huge wedge of rock and soil and forest, thrust northward into the acute angle formed by the Hancock and Ashford brooks, a good name to the mountain, and a fitting memorial to the man. On the same day in September, 1766, when Richard Stratton gave his son, Isaac, his farm in South Williamstown, he also gave his second son, Daniel, for £5, "together with that parental love and affection which I have and do bear," etc., a good farm in the White Oaks, consisting of first-division fifty-acre lot No. 51, with parts of two meadow lots adjoining the main lot, and two oak lots convenient of access to the homestead. It has been noted already that the father also gave on similar terms to his third son, Ebenezer, an excellent farm on Green River, on which this son lived and died, the road leading to which has recently been christened by the town the "Stratton road."

ISAAC STRATTON'S HOUSE.
Built 1785.

9. Not much inferior in point of social consideration to Daniel Burbank was Thomas Roe, from Canaan, Connecticut, who bought of Asa Douglas, then of that place, for £30, in December, 1764, the fifty-acre lot next south of Burbank's, and the last in that tier of lots. Then follow in that direction the 100-acre lots, on which the Demings first sat down. The deed from Douglas to Roe was executed in Canaan, when the latter was twenty-eight years old, and his wife, Mary Welles, was three years younger. She was from Hartford. They undoubtedly began on their new lot in the spring of 1765. The deed was executed in Canaan before John Beebe, Justice of the Peace. Here they lived to have twelve children, of whom the eldest was Elisha, born Dec. 5, 1768. Their lot, No. 58, ran back to the Ashford Brook on the east, and was flanked on that

side by Deer Hill, one of the foothills of the Greylock group; and Elisha Roe, as well as Samuel Burbank, reported in their old age to the youngsters that they used to see the deer sport and graze on the swell over the brook.   Hence the name "Deer Hill."

Both Thomas and Mary Roe were members of the first church here when Mr. Swift was settled in 1779; and as there is no list of the church-members previous to that time, and as, after Mr. Welch went away to the army in the autumn of 1775, all church matters were in confusion for four years, it is best to regard Mr. Swift's flock of 1779 as the primitive sheep of the place.   Forty of these were husbands and wives, of whom eleven couples continued for life in the communion of the church, and nine couples were dismissed, or removed from the town.   Of the remaining twenty-one, nine continued in their relation to the local church till their death, and twelve withdrew elsewhere.   Tradition still continues to whisper kind words about the family of Thomas Roe at the south part, but the inexorable silence will soon set in.   The first and only well-authenticated case of "bundling" in the early times of West Hoosac has been preserved in connection with the hospitable house of Thomas Roe.   Old Aaron Deming told Dan Foster, who owned and occupied the Roe place during a long and reputable life, that he slept in the Roe house the first night he ever slept in the town, and that he found a couple there who were sparking and bundled; and that he slept with them on the same bed, the young lady on the front side, and the "Sparker" next, and he on the outside; "But I didn't covet her!"   The second son, Welles Roe, born Dec. 29, 1779, was killed while driving into the barn on a load of hay, after a manner somewhat common in New England in the olden time.   The eldest son, Elisha, married Electa Hill, of Goshen, Connecticut, a daughter of Ambrose and Lucy Beach Hill.   They moved to Medina, New York, and had eleven children between 1799 and 1819.   Four of these were still living in 1885.   One of them, Mrs. Roxanna Roe Pratt, at that date resided at 3823 Ellis Avenue, Chicago, and communicated with parties in Williamstown on points relating to her ancestry.   Elisabeth Roe, a sister of Elisha and Welles, married, in 1793, Rev. Aaron Simmons, a Baptist minister; and another sister married Mr. Martin, of Bennington; and still another, Mr. Calkins, of Waterbury, Vermont.   The following letter, this day received from Mrs. Roxanna Roe Pratt, a granddaughter of Thomas Roe, herself born on the old farm in 1812, printed exactly as she wrote it, may interest somebody long after both writer and recipient (to use her words) "have past to their long home": —

PROFESSOR PERRY,   CHICAGO, May 23, 1893.

Dear Sir, Your letter in answer to my daughters husband Mr. Steele was received with many thanks, for your kindness in giving us the information concerning the Roe family, Thomas Roe was my Granfather, I was the daughter of his son Elisha Roe. You were correct in the number of children of my Grandfather, my Father had eleven children. I was the youngest of five girls, and all have past to their long home, but myself only waiting until the shadows are a little longer grown. I have the Old family Bible of my Grandfathers, it is so old that some of letters and dates are Illegible. I know my Grandfather was in the Revolutionary war, but have no proof of it, but through you, my older brothers used to play Soldiers with his Regimentals I was quite young when they died. I think my Grandfather was eighty seven, and my Grandmother eighty two, I remember them very well, The reason of this request, my daughters wished to join the Daughters of the Revolution. There is a large Society of them in this city, of all the prominent familes of the eastern states, and are quite Enthusiastic so all join that can, You remember my daughter Mrs Sidley in one of her visits to see her son William while he was in College, told me of your kindness in taking her to ride down through South Williamstown, by the old Homestead, and I feel very much gratified for your kindness in so doing, my Grandson William is a lovely man, he is a Lawyer in a very prominent firm here, and doing very nicely.

He and his Mother sends their kindest regards to you, hoping to see you this summer at our Worlds Fair, and they will give you a most cordial welcome at their home, Please excuse my long epistle explaining family matters, you can see the Old hand a little shaky. again thanking you I remain your friend

MRS ROXANNA PRATT.

10. In one of the preceding chapters we have learned some interesting facts in relation to Samuel Kellogg, who, by the time the first meeting-house was built in 1768, was well established on his farm, situated just half-way between the east end of the village and the east boundary of the town, and who would doubtless consider himself, and be considered by others, entitled to a pew of, at least, the average respectability; especially as he and his wife, Chloe Bacon, were both in personal covenant with the church, and as they had had three children when the "seating of the meetinghouse" took place. Samuel Kellogg, the son of Benjamin, was born in old Hadley (long the seat of the family), June 9, 1734, and, like many another young man of his time, dropped down the Connecticut River into the state below, and crept back into Massachusetts by the Housatonic. The fact is, the direct mountain barrier in Massachusetts between the Connecticut and the Hoosac and the Housatonic was, for a long time, too formidable for direct assault. Kellogg came up from Canaan, Connecticut, in 1761, along a path that had been already, for ten years, pretty well frequented by

young men both in peace and war. The place where he sat down,
after some shiftings, was on the rude path between Fort Massachusetts and West Hoosac Fort, midway between the two. It was the
present road. It was the path, in reference to which the West
Hoosac proprietors voted, on the 19th of April, 1762, "To clear
a road to the East town for a cart to get along." The surveyors,
in laying out the fifty-acre lots of the first division, caused ten of
those lots to abut at their north end upon this road, while they
stretched upon the south towards Saddle Mountain; and north of
this road to the Hoosac River were two fifty-acre lots (Nos. 26 and
27) and several meadow lots. Kellogg began on the north end of
No. 19, but still on the south side of the fort road, because the land
was a little higher on that side. His first log house stood a little
back of some present poplar trees planted by his son, and now (1893)
very old. He bought, at various times, adjoining lands on both
sides the road, and extending northwards as far as the river, to and
along which it was only possible to pass, at first, by jumping from
one prostrate log to another on account of the wetness of the land,
until he had compacted there a farm of about 170 acres.

Of course, the first thing for him to do, as for each other pristine
settler throughout the town, was to chop down some trees at some
selected point, and thus at once to make a place, and get the materials for a log cabin for shelter and an incipient home; and the next
thing was to clear off more ground for some arable land. All this
involved hard labor, and much of it, and the time could not be
essentially hastened; and nothing but the plough could determine,
beyond all question, the quality of the soil. Kellogg found his land
south of the fort road, and near it, to be very clayey upon trial.
When he came to be able to put up a framed house, and a two-story
one at that, on his slowly expanding arable acres, he selected a site
on the opposite side of the road, where the land, too, proved to be,
and has continued to be till this day, of a more tractable and fertile
quality.

Pretty direct and reliable tradition maintains that Samuel Kellogg, while subduing his homestead in the early years, sometimes
felt obliged to take refuge o' nights in one or other of the two forts
which were about equally accessible to him. The Indians continued
to prowl along their old war-paths even after the general Peace of
Paris of 1763. In the course of twenty years or so, Kellogg became
possessed of another farm southeast of his homestead and at more
than a mile interval from it, on the high and excellent land toward
Saddle Mountain, partly in the present town of North Adams, to

which and across which ran then, as now, a road parallel to the river-road, hugging the hills. Samuel Kellogg, Junior, inherited, on his father's death in 1788, both the homestead and the hill-farm, and some account of these lands, as typical of others like them through-out the town, may, perhaps, be found on pages to follow. The elder Kellogg is believed by his descendants to be in the direct line of Joseph Kellogg, one of the original settlers in old Hadley in 1660, a Puritanic family, and, as first exemplified in Williamstown, intelli-gent and enterprising and prosperous and patriotic.

Samuel Kellogg was prominent among the proprietors here from the first, sometimes presided at their meetings, and more often was assessor or other officer, and chairman of their important committees. As the questions that slowly culminated in the American Revolution were developed one after another, he took upon them a decidedly patriotic stand, perhaps in part on account of the warm Scotch blood that flowed in his veins, and certainly in sympathy with his relatives of the same name in Hadley and Hatfield. As the war drew on, he went to Boston several times as a member of the local "Committee of Safety" in Williamstown, and on other business connected with the colony; and he was in the battle of Bennington with nearly every other able-bodied man of the town. His wife's father, Daniel Bacon, was killed in that battle, as were two other citizens of the town. It is believed by his grandson, Giles Bacon Kellogg, that he was commissioned a justice of the peace here under the Crown before the war broke out, and that he bore the title of "Esquire" from that source; at any rate, he served as a justice and bore that title after the war was over; and there is very little, if any, doubt that he tried in that capacity a gang of counterfeiters that had operated, or were supposed to have operated, in the depths of the Hopper. They were betrayed by the smoke arising from their fires, and were arrested on legal process issued by him. Giles B. Kellogg (Williams College, 1829) writes as follows: "I know there was a mysterious chest kept locked or nailed up in the closet of the southeast chamber of our house, which was said to contain the tools taken from the counterfeiters and delivered to grandfather. I never heard what became of the counterfeiters or knew what became of the tools."

Samuel Kellogg died when he was fifty-four years old, leaving much of his property and of his position to his son of the same name, who was born Sept. 29, 1766. The father had a half-brother, Eben-ezer Kellogg, who outlived him more than forty years, and who made his home with him the latter part of his life, and who exem-plifies a sort of character considerably common in New England

during the last part of the last century and the beginning part of
this.   His wife was Filene Fuller, and they lived at the eastward
till after her death, when, having no children, he came over the
mountain to his brother's, and never after removed, but died here
about 1831.   He was a man of fine physical frame and of no ordinary
intelligence, and was exceedingly fond of the unbroken forests.   He
was a great hunter and fisherman, and claimed to be a skilful root-
doctor.   After his brother's death, he would sometimes leave his
nephew's house and be absent for a week at a time, hunting and fishing and searching for roots in the woods and mountains.   He came
and went easily, making no reports of his journeys, nor seeming to
think of them as worthy of any chronicle.   But he had a good memory of the earlier times and persons, was fond of reporting the
epitaphs of the Kelloggs in the old Hadley burying-ground, and
some of the facts above noted in relation to Samuel Kellogg have
come down through this singular informant.

   11. Daniel Bacon, the father-in-law of Samuel Kellogg, was from
Middletown, Connecticut, a blacksmith by trade, son of Nathaniel
Bacon, 2d, of Middletown, and the best known of the three men
from Williamstown killed in the battle of Bennington.   His daughter Chloe married Kellogg, in March, 1764, and some time after her
husband's death, in 1788, she married Thomas Henderson, a farmer
of Bennington, and lived there until 1829, when she died, aged
eighty-five.   She was, accordingly, twenty-three years old when she
married Kellogg, and her father must have been older than the
average incomer when he settled here.   His ultimate farm consisted of two fifty-acre lots of the first division, — Nos. 61 and
63, — adjoining end to end, and lying directly east of Taylor's
Crotch.   His nearest neighbor was Absalom Blair, who was with
him and Kellogg in Bennington Battle.   Bacon's father preceded
him in the buying and selling of lands in Berkshire, as appears
from certain deeds in the old registry.   For example, Nathaniel
Bacon, 2d, of Middletown, gave, under the usual formula, his lots in
"New Framingham" (Lanesboro) to his son Jacob, 20 Aug., 1761;
and this Jacob lived, in 1765, in "Yokuntown" (Lenox), and, still
later, sold the lands in Lanesboro to Elijah Hurlburt.   Daniel came
to Williamstown before Jacob did, and in September, 1766, bought
of Samuel Payen, of Water Street, fifty-acre lot 61, for £23; and
apparently, some time after, bought No. 63, adjoining, for £40, of
Aaron Bacon, who may likely have been another brother, though we
know little about him.   The description of No. 63 in the deed from
Aaron to Daniel is worth quoting: "bounded West on highway,

East on land belonging to Jonathan Kilborn, South on land belonging to Josiah Wright, North on a highway." This second "highway" is what is now called the "Blair road." The cellar of Bacon's original house, on No. 63, is still visible enough, near a spring of living water, on the south side of the lot. There is an old plum tree or two still growing near the cellar-wall. The next house built on that lot was on a knoll considerably further north, — a brick house, in which Captain Isaac Latham lived for many years, — but the present farm-house is still further north, and on the very edge of the Blair road. Daniel Bacon seems to have been a stirring man, and ultimately reached the rank of "Sergeant" in his militia company, and would doubtless have been fairly seated in the meeting-house by 1768, which was nine years before his honored death.

Though in somewhat rude lines, Jacob Bacon also left deeply cut memorials of himself in the town of his final choice of residence. He lived and died on what is now "Farm B," belonging to John B. Gale (Williams College, 1842), originally No. 11 of the first division of the fifty-acre lots, on the Green River road. He died Dec. 27, 1819, in his eightieth year. His wife, Lois, died Nov. 23, 1818, in her fifty-ninth year. Their son Stephen, born Feb. 28, 1771, made his home well up into the Hopper, where his posterity have resided ever since. His wife's name was Mehitable. They were married Feb. 2, 1789, when the groom was not quite eighteen. Their son Stephen was born Oct. 7, 1804, and practically spent his life on the Upper Hopper Brook. He once told the present writer, that, when he was a small boy, Aaron Wright lived still further up the brook than the Bacon place; indeed, somebody has lived beyond the Bacons during the whole of this century, Stephen Pettitt being the last long-lived and well-known occupant of this obscure *ultima Thule*. The second Stephen Bacon said, also, once, to the writer, that he remembered his grandfather Jacob perfectly well, that he visited him often on "Farm B," as it was then, and that he once gave him a penny! The present Stephen Bacon, the third of that name in regular succession, an intelligent and enterprising and excellent man, is still cultivating the ancestral acres, and many more well-rounded ones in extension of them; in fact, the Upper Hopper would no longer be itself without some hospitable family, with that well-known name to give its greeting, and, perchance, its succor, to the passing wayfarer towards, or in return from, the summit of Greylock. Still, it was an old soldier of Fort Massachusetts, Elkanah Parris, becoming a Quaker after the Peace of Paris, leaving his own-built "regulation" house in the village, on Green River (still standing), who, with his wife Grace, and four children, first followed up the beautiful brook, and chose the site and built the house, with its white-oak sills from north of the Hoosac, in which four generations of the Bacons have already dwelt.

Besides this Parris house, called now for three-quarters of a cen_ tury the "Bingham house," and which is still owned and occupied by Chloe Bingham, there are two other original "regulation" houses standing intact in this village, very similar to this one; namely, the "Simonds house," originally built on house lot 22, but long ago

THE "REGULATION" HOUSE OF ELKANAH PARRIS.

moved across the street to a high position opposite, and now forming the west end of the home of Mrs. Patrick Kelly; and the second one, now forming the L part of the old Bissell Sherman house, itself erected in 1797. The General Court required, in 1750, of each pur_ chaser of a house lot, in order to maintain his landed rights in the "propriety," that he build a house on it, within a specified time, "at least 18 feet long and 7 foot stud."

12. It was just fifty years after the big immigration into New England of the Scotch-Irish Presbyterians, in 1718, that the first meeting-house was built in Williamstown. In the mean time, the

original Worcester contingent had colonized Blandford and Coleraine
bodily, and large numbers of families had gone into Western and
other towns in Worcester County, and there was a considerable tendency, from the original New Hampshire settlements, of these people
into these towns of western Massachusetts; and Berkshire County
at last, and even Williamstown, felt the impulse of their coming.
Absalom Blair, with Martha Young, his wife, both from Western,
and she a sister of the Williamstown Youngs, who have been already
considered, were among the first of the Scotch-Irish people to settle
in Williamstown, and the very first to become anywise prominent
here. Abraham Blair was one of the soldiers who distinguished
himself for bravery and endurance in the famous siege of the Irish
Londonderry in 1689, and he was made free of taxes thereafter anywhere within the British dominions. His son Robert, then thirty-
four years old, was one of the Worcester incomers of 1718, and died
there Oct. 14, 1774, in the ninety-first year of his age. His wife,
Isabel, died nine years before, aged eighty-two. They left a very
large posterity in Worcester and in western Massachusetts generally.
There was a Robert, Junior, in Worcester, who had sons, — Robert
and David, — and these also had very large families. There were
other Blairs besides Robert — a plenty of them — in the great
immigration of 1718. There was James Blair, "a man of gigantic
stature and of fearless courage," who was one of the pristine settlers
of Londonderry, New Hampshire. Ensign David Blair died in
Western in 1804, aged ninety-six. He was, consequently, ten years
old at the incoming. John Blair also died in Western (now Warren)
in 1796, aged eighty-six, and was thus eight years old in 1718. He
was the father of Ezekiel Blair, born in April, 1742, who came to
Williamstown and bought his farm in 1764. Blandford, also, was
full of Blairs, among others Deacon Robert, of the Presbyterian
church there, who owned and lived on the "Gore," and died there
in 1802.

Absalom Blair, who came ultimately to be Captain in his militia
company, a patriotic man throughout the Revolution, the father of
ten children, was born in November, 1742, and died in April, 1811,
at the age of sixty-nine. His widow survived him eighteen years.
He settled on Green River but a little way below its crotch, and the
broad and fertile farm went by the name of "Blair's" for more
than a century. It consisted of two or three meadow lots and two
fifty-acre lots. The Green River was bridged to reach the house,
which stood on meadow lot No. 62, on the north side of the road
where is now an orchard, while the new and better house was built

on higher ground on the south side of the road opposite to the old one. This Blair road, about half a mile long, running due east, strikes at right angles the Stratton road running due south from the east end of the Main Street at Markham's. Absalom Blair seems to have possessed the main characteristics of the Scotch-Irish people in New England: namely, they were rather rough in speech and manner, wilful even if not imperious in temper; while not broadly intelligent, penetrating in intellect; industrious and frugal; of strong prejudices not unlike grudges; taking easily to non-monarchical forms of government, and lurching heavily against all classes specially privileged by law; as compared with the descendants of the Pilgrims and the Puritans not peculiarly religious, but perhaps peculiarly attached to their old Presbyterian forms. As a rule, too, they had very large families, and were apt to live till they were very old; and as a general thing, they did not seem to put up into as high a notch on the scale of the virtues as it might always well hang in the virtue of personal cleanliness!

Absalom Blair's oldest son, and the inheritor of his farm, and the transmitter of his name in this town to this day, was William Blair, born in October, 1765. He was old enough at the time of the battle of Bennington — namely, twelve years old — to be set by his anxious mother, who lived to tell the tale to the next generation, to listen intently out of doors that August afternoon for sounds from the northward. The boy asseverated at the time, and ever afterward, and his mother believed him and reported it down to her old age (she died in 1829), and his father on his return did not discredit it, that he heard distinctly, at considerable intervals, volleys of what he supposed were cannon; and although cannon played a relatively small part in the battle of Bennington, they were fired a good many times, and especially a good many times in the second fight; and so the boy's testimony becomes credible, particularly as confirmed by that of Samuel Burbank, who, though two miles further south, compensated that disadvantage by keeping his ear to the ground for long spaces of time.

William Blair married the most interesting girl there was in Williamstown at the time; and she continued to be, perhaps, the most interesting woman in Williamstown till her death, June 26, 1864, in her ninety-second year. Her name was Sally Train, and she became Mrs. Blair July 17, 1792. He was twenty-five, and she was eighteen. Her mother was the first child born in Williamstown, Rachel Simonds, born April 8, 1753, whose own childhood was nurtured amid constant hazards, French and Indian stratagems, frequent removals for greater safety from the home on the west side of Hemlock Brook to the fort upon the east side, — including stays in the fort for months together; when she was three years and a half old, three men from the fort were killed by Indians on the banks of the brook within a stone's throw of either home or fort; and as she grew up towards womanhood under kindlier conditions, and in a larger and better home, as there were apparently no eligible young men for her to marry, she married Thomas Train, who had been a soldier or officer in both forts, an excellent man, but twenty or twenty-five years her senior. We have already, in another connection, pointed out the place of their brief home together as marked at present by the sturdy elm tree, and told the story of his strange journey to Virginia and sudden death there, leaving here a youthful widow with her infant daughter, Sally Train.

Mrs. Train remained a widow but for a few years with her little daughter — both young together — when she was married to Benjamin Skinner, a young man who came up here from Colchester in 1775 with an older brother, Tompson J. Skinner, sons of the Rev. Thomas Skinner, of West Chester, a parish in Colchester. The older brother was destined to play a great part in Williamstown, and to become celebrated in both senses of that word throughout Massachusetts; the younger one, who was less gifted and consequently overshadowed, became, notwithstanding, a very useful and prominent man during a long life. Mrs. Train's second marriage proved happy and fruitful; and Sally grew up with the elder of the Skinner children, of whom there were, in all, three daughters and four sons. Each of the daughters married distinguished gentlemen, and two of the sons filled also large spaces in the public eye. The other two sons are mentioned in an uncomplimentary way in the will of Colonel Benjamin Simonds, who was their grandfather. The epitaph of Mrs. Skinner is quotable: "Mrs. Rachel Skinner, amiable consort of Mr. Benjamin Skinner, b. 8 April 1753, died 29 Nov. 1802." Mr. and Mrs. Skinner united with the church together in 1780. He became one of the deacons in 1802, and continued as such till his death in 1828, aged seventy-eight. He was also appointed postmaster in 1819. Just a year after the death of his first wife, he married Deodama Noble; and one son, George Noble Skinner (Williams College, 1827), was the sole fruit of that union. "Aunt Skinner," as she was always called in her old age, is still remembered by many persons not yet called old.

Mrs. Sally Train Blair assumed the responsibilities as mistress at the Blair farm on her early marriage to William Blair, or rather, shared them at first with her mother-in-law, Martha Young Blair, who survived the marriage of her eldest son for thirty-six years, and continued to sustain these responsibilities with unusual cheerfulness and vigor, until they were shared in her old age by her unmarried daughter, Maria Blair, who was born in November, 1803.   Besides this daughter there were two others, Alice and Harriet, and six sons, two of whom, Bernard, 1825, and George Train, 1833, were graduates of Williams College.   The latter, taking up his residence in Troy directly after graduation, studied law, held the office of city clerk for several years, was chosen surrogate and held the office for ten years, was appointed postmaster of Troy in 1861, and in 1865 paymaster in the United States army.   He came to Williamstown on business in 1867, was taken suddenly ill, and died amid the familiar scenes of his youth, April 3, aged fifty-seven.   Bernard Blair, the only other graduate of that surname in the first century of the College, spent his entire life after leaving college in Salem, New York, both studying and practising law there, was elected a member of the Twenty-seventh Congress from that district, and usefully served his generation as president of a local bank and railroad, and in all other relations of life.   Edwin Blair, another brother, ultimately came to carry on the farm, and to furnish a home for his maiden sister Maria ; but not succeeding well financially, and marrying also late in life, he became melancholic, and committed suicide.   At the present writing, Deacon Henry Blair, born in May, 1812, and the last survivor of the children of William and Sally, and Austin Blair, his son, named for his uncle, Austin Wing Blair, who was the youngest child of William and Sally, are the only men left in Williamstown of that once prevalent name.   Alice Blair, the oldest child of William and Sally, born in September, 1796, still remembered by at least one old lady in Williamstown (Mrs. James Smedley) as a beautiful young lady riding gracefully, was married to Hiram Bacon of the family but just now characterized in these pages, and they removed with their family to Indiana in 1822.   Many of the later descendants of the Blairs, and also of the Kelloggs and other families, migrated to Georgia, Vermont, and settled down there.

13. William Horsford has perhaps been postponed in this imaginary order of seating to a later place than was his due accorded to him by the committee at the time.   He was a very early comer. He was one in a select company of soldiers sent up hither by the colony of Connecticut as the best place at which to guard its own frontiers from the French and Indian raiders from Canada.   It was easy for these to drop down the Housatonic into Connecticut, if they

could once get by the two forts on the Hoosac, and the watershed a few miles to the south of them. One such raid actually penetrated through Stockbridge into the border towns below. But William Horsford and his brother Josiah and Nehemiah Smedley and Allen Curtiss and John and Jonathan Kilbon, all from Litchfield or its immediate vicinity, had been up to West Hoosac to prepare for themselves and their families a new home on the soil some considerable time before they, with others, enlisted into this select company of militia. It was in the latter part of the lull between the Peace of Aix-la-Chapelle and the fresh outbreak of the war in 1754. It was, indeed, their individual sense of the hazards of proceeding under their purchase of houselot-rights, some of which had been vended by Massachusetts in Litchfield and its neighborhood, that led these young men to return to Connecticut and to report on the prospect of things here, and then to enlist with many more under public authority and come back to help garrison the West Hoosac Fort. Not a great deal more was done in the way of subduing fresh house lots, although a few kept along with their work in summer, having the two forts as a base of safety and supplies, until the news came of the battle of Quebec in 1759. Then soon all was astir again. Seventeen hundred and sixty marks the beginning of settlements in West Hoosac on a considerable scale.

William Horsford married in Litchfield, in 1759, Esther Smedley, born March 20, 1737, eldest sister to Nehemiah Smedley; and their first-born, Esther, saw the light in West Hoosac, May 19, 1760. Some, who were ignorant of the facts in regard to Benjamin Simonds, who already had four children native to this soil, used to claim that Esther Horsford was the first child of English parentage born in the town. Eight brothers and sisters followed in due succession, including Rhoda, the last, born May 23, 1779. The mother of these children died March 1, 1791. The primitive record ends, — "Elisabeth Horsford the aged Died May 28, 1781." This was unquestionably the mother of William and Josiah Horsford, who had accompanied, or at least followed, them into the wilderness.

The original holder of house lot 44, the lot directly north across Main Street from the West College, was Josiah Dean, of Canaan, Connecticut, and he sold the lot, "and all appertaining to it, that is, $\frac{3}{48}$ part of West Hoosuck," to Daniel and William Horsford, both of Canaan, for £260 of then lawful Connecticut money, *Nov. 1, 1752.* William bought out Daniel's share, that is, one half of No. 44 and all after-drafts, for £26 of Massachusetts money (which was then silver), Feb. 2, 1761. Daniel is called in this deed "Senior" —

undoubtedly father to William and Josiah, and husband to "Elisabeth Horsford the aged." The interesting point to notice is, that, the day before this sale to the Horsfords, namely, *Oct. 31, 1752,* Samuel Smedley, of Litchfield, bought of Ezekiel Hinds, of Stockbridge (then of Fort Massachusetts), for £27, house lot 1 "and all appertaining," etc. Samuel Smedley was the father of Nehemiah; and the latter came into full possession of No. 1, March 21, 1758, in consequence of the father's death in the mean time and by virtue of a deed then executed to him by the widow and the eldest son, John, jointly. Scarcely any doubt can remain upon a mind weighing closely all the dates and circumstances, that it was in the spring of 1753 when these Connecticut young men first crossed the watershed between the Housatonic and the Hoosac, and made some little beginnings on their respective lots, — the main fact of their coming about that time, and for that very purpose, being clearly testified to long afterwards by Nehemiah Smedley's oldest son, Levi, born in 1764. It will perhaps be remembered by the careful reader of the preceding chapters, that the first proprietors' meeting was convened Dec. 5, 1753, at the house of Seth Hudson on house lot 9. The proprietors certainly present at that time were Allen Curtiss, Isaac Wyman, Seth Hudson, Jonathan Meacham, Ezekiel Foster, Jabez Warren,. Samuel Taylor, Gideon Warren, Thomas Train, Josiah Dean, and Ebenezer Graves. It must not be inferred from the attendance of these eleven men at that meeting, that all of them had already built houses on their house lots; most of them, indeed, were then lodged in Fort Massachusetts as soldiers, as was Isaac Wyman, then commanding there, and yet made clerk and treasurer of the proprietors at that time; the only houses that are certainly *known* to have been already built on the house lots at the date of that meeting were Simonds's on No. 22, Curtiss's on No. 13, and Hudson's on No. 9; each of these three was on one side or the other of Hemlock Brook; and Elisha Higgins, a soldier in Fort Massachusetts, had purchased, for £20, No. 12, directly on the brook the north side of Main Street, as Curtiss's lot was opposite on the south side. Higgins's purchase was Oct. 12, 1753. Higgins subsequently bought house lot 17, and made it his permanent homestead. This is the second lot west of Curtiss's, fairly on the present Danforth plateau south side of Main Street.

When William Horsford came back to West Hoosac to stay, which was about the time when Allen Curtiss went back to Canaan to stay, although the latter did not sell out his house lot 13 until March, 1762, the former began to buy and sell lots all over the town (as did also his compeers), though he never sold his homestead house lot 44 until he left the town for good in the last decade of the century. As his family increased, he put up on 44 a good-sized framed house, which is still standing enlarged in another part of the village. He was active in all the affairs of the propriety till the incorporation of the town in 1765, in all whose further affairs he was patriotic and influential for about thirty years longer. Why he went, whither he went, and exactly when he went are questions that cannot now be answered. His wife died here in 1791, and after that there has been found no note or sign of him in Williamstown. On the popular subscription-paper for the new meeting-house, started in September, 1796, the original of which is in the writer's possession, Horsford's name does not appear, although had he been at that time a resident, it would naturally and almost certainly be found there, inasmuch as the second meeting-house was built by the proprietors as well as the first one, and yet by subscription. Both Horsford and his wife united with the church in 1781. She died in its communion ten years later; while the letter " r " appended to his name in the manual shows that he had " removed to distant parts." It is to be presumed, and will probably some day be ascertained, that he passed on with many of his neighbors, and perhaps some or all of his children, into the new state of Vermont. The attractive house lot 44 passed shortly into possession of General Samuel Sloan, who soon built upon its front the fine residence now occupied by the president of the College. The west corner of that front was set off from the rest of the lot for some purpose or other a long time ago; and about 1860 the Catholics bought it and erected upon it their present handsome church.

14. Josiah Horsford, the brother of the foregoing, was only a little younger than he, and the lives of the two in most respects ran parallel with each other. Josiah's wife was Jemima Smedley, sister of William's wife; they too had nine children, each of whom, as a rule, was about two years younger than the corresponding child in the brother's family; Josiah bought early and kept long house lot No. 42, the lot next west of his brother's, and the nucleus of the present old house standing on its front was built by Josiah Horsford, — probably his " regulation house " erected in 1761; and the last visible tracks made by Josiah's family, while in general coeval with those of the other family, in one important respect, soon to be noted, were in contrast with them. Jemima Smedley Horsford joined the church in 1781, the same year as her sister and husband, but her own husband never became a member; she was regularly

dismissed to unite with some other church (such was the custom),
in all probability a church to the northwards. Josiah Horsford,
unlike his brother, had two sons who remained and married here, —
Josiah, Junior, whose wife was Sevelle, and who had four children
between 1790–1801, and Roswell, who married Elizabeth Morse in
February, 1792. The great service of Josiah Horsford was as proprietors' clerk, succeeding Richard Stratton in 1765, and continuing
until the proprietors' meetings were practically suspended in 1774,
under the double pressure of the oncomings of the Revolution, and
the consequent growth of the town organization as such. The ill-
spelled records in Horsford's own hand during that quarrelsome
interval of nine years, show him to have been a man of character
and influence and persistence. However, he did not hold on to
his homestead, as did his brother William. Like him, Josiah had
vigorously bought and sold lands in all parts of the town in specu-
lative times; for example, he bought of Rev. Whitman Welch, for
£25, in October, 1767, house lot 36, the original minister's lot, that
cornered on the "Square," and that early came to be the site of the
chief public house of the village and has continued so ever since;
and he sold the same year, in May, 100-acre lot No. 47, to Nehemiah
Williams, which holds the big rock on the northern slope of Northwest Hill.

But it may well have been that his pecuniary fortunes decayed
in his old age; and it may possibly have been that he became
addicted to strong drink. At any rate, the homestead was sold in
the spring of 1796 to the Whitman brothers of Hartford, who immediately opened a store for the sale of dry-goods and groceries in the
east end of the house, afterwards building two stores in succession
attached to the house at the east end, and at last the present store
detached from the house and a little further to the east; and in these
stores a mercantile business was kept up, in the name and interest of
the Whitman family, for over sixty years. For many years now
lately past, Charles H. Mather has owned and occupied, as a merchant, the last-named of these stores. In a promiscuous lot of old
papers and bills belonging to the Whitmans, that were not long ago
discovered in the house last occupied by them, was found a bill
to Josiah Horsford for liquors sold him "per son Ambrose" as late
as 1803. Ambrose was Josiah Horsford's youngest son, born Dec. 31,
1781, and was consequently twenty-one years old when he procured
the stimulants at Whitman's store as agent for his father. This is
absolutely all we know of Ambrose Horsford; and the last glimpse
we get of the sturdy old pioneer, and proprietors' clerk, and Revolu-

tionary soldier, Josiah Horsford, the never-to-be-forgotten, is in playing the rather passive rôle of sending his grown-up son to the store for strong drink, and getting it charged. William and Josiah Horsford were steadily so prominent here, as much to overshadow their near relatives of the same name and from the same place (Canaan, Connecticut), who played no insignificant part in West Hoosac and early Williamstown. John and Daniel Horsford bought of Ephraim Williams, Junior (the founder), house lot No. 10, for £30, April 14, 1753. The same parties sell the same house lot in September, 1765, to Daniel Horsford, Junior, for £70, — an increase of value in twelve years of 133 per centum. John Horsford, Bloomer, bought of Seth Hudson, Gentleman, house lot No. 9, which was Hudson's original draft, and directly opposite Colonel Williams's original drafts, Nos. 8 and 10.

15. At this distance of time, and in the writer's real ignorance of the exact condition of things in 1768, it seems quite likely that the two junior members of the building and seating committee would not postpone provision for themselves and their families to a point later than that to which we have now come. We have already learned quite a good deal about Benjamin Simonds, and something about Mary Davis, of Northampton, his wife. They were married in Northampton by the famous Joseph Hawley, Justice of the Peace, April 23, 1752. They had, when the meeting-house was done, eight children, — 1753–1768. They lived, then, very near to the new place of worship, namely, on the south side of Main Street, in a house that they had built themselves on house lot No. 3, and in which they had kept a tavern, at least, since 1763, — the first tavern in the hamlet. They owned, in 1765, six other house lots close by, on both sides of Hemlock Brook, including No. 22, their original purchase, and on which they built their first house, whose precise site can be pointed out to this day, and some of the stones of whose cellar or underpinning are now scattered on the surface of the ground. Simonds was enterprising, and already experienced. He was now forty-two years old. He had the confidence of his fellow-settlers to a remarkable degree. Neither he nor his wife ever became members of the church; but, in connection with the Searles, the Meachams, and the Strattons, they represented the indefinable East-of-the-Mountain sentiment, in contradistinction from the peculiar Connecticut sentiment, voiced (we may suppose) by the Welches, the Horsfords, and the Smedleys. We cannot infer what the differences between these were, but we perceive considerable signs of collision between them.

Simonds was laying the foundations in his increasing property, in his general enterprise and public spirit, in his broadening acquaintance as a tavern-keeper, and in his early experience and constant interest in militia affairs, for the astonishing influence, both military and civil, that he exerted in the two decades following. We shall recur to this in the next chapter; here we wish only to indicate a few facts of his personal and family history not heretofore touched upon. The following table is extracted mainly from the family Bible still preserved in the line of his descendants, the Blairs: —

BENJAMIN AND MARY SIMONDS, THEIR CHILDREN.

1. Rachel, born April 8, 1753. She became Mrs. Thomas Train & later Mrs. Benj. Skinner.
2. Justin, born Feb. 17, 1755. Nothing is now, known of his after life.
3. Sarah born July 8, 1757. She became Mrs. Ithamar Clark of Pownal.
4. Marcy born Dec. 2, 1759. She became Mrs. Charles Kellogg.
5. Joseph, born April 8, 1762. He was named from his grandfather Simonds.
6. Prudence, born Dec. 4, 1763. She became Mrs. Jonathan Bridges.
7. Ablina, born Oct. 8, 1765. She became Mrs. Joseph Osborne, later Mrs. Paddock.
8. Electa, born in 1768. She became Oct. 21, 1787, Mrs. Thaddeus Edwards.
9. Polly, born in 1771. She became Mrs. Perley Putnam.
10. Benjamin born in 1773. He died June 16, 1786.

The epitaph of Benjamin Simonds is as follows: —

This monument erected in memory of Col. Benjamin Simonds, one of the first settlers in Williamstown, and a firm supporter of his country's Independence. He was born Feb. 23, 1726, and died April 11, 1807.

The epitaph of the mother of his children is as follows: —

Mary Simonds, wife of Col. Benjamin Simonds, died 7 June, 1798, in the 70 year of her age.

The inscription on the tombstone of Colonel Simonds's second wife, who was the widowed mother of Perly Putnam, one of the sons-in-law of Simonds, runs as follows : —

IN MEMORY OF
ANNA
WIFE OF COL. BENJ SIMONDS
AND RELICT OF
ASA PUTNAM OF BRATTLEBORO' VT.
DIED APRIL 3, 1807, AGED 61 YEARS.

The formal contract of marriage between Colonel Simonds and Mrs. Putnam, drawn by Daniel Dewey, Esq., and entitled "Articles of Agreement," bears date Nov. 4, 1798. Tompson Joseph Skinner, Esq., is in this paper the party of the third part, widow Anna Putnam is the party of the second part, and Benjamin Simonds, Esq., is the party of the first part. She is to have $600 in six annual instalments, if she survive her husband; she "shall have decent and convenient accommodations in his now dwelling house for and during the term of one year next after his decease"; "his executors and administrators shall during that time support and maintain the said Anna in a decent and reputable manner suitable to her habits and circumstances of life; and shall likewise as soon as convenient after the decease of the said Benjamin furnish the said Anna with a decent suit of mourning," etc. "As a jointure in lieu of dower," said Benjamin covenants to give "three acres of land to be taken off the east end of Oak Lot No. 53, and to be included between two parallels across the east end of said lot to the use of the said Benjamin and Anna for and during their joint lives, remainder over to the use of the said Anna to take effect immediately on the decease of the said Benjamin, for and during her natural life, to her own proper use, behoof, and benefit, with full power and liberty for the said Anna to cut, fell down, carry away and dispose of any wood or timber growing on said land," etc. Anna Putnam had an estate of her own, and the "Agreement" covenants that she shall hold, enjoy, and bequeath the same as though she were *feme sole* during said intended intermarriage; and if she die intestate, her property to go to her children. T. J. Skinner was to be trustee of the said Anna, to manage her property, etc.

John Putnam, of Buckinghamshire, England, which was the county of John Hampden at the same time, emigrated to Massachusetts in 1634, and settled in Danvers, where many of his descendants are still living. Asa Putnam, of Brattleboro, was of the fifth generation from John, through the latter's son Nathaniel, while General Israel Putnam stood in the line of Thomas, another of John's sons. Asa Putnam was the son of Josiah Putnam, of Western, now Warren, Massachusetts. Josiah was own cousin of General Israel Putnam. Josiah's son, Captain Josiah, who died in 1835, aged eighty-six, own brother of Asa, sent two of his sons, William and James, from Western to Williams College, at the outset of the institution. William entered in 1793, when the College opened, but died three years later, and without graduating. James, who was younger, entered later, but was not graduated. It is probable that Rufus

Putnam (Williams College, 1804), was a brother of these two. At any rate, he was from Western, was a lawyer by profession, and died in Rutland, Vermont, in 1847, aged sixty-four. The way to Williamstown was thus paved for the Putnams. Asa Putnam, a farmer, born in Western in 1742, died in Brattleboro, in September, 1795, aged fifty-three. Mrs. Anna Putnam brought three of her nine children, the three youngest, into Colonel Simonds's family on her intermarriage with him; while her eldest son, Perly Putnam, was already settled in Williamstown as the husband of Polly Simonds. These three children were Sewell, Sylvia, and Harvey. The last-named, youngest of all, was born in Brattleboro, Jan. 5, 1793. He was four years old when he came to Williamstown, and lived with his mother till her death in 1807. Shortly after this, he removed to Skaneateles, New York, where he was apprenticed to his elder brother Perly to learn the saddle and harness-making trade. Two years at this, and then he entered the law office there of Daniel Kellogg, also from Williamstown, and a son of that Samuel Kellogg who has already been characterized at length in these pages. Harvey Putnam studied his profession before he was admitted to practise it, as long as Jacob served for Rachel, and then he, too, like Jacob, married, not indeed his own cousin, but one of the own granddaughters of Colonel Simonds, Myra Osborne. This marriage took place at Skaneateles, Aug. 5, 1817. Western New York witnessed thereafter, in the person of Harvey Putnam, a distinguished lawyer, a reputable member of Congress repeatedly elected, and an excellent judge in different positions, till his death, in 1855. James O. Putnam, of Buffalo, long in the public and diplomatic service of his state and country, is his son. Harvey Putnam was of medium size and a very light complexion; he had a quick and elastic step, and a movement that gave one the impression that he was in a hurry; he was for thirty years a member and officer of the Presbyterian church; and one of his daughters was married to John B. Skinner, 2d (Williams College, 1842), son of Samuel Skinner (Williams College, 1816), and grandson of Deacon Benjamin Skinner.

When Colonel Simonds made his last will and testament in 1803, and its two codicils also in the two successive years, these were all witnessed formally by Ephraim Seelye (his nearest neighbor across the road), and the two other Putnam children, Sewell and Sylvia. The last-named was a member of the family, seventeen years old, when her mother and the Colonel both died in April, 1807; and in her old age caused to be communicated to the writer her recollection that the Colonel did not care to live after her mother died, and, in fact, dropped away eight days later. Mrs. Simonds was born in 1746, the year of Simonds's captivity in Canada, and was consequently twenty years younger than her second husband, yet he outlived her, and mourned her loss in his eighty-second year. Sylvia Putnam married Mr. Z. A. Hamilton, and lived about forty years in Aurora, New York, and died in October, 1883, aged ninety-four, with her daughter, Mrs. Salmon Johnson, in Cattaraugus, New York. She was the mother of General Charles S. Hamilton, of Wisconsin. The present writer had the pleasure of sending her, when she was about ninety years old, a photograph of Colonel Simonds, taken from an original portrait referred to in his will, and painted by W. Jennys in 1796. She recognized the picture instantly, and it moved her deeply; and as the Colonel's portrait, after many mutations, had then come to be the property of the sender and hung in his study, she proposed to Mrs. Johnson to send to him an original portrait of her own mother, which, she said, had hung beside the Colonel's in her early home in Williamstown. Accordingly, after a separation of about seventy-five years, the two portraits were united again in Williamstown for a number of years. It later appeared, however, that Mrs. Hamilton had previously promised her mother's portrait to her great-granddaughter, Harriet O. Putnam, of Buffalo, in whose hands it is at the present time. Mrs. Hamilton communicated other pleasant recollections of Colonel Simonds in her girlhood: such as, for example, he always wore his military costume more or less complete till the last, as it appears in his portrait,—the cocked hat and powdered wig, the white neck-kerchief and frilled shirt-bosom, the regimental coat and buttons, and also the short clothes and knee-buckles; he always went to church in full costume; and he occasionally offered family prayers, standing by the back of his chair. The late Dr. Morgan, of Bennington, told the writer that when he was a small boy riding past with his father, he had repeatedly seen the Colonel sitting in summer in his front doorway in his military toggery, being saluted by, and saluting in turn, the passers-by.

The Colonel's will lets a good deal of light into the condition of things in his family at the opening of the century. It was drawn by Judge Daniel Dewey, who was appointed one of the two executors, Jonathan Bridges, one of his sons-in-law, being the other. When the will came to probate in May, 1807, the latter in a good hand waived administration on the estate of Benjamin Simonds, and requested the judge that Daniel Dewey might be appointed sole executor of said will. The first clause directs his executors "particularly to pay to my beloved wife, Anna Simonds, six hundred dollars at the several times and in the manner specified in the contract made with her before our intermarriage,"—a copy of which contract was deposited with the will. Anna, his wife, was also "to have the use of the house in which I now live, and of the eight acres of land adjoining for one year," and then all real estate was to be sold to carry out the other provisions of the will. By the second codicil, added in March, 1805,—"I give and bequeath to my said wife, Anna Simonds, my chaise with the harness and horse which I use in the chaise, to keep and use during her natural life."

Colonel Simonds had had three sons in all, but Justin and Benjamin had both died before the will was made, leaving only Joseph, who was born in 1762, and was consequently forty-one years old in 1803. Mrs. Sylvia Hamilton had the impression, in her old age, that Joseph Simonds was a ne'er-do-well; at any rate, she remembered very little about him, and certainly very few echoes of the man have reached down to the present time. The grandfather, Joseph Simonds, made a very distinct impression upon his generation by uniting with the Scotch-Irish in the founding of Londonderry, New Hampshire, by helping to settle the so-called "English Range" in that town, and becoming an early leader there, and also later by becoming one of the pioneers and leaders in the settlement of "Ware River" in Massachusetts, whence his son Benjamin enlisted for Fort Massachusetts in 1745; but this Joseph, though named after his grandfather, and having before him as an example the great enterprise and success of his father, seems to have amounted to but little, and is thus mentioned in his father's will: "Unto my son, Joseph Simonds, I will and bequeath my clock and the case which contains it, my desk and book-case, and my firelock and side arms and my powder Flask and all the ammunition I have on hand, also all my wearing apparel of every description including buckles and buttons."

When this will was drawn, his eldest daughter, Rachel Train-Skinner, had recently died, and also his second daughter, Sarah (Mrs. Ithamar Clark), and her husband, too; and these facts help to explain the terms of the main clause of the will, which was to this effect; namely, that the rest of his estate, real and personal, should be divided into equal parts,— one each to go to Benjamin Skinner (Rachel's second husband), Joseph Simonds, Charles and Marcy Kellogg, Jonathan and Prudence Bridges, Joseph and Ablina Osborne, Thaddeus and Electa Edwards, Perly and Polly Putnam, and to the five sons of Sarah Clark, deceased,— eight equal parts in all, but Benjamin Skinner and Jonathan Bridges had already had $1000 each, and this sum was to be deducted from their shares respectively; but "all other sums of money and other things by me given to my said son or any of my daughters shall not be taken into consideration" in this division. By the first codicil to the will, the eight shares were to amount to $1000 each and no more, and the residue was to go to his son, Joseph Simonds; and by the same, all claims of Rachel Skinner's children (said Rachel having received her portion) are cut off by one dollar to each. By the second codicil, Joseph Osborne having died since the execution of the will, his daughter Ablina was to have the whole share. "I likewise give to my daughter, Polly Putnam, my Portrait." "And to my granddaughter, Sally Blair, the wife of William Blair, my large family Bible in two folio volumes after the expiration of one year from my decease, until which time it is my desire that it remain with my said wife."

This Bible has already become an heirloom in the Blair family in Williamstown, being the property, at present, of Deacon Henry Blair, to be inherited by his eldest son, Austin Blair. The portrait passed over by gift, or otherwise, from the Putnams to the Osbornes and their heirs, and by these latter courteously and generously transmitted to the writer, whose family are in the direct line of Colonel Simonds through Jonathan and Prudence Bridges, to the eldest of whom, Grace Perry, the portrait is destined to fall. This can always be identified by many infallible marks and scars, but chiefly by the signature of the artist himself upon the back of the canvas, " W Jennys pinx' 1796."

Among "the five sons of Sarah Clark deceased," entitled to one share out of the eight, into which their grandfather's general estate was to be divided for distribution, was one, Dr. Billy J. Clark, who became distinguished, and will always be remembered for signal services rendered to the cause of temperance in this country. Some account of his early life, and of the circumstances under which he conceived an invincible repugnance to the drinking of intoxicants, has been put down on the pages of an earlier chapter of this book. From a country tavern, kept by his father, near Centre Pownal, where this repugnance was engendered, he passed to the study of medicine, married Joanna Paine, settled down for a forty years of most successful practice in Moreau, New York, but closed his career in the neighboring town of Glens Falls as an apothecary, and as a temperance leader and organizer. Appleton's Cyclopædia has this to say of this son of " Sarah Clark deceased ": "The earliest organization to stem the tide of intemperance in this Republic would seem to have

been that of 'The Temperate Society of Moreau and Northumberland,' which was instigated by Dr. B. J. Clark, of Moreau, in March,
1808, and constituted by the signature of forty-three members, mainly
substantial farmers of the two towns named.   Their constitution
stipulated, that ' no member shall drink rum, gin, whiskey, wine, or
any distilled spirits, or composition of the same, or any of them,
except by the advice of a physician, or in case of actual disease (also
excepting wine at public dinners), under penalty of twenty-five
cents.   Provided that this article shall not infringe on any religious
ordinance.'   And further,
that ' no member shall be
intoxicated under penalty of
fifty cents.'   And again:
' no member shall offer any
of said liquors to any other
member, or urge any other
person to drink thereof,
under penalty of twenty-five
cents for each offence.'
Through Dr. Clark's energy
and perseverance, a special
act of the New York Legislature was obtained, incorporating the Saratoga County
Medical Society, the first
organization of the kind in
the state.   He was also a
member of the New York
Electoral College in 1848.
He was born in Northamp-

ton in January, 1778.   A few years later his parents removed to
Williamstown (his mother's birthplace and grandparents' residence),
where he attended the free school founded under Colonel Williams's
will.   At the age of seventeen he commenced his medical studies
with Dr. Gibbs in Pownal, and continued them with Dr. Wicker in
Easton, New York, and commenced his practice, in Moreau, in 1799.
His wife died in January, 1839, and not long after he moved to
Glens Falls, where he died, greatly honored, in September, 1866, in
his eighty-ninth year.   His son Walter was a member of Williams
College in 1831, but was not graduated.   His four brothers, referred
to with himself in Colonel Simonds's will, were Ira, Isaac, Chester,
and Sereno.

If Billy J. Clark proved himself to be the most distinguished scion of the Sarah Simonds branch of the large paternal tree, what shall be said of John B. Skinner as illustrating and making famous the elder and double Rachel Simonds branch of the same tree? We have already spoken of the Blairs as springing from Sally Train, the only child of Rachel Simonds by her first husband, to whom the Colonel expressly willed his "large family Bible in two folio volumes"; we have also noted the disparaging mode of reference in the Colonel's will to the children of Rachel Skinner, of whom there were five in all, the two eldest sons in which group, Harry and William, having already given marked signs of intemperance and inefficiency; but there were two younger boys, Samuel and John Burr, respectively nine and five years old when the will was drawn, who showed them-selves in after life to be men of very different character. Samuel Skinner, born in 1794 (Williams College, 1816), studied law with his sister's husband, Samuel A. Talcott, of whom we shall learn more by-and-bye, till 1819, when he settled down in his profession at Leroy, New York, where he died in 1852. Durfee's "Annals of Williams" has this to say of him: "Mr. Skinner was a well-read, safe, and careful lawyer, devoted to the interests of his clients, distinguished for fairness in practice, and diligence and uprightness in business. He acquired a handsome fortune, and left an unsullied name. He was for many years a ruling elder in the Presbyterian church at Leroy, an active, liberal, and devoted Christian, possessing uncommon gifts for the duties of the office. He exerted a wide influence in the community, which is still felt, and where his memory is cherished with the deepest tenderness."

While the above picture is not in terms overdrawn, John Burr Skinner, born in 1799, the youngest child of Deacon Benjamin and Rachel Train-Skinner, became a much more famous and deeply influential man and lawyer than his brother. In partial explanation of his remarkable career, it should here be premised that Deacon Skinner was a Jeffersonian Democrat and a devoted Freemason; he was a man of fine appearance, with a clear and penetrating voice, of warm feelings readily expressing themselves in manly tears, and a natural leader in all church matters and a frequent and acceptable lay reader in public church worship. In an atmosphere diffused by such a positive man as this, John Burr Skinner grew up, to say nothing of the natural influence of his uncle, General T. J. Skinner, who was a consummate speaker and adroit politician, and the political leader of his party for many years in Berkshire County. After his graduation at Williams in 1818, young Skinner naturally drifted

into democratic circles; he entered the law office of Hon. Daniel
Buel, of Troy, New York, where he formed a life-long friendship
with his fellow-student, the late William L. Marcy, governor of New
York and secretary of state under President Pierce. He completed
his preparatory studies at the then celebrated law school of Judges
Gould and Reeves, at Litchfield, Connecticut; and soon after established himself as a lawyer in the hamlet of Wyoming, New York,
in the present county of Wyoming, both of which names were given
by himself to their respective localities. His cousin, James O. Putnam, said of him : —

His success, solid and brilliant, was assured from the first. His industry, his
fidelity to professional trusts, his learning and his marvellous power before juries,
gave a leadership at the circuits which he never lost. The jury trial was the
favorite theatre of his professional contests, and it was as the advocate that he
was without a peer. The methods of conducting litigation in his time differed
from the present. Then the great object was to secure a verdict from the twelve
men. On their decision hung the issues of life and death and fortune. This
made the counsel who could carry the jury, whether by magic or storm, an indispensable ally. Appeals were comparatively few. Now-a-days when the jury in
so many trials is but an incident, and law, as has been said with much humor
and some wisdom, is the power of decision of the last judge that can hear the
case, the eloquent advocate holds a position less relatively important in the trial
of causes. But Judge Skinner was learned as a lawyer, as well as eloquent
as an advocate, and it was this rare combination that gave him a position so
distinguished before the courts.

Ex-President Fillmore, who presided at a meeting of the Bar of
Erie County, convened to give some expression of its sentiment on
the occasion of his death, in 1871, said : —

My acquaintance with Mr. Skinner commenced in 1829, when he and I were
both members of the Assembly. That was my first year, but I think it was his
third year, and he had then an enviable reputation for so young a man in that
distinguished body, as yet free from the suspicion of bribery, and adorned by
the talents of such men as John C. Spencer, Erastus Root, Benj. F. Butler,
Frank Granger, and of others. The revision of our statutes, the great work
which did so much to methodize and relieve them from the cumbrous language
and accumulated contradictions and inconsistencies of years, was then just completed, and in that great work Judge Skinner bore a conspicuous part. I know
he was listened to with confidence and respect, and no member of the House
seemed to exert a more salutary influence. My subsequent acquaintance with
him was mainly at the Bar. Here he was distinguished for his legal arguments
and forensic eloquence. I have often felt a tremor of anxiety when I have had
to meet him. He was a man religiously devoted to the interest of his client,
without ever compromising his own conscience or dignity. He prepared his
case with great labor and assiduity, and whatever could be said in favor of his
client's interest he presented with great clearness and force, and when that was

done he conceived that he had discharged his professional duty, and he patiently waited the result. The highest encomium that can ever be passed upon a man of his profession may with great propriety be passed upon him, and that is, he was a learned, conscientious lawyer.

Hon. James R. Doolittle, late United States senator from Wisconsin, had this to say, two years after Judge Skinner's death: —

The late John B. Skinner, as a lawyer and advocate, had few equals, and no superior, for many years, in western New York. To uniform courtesy, untiring industry, unflinching and incorruptible fidelity to his clients, you must add great tact and knowledge of human nature, as well as great legal learning, and oftentimes the highest order of eloquence, to make a just estimate of his character. It was before a jury that he was, in some respects, unequalled. His efforts there were entirely extemporaneous. Those who have had great opportunity to hear the most eloquent of American orators, say there were occasions when those extemporaneous efforts of Mr. Skinner, in true eloquence and power, surpassed all his contemporaries. When fully roused, his language was pure English, — chaste, elegant, and concise. He spoke without apparent effort, with a directness, earnestness, and naturalness that seemed almost inspired. His mind, like his person, was high-wrought and of the finest mould. All his appeals and all his conversations were addressed to the better part of our nature. With truth it may be said, no one ever heard him at the Bar, or held private conversation with him, who did not feel his nobler sentiments strengthened and elevated by his influence.

Judge Martin Grover, of the Court of Appeals of the state of New York, who knew him very thoroughly on the circuit, and otherwise, from 1836 onwards for twenty years, embodied his recollections, in 1873, in a paper prepared for the Buffalo Historical Society. We quote: —

Mr. Skinner attended all the circuits in Livingston, Allegheny, Cattaraugus, Chautauqua, and Genesee counties, and his presence was regarded almost as essential as that of the Judge. There were then no railroads in any part of the district, and Mr. Skinner travelled from one country town to another, in company with the Judge, each with his own horse and sulky. Extensive study and large experience had made Mr. Skinner perfectly familiar with, and master of, nearly every legal question presented, and he was, therefore, able to take a leading part in nearly every case tried. His clear intellect and capacity for quick comprehension enabled him to try a cause with great ability, without any previous preparation, and with but little consultation with his client and the other counsel. He would grasp the entire case at once and adopt the correct mode of conducting the trial. He was very sagacious in the examination of witnesses. An adverse witness rarely succeeded in baffling him, and, as a general rule, he would derive an advantage for his client from the reluctance of such a witness to disclose the whole truth. But his great power was in summing up to the jury. In this I have never seen one superior and scarcely ever his equal. His clear statements and close logical arguments usually convinced the

understanding of his hearers, and when to these were added his powers of persuasion, the effect was overwhelming.   He possessed in an eminent degree the
highest powers of an orator.   In listening to him no one could doubt his entire
sincerity, and when he appealed to the highest and noblest principles of humanity it was the outpouring from the heart.   His words went directly to the hearts
of the audience.   His control of their emotions was, for the time, complete.
Nothing seemed to give him greater pleasure than the exertion of these high
powers in the cause of justice.   He was a gentleman of the old school, and
exhibited these traits in all his conduct during a trial.   Always courteous to
the Bench, though firm and earnest in insisting upon the rights of his client,
his uniform politeness to the adverse party — counsel and witnesses — had a
strong tendency to restrain undue exhibitions of passion, too frequently witnessed upon exciting trials.

His early friend and fellow-student, Governor Marcy, appointed
Mr. Skinner, in 1838, to the office of judge of the eighth circuit,
who, at that time, had equity jurisdiction as vice-chancellor; but
he declined the appointment.   President Pierce nominated him for
United States District Attorney for the northern district of New
York; a position which he also declined.   In the mean time, in
1846, the governor of New York appointed him Judge of the county
court of Wyoming, under the new constitution of that state, a place
which he held but for a few months, until the election, which inau-
gurated the new elective judiciary system.   He failed of his election
under that system, on political grounds, which are clearly unfolded
by his kinsman, James O. Putnam.

During the period of Mr. Skinner's service in the Legislature, a new element
appeared in western New York politics, a sort of Nile inundation, breaking up
and sweeping away all old political organizations.   I refer to Anti-Masonry.   It
took the form of a political party, and from the start was at the white heat of
popular passion.   The tide kept rapidly rising, and floated out on the sea of
popular favor all the men of that generation in the career of politics in western
New York.   To be an Anti-Mason was to be in the realm of possibilities for any
position within the gift of the local constituency.   To be of the opposition was
to be whelmed under a flood of majorities which made hopeless, almost down to
the present day, all its political aspirations through popular election.   Mr. Skinner's father was a Mason, and that fact powerfully influenced him.   He could
not be floated off on any impulsive tide, and he would not hold an organization
responsible for a crime, atrocious as it was, of a few individual members.   He
united with the opposition to the Anti-Masonic party, and when the Anti-
Masonic was merged in the Whig party, his attitude remained unchanged in the
Democratic organization.   The result was that the standard majority of about
3000 in "old Genesee," Anti-Masonic and Whig for forty years, was as Ossa on
Pelion and both on Atlas, over the hopes and candidacy of every man of the
minority for political promotion.   Mr. Skinner was often the candidate of his
party for high honors, but the contest was always a forlorn hope, and he led it
with characteristic courage and devotion.

No other native of Williamstown certainly, perhaps it may be said no other graduate of Williams College, ever gained the breadth and constancy and solidity of reputation, at once as a lawyer and as an orator, and as a genial friend and gentleman, and as a high officer and representative of a great national church, that was acquired by John B. Skinner (Williams College, 1818), 1799–1871, the most honored among the many honored descendants of Colonel Benjamin Simonds. Let us listen for a moment to what a clergyman, Rev. J. E. Nassau, who knew him thoroughly, said of him two years after his death: "He was a person of the finest sensibilities, that manifested themselves continually in his domestic, Christian, and professional life and intercourse. I have often seen him profoundly affected and moved even to tears in religious meetings and public addresses, and even in common conversation upon topics that greatly interested him. And nothing took deeper hold of his emotion than the grand elemental truths of the Bible, the permanent interests of the Church, the sorrows and joys of friends, or the vital interests of the Country."

After his removal to Buffalo in 1860, — except an interval of eighteen months of foreign travel, in the course of which he lost, by death in Switzerland, his only child (Mrs. Letchworth), and his only grandchild, — Judge Skinner passed the last ten years of his life in the varied duties of a useful and honored citizenship. His last years, with the exception of the great sorrow just referred to, were serene and happy. A paragraph from an address made by him before the American Bible Society in New York, will exhibit some of the traits of the man and the orator: —

But I have touched only a single point; — such a view of this subject would be like that relief which should take the hopeless, drowning man from the fatal wreck, and carry him within view of the cheering light, and within sound of the glad voices of sympathy and kindred, and leave him there to die unblest. I have not referred to the power of the Gospel to break the fetters in which pride and avarice and selfishness have bound up the charities of the soul; nor to those fountains of benevolence which this week commemorates, and which, springing from this source, have sent forth their gushing waters over the dry earth, producing moral beauty and verdure and loveliness. I have not alluded to that noble institution in the father-land, whose jubilee has just been celebrated, and which has shed its radiance over every clime, and whose light, mingling with ours, beams from those bright spots indicated on your missionary map, which a kindred institution has rescued from the desert. I have not spoken of that boon of sympathy and brotherhood which has reclaimed the drunkard, and sought out the abandoned, and carried the hopes of life to the lost. These are the fruits of that Tree of Life whose leaves are for the healing of the nations. Nay, this influence is the voice of the Son of God in the sepulchre of Lazarus. It penetrates

the grave, and rescues its tenants from corruption and the worm ; it clothes them
with a robe of spotless righteousness ; it furnishes them with a passport to that
city that hath foundation, to those joys which "eye hath not seen, nor ear
heard, nor hath entered into the heart of man to conceive."

Colonel Simonds's third daughter, Marcy, born Dec. 2, 1759, became the wife of Charles Kellogg, and they the ancestors of a considerable number of distinguished men and of admirable women, but
not of men so much distinguished as some of those springing from
each of her elder sisters. The several Kellogg families have played
a prominent part in the story of Williamstown, and in that of the
College too, even down to the present time. They all sprang from
Samuel of Hatfield, through Nathaniel, his eldest son, who settled
and remained in Colchester, Connecticut, whence came to Williamstown Charles and Nathaniel, brothers of the fifth generation from
Samuel of Hatfield. The Samuel Kellogg already characterized
in these pages, who came to Williamstown considerably earlier than
these two brothers, was of the same lineage with them, while the
exact degree of kinship has not been ascertained. The two lines
came together again, as we shall shortly see. Charles Kellogg
probably married Marcy Simonds in 1775; if so, she could not have
been more than sixteen years old; the births of five of their children,
born in Williamstown, are recorded in the old proprietors' book; and
of these, Justin was born Jan. 17, 1781. Charles Kellogg was the
first innholder of record in the old Mansion House, which was
burned down in October, 1872, and which had a sort of history very
closely interwoven with that of the town and the College; and so,
for a time at least, the son-in-law followed the vocation of the
wife's father here, but he moved on about the opening of this century into the new promised land of Washington County, New York,
and settled in Middle Granville, where he died in 1828, aged seventy-eight. His son, Justin, went early from Granville to Troy,
and became a merchant there, highly esteemed and prosperous, was
for many years a Justice of the Peace, and a prominent member of
the Presbyterian church. He was killed by the overturning of a
stage-coach, while descending Oak Hill near Buskirk's Bridge, in
May, 1839, in his fiftieth year. He left two daughters, Adeline and
Harriet; the first of whom, born in 1816, a well-educated and beautiful woman, intermarried, in 1836, with Giles B. Kellogg (Williams
College, 1829), a grandson of the first Samuel Kellogg of Williamstown. Two lines were thus happily united. Justin Kellogg
(Williams College, 1865), a well-known lawyer of Troy, and at the
present time an alumni-trustee, as was also his father before him

in 1868–78, and Giles Kellogg (Williams College, 1876), now a business man in Boston, were sons of this intermarriage and represent, among her other numerous posterity, Marcy Simonds, who died in Middle Granville in 1834, aged seventy-eight. Justin A. Kellogg, of Indianapolis, is another scion of this widely extended stock, — a descendant of Marcy and Charles Kellogg.

Prudence, the fourth daughter of Colonel Simonds, born Dec. 4, 1763, was married before she was nineteen years old to Jonathan Bridges, who was ten years older, and who migrated hither from Colchester, Connecticut, just as the embers of the Revolutionary War were being raked in. Jonathan left two brothers in Colchester, Samuel and Amasa; Samuel always remained there, and sent his son, Samuel A., to Williams College, from which he was graduated in 1826, and became a prominent man in Pennsylvania, a member of Congress, LL.D. in 1876, and trustee in Muhlenburg College; and Amasa, a blacksmith, came much later than his brother to Williamstown, and lived (always poor) both on the crest of Northwest Hill and afterwards at its foot in a small house built by him, and but recently removed by Colonel A. L. Hopkins. After the birth of three children in Williamstown, Jonathan Bridges removed to Adams, where three others were added to his family, and then he returned here and bought the farm north of the Hoosac River, which has been owned and occupied by his descendants — Samuel and Edwin and Charles in succession — down to the present time. Four more children were born to Jonathan and Prudence during their second sojourn on the Hoosac, of whom the last was Lucy, born Feb. 2, 1808, and still living in 1893. Jonathan died in 1818, and Prudence in 1844. As a rule, the posterity of the latter have not shown the conspicuous talents nor gained the usual prominence of the posterity of her three older sisters; indeed, she herself, though a kindly and painstaking woman devoted to the interests of her family, showed in her old age symptoms and even evidences of a sort of harmless insanity; and her eldest son, Elam, died in an insane hospital in Utica, in 1847. She herself passed all the latter years of her life in the family of her youngest daughter, Lucy Bridges Smedley, and died under her loving and watchful care in her eighty-first year. Mrs. Smedley's eldest daughter helped to care for and to comfort her grandmother in her latest years; and it is noteworthy, and most gratifying to a father's love to note, that the eldest son of this granddaughter, Bliss Perry (Williams College, 1881), and professor both in his own Alma Mater and in Princeton College, has been thus far the only one of the descendants of

Prudence Simonds who has enjoyed and maintained what is rightly and usually termed a public reputation. He has already distinguished himself both as public teacher, and a literary worker on the highest fields.

Ablina Simonds, the fifth daughter of the Colonel, born Oct. 8, 1765, the year of the incorporation of West Hoosac as Williamstown, married, when she was but just over nineteen, Joseph Osborne, who was an enterprising citizen here for many years; and who, if he were the Joseph Osborne " of the mountain land west of Sheffield, yeoman," who sold land to Nathan Benjamin of "said mountain land" in 1764, must have been much older than his wife. They were married Dec. 2, 1784. Three children of this union, Emmet and Melissa and Julia, were all baptized here the 21st of July, 1793, on the occasion of both their parents uniting with the church. The fourth and last child, Myra, was born Dec. 6, 1795. Both parents were living when Colonel Simonds made his will; but in the second codicil of the same, drawn in March, 1805, Joseph Osborne's death is mentioned, and a direction given that his widow receive the whole share intended for them both. Mrs. Osborne afterwards married Judah Paddock, Esq., of Skaneateles, New York, but there were no more children. Emmet Osborne, the only son, — what generation is wholly without such, — proved to be "a ne'er-do-weel." Melissa Osborne, born Nov. 20, 1787, was married to Pharez Gould in due time, and one son and one daughter were the offspring of this union. Miss Gould became Mrs. Addison G. Jerome, of New York, and she, in turn, the mother of Eugene Murray Jerome (Williams College, 1867), who is now with a beautiful family a highly respected and influential resident of Williamstown; and Mr. Gould became the father of the late lamented Edward Osborne Gould (Williams College, 1867), who was a broker in New York, and died in 1883.[1] Julia Osborne married, in 1816, Alfred Northam, born in Williamstown in 1788, and a graduate of Williams in the class of 1808. He was the eldest son of Timothy Northam and Rebekah Meacham. He studied law with Daniel Kellogg at Skaneateles, New York, and became a partner with him in the practice of that profession. After a residence there of about fifteen years, he removed to Syracuse, where he acted as Justice of the Peace for several years, and where,

[1] Ned Gould, as he was called in College, and by his *confrères* generally, was an extremely genial student and man. Colonel Simonds had willed his own portrait to the Putnams, but it had passed over in some way to the Osbornes, and Gould claimed it as his own, and gave it to me. He said, "Now, Professor, if I should ever get married and beget sinners of my own, you'll have to give this back!" He died a bachelor.

in November, 1832, in her fortieth year, his wife committed suicide in the night by opening the jugular vein. This is said to have given his system such a shock that he never fully recovered from it. He removed, however, the same year to Peoria, Illinois, but returned to Syracuse in 1840, and was cared for in his old age by Mrs. Jerome, a niece of Mrs. Northam's, at Lockport, where he died in 1858, and where some of Mrs. Jerome's children remember him vividly as swinging his cane with vehemence to keep them off from his gouty feet! Mrs. Julia Northam never had any children. Miss Myra Osborne, the youngest of the Colonel's grandchildren in this family, was united in marriage with Harvey Putnam in 1817, the youngest of his step-sons. A great-great-grandson of the Colonel, through James O. Putnam, is now (1893) in attendance upon the Yale Theological Seminary in the same class with another of his great-great-grandsons, a son of the present writer, Carroll Perry.

The Colonel's sixth daughter, Electa Simonds, born in 1768, married, when she was nineteen, Thaddeus Edwards, and died in Skaneateles without children in 1841. She was a fleshy woman, the largest of all of Colonel Simonds's daughters. Polly, the youngest daughter, born in 1771, married in due season, that is to say, early, Perly Putnam, the eldest son of her stepmother. He was a harness-maker by trade, and lived for some years on the house lot originally bought and occupied by his father-in-law, No. 22, and still occasionally called by old people the "Putnam lot." He migrated with his family to Skaneateles, where his youngest brother, Harvey, was apprenticed to him, where his family was brought up, and where both the parents died. Their son, Henry, inherited at first his grandfather's portrait from his mother, to whom it was specifically willed, whence it passed into the hands of the Osborne cousins. Contrary to the wishes and judgment of both families, their daughter, Mary, a name that now began to expel the more common "Polly," was wooed and won (in a clandestine way) by Thaddeus Edwards, 2d, a nephew of the husband of Electa Simonds; and another daughter, Electa Putnam, became the second wife of James Northam, of Williamstown, a brother of Alfred Northam, who was the husband of Julia Osborne. Thus the Northams, the heads of whose families all came from Colchester to Williamstown, were intermingled with the older Meacham and Simonds families.

In connection with this account of all the children of Benjamin Simonds, and of his last will and its two codicils, it will be appropriate to copy the "Inventory of his estate, whereof he died seized and possessed" in 1807. The appraisers were Deodatus Noble,

Ephraim Seelye, and Asa Northam; and these, as such appraisers, took oath before Joshua Danforth, Justice of the Peace. The "shares" mentioned in Simonds's will had all been distributed to his children previous to his death.

7 acres of land with dwelling house and barn	$600
1 Chaise and harness	75
1 horse $35 2 cows $42	77
Clock and Case $35 watch $15	50
Silver hilted sword $10 cherry desk $12	22
Case of drawers $25 Feather bed and pillows $12	37
2 woolen rugs $1.50 7 woolen blankets $2.50	4
Wig .50 Old Beaver Hat $1 Great Coat $2	3.50
Black Coat vest and Breeches $15 arm Chair .50	15.50
7 pewter plates $1.25 silver shoe buckles $1.50	2.75
Pair knee buckles .50 6 silver tea spoons $4.50	5.
Ivory headed cane .75 2 cotton sheets $2.25	3.
2 linen sheets $2.50 Pair linen pillow-cases .50	3.
6 linen sheets $6 2 pair table linen $1.50	7.50
Carving knife and fork .40 warming pan $1	1.40
5 iron spoons .50 4 pans .40 2 skimmers .12	1.02
Brass kettle $10 7 barrels Cyder $10	20.
½ barrel Pork and barrel $8 10 bushels Wheat $12.50	20.50
Brown's Family Bible 2 vol. fol.	6.
Tin stove .25 small chest .50 axe $1 shovel and tongs .50	2.25
Iron fetters .50 2 linen shirts 1.50 2 pair hand irons $1	3.
And many other items aggregating	$1039.70

16. When the new meeting-house was built and seated, in 1768, the youngest member of the building and seating committee, Nehemiah Smedley, was thirty-five years old. Some account of his ancestry and immediate parentage, of his brothers and sisters, — of whom there were ten, — and of his own movements from Litchfield to West Hoosac, both as a soldier first and a settler afterwards, has already been given in these pages. We reserve till the next chapter all references to his conspicuous Revolutionary services. The enterprise and business capacity and general good judgment of this comparatively young man were recognized by the proprietors in his selection to serve upon these two important committees. No portrait or other likeness at all of this Smedley has been preserved to posterity. Strange to say, no headstone was ever erected over his grave, and even the place of his burial, within the limits of the graveyard, is unknown. He was not even a member of the church, in which his son and grandson served an aggregate of seventy-five years as deacons, and in which one of his great-great-grandsons is now a deacon. His personal education was slight, as is manifested

in his personal papers, all of which are preserved, and are the property of the writer; and yet, it may well be questioned whether any one of the original proprietors of Williamstown — save only each of his two senior colleagues of the church-building committee — exerted upon the town a more wholesome and pervasive influence. He made such an opening here as rendered feasible and desirable the subsequent coming and settling of five brothers and four sisters. He acquired property easily, and both retained and increased it. He built his first house and planted his first orchard on the front of house lot No. 1, and the next door to the west of him was the first tavern-stand of the little hamlet; and it is quite possible, perhaps even probable, that the first five or six families who settled in Bennington (about twenty persons in all) in June, 1761, who certainly came over the Hoosac Mountain on horseback in that month, and passed through West Hoosac, and so on through Pownal, tarried over night at this tavern and in the small houses adjacent to it. At any rate, Mary Harwood, then just sixteen years old, was in that little company, which was led by Peter Harwood, her brother, ten years older than herself. Another brother, Eleazar, two years younger than Peter, was also along; and two brothers Robinson, Leonard and Samuel, Junior, from Hardwick, and Samuel Pratt and Timothy Pratt from Amherst, were the only other adults in the party. It is much more likely than not that a part of these persons lodged one night in the tavern, another part in the West Hoosac Fort opposite, and still other persons in one or more of the houses on Hemlock Brook close by.

It is possible that Nehemiah Smedley opened his bachelor hall to one or more of these pioneers into the regions beyond, and that thus, or otherwise, he gained, at this time, a speaking acquaintance with Mary Harwood. If not, then such acquaintance was not long delayed; for in two years time, at most, Mary Harwood became Mrs. Smedley, and mistress of the "regulation" house on No. 1. Levi Smedley, their first-born, enlivened the scene in the aforetime bachelor hall on Oct. 8, 1764. Seven other children rapidly followed, about half of them born in the new and large house (still standing) near the junction of the Green and Hoosac rivers. Indeed, the heavy oak timbers of this new house were lifted into their place on the eighth birthday of little Levi; that is to say, Oct. 8, 1772, and Harwoods and other friends from Bennington came down to the "raising." The war was drawing on; and Captain Smedley, twelve years older than his wife, was away from home much of the time for several years, which, of course, in such times, increased the cares and anxieties of the mother with her little flock; and just eight days before she became thirty-seven years old, she passed away into a realm unvexed by wars, and leaving her youngest born, Samuel, but nine months old.   In less than a year thereafter, Captain Smedley married an old acquaintance and neighbor of the Smedleys in Litchfield, Mrs. Lyman Gibbs, and one son crowned this marriage also, James, born Dec. 23, 1783.

Nehemiah himself was drawing near to his earthly end.   He had led a life of hardships and exposure, and of unintermitted activities. He was one of the first to perceive that the system of house lots of ten acres each, and the rest of the farm made up of lots drawn by the homestead in different parts of the town, was ill-adapted to a community of farmers; and he early cast his eyes about to see where he could aggregate a good farm not far from the "Square," in which he could have all the requisite kinds of land in essential contiguity around his homestead.   This end was essentially accomplished in 1765.   The first-division fifty-acre lot No. 28 lay a little to the east of the Green River "on the road to the east town," and was owned by John Moffat, painter, of Boston, the original drawer of house lot 46, which, in turn, had drawn this fifty-acre lot.   Smedley evidently went to Boston to buy this lot, the consideration for which was £50 lawful money, and the deed to convey which was signed in Boston by Moffat, and witnessed there by Belcher Noyes, and William Smibert of that town, June 21, 1765.   Earlier in the same year, two meadow lots adjoining this lot were secured, — No. 12 from Ephraim Seelye for £13, and No. 13 from William Horsford for £30, — both of these meadow lots extending north across the Hoosac to the old Mohawk trail, later developed into the "north road to the east town."   The autumn before he had bought meadow lot No. 10 for £20, which was near, but not adjacent to the others, and which lay mostly north of the river.   In October, 1766, he bought, also, fifty-acre lot No. 29, which lies directly opposite the home lot on the south side of the road, and comes up to the bridge over Green River at the east end of the house lots.   This purchase virtually completed what has been called for a century and a quarter the "Smedley farm," though he bought of Rev. Whitman Welch, May 4, 1775, eighteen and three-fourth acres more of land contiguous to what he held before, and a little afterwards oak lot No. 18, containing nineteen acres.   When he died, in 1789, in his fifty-seventh year, the public inventory of his estate sets down the "Homestead Farm," as containing 177 acres, which, with the "Dwelling House and Barn," were valued at £1300 ($4333.33); one sixty-acre lot at £60 ($200);

one pine lot containing about three acres, at £4 ($13.33) ; the live stock at £92 19s. ($309) ; and furniture and all other items at £109 14s. ($368). Total, $5224.66.

When Smedley made his will, Dec. 17, 1787, " being weak in body but of sound mind and memory (blessed be God!)," he made his eldest son sole executor, who had just passed into his twenty-fourth year, and who gave bonds in the sum of £1000. Two of his near neighbors, Samuel Kellogg and Ira Baker, owning the farms next to his to the eastward, signed Levi Smedley's bond, and the same, with William Wells, witnessed the will. The testator lived about two years after his will was drawn, and the same was approved by the Judge of Probate March 2, 1790. The father's methods of doing business are shown in the accounts of his executor; namely, the debts due to the estate at the testator's death were £6 5s. 0d., all but nine shillings for hay sold to sundry persons; the nine shillings were owed by William Towner, Esq. The debts owed by the estate were £4 8s. 0d., more than half of which was due to Dr. Sheldon, his attending physician, and eight shillings to Dr. Porter, presumably for counsel. Tradition has it that Nehemiah Smedley died of consumption, and alleges as corroborative proof that it was noticed long before his death, that when he crossed the Hoosac in his boat to those parts of his farm north of that river, and returned, the matter he expectorated sank into the water instead of floating, which was supposed to be sure proof of the presence of blood from the lungs.

After the father's death, the two eldest sons carried on the large farm, for many years in company, and both brought up large families under the one roof in harmony; but they finally resolved to divide between themselves the farm which they had jointly increased by considerable purchases of land, and especially by the " Luce lot," at the same time resolving to take no outside counsel over the division, and to make no after complaints about it in any case. This mutual understanding was carried out in the letter and spirit of it to a good old age of both parties. Levi naturally took the homestead, and died in 1849, aged eighty-five. He and his wife, Lydia Gibbs from Litchfield, united with the church in 1792, and he became a deacon in 1828, and served twenty-one years. Elijah Smedley and his wife, Lucy Gibbs, a cousin of the other, united with the church in 1793. After the division, these lived in a house southeast of the old homestead, and both died there in an honored old age. Asahel Foote (Williams College, 1827) married their daughter Mary, assumed the care of the farm, taught a successful private school in the house for many years, became a deacon in the church

in 1838, and died in the old house in 1882. Charles Rollin Foote
(Williams College, 1859), now a citizen of California, was their only
son. Besides Levi and Elijah, Captain Nehemiah Smedley had four
other sons, Moses, Elisha, Samuel, and James. The two first mentioned migrated early to Hinesburg, Vermont. Any other air than
that of Williamstown does not seem to be wholesome to the Smedleys, either physically or morally. George, the son of Elisha,
returned to Williamstown in 1856, and bought the Kellogg farm,
next east of the old homestead. Frederic George (Williams College, 1864), now a prosperous lawyer in New York, still owning
and occupying in summer the old Kellogg farm, is his only son.
Frederic Miller Smedley (Williams College, 1893) is the only son
of Frederic George. Samuel, who went from here to New Lisbon,
Otsego County, New York, did not leave behind him there a savory
reputation; but James, the youngest son of Nehemiah, who married
Emily Wheelock, daughter of John Wheelock, who was a drummer-
boy in the Revolution, became, like his father-in-law, a pious man
and a good citizen, both in Hinesburg, Vermont, and in Lockport,
New York. Of the children of Deacon Levi Smedley, Levi, born
in 1795, inherited the farm in due time, lived a long and useful life
upon it, represented his town in the General Court for one year, and
did good service in forwarding the cause of the Hoosac Tunnel, then
before the Legislature. He did not, however, show the vigor and
enterprise as a farmer and citizen that the good deacon exhibited
before him; and the good deacon himself was, perhaps, inferior in
those respects to the good Captain Nehemiah. The "Western
fever" struck, at last, Chauncy, Levi's son, after he had owned and
operated the ancestral acres for half a lifetime, and he sold out
and migrated to Illinois, and his son, Leveus Smedley, is now a
farmer in Indiana. The deacon's youngest son, James, born Dec. 1,
1804, spent his whole life in Williamstown, except for two brief
intervals, and died on Good Friday, 1892, in his eighty-eighth year.

Like his fathers before him, he, too, dwelt among his own people.
His lot in life was comparatively obscure, not succeeding well in the
medical profession, which he learned in his youth, on account of
abnormally quick sensibilities, which would not allow him to sleep
whenever he had a critical case on his hands. He lacked a needful
confidence in his own knowledge and judgment, and necessarily,
after a little, the medical confidence of the communities in which he
practised. He enjoyed, however, the moral confidence of those communities to a remarkable degree, and to an extreme old age. He
fell back early on the life of a small farmer and fruiterer; and was

half-way through the eighty-eighth year when his call came. He was chosen a deacon in the church in 1838, and served in conjunction with his father for eleven years, and then onward for forty-three years longer. During the long period of fifty-four years of an unbroken deaconate, this good man was not absent from his place at the memorial table more than two or three times all told. Next to the native church, of which he stood an unblemished member for just seventy years, his interest centred in Williams College, which he watched very closely all his life. He attended the commencement of 1810, and all the succeeding commencements but five up to and including that of 1890. He studied one year in College, and then passed to the medical school at Pittsfield, at that time a department of the College, at which he was regularly graduated in 1829. He knew, personally, each of the six successive presidents of the College from the first, and could well describe their looks and characteristics. He had a remarkable memory for the names and faces and residences of the students of many generations, and they, in turn, were fond of seeing him and hearing his fluent accounts of the men and days of old.

The following appreciative words are from the admirable funeral sermon preached by Rev. Dr. John Bascom : —

Deacon Smedley was a plain, simple-hearted, and very devout man. He was an excellent illustration of the strength of character and breadth of influence which are secured by an unfailing hold in the invisible things which pertain to the Kingdom of Heaven. His long life and very long deaconry, without quite covering the early era of the Williamstown church, fully embraced and expressed its spirit and methods. He clung tenaciously to the good men, the memories, and the religious experiences of his youth. The definite and very positive faith of those early times, with a periodic fervor of enforcement, were with him the familiar type of an earnest Christian life. The less stringent but more comprehensive beliefs, the less incisive but more inclusive religious action, we are slowly approaching, had the appearance, to him, somewhat of the subterfuges of a lax and shifty generation. Deacon Smedley was a fine example of one of the many forms of profitable and commanding character, which are built up, each in its own fashion, by the progress of our very variable and very complex Christian faith.

Deacon Smedley married Lucy Bridges, a granddaughter of Colonel Simonds, and thus, in one way, these two sturdy stocks were engrafted into each other; and her brother, Samuel Bridges, intermarried also with Irene Smedley, a sister of the deacon; and a number of the present families in Williamstown sprang from these two unions. The deacon's eldest daughter, Mary, married A. L. Perry (Williams College, 1852) ; and Grace Perry (Wellesley, 1881), Bliss

Perry (Williams, 1881), Walter Perry (Williams, 1887), and Carroll Perry (Williams, 1890) are of that line; while Lucy, the
deacon's youngest daughter, was united in marriage to Jonathan
Wadhams (Williams College, 1867).   Another of Deacon James's
sisters, Lydia, born and bred like him by the riverside, married Noah
Sheldon (Williams College, 1815); and two of their sons, Charles
and Samuel (both Williams College, 1847), were honored in their
graduation, one with the Philosophical Oration, and the other with
the Salutatory.   Another of these sisters married Manning Brown,
a native of Cheshire, and a successful farmer and manufacturer in
Williamstown and Adams; and their son, Timothy M. Brown (Williams College, 1859), has long been a prominent citizen and lawyer
in the city of Springfield on the Connecticut River.   Deacon James
Smedley's widow, her son William and wife, who care for her in
her extreme age, and two orphan children of her youngest son,
Edward, who was in the Signal Corps on Commodore Farragut's flag-
ship in the battle of Mobile Bay, a son and a daughter, are the only
persons in Williamstown bearing the name of Smedley as the nineteenth century draws to a close.   What a contrast in point of numbers as compared with the close of the eighteenth century here!

17. There came to Williamstown in 1764, from Weathersfield,
Connecticut, a man by the name of Josiah Wright.   His wife's name
was Abigail, and both became members of the Williamstown church,
it is to be presumed, by letter.   They had a son, Josiah Wright,
Junior, and probably several other sons.   There was a Gideon Wright
and his wife Sarah, who were also very early members of the church;
and it is not to be doubted that a pew was set aside in the meeting-
house of 1768 for the Wright family.   There is an epitaph in the old
burial-ground by the Hemlock Brook, — "Mr. Jonathan Wright, who
died April 10, A.D. 1766 in the 30th year of his age."   Justice Wright
and his wife, Mercy, had children born in town, 1779–1782; and Stephen Bacon, 2d, told the writer that when he was a small boy — that
is, at the beginning of this century — there was an Aaron Wright,
who lived on the Upper Hopper Brook above Bacons'.   But, as we
shall see shortly, interest in the Wright family turns rather on a
locality than on persons particular.   Josiah Wright, Junior, bought
of Samuel Clark in July, 1772, for £5, the meadow lot No. 63, which
is the meadow lot directly south of Blair's (now Hubbell's).   As we
have seen before, Blair's original house stood north of the road, in
what is now an orchard; and there is some considerable evidence
that Wright owned meadow lot No. 62 as well as 63, and, at any
rate, his access to 63 must have been past the present Hubbell build-

ings to the south. However this may be (and it is not important),
it is certain that Josiah Wright's son settled not long after his
arrival in town on first-division fifty-acre lot No. 61, the northern
end of which comes up to the Blair road before that road turns
sharply north into the Stratton road. The eastern side of Wright's
lot 61 flanks what was then Aaron Bacon's lot 63 (these were both
fifty-acre lots), and Bacon must have come out to the Blair road
very near where the senior Wright built his first house. This house
was superseded after a while by a brick house, which has only lately
been taken down, and about which cluster a series of weird traditions, which the future novelist of the town (may God speed his
coming!) may likely enough work up into a tale that shall outlive
these imperfect records now being woven into a loose fabric that
may ravel out in time.

It is not at all certain, hardly probable, that the brick house
was built while the elder Wright was still in the saddle there. If
not, it was certainly built by one or more of his sons. The family
remained in possession, and gradually acquired a bad reputation.
The father and mother moved on to Arlington, Vermont, where
Abigail died in February, 1795, and Josiah in February, 1799, he in
his eighty-seventh year and she in her seventy-ninth; and at some
time between the close of the war and the close of the century, the
inmates of the brick house were thought so ill of by their neighbors
that the latter lent a ready ear to a story of murder committed by
the former, and repeated it over, little by little, with ghostly details
and additions, to their children, from several of whom the writer
has derived it directly, though, of course, with quaint and considerable variations. This is not history, nor does it aspire to become
such; but there must have been some basis of fact, and surely a
stiff basis of locality, for a story that has been told under breath,
and not without shudders, for several generations, in the Blair family and in the Williams family, — the two nearest neighbors, — and
also in the Corbin and other families at the South Part. It is the
only tale of robbery and murder and ghosts that connects itself,
even in dimmest outline, with the early story of Williamstown, and
runs in general in something like the way following: The Wrights
had become considerably indebted to a certain pedlar driving one
horse, who frequented those parts in quest of the usual driblets of
gain. The neighbors had seen him drive up to the brick house, had
watched for his return, and had not discovered it. In the mean
time, mysterious movements were observed in and around the house.
Lights were seen at unusual times, and in usually unfrequented

parts of the house. The suspicions of the neighbors, that something wrong was going on in and around the Wright house, were thoroughly aroused, and these suspicions were mutually inflamed by communicating them. In a day or two, all was still and apparently abandoned at the brick house. Neighbors combined in fear and dread, but with all due resolution, to search for the body of the pedlar and for his various effects. Possible places of interment or hiding away were scrutinized, sheds and barn and cellar were examined, and nothing was found anywhere of a questionable character, until at last the pedlar's horse was discovered in the best room of the brick house, with cloths wrapped round his hoofs, apparently so that his stampings on the floor might not be heard by the neighbors, before the inmates had gotten a good ways off from the premises. No stampings or neighings from the real horse had then been heard by anybody; but years and years afterwards, and to many successive occupants of the house, mysterious sounds issued from that room, slight but distinct, treadings on that floor, deadened as if falling on cloths, and neighings, not equine and earthly, but stifled and supernatural, as if the ghost of the pedlar had come back to seek for his horse, and the horse had greeted his old master with at least the distant echoes of accustomed sounds. There are old people, still living, who have confessed, in the writer's hearing, to strange perturbations of mind as they have entered or quitted, or even thought of (in the night), the square room of the old brick house above Blair's.

18. Titus Harrison was from Litchfield, and owned, in 1765, house lot No. 39, the third lot east from South Street, and the one on which Eli Porter lived a great many years, and on which the late Dr. Samuel Duncan built the present house owned by his children. Harrison soon quitted the Main Street, even if he ever occupied his house lot 39, and established himself on Water Street, where he utilized, for the first time, the successive falls in the Green River at that point, for milling purposes. He built a house there on the bank of the river, and had for near neighbors Joseph Osborne and Samuel Payen. The last-named was a carpenter from Dutchess County, New York, who, like many others before and after him, was drawn towards the mill-privileges on the lower course of Green River. There are three or four of these natural falls in the stream, near the east end of the Main Street and to the south of it, and one (lower down) to the north of it. The last one was not utilized for a water-privilege till after the Civil War, when the Arnold brothers, of North Adams, and other capitalists, using Professor

Chadbourne as a sort of partner, or rather agent, availed themselves of it, in connection with a local fall in the Hoosac, to obtain power for the present large cotton-mill at their junction; but the falls above drew attention to themselves at the very first, and occupied the minds of many projectors and many purchasers before Titus Harrison first practically made them tell. The standing difficulty was, that first-division fifty-acre lot No. 30, which covered all the land contiguous to the falls on both sides of the river, was about sixty feet below the nearest point of access to the Main Street from any prospective mill or mills, and this point of access was a regular jumping-off place at that, — rocky and precipitous. In June, 1761, Gideon Warren, formerly a soldier at Fort Massachusetts, but then a yeoman of West Hoosac, sold to Samuel Payen, for £6, "two acres on Green river, part of a lot known as No. 30, beginning at the N.W. corner of M. L. 47, thence North 20 rods, thence East 16 rods across Green river, thence South 20 rods on the east side of the river, thence West across the river 16 rods to the place of beginning, with privilege of flowing the river bank as hie up as ye top of ye upper falls"; "and also a strip of land two rods wide by the west side of said river beginning at the north side of said land I sold to said Payn, and running north by said river to the mouth of the brook [Phebe's Brook], and up the hill to the lot now enclosed and so out to the main road or Highway, to be a highway for the use of the town." Isaac Stratton and Daniel Stratton sign this deed as witnesses.

This was a very important deed. Gideon Warren and Samuel Payen solved the mill question, opened up Water Street into Main just as it runs to-day, and went part way towards justifying the location of the house lots as a site for a permanent village. There can be little or no doubt that the commissioners sent up by the General Court in the spring of 1750 to lay out the house lots — that is, the prospective village — were a good deal controlled in their selection of a site, in many respects unfortunate, by the situation of these Green River Falls. If they had carried fully out their original scheme of a uniform rectangle, one quarter of the lots in number coming into each angle of their Greek cross constituted by the Main Street and North and South Streets bisecting it, these falls would have fallen into two individual house lots, otherwise almost worthless on account of the high and abrupt wall dividing the Main Street from the tumbling stream. Hence, they threw out five house lots altogether from the east end of the southeast quarter of their rectangle, and ran one lot (No. 57) parallel with the Main Street, while all the rest

were at right angles to it. At the same time the falls might serve
the hamlet fairly well, though they were at one extreme corner of it.
The plot was laid out too long for its width (one mile and three-
eighths), and on very uneven ground, apparently for the purpose of
bringing as many lots as possible into contiguity with running water,
and also of bringing the whole plot into neighborhood with those
successive mill-privileges.   Posterity will never find fault, on the
whole, with the commissioners of 1750.   They had a difficult task
to fulfil.   They did not know whether or not wells could be successfully sunk into, or through, or towards the limestone rock.   They
managed to get in sixty-three house lots of ten acres each (and
more), twenty-one of which were traversed by one or other of the
two tributaries of Hemlock Brook, or by the united stream; the
Green River skirts the eastern ends of both the eastern quarters of
the quadrangle in their entire extent; and there are, at least, eight
or ten copious springs of water within the designated area.   For
some reason Gideon Warren did not feel warranted in facing the
practical difficulties involved in his mill-privileges, so he sold them
to Payen with a way out into the street above; three years later he
sold off from his lot No. 30 eleven acres more from the southern end
to James Meacham; and the very last glimpse that we reach of our
old soldier and early settler, Gideon Warren, is as proprietors' clerk
in the brand-new town of Pittsford, Vermont, March 19, 1771.

Neither did Samuel Payen ever reach the point of opening an
actual sawmill for logs, or a grist-mill for grain to be ground for toll,
on his new Green River privileges.   He was enterprising and apparently well-to-do; he bought of Titus Harrison, at one time, October,
1765, first-division fifty-acre lot 61, and second-division fifty-acre lot
30, and 100-acre lot 46, all drawn in succession by Harrison's house
lot 39; he bought, also, of Jedidiah Smedley, the next year, a part
of Smedley's home lot No. 30 on upper Water Street, what is now
Gale's " Farm A "; he seems to have been the most influential man
on Water Street up to his time; he doubtless co-operated with the
then owner of that stretch of house lot 57, across which the proposed
road up the steep hill from Water Street must pass into Main, for it
was alike the interest of both parties, and of all parties, to have the
road built; nevertheless, it was reserved for Titus Harrison, the next
owner of the privileges, to erect the mills, and set things agoing on
Water Street.   He gradually bought a large estate in lands in that
vicinity, — three meadow lots, at one time, on Green River, of Judah
Williams, for £168, in 1782.   He sets himself down as " Miller " in
his deeds.   He was probably past middle life when he migrated from

Litchfield to Williamstown. He had many sons and daughters; and while neither he nor they were professing Christians in 1768, he was too prominent a proprietor to be passed by in the pew-distribution, and his family was large enough to fill up the pew. His wife, Anna, could not write, but made her mark upon the deeds, by which, near the close of the decade of the eighties, he began to divide, among his sons, his real estate, including his grist-mill. The cares of a large business were likely enough a burden to him. He gave to his son, Noah, the thirty acres bought of Judah Williams. He deeds to his sons, Almond and Truman, his remaining lands on Green River, which amounted to eighty-two acres, in consideration of their joint bonds for the fulfilling of certain specified purposes. This act conveyed the grist-mill, whose wheel has not ceased to turn, nor its stones to revolve, from that day to this. As is usual and inevitable in such cases, Titus Harrison's sons crowd him out of the field of view thereafter, and off from the records of the time.

Noah Harrison and his wife, Huldah, brought up a family of children on Water Street who did credit in life to their parents and grandparents. Lois, the eldest of these, married Hendrik Willey, who operated for a time a small woollen-mill (the first one of its kind in the town) on one of the Green River falls next above the one where stood and stands the grist-mill. John Willey, a brother of this Hendrik, took out in marriage Julia Stratton, Deacon Ebenezer's daughter, who lived a little east of the Green River mills on the present Stratton road. Polly Harrison, another daughter of Noah, was married in due time to Asahel Stratton. Almond Harrison, another son of Titus, bore a very considerable part for a lifetime in the measures and enterprises of his town. He married Jerusha Bacon, a daughter of old Jacob Bacon, of whom we have already spoken, and the fortunes of the two families became much intermingled. His home farm, on which he built a brick house still standing, is the one next but one north of the Stone Church on the Green River road; and he brought up a large family there. He also bought of Ephraim Seelye, the land-grabber, 1300 acres on Bald Bluffs for $1000, and gradually cleared up the land there, built a good log-house near what has long been the Greylock summer camp, where the stones of the cellar and the cellar itself may still be seen, and in which a succession of respectable tenants helped him to raise there good crops of wheat and other cereals. He sold this land after a time for about what he gave for it to his brother-in-law, Stephen Bacon, who improved the road to it, and thus accustomed his family to the slopes of the Hopper and to the Hopper itself, which has supported the Bacons in plenty for three or four generations. Almond Harrison, however, who had a cider-mill near his homestead, transformed it afterwards into a cider-brandy still, the frame of which is yet doing duty *in situ* as a barn, and became himself addicted to that stimulant to his ruin, so that Deacon Levi Smedley was appointed guardian of his children and their property.

Chloe Harrison, Almond's eldest child, born in 1785, was married to Oliver Barrit, a son of Peter Barrit, of the North Part of the town. Almy, the second daughter, married Dr. Ebenezer Stratton, Deacon Ebenezer's son, and the doctor died in his father's house on Stratton road, and Ebenezer Harrison Stratton (Williams College, 1828), in 1893 the oldest living graduate of the College except David Dudley Field, notes in his name the two families of his birth-place from which he sprang, in which place there is now no person of either name. Jerusha and Lucy Harrison were married respectively to a Dr. Thacher and a Mr. Walker, both of whom lived in Manchester, Vermont, and the writer had the privilege, many years ago, of talking over with Mrs. Walker the matters of auld lang syne in Williamstown. Clement Harrison, the oldest son of Almond, born Feb. 8, 1789, inherited the Green River farm of his father and its appurtenances, and did not escape unscathed the temptations arising in connection with the cider-brandy still; but he reformed, abandoned the bad associations of place and neighborhood, purchased the Fort Massachusetts farm in North Adams originally owned by Colonel Ephraim Williams, united with the Methodist church there, and died in a prosperous and honored old age. It was he who first pointed out to the present writer, when he was a senior in College, the lines of the old fort, over which he had often guided the plough with his own hands, and permitted him to remove to the College the last headstone remaining complete in the little old burial-ground attached to the fort. Six years afterwards, the same persons scrutinized the site of the fort a second time more carefully, with reference to planting an elm tree in the centre of the open parade-ground of the fort. The owner of the farm felt sure that he designated very nearly the exact spot, and the other party opened the ground for the tree then and there; but the present tree was set a year later (1859), because the first one did not thrive in its new environment. Bradford Harrison, the son and successor of Captain Clement, though he had the blood of the good old Pilgrim governor in his veins, recurred to the habits engendered by the cider-brandy still on the Green River farm of his grandfather.

Joel Harrison, a younger brother of Clement, who married Eliza Wells, a sister of Mrs. Truman Paul, migrated, with others, into the state of New York, where he became a General in the militia. Three of Clement Harrison's brothers, Almond and Salmon and John, all married daughters of the Hickox family living on Bee Hill, where dwelt also, at that time, Colonel William Waterman, the father of a large and reputable family here. At the wedding of John Harrison, who had joined the church in 1826, Mrs. Hickox, the mother of the bride, enlarged to Colonel Waterman, a neighbor and a guest, on the general merits of the incipient son-in-law, adding, "And what is more, Colonel, he can make just as good a prayer as Mr. Gridley!" Rev. Ralph W. Gridley was the peculiarly fervent and excellent pastor of the church from 1816 to 1834.

19. If the lines here drawn of most of the old settlers and their families seem stiff and hard and become monotonous to the modern reader, it may be in part because of the nature of the meagre records from which even the outlines of these pictures are derived. Only now and then there steps into view from out the general dimness of the old time a man or woman about whose person plays, if not a fuller, at least a rosier, light. Such is certainly the fact in regard to Elkanah Parris and his wife, Grace Parris. We know but little about either of them, and never shall know; but the little we do know begets a strong desire to know more. They had at least four children born in town, and these between the dates 1763–1770. He was a soldier in Fort Massachusetts for a considerable time. He appears in the scanty records in intimate and repeated relations with Daniel Donalson of Coleraine, one of the Scotch-Irish immigrants of 1718, when he was about twelve years old. Donalson became the original proprietor of house lot No. 63, the one lying nearest to the last stretch of Green River, but he seems never to have become a resident, although he too was a soldier in Fort Massachusetts, and as such became interested in West Hoosac. After a little, he sold his lot to John Chamberlin, of Stockbridge, for £13. The deed bears date Oct. 10, 1751. Elisha Chapin and Samuel Brown witnessed it. Chapin and Chamberlin were fellow-soldiers with Donalson in the line of forts, and Brown was a leading citizen of Stockbridge. Chamberlin sells the lot and all its after-drafts to Elkanah Parris, expressly designated in the deed as of "Fort Massachusetts," and received therefor £38. When the propriety became a town in 1765, this lot is set down as belonging to Elkanah Parris; and six years later, it is put down in the name of "Daniel Donalson *per* Elkanah Parris."

Instead of building his "regulation house" on his house lot .63, which lies on relatively high ground above the river, he preferred for some reason to build it upon the other side of the Main Street, and outside of any house lot, on the low bank close by the river, and on land then of little or no value, belonging to fifty-acre lot No. 30. There it stands to-day almost precisely as he built it. The motive in placing it down there rather than on the high and sightly ground, later occupied by the fine two-story brick house still in excellent condition, was in all likelihood the facility of getting water. However, he did not stay there very long, perhaps because the ice in the spring freshets as Green River then was may have threatened the east end of his house; the river has worn its way to the east at that point more than three times its breadth since Parris built his house there, and in 1869 a sudden "flood" not only carried away the bridge entire, but also cut a passage through the bank at its east end considerably wider than the bridge was long. For some reason, at any rate, Parris moved about half a mile to the east, near to Samuel Kellogg's house, probably into the house afterwards occupied by Lieutenant Sampson Howe, on the south side of the road. Whether it were the Quaker principles which he imbibed and professed after the close of the French and Indian War, or a natural love for solitude and contemplation amid the vast works of God, he moved next into the Hopper, and built the good house with its white-oak sills, now owned and occupied by Stephen Bacon, 3d. His is the only well-authenticated Quaker family that ever dwelt in Williamstown. He owes to this circumstance, and to the contrast between his early life in the line of forts, and in marches between them and very likely also to Ticonderoga and Crown Point and his later life in the great gorge crowned by Greylock, a weird distinction and a sort of halo that will never wholly fade out. There are those who are willing to take the risks of the conjecture, that his wife, Grace Parris, was a quiet and beautiful woman. That he was a kindly and neighborly man seems to be shown by the frequent recurrence of his autograph as a witness in the deeds and other documents of his time. He owned, at one time, the whole of house lot 57, and sold the west end of it to Isaac Searle for £15; and in 1771 the whole lot is put down to Caleb Parris.

20. Perhaps the last family to be provided for in the narrow quarters of the new meeting-house, was that of Asa Johnson, who was from Canaan, Connecticut, and who fixed himself about 1762 on a sightly swell just north of the house lots and near to the first, but soon abandoned, burial-ground. The old county road ran past

his house from Pittsfield to Bennington. That portion of the county road that passed over "Johnson Hill," as it has been recently proposed that that broad and comely height should be named, was long ago discontinued; but several elegant residences now crown the hill, conspicuous among them those of Mr. Jerome, Professor Hewitt, and Mrs. Huntoon. Asa Johnson and Thankful, his wife, had a daughter born to them in Canaan, named Hannah, on the 29th of October, 1760. When they arrived in West Hoosac a year or two later, he seems to have shown a certain enterprise and vigor in buying and selling lots, and in various dealings with the leading settlers who had preceded him; but evidence of bad management and want of thrift soon begins to peer out between the lines of various old records; he gets heavily into debt to Robert Henry, of Albany, a merchant there, from whom other settlers also purchased their supplies in part; in September, 1766, Henry sued Johnson, and obtained judgment against him in £141 11s. 11d. debt, and £3 11s. costs; Samuel Kellogg, Richard Stratton, and Jonathan Meacham took oath to apprise the real estate in order to satisfy this execution; Johnson sold in November, in part satisfaction of this debt, to Benjamin Simonds for £37 10s., meadow lots 29 and 32, oak lot 15, and pine lot 3; but the large debt would not wholly down, until in 1770 he sold to Henry directly, for £45, his homestead, twelve and one-half acres, the remnant that was left to him of fifty-acre lot No. 37, including his dwelling-house and outbuildings. This patch is bounded in the deed as follows: "northerly on land of said Robert Henry, westerly on William Hosford's land, southerly on the burial yard, and easterly on the County Road." This patch of land soon fell into the hands of Robert Hawkins, of New Milford, Connecticut, and later was long occupied as a home by Solomon Wolcott, of Colchester, and later still, by Colonel Samuel Tyler, who lived for some time in the same house with Wolcott. The writer remembers the old house well, and it was taken down not far from 1852. Asa Johnson and his wife removed from Williamstown, poor, but not discouraged, to what is now Rutland, Vermont, and their daughter, Chloe, was born there Oct. 3, 1770, the third white child to be born in Rutland, the two previous births having happened within ten days before, — William Powers on September 23, and William Mead on the next day. Rutland, however, had been a focus of Indian travel, and of white men's military marches, long before 1770. After Fort Dummer was built in 1724, Rutland lay in the most accessible path from the Connecticut River to Lake Champlain. Massachusetts sold goods at Fort Dummer cheaper than the French sold the same

in Canada; and hence a brisk Indian trade across the highlands of
Vermont. Three times in the course of the year 1759, brave sights
were seen at the crossing of the Otter Creek in what is now Centre
Rutland : first, 800 New Hampshire troops with axes and shovels
and hoes, cutting down trees and levelling hummocks, and making
a military road from Charleston, New Hampshire, to Crown Point,
in order the better to co-operate with General Amherst, in his part
towards the conquest of Canada; second, soon after, 400 fat cattle
in five droves, passing over this new road to diminish (if possible)
the scurvy in the great garrison at Crown Point; and third, Major
Robert Rogers, the great ranger and indomitable forester, with a
new corps of rangers, recruited at Charleston, on his return from the
exploit of destroying the Indian village of St. Francis on the St.
Lawrence, the pest of New England, and now after two months'
absence on his way to rejoin Amherst at Crown Point.

It only remains in this long chapter to quote *verbatim* the different orders taken, in well-warned proprietors' meetings, in relation to
the erection and occupation of this first meeting-house of 1768.

Voted to Build a meeting House also voted that Said meeting House be forty
feet in Length and thirty feet in Breadth. Voted to finish Said House in two
year. Voted Said House be Studed and Bracesed. Voted to plaister as far as
is Needed. Voted to lay the uper floer on the top of the jice and Laith and
Plaister on the under Side of the jice. Voted and Chose Nehemiah Smedley
Samuel Sanford Richard Stratton a Commetree to finish Said meeting House.
Voted to Raise three Pounds on Each Right to Build Said meeting House. Voted
to Leave the Rest of Said work of ᵈ House to the Discrestion of Said Commetree. [Dec. 9, 1766.]

Voted and Chose Benjamin Simonds a Commete man in the Room of mr
Samuel Sanford for Building the meeting House. [March 11, 1768.]

Voted to appoint a Place to Sett up a meeting House. Voted by Intrest and
to Sett it on the Square 9880 acres the Contray by Intrest 5035 acres. Voted to
Leave it to the Discression of the Commetee to provide for the Raising Sᵈ House.
[April 18, 1768.]

Voted to Give Instructtions to the meeting House Commetee Concerning the
Pew Ground also Voted to Build Pews. Voted that Said Commetee go on and
Build Pews according to their Dischression and then Seet said House. [Nov.
7, 1768.]

Voted to Raise one Pound on Eaich Proprietor Right to finish the meeting
House and Some other old Rearriges. Voted Excepted accounts as follows
to Benjamin Simonds and Nehemiah Smedley for finishing the meeting House
£4 8s. 3d. [Oct. 9, 1769.]

Voted to Build 2 Pews at the East End of the meeting House. Voted Not
to Except the meeting House as finished. [April 13, 1770.]

INDEX.

Norwood Press:
J. S. Cushing & Co. — Berwick & Smith.
Boston, Mass., U.S.A

CPSIA information can be obtained
at www.ICGtesting.com
Printed in the USA
BVHW052151051118
532208BV00013B/841/P